*Sixth Edition*

# CURRICULUM
## FOUNDATIONS, PRINCIPLES, AND ISSUES

**Allan C. Ornstein**
*St. John's University*

**Francis P. Hunkins**
*University of Washington, Emeritus*

**PEARSON**

Boston   Columbus   Indianapolis   New York   San Francisco   Upper Saddle River
Amsterdam   Cape Town   Dubai   London   Madrid   Milan   Munich   Paris   Montreal   Toronto
Delhi   Mexico City   Sao Paulo   Sydney   Hong Kong   Seoul   Singapore   Taipei   Tokyo

**Vice President and Editorial Director:** Jeffery W. Johnston
**Senior Acquisitions Editor:** Meredith Fossel
**Editorial Assistant:** Andrea Hall
**Vice President, Director of Marketing:** Margaret Waples
**Senior Marketing Manager:** Christopher Barry
**Senior Managing Editor:** Pamela D. Bennett
**Project Manager:** Kerry Rubadue
**Senior Operations Supervisor:** Matthew Ottenweller

**Senior Art Director:** Diane Lorenzo
**Text Designer:** Aptara®, Inc.
**Cover Designer:** Jodi Notowitz
**Permissions Administrator:** Rebecca Savage
**Full-Service Project Management:** Penny Walker; Aptara®, Inc.
**Composition:** Aptara®, Inc.
**Printer/Binder:** Edwards Brothers
**Cover Printer:** Lehigh-Phoenix Color/Hagerstown

Credits and acknowledgments borrowed from other sources and reproduced, with permission, in this textbook appear on appropriate page within text.

If you purchased this book within the United States or Canada you should be aware that it has been imported without the approval of the Publisher or the Author.

Every effort has been made to provide accurate and current Internet information in this book. However, the Internet and information posted on it are constantly changing, so it is inevitable that some of the Internet addresses listed in this textbook will change.

10 9 8 7 6 5 4 3 2 1

ISBN 10:    0-13-289949-3
ISBN 13: 978-0-13-289949-9

*To all those who are dear to me and understand me: Jason, Joel, Stacey—and to my soulmate and wife, Esther. Love always.*

**—Allan**

*To my wife, Dr. Patricia A. Hammill, my love, my friend and my fellow educator, who views life as the ultimate experience. Also to my daughter, Leah D. Hunkins, and my son, Frank P. Hunkins, whom I admire and love. And, finally, to my grandchildren, Blake Francis Hunkins, Flora Eudia Hunkins, and Samuel James Lindsay-Hunkins: love and sincere wishes for good learning.*

**—F. P. H.**

# ABOUT THE AUTHORS

**Allan C. Ornstein** is a professor of education at St. John's University. He is a former Fulbright-Hayes Scholar and has been a consultant for more than 60 different government and education agencies, including the American Federation of Teachers, the National Association of Secondary School Principals, and the Educational Testing Service. Dr. Ornstein has published more than 400 articles and 55 books, recently including *Contemporary Issues in Curriculum*, Fifth Edition.

**Francis P. Hunkins** was a professor of education specializing in general curriculum, curriculum development, curriculum issues, and curriculum theory in the College of Education at the University of Washington for 35 years. Since retiring, Dr. Hunkins has remained active in writing educational textbooks. As a past president, he also remains active in the Association for Teaching and Curriculum.

During his tenure at the University of Washington, Dr. Hunkins served as chairperson of the area of curriculum and instruction (1995–2000). He also consulted widely with school systems around the country. He twice was a visiting scholar at Monash University in Australia and was also a visiting scholar at the Hong Kong Institute of Education in 1999.

Over his career, he has written 21 educational textbooks and numerous articles for educational journals. He makes his home with his wife, Dr. Patricia A. Hammill, in the Seattle area.

# CURRICULUM TIPS

# PREFACE

*Curriculum: Foundations, Principles, and Issues,* Sixth Edition, is a book for researchers, theoreticians, and practitioners of curriculum. It is a basic text for those studying curriculum planning, development, implementation, and evaluation, as well as a reference for teachers, supervisors, and administrators who participate in curriculum making.

The book is a comprehensive and thoroughly documented overview of the foundations, principles, and issues of curriculum. *Foundations* are the areas of study outside curriculum that have an impact on the field; *principles* are the means and methods used in reflecting about the totality of curriculum and in designing, developing, implementing, and evaluating curriculum; *issues* are the current and evolving educational, political, and social dynamics that influence the curriculum field.

## NEW TO THIS EDITION

The sixth edition has been thoroughly updated to address current trends in curricula. All chapters have been revised and updated, and new discussions on leaders in the field as well as explorations of global topics have been added:

- New content on social foundations provides the basis for helping educators formulate excellent curricula.
- Major discussions on international testing are presented.
- A new chapter on international scenes in education (Chapter 10) helps educators consider how the educational systems of other countries compare to their own.
- Updates to the scientific models in curriculum evaluation are included (Chapter 9).
- Updates to discussion on major learning theories and principles (Chapter 4).
- MyEdLeadershipLab™ is integrated in the student text, enhancing the teaching and learning experiences.

## OVERVIEW OF THE TEXT

The book consists of a one-chapter introduction to the field plus three major parts. Part I, *Foundations of Curriculum*, has four chapters: one each on the curriculum's philosophical, historical, psychological, and social foundations. Part II, *Principles of Curriculum*, is composed of chapters on curriculum design, development, implementation, and evaluation. Part III, *Curriculum Issues and the World Scene*, consists of one chapter, *International Scenes in Education*.

This book differs from other curriculum texts in several ways. Most texts focus on either theory or practice. Some texts advance a particular political or social position. Others approach the field of curriculum as an administrative challenge. This text provides a balanced and comprehensive view of the field of curriculum. We have avoided taking a particular philosophical, educational, political, or social stance. Instead, we have aimed at providing a complete view of the field of curriculum so that readers can consider choices and formulate their own views on curriculum foundations, principles, and issues. In short, we have supplied a mix of materials to help researchers and practitioners develop their own interpretations of the field—past, present, and future.

The book provides three instructional and learning tools: Curriculum Tips, Focusing Questions, and overview tables. Curriculum Tips give practical meaning to the research and insights into the curriculum process. The Focusing Questions at the beginning of each chapter orient the reader and set the stage for the chapter's main ideas. The overview tables make learning more meaningful and provide recaps of the major concepts and principles discussed in the chapter.

## MyEdLeadershipLab™

Help your students bridge the gap between theory and practice with MyEdLeadershipLab™. MyEdLeadershipLab™ connects your course content to video- and case-based real-world scenarios, and provides the following:

- *Building Ed Leadership Skills* exercises that offer opportunities for candidates to develop and practice skills critical to their success as school leaders. Hints and feedback provide scaffolding and reinforce key concepts.
- *Assignments and Activities* assess candidates' understanding of key concepts and skill development. Suggested responses are available to instructors, making grading easy.
- *Multiple-Choice Quizzes* help candidates gauge their understanding of important topics and prepare for success on licensure examinations.

Access to MyEdLeadershipLab™ can be packaged with this textbook or purchased as a stand-alone feature. To find out how to allow student access to this Web site and gain access as an instructor, go to www.MyEdLeadershipLab.com, e-mail us at edleadership@pearson.com, or contact your Pearson sales representative.

## ACKNOWLEDGMENTS

Every textbook results from the participation of many people. We are grateful to all. We particularly thank those who reviewed the manuscript: Linda S. Behar-Horenstein, University of Florida; Doug Feldmann, Northern Kentucky University; and Ava J. Muñoz, University of Texas at Arlington.

—A. C. O.
—F. P. H.

# BRIEF CONTENTS

# CONTENTS

# 1

■ ■ ■

# The Field of Curriculum

## FOCUSING QUESTIONS

1. Why is it necessary to understand the field of curriculum?
2. What approach to curriculum do most educators adopt? Why?
3. How do you define *curriculum*?
4. Why do most theorists define *curriculum* in terms of generic principles or processes, not specific subject matter?
5. What fundamental questions guide the field of curriculum?
6. How do the foundations of education influence curriculum? Which foundation areas are most important? Why?
7. What are the differences between *curriculum development* and *curriculum design*?
8. How can theory and practice be integrated into the planning of curriculum?
9. What roles do principals and teachers play in curriculum planning?

Curriculum as a field of study has been characterized as elusive, fragmentary, and confusing. Certainly the field can be all that at times, but curriculum as a field of study is crucial to the health of schools and society. Whether we consider curriculum narrowly, as subjects taught in schools, or broadly, as experiences that individuals require for full participation in society, there is no denying that curriculum affects educators, students, and other members of society.

Given the plethora of books, articles, and treatises on curriculum, many people in the field feel frustrated with the continuing confusion. However, the field of curriculum is intended not to provide precise answers but to increase our understanding of its complexities. Curriculum results from social activity. It is designed for both present and emerging purposes. Curriculum is a dynamic field.[1]

Analyzing the concept of curriculum in a broad context illuminates what we mean by curriculum, what it involves, and who is involved in and served by the curriculum. We thus look at curriculum in terms of approach (an orientation or perspective) and definition. We also consider the relationships and differences among curriculum's foundations and domains, its theory and practice, and the roles of participants in the field of curriculum.

## CURRICULUM APPROACHES

Our approach to curriculum reflects our perceptions, values, and knowledge. A curriculum approach reflects a *holistic* position, or a *metaorientation,* encompassing curriculum's foundations (a person's philosophy, view of history, view of psychology and learning theory, and view of social issues), curriculum domains (common, important knowledge within the field), and curricular theory and practice. An approach expresses a viewpoint about curriculum's development and design; the role of the learner, teacher, and curriculum specialist in planning curriculum; the curriculum's goals; and the important issues that must be examined.

A curriculum approach reflects our views of schools and society. By understanding our curriculum approach and that of our school or school district, it is possible to conclude whether our professional view conflicts with the formal organizational view.

Although schools, over time, tend to commit to a particular curriculum approach, many educators are not strongly committed to one approach. Rather, they emphasize one approach in some situations and advocate other approaches in other situations. Curriculum textbook writers sometimes adhere to more than one curriculum approach. Curriculum specialists, even curriculum students, must examine their approaches.

Curriculum approaches can be viewed from a technical/scientific or nontechnical/nonscientific perspective. Technical/scientific approaches coincide with traditional theories and models of education and reflect established, formal methods of schooling. Nontechnical/nonscientific approaches evolved as part of avant-garde and experimental philosophies and politics; they tend to challenge established, formalized education practices and be more fluid and emergent.

The remainder of this section outlines five curriculum approaches. The first three may be classified as technical or scientific and the last two as nontechnical and/or nonscientific.

### Behavioral Approach

Rooted in the University of Chicago school (from Franklin Bobbitt and W. W. Charters to Ralph Tyler and Hilda Taba), the behavioral approach is the oldest and still the dominant approach to curriculum.[2] Logical and prescriptive, it relies on technical and scientific principles and includes paradigms, models, and step-by-step strategies for formulating curriculum. This approach is usually based on a plan, sometimes called a *blueprint* or *document*. Goals and objectives are specified, content and activities are sequenced to coincide with the objectives, and learning outcomes are evaluated in relation to the goals and objectives. This curriculum approach, which has been applied to all subjects since the early 1920s, constitutes a frame of reference against which other approaches to curriculum are compared. The approach has also been called logical, conceptual-empiricist, experientialist, rational-scientific, and technocratic.[3]

The behavioral approach started with the idea of efficiency, influenced by business and industry, and the scientific management theories of Frederick Taylor, who analyzed factory efficiency in terms of time-and-motion studies and concluded that each worker should be paid on the basis of his or her individual output, as measured by the number of units produced in a specified period of time. Efficient operation of schools became a major goal in the 1920s. (Some critics have termed Taylor's approach *machine theory*.)

Ensuring efficiency in schools often meant eliminating small classes, increasing student–teacher ratios, hiring fewer administrators, reducing teacher salaries, maintaining or reducing operational costs, and so on, and then preparing charts and graphs to show the resultant cost reductions. Raymond Callahan later branded this approach the "cult of efficiency."[4] The goal was to reduce teaching and learning to precise behaviors with corresponding measurable activities.

Bobbitt set out to organize a course of studies for the elementary grades: "We need principles of curriculum making. We did not know that we should first determine objectives from a study of social needs. . . . We had not learned that [plans] are means, not ends."[5] He developed his approach in the early 1920s in *How to Make a Curriculum,* in which he outlined more than 800 objectives and related activities to coincide with predetermined student needs. These activities ranged from teeth and eye care to keeping home appliances in good condition to spelling and grammar.[6] Bobbitt's methods were sophisticated for his day; however, taken out of context, his machine analogy and his list of hundreds of objectives and activities were easy to criticize.

It was left to Tyler, who took a number of Bobbitt's courses at the University of Chicago, to recognize the need for behavioral objectives that were not so small or lockstep. He combined basic techniques of curriculum, instruction, and evaluation into a simple plan. Tyler advocated using a school's (or school district's) philosophy "in making decisions about objectives." Tyler's approach combined behaviorism (objectives were important) with progressivism (the learner's needs were emphasized). Tyler was influenced by Edward Thorndike, John Dewey, and the "scientific movement of curriculum [making] during the . . . thirty years" prior to his classic text.[7]

Today few educational behaviorists continue the tradition of Ivan Pavlov's and John Watson's stimulus–response (S–R) theories, but many formulate precise objectives and evaluate programs according to those objectives, urging accountability plans, outcome-based education, and standards-based education. Many still rely on direct instruction, practice and drill, monitoring students, and prompt feedback. Behaviorism has evolved over the years to address the complexities of human learning; it now allows for research that investigates the mind's depths.[8] Most behaviorist educators now perceive learners as cognitive individuals functioning within a social context. Individual students experience and respond to the same curriculum in different ways, depending on their cultural interpretations and prior life activities. The behavioral approach to curriculum, with its dependency on technical means of selecting and organizing curricula, is likely to continue to serve us well in the future.

## Managerial Approach

Reminiscent of organizational theory, the managerial approach considers the school as a social system in which students, teachers, curriculum specialists, and administrators interact. Educators who rely on this approach plan the curriculum in terms of programs, schedules, space, resources and equipment, and personnel. This approach advocates selecting, organizing, communicating with, and supervising people involved in curriculum decisions. Consideration is given to committee and group processes, human relations, leadership styles and methods, and decision making.[9]

An offshoot of the behavioral approach, the managerial approach also relies on a plan, rational principles, and logical steps. It tends to focus on curriculum's supervisory and administrative aspects, especially the organizational and implementation process. (See Curriculum Tips 1.1.)

Advocates of the managerial approach are interested in innovation and in how curriculum specialists, supervisors, and administrators can facilitate change. The curriculum specialist or supervisor (sometimes the same person) is considered a practitioner, not a theorist—a change agent, resource person, and facilitator. This person reports to an administrator and adheres to the school's mission and goals. The school may resist or support change.[10] If the school is innovative or reform minded, then the school culture tends to create and sustain a culture for change. If the school emphasizes the "three R's" (reading, writing, and arithmetic), the curriculum specialist introduces plans accordingly. Managers communicate a desire for change or stability to subordinates (teachers).

The managerial approach is rooted in the organizational and administrative school models of the early 1900s, a period that combined a host of innovative plans involving curriculum and instruction that centered around individualization, departmentalization, nongrading, classroom grouping, homeroom and work–study activities. It was an era when superintendents introduced school-district plans to modify schools' horizontal and vertical organization. The plans'

---

**CURRICULUM TIPS 1.1    The Role of the Curriculum Supervisor**

Regardless of the curriculum approach, a curriculum supervisor or specialist performs certain roles and many important tasks within the school or school district, such as the following:

1. Help develop the school's or community's *educational goals.*
2. *Plan curriculum* with students, parents, teachers, and support personnel.
3. Coordinate or evaluate a *survey of student needs.*
4. *Design programs* of study by grade level and/or subject.
5. Plan or *schedule classes;* plan the school calendar.
6. Develop or help staff to write *behavioral objectives* for subject areas.
7. Prepare *curriculum guides* or teacher guides by grade level or subject area.
8. Formulate or revise *resource units* and unit plans.
9. Help select and evaluate *textbooks.*
10. Organize, select, or order instructional *materials* and *media.*
11. Serve as a *resource agent* for teachers.
12. *Observe teachers* and hold pre- and postobservation conferences.
13. Help teachers *implement curriculum* in the classroom.
14. Help redefine or *improve content.*
15. Work with staff in *writing grants.*
16. Encourage curriculum *innovation;* serve as a change agent.
17. *Conduct curriculum research* and/or work with curriculum consultants within the school.
18. Develop standards for curriculum and instructional *evaluation.*
19. Coordinate or *plan staff development* programs.
20. *Work with supervisors,* subject chairs, resource personnel, testing and technology specialists, and teachers within the school (and school district).

---

names usually reflected the school district's name or organizational concept, as in Batavia (NY) Plan, Denver Plan, Portland Plan, Platoon Plan, and Study Hall Plan. Superintendents and associate superintendents were involved in curriculum leadership, often developing a plan in one school district and also implementing it in another. Many administrators combined managerial and curriculum leadership skills.[11]

The managerial approach became the dominant curriculum approach in the 1950s and 1960s. During this period, principals were seen as curriculum leaders, instructional leaders, and managers. Midwest school administrators and professors with administrative backgrounds dominated the field of curriculum in setting policies and priorities, establishing the direction of change, planning and organizing curriculum, and carrying out it instruction.

These administrators were politically active. They used supervisory and curriculum associations and their respective journals and yearbooks as platforms for their ideas. Many, such as William Alexander, Robert Anderson, Leslee Bishop, Gerald Firth, Arthur Lewis, John McNeil, and J. Lloyd Trump, became curriculum professors at major universities; others became active as board directors and executive committee members of professional organizations that had major impact on curriculum, supervision, and administration. Many published curriculum books that expressed their managerial views.[12]

These school administrators were less concerned about content than about organization and implementation. They were less concerned about subject matter, methods, and materials than about improving curriculum in light of policies, plans, and people on a systemwide basis. They envisioned curriculum changes as they administered resources and restructured schools.

Many of today's ideas about school reform and restructuring derive from the 1950s and 1960s: A current emphasis on standards and high-stake testing reflects an earlier emphasis on state control of schools. Many current plans related to school-based management and empowerment are based on the previous era's career ladder, team teaching, and differential staffing models. Much of the new legislative and administrative support for improving curriculum and instruction is based on the changing roles of the superintendent and principal as curriculum and instructional leaders that blossomed during the 1950s and 1960s.

## Systems Approach

A managerial view that emphasizes organizing people and policies led to an emphasis on organizing curriculum into a system. The organization's units and subunits are viewed in relation to the whole. The curriculum plan often entails organizational diagrams, flow charts, and committee structures. Sometimes referred to as *curriculum engineering,* the approach includes the processes by which *engineers,* such as superintendents, directors, coordinators, and principals, plan the curriculum, the curriculum's *stages* (development, design, implementation, and evaluation), and the curriculum's *structures* (subjects, courses, unit plans, and lesson plans).

Systems theory, systems analysis, and systems engineering influenced the systems approach to curriculum. School managers widely employ concepts developed by social scientists when they discuss administrative and organizational theory. The military, business, and industry use the systems approach to ensure that people master the tasks they must perform.[13]

In the systems approach to curriculum, the parts of the school or school district are examined in terms of their interrelatedness. Departments, personnel, equipment, and schedules are planned to change people's behavior. Information is usually communicated to administrators, who then consider choices.

A school district's organizational chart represents a systems approach, showing line–staff relationships of personnel and how decisions regarding special areas (i.e., curriculum, instruction, testing and evaluation, personnel, and budgeting) are made. In large school districts (50,000 or more students), teachers, supervisors, and principals at the school or local level often seem distant from top administration at the school-district or central level. In small school districts, the central office is less bureaucratic (and less distant from the local level) because there are fewer layers. Two educators have written, "The organizational hierarchy of larger school districts [is] cumbersome, and those with 100,000 or more students (0.01 percent of all school districts) often have charts extending off the page. Most readers would have difficulty understanding [or following] these charts, not because they are unknowledgeable" but because of the complex systems and hierarchical arrangements of large (city or county) school districts.[14]

RAND Corporation developed one application of the systems approach that has rapidly spread from government to business agencies. Called the Planning, Programming, Budgeting System (PPBS), it integrates planning, programming, and budgeting into the system's structure, functions, and capabilities. In our case, the system is curriculum.

Currently, many schools use a systems approach, known as *total quality management* (TQM), based on Ed Deming's 14 points for improving the system in which people work. This approach, also drawn from industry, represents a paradigm shift emphasizing client priority (in our case, students), extensive data collection and analysis, self-monitoring and inspection, collaboration, communication, cooperation, and team responsibility.[15]

When applying TQM to curriculum development and implementation, participants realize that their function depends on acquiring and applying what is called *profound knowledge.* Such knowledge is based on four components: systematic thinking, theory of variation, theory of knowledge, and knowledge of psychology. *Systematic thinking* enables people to realize that their actions interact with others' actions and that the total organization entails the dynamic interaction of many subprocesses. The *theory of variation* recognizes that curriculum activity entails common and special causes and effects. A school is a community in which people exhibit individual differences. They must learn to communicate, cooperate, respect others' opinions, and reach a consensus. According to the *theory of knowledge,* the knowledge possessed by the people within the system is essential to curricular success. The *knowledge of psychology* supports TQM by optimizing the participation and learning of students and teachers. To use this approach successfully, individuals must understand, respect, and care for one another.

George Beauchamp described the first systems theory of curriculum. He postulated five equally important components of education: (1) administration, (2) counseling, (3) curriculum, (4) instruction, and (5) evaluation.[16] Many professors of education (outside of curriculum) do not accept this notion of equal components; they view their own field as most important. For example, school administrators often delegate supervisors to take care of curriculum matters, especially if the administrators view their leadership role as chiefly managerial. Curriculum specialists usually view curriculum as the major component and see related fields such as teaching, instruction, and supervision as subsystems that help implement the curriculum.[17] However, Beauchamp was trying to convey that the five components of education draw their ideas from psychology, sociology, history, philosophy, and so on. In any event, practitioners should use whichever procedures are most helpful and applicable to the real world.

Curriculum specialists who value the systems approach view curriculum broadly and are concerned with curriculum issues relevant to the entire school or school system, not just particular subjects or grades. They are concerned with theory in which the curriculum is related across different programs and content areas, the extent to which the curriculum reflects the school's (or school system's) organization, the participants' needs and training, and various methods for monitoring and evaluating results. Long-term planning is fused with short-term, or incidental, planning.

## Academic Approach

Sometimes referred to as the *traditional, encyclopedic, synoptic, intellectual,* or *knowledge-oriented approach,* the academic approach attempts to analyze and synthesize major positions, trends, and concepts of curriculum. This approach tends to be historical or philosophical and, to a lesser extent, social or practical. The discussion of curriculum development is usually scholarly, theoretical, and concerned with many broad aspects of schooling, including the study of education.

This approach is rooted in the works of John Dewey, Henry Morrison, and Boyd Bode,[18] and became popular during the 1930s and carried through the 1950s. The influx of new topics related to curriculum during this period expanded the field to include many trends and issues and led to the integration of various instructional, teaching, learning, guidance, evaluation, supervision, and administrative procedures.

After the 1950s, interest in curriculum centered on the structure of disciplines and qualitative methods. The academic approach lost some of its glamour. The texts that continued to reflect this approach in the second half of the 20th century (such as those by William Schubert, Daniel and Laurel Tanner, and Robert Zais)[19] tended to overwhelm the beginning curriculum student, who usually lacked sufficient background knowledge. But curriculum scholars continue to use this approach when talking to one another. Schubert and, more recently, James Sears and J. Dan Marshall have reviewed how curriculum scholars have influenced curriculum thought and shaped the field. The acquisition of the field's knowledge and ideas is shown through doctoral study and mentorship.[20]

The academic approach has partly returned in the current focus on the nature and structure of knowledge as current curricularists address curriculum from a postmodern academic perspective. Attention is now on understanding how knowledge can be constructed, deconstructed, and then reconstructed. As William Pinar noted, academics and schools must strive to comprehend the field of curriculum.[21] However, it is doubtful that the academic approach will become popular among practitioners.

The academic approach to curriculum addresses much more than subject matter and pedagogy. Academics cover numerous foundational topics (usually historical, philosophical, social, and political), thus presenting an overview of curriculum. They consider areas of study not usually included in curriculum deliberation and action, such as religion, psychotherapy, literary criticism, and linguistics. To many educators, such fields seem very foreign at first. However, educators are beginning to realize the need to perceive curriculum as diverse discourse. Everyone involved in the academic approach to curriculum is in the "business" of words and ideas.[22]

## Humanistic Approach

Some curriculum leaders contend that the preceding approaches are too technocratic and rigid. They contend that curricularists who try to be scientific and rational miss the personal and social aspects of curriculum and instruction; ignore subject matter's artistic, physical, and cultural aspects; rarely consider the need for self-reflectiveness and self-actualization among learners; and overlook the sociopsychological dynamics of classrooms and schools. This view is rooted in progressive philosophy and the child-centered movement of the early 1900s (first spearheaded at the University of Chicago when Dewey, Charles Judd, and Francis Parker developed progressive teaching methods based on the student's natural development and curiosity).[23]

In the 1920s and 1930s, the progressive movement moved east and was dominated by Teachers College, Columbia University, and by such professors as Boyd Bode, Frederick Bosner, Hollis Caswell, L. Thomas Hopkins, William Kilpatrick, Harold Rugg, and Dewey (who was by then at Columbia).[24] This approach gained further impetus in the 1940s and 1950s with the growth of child psychology and humanistic psychology (which deals with valuing, ego identity, psychological health, freedom to learn, and personal fulfillment).

Mainly at the elementary school level, curriculum activities emerged from this approach, including lessons based on life experiences, group games, group projects, artistic endeavors, dramatizations, field trips, social enterprises, learning and interest centers, and homework and tutoring stations (or corners). These activities include creative problem solving and active student participation. They emphasize socialization and life adjustment for students, as well as stronger family ties and school–community ties. They are representative of Parker, Dewey, Kilpatrick, and Carleton Washburne's ideal school and the kinds of curriculum activities they put into practice. Such activities are still practiced in the Parker School in Chicago; Dewey's lab school at the University of Chicago; Washburne's school district in Winnetka, Illinois; Kilpatrick's Lincoln School of Teachers College, Columbia University; many other private and university lab schools; and some recent charter schools.

Various developmental theories (e.g., those of Frederick Erikson, Robert Havighurst, and Abraham Maslow) and child-centered methods (e.g., those of Friedrich Froebel, Johann Pestalozzi, and A. S. Neill) for curriculum derive from the humanistic approach, which considers informal as well as formal curricula. This approach considers the whole child, not only the cognitive dimension. The arts, the humanities, and health education are just as important as science and math.

Curriculum specialists who believe in this approach tend to put faith in cooperative learning, independent learning, small-group learning, and social activities, as opposed to competitive, teacher-dominated, large-group learning. Each child has considerable input into the curriculum and shares responsibility with parents, teachers, and curriculum specialists in planning classroom instruction. In schools that adopt this approach, curriculum leaders and supervisors tend to permit teachers more input into curriculum decisions, and the ideas of professional collegiality and mentor systems are more pronounced. Curriculum committees are *bottom up* instead of *top down,* and students often are invited into curriculum meetings to express their views.[25]

The humanistic approach became popular again in the 1970s as relevancy, radical school reform, open education, and alternative education became part of education's reform movement. Today, however, demands for educational excellence and academic productivity have resulted in an emphasis on cognition, not humanism, and on subjects such as science and math, rather than art and music. Nevertheless, the humanistic approach may gain adherents as people come to realize the interdependence of cognition and affect.[26] Education must focus on both the personal and interpersonal, and requires overcoming a long tradition of regarding cognition as something separate from feeling. To be sure, the student's self-concept, self-esteem, and personal identity are essential factors in learning, which involves social and moral, not just cognitive, aspects.

## Reconceptualist Approach

To some curriculum scholars, the reconceptualist approach to curriculum largely extends the humanistic approach. Others argue that reconceptualism is concerned chiefly with change and reform. Still others argue that reconceptualists lack an approach because they lack a model for developing and designing curriculum.

Reconceptualists focus on education's larger ideological issues. They investigate and influence society's social, economic, and political institutions. Reconceptualists are more interested in theory than practical applications. Pinar has gone so far as to state that the era of curriculum development has passed.[27] Pinar's viewpoint would be considered impractical by a practitioner who has to deal with the selection and organization of content. However, Pinar is addressing not practitioners, but other theorists—an example of the divide that exists between theorists and practitioners.

Some curricularists who associate with the reconceptualists' camp contend that there is no one precise, certain way to create curricula; curriculum development is more like a communal conversation.[28] Curriculum development is not a closed system, but remains open.

Reconceptualists are interested in curricula's interactions with political, economic, social, moral, and artistic forces.[29] They see the school as an extension of society and students as capable of changing society. Many reconceptualists see current curricula as overly controlling and designed to preserve the existing social order and its inequalities.

Reconceptualists have brought greater diversity to curricular dialogue. Reconceptualism is rooted in the philosophy and social activism of such early reconstructionists as George Counts, Harold Rugg, and Harold Benjamin.[30] Like today's reconceptualists, these scholars urged curricularists to rethink curriculum. However, reconceptualists are more likely to speak in terms of inequality, discrimination, and oppression—for example, with regard to class, gender, and race.

## DEFINITION OF CURRICULUM

What is curriculum? What is its purpose? How does it affect students and teachers? By and large, the way we define curriculum reflects our approach to it. We can specify five basic definitions of curriculum.

First, curriculum can be defined as a *plan* for achieving goals. This position, popularized by Tyler and Taba, exemplifies a linear view of curriculum. The plan involves a sequence of steps. Today most behavioral and some managerial and systems people agree with this definition. For example, J. Galen Saylor defines curriculum as "a plan for providing sets of learning opportunities for persons to be educated."[31] David Pratt writes, "Curriculum is an organized set of formal education and/or training intentions."[32] Jon Wiles and Joseph Bondi view curriculum as a four-step plan involving purpose, design, implementation, and assessment. The curriculum worker wants the plan's "intent" to be realized as fully as possible.[33]

Second, curriculum can be defined broadly as dealing with the learner's *experiences*. By this definition, almost anything planned in or outside of school is part of the curriculum. This definition is rooted in Dewey's definition of experience and education and in Hollis Caswell and Doak Campbell's view from the 1930s that curriculum is "all the experiences children have under the guidance of teachers."[34] Humanistic curricularists and elementary school curricularists subscribe to this definition, which textbook writers have interpreted more broadly over the years. Gene Shepherd and William Ragan state, "The curriculum consists of the ongoing experiences of children under the guidance of the school." It represents "a special environment . . .

for helping children achieve self-realization through active participation within the school."[35] Elliot Eisner describes the curriculum as a "program" that a school "offers to its students," a "preplanned series of educational hurdles and an entire range of experiences a child has within the school."[36] Marsh and Willis view curriculum as all the "experiences in the classroom [that are] planned and enacted." However, they note a difference between what the school plans and what the teacher enacts.[37]

According to a third definition, less popular than the first two, curriculum is a _system_ for dealing with people. The system can be linear or nonlinear. A linear system plots out the means to a desired end. In contrast, a nonlinear system permits the curriculum specialist to enter at various points of the model, skip parts, reverse order, and work on more than one component at a time. Many managerial and systems curricularists adopt this definition.[38]

Fourth, curriculum can be defined as a _field of study_ with its own foundations, knowledge domains, research, theory, principles, and specialists. Those who adopt this definition tend to discuss curriculum in theoretical rather than practical terms. They are concerned with broad historical, philosophical, or social issues. Academics often subscribe to this view of curriculum—for example, William Reid, Schubert, and the Tanners.[39]

Finally, curriculum can be defined in terms of _subject matter_ (math, science, English, history, and so on) or content (the way we organize and assimilate information). We can also talk about subject matter or content in terms of _grade levels_. People who adopt this definition emphasize the facts and concepts of particular subject areas. Most U.S. school districts subscribe to this definition. Yet, university courses in elementary and secondary school curriculum rarely are subject specific (e.g., on math or biology curricula); they emphasize generic principles of curriculum that cut across and encompass most, if not all, subjects.

## The Challenges of Definition

Definitional debates take time and energy, but they address important curriculum issues. The language of curricularists is neither philosophically nor politically neutral.[40] Variations in the way curriculum is defined provide needed scope and diversity. The more precise one's definition of curriculum and the more a person relies on a preconceived plan or document, the greater the tendency to omit or miss relevant (but hard to observe) sociopsychological factors related to teaching and learning. Ronald Doll points out, "Every school has a planned, formal acknowledged curriculum," but it also has "an unplanned, informal and hidden one" that must be considered.[41] The _planned_, formal curriculum focuses on goals, objectives, subject matter, and organization of instruction; the _unplanned_, informal curriculum deals with sociopsychological interaction among students and teachers, especially their feelings, attitudes, and behaviors. We must also realize the power of the _hidden_ curriculum—the part of the curriculum that, while not written, will certainly be learned by students. If we define curriculum too narrowly, we overlook what Eisner has called the _null curriculum_, subject matter and experiences that are not taught.[42] Not everything that goes on in school can or should be discussed in terms of curriculum.

Other critics, such as Larry Cuban and Atfie Kohn, have argued that with the current emphasis on testing, the curriculum has become _narrow_ and _bland_. Certain subjects, such as reading and math, are emphasized at the expense of subject matter that has moral, creative, and emotional value.[43] Teaching to the text seems to placate the public, especially if such actions lead to improvement of student test scores. The focus on facts for the purpose of testing is often at the expense of discussion topics and questions that ask, Why? What if?

This narrowing of the curriculum, however, coincides with Taylor's machine theory and Bobbit and Charter's school of scientific curriculum making. This guide to curriculum making was and is still advocated by educators who want to concentrate on precise objectives and subject matter and purposeful activities that correspond to the desired objectives and subject matter.

### Background Issues for Defining the Field

Content or subject matter issues are relevant, too. Is it appropriate to talk about a social studies or math curriculum or about curriculum in general? Are there principles of curriculum that apply to all subjects or principles that apply only to specific subjects? Should subject matter be organized around separate disciplines or based on interdisciplinary and core approaches? To what extent is subject content a matter of student, professional, or parental choice? Should it be determined by the community, state, or nation? How should subjects be organized—around behavioral objectives, student activities, social or community values, future jobs? Which content should be graded? What portion of subject matter should be classified as general, specialized, or elective? What is the appropriate mix of required versus optional subjects? What is the appropriate stress on facts, concepts, and principles of subject matter? As Beauchamp writes, "The posture . . . one assumes with respect to the content of a curriculum inevitably will be of great influence upon . . . theory and planning."[44] Actually, that posture influences everything that follows, including developing, implementing, and evaluating the curriculum.

Other issues are related to people. Who are the major participants? To what extent should students, teachers, parents, and community members be involved in curriculum planning? Why are school administrators assuming greater roles in curriculum matters and curriculum specialists assuming fewer roles? What are the roles and responsibilities of researchers and practitioners in curriculum making? How do we improve their communication?

### Fundamental Questions

Asking the right questions is crucial for addressing basic concerns in curriculum and for determining the basic concepts, principles, and research methods of the field. If we ask the wrong questions, the discussions that follow—and even the answers—are of little value. The danger in listing a host of fundamental questions, however, is that they tend to become translated as a set of principles or steps to be blindly followed. However, appropriate questions can be used as a base for raising issues and problems that curriculum specialists must address, whether they deal in theory, practice, or both.

The first list of fundamental questions was formulated by a famous 12-person committee on curriculum making, headed by Harold Rugg and organized in 1930 for the Twenty-sixth Yearbook of the National Society for the Study of Education (NSSE). This group of curriculum specialists, perhaps the most prestigious ever convened to present a general system on the principles of curriculum making, started the second volume of the yearbook with 18 "fundamental questions" to serve as a basis for "viewing . . . the issues and problems of curriculum" for that era.[45] These questions centered around subject matter, learning, and the guiding objectives, activities, materials, and outcomes of the curriculum, as well as the role of school in American society.

A more recent set of questions was presented more than 50 years later and is shown in Table 1.1. These questions focus on the place and function of subject matter, the methods and materials for facilitating learning, the role of the curriculum specialist, and the relationship between curriculum, instruction, supervision, and government levels of curriculum making.

These fundamental questions help establish what Tyler called curriculum's "rationale," Saylor, Alexander, and Lewis later called its "purpose," and Schubert more recently called the "paradigm" that governs inquiry in the field of curriculum.[46] Curriculum specialists can delineate important theories, concepts, and methods in the field by asking, What? Who? and How?

## FOUNDATIONS OF CURRICULUM

Debate continues regarding curriculum's meaning, foundations, and knowledge domains. Current knowledge concerning curriculum is "widely scattered" and either "unknown or unread" by most who teach or practice curriculum.[47] Some people believe that the field lacks purpose and direction because it has extensively "adapted and borrowed subject matter from a number of

| **Table 1.1**    Fundamental Questions about Curriculum |
| --- |

1. How is curriculum defined?
2. What philosophies and theories are we communicating, intentionally or not, in our curriculum?
3. What social and political forces influence curriculum? Which ones are most pertinent? Which impose limitations?
4. How does learning take place? What learning activities will best meet our learners' needs? How can these activities best be organized?
5. What are the domains of curriculum knowledge? What types of curriculum knowledge are essential?
6. What are a curriculum's essential parts?
7. Why do changes in curriculum occur? How does change affect the curriculum?
8. What are the curriculum specialist's roles and responsibilities?
9. How is the curriculum best organized?
10. What are the roles and responsibilities of the teacher and student in organizing curriculum?
11. What are our aims and goals? How do we translate them into instructional objectives?
12. How do we define our educational needs? Whose needs? How do we prioritize these needs?
13. What subject matter is most worthwhile? What are the best forms of content? How do we organize them?
14. How do we measure or verify what we are trying to achieve? Who is accountable? For what and to whom?
15. What is the appropriate relationship between curriculum and instruction? Curriculum and supervision? Curriculum and evaluation?

*Source:* Allan C. Ornstein, "The Theory and Practice of Curriculum," *Kappa Delta Pi Record* (Fall 1987), p. 16.

[other] disciplines," including its major "principles, knowledge and skills."[48] This is basically the same criticism that Joseph Schwab made in 1969, when he complained that the field was "moribund [because] it has adopted theories from outside the field of education."[49] However, the field's lack of unity also suggests flexibility and richness.

The foundations of curriculum set the external boundaries of the knowledge of curriculum and define what constitutes valid sources from which to derive the field's theories, principles, and ideas. Curriculum's commonly accepted foundations are philosophical, historical, psychological, and social. (Cultural, political, and economical foundations may be included within or apart from social foundations.) Although curriculum writers generally agree on the four foundation areas, few attempt to analyze these areas in depth.

Herbert Kliebard claims that the field of curriculum is synoptic. Curriculum specialists bring perspectives from other fields to bear on curriculum. They use concepts, methods, and research tools of philosophers, historians, psychologists, sociologists, economists, and political scientists.[50]

Regardless of their approach, curriculum specialists rely on the foundation areas to study and practice curriculum. This text examines four foundation areas (in four chapters) with the intention of presenting important sources of information from other fields that are pertinent to curriculum.

## CURRICULUM DOMAINS

Whereas curriculum's foundations represent the field's *external* boundaries, curriculum's domains define the field's internal boundaries—the accepted knowledge *within* the field presented in published articles and books. Although curriculum specialists generally agree on the foundation areas, they often disagree on curriculum's knowledge domains. Many efforts have been made to determine these domains. However, much literature on the subject is largely unread,[51] and in other cases it is considered diffuse and fragmentary.

The lack of consensus of the curriculum domains is illustrated by the experts themselves. Beauchamp divided curriculum knowledge into planning, implementation, and evaluation.[52] Fenwick English viewed curriculum in terms of ideological (philosophical–scientific), technical (design), and operational (managerial) issues.[53] Edmund Short listed curriculum's domains as policy making, development, evaluation, change, decision making, activities or fields of study, and forms and language of inquiry.[54]

Linda Behar established an empirical format for identifying *curriculum domains* (broad areas of knowledge based on the most influential curriculum textbooks over a 20-year period) and *curriculum practices* (precise activities teachers and curriculum specialists engage in while inquiring about planning or implementing the curriculum). As many as 49 curriculum practices were validated and then rated in importance by U.S. curriculum professors. These practices were grouped into nine curriculum domains: (1) curriculum philosophy, (2) curriculum theory, (3) curriculum research, (4) curriculum history, (5) curriculum development, (6) curriculum design, (7) curriculum evaluation, (8) curriculum policy, and (9) curriculum as a field of study.[55] The nine domains help establish recommended content for a curriculum text, because the domains outlined were based on assessing the most influential texts in the field over a 20-year period.

Allan Glatthorn describes seven types of curriculum: (1) *recommended curriculum* delineated by scholars and professional organizations; (2) *written curriculum* that appears in state and school district documents; (3) *taught curriculum* that teachers attempt to implement; (4) *supported curriculum* that helps implement or deliver the curriculum resources such as textbooks and computers; (5) *assessed curriculum* that is tested and evaluated; (6) *learned curriculum,* what the students actually learn; and (7) *hidden curriculum,* unintended curriculum.[56] Traditionally, teachers have been most influenced by learned and assessed curriculum—making their curriculum decisions on the basis of students' needs and responses to the taught curriculum. Since 2000, the standards-education movement has resulted in school administrators becoming increasingly concerned with aligning the *written curriculum* (content) with the *assessed curriculum* (especially as assessed through high-stakes tests).

Despite this lack of consensus, however, it is important to establish a framework for conceptualizing the domains of curriculum—that is, the significant and indispensible curriculum knowledge necessary to conduct research and make theoretical and practical decisions about curriculum. The problem is that few curriculum writers can agree on the domains of curriculum knowledge; in some cases, no framework exists that connotes curriculum as a distinct enterprise with its own boundaries, internal structures, relations, and activities. We maintain that, of all the domains of curriculum knowledge, the *development* and *design* of the curriculum—what some observers refer to as the *theoretical aspects* and what others call the *technical aspects* of curriculum—are crucial for any text.

## Curriculum Development

We maintain that, of all domains of curriculum knowledge, curriculum *development* and *design* (its theoretical or technical aspects) are most crucial in any curriculum text. Analyzing curriculum in terms of development is the traditional and most common approach to the field. The idea is to show how curriculum is planned, implemented, and evaluated as well as what people, processes, and procedures are involved in constructing the curriculum. Such development is usually examined in a logical step-by-step fashion, based on behavioral and managerial approaches to curriculum and rooted in scientific principles of education. Many curriculum texts today use the terms *development* and *plan* in their titles and thus reflect this thinking.

Most curriculum textbooks offer some development model, outline, or plan. Starting with a philosophy or set of objectives, this model includes student assessment, content selection and organization, implementation, and evaluation. The number of steps ranges from four (Tyler, Saylor and Alexander, Wiles and Bondi) to seven (Taba) or more (Doll). More concerned with standards, Glatthorn and David Squires emphasize the need to align the curriculum with what is being tested.[57]

All these development models attempt to show the relationship of curriculum to various decisions, activities, and processes. They provide guideposts. The models tend to be graphically or pictorially illustrated. They show input, transformations, and output and treat curriculum as a system composed of subsystems. Theoretical and scientific, the development models are conceived in technical terms. One must have knowledge of the field to fully appreciate and understand them. Such models tend to ignore processes that are not easily observed, measured, or controlled. They sometimes ignore attitudes, emotions, feelings, and beliefs linked to teaching and learning.

By adopting development models, curricularists tend to constrain curriculum choices. They sometimes forget that the path to curriculum development is strewn with qualitative judgments, concessions to social and political realities, and the need to serve diverse students and teachers. However, some curricularists argue that being systematic doesn't preclude flexibility, and that their models consider multiple variables and permit choices.

This textbook gives considerable attention to nontechnical models. Doll notes that postmodernists often say that there are no universal principles; everything is relational or contextual.[58] Similarly, William Reid claims that we must go beyond rational and logical methods and rethink the curriculum in terms of aesthetics, morality, and spirituality.[59] In contrast, technical models sometime discourage change, which they treat as disruptive and inefficient.

A system of curriculum development can be open or closed. Open systems are dynamic and evolutionary; they develop through change. Closed systems are static and unable to accommodate change. Perhaps everyone involved should think of curriculum development as an open system—a journey, rather than a destination.

## Curriculum Design

*Curriculum design* refers to the way we conceptualize the curriculum and arrange its major components (subject matter or content, instructional methods and materials, learner experiences or activities) to provide direction and guidance as we develop the curriculum. Most curriculum writers do not have a single or pure design for curriculum. They are influenced by many designs and approaches; they draw bits and pieces from different designs.

In general, a curriculum design should provide a basic frame of reference, a template if you wish, for planning what the curriculum will look like after engaging in curriculum development. If we liken a curriculum to a painting, *design* refers to how we want our artistic composition arranged. Whereas a curriculum design is influenced to some extent by the writer's curriculum approach, just as a painting is influenced to some degree by the artist's approach, it is the writer's views of the world and his or her views of teaching, learning, and instruction that are key to design selection.

The way people design a curriculum is partly a product of their view of curriculum. For example, those who view curriculum in behaviorist terms and favor a prescribed plan and set of learning outcomes produce different curriculum designs than those who view curriculum as a system of managing people and organizing procedures. Those who view teaching and learning in primarily psychological terms present different curriculum designs than those who view it in social or political terms. Whereas curriculum development tends to be technical and scientific, curriculum design is more varied because it is based on curricularists' values and beliefs about education. If academic knowledge is paramount to a curricularist, his or her design most likely stresses disciplined knowledge. If, instead, students' overall growth is central, the curricularist designs with social and psychological concerns in mind. In general, curriculum design should provide a framework for planning what the curriculum will look like after curriculum development.

For most of the 20th century, curriculum specialists who started out as teachers were content oriented, emphasizing the core academic disciplines. Many people believe that we need designs that focus more on the student and less on the content, but such designs have not gained wide acceptance. It is not likely that schools will become more receptive to novel and radical designs in the near future. After all, schools socialize students in accordance with a society's norms and are, therefore, inherently conservative. Moreover, we as educators are in the midst of high-stakes testing and standards, which emphasize knowledge and information—what most of us in the field of teaching simply call *content*.

## Planned and Unplanned Curriculum

What students learn in school extends beyond the *planned* (*formal*) curriculum. The planned curriculum translates the school's goals into the subjects that students are expected to learn, the measured objectives of the courses and lessons (often stated in the teachers' unit plans and lesson plans), and the subject's assigned readings. However, a school also transmits an *unplanned* (*informal*) curriculum, one that is not intended or stated.[60]

Eisner also distinguishes between the planned and the operational curriculum. The planned curriculum is developed after considering several options and is usually prepared by a curriculum committee of the school or school district. The *operational* curriculum emerges in the classroom as a result of the actual situation and requires that teachers make adjustments as needed.[61]

Then, there is the *hidden* curriculum, which arises from interactions among students and between students and teachers. Too often, curriculum texts ignore the powerful influence of the hidden curriculum, which is built around the peer group and often competes with the teacher's planned curriculum. It influences thinking and behavior in classrooms, sometimes even conflicting with the primary goals and values of the school and larger society.

When teachers and schools put too much emphasis on grades, the hidden curriculum elevates correct answers over understanding, facts over ideas, conforming behavior over independent behavior, and getting on the honor roll over helping others. Critics argue that the hidden curriculum teaches students that "beating the system" or "winning" is more important than anything else.[62]

As part of the socialization process, schools and society require that students conform and remain largely passive and compliant in the classroom. Students must stay in their seats, raise their hands and wait to be called on, line up as required, and so on. Children are socialized to follow rules and regulations.

Phillip Jackson summarizes schools' hidden curriculum: "It is expected that children will adapt to the teacher's authority by becoming 'good workers' and 'model students.' The transition from classroom to factory or office is made easier by those who have developed 'good work habits' in their early years."[63] John Holt also describes the socialization process: The aim of teachers and schools is to create student "producers," not thinkers, to reward right-answer-oriented students and discourage creative or divergent responses.[64] Producers follow rules and conform to teachers' expectations. Thinkers raise questions, come up with novel answers, and grapple with ideas. In an era of curriculum standards and high-stakes testing, the emphasis too often is on fact accumulation rather than critical thinking.

As previously mentioned, Eisner also distinguishes between the *implicit* curriculum (what the school teaches as having cognitive and social value) and the *null* curriculum (omitted content and values). For example, the public school curriculum generally avoids topics dealing with death, sex, and spirituality. Schools also may neglect nonverbal and nonliteral thinking, such as "visual, auditory and metaphoric . . . forms of expression."[65] Omissions should arise from objective criteria, not ignorance or bias.

To some extent, the null curriculum goes back to William Reid's point that curriculum involves deliberate choices; educators are inclined to emphasize agreed-on content and perspectives and systematically omit others.[66] For researchers, the curriculum can be viewed in terms of *content analysis*—that is, the attempt to sample, record, and justify the knowledge and information.[67] Certain facts, ideas, and values are represented and considered "commonly shared content"; the norms and rules that govern are *implicit.* Other data are omitted; this exclusion coincides with the null curriculum and unplanned curriculum.

The point is, whether we use terms such as *unplanned, hidden,* or *null curriculum,* certain subjects have always been considered more important than others. This controversy can be traced back to John Dewey and Boyd Bode (also a progressive educator), who reminded us that all subjects, including literature, art, music, dance and vocational education, serve as means to an end, expand the learner's understanding of culture, and enhance the learner's sensitivities and appreciation of the norms and values of society.[68]

Although Dewey and Bode never used the aforementioned curriculum terms, they were concerned that certain subjects would be deemphasized and the spirit of individual creativity would be curtailed because of content omission; moreover; the idea of democracy would be left to the care of itself and be divorced from educational leadership.

## THEORY AND PRACTICE

A field of study involves theoretical and practical knowledge. By *theory,* we mean the most advanced views within a field. Theory often establishes the field's framework and helps researchers and practitioners analyze and synthesize data, organize concepts and principles, suggest new ideas and relations, and speculate about the future. According to Beauchamp, *theory* may be defined as the knowledge and statements that "give functional meaning to a series of events [and] take the form of definitions, operational constructs, assumptions, postulates, hypotheses, generalizations, laws or theorems." Curriculum theory involves "decisions about . . . the use of a curriculum, the development of curriculum, curriculum design and curriculum evaluation."[69] This definition suggests a scientific and technical approach to curriculum.

Good curriculum theory describes and explains the concepts, principles, and relationships that exist within the field. It also has predictive value; rigorous laws yield high probability and control. Good theory also prescribes actions to be taken. However, it is impossible to fully predict educational outcomes. Like other aspects of education, curriculum involves judgments, hunches, and insights that are not always conducive to laws, principles, or generalizations. Often, a curriculum does not emerge as a tightly regulated and concise set of enterprises, but evolves as one action or choice that leads to another.

Nonetheless, all curriculum texts should try to incorporate theory, to be systematic in their approach, and to establish worthwhile practices. As expressed by Taba, "Any enterprise as complex as curriculum requires some kind of theoretical or conceptual framework of thinking to guide it."[70]

### From Theory to Practice

The test of good theory is whether it can guide practice. Good practice, in turn, is based on theory. By *practice,* we mean applied procedures, methods, and skills. Successful teaching results in procedures, methods, and skills that can be effectively applied in different situations.

People directly involved with curriculum must deal with practice. These people include administrators, supervisors, and teachers; curriculum developers and curriculum evaluators; textbook authors and test makers; and individuals assigned to curriculum committees, accrediting agencies, school boards, and local, regional, state, and federal educational agencies. Theories should be workable for these practitioners, make sense, have explanatory power, and be applicable to the real world of classrooms and schools. (See Curriculum Tips 1.2.)

According to Elizabeth Vallance, "Much ado [is] made about the split between theory and practice in the dialogues and concerns about professional curriculum workers." The crux of the matter is to provide "practical answers to very practical questions having to do with design, development, implementation, and evaluation of curricula." The distinctions between theory and practice are secondary to Vallance because both aspects of curriculum focus on the "same curriculum problems."[71]

The problem is that most curricularists, including those who write textbooks, have difficulty fusing theory and practice. This is true even though many curriculum books emphasize theory and practice[72] or principles and processes.[73] Perhaps curricularists have difficulty connecting theory and practice because their methods of inquiry lend themselves more to theoretical discussions than to practical matters. Although theory is recognized by professors of curriculum as a worthwhile endeavor, good practice is often misconstrued by theoreticians as a "cookbook" or as simple "do's" and "don'ts" that are unimportant.

Decker Walker notes that theory should provide a framework with which to conceptualize and clarify important problems and techniques. He states, however, that "curriculum theories . . . that are correct and complete to serve as . . . a basis for practical decisions do not exist." Educators, including curricularists, tend to embrace "theory as an ideology," even though much of what they say is based on their philosophical or social lens and closes us to "other aspects of reality and other values."[74]

Most curriculum texts are more theoretical than practical, but so are education textbooks in general. Despite their claims, curricuralists seem unable to make the leap from theory to practice, from the textbook and college course to the classroom and school (or other organizations). Good theory in curriculum (and in other fields of education) often gets lost as practitioners (say, teachers) try to apply what they learned in college to the job setting in a search for practical solutions to common everyday problems.

## CURRICULUM TIPS 1.2   Translating Theory into Practice

To progress toward successfully blending curriculum theory and practice, we must recognize certain basic steps:

1. *Read the literature.* Any attempt to merge theory and practice must be based on knowledge of the professional literature.
2. *Identify the major terms.* Curriculum theorists and practitioners must identify and agree on the major constructs, concepts, and questions for discussion.
3. *Check the soundness of existing theories.* Existing theories must be analyzed in terms of their validity, accuracy, assumptions, logic, coherence, generalizability, values, and biases.
4. *Avoid fads.* Fads and "hot topics" must not be introduced to practitioners under the guise of a new theory, reform, or innovation. When a professional publication or conference introduces a new program or method, that program or method should be evaluated before being adopted.
5. *Align theory with practice.* Theory must be considered within the context of classrooms and schools; it must be readily applicable.
6. *Test theory.* If a theory is credible and makes sense, it must be empirically tested by trying it in practice and by measuring the results. A theory should first be applied on a small scale and involve a comparison of experimental and control schools.
7. *Interpret theory.* A theory must be tested in realistic situations. It must be evaluated in schools for at least one year and ideally for three years.
8. *Modify theory; reduce its complexity.* A theory is a generalizable construct supported by language or quantitative data. Nonetheless, theory must be modified from paper to practice, from the abstract to the concrete world, and from complex concepts to lay terms. When we put theory into practice, we involve many people and resources to make it work. Theory must be modified to suit people if it is to move from idea to action.

The problem of translating theory into practice is further aggravated by practitioners who feel that practical considerations are more worthwhile than theory; most teachers and principals view theory as unpractical and "how-to-do" approaches as helpful. In short, many theoreticians ignore the practitioners, and many practitioners ignore the theoreticians. Moreover, many theoretical discussions of curriculum are divorced from practical application in the classroom, and many practical discussions of curriculum rarely consider theoretical relationships.[75]

Practice involves selecting strategies and rules that apply to various situations. Adopting the right method for the appropriate situation is not an easy task and involves a good deal of common sense and experience. Good curriculum practice includes understanding the constraints and specifics operating within the school and comprehending the school's priorities and the needs of the students and staff. Also, successful practitioners can develop, implement, and evaluate the curriculum. They can select and organize (1) goals and objectives; (2) subject matter; (3) methods, materials, and media; and (4) suitable learning experiences and activities and then (5) assess these processes.

In an attempt to blend theory and practice in curriculum, curriculum specialists have relied on teacher-authored articles, teacher-professor research teams, teachers' voices and stories, case studies and scenarios, planning guides, computerized media, blogs, wikis and podcasts. These so-called theoretical and practical features fall short and don't really get to the heart of the problem, because the courses are not tightly integrated with fieldwork or school-based internships. Faculty members often lack knowledge in either theory or practice because of their own professional background and experiences. The result is that most newly hired curriculum workers in schools sink or swim on their own, relying on a mix of experience, personality, common sense, and luck.

In a final analysis, it is up to the curriculum specialist to recognize that the theoretician and practitioner have different agendas and perceptions of what is important. The practitioner does not function as the mere user of the theoretician's or researcher's product, and the theoretician is often interested in knowledge that has little value to practitioners. One role for the curriculum specialist, what some educators call the *reflective practitioner,* is to generate dialogue between the theoretician and practitioner and establish modes of collaboration that can benefit both groups.[76]

## Curriculum Certification

In most states, curriculum lacks certification (specified requirements). This situation increases the difficulty of defining and conceptualizing the field and agreeing on curriculum courses at the level of higher education. The closest thing to certification is an endorsement or license (issued by the state department of education and sometimes by a city school district) as a supervisor or principal. We need people qualified to serve as curriculum generalists and specialists, both as resource agents and decision makers, as well as people who can maintain a balanced curriculum in terms of goals, subject matter, and learning activities when special-interest groups seek to impose their brand of education. Currently, minimum requirements for curriculum personnel vary within and between states, and curriculum programs vary considerably among colleges and universities. Because there are no licensing requirements or state or professional regulations, each school of education usually decides on its own program requirements and the courses it offers to meet these requirements. The result is a proliferation of elective courses in curriculum programs and a lack of specialized and general agreed-on courses. Even when curriculum course titles are similar, wide differences in content and level of instruction are common.

Ironically, the curriculum field is very unclear as to its curriculum. Although there are many curriculum programs at the university level, there is little guarantee that people who graduate from such a program will know how to develop, implement, and evaluate a curriculum or know how to translate theory into practice. Some curriculum students (especially those in administration) may not have taken courses in development, implementation, or evaluation. No test or screening device helps school systems or school board officials assess the abilities of curriculum personnel. This also adds to the problem of defining the roles and responsibilities of curriculum specialists and generalists.

Professionals are certified in such fields as teaching, counseling, school psychology, supervision, and administration. Job descriptions and related course requirements are defined. In contrast, curriculum jobs are not well defined, and there are few certification requirements or licenses. Curriculum positions are available in schools, universities, and local, regional, state, and federal education agencies, but without certification, people other than curriculum experts can obtain those positions—in some cases having been exposed to only one or two curriculum courses.

Many curriculum specialists who work in schools are certified in other fields. Similarly, most professors of curriculum have never been required to meet any state or national standards or pass any certification tests with regard to curriculum.

The lack of certification weakens curricularists' role in the schools and their influence at the university level. In still other cases, school principals who are expected to be curriculum leaders may not have had more than one or two curriculum courses at the university level because their certification requirements often limit such courses to one or two. It also encourages local and state policy makers and legislators to develop and design the school curriculum; these non-experts impose standards and approve programs in terms of goals, content, and subject matter. This is especially true in large states such as California, Florida, Illinois, New York, and Texas, where pressure groups often influence standards, programs, and textbook adoptions. Because the field lacks professional certification, the responsibilities of curriculum leaders are vague and diffuse, and a strong and organized constituency is lacking at the K-12 school and university levels.

Although there are hundreds of educational leadership programs across the country, it is difficult to a know just how many reflect a strong curriculum focus or whether they incorporate the latest research findings. First, there is little relationship between university preparation programs, leadership certification and license requirements. Most states have ineffectual accreditation requirements—"making it easy for weak programs to produce hundreds . . . and thousands of underprepared candidates for school leadership [and curriculum] positions." Programs are usually evaluated according to "the number of graduates who pass certification exams," and not on the features of the program or whether the candidates who take positions are competent.[77]

Of the top 500 or more leadership programs across the country, many have become mills—concerned mainly with student enrollments and revenues. Academic integrity and admissions requirements have been ignored or watered down, and continuous evaluation and improvement of the programs are missing ingredients.

It would behoove the field's professional organizations (e.g., the Association for Supervision and Curriculum Development), leading curriculum journals (e.g., the *Journal of Curriculum Studies* and the *Journal of Curriculum and Supervision*), leading curriculum professors (e.g., the "100 Professors of Curriculum" at AERA), and practitioners at the central school districts and state departments of education who develop curriculum to pressure local and state agencies to formulate curriculum policy and certification.

## THE ROLES OF THE CURRICULUM WORKER

Much has been written about the curriculum worker's roles and responsibilities. The term *curriculum worker* (used interchangeably with *curriculum supervisor, curriculum leader, curriculum coordinator,* and *curriculum specialist*) encompasses various educators, from teachers to superintendents. Anyone involved in curriculum development, implementation, or evaluation is a curriculum worker. A *curriculum supervisor*—usually a chairperson, assistant principal, or principal—generally works at the school level. A *curriculum leader* can be a supervisor or administrator: a chairperson, principal, or director or associate superintendent of curriculum. A *curriculum coordinator* usually heads a program at the school-district, regional, or state level; the program may be a special government-funded program or a traditional subject-area program such as a math or English program. A *curriculum specialist* is a technical consultant from the district level, a regional or state department of education, or a university. A curriculum specialist provides advice or in-service assistance, sometimes in the classroom but usually at meetings, conferences, or staff sessions. Most of these terms, as well as the related responsibilities and functions, depend on the philosophy and organization of the school district (or state education agency) and the administration's personal preferences and views. The terms are also rooted in the ASCD's original mission and practice, when it emphasized curriculum and supervision, as opposed to today's emphasis on curriculum, teaching, and learning.

There is further confusion regarding whether curriculum planning or development takes place at the local, state, or national level. In the past, emphasis on curriculum development was at the school or school-district level. Since the mid-1980s, the school-reform movement has shifted some curriculum responsibilities to the state level, and there is serious talk of movement to the national level. The state and national testing and standards movement that began in the 1990s and accelerated in the 21st century encourages this reform notion of curriculum. (Most other nations have a national ministry of education with major curriculum responsibilities.)

In the past, curriculum roles were defined at the local level, and decisions to groom curriculum leaders were made at the subject chair's and principal's level. Most school districts depend on teachers and supervisors to develop curriculum (usually without pay, unless they meet in the summer). Also, parents are included in many curriculum committees at the school level. Staff limitations make it unlikely that the central office of the school district will provide curriculum specialists, especially specialists who aren't burdened with other responsibilities. Only large school districts can afford to have a curriculum department with a full staff of specialists. In such school districts, most curriculum development takes place at the district level; teachers often complain that their professional input is minimal, consisting of nothing more than implementing predetermined and prepackaged materials from the district office.

## The Curriculum Worker's Responsibilities

What are a curriculum worker's responsibilities? Assigned responsibilities within the school structure are important, but they are unclear because different people (teachers, supervisors, principals, district personnel, and others) are usually expected to serve as curriculum workers. Each position holder has different professional responsibilities, needs, and expectations and must make adjustments. For example, teachers must, of course, provide instruction, and principals must manage a school and assist teachers.

The teacher works with supervisors and administrators as part of the curriculum team. Early identification of teachers who can serve as curriculum workers is essential for the teacher's growth and the school's (and school district's) vitality. The following clarifies the responsibilities of curriculum workers:

1. Develop *technical methods* and tools to carry out curriculum planning in the school (school district or state agency).
2. Blend *theory* building with *practice;* obtain curriculum knowledge and apply it in the real world of classrooms and schools.
3. Agree on what is involved in curriculum *development* and *design,* including the relationships among the curriculum's elements.
4. Agree on the relationships among *curriculum, instruction,* and *supervision,* including their interdependencies.
5. Be a *change agent* who considers schools within the context of society. Balance the demands and views of the local community with state and national goals and interests.
6. Create a *mission or goal statement* to provide direction and focus behavior within the organization.
7. Be open to new *curriculum trends* and thoughts. Examine various proposals and suggest modifications. Do not fall victim to fads or particular pressure groups.

8. Confer with parental, community, and professional groups. Develop skills in human relations and in *working with individuals and groups.*

9. Encourage colleagues and other professionals to *solve professional problems.* Innovate; become familiar with and use new programs and ideas.

10. Develop a program for continuous *curriculum development, implementation,* and *evaluation.*

11. Balance different *subject areas and grade levels,* and integrate them into the total curriculum. Pay close attention to scope and sequence by subject and grade level.

12. Understand current *research in teaching and learning,* as well as new programs relevant to target students.

### The Student's Role

Student involvement in curriculum planning can be traced to the ideas of Kilpatrick and Rugg, who were child- and activity-centered in outlining the roles and concepts of curriculum making. Discussed freely in the 1920s and 1930s, the premise of student involvement was to plan themes, units, lesson plans, and school projects that allowed for considerable student input. Dewey, however, downplayed the students' role because he felt students would express interest in certain topics in order to please their teachers. In the final analysis, it was the teacher's responsibility to plan and implement curriculum and to be "aware more than the children themselves of what the children want and need."[78]

Whereas Tyler did not clearly describe the student's role in *Basic Principles of Curriculum and Instruction,* his colleague Taba was clear about student involvement. According to Taba, curriculum making should start with "diagnosing the needs of students."[79] She considered curriculum "as a plan for learning." Therefore, knowledge of the students and their potential contributions had a "bearing on shaping [the] curriculum." Because learning was developmental, the curriculum should proceed "only after some information is obtained regarding . . . ideas, forms of thought, feelings, habits and skills of students."[80]

More recently, Doll has spoken of student involvement in curriculum planning related to students' rights and the fact that students are the program's recipients. Students should be consulted at least "informally in classroom and school activities [since they] offer important clues about actions to be taken."[81] Peter Oliva feels students should participate in curriculum development, subject to "a number of variables such as intelligence, motivation and knowledge" and, most importantly, their "maturity." He distinguishes between input from high school students and younger students.[82]

The authors' view is that students are neither experts nor professionals, so their role in curriculum planning should be limited to providing information. Teachers who encourage student or parental input in curriculum planning run the risk of reducing their influence and getting bogged down on tangental subjects.

### The Teacher and the Curriculum

Although Doll views the curriculum expert primarily as a subject chair or principal, he is concerned with the teacher's role in planning and implementing the curriculum at the classroom, school, and district levels. In his opinion, the teacher should be involved "in every phase" of curriculum making, including the planning of "specific goals, . . . materials, content, and methods." Teachers should have a curriculum "coordinating body" to unify their work and develop "relationships with supervisors [and] other teachers" involved in curriculum.[83]

Oliva has a broader view of the teacher's role. For him, teachers are the "primary group in curriculum development." They constitute the "majority or the totality of the membership of curriculum committees and councils." Their role is to develop, implement, and evaluate curriculum. In his words, teachers work in committees and "initiate proposals, . . . review proposals, gather data, conduct research, make contact with parents and other lay people, write and create curriculum materials, . . . obtain feedback from learners, and evaluate programs."[84]

Doll's and Oliva's views suggest a *bottom-up* approach to curriculum, in which the teacher plays a major role. Taba popularized the bottom-up view in her classic text on curriculum development.[85] Rugg introduced the view that teachers must be released from classroom duties to "prepare courses of study, and assemble materials, and develop outlines of the entire curriculum." Later, Caswell and Campbell envisioned teachers participating in curriculum committees at the school, district, and state levels during summers and sometimes to fulfill special assignments during the school year.[86]

Carl Glickman takes a broad view of teacher involvement in curriculum. He considers three levels. In level 1, the teachers' role is *maintenance,* whereby they rely on prescribed textbooks, workbooks, and printed materials. Teachers at level 2 are *meditative,* and curriculum planning is confined to refining or modifying the agreed-on content. In level 3, what he refers to as a *creative* or *generative* stage, the curriculum is examined at the departmental or school level; the content is changed regularly, teachers are considered to be professionals, and they have greater responsibility for curriculum decisions.[87]

James Beane advocates a lesser role for the teacher. Although teachers may emerge as curriculum leaders, the "major responsibility of administrative and supervisory personnel should be to provide leadership and assistance in curriculum development and implementation." Other aspects of curriculum work, such as "budget development, grant writing, and interaction with school boards," should be carried out by supervisors and administrators "in such a way as to facilitate curriculum planning." Nonetheless, the school district has the ultimate responsibility to employ support personnel who have skill in curriculum planning, and such personnel may include "teachers, school officials, and citizens."[88]

Glatthorn is even more top-down. He makes little provision for teacher input, and discusses the role of "coordinators" at the district level and that of principals, assistant principals, and chairs at the school level. He envisions a "teacher specialist" as a member of a subject or grade-level team only at the elementary school level, and in that case confined mainly to reading and math.[89]

Based on traditional theories of social organization and open systems and our current knowledge of effective schools, we see the teacher's role in curriculum making as central. We see teachers as part of a professional team, working with supervisors, administrators, and other colleagues at the school, district, and state level. In small and medium-size school districts, parents also participate in curriculum committees (although the authors have expressed previous reservation). In our view, the teacher sees the curriculum as a whole and serves as a resource and agent: developing the curriculum in committees, implementing it in classrooms, and evaluating it as part of a technical team. To guarantee curriculum continuity, integration, and unity across subjects and grade levels, teachers must be actively involved in the curriculum. The experienced teacher has a broad and deep understanding of learning, students' needs and interests, and effective content, methods, and materials. The teacher (not the supervisor or administrator) has the best chance of implementing the curriculum at the classroom level. Supervisors and administrators should act as facilitators by lending support, coordinating, and communicating with others in the school. The teacher should play the major role in planning, implementing, and evaluating the curriculum at the local school level.

## The Principal and the Curriculum

Although there is consensus in the literature that the principal should be a leader in curriculum and instruction, there is considerable disagreement regarding the principal's specific roles. Surveyed principals often say that they consider curriculum and instruction top priorities and recognize the need to spend more time on these areas of development.[90]

However, Glatthorn notes that "most experts who have examined school leadership [or the principal's role] have focused unduly on the principal as a leader of instruction, ignoring the role of curriculum leader."[91] Given the national and state standards movement and the need to upgrade the curriculum to meet these standards, school principals' attention has increasingly focused on curriculum, especially on aligning curriculum with state standards and high-stakes tests, which can jeopardize schools' reputations as well as principals' and teachers' jobs.

However, data suggest that teachers do not view curriculum-instructional leadership as a major responsibility of principals, do not see much evidence of such leadership on the part of principals, and are reluctant to accept principals in this leadership capacity.[92] Often, teachers believe that principals are incapable of providing such leadership and don't want their assistance in these technical areas, which teachers consider more appropriate for peer coaching and collegial staff development.[93]

Historically, principals have spent only about 15 to 20 percent of their time coordinating activities in curriculum and instruction (combined)[94] and have spent only 3 to 10 percent of their time observing teachers in the classroom.[95] Principals have contended that dealing with the school's daily operation, especially writing memos, attending meetings, and speaking on the telephone, takes up most of their time.

Thelbert Drake and William Roe, who have been writing about principals since the early 1980s, also note a wide discrepancy between actual and desired amount of time on leadership tasks. Of the 14 most common tasks rated by school principals, curriculum development was considered the second most important. However, on average, principals spent only 7.9 percent of their professional time on curriculum development.[96] Two administrators have listed 74 items principals must attend to in order to begin a school year effectively, none of which deal with curriculum or instruction.[97]

Thus, principals look to assistant principals or chairpersons to meet responsibilities of curriculum, instruction, and program development.[98] Most secondary school principals rely on other staff members (teachers and supervisors) to plan, implement, and evaluate the curriculum. Principals must deal with many problems and issues involving students, teachers, and parents. Curriculum gets pushed to the background.

Although the National Association of Elementary School Principals and the National Association of Secondary School Principals envision the principal as a curriculum and instructional leader—and this theme continually appears in their journals (which principals read)—the realities of a principal's job do not permit a focus on these leadership areas. Principals have the knowledge and experience to know what works in schools. Yet, many principals take notice of curriculum only to the extent that it raises the level of learning in their school or improves test scores.

## Changing Professional Roles: Standards and Testing

As the states have mandated curriculum standards and high-stakes testing, and as the federal government moves toward national assessment, teachers' individual and collective thinking about curriculum content and what is worth teaching and how it should be taught has diminished. Similarly, the role of the principal as a curriculum or instructional leader has been diminished. Critics such as Michael Apple refer to this trend as *deprofessionalism,* and James Popham refers it as *professional impotence.*

In short, the states and federal government are reducing curriculum decision making at the local or school-district level and moving in the direction of indirectly controlling curriculum decisions. When aligned with state standards, high-stakes tests can be used to determine whether teachers and principals are implementing the curriculum. In the states without a mandated curriculum, the teachers wind up teaching toward the test. According to Carl Glickman, "the test itself becomes the curriculum."[99] Curriculum alignment is turned *upside down*. Instead of starting with the curriculum and aligning instruction and assessment with the curriculum, the opposite happens: Teachers (and principals) start with the statewide test and align curriculum and instruction to the test.

In states where curriculum content is recommended or required, usually accompanied by formal and written standards, teachers tend to follow in lockstep; moreover, instructional leaders become "inspectors," or "cops," who observe and evaluate teachers. They ensure teachers are on task and following the recommended or required standards and that students are being taught prescribed content and are being prepared for the high-stakes tests that are being used to evaluate students.

The irony is, according to Popham, teachers and principals know very little—if not next to nothing—about educational testing and measurements because they have not been trained in assessment methods. Given that students' test scores have become significant today, educators "who choose to remain unaware of assessments' key concepts [and techniques] are being dangerously naïve" and are inviting "professional suicide."[100] In an era of high-stakes testing, it is essential that educators involved in curriculum, teaching, and supervision not necessarily know how to carry out testing and measurement procedures, but at least understand and be able to interpret those *concepts* and techniques.

Although the reliability and validity of these tests can be questioned, government and business officials view this criticism as excuses and do not want to hear this discussion. In an age of global competitiveness and accountability, we are told the data systems provide us with knowledge about evaluating student learning and assessing teacher effectiveness. Nevertheless, as professionals, educators must refrain from "gaming" the system: teaching toward the test, "cooking results," and manipulating which students take the exams. Finally, they must defend themselves from being bullied or pressured into unethical behavior because of the consequence of the exams and the fear at possibly losing their jobs.

## Conclusion

We presented different definitions of curriculum, discussed the relationship between curriculum foundations and domains, illustrated how theory and practice interrelate within the field of curriculum, and described the curriculum worker's roles and responsibilities. In effect, we have told readers that they can focus on approaches and definitions, foundations and domains, theory and practice, of curriculum and instruction. No one can fully integrate the field of curriculum. Each individual should consider different definitions, approaches, development and design models, and curriculum roles.

---

### MyEdLeadershipLab™

Go to Topic 1: *Defining Curriculum,* on the MyEdLeadershipLab™ site (www.MyEdLeadershipLab. com) for *Curriculum: Foundations, Principles, and Issues,* Sixth Edition where you can:

- Find learning outcomes for *Defining Curriculum* along with the national standards that connect to these outcomes.
- Complete Assignments and Activities that can help you more deeply understand the chapter content.
- Apply and Practice your understanding of the core skills identified in the chapter with the Building Leadership Skills unit.
- Prepare yourself for professional certification with a Practice for Certification quiz.

---

## Endnotes

1. Allan C. Ornstein, Edward Pajak, and Stacey B. Ornstein, *Contemporary Issues in Curriculum,* 4th ed. (Boston: Allyn & Bacon, 2007); and Jon Wiles, *Curriculum Essentials,* 2nd ed. (Boston: Allyn & Bacon, 2005).

2. Franklin Bobbitt, *The Curriculum* (Boston: Houghton Mifflin, 1918); W. W. Charters, *Curriculum Construction* (New York: Macmillan, 1923); Ralph W. Tyler, *Basic Principles of Curriculum and Instruction* (Chicago: University of Chicago Press, 1949); and Hilda Taba, *Curriculum Development: Theory and Practice* (New York: Harcourt Brace Jovanovich, 1962).

3. William Pinar, "Notes on the Curriculum Field," *Educational Researcher* (September 1978), pp. 5–12; William H. Schubert, *Curriculum Books: The First Eighty Years*

(Lanham, MD: University Press of America, 1980); and James T. Sears and J. Dan Marshall, eds., *Teaching and Thinking about Curriculum* (New York: Teachers College Press, Columbia University, 1990).

4. Raymond Callahan, *Education and the Cult of Efficiency* (Chicago: University of Chicago Press, 1962).

5. Bobbitt, *The Curriculum,* p. 283.

6. Franklin Bobbitt, *How to Make a Curriculum* (Boston: Houghton Mifflin, 1924), pp. 14, 28.

7. Tyler, *Basic Principles of Curriculum and Instruction,* p. 4.

8. Linda Darling-Hammond and Jon Snyder, "Curriculum Studies and the Traditions of Inquiry: The Scientific Tradition," in Philip W. Jackson, ed., *Handbook of Research on Curriculum* (New York: Macmillan Publishing Co., 1992), pp. 41–78; and Thomas Good and Jere E. Brophy, *Looking in Classrooms,* 9th ed. (Boston: Allyn & Bacon, 2003).

9. Andy Hargreaves and Dean Funk, *Sustainable Leadership* (Indianapolis, IN: Jossey-Bass, 2005); Allan C. Ornstein, "The Field of Curriculum: What Approach?" *High School Journal* (April–May 1987), pp. 208–216; and Edward Pajak, "Clinical Supervision and Psychological Functions," *Journal of Curriculum and Supervision* (Spring 2002), pp. 189–205.

10. Michael Fullan, *Leadership and Sustainability* (Thousand Oaks, CA: Corwin Press, 2005); and Dennis Sparks, *Leading for Results,* 2nd ed. (Thousand Oaks, CA: Corwin Press, 2007).

11. Allan C. Ornstein, *Teaching and Schooling in America: Pre and Post September 11* (Boston: Allyn & Bacon, 2003).

12. Leslee J. Bishop, *Staff Development and Instructional Improvement* (Boston: Allyn and Bacon, 1976); Gerald R. Firth and Richard Kimpston, *The Curriculum Continuum in Perspective* (Itasca, IL: Peacock, 1973); Robert S. Gilchrist, *Using Current Curriculum Developments* (Alexandria, VA: Association for Supervision and Curriculum Development, 1963); Arthur J. Lewis and Alice Miel, *Supervision for Improved Instruction* (Belmont, CA: Wadsworth, 1972); John McNeil and William H. Lucio, *Supervision: A Synthesis of Thought and Action,* 2nd ed. (New York: McGraw-Hill, 1969); J. Lloyd Trump and Dorsey Baynham, *Focus on Change* (Chicago: Rand McNally, 1961); and Glenys G. Unruh and William A. Alexander, *Innovations in Secondary Education,* 2nd ed. (New York: Holt, Rinehart and Winston, 1971).

13. Lee G. Bolman and Terrence E. Deal, *Reframing Organizations,* 3rd ed. (Indianapolis, IN: Jossey-Bass, 2003); and Bruce Joyce, Marsha Weil, and Beverly Showers, *Models of Teaching,* 7th ed. (Boston: Allyn and Bacon, 2004).

14. Fred Lunenburg and Allan C. Ornstein, *Educational Administration: Concepts and Practices,* 5th ed. (Belmont, CA: Wadsworth, 2008), p. 323.

15. Leo H. Bradley, *Total Quality Management for Schools* (Lancaster, PA: Technomic, 1993); and William G. Ouchi, *Theory Z: How American Business Can Meet the Japanese Challenge* (New York: Avon Books, 1993).

16. George A. Beauchamp, *Curriculum Theory,* 4th ed. (Itasca, IL: Peacock, 1981).

17. Allan C. Ornstein, "Curriculum, Instruction, and Supervision—Their Relationship and the Role of the Principal," *NASSP Bulletin* (April 1986), pp. 74–81. See also Michael Fullan, Peter Hill, and Carmel Crevola, *Breakthrough* (Thousand Oaks, CA: Corwin Press, 2006); and Thomas J. Sergiovanni, *Rethinking Leadership,* 2nd ed. (Thousand Oaks, CA: Corwin Press, 2006).

18. John Dewey, *Democracy and Education* (New York: Macmillan, 1916); Henry C. Morrison, *The Practice of Teaching in the Secondary School* (Chicago: University of Chicago Press, 1926); and Boyd H. Bode, *Modern Educational Theories* (New York: Macmillan, 1927).

19. William H. Schubert, *Curriculum: Perspective, Paradigm and Possibility* (New York: Macmillan, 1986); Daniel Tanner and Laurel N. Tanner, *Curriculum Development: Theory into Practice,* 2nd ed. (New York: Macmillan, 1980); and Robert S. Zais, *Curriculum: Principles and Foundations* (New York: Harper & Row, 1976).

20. William H. Schubert et al., "A Genealogy of Curriculum Researchers," *Journal of Curriculum Theorizing* (Vol. 8, 1988), pp. 137–183; and James T. Sears and J. Dan Marshall, "Generational Influences on Contemporary Curriculum Thought," *Journal of Curriculum Studies* (March–April 2000), pp. 199–214.

21. William F. Pinar, William M. Reynolds, Patrick Slattery, and Peter M. Taubman, *Understanding Curriculum* (New York: Peter Lang, 1995); and William Pinar, *Contemporary Curriculum Discourses* (New York: Peter Lang, 1999).

22. Maxine Greene, "Imagining Futures: The Public School and Possibility," *Journal of Curriculum Studies* (March–April 2000), pp. 267–280; William A. Reid, "Rethinking Schwab: Curriculum Theorizing as Visionary Activity," *Journal of Curriculum and Supervision* (Fall 2001), pp. 29–41; and Pinar, *Contemporary Curriculum Discourses.*

23. John Dewey, *The Child and the Curriculum* (Chicago: University of Chicago Press, 1902); Charles Judd, *The Evolution of a Democratic School System* (Boston: Houghton Mifflin, 1918); and Francis W. Parker, *Talks on Pedagogics* (New York: Kellogg, 1894).

24. Boyd Bode, *Progressive Education at the Crossroads* (New York: Newson, 1938); Frederick G. Bosner, *The Elementary School Curriculum* (New York: Macmillan, 1920); Hollis L. Caswell, *Program Making in Small Elementary Schools* (Nashville, TN: George Peabody College for Teachers, 1932); L. Thomas Hopkins and James E. Mendenhall, *Achievement at the Lincoln School* (New York: Teachers College Press, Columbia University, 1934); William H. Kilpatrick, *Foundations of Method* (New York: Macmillan, 1925); and Harold Rugg and Ann Shumaker, *The Child-Centered School* (New York: World Books, 1928).

25. Michael Fullan, *The Moral Imperative of School Leadership* (Thousand Oaks, CA: Corwin Press, 2003); and Robert D. Ramsey, *Lifelong Leadership by Design* (Thousand Oaks, CA: Corwin Press, 2009).

26. Elliot W. Eisner, *The Kind of Schools We Need* (Portsmouth, NH: Heinemann, 1998).

27. Pinar et al., *Understanding Curriculum.*

28. Richard F. Elmore, *School Reform from the Inside Out* (Cambridge, MA: Harvard Education Press, 2004); Michael Fullan, *What's Worth Fighting For in the Principalship,* 2nd ed. (New York: Teachers College Press, Columbia University, 2008).

29. Daniel L. Duke, *The Challenges of School District Leadership* (New York: Routledge, 2010); Milbrey M. McLaughlin and Joan E. Talbot, *Building School-Based Teacher Learning Communities* (New York: Teachers College Press, 2006); and Allan Ornstein*, Class Counts: Education, Inequality and the Shrinking Middle Class* (Lanham, MD: Rowman & Littlefield, 2007).

30. George S. Counts, *Dare the School Build a New Social Order?* (New York: John Day, 1932); Harold O. Rugg, ed., *Democracy and the Curriculum* (New York: Appleton-Century, 1939); Harold O. Rugg et al., *American Life and the School Curriculum* (Boston: Ginn, 1936); and Harold Benjamin, *The Saber-Tooth Curriculum* (New York: McGraw-Hill, 1939).

31. J. Gaylen Saylor, William M. Alexander, and Arthur J. Lewis, *Curriculum Planning for Better Teaching and Learning,* 4th ed. (New York: Holt, Rinehart and Winston, 1981), p. 10.

32. David Pratt, *Curriculum Design and Development* (New York: Harcourt Brace, 1980), p. 4.

33. Jon Wiles and Joseph Bondi, *Curriculum Development: A Guide to Practice,* 8th ed. (Boston: Pearson, 2011), p. 142.

34. John Dewey, *Experience and Education* (New York: Macmillan, 1938); and Hollis L. Caswell and Doak S. Campbell, *Curriculum Development* (New York: American Book Company, 1935), p. 69.

35. William B. Ragan and Gene D. Shepherd, *Modern Elementary Curriculum,* 4th ed. (New York: Holt, Rinehart and Winston, 1971), pp. 3–4.

36. Elliot W. Eisner, *The Educational Imagination,* 3rd ed. (Columbus, OH: Merrill, 2002), p. 26.

37. Colin J. Marsh and George Willis, *Curriculum: Alternative Approaches, Ongoing Issues,* 3rd ed. (Columbus, OH: Merrill, 2003), p. 4.

38. David G. Armstrong, *Curriculum Today* (Columbus, OH: Merrill, 2003); Ronald C. Doll, *Curriculum Improvement: Decision Making and Process,* 9th ed. (Boston: Allyn & Bacon, 1996); and Peter F. Oliva, *Developing the Curriculum,* 7th ed. (Boston: Pearson, 2009).

39. William A. Reid, *Curriculum as Institution and Practice* (Mahwah, NJ: Erlbaum, 1999); Schubert, *Curriculum: Perspective, Paradigm and Possibility;* and Tanner and Tanner, *Curriculum Development: Theory into Practice.*

40. Arthur W. Applebee, *Curriculum as Conservation* (Chicago: University of Chicago Press, 1996); and Ian Westbury et al., *Teaching as a Reflective Practice* (Mahwah, NJ: Erlbaum, 2000).

41. Doll, *Curriculum Improvement: Decision Making and Process,* p. 5. See also Carol Ann Tomlinson et al., *The Parallel Curriculum* (Thousand Oaks, CA: Corwin Press, 2008).

42. Eisner, *The Educational Imagination.*

43. Larry Cuban, *Hugging the Middle: How Teachers Teach in an Era of Testing and Accountability* (New York: Teacher's College Press, Columbia University, 2008); Alfie Kohn, *The Schools Our Children Deserve* (Boston: Houghton Mifflen, 1999).

44. Beauchamp, *Curriculum Theory,* p. 81.

45. Harold Rugg, "Introduction," in G. M. Whipple, ed., *The Foundations of Curriculum Making,* Twenty-sixth Yearbook of the National Society fo the Study of Education, Part II (Bloomington, IL: Public School Publishing, 1930), p. 8.

46. Tyler, *Basic Principles of Curriculum and Instruction;* Saylor, Alexander, and Lewis, *Curriculum Planning for Better Teaching and Learning;* and Schubert, *Curriculum: Perspective, Paradigm, and Possibility.* See also Elliot W. Eisner, "Those Who Ignore the Past," *Journal of Curriculum Studies* (March–April 2000), pp. 343–357.

47. Carmen L. Rosales-Dordelly and Edmund C. Short, *Curriculum Professors' Specialized Knowledge* (New York: Lanham, 1985), p. 23.

48. Oliva, *Developing the Curriculum,* p. 15.

49. Joseph J. Schwab, "The Practical: A Language of Curriculum," *School Review* (November 1969), p. 1.

50. Herbert Kliebard, "Curriculum Theory as Metaphor," *Theory into Practice* (Winter 1982), pp. 11–17; and Herbert Kliebard, "Problems of Definition of Curriculum," *Journal of Curriculum and Supervision* (Fall 1989), pp. 1–5.

51. William M. Reynolds, "Comprehensiveness and Multidimensionality in Synoptic Curriculum Texts,"*Journal of Curriculum and Supervision* (Winter 1990), pp. 189–193; and Sears and Marshall, "Generational Influences on Contemporary Curriculum Thought."

52. Beauchamp, *Curriculum Theory.*

53. Fenwick W. English, "Contemporary Curriculum Circumstances," in F. W. English, ed., *Fundamental Curriculum Decisions* (Alexandria, VA: Association for Supervision and Curriculum Development, 1983), pp. 1–17.

54. Edmund C. Short, "Curriculum Decision Making in Teacher Education," *Journal of Teacher Education* (July–August 1987), pp. 2–12; Edmund C. Short, "Organizing What We Know about Curriculum," unpublished paper, 1984.

55. Linda Behar, "A Study of Domains and Subsystems in the Most Influential Textbooks in the Field of Curriculum 1970–1990," unpublished doctoral dissertation. Loyola University of Chicago, 1992.

56. Allan A. Glatthorn and Jerry M. Jailall, *The Principal as Curriculum Leader,* 3rd ed. (Thousand Oaks, CA: Corwin Press, 2008).

57. Glatthorn and Jailall, *The Principal as Curriculum Leader;* David A. Squires, *Aligning and Balancing the Standards-Based Curriculum,* 3rd ed. (Thousand Oaks, CA: Corwin Press, 2008).

58. William E. Doll, *A Post-Modern Perspective on Curriculum* (New York: Teachers College Press, Columbia University, 1993); Marsh and Willis, *Curriculum: Alternative Approaches.*

59. Eisner, *The Educational Imagination.*

60. James A. Beane et al., *Curriculum Planning and Development* (Boston: Allyn & Bacon, 1986); and Marsh and Willis, *Curriculum: Alternative Approaches, Ongoing Issues.*

61. Eisner, *The Educational Imagination.*

62. Alfie Kohn, "Fighting the Tests: A Practical Guide to Rescuing Our Schools," *Phi Delta Kappan* (January 2001), pp. 348–357.

63. Philip W. Jackson, *Life in Classrooms* (New York: Holt, 1968), p. 32. See also Philip W. Jackson, *The Practice of Teaching* (New York: Teachers College Press, Columbia University, 1986).

64. John Holt, *How Children Fail* (New York: Putnam, 1964). See also John I. Goodlad, *A Place Called School* (New York: McGraw-Hill, 1984); and Peter McLaren, *Life in School,* 5th ed. (Boston: Allyn & Bacon, 2007).

65. Eisner, *The Educational Imagination,* p. 98.

66. William A. Reid, *The Pursuit of Curriculum* (Norwood, NJ: Ablex, 1992).

67. Klaus Krippendorff, *Content Analysis: An Introduction to Its Methodology* (Beverly Hills, CA: Sage, 1980).

68. John Dewey, *Democracy and Education* (New York: Macmillan, 1916); Boyd H. Bode, *Modern Educational Theories* (New York: Macmillan, 1927).

69. Beauchamp, *Curriculum Theory,* p. 58.

70. Taba, *Curriculum Development: Theory and Practice,* p. 413.

71. Elizabeth Vallance, "Curriculum as a Field of Practice," in F. W. English, ed., *Fundamental Curriculum Decisions* (Alexandria, VA: Association for Supervision and Curriculum Development, 1983), p. 155.

72. John F. Miller and Wayne Seller, *Curriculum: Perspectives and Practice* (New York: Longman, 1985); Tanner and Tanner, *Curriculum Development: Theory into Practice;* and Wiles and Bondi, *Curriculum Development: A Guide to Practice.*

73. Doll, *Curriculum Improvement: Decision Making and Process;* and Oliva, *Developing the Curriculum.*

74. Decker Walker, *Fundamentals of Curriculum* (New York: Harcourt Brace, 1990), p. 200.

75. Andy Hargreaves and Shawn Moore, "Curriculum Integration and Classroom Relevance: A Study of Teacher Practice," *Journal of Curriculum and Supervision* (Winter 2000), pp. 89–112; and Allan C. Ornstein and Francis P. Hunkins, "Theorizing about Curriculum Theory," *High School Journal* (December–January 1989), pp. 77–82.

76. Reba N. Page, "Common Sense: A Form of Teacher Knowledge," *Journal of Curriculum Studies* (September–October 2001), pp. 525–533; and Diane Y. Silva, "Collaborative Curriculum Encounters," *Journal of Curriculum and Supervision* (Summer 2000), pp. 279–299.

77. Michelle D. Young, "Why Not Use Research to Inform Leadership Certification and Program Approval," *UCEA Review,* Summer 2010, p. 5.

78. John Dewey, "Comments and Criticisms by Some Educational Leaders in Our Universities," in G. M. Whipple and L. C. Mossman, eds., *The Activity Movement,* Thirty-third Yearbook of the National Society for the Study of Education, Part II (Bloomington, IL: Public School Publishing, 1934), p. 85.

79. Hilda Taba, *Curriculum Development* (New York: Harcourt, 1962), p. 12.

80. Ibid., pp. 12–13

81. Doll, *Curriculum Improvement: Decision Making and Process,* p. 25.

82. Oliva, *Developing the Curriculum,* p. 91.

83. Doll, *Curriculum Improvement: Decision Making and Process,* p. 334.

84. Oliva, *Developing the Curriculum,* p. 120.

85. Taba, *Curriculum Development: Theory and Practice.*

86. Caswell and Campbell, *Curriculum Development;* and Harold Rugg, "The Foundations of Curriculum Making," in G. Whipple, ed., *The Foundations of Curriculum Making,* Twenty-sixth Yearbook of the National Society for the Study of Education, Part II (Bloomington, IL: Public School Publishers, 1930), pp. 439–440.

87. Carl Glickman et al., *Supervision and Instructional Leadership,* 8th ed. (Boston: Allyn & Bacon, 2010).

88. James A. Beane, Conrad F. Toepfer, and Samuel J. Alessi, *Curriculum Planning and Development* (Boston: Allyn & Bacon, 1986), pp. 355, 358.

89. Allan A. Glatthorn, *Curriculum Leadership* (Glenview, IL: Scott Foresman, 1987), pp. 148–149.

90. Jo Blasé, Joseph Blasé, and Peggy Kirby, *Bringing Out the Best in Teachers: What Effective Principals Do* (Thousand Oaks, CA: Corwin Press, 2008); Gordon A. Donaldson, *Cultivating Leadership in Schools,* 2nd ed. (New York: Teachers College Press, Columbia University, 2006); and Theodore Kowalski, *The School Principal* (New York: Routledge, 2010).

91. Glatthorn and Jailall, *The Principal as Curriculum Leader,* p. 24.

92. Michael Fullan, *Leading in a Culture of Change* (San Francisco: Jossey-Bass, 2001); and Kenneth A. Strike, *Ethical Leadership in Schools* (Thousand Oaks, CA: Corwin Press, 2007).

93. Dale L. Brubaker, *Revitalizing Curriculum Leadership,* 2nd ed. (Thousand Oaks, CA: Corwin Press, 2004); Thomas Hatch, *Managing to Change* (New York: Teachers College Press, Columbia University, 2009), Elizabeth A. Hebert, *The Boss of the Whole School* (New York: Teachers College Press, Columbia University, 2006); and Adrian Rogers and Deborah Bainer Jenkins, *Redesigning Supervision* (New York: Teachers College Press, Columbia University, 2010).

94. William L. Boyd, "What School Administrations Do and Don't Do," *Canadian Administrators* (April 1983), pp. 1–4; and James T. Scarnati, "Beyond Technical Competence: Nine Rules for Administrators," *NASSP Bulletin* (April 1994), pp. 76–83.

95. Daniel Duke, *School Leadership and Instructional Improvement* (New York: Random House, 1987); Forest W. Parkay, Eric J. Anxril, and Glen Hass, *Curriculum Planning: A Contemporary Approach,* 9th ed. (Boston: Allyn & Bacon, 2010).

96. Thelbert L. Drake and William H. Roe, *The Principalship,* 6th ed. (Columbus, OH: Merrill, 2003).

97. Beverly Findley and Dale Findley, "Gearing Up for the Opening of the School Year: A Check List for Principals," *NASSP Bulletin* (September 1998), pp. 57–62.

98. Boyd, "What School Administrators Do and Don't Do"; and Ernestine Riggs and Ana G. Serafin, "The Principal as Instructional Leader," *NASSP Bulletin* (November 1998), pp. 78–85. See also Thomas J. Servioanni, *The Principalship: A Reflective Practice Perspective,* 6th ed. (Boston: Allyn & Bacon, 2009).

99. Glickman et al. *Supervision and Instructional Leadership,* p. 360.

100. W. James Popham, "Assessment Illiteracy: Professional Suicide," *UCEA Review*, Summer 2010, p. 1.

# 2

■ ■ ■

# Philosophical Foundations of Curriculum

## FOCUSING QUESTIONS

1. How does philosophy influence curriculum workers?
2. In what way is philosophy the main curriculum source?
3. In terms of knowledge and values, what are the differences among idealism, realism, pragmatism, and existentialism?
4. In terms of content and methods, what are the differences among perennialism, essentialism, progressivism, and reconstructionism?
5. Can schools promote equality and excellence at the same time? Why or why not?
6. In what ways are reconstructionists both realistic and idealistic? Mainstream and radical?
7. Which philosophical orientation is likely to most influence the curriculum field in the future? Why do you think this is so?
8. Which philosophical orientation appears most contrary to mainstream education?

Philosophy is central to curriculum. The philosophy of a particular school and its officials influences the goals, content, and organization of its curriculum. Usually, a school reflects several philosophies. This diversity enhances the curriculum's dynamics. Studying philosophy allows us not only to better understand schools and their curricula, but also to deal with our own personal beliefs and values.

Philosophical issues have always had an impact on schools and society. Contemporary society and its schools are rapidly changing. The special need for continuous reappraisal calls for a philosophy of education. As William Van Til puts it, "Our source of direction is found in our guiding philosophy. . . . Without philosophy, [we make] mindless vaults into the saddle" and we have a tendency to "ride madly off in all directions."[1] To a large extent, our philosophy of education determines our educational decisions, choices, and alternatives.

Philosophy deals with the larger aspects of life and the way we organize our thoughts and interpret facts. It is an effort to understand life—its problems and issues in full perspective. It involves questions and our own point of view as well as the views of others; it involves searching for defined values and clarifying our beliefs.

## PHILOSOPHY AND CURRICULUM

Philosophy provides educators, especially curriculum workers, with a framework or frameworks for organizing schools and classrooms. It helps them determine what schools are for, what subjects have value, how students learn, and what methods and materials to use. It clarifies education's goals, suitable content, teaching and learning processes, and the experiences and activities that schools should emphasize. Philosophy also provides a basis for deciding which textbooks to use, how to use them, and how much homework to assign, how to test students and use the test results, and what courses or subject matter to emphasize.

L. Thomas Hopkins writes the following:

> Philosophy has entered into every important decision that has ever been made about curriculum and teaching in the past and will continue to be the basis of every important decision in the future.
>
> When a state office of education suggests a pupil-teacher time schedule, this is based upon philosophy, either hidden or consciously formulated. When a course of study is prepared in advance in a school system by a selected group of teachers, this represents philosophy because a course of action was selected from many choices involving different values. When high school teachers assign to pupils more homework for an evening than any one of them could possibly do satisfactorily in six hours, they are acting on philosophy although they are certainly not aware of its effects. When a teacher in an elementary school tells a child to put away his geography and study his arithmetic, she is acting on philosophy for she has made a choice of values. . . . When teachers shift subject matter from one grade to another, they act on philosophy. When measurement experts interpret their test results to a group of teachers, they act upon philosophy, for the facts have meaning only within some basic assumptions. There is rarely a moment in a school day when a teacher is not confronted with occasions where philosophy is a vital part of action. An inventory of situations where philosophy was not used in curriculum and teaching would lead to a pile of chaff thrown out of educative experiences.[2]

Hopkin's statement reminds us how important philosophy is to all aspects of curriculum making, whether we know that it is operating or not. Indeed, almost all elements of curriculum are based on a philosophy. As John Goodlad points out, philosophy is the beginning point in curriculum decision making and the basis for all subsequent decisions. Philosophy becomes the criterion for determining the aims, means, and ends of curriculum.[3] It is crucial for nearly all decisions regarding teaching and learning.

### Philosophy and the Curriculum Worker

Our philosophy reflects our background and experiences. Our decisions are based on our worldview, attitudes, and beliefs. Philosophy guides action.

No one can be totally objective, but curriculum workers can broaden their knowledge and understanding by considering problems from various perspectives. Someone who rigidly adheres to a particular personal philosophy may come into conflict with others. Ronald Doll notes, "Conflict among curriculum planners occurs when persons . . . hold [different] positions along a continuum of beliefs and . . . persuasions." The conflict may become so intense that "curriculum study grinds to a halt." Usually, the differences can be reconciled "temporarily in deference to the demands of a temporary, immediate task. However, teachers and administrators who are clearly divided in philosophy can seldom work together in close proximity for long periods of time."[4]

At the same time, curriculum workers who lack a coherent philosophy can easily lack clarity and direction. A measure of positive conviction is essential for prudent action. Ideally, curriculum workers have a personal philosophy that can be modified. They base their conclusions on the best evidence available, and they can change when better evidence surfaces. Indeed, mature people are more capable of examining their philosophy and appreciate other points of view, especially when facts or trends challenge their original beliefs and values.

## Philosophy as a Curriculum Source

Philosophy's function can be conceived as either (1) the starting point in curriculum development or (2) a function interdependent with other functions in curriculum development. John Dewey represents the first school of thought. He contended that "philosophy may . . . be defined as the general theory of education" and that "the business of philosophy is to provide" the framework for schools' "aims and methods." For Dewey, philosophy is a way of thinking that gives meaning to our lives.[5] It is not only a starting percentage for schools, it is also crucial for all curriculum activities. "Education is the laboratory in which philosophic distinctions become concrete and are tested."[6]

In Ralph Tyler's curriculum framework, philosophy is commonly one of five criteria used in selecting "educational purposes." The relationships between philosophy and the other criteria—studies of learners, studies of contemporary life, suggestions from subject specialists, and the psychology of learning—are shown in Figure 2.1. Influenced by Dewey, Tyler seems to place more importance on philosophy than on other criteria for developing educational purposes. He writes, "The educational and social philosophy to which the school is committed can serve as the first screen for developing the social program." He concludes that "philosophy attempts to define the nature of the good life and a good society" and that the educational philosophies in a democratic society are likely "to emphasize strongly democratic values in schools."[7]

For Goodlad, we must agree on the nature and purpose of education before we can pursue curriculum's philosophy, aims, and goals. According to Goodlad, the school's first responsibility is to the social order (which he calls the *nation–state*), but our society emphasizes individual growth.[8] Society versus the individual has been a major philosophical issue in Western society for centuries and was also important in Dewey's works. As Dewey stated, we wish "to make [good] citizens and workers" but also want "to make human beings who will live life to the fullest." American Education, in this century, can be viewed as a process that fosters both the growth of individuals and a good society. For Dewey and Goodlad, education is growth—and the meaning that growth has for the individual and society; it is a never-ending process, and the richer the child's growth, the better the quality of the educational process and society in general.

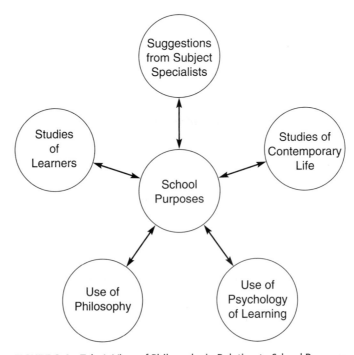

**FIGURE 2.1**   Tyler's View of Philosophy in Relation to School Purposes

## MAJOR PHILOSOPHIES

Four major philosophies have influenced U.S. education: idealism, realism, pragmatism, and existentialism. The first two philosophies are traditional; the last two are contemporary.

### Idealism

Plato is often credited with formulating *idealist* philosophy, one of the oldest that exists. The German philosopher Hegel presented a comprehensive view of the historical world based on idealism. In the United States, transcendentalist philosophers Ralph Waldo Emerson and Henry Thoreau outlined an idealist conception of reality. In education, Fredrich Froebel, the founder of kindergarten, was a proponent of idealist pedagogy. William Harris, who popularized the kindergarten movement when he was superintendent of schools in St. Louis, Missouri, and who became U.S. Commissioner of Education at the turn of the 20th century, used idealism as a source for his administrative philosophy. To most educators, idealism's leading U.S. proponent is J. Donald Butler. To the authors, however, a better known person is William Bennett, a strong believer in values and virtues.[9]

Heavily influenced by Plato and Augustine, U.S. idealists agree that the highest aim is the search for truth and enduring values. As expressed in Plato's *Republic* and later Christian doctrine, Plato believed that ideas could be integrated into universal concepts and a meaningful whole. Truth can be found through reasoning, intuition, and religious revelation.[10] Some idealists, such as Kant, believe it is possible to achieve moral clarification but not possible to arrive at absolute or universal truths. Perhaps the most influential idealist, Hegel thought that one could progress toward truth by continually synthesizing thesis and antithesis, thereby arriving at ever-higher levels of understanding.

To idealists, learning is a primarily intellectual process that involves recalling and working with ideas; education is properly concerned with conceptual matters. The idealist educator prefers a curriculum that relates ideas and concepts to one another. The curriculum is hierarchical; it constitutes humankind's cultural heritage and is based on learned disciplines, as exemplified by the liberal arts curriculum. At the top of the hierarchy are the most abstract subjects: philosophy and theology. Mathematics, too, is important because it cultivates abstract thinking. History and literature rank high because they offer moral and cultural models. Language is also important because it enables communication and conceptual thought. Lower on the curricular ladder are the sciences, which deal with particular cause-and-effect relationships.

### Realism

Aristotle is often linked to the development of *realism,* another traditional school of thought. Thomas Aquinas's philosophy, which combined realism with Christian doctrine, developed an offshoot of realism called *Thomism,* in which much of contemporary Catholic education is rooted. Johann Pestalozzi's instructional principles, which began with concrete objects and ended with abstract concepts, were based on realism. Such modern educators as Harry Broudy and John Wild are leading realists.[11]

Realists view the world in terms of objects and matter. People can come to know the world through their senses and their reason. Everything is derived from nature and is subject to its laws. Human behavior is rational when it conforms to nature's laws and when it is governed by physical and social laws.

Aristotle believed that everything had a purpose and that humans' purpose is to think. In Buddhism, however, true peace is derived not from thinking about something but from thinking about nothing. For Aristotle, and later Aquinas, the universe is ordered; things happen for a purpose and education should illuminate purpose. Aristotle encourages people to live a rational life of moderation, to strive for the "golden mean," a compromise between extremes.

Like idealists, realists stress a curriculum comprising separate content areas, such as history and zoology. Also like idealists, realists rank the most general and abstract subjects at the top of the curricular hierarchy. Lessons that cultivate logic and abstract thought are stressed. The three R's are basic to education.[12] Whereas idealists consider the classics ideal subject matter because they convey enduring moral truths, realists value the sciences as much as the arts.

## Pragmatism

In contrast to the traditional philosophies, *pragmatism* (also referred to as *experimentalism*) is based on change, process, and relativity. Whereas idealism and realism emphasize subject matter, pragmatism construes knowledge as a process in which reality is constantly changing. Learning occurs as the person engages in problem solving, which is transferable to a wide variety of subjects and situations. Both the learner and the learner's environment are constantly changing. Pragmatists reject the idea of unchanging and universal truths. The only guides that people have when they interact with their social world or environment are established generalizations, assertions subject to further research and verification.

To pragmatists, teaching should focus on critical thinking. Teaching is more exploratory than explanatory. The method is more important than the subject matter. The ideal teaching method is concerned not so much with teaching the learner what to think as with teaching the learner to critically think. Questions such as Why? How come? and What if? are much more important than What? Who? or When?

Scientific developments around 1900 fostered pragmatic philosophy. Society increasingly accepted scientific explanations for phenomena. In 1859, Charles Darwin's *The Origin of Species* shook the foundations of the religious, human-centered worldview. Mathematician Charles Peirce and psychologist William James developed the principles of pragmatism, which (1) rejected the dogmas of preconceived truths and eternal values and (2) promoted testing and verifying ideas. Truth no longer was absolute or universal.[13]

The great educational pragmatist was Dewey, who viewed education as a process for improving the human condition. Dewey saw schools as specialized environments within the larger social environment. Ideally, curriculum was based on a child's experiences and interests and prepared the child for life's affairs.[14] The subject matter was interdisciplinary. Dewey emphasized problem solving and the scientific method.

## Existentialism

Whereas pragmatism is mainly a U.S. philosophy that evolved just prior to 1900, *existentialism* is mainly a European philosophy that originated earlier but became popular after World War II. In U.S. education, Maxine Greene, George Kneller, and Van Cleve Morris are well-known existentialists who stress individualism and personal self-fulfillment.[15]

According to existentialist philosophy, people continually make choices and thereby define themselves. We are what we choose to be; in doing so, we make our own essence, or self-identity. Hence, the essence we create is a product of our choices; this varies, of course, among individuals. Existentialists advocate that students be free to choose how and what they study. Critics argue that such free choice would be too unsystematic and laissez-faire, especially at the elementary school level. Existentialists believe that the most important knowledge is knowledge of the human condition. Education should develop consciousness of choices and their significance.[16] Existentialists reject the imposition of group norms, authority, and established order. They recognize few standards, customs, or opinions as indisputable.

Some critics (mainly traditionalists or conservatives) claim that existentialism has limited application to schools because education in our society—and in most other modern societies—involves institutionalized learning and socialization, which require group instruction, restrictions on individuals' behavior, and bureaucratic organization. Schooling is a process that limits students' freedom and is based on adult authority and generally accepted behavior and beliefs. As students, most of us follow rules; as teachers, most of us enforce rules. The individual existentialist, exerting his or her will and choice, will encounter difficulty in school—and other formal organizations.

**Table 2.1**    Overview of Major Philosophies

| Philosophy | Reality | Knowledge | Values | Teacher's Role | Emphasis on Learning | Emphasis on Curriculum |
|---|---|---|---|---|---|---|
| Idealism | Spiritual, moral, or mental; unchanging | Rethinking latent ideas | Absolute and eternal | To bring latent knowledge and ideas to consciousness; to be a moral and spiritual leader | Recalling knowledge and ideas; abstract thinking is the highest form | Knowledge based; subject based; classics or liberal arts; hierarchy of subjects: philosophy, theology, and mathematics are most important |
| Realism | Based on natural laws; objective and composed of matter | Consists of sensation and abstraction | Absolute and eternal; based on nature's laws | To cultivate rational thought; to be a moral and spiritual leader; to be an authority | Exercising the mind; logical and abstract thinking are highest form | Knowledge based; subject based; arts and sciences; hierarchy of subjects: humanistic and scientific subjects |
| Pragmatism | Interaction of individual with environment; always changing | Based on experience; use of scientific method | Situational and relative; subject to change and verification | To cultivate critical thinking and scientific processes | Methods for dealing with changing environment and scientific explanations | No permanent knowledge or subjects; appropriate experiences that transmit culture and prepare individual for change; problem-solving activities |
| Existentialism | Subjective | Knowledge for personal choice | Freely chosen; based on individuals' perception | To cultivate personal choice and individual self-definition | Knowledge and principles of the human condition; acts of choosing | Choices in subject matter, electives; emotional, aesthetic, and philosophical subjects |

An existentialist curriculum consists of experiences and subjects that lend themselves to individual freedom and choice. For example, the arts are stressed because they cultivate self-expression and portray the human condition and situations involving choices. Teachers and students discuss their lives and choices.[17] In particular, literature, drama, filmmaking, music, and art reflect self-expressive activities and illustrate emotions, feelings, and insights—all conducive to existentialist thinking. (See Table 2.1.)

## EDUCATIONAL PHILOSOPHIES

Four agreed-on philosophies of education have emerged: perennialism, essentialism, progressivism, and reconstructionism. Each of these philosophies has roots in one or more of the four major philosophical traditions. For example, perennialism draws heavily on realism, essentialism is rooted in idealism and realism, and progressivism and reconstructionism stem from pragmatism. Some reconstructionism has links to existentialist views.

### Perennialism

*Perennialism,* the oldest and most conservative educational philosophy, is rooted in realism. It dominated much of American education from the colonial period to the early 1990s. At the elementary school level, the curriculum stressed the three R's as well as moral and religious training; at the secondary level, it emphasized such subjects as Latin, Greek, grammar, rhetoric, logic, and geometry.

As a philosophy of education, perennialism relies on the past and stresses traditional values. It emphasizes knowledge that has stood the test of time and cherished values of society. It is a plea for the permanency of knowledge and values that have stood the test of time—an unchanging view of the human nature, truth, and virtue. Robert Hutchins, a long-time advocate of perennialism, has noted that a person's function is "the same in every society. . . . The aim of the educational system is the same in every age and in every society where such a system can exist. That aim is to improve people."[18]

For perennialists, human nature is constant. Humans have the ability to reason and to understand nature's universal truths. The goal of education is to develop the rational person and uncover universal truths by developing students' intellect and moral character.

The perennialist's curriculum is subject centered; it relies heavily on defined disciplines or logically organized bodies of content, emphasizing language, literature, mathematics, and sciences. Teachers are viewed as authorities in their fields. They stimulate discussion and students' rational powers. Teaching is based primarily on the Socratic method: oral exposition, lecture, and explication. Here is one curriculum for all students, with little room for elective subjects or vocational or technical subject matter. Character training is also important as a means of developing the student's moral and spiritual being.

**PERMANENT STUDIES.**   According to perennialists, the liberal arts comprise our intellectual heritage, as exemplified by Robert Hutchins's book series *Great Books of the Western World.* The series covers the foundations of Western thought and its scientific and cultural knowledge. By studying the great ideas of the past, we can better cope with the present and future. Students read and discuss the works of great thinkers and artists such as Plato, Aristotle, and Shakespeare in order to cultivate their intellect. Students are encouraged to learn Latin and Greek so that they can read ancient classics in their original language. In addition to the classics and the study of language, Hutchins urges the study of the three R's, grammar, rhetoric, logic, advanced mathematics, and philosophy.[19] This curriculum treats human nature as rational and knowledge as unchanging. For Hutchins, this type of education is not "specialized," "preprofessional," or "utilitarian." It is broad-based, academic, and "calculated to develop the mind."[20] It is a universal, broad education that prepares the individual to think, to prepare for many jobs, and to deal with life. By studying the great ideas of the past, we can better cope with the future.

**THE PAIDEIA PROPOSAL.**   Mortimer Adler's book *The Paideia Proposal* revived perennialism. Adler advocated three types of learning that improve the intellect: acquisition of *organized knowledge,* to be taught by didactic instruction; development of *basic learning skills* through coaching and presentation of *ideas;* and acquisition of *values,* to be taught by the Socratic method.[21] Further outlined in Table 2.2, these three types of learning are the same that Dewey outlined in *Democracy and Education* (1916) and Ralph Tyler later presented in *Basic Principles of Curriculum and Instruction* (1949).

Adler considers a broad liberal education the best education for *all* students. He advocates that the same curriculum and quality of teaching be provided to all students. He considers an academic curriculum to have more practical value than vocational or specialized training. Such a curriculum, he believes, prepares students for a wide range of jobs. Adler considers these subjects indispensable: language, literature, fine arts, mathematics, natural sciences, history, and geography. Although it emphasizes fundamental subjects, *The Paideia Proposal* does not present subject matter as an end in itself, but as the context for developing intellectual skills that include the three R's, speaking, listening, observing, measuring, estimating, and problem solving. Together, the fundamental subjects and intellectual skills lead to a higher level of learning, reflection, and awareness. For Adler, as for Hutchins, education's purpose is to cultivate significant knowledge and thinking skills, to read the best books—"great books," as they were called by Hutchins—which are recommended by the Paideia program.

| **Table 2.2** The Paideia Course of Study | | |
|---|---|---|
| **Curriculum/Instructional Concentration** | **Method** | **Content** |
| Acquisition of knowledge | Didactic instruction, teaching by telling<br>Lectures, explanations<br>Standard questions<br>Laboratory demonstrations<br>Use of textbooks | Language<br>Literature<br>Math<br>Science<br>History, geography<br>Fine arts |
| Learning (intellectual) skills | Coaching<br>Exercises, problems<br>Supervised practice<br>Use of computers and other instructional tools | Reading, writing, speaking, listening<br>Observing, measuring, estimating<br>Critical judgment |
| Ideas and values | Socratic questioning<br>Active participation<br>Philosophical essays and debates<br>Creative products | Discussion of major books, not textbooks<br>Interdisciplinary subject matter (literature, history, science, philosophy, etc.)<br>Involvement in linguistic and artistic activities |

*Source:* Information from Mortimer J. Adler, *The Paideia Proposal: An Educational Manifesto* (New York: Macmillan, 1982), pp. 23–32.

Perennialism appeals to a small group of educators who stress intellectual meritocracy. Such educators emphasize testing, tougher academic standards and programs, and identification of gifted and talented students. They advocate a uniform curriculum, usually liberal arts, with few electives. For perennialists, educational equality results from providing all students with high-quality academic education; they believe tracking some students into a vocational curriculum would deny them an equal education.

**RETURNING TO THE LIBERAL ARTS.** In *The Closing of the American Mind,* Allan Bloom voiced concern about a lack of universal standards and subjects within education.[22] Like other perennialists, he asserts that cultural relativism—with its emphasis on trivial pursuits, quick fixes, and relevancy—has degraded U.S. education. According to Bloom, U.S. schools fail to foster critical thinking. Deprived of a serious liberal arts and science education, unfamiliar with the great works and ideas of the past, U.S. students lack mental depth. We have rejected universal standards of morality and excellence. Like Hutchins before him, Bloom seeks to reestablish the benefits of reading classics and obtaining a liberal arts education. Bloom calls for intellectually challenging education that helps preserve what is best in the national culture.[23]

On a national level, Bloom contends we are heading for *educational nihilism*—a disrespect for tough academics and critical thought. Our schools, and especially universities, are not places where serious thought occurs. Our educational institutions fail in their fundamental task of educating people and providing a place for serious learning and scholarship. We have welcomed the false doctrine of equality and have rejected universal standards of excellence. We refuse to take a position on what is right and wrong based on standards of truth (of course, we can argue whose truth); rather, we welcome easy or no-fault choices.

Indeed, if we want to ask ourselves how and where we went wrong, why we are in social and economic decline, Bloom offers a conservative analysis and sense of fundamental reform.

To remedy American education and to neutralize the problems caused by cultural relativism, Bloom, as did Hutchins more than 60 years ago, seeks to reestablish the idea of an educated person along the line of great books and great thinkers and to reestablish the virtues of a liberal education. Bloom, in a more recent publication, reiterates his call for an education that is more challenging and prizes that which is crucial to the well being of the national culture.[24]

## Essentialism: Reaffirming the Best and Brightest

As noted previously, in perennialism the stress is on preserving the best knowledge, values, dispositions, and mores of societies from the distant and recent past. Education's challenge is to offer curricula that enable students to comprehend their history and culture. Education aims to foster in students, our future citizens, a reaffirmation of commitment to their society and a renewal of valuing their culture's contributions.

Essentially, perennialism is a Western philosophy tracing its roots back to Aristotle's development of realism. Over the centuries, other Western thinkers have contributed to this philosophy. Today, some may argue that some educators have used this philosophy to tout Western culture's contributions to society. Indeed, this zealous pride seems to be behind some educators' and members of the public's demands that American students must be number one in the world. We must claim the best and the brightest.

Like perennialists, many essentialists emphasize mastering the skills, facts, and concepts that form the basis of the subject matter. Hyman Rickover writes, "For all children, the educational process must be one of collecting factual knowledge to the limit of their absorptive capacity."[25] A curriculum that takes students' interests or social issues into account is regarded as wasteful, as are teaching methods that rely on psychological theories. Arthur Bestor declares, "Concern with the personal problems of adolescents has grown so excessive as to push into the background what should be the schools' central concern, the intellectual development of its students."[26] The school is viewed as sidetracked when it focuses on students' social and psychological problems rather than cognition. (Most current task force reports on academic excellence, incidentally, agree with this assessment.) Discipline, training, homework, and serious study are emphasized. According to Rickover, "The student must be made to work hard, and nothing can really make it fun."[27]

The role of the essentialist teacher follows perennialist philosophy. The teacher is considered a master of a particular subject and a model worthy of emulation. The teacher is responsible for the class and decides on the curriculum with minimal student input. The teacher is respected as an authority, exhibits high standards, and expects the same from students.

Essentialism is reflected in the current public demand to raise academic standards. It is evidenced in reports such as *A Nation at Risk* and, more recently, No Child Left Behind (NCLB). (Other reports on excellence are discussed in Chapter 5.) Recent proposals outlined in Ernest Boyer's *High School* (1983), Theodore Sizer's *Horace's Compromise* (1987; also about high schools), and Richard Allington's *Schools That Work* (2006; focuses on elementary schools) also reflects essentialism. Although current essentialist philosophy is more moderate than it was in the 1950s during the post-Sputnik era (e.g., it somewhat accommodates less able students), it still emphasizes academics (not play) and cognitive thinking (not the whole child).

**FROM BACK-TO-BASICS TO STANDARDS.**  Automatic promotion of marginal students, a dizzying array of elective courses, and textbooks designed more to entertain than to educate are frequently cited as reasons for the decline in students' basic skills. The call is for a return to basics. Annual Gallup polls have asked the public to suggest ways to improve education; since 1976, "devoting more attention to teaching the basics" and "improving curriculum standards" have ranked no lower than fifth in the list of responses; in the 1980s and 1990s, these suggestions consistently ranked among people's top three suggestions.[28]

By 2009, 44 states had standards in the four high school academic areas (English, history, math, and science) and 46 states had K–12 standards in language arts and math. Students in

26 states did not graduate from high school without passing statewide tests (although standards vary among states). Twenty-two states required elementary school students to pass standardized tests in order to be promoted but offered extra instruction via after-school classes and summer school, as well as providing for retaking tests.[29] Similarly, numerous states implemented pay-for-performance incentives tied to increased student achievement. The incentives included bonuses for outstanding teachers, rewards for all teachers whose schools met improvement targets, and extra pay for inner-city teachers whose students showed academic improvement. Bonuses for teachers and administrators ranged from $1,000 to $5,000 for teachers to $25,000 to $35,000 for principals.[30] The bonus package for New York City teachers, implemented in 2007, is capped at $3,000. However, what is missing on a nationwide basis is bonuses for science and math teachers, which are essential if we are to compete on a global basis. (The 2005 landmark report *Rising Above the Gathering Storm* addresses this issue somewhat by recommending scholarships for math and science students who plan to teach.)

As an offshoot of this movement, more than 40 states required beginning teachers to demonstrate competence in basic skills (spelling, grammar, mathematics), their academic subject (English, social studies, science, etc.), or pedagogical practices in order to receive certification. Two major concerns are (1) the persistent achievement gap between African American and Hispanic students on the one hand and Asian and white students on the other, and (2) the gap between minority and white teachers with regard to passing simple teaching tests.[31]

The back-to-basics movement and now the standards movement have fostered essentialist curricula with heavy emphases on reading, writing, and math at the elementary level. "Solid" subjects—English, history, science, and math—are required in all grades. *English* means traditional grammar, not linguistics or nonstandard English; it means Shakespeare, not *Lolita* or *South Park*. *History* means U.S. and European history and perhaps Asian and African history, but not African American history or ethnic studies. *Science* means biology, chemistry, and physics, not ecology. *Math* means old, not new, math. Elective courses, minicourses, even integrated social science and general science courses are considered too "soft." In many cases, the curriculum content is aligned with high-stakes tests. State and national standards are emphasized, with textbooks that correspond to standards and tests being favored.

Proponents of the movement are concerned that illiterate students graduate; high school and college diplomas fail to represent academic performance; minimum standards are lacking; and students lack the basic skills and knowledge they need to survive in the job market. Some of these advocates are college educators who would eliminate open admissions, credit for life experiences or remedial courses, and grade inflation. They demand reasonable high school and college standards and advocate using tests to monitor educational standards over time and to pressure students, teachers, and parents to fulfill their responsibilities.[32]

Although the movement is spreading and state legislators and the public seem convinced of the need for minimum standards, unanswered questions remain. What standards should be considered minimum? What should we do with students who fail to meet these standards? Are we punishing students for schools' inability to educate them? How will the courts and then the school districts deal with the fact that proportionately more minority than white students fail competency tests? Is the issue minimum competency or equal educational opportunity?

**EMPHASIZING CONTENT, DEEMPHASIZING PROCESS.** E. D. Hirsch's *Cultural Literacy,* a national best-seller, focuses on the background knowledge necessary for cultural (Hirsch calls it *functional*) literacy and effective communication in the United States. Hirsch has compiled some 5,000 "essential" items from history, geography, literature, science, and technology.[33] More than 80 percent of the total items refer to events, people, or places from previous centuries, and about 25 percent deal with the classics. Instead of emphasizing critical thinking or process, Hirsch stresses information at all grade levels of schooling. We don't have to know the finer details, but there should be some minimum level of understanding and competence, depending on the subject area and topic, for effective communication. Hirsch maintains that students who are unable to master the common knowledge cannot become intelligent readers and cannot speak properly (or formally).[34] He also stresses the importance of scientific information at all levels of schooling; moreover, he has written a series of follow-up books on essential knowledge for every grade level. Knowing the facts, for him and a growing number of present-day essentialists (Lynne Cheney, William Bennett, Chester Finn, Diane Ravitch, et al.), increases the students' capacity to comprehend what they read, see, hear, and discuss. The need for background knowledge is judged important for future communication and specialization. Finally, Hirsch argues that we have overlooked content and stressed process—or thinking skills—with little regard for subject matter. The outcome has been a decline in national literacy. For traditional educators, an educated person must have command of knowledge; the goal of education is to transmit adult society's shared knowledge and values to youth. Without this transmission, traditionalists argue, U.S. society will become fragmented, and its ability to accumulate information and communicate it to various segments of the populace will be diminished.

Although the teacher understands the value of many subjects, he or she feels there is the need for students to understand certain *ideas* and *values*, some rooted in 3000 years of philosophy, literature, art, music, theater, and so on. Without certain agreed-on content (what Arthur Bestor and Allan Bloom call the *liberal arts,* what E. D. Hirsch and Diane Ravitch call *essential knowledge,* and what Robert Hutchins and Mortimer Adler call the *Great Books*), our heritage would crumble and we would be at the mercy of chance and ignorance; moreover, our education enterprise would be subject to the whim and fancy of local fringe groups.

**EXCELLENCE IN EDUCATION.**   The back-to-basics movement led to a demand, in the 1980s, for educational excellence and tougher academics. Today, this demand is part of a broader theme of military defense and technological and economic competition. *A Nation at Risk* (which appeared in the mid-1980s), *National Goals for Education* (initially published in 1990 and revised in 1994 and 1998), NCLB (published in 2001), and "Race to the Top" in 2010 all called for improved U.S. education and emphasized international "competition" and "survival"—themes reminiscent of the post-Sputnik era and, eventually, of the development of the national standards movement.[35]

Overall, the trend is for higher achievement (not just minimum competency) for all children (not just college-bound students) in the academic areas. Cognitive achievement is stressed, along with rigorous grading, testing, and discipline. Some advocates of this approach promote intellectually demanding high school content such as calculus, physics, and advanced foreign languages. Some would make computer skills the fourth R—because they consider these skills essential in a technological world. The emphasis is on academic and economic productivity. The vitality of the U.S. economy and U.S. political hegemony are linked to strengthening the nation's educational institutions.

Other educators allow wider latitude in defining excellence and permit various models or criteria of excellence. Still many criticize the overemphasis on mathematical and scientific excellence in the schools and the consequent underemphasis or ignoring of other conceptions of excellence—linguistic, humanistic, musical, spatial, kinesthetic, moral, interpersonal, intrapersonal, and information-processing areas.[36] Some are also concerned that equity and equality will be swept under the rug, with too much stress on academic standards at the expense of moral knowledge, community service, and caring—in general, on cognitive excellence—and a return to post-Sputnik-type emphasis on academically talented students but not low-achieving students or high school dropouts.[37] Some fear that this emphasis on excellence will lead to disappointment; they say it is wrong to assume that increased testing and more course requirements will automatically raise the level of student performance. Students, teachers, and parents must also be motivated, and technical and financial support at the school and school district level must be evidenced. (See Curriculum Tips 2.1.)

## Progressivism

Progressivism developed from pragmatic philosophy, as a backlash against perennialist thinking in education. The progressive movement in education was part of the larger social and political reform movement that characterized U.S. society around 1900. It grew out of the political thought of progressives such as Robert LaFollette, Theodore Roosevelt, and Woodrow Wilson and out of the muckraker movement of the 1910s and 1920s. Progressivism is considered a contemporary reform movement in educational, social, and political affairs.

Progressivism's educational roots can be traced back to the reform writings of Thomas Jefferson and Benjamin Rush in the 18th century, Horace Mann and Henry Barnard in the 19th century, and John Dewey in the early 20th century.[38] In *Democracy and Education,* Dewey claims that democracy and education go hand in hand. He viewed the school as a miniature democratic society in which students learn the skills necessary for democratic living.[39]

According to progressivist thought, these skills include problem-solving and scientific methods. Schools should nurture cooperation and self-discipline and transmit the society's culture. Because reality is constantly changing, Dewey saw little need to focus on a fixed body of knowledge. Progressivism emphasized *how* to think, not *what* to think. Traditional education, with its "method of imposition from the side of the teacher and reception [and] absorption from the side of the pupil," Dewey wrote, "may be compared to inscribing records upon a passive phonographic disc to result in giving back what has been inscribed when the proper button is pressed in recitation or examination."[40]

---

### CURRICULUM TIPS 2.1  Recognizing and Rewarding Academic Excellence

Along with higher academic standards, schools are introducing academic incentives for greater student achievement. Here are some ways to motivate and reward high-achieving students:

1. Involve parents in their children's learning, especially in early grades. Provide classes that show parents how to help children learn, motivate them, and encourage academic initiative and independence.
2. Display past and current scholars, such as straight-A students, National Merit finalists, and valedictorians on an Academic Honors Wall. Display photographs permanently.
3. Recognize improvement and achievement by expanding honor rolls, sending personalized letters to parents, and printing names in school newsletters.
4. Each quarter or semester, have teachers select top scholars from their respective grade levels. Award certificates, plaques, medals, trophies, savings bonds, or classic books.
5. Conduct a special academic assembly each semester. Recognize high-achieving students in local newspapers and magazines. Honor students (and their parents) with a special luncheon or dinner.
6. Develop enrichment classes (at the elementary level) and advanced-level and honor programs at the secondary level for the talented and academically gifted.
7. Develop homework and tutoring programs for at-risk students as well as average students who may need assistance in one or two subjects. Use high-achieving students as peer tutors.
8. Recognize academic students at least as much as the school's athletes. Form academic clubs that provide status and publicity for the participants.
9. Cooperate with local business and industry to publicize or award high-achieving students.
10. Make school videos of student leaders, including past and present high achievers, and associate academic excellence with successful alumni.
11. Be sensitive to too much academic competition among students. Try to maintain a balance between cognitive and social goals and to recognize deserving (not necessarily only A) students.
12. Implement study clubs, reading clubs, or special skills clubs on Saturdays or during the summer for students who need extra help in selected areas or who are studying for National Assessment of Educational Progress (NAEP), ACT, or SAT tests.

For Dewey and other progressivists, the curriculum should be interdisciplinary and teachers should guide students in problem solving and scientific projects. Dewey saw the teacher as the "leader of group activities" and allowed students to analyze and interpret data and to draw their own conclusions. The teacher and students planned activities together (although Dewey affirmed that final authority rested with the teacher).

However, William Kilpatrick, his former student and later colleague at Columbia University (Dewey left the University of Chicago for Columbia University in 1904) envisioned a greater role for students in curriculum making, and in the 1920s and 1930s he urged elementary school teachers to plan and organize around social activities, group enterprises, and group activities. Kilpatrick encouraged teachers to allow students to say what they think and to think for themselves, not just please the teacher. In comparing Dewey and Kilpatrick, the latter was more progressive and, unlike Dewey, was heavily involved in many social issues related to schools and society and edited the leftist journal *New Leader*. Whereas Dewey sought a new curriculum with organized subjects based on the child's experiences, Kilpatrick maintained that the child's needs and interests were uncertain and rejected the notion of a fixed curriculum. Dewey was a chore to read, often writing 25- to 30-word sentences. Kilpatrick interpreted Dewey and made his ideas more manageable for the average reader.

The progressive movement split into several groups: the child centered, activity centered, creative, and neo-Freudian. Dewey criticized progressivist educators who devalued knowledge or thought it had little value but also progressivists who rejected adult authority over schoolchildren. He declared "progressive extremists" and "laissez-faire" philosophies to be destructive to the ideas of progressivism, and warned, "Any movement that thinks and acts in terms of an ism becomes so involved in reaction against other isms that it is unwittingly controlled by them."[41]

Boyd Bode, another leading progressivist, warned his associates of an impending crisis in *Progressive Education at the Crossroads.*[42] The movement had "nurtured the pathetic hope that it could find out how to educate by relying on such notions as interests, needs, growth and freedom," he wrote. Its "one-sided devotion to the child" actually betrayed the child by depriving him or her of appropriate subject matter. Unless progressivism changed course, it would be "circumvented and left behind."[43] Bode's words proved prophetic. More and more progressive thinkers responded to the growing criticism with self-justifying theories and impractical methods that most school districts simply ignored.

Progressivists were united in opposing (1) authoritarian teaching, (2) overreliance on textbook methods, (3) memorization of factual data by constant drill, (4) static aims and materials that fail to take account of a changing world, (5) intimidation or corporal punishment as a form of discipline, and (6) attempts to separate education from individual experiences and social reality. However, according to Lawrence Cremin, the movement's inability to reach a consensus on the purpose of schooling, or even establish a set of pedagogical principles, led to its downfall.[44]

Progressivists rejected rote learning, lesson recitations, and textbook authority. They also criticized conventional subject matter and experimented with other approaches to curriculum. Progressive education focused on the learner rather than the subject, emphasized activities and experiences rather than verbal or mathematical skills, and encouraged cooperative group-learning activities rather than competitive individual learning. Progressivism also cultivated a cultural relativism that often clashed with traditional philosophy and values.

Although progressive education waned in the 1940s and 1950s with the advent of essentialism, the philosophy has continued to leave a mark. Contemporary progressivism manifests as calls for a relevant curriculum, humanistic education, and radical school reform.

**RELEVANT CURRICULUM.** As the 1960s unfolded, students took a more active role in their education and demanded a more progressive and student-centered curriculum. Students and educators now argued that students must be motivated and interested in the learning task and the classroom should build on life experiences and interesting activities. They demanded relevance, advocating (1) individualized instruction (e.g., independent study and special projects), (2) revised and new courses of interest to students (e.g., courses on sex education, drug addiction, race relations, and urban problems), (3) educational alternatives (e.g., electives, minicourses, open classrooms), (4) the extension of the curriculum beyond the school's walls (e.g., work–study programs, credit for life experiences, off-campus courses, external degree programs), and (5) the relaxation of academic standards and admission standards to schools and colleges.[45]

**HUMANISTIC CURRICULUM.**   The humanistic curriculum began as a reaction to a perceived overemphasis on subject matter and cognitive learning in the 1960s and 1970s. In his best-selling book *Crisis in the Classroom,* Charles Silberman advocated humanizing U.S. schools.[46] He charged that schools are repressive and that they teach students docility and conformity. He suggested that elementary schools adopt the methods of British infant schools and that secondary schools incorporate independent study, peer tutoring, and community and work experiences.

The humanistic model of education, which stems from the human potential movement in psychology, reflects the work of Arthur Jersild, Arthur Combs, and Donald Snygg. Jersild linked good teaching with knowledge of self and students. Combs and Snygg explored the impact of self-concept and motivation on achievement.[47] They considered self-concept the most important determinant of behavior.

A humanistic curriculum emphasizes affective, rather than cognitive, outcomes. It draws heavily on the works of Abraham Maslow and Carl Rogers.[48] Its goal is to produce "self-actualizing people," in Maslow's words, or "total human beings," in Rogers's. The works of both psychologists are laced with terms such as *maintaining, striving, enhancing, experiencing, independence, self-determination, integration,* and *self-actualization.* A humanistic curriculum emphasizes happiness, aesthetics, spirituality, caring, and empathy.

By the end of the 20th century, the humanistic teacher was depicted by William Glasser's "positive" and "supportive" teacher who could manage students without coercion and teach without failure.[49] It was also illustrated by Robert Fried's "passionate" teacher and Vito Perrione's "teacher with a heart"—teachers who live to teach young children and refuse to submit to apathy or criticism that may infect the school in which they work.[50] These teachers are dedicated and caring, they actively engage students in their classrooms, and they affirm their identities. The students do not have to ask whether their teacher is interested in them, thinks of them, or knows their interests or concerns. The answer is definitely yes.

The humanistic teacher is also portrayed by Theodore Sizer's mythical teacher "Horace," who is dedicated and enjoys teaching, treats learning as a humane enterprise, inspires his students to learn, and encourages them to develop their powers of thought, taste and character.[51] Yet the system forces Horace to make a number of compromises in planning, teaching, and grading, which he knows that, if we lived in an ideal world (with more than 24 hours in a day), he would not make. He hides his frustration. Sizer simply states, "Most jobs in the real world have a gap between what would be nice and what is possible. One adjusts."[52] Hence, most caring and dedicated teachers are forced to make some compromises, take some shortcuts, and make some accomodations. As long as no one gets upset and no one complains, the system permits a chasm between rhetoric (the rosy picture) and reality (slow burnout).

There is also the humanistic element in Nel Noddings' ideal teacher, who focuses on the nurturing of "competent, caring, loving, and loveable persons." To that end, she describes teaching as a caring profession in which teachers should convey to students a caring way of thinking about one's self, siblings, strangers, animals, plants, and the physical environment. She stresses the affective aspect of teaching: the need to focus on the child's strengths and interests, the need for an individualized curriculum built around the child's abilities and needs.[53] Caring, according to Noddings, cannot be achieved by a formula or checklist. It calls for different behaviors for different situations, from tenderness to tough love. Good teaching, like good parenting, requires continuous effort, trusting relationships, and continuity of purpose—the purpose of caring, appreciating human connections, and ideas from a historical, multicultural, and diverse perspective.[54]

Actually, the humanistic teacher is someone who highlights the personal and social dimension in teaching and learning, as opposed to the behavioral, scientific, or technological aspects. We might argue that everything that the teacher does is "human" and the expression *humanistic teaching* is a cliché.

Advocates of humanistic education contend that the present school curriculum has failed miserably. Teachers and schools, they say, overemphasize cognitive ability and seek to control students not for the students' benefit but for the benefit of adults. They see the schools as unconcerned about affective processes, self-knowledge, and higher domains of consciousness.

Humanists seek more meaningful relationships between students and teachers. They would foster student independence, self-direction, and acceptance of self and others. In their view, teachers should facilitate student self-understanding and psychological health. The teacher's role is to help learners cope with their psychological needs and problems.

A drawback to the humanistic approach is its lack of attention to intellectual development. When asked to judge their curriculum's effectiveness, humanists generally rely on testimonials and subjective assessments by students and teachers. They may also present materials such as student paintings and poems or speak of "marked improvement" in student behavior and attitudes. They present very little empirical evidence to support their stance. (See Curriculum Tips 2.2.)

**RADICAL SCHOOL REFORM.**    Since the late 1960s and now in the 21st century, *radical romanticists* (or *neoprogressives*) have criticized the educational establishment. The criticisms originally appeared in major publications such as *Atlantic Monthly* and *New York Times Magazine*. The radical critics also wrote popular books on their views.

---

### CURRICULUM TIPS 2.2    Affective Methods to Enhance Learning

Progressive philosophy and humanistic education increase students' self-understanding, personalize and individualize learning, and provide academic experiences that take students' personal needs and interests into account. The classroom is characterized by activity, not passivity; cooperation, not competition; and many learning opportunities other than textbooks and teacher-dominated situations. The following guidelines can help teachers and curriculum workers provide leadership within progressive and humanistic approaches.

1.  Demonstrate interest in and concern for each student.
2.  Challenge students to be actively involved in their own learning; encourage self-direction and self-control.
3.  Help students define personal goals; recognize their efforts in pursuit of a chosen goal.
4.  Structure learning activities so that students can accomplish their personal goals.
5.  Relate content to students' personal goals, needs, and interests.
6.  Match task requirements to students' age, development, and abilities.
7.  Offer constructive feedback.
8.  Test students if necessary, but delay grading their performance (say, until the fourth or fifth grade).
9.  Use local resources to obtain information and solve problems. Actively involve students in learning that involves different materials, people, and places.
10. Provide alternative ways to learn; minimize memory, rote, and drill activities.
11. Help students achieve competence and mastery; let them know that their learning results from their own efforts.
12. Recognize student improvement and achievement.
13. Encourage students to share materials and resources and to work in groups.
14. Encourage students to contribute their ideas and feelings, to accept and support one another, and to be considerate of those who need help.

Early prominent radicals such as Edgar Friedenberg, John Holt, Paul Goodman, and A. S. Neill expressed disdain for established schooling methods, compulsory schooling, adult authority, and school rules. The later crop of radicals, such as Ivan Illich, Henry Giroux, and Peter McLaren, expressed contempt for the society within which schools exist. All these critics essentially viewed students as prisoners, teachers as prison guards or system lackeys, and schools as prisons where students are intellectually and emotionally confined. They considered schools highly discriminatory places that (1) sort and track students for various jobs that perpetuate class differences and (2) perpetuate a culture of production and consumption that benefits the few and exploits the many.[55]

Friedenberg has argued that teachers "dislike and distrust" their students and "fear being involved with young people in any situation that is not under their complete control." Teachers feel "repressed hostility," suppressed anger, and jealousy toward their students because of students' youthful energy and freedom.[56]

Holt's book *How Children Fail* is his most influential text. It contains nothing positive about teachers or schools. Holt describes teachers as enforcing rigid rules and schoolchildren as learning to be stupid and learning how to focus on right answers. He goes into great detail about how children adapt strategies of fear and failure to please their teachers. The "successful" students become cunning strategists in a game of beating the system and outwitting the teacher—figuring out how to get away with the least amount of work, getting the answer out of the teacher, or faking the answer.[57]

Goodman's thesis is that our society is sick, full of false values that have produced sick schools. He contends that schools exist primarily to channel people into jobs and to provide a market for textbook companies, building contractors, and teachers. Elementary schools provide a "baby-sitting service" for parents and keep kids off the street. Secondary schools are "the arm of the police, providing cops and concentration camps paid for in the budget under the heading of 'Board of Education.'" From kindergarten to college, schools teach youth to adjust to a sick society and provide "a universal trap [in which] democracy begins to look like regimentation."[58] Goodman's solution is to eliminate compulsory education, which he refers to as "miseducation," and "drastically cut back formal schooling because the present extended tutelage is against nature and arrests growth."[59]

Neill, a romantic progressivist, recounted the way he operated his school Summerhill in Suffolk, England: "We set out to make a school in which we should allow children to be themselves. In order to do this, we had to renounce all discipline, all direction, all suggestion, all moral training. . . . All it required was what we had—a complete belief in the child as a good, not an evil, being. For almost forty years, this belief in the goodness of the child has never wavered; it rather has become a final faith."[60] Neil considered children "innately wise and realistic." If left to themselves, they will develop as normal adults. Those "who are to become scholars will be scholars"; those "who are only fit to sweep the streets will sweep streets."[61] Neill was not concerned with formal instruction; he did not believe in exams or homework. Those who want to study will study; those who prefer not to study will not. Neill's criterion for success was an ability to "work joyfully" and "live positively." By this contention, most Summerhill students allegedly succeeded. A few years after his death, Summerhill closed—indicating that it was perhaps Neill's personality, not his philosophy, that was the key to Summerhill's story.

Illich argued for a new society that could emerge only after deschooling.[62] He advocated eliminating schools, thereby liberating people from institutional and capitalistic indoctrination. Society would no longer discriminate on the basis of one's degree of formal education. In lieu of school, Illich recommended small learning networks characterized by (1) *educational objects* (shops, libraries, museums, art galleries, and so on) open to learners, (2) *peer matching* (identifying and bringing together students who wish to engage in a particular learning activity), (3) *skill exchanges* (exchanges between those who are competent in a particular skill and wish to teach it and those who wish to learn it), and (4) *educators at large* (counselors who advise students and parents, and intellectual initiators and administrators who operate the networks).

Giroux posits that public education is in a dire state that negatively affects all society. In this view, a change in the nature of democracy has produced a crisis in education.[63] Giroux interprets democracy from a Marxist viewpoint. Essentially, he views current democracy as exclusive rather than inclusive: Many do not benefit from the system. Giroux laments the "refusal to grant public schooling a significant role in the ongoing process of educating people to be active and critical citizens capable of fighting for and reconstructing democratic public life."[64]

McLaren goes further as an ideolog. He states that capitalist schooling is generally perverse in that it strives, through its curriculum, to create a culture of desire. Instead of nurturing consensus, it hides inequality and intolerance. He writes, "Perverts cannot tolerate difference," so they present an illusion of harmony.[65] McLaren rejects a goal of shaping students into productive, loyal citizens. The exhortation that students "be all that they can be [is] situated within a total obedience to normative codes of conduct and standardized regimes of valuing."[66] According to McLaren, education as presently structured is not empowering. Students are treated as objects of consumption and taught to become consumers.[67] Schools mold students to conform to society's capitalist inequities.

## Reconstructionism

Reconstructionist philosophy is based on socialistic and utopian ideas of the late 19th and early 20th centuries; yet the Great Depression gave it new life. The progressive educational movement was at the height of its popularity then, but a small group of progressive educators became disillusioned with U.S. society and impatient for reform. Members of this group argued that progressivism overemphasized child-centered education and mainly served the middle and upper classes with its play theories and private schools. They advocated greater emphasis on society-centered education that addressed the needs of all social classes.

At the 1932 annual meeting of the Progressive Education Association, George Counts urged progressive educators to consider the era's social and economic problems and use the schools to help reform society. In his speech "Dare the School Build a New Social Order?" (later published as a book), Counts criticized his progressive colleagues for not being more involved in social and economic issues, and that many of their progressive ideas had led to "play schools" for upper-middle- and upper-class children. He suggested that progressive educators became more socially involved in the issues of the day (and, if the authors may add, as the early 20th-century muckrakers were involved in social and economic issues). He also suggested that teachers organize into unions and teachers and schools become agents of social reform.

Counts stated, "If Progressive Education is to be genuinely progressive, it must . . . face squarely and courageously every social issue, come to grips with life in all its stark reality, establish an organic relation with the community, develop a realistic and comprehensive theory of welfare, fashion a compelling and challenging vision of human destiny, and become less frightened than it is today at the bogeys of imposition and indoctrination."[68] According to Counts, progressive education had ignored the social problems of the 1920s and 1930s, which included discrimination, poverty, and unemployment.

Theodore Brameld, often credited with coining *reconstructionism* in 1950 (actually, Dewey coined the term),[69] asserted that reconstructionism is a crisis philosophy and, therefore, suited to today's society, which is in crisis.[70] According to Brameld, students and teachers must improve society. Classroom political neutrality, disguised as objectivity and scientific inquiry, does not suit the democratic process. Brameld writes, "Teachers and students have a right to take sides, to stand up for the best reasoned and informed partialities they can reach as a result of free, meticulous examination and communication of all relevant evidence." In particular, teachers must measure up to their social responsibilities. "The immediate task before the [teaching] profession is to draw upon this strength and thus to strengthen control of the schools by and for the goal-seeking interests of the overwhelming majority of mankind."[71]

Curriculum must be transformed in keeping with a new social-economic-political education; it must incorporate reform strategies. For reconstructionists, analysis, interpretation, and evaluation of problems are insufficient; students and teachers must effect change. Society is always changing, and the curriculum has to change. A curriculum based on social issues and services is ideal.

In the 1960s, the heyday of the War on Poverty and the Civil Rights Movement, reconstructionism focused on issues related to equality and equity, such as compensatory funding and school desegregation. Proponents of this era include Christopher Jencks, Jonathan Kozol, Gary Orfield, and William Wilson.[72] These reconstructionists advocated a program of education that (1) critically examines a society's cultural heritage, (2) examines controversial issues unabashedly, (3) commits to bringing about constructive social change, (4) cultivates a future-oriented attitude that considers school reform, and (5) enlists students and teachers to enhance educational opportunities for *all* children and youth. In such a program, teachers are considered agents of social change. They organize not to strengthen their professional security but to encourage widespread experimentation in the schools and to challenge society's outdated structures. They are the vanguard of a new social order.

Today *critical pedagogy*, which is rooted in reconstructionist philosophy and the ideas of Counts and Brameld, begins with the idea that students have the capacity to think, question, and be critical. Teachers and schools need to educate students to be informed citizens and agents for change. The students must be viewed as the major resource for promoting and protecting democracy, informed and educated in the Jeffersonian sense that no democracy can exist without an educated populace. The schools are seen by critical pedagogists as a means to educate students in the ideas of democracy and to encourage then to question textbooks, teachers, and political pundits. Instead of schools serving as an agent for the capitalist and corporate world and thus maintaining a dominant and subordinate class system (ideas promoted by radical and neomarxist educators such as Apple, Giroux, and McLaren), they are viewed ideally as an institution for encouraging social reform and social justice.

**INTERNATIONALISTS.** Today's reconstructionist educators tend to be sensitive to global issues, which they analyze as part of the larger social order. Historically, the United States has taken a relatively isolationist position, but interdependence among nations no longer allows Americans to remain ignorant of developments in distant countries. Educators now feel the need to emphasize understanding other nations and cultures.

Such terms as *global village, global interdependence, shrinking world,* and *greenhouse effect* reflect new global concerns. This group of curriculum experts is seeking an *international component* in U.S. curricula. Students would acquire knowledge and skills essential for global peace and cooperation.[73] Joel Spring advocates such an international curriculum component. He maintains that students must acquire an awareness of global events and an understanding of "worldwide systems." These systems are social, political, economic, physical, cultural, communicative, and historical.[74] This new curriculum would focus on the Earth's ecosystem and world problems. According to Spring, it might address Western imperialism, Arab nationalism, and the growing economic influence of China and India.

As technology increasingly links different countries, curriculum's international component is likely to increase. In *The World Is Flat,* Thomas Friedman points out that computers, broadband and cellular networks, and the Internet have leveled the economic playing field. Global trade indicates continuous growth in investments and jobs in China, India, Brasil, and other emerging markets, the slow demise of American workers who are unable to compete in a global economy,[75] and the slow transfer of trillions of dollars to the Asian rim over the next 10 years. If your job can be digitized, it may only be a short time before it becomes movable to the other side of the world—with people willing to work for two-thirds less than the American scientist, engineer, or accountant.

Americans cannot be ignorant of the world and their place in it, especially after the events of September 11, 2001. Our gross national product, standard of living, and security are connected to the world community and influenced by global activities.

In *Class Counts,* Allan Ornstein maintains "there are some 2 to 2.5 billion people marginally existing on either $1 or $2 a day, and another 1.5 to 2 billion people [worldwide] earning between $2 and $3.50 a day, and the number is growing because of the 'population bomb.' The U.S. represents 4 percent of the world population, consumes 25 percent of the world's resources and produces 38 percent of the world's gross domestic product."[76] How much of a divide between "haves" and "have nots" can the world tolerate without instability?

Ornstein continues to outline the global economic landscape. It's not a pretty picture. The American workforce has lost its place in the sun, along with its industrial model. It was good while it lasted, and we were the envy of the rest of the world. They were good days, but now it is coming to an end. "We need to understand that America as a nation is moving into the slow lane. Our last cutting-edge industries—semiconductors, telecommunications, computer software, nanotechnology, and Internet services—are slowly moving into the Asian rim where talented technical specialists are cheaper and in abundance."[77] Similarly, U.S. science and technology companies are being challenged by the technological and entrepreneurial growth of Europe and emerging nations. It's happening all around us; it is reflected in our unemployment and underemployment trends (totaling 20 percent in 2010), individual plastic debts (averaging some $10,000 per person), and the national debt (some $14 trillion), plus the fact that the Chinese (and a few other nations) have to lend us trillions to keep us from drowning.

Linda Darling-Hammond uses the words *flat-world* in her recent book to comment on U.S. education and globalization in the 21st century. She warns that the United States is falling behind in the world's ranking of science and math and that lack of equality of educational opportunity for low-income and minority students has dire consequences in a competitive and global economy. Everyone benefits when all students have equal and fair opportunities to achieve their human potential.[78] Keep in mind that the U.S. dropout rate is the highest among industrialized nations, approaching 15 percent and as high as 35 percent in big cities. Also consider that the United States regularly falls in the bottom half, and often the bottom 20 percent, among their industrialized counterparts on international tests in math and science (see Chapter 5).

The education and economic crisis we now face will become a generational journey we will face for the remaining century, as we try to transform ourselves and cope with the coming storm. "This crisis will not be solved by rallies in the streets (a liberal response) or by paying executives more money (a conservative response). It will be resolved by painful changes involving a shared moral foundation and a sense of justice, adopting new education policies that provide education and equity for all students and new work-related policies that protect American workers from the Walmarts of America (average wage of $8 per hour) and from foreign competition, providing progressive taxes and regulating the big banks, and marching to the ballot boxes in record numbers in order to elect people willing to make these kinds of changes."[79]

**RECONCEPTUALISTS.**    Reconceptualists view the technical or Tylerian approach to curriculum development as overly narrow.[80] They have criticized most curricularists for using a technocratic, bureaucratic approach that is insensitive to people's feelings and experiences. Reconceptualists include the intuitive, personal, mystical, linguistic, political, social, and spiritual in their approach to curriculum. They believe that current society is marked by alienation, a failure to accommodate diversity, and indifference to people's needs.[81] In their view, a more traditional and technical approach to curriculum perpetuates inequities within and outside the school.

According to William Pinar, the field of curriculum has already been reconceptualized.[82] Postmodernists may argue, instead, that the field simply is always developing. Reconceptualists have brought aesthetic and existentialist views into the field. They tend to be socially sensitive and politically concerned intellectuals who stress broad problems and issues of society.

Reconceptualists accept many aspects of progressive philosophy, including learner-centered, relevant, humanistic, and radical school-reform models. However, they are more concerned with personal self-knowledge, particularly mystical, spiritual, and moral introspection.

The reconceptualist curriculum emphasizes language and communication skills, personal biographies, art, poetry, dance, drama, literature, psychology, and ethics. Maxine Greene advocates such a curriculum, which stresses "personal expression," "aesthetic ideas," "intellectual consciousness," and "reflective self-consciousness."[83] Paulo Freire contends that reconceptualist curricula focus on human problems and have the potential to "transform the world."[84] According to Pinar, a reconceptualist curriculum deals with "personal becoming," "affiliative needs," "sensitivity," and "enjoyment."[85]

Reconceptualist views reflect reconstructionist philosophy. Rooted in the school of Dewey, Counts, and Rugg, many reconceptualist ideas deal with socioeconomic relationships, gender and racial roles and attitudes, the relationship between labor and capital, and the consequences of political power. Reconceptualists are concerned about technocratic and bureaucratic systems that oppress and dehumanize individuals. Many see schools as an instrument of society that coerces students through various customs, mores, and practices.

Some reconceptualists have been labeled neo-Marxists. Michael Apple, for one, speaks of schools' (and society's) political, economic, and cultural domination of the individual. Such domination "is vested in the constitutive principles, codes, and especially the common sense consciousness and practices underlying our lives, as well as by overt division and manipulation."[86] In other words, society's structures and institutions, including schools, perpetuate the social, political, and economic system. Apple points out that just as there is "unequal distribution of economic capital in society, so, too is there a similar system of distribution surrounding cultural capital." In technological societies, schools are "distributors of this cultural capital."[87] They distribute knowledge in a way that suits those in power. Poor and working-class students are discriminated against in schools and society because they lack power; critical knowledge is passed on to those children whose parents possess political and economic power.

Illich outlines a less institutionalized, formal, and discriminatory curriculum aimed at "emancipation." He advocates a "grass-roots" curriculum that engages students, teachers, and community members.[88] Similarly, Freire advocates "pedagogy for the oppressed" (the poor) and describes how people can be empowered to take action and overcome oppression. When they reach a "critical transforming stage," they can change the social order. Freire calls for dialogue among students and adults sensitive to change. The curriculum should focus on community, national, and world problems and be interdisciplinary.[89]

In general, reconceptualists such as Illich and Freire emphasize the social sciences—history, political science, economics, sociology, and, to some extent, psychology and philosophy—not the hard sciences. The goal is to develop student self-realization and freedom so that students will liberate themselves and others from society's restrictions. James Macdonald views the reconceptualist agenda as "utopian," a "form of political and social philosophizing."[90] For Maxine Greene, the curriculum instills "intellectual and moral habits," "critical understanding," "existentialist renewal," and "discovery of 'otherness,'" so that students become more accepting of diversity.[91] All who are oppressed—youth, the poor, members of minorities, women, and so on—are considered potential agents for change. In essence, reconceptualism is an updated version of old reconstructionism, which viewed students and teachers as agents of change. In reconceptualism, however, the teacher sometimes is viewed as an agent of oppression, a representative of the larger coercive society.

**EQUAL EDUCATIONAL OPPORTUNITY.**   The U.S. notion of equality is rooted in the Constitution, written nearly 200 years before reconstructionism emerged as a philosophy. U.S. public schools grew out of the concept of equal opportunity and the notion of universal, free education. Horace Mann spearheaded the rise of the "common school." He asserted, "Education beyond all other devices of human origin is the greatest equalizer of the condition of men—the balance-wheel of the social machinery."[92] Equal opportunity in this context would not lead to equal outcomes or a classless society.

As David Tyack has written, "For the most part, working men did not seek to pull down the rich; rather they sought equality of opportunity for their children, an equal chance at the main

**Table 2.3** Overview Of Educational Philosophies

| Educational Philosophy | Philosophical Base | Aim of Education | Knowledge | Role of Education | Curriculum Focus | Related Curriculum Trends |
|---|---|---|---|---|---|---|
| Perennialism | Realism | To educate the rational person; to cultivate the intellect | Focus on past and permanent studies; mastery of facts and timeless knowledge | Teacher helps students think rationally; based on Socratic method, oral exposition; explicit teaching of traditional values | Classical subjects; literary analysis; constant curriculum | Great books; Paideia proposal; returning to the liberal arts |
| Essentialism | Idealism, realism | To promote the intellectual growth of the individual; to educate the competent person | Essential skills and academic subjects; mastery of concepts and principles of subject matter | Teacher is authority in particular subject area; explicit teaching of traditional values | Essential skills (three R's) and essential subjects (English, science, history, math, and foreign languages) | Back to basics; cultural literacy; excellence in education |
| Progressivism | Pragmatism | To promote democratic, social living | Knowledge leading to growth and development; a living-learning process; focus on active and relevant learning | Teacher is guide for problem solving and scientific inquiry | Based on students' interests; addresses human problems and affairs; interdisciplinary subject matter; activities and projects | Relevant curriculum; humanistic education; radical school reform |
| Reconstructionism | Pragmatism | To improve and reconstruct society; to educate for change and social reform | Skills and subjects needed to identify and ameliorate society's problems; active learning concerned with contemporary and future society | Teacher serves as an agent of change and reform; acts as a project director and research leader; helps students become aware of problems confronting humankind | Emphasis on social sciences and social research methods; examination of social, economic, and political problems; focus on present and future trends as well as on national and international issues | International education; reconceptualism; equality of educational opportunity |

chance."[93] In the 19th and early 20th centuries, equal opportunity meant an equal start for all children, but it was assumed that some would go further than others. Differences in backgrounds and abilities, as well as motivation and luck, would create differences in outcomes among individuals, but the school would assure that children born into any class would have the opportunity to achieve the same status as children born into other classes. "Schools represented the means of achieving the goal . . . of equal chances of success" relative to all children in all strata.[94]

Schools did not fully achieve this goal because school achievement and economic outcomes are highly related to social class and family background.[95] However, without public schools, social mobility would have been less. The failure of the common school to provide social mobility raises the question of the role of the school in achieving equality—and the question of just what the school can do to affect economic outcomes.

The modern view of educational equality, which emerged in the 1950s and continued through the 1990s, goes much further than the old view. James Coleman has outlined five factors relevant to equal or unequal educational opportunity (all but the first reflect reconstructionist philosophy): (1) offering the same curriculum to all children, with the intent that school facilities be equal, (2) schools' racial composition, (3) intangible characteristics such as teacher morale and teachers' expectations of students, (4) cognitive and economic outcomes for students with *equal* backgrounds and abilities, and (5) cognitive and economic outcomes for students with *unequal* backgrounds and abilities.[96]

When we view educational equality or inequality in terms of cognitive and economic outcomes, we start comparing racial, ethnic, and religious groups. Such comparisons raise controversial issues, including how much to invest in human capital, how to determine the cost-effectiveness of social and educational programs, who should be taxed and how much, whether slow learners should receive more attention than fast learners, and whether affirmative action constitutes reverse discrimination.[97]

In his classic text on excellence and equality, John Gardner writes, "Extreme equalitarianism—or what I would prefer to say equalitarianism wrongly conceived—which ignores differences in native capacity and achievement, has not served democracy well. Carried far enough, it means . . . the end of that striving for excellence which has produced mankind's greatest achievements." At the same time, he notes, "No democracy can give itself over to extreme emphasis on individual performance and still remain a democracy. . . . A society such as ours has no choice but to seek the development of human potentialities at all levels. It takes more than an educated elite to run a complex, technological society. Every modern industrialized society is learning that hard lesson."[98]

The issues raised by Gardner have received considerable attention over the past 25 years. That attention has resulted in legislation aimed at educational equality. Among other educators, reconstructionists have raised issues such as school desegregation, compensatory education, multicultural education, disability education, more effective schooling, and affirmative action. (See Table 2.3.)

## Conclusion

Philosophy directs our actions. In the absence of a coherent philosophy, an educator is unduly influenced by external pressures. To a large extent, curriculum reflects philosophy. Dewey was so convinced of the importance of philosophy that he viewed it as the all-encompassing aspect of the educational process—as necessary for "forming fundamental dispositions, intellectual and emotional, toward nature and fellow man."

Major philosophical viewpoints have emerged within the curriculum field: idealism, realism, pragmatism, and existentialism. These viewpoints range from traditional and conservative to contemporary and liberal. They have influenced educational theories: perennialism and essentialism (which are traditional and conservative) and progressivism and reconstructionism (which are contemporary and liberal). (See Table 2.4.) Few schools adopt a

**Table 2.4**   Traditional and Contemporary Education Philosophies

| Traditional Philosophy (Perennialism, Essentialism) | Contemporary Philosophy (Progressivism, Reconstructionism) |
|---|---|
| **Society and Education** | |
| 1. Formal education begins with the school; schools are considered the major institution of the child's education. | 1. Formal education begins with the family; the parents are considered the most important influence in the child's education. |
| 2. School transmits the common culture; individual's major responsibility is to society, performing societal roles; conformity and cooperation are important. | 2. School improves society; individual's fulfillment and development can benefit society; independence and creativity are important. |
| 3. Education promotes society's goals; it involves authority and moral restraint. | 3. Education involves varied opportunities to develop one's potential and engage in personal choices. |
| 4. Certain subjects and knowledge prepare students for democracy and freedom. | 4. Democratic experiences in school help prepare students for democracy and freedom. |
| 5. Education is formulated mainly in cognitive terms; focuses on academic subjects. | 5. Education is concerned with social, moral, and cognitive terms; focus on the whole child. |
| 6. Values and beliefs tend to be objective and, if not absolute, based on agreed-on standards or truths. | 6. Values and beliefs are subjective, based on the individual's view of the world. |
| **Knowledge and Learning** | |
| 7. Emphasis on knowledge and information. | 7. Emphasis on resolving problems and functioning in one's social environment. |
| 8. Emphasis on subjects (content). | 8. Emphasis on students (learners). |
| 9. Subject matter selected and organized by teacher. | 9. Subject matter planned by teacher and students. |
| 10. Subject matter organized in terms of simple to complex, centered on the past. | 10. Subject matter organized in terms of understanding relationships, centered on present or future. |
| 11. Unit or lesson plans organized according to topics or concepts. | 11. Unit or lesson plans organized according to problems or student interests. |
| 12. Subject matter compartmentalized according to distinct fields, disciplines, or study areas. | 12. Subject matter integrated; includes more than one related subject. |
| **Instruction** | |
| 13. Textbooks and workbooks dominate; teaching and learning largely confined to classroom. | 13. Varied instructional materials; teaching and learning include community resources. |
| 14. Whole-group learning, fixed schedules, and uniform time periods. | 14. Whole, small, and individualized groups, flexible schedules, and adjustable time periods. |
| 15. Homogeneous grouping; tracking of students into special programs. | 15. Heterogeneous grouping; some tracking of students but widely differentiated programs. |
| 16. Students passively assimilate what teacher or textbook says. | 16. Students actively seek information that can be used or applied. |
| 17. Emphasis on uniformity of classroom experiences and instructional situations. | 17. Emphasis on variability of classroom experiences and instructional situations. |
| **Purpose and Programs** | |
| 18. Emphasis on liberal arts and science. | 18. Mix of liberal arts, practical, and vocational subjects. |
| 19. Emphasis on specialization or scholarship. | 19. General emphasis for the layperson. |
| 20. Curriculum prescribed; little room for electives. | 20. Curriculum based on student needs or interests; room for electives. |
| 21. Excellence and high standards; special consideration for high achievers | 21. Equality and flexible standards; special consideration for low achievers. |

*Source:* Information from Allan C. Ornstein, "Philosophy as a Basis for Curriculum Decisions," *High School Journal* (December–January 1991), pp. 106–107.

single philosophy; most combine various philosophies. We believe that no single philosophy, old or new, should exclusively guide decisions about schools and curriculum. The most important thing is that a school's approach to curriculum be politically and economically feasible and that it serve the needs of students and society.

Too often, teachers and administrators plan and implement behavioral objectives with minimal regard to a school's overall philosophy. Curriculum workers must help develop and design school practices in harmony with the philosophy of the school and community.

---

## MyEdLeadershipLab™

Go to Topics 2 and 10: *Curriculum*: *Impact on Outcomes* and *Textbook as Curriculum*, on the MyEdLeadershipLab™ site (www.MyEdLeadershipLab.com) for *Curriculum*: *Foundations, Principles, and Issues,* Sixth Edition where you can:

- Find learning outcomes for *Curriculum: Impact on Outcomes* and *Textbook as Curriculum* along with the national standards that connect to these outcomes.
- Complete Assignments and Activities that can help you more deeply understand the chapter content.
- Apply and Practice your understanding of the core skills identified in the chapter with the Building Leadership Skills unit.
- Prepare yourself for professional certification with a Practice for Certification quiz.

---

## Endnotes

1. William Van Til, "In a Climate of Change," in R. R. Leeper, ed., *Role of Supervisor and Curriculum Director in a Climate of Change* (Washington, DC: Association for Supervision and Curriculum Development, 1965), p. 18.

2. L. Thomas Hopkins, *Interaction: The Democratic Process* (Boston: D. C. Heath, 1941), pp. 198–200.

3. John I. Goodlad et al., *Curriculum Inquiry* (New York: McGraw-Hill, 1979).

4. Ronald C. Doll, *Curriculum Improvement: Decision Making and Process,* 9th ed. (Boston: Allyn & Bacon, 1996), p. 27.

5. John Dewey, *Democracy and Education* (New York: Macmillan, 1916), pp. 186, 383–384.

6. Ibid., p. 384.

7. Ralph W. Tyler, *Basic Principles of Curriculum and Instruction* (Chicago: University of Chicago Press, 1949), pp. 33–34.

8. John I. Goodlad, *What Schools Are For* (Bloomington, IN: Phi Delta Kappan Educational Foundation, 1979). See also John I. Goodlad, *A Place Called School* (New York: McGraw-Hill, 1984).

9. J. Donald Butler, *Idealism in Education* (New York: Harper & Row, 1966).

10. Howard A. Ozman and Samuel Craver, *Philosophical Foundations of Education,* 8th ed. (Columbus, OH: Merrill, 2008).

11. Harry S. Broudy, *Building a Philosophy of Education* (Englewood Cliffs, NJ: Prentice Hall, 1961); and John Wild, *Introduction to a Realist Philosophy* (New York: Harper & Row, 1948).

12. Broudy, *Building a Philosophy of Education;* and William O. Martin, *Realism in Education* (New York: Harper & Row, 1969).

13. Ernest E. Bayles, *Pragmatism in Education* (New York: Harper & Row, 1966); and John L. Childs, *Pragmatism and Education* (New York: Holt, Rinehart and Winston, 1956).

14. John Dewey, *Experience and Education* (New York: Macmillan, 1938).

15. Maxine Greene, *Existential Encounters for Teachers* (New York: Random House, 1967); George F. Kneller, *Existentialism in Education* (New York: Wiley, 1958); and Van Cleve Morris, *Existentialism and Education* (New York: Harper & Row, 1966).

16. Harold Soderquist, *The Person and Education* (Columbus, OH: Merrill, 1966); and Donald Vandenberg, *Human Rights in Education* (New York: Philosophical Library, 1983). See also Israel Scheffler, *Of Human Potential: An Essay in the Philosophy of Education* (Boston: Routledge & Kegan Paul, 1986).

17. Maxine Greene, *Landscapes of Learning* (New York: Teachers College Press, Columbia University, 1978); Barbara McKean, *A Teaching Artist at Work* (Portsmouth, NH: Heinemann, 2006); and Seymour B. Sarason, *Teaching as a Performing Art* (New York: Teachers College Press, Columbia University, 1999).

18. Robert M. Hutchins, *The Conflict in Education* (New York: Harper & Row, 1953), p. 68.

19. Robert M. Hutchins, *The Higher Learning in America* (New Haven, CT: Yale University Press, 1936).

20. Robert M. Hutchins, *A Conversation on Education* (Santa Barbara, CA: The Fund for the Republic, 1963), p. 1.

21. Mortimer J. Adler, *The Paideia Proposal: An Educational Manifesto* (New York: Macmillan, 1982); Mortimer J. Adler, *Paideia Problems and Possibilities* (New York:

Macmillan, 1983); and Mortimer J. Adler, *The Paideia Program: An Educational Syllabus* (New York: Macmillan, 1984).

22. Allan Bloom, *The Closing of the American Mind* (New York: Simon & Schuster, 1987).

23. Allan Bloom, in Brad Miner, ed., *Good Order: Right Answers to Contemporary Questions* (New York: Simon & Schuster, 1995).

24. Ibid.

25. Hyman G. Rickover, "European vs. American Secondary Schools," *Phi Delta Kappan* (November 1958), p. 61.

26. Arthur Bestor, *The Restoration of Learning* (New York: Knopf, 1955), p. 120.

27. Rickover, "European vs. American Secondary Schools," p. 61.

28. Stanley M. Elam, "The Gallup Education Surveys," *Phi Delta Kappan* (September 1983), p. 26. See also Gallup polls published in the September or October issues of *Phi Delta Kappan,* 1984 to 2003.

29. Allan C. Ornstein, Edward Pajak, and Stacey B. Ornstein, *Contemporary Issues in Curriculum,* 5th ed. (Boston: Allyn and Bacon, 2011). Also see Phyllis Tashlik, "Changing the National Conversation on Assessment," *Phi Delta Kappan* (March 2010), pp. 55–59; Thomas Toch, "National Standards Closer to Reality," *Phi Delta Kappan* (September 2009), pp 72–73.

30. Julia E. Koppich, "Teacher Unions and New Forms of Teacher Conversation, *Phi Delta Kappan* (May 2010), pp 22–26; Gary W. Ritter and Nathan C. Jensen, "The Delicate Task of Developing an Attractive Merit Pay Plan for Teachers," *Phi Delta Kappan* (May 2010), pp. 32–37; and Rick Stiggins, "Assessment for Learning," *Phi Delta Kappan* (February 2009), pp. 419–421.

31. Christopher Jencks and Meredith Phillips, eds., *The Black-White Test Score Gap* (Washington, DC: Brookings Institution, 1998); Gary Orfield and Mindy Kornhaber, eds., *Raising Standards or Raising Barriers?* (Washington, DC: Brookings Institution, 2001); and Ornstein, *Class Counts: Education, Inequality and the Shrinking Middle Class.*

32. Lorin Anderson, "Upper Elementary Grades Bear the Brunt of Accountability," *Phi Delta* Kappan (February 2009), pp. 413–418; Donald B. Gratz, "Looming Questions in Performance Pay," *Phi Delta* Kappan (May 2010), pp. 16–21; and Daniel U. Levine and Allan C. Ornstein, "Research on Classroom and School Effectiveness," *Urban Review* (July 1989), pp. 81–95. See also Sharon L. Nichols and David C. Berliner, *Collateral Database: High Standards Corrupt America's Schools* (Cambridge, MA: Harvard Education Press, 2007).

33. E. D. Hirsh, *Cultural Literacy: What Every American Needs to Know,* rev. ed. (Boston: Houghton Mifflin, 1987).

34. E. D. Hirsch, *The Knowledge Deficit* (New York: Houghton Mifflin, 2006).

35. Allan C. Ornstein, "The National Reform of Education," *NASSP Bulletin* (May 1992); Richard W. Riley, "Education Reform through Standards and Partnerships: 1993–2000," *Phi Delta Kappan* (May 2002), pp. 700–707; Joan Richardson, "Quality Education: An Interview with Secretary of Education Arne Duncan," *Phi Delta* Kappan (September 2010), pp. 24–29; Also see Sara Schwartz Chrismer et al., *Assessing NCLB: Perspectives and Prescriptions* (Cambridge, MA: Harvard Education Press, 2007); and Arne Duncan, "Education Reform's Moon Shot," *Washington Post,* July 24, 2009.

36. Howard Gardner, "National Education Goals and the Academic Community," *Education Digest* (February 1990), pp. 41–43; and Maxine Greene, "Imagining Futures: The Public School and Possibility," *Journal of Curriculum Studies* (March–April 2000), pp. 267–280.

37. John I. Goodlad, "Kudzu, Rabbits and School Reform," *Phi Delta Kappan* (September 2002), pp. 16–23; and Nel Noddings, *Educating Moral People: A Caring Alternative to Character Education* (New York: Teachers College Press, Columbia University, 2002). See also Evans Clinchy, *Rescuing the Public Schools* (New York: Teachers College Press, Columbia University, 2007).

38. R. Freeman Butts, *Public Education in the United States* (New York: Holt, Rinehart and Winston, 1978); Lawrence A. Cremin, *The Transformation of the School* (New York: Knopf, 1961); and Allan C. Ornstein, *Teaching and Schooling in America: Pre– and Post–September 11.* (Boston: Allyn & Bacon, 1993).

39. John Dewey, *Democracy and Education* (New York: Macmillan, 1916).

40. John Dewey, "Need for a Philosophy of Education," *New Era in Home and School* (November 1934), p. 212.

41. John Dewey, *The Child and the Curriculum* (Chicago: University of Chicago Press, 1902), pp. 30–31.

42. Boyd H. Bode, *Progressive Education at the Crossroads* (New York: Newson, 1938).

43. Ibid., p. 44.

44. Cremin, *The Transformation of the School.* Also see Joel Spring, *The American School: 1642–1990* (New York: Longman, 1990).

45. Herbert Kohl, *The Open Classroom* (New York: Random House, 1969); and Jonathan Kozol, *Free Schools* (Boston: Houghton Mifflin, 1972). See also C. M. Bowers and David J. Flinders, *Responsive Teaching* (New York: Teachers College Press, Columbia University, 1990).

46. Charles A. Silberman, *Crisis in the Classroom* (New York: Random House, 1971).

47. Arthur T. Jersild, *In Search of Self* (New York: Teachers College Press, 1952); Arthur T. Jersild, *When Teachers Face Themselves* (New York: Teachers College Press, 1955); and Arthur Combs and Donald Snygg, *Individual Behavior,* 2nd ed. (New York: Harper & Row, 1959). See also Arthur Combs, ed., *Perceiving, Behavioring, Becoming* (Washington, DC: Association for Supervision and Curriculum Development, 1962); and Arthur W. Combs, *A Personal Approach to Teaching* (Boston: Allyn & Bacon, 1982).

48. Abraham H. Maslow, *Toward a Psychology of Being* (New York: Van Nostrand Reinhold, 1962); Abraham H. Maslow, *Motivation and Personality,* 2nd ed. (New York:

Harper & Row, 1970); Carl R. Rogers, *Client-Centered Therapy* (Boston: Houghton Mifflin, 1951); Carl R. Rogers, *On Becoming a Person* (Boston: Houghton Mifflin, 1961); and Carl R. Rogers, *Freedom to Learn for the 1980s,* 2nd ed. (Columbus, OH: Merrill, 1983).

49. William Glasser, *Schools Without Failure* (New York; Random House, 1961).

50. Robert Fried, *The Passionate Teacher;* Vito Perrione, *Teacher with a Heart* (New York: Teachers College Press, Columbia University, 1998).

51. Theodore R. Sizer, *Horace's Compromise* (Boston: Houghton Mifflin, 1985).

52. Ibid., p. 20.

53. Nel Noddings, *The Challenge to Care in Schools* (New York: Teachers College Press, Columbia University, 1992).

54. Ibid.

55. Richard F. Elmore, *School Reform from Inside Out* (Cambridge, MA: Harvard Education Press, 2004); Jeanne Oaks, *Keeping Track* (New Haven, CT: Yale University Press , 1985); and Joel Spring, *Political Agendas for Education* (Mahwah, NJ: Erlbaum, 2005).

56. Edgar Z. Friedenberg, *The Vanishing Adolescent* (Boston: Beacon Press, 1959), pp. 26, 91, 110. See also Edgar Z. Friedenberg, *Coming of Age in America* (New York: Random House, 1967); and Peter McLaren, "Education as a Political Issue: What's Missing in the Public Conversation," in Joel L. Kincheloe and Shirley R. Steinberg, eds., *Thirteen Questions,* 2nd ed. (New York: Peter Lang, 1995), pp. 265–280.

57. John Holt, *How Children Fail* (New York: Pitman, 1964).

58. Paul Goodman, *Compulsory Mis-Education* (New York: Horizon Press, 1964), pp. 20–22.

59. Paul Goodman, *New Reformation* (New York: Random House, 1970), p. 86.

60. A. S. Neill, *Summerhill: A Radical Approach to Child Rearing* (New York: Hart, 1960), p. 4.

61. Ibid., pp. 4, 14.

62. Ivan Illich, *Deschooling Society* (New York: Harper & Row, 1971).

63. Henry A. Giroux, *Teachers as Intellectuals* (Westport, CT: Bergin & Garvey, 1988); and Henry A. Giroux, Colin Lankshear, Peter McLaren, and Michael Peters, *Counternarratives* (New York: Routledge, 1996).

64. Giroux, *Teachers as Intellectuals,* p. 296. Also see Henry Giroux, "Charting Disaster," *Truthout* (June 21, 2010).

65. Peter McLaren, "Critical Pedagogy and the Pragmatics of Justice," in Michael Peters, ed., *Education and the Postmodern Condition* (Westport, CT: Bergin & Garvey, 1995), p. 91.

66. Ibid., p. 92.

67. Peter McLaren, "A Pedagogy of Possibility," *Educational Researcher* (March 1999), pp. 49–54; and Peter McLaren, *Life in School,* 5th ed. (Boston: Allyn & Bacon, 2007); and Peter McLaren, *Pedagogy and Praxis* (Boston: Sense Publishers, 2007).

68. George S. Counts, *Dare the School Build a New Social Order?* (New York: Day, 1932), pp. 7–8. See also Robert R. Sherman, "Dare the School Build a New Social Order—Again?" *Educational Theory* (Winter 1986), pp. 87–92.

69. John Dewey, *Reconstruction in Philosophy* (New York: Holt, 1920).

70. Theodore Brameld, *Ends and Means in Education* (New York: Harper & Row, 1950); and Theodore Brameld, *Patterns of Educational Philosophy* (New York: World, 1950).

71. Theodore Brameld, "Reconstructionism as Radical Philosophy of Education," *Educational Forum* (November 1977), p. 70.

72. Christopher Jencks et al., *Inequality: A Reassessment of the Effect of Family and Schooling in America* (New York: Basic Books, 1972); Jonathon Kozol, *Death at an Early Age* (Boston: Houghton Mifflin, 1964); Kozol, *Savage Inequalities* (New York: Crown, 1991); Gary Orfield et al., *Status of School Desegregation: 1968–1986* (Washington, DC: National School Boards Association, 1989); and William J. Wilson, *The Truly Disadvantaged* (Chicago: University of Chicago Press, 1987).

73. Ruud J. Garter, "International Collaboration in Curriculum Development," *Educational Leadership* (December–January 1987), pp. 4–7; David Hill, "Rediscovering Geography: Its Five Fundamental Themes," *NASSP Bulletin* (December 1989), pp. 1–7; and Jon Nixon, "Reclaiming Coherence: Cross-Curriculum Provision and the National Curriculum," *Journal of Curriculum Studies* (March–April 1991), pp. 187–192.

74. Joel Spring, *How Educational Technologies Are Shaping Global Society* (Mahwah, NJ: Erlbaum, 2004); and Joel Spring, *Pedagogies of Globalization* (Mahwah, NJ: Erlbaum, 2006).

75. Thomas Friedman, *The World Is Flat* (New York: Farrar, Strauss, and Giroux, 2005).

76. Ornstein, *Class Counts.*

77. Ibid. p. 203

78. Linda Darling-Hammond, *The Flat World and Education* (New York: Teachers College Press, Columbia University, 2009).

79. Ornstein, *Class Counts*, p. 204.

80. Elliot W. Eisner, "Curriculum Ideologies," in Philip W. Jackson, ed., *Handbook of Research on Curriculum* (New York: Macmillan Publishing Company, 1992), pp. 302–326.

81. Elliot W. Eisner, "What Does It Mean to Say a School Is Doing Well?" *Phi Delta Kappan* (January 2001), pp. 367–372; and Goodlad, "Kudzu, Rabbits, and School Reform," pp. 16–23.

82. Referenced in Patrick Slattery, *Curriculum Development in the Postmodern Era* (New York: Garland Publishing, Inc., 1995). See also William F. Pinar, *Contemporary Curriculum Discourses* (New York: Peter Lang, 1999).

83. Maxine Greene, "Interpretation and Re-Vision: Toward Another Story," in J. T. Sears and J. D. Marshall, eds., *Teaching and Thinking about Curriculum* (New York: Teachers College Press, Columbia University, 1990), pp. 75–78; and Maxine Greene, *Variations on a Blue Guitar*

(New York: Teachers College Press, Columbia University, 2002).

84. Paulo Freire, *Pedagogy of the Oppressed* (New York: Herder & Herder, 1970), pp. 75, 100, 108; and Paulo Freire, *The Politics of Education: Culture, Power and Liberation* (Westport, CT: Bergin & Garvey, 1985).

85. William Pinar, "Sanity, Madness, and the School," in W. Pinar, ed., *Curriculum Theorizing: The Reconceptualists* (Berkeley, CA: McCutchan, 1974), pp. 364–366, 369–373, 381; and William Pinar et al., *Understanding Curriculum* (New York: Peter Lang, 1995).

86. Michael W. Apple, *Ideology and Curriculum* (Boston: Routledge & Kegan Paul, 1979), p. 4. See also Michael W. Apple, *Teachers and Texts,* rev. ed. (Boston: Routledge & Kegan Paul, 2004).

87. Michael Apple and Nancy R. King, "What Do Schools Teach?" in R. H. Weller, ed., *Humanistic Education* (Berkeley, CA: McCutchan, 1977), p. 30. See also Michael Apple et al., eds., *International Handbook of Critical Education* (New York: Routledge, 2009).

88. Illich, *Deschooling Society.* See also Michael W. Apple and James A. Beane, *Democratic Schools: Lessons in Powerful Education* (Portsmouth, NH: Heinemann, 2007).

89. Paulo Freire and Donaldo Macedo, *Literacy: Reading the Word and the World* (Westport, CT: Bergin & Garvey, 1989); and Freire, *Pedagogy of the Oppressed.*

90. Macdonald, "Curriculum and Human Interests," in W. Pinar, ed., *Curriculum Theorizing: The Reconceptualists* (Berkeley, CA: McCutchan, 1975), p. 293. See also Raymond A. Morrow and Carlos A. Torres, *Reading Freire and Habermas* (New York: Teachers College Press, Columbia University, 2002).

91. Greene, "Imagining Futures: The Public School and Possibility."

92. Horace Mann, *The Republic and the School,* rev. ed. (New York: Teachers College Press, Columbia University, 1957), p. 39.

93. David B. Tyack, *Turning Points in American Educational History* (Waltham, MA: Blaisdell, 1967), p. 114.

94. Henry M. Levin, "Equal Educational Opportunity and the Distribution of Educational Expenditures," in A. Kopan and H. J. Walberg, eds., *Rethinking Educational Equality* (Berkeley, CA: McCutchan, 1974), p. 30. See also Ornstein, *Class Counts.*

95. See James S. Coleman et al., *Equality of Educational Opportunity* (Washington, DC: U.S. Government Printing Office, 1966); and Jencks et al., *Inequality: A Reassessment of the Effect of Family and Schools in America.* See also Christopher Jencks and Meredith Phillips, eds., *The Black-White Test Score Gap* (Washington, DC: Brookings Institution Press, 2000).

96. James S. Coleman, "The Concept of Equality of Educational Opportunity," *Harvard Educational Review* (Winter 1968), pp. 7–22.

97. Nathan Glazer, *We Are Multiculturalists Now* (Cambridge, MA: Harvard University Press, 1997); John McWhorter, *Losing the Race* (New York: Simon & Schuster, 2000); and Lois Weis, *The Way Class Works* (New York: Routledge, 2007).

98. John W. Gardner, *Excellence: Can We Be Equal and Excellent Too?* (New York: Harper & Row, 1961), pp. 17–18, 83, 90.

# 3

■ ■ ■

# Historical Foundations of Curriculum

## FOCUSING QUESTIONS

1. Why is it important to know curriculum's historical foundations?
2. How did U.S. schools modify European educational ideas?
3. How did U.S. democratic ideas contribute to the rise of public schooling in the United States?
4. In what ways did U.S. nationalism influence the curriculum during the first half of the 19th century?
5. How did 19th-century European pioneers of pedagogy influence the U.S. school curriculum?
6. What unique problems were evidenced in the 19th century as the elementary (or secondary) school curriculum developed?
7. How did the Committee of Fifteen and the Committee of Ten influence 20th-century curriculum?
8. How did scientism in education influence curriculum making?
9. What roles can historians of curriculum play within the field of curriculum?
10. What value do you give to a historical sense of curriculum?

A knowledge of curriculum's history provides guidance for today's curriculum makers. We begin our discussion with the colonial period and proceed through the 18th, 19th, and 20th centuries. Most of our discussion focuses on the past 100 years.

## THE COLONIAL PERIOD: 1642–1776

Curriculum's historical foundations are largely rooted in the educational experiences of colonial Massachusetts. Massachusetts was settled mainly by Puritans, who adhered to strict theological principles. The first New England schools were closely tied to the Puritan church. According to educational historians, a school's primary purpose was to teach children to read the Scriptures and notices of civil affairs.[1] Reading was the most important subject, followed by writing and spelling, which were needed for understanding the catechism and common law. Since colonial days, therefore, reading and related language skills have been basic to American education and the elementary school curriculum.

## Three Colonial Regions

Schools in colonial Massachusetts derived from two sources: (1) 1642 legislation required parents and guardians to ensure that children could read and understand the principles of religion and the laws of the Commonwealth and (2) the "Old Deluder Satan" Act of 1647, which required every town of 50 or more families to appoint a reading and writing teacher. Towns of 100 or more families were to employ a teacher of Latin so that students could be prepared to enter Harvard College.[2] Except for Rhode Island, the other New England colonies followed Massachusetts's example. These early laws reveal how important education was to the Puritan settlers. Some historians consider these laws to be the roots of U.S. school law and the public school movement. The Puritans valued literacy partly as a way of preventing the formation of a large underclass, such as existed in England and other parts of Europe. They also wanted to ensure that their children would grow up committed to the religious doctrines.

Unlike New England, the middle colonies had no language or religion in common. George Beauchamp writes, "Competition among political and religious groups retarded willingness to expend the public funds for educational purposes."[3] No single system of schools could be established. Instead, parochial and independent schools related to different ethnic and religious groups evolved. Schools were locally rather than centrally controlled. The current notion of cultural pluralism thus took shape some 250 years ago.

Until the end of the 18th century, educational decisions in the southern colonies were generally left to the family. On behalf of poor children, orphans, and illegitimate children, legislation was enacted to ensure that their guardians provided private instruction—for example, in vocational skills. However, the plantation system of landholding, slavery, and gentry created great educational inequity. In general, the white children of plantation owners were privately tutored, but poor whites received no formal education. Unable to read and write, many poor whites became subsistence farmers like their parents. The law prohibited slave children from learning to read or write. The South's economic and political system "tended to retard the development of a large-scale system of schools. This education [handicap] was felt long after the Civil War period."[4]

Despite the regional variations, the schools of New England, the middle Atlantic colonies, and the South all were influenced by English political ideas. Also, despite differences in language, religion, and economic systems, religious commitment was a high priority in most schools. "The curriculum of the colonial schools consisted of reading, writing, and [some] arithmetic along with the rudiments of religious faith and lessons designed to develop manners and morals."[5] It was a traditional curriculum, stressing basic skills, timeless and absolute values, social and religious conformity, faith in authority, knowledge for the sake of knowledge, rote learning, and memorization. The curriculum reflected the belief that children were born in sin, play was idleness, and children's talk was gibberish. The teacher applied strict discipline. This approach to the curriculum dominated American education until the rise of progressivism.

## Colonial Schools

Schools were important institutions for colonial society. However, a much smaller percentage of children attended elementary or secondary school than do today.

**TOWN SCHOOLS.**   In the New England colonies, the town school was a locally controlled public elementary school. Often it was a crude, one-room structure dominated by the teacher's pulpit at the front of the room and attended by boys and girls of the community. Students sat on benches and studied their assignments until the teacher called on them to recite. The children ranged in age from 5 or 6 to 13 or 14. Attendance was not always regular; it depended on weather conditions and on the extent to which individual families needed their children to work on their farms.[6]

**PAROCHIAL AND PRIVATE SCHOOLS.**   In the middle colonies, parochial and private schools predominated. Missionary societies and various religious and ethnic groups established elementary schools for their own children. Like the New England town schools, these schools focused on reading, writing, and religious sermons. In the South, upper-class children attended private schools oriented toward reading, writing, arithmetic, and studying the primer and Bible; less fortunate children might attend charity schools, where they learned the "three R's," recited religious hymns (which was less demanding than reading the Bible), and learned vocational skills.

**LATIN GRAMMAR SCHOOLS.**   At the secondary level, upper-class boys attended Latin grammar schools, first established in Boston in 1635, as preparation for college. These schools catered to those who planned to enter the professions (medicine, law, teaching, and the ministry) or become business owners or merchants.[7] A boy would enter a Latin grammar school at age 8 or 9 and remain for 8 years. His curriculum focused on the classics. "There were some courses in Greek, rhetoric, . . . and logic, but Latin was apparently three-quarters of the curriculum in most of the grammar schools, or more."[8] The other arts and sciences received little or no attention. "The religious atmosphere was quite as evident . . . as it was in the elementary school," with the "master praying regularly with his pupils" and quizzing them "thoroughly on the sermons."[9] The regimen of study was exhausting and unexciting, and the school served the church. As Samuel Morrison reminds us, the Latin grammar school was one of colonial America's closest links to European schools. Its curriculum resembled the classical humanist curriculum of the Renaissance (when schools were intended primarily for upper-class children and their role was to support the era's religious and social institutions).[10]

**ACADEMIES.**   Established in 1751, the academy was the second American institution to provide education. Based on Benjamin Franklin's ideas and intended to offer a practical curriculum for those not going to college, it had a diversified curriculum of English grammar, classics, composition, rhetoric, and public speaking.[11] Latin was no longer considered a crucial subject. Students could choose a foreign language based on their vocational needs. For example, a prospective clergyman could study Latin or Greek, and a future businessman could learn French, German, or Spanish. Mathematics was taught for its professional uses rather than as an abstract intellectual exercise. History, not religion, was the chief ethical study. The academy also introduced many practical and manual skills into the formal curriculum: carpentry, engraving, printing, painting, cabinet making, farming, bookkeeping, and so on. These skills formed the basis of vocational curriculum in the 20th century.

**COLLEGES.**   Most students who graduated from Latin grammar schools went to Harvard or Yale University. College was based on the Puritan view that ministers needed to be soundly educated in the classics and scriptures. The students had to demonstrate competency in Latin and Greek and the classics. As is the case today, secondary education prepared students for college. Ellwood Cubberley writes, "The student would be admitted into college 'upon Examination' whereby he could show competency 'to Read, Construe, Parce Tully, Vergil and the Greek Testament; and to write Latin in Prose and to understand the Rules of Prosodia and Common Arithmetic' as well as to bring 'testimony of his blameless and inoffensive life.'"[12]

The Harvard/Yale curriculum consisted of courses in Latin, grammar, logic, rhetoric, arithmetic, astronomy, ethics, metaphysics, and natural sciences. The curriculum for the ministry or other professions also included Greek, Hebrew, and ancient history.

## Old Textbooks, Old Readers

The hornbook, primer, Westminster Catechism, Old Testament, and Bible were considered textbooks. Until the American Revolution, most elementary textbooks were of English origin or directly imitated English textbooks.[13] Children learned the alphabet, the Lord's Prayer, and some syllables, words, and sentences by memorizing the *hornbook,* a paddle-shaped board to which was attached a sheet of parchment covered with a transparent sheath made from flattened cattle horns.

When the *New England Primer* was published in the 1690s, it replaced the English primer. The first American basal reader, it would remain the most widely used textbook in the colonies for more than 100 years; more than 3 million copies were sold. Religious and moral doctrines permeated the *New England Primer*. The somber caste of Puritan religion and morals was evident as students memorized sermons and learned their ABCs through rote and drill:

> A— *In Adam's Fall*
> *We sinned all*
> B— *Thy Life to mend*
> *This book attend*
> C— *The Cat doth play*
> *And after slay . . .*
> Z— *Zacheus he*
> *Did climb the tree*
> *His Lord to see.*[14]

In 1740, Thomas Dilworth published a *New Guide to the English Tongue,* which combined grammar, spelling, and religious instruction. It was followed a few years later by *The School Master's Assistant,* a widely used mathematics text.

Years later Noah Webster, an ardent cultural nationalist, wrote a letter to Henry Barnard (then Connecticut's Commissioner of Education), in which he described the narrowness of the elementary curriculum and the limited use of textbooks:

> [B]efore the Revolution . . . the books used were chiefly or wholly Dilworth's Spelling Books, the Psalter, Testament, and Bible. No geography was studied before the publication of Dr. Morse's small books on that subject, about the year 1786 or 1787. No history was read, as far as my knowledge extends, for there was no abridged history of the United States. Except the books above mentioned, no book for reading was used before the publication of the Third Part of my Institute, in 1785. . . . The introduction of my Spelling Book, first published in 1783, produced a great change in the department of spelling. . . . No English grammar was generally taught in common schools when I was young, except that in Dilworth, and that to no good purpose.[15]

## THE NATIONAL PERIOD: 1776–1850

A new mission for education, which began to emerge during the Revolutionary period, continued throughout the early national period. Many leaders began to link free public schooling with the ideas of popular government and political freedom. President Madison wrote, "A popular government without popular information, or the means of acquiring it, is but a prologue to a farce or a tragedy or perhaps both." Thomas Jefferson expressed a similar belief when he asserted, "If a nation expects to be ignorant and free in a state of civilization, it expects what never was and never will be."

Life, liberty, and equality were emphasized in the era's great documents: the Declaration of Independence, the Bill of Rights, and the 1785 Northwest Ordinances (which divided the Northwest Territory into townships and reserved the 16th section of "every township for the maintenance of public schools"). The ordinances reaffirmed that "schools and the means of education shall forever be encouraged" by the states. The federal government thus committed to advancing education while assuring the constitutionally guaranteed autonomy of state and local schools. As a result of these ordinances, the federal government gave 39 states more than 154 million acres of land for schools.[16]

By 1800, secular forces had sufficiently developed to challenge and ultimately reduce religious influence over elementary and secondary schools. These secular forces included the development of democracy, the development of a strong federal government, emerging cultural nationalism, the idea of religious freedom, and new discoveries in the natural sciences.

## Rush: Science, Progress, and Free Education

Dr. Benjamin Rush (1745–1813) represented this new era. In 1791, he wrote that the emphasis on the classics prejudiced the masses against institutions of learning. As long as Latin and Greek dominated the curriculum, universal education beyond the rudiments was wishful thinking. Education should advance democracy and the exploration and development of natural resources. "To spend four or five years in learning two dead languages, is to turn our backs upon a gold mine, in order to amuse ourselves catching butterflies." If the time spent on Latin and Greek was devoted to science, this champion pragmatist continued, "the human condition would be much improved."[17]

Rush outlined a plan of education for Pennsylvania and the new nation: free elementary schools in every township consisting of 100 or more families, a free academy at the county level, and free colleges and universities at the state level for society's future leaders. Tax dollars would pay for the expenses, but the educational system ultimately would reduce taxes because a productive, well-managed workforce and entrepreneur force would result. (Thirty years later Horace Mann would make the same argument when he spearheaded the common school movement.) Rush's curriculum emphasized reading, writing, and arithmetic at the elementary school level; English, German, the arts, and, especially, the sciences at the secondary and college level; and good manners and moral principles at all levels.

## Jefferson: Education for Citizenship

Thomas Jefferson (1743–1826) had faith in agrarian society and distrusted the urban proletariat. A man of wide-ranging interests, which included politics, architecture, agriculture, science, art, and education, Jefferson believed that the state must educate its citizenry to ensure a democratic society. In "A Bill for the More General Diffusion of Knowledge," introduced in the Virginia legislature in 1779, Jefferson advocated a plan that provided educational opportunities for both common people and landed gentry "at the expense of all."[18] To Jefferson, formal education should not be restricted to particular religious or upper-class groups. Public taxes should finance schools. Jefferson's plan divided Virginia's counties into wards, each of which would have a free elementary school for the teaching of reading, writing, arithmetic, and history. The plan also provided for the establishment of 20 secondary-level grammar schools, to which poor but gifted students could receive scholarships. The students in these 20 schools would study Latin, Greek, English, geography, and higher mathematics. On completing grammar school, half the scholarship students would receive positions as elementary or ward school teachers. The 10 scholarship students of highest achievement would attend William and Mary College. Jefferson's plan promoted continuing education for the brightest students as well as equal opportunity for economically disadvantaged students.

Neither Jefferson's proposal for Virginia nor Rush's proposal for Pennsylvania was enacted. Nonetheless, the bills indicate educational theorizing characteristic of the young nation. Coupled with Franklin's academy and its practical curriculum based on business and commercial principles rather than classical and religious principles, these bills promoted education aimed at good citizenship and social progress. Rush, Jefferson, and, to lesser extent, Franklin proposed universal education and methods for identifying students of superior ability, who were to receive free secondary and college educations at public expense.

## Webster: Schoolmaster and Cultural Nationalist

The United States differed from most new countries struggling for identity in that it lacked a shared cultural identity and national literature. In its struggle against the "older" cultures and "older" ideas, the new nation went to great lengths to differentiate itself from the Old World and especially

England.[19] Noah Webster (1758–1843) urged Americans to "unshackle [their] minds and act like independent beings. You have been children long enough, subject to the control and subservient to the interests of a haughty parent. . . . You have an empire to raise . . . and a national character to establish and extend by your wisdom and judgment."[20]

In 1789, when the Constitution became the law of the land, Webster argued that the United States should have its own system of "language as well as government." Great Britain's language, he argued, "should no longer be our standard; for the taste of her writers is already completed, and her language on the decline."[21] By the act of revolution, the American people had declared their political independence from England. Now they needed to declare their cultural independence as well.

Realizing that a distinctive national language and literature conveyed a sense of national identity, Webster set out to reshape U.S. English. Moreover, the expression "American English" (as opposed to the British dialect) was coined by Webster. He believed that a uniquely U.S. language would (1) eliminate the remains of European usage, (2) create a uniform U.S. speech free of localism and provincialism, and (3) promote U.S. cultural nationalism.[22] A U.S. language would unite citizens. However, such a language would have to be phonetically simple to render it suitable to the common people. As children learned the U.S. language, they also would learn to think and act as Americans. Because the books read by students would shape the curriculum of U.S. schools, Webster spent much of his life writing spelling and reading books. His *Grammatical Institute of the English Language* was published in 1783. The first part of the *Institute* was later printed as *The American Spelling Book,* which was widely used throughout the United States in the first half of the 19th century.[23] Webster's *Spelling Book* went through many editions; it is estimated that 15 million copies had been sold by 1837. In fact, it outsold every book in the 19th century except the Bible. Webster's great work was *The American Dictionary,* which was completed in 1825 after 25 years of laborious research.[24] Often termed the "schoolmaster of the Republic," Webster helped create a sense of U.S. language, identity, and nationality.

### McGuffey: The Readers and American Virtues

William Holmes McGuffey (1800–1873), who taught most of his life in Ohio colleges, also entered the debate on U.S. cultural nationalism. His five *Readers* were the most popular textbooks in the United States during his era. (An estimated 120 million copies were sold between 1836 and 1920.)[25] McGuffey gratefully acknowledged U.S. "obligations to Europe and the descendants of the English stock" in science, art, law, literature, and manners. However, the United States had made its own contributions to humankind; they "were not literary or cultural, but moral and political." The seeds of popular liberty "first germinated from our English ancestors, but it shot up to its fullest heights in our land."[26] The United States had shown Europe that "popular institutions, founded on equality and the principle of representation, are capable of maintaining governments" and that it was practical to elevate the masses "to the great right and great duty of self-government."[27]

McGuffey's *Readers* extolled patriotism, heroism, hard work, diligence, and virtuous living. Their tone was moralistic, religious, capitalistic, and nationalistic. The selections of American literature included orations by George Washington, Patrick Henry, Benjamin Franklin, and Daniel Webster. Through his *Readers,* McGuffey taught several generations of Americans. He also provided the first graded *Readers* for U.S. schools and paved the way for a graded system, which began in 1840. Along with his *Pictorial Primer,* many of his *Readers* are used even today in some rural, conservative, and/or fundamentalist schools. (See Curriculum Tips 3.1.)

## NINETEENTH-CENTURY EUROPEAN EDUCATORS

Although widely criticized, European thought greatly influenced U.S. education. At the college level, German educators influenced the fields of natural science, psychology, and sociology; many of our research-oriented universities were based on the German model. At the K–12 level, progressive ideas from German and Swiss thinkers led to curricular and instructional methods

---

**CURRICULUM TIPS 3.1    The Need for Historical Perspective**

All professional educators, including curriculum specialists, need an understanding of history to avoid repeating the mistakes of the past and also to better prepare for the future.

1. The development of ideas in education is part of our intellectual and cultural heritage.
2. A truly educated person has a sense of historical context.
3. An understanding of various theories and practices in education requires an understanding of historical foundations.
4. An understanding of historical foundations in education helps us integrate curriculum, instruction, and teaching.
5. History illuminates current pedagogical practices.
6. In developing a common or core curriculum, a historical perspective is essential.
7. With a historical perspective, curriculum specialists can better understand the relationship between content and process in subject areas.
8. References to history, especially case examples, contribute to academic education's moral dimension.
9. The history of education permits practitioners to understand relationships between what students of the past learned and what students now learn.
10. The study of education history is important for the purposes of education theory and research.

---

that were psychologically oriented and considered students' needs and interests. English models of schooling also affected U.S. education.

The theme of reform characterized much of the era's educational discourse. The limitations of the "traditional curriculum and typical school of this era were recognized by educational leaders in Europe and America, and many of the features that were now firmly established in [curriculum] theory and practice can be traced to the ideas of the men and women who were ahead of their time."[28] The traditional curriculum, which emphasized Latin, Greek, and the classics, became less popular. New pedagogical practices replaced rote learning, memorization, and corporal punishment.

## Pestalozzi: General and Special Methods

Early U.S. education was strongly influenced by Johann Heinrich Pestalozzi (1746–1827), a Swiss educator. According to one educational historian, Pestalozzi "laid the basis for the modern elementary school and helped to reform elementary-school practice."[29] Pestalozzi maintained that education should be based on the child's natural development. His basic pedagogical innovation was his insistence that children learn through the senses. He deplored rote learning and advocated linking the curriculum to children's home experiences.

Pestalozzi proposed a "general" method and a "special" method. The general method called for educators who provided children with emotional security and affection. The special method considered children's auditory and visual senses. Pestalozzi devised the "object" lesson, in which children studied common objects, such as plants, rocks, and household objects. Children would determine an object's form, draw the object, and then name it. From these lessons in form, number, and sound came more formal instruction in the three R's.

William McClure and Joseph Neef—and later Horace Mann and Henry Barnard—worked to introduce Pestalozzi's ideas into U.S. schools.[30] Pestalozzi's basic concepts of education became part of progressive schooling and later appeared in the movement for curriculum relevancy and humanistic curriculum.

## Froebel: The Kindergarten Movement

Friedrich Froebel (1782–1852), a German educator, developed what he called "kindergarten" (children's garden). He focused on the 3- and 4-year-old children and believed that their schooling should be organized around play and individual and group interests and activities. Froebel encouraged a child-centered curriculum based (like Pestalozzi's) on love, trust, and freedom. Songs, stories, colorful materials, and games were part of the formal curriculum. The children could manipulate objects (spheres, cubes, and circles), shape and construct materials (clay, sand, cardboard), and engage in playful activities (build castles and mountains, run, and otherwise exercise).[31]

Together, these activities made up the learning environment and provided a secure and pleasant place where children could grow naturally. German immigrants brought the kindergarten concept to the United States. Margaret Schurz established the first U.S. kindergarten in Watertown, Wisconsin, in 1855. William Harris, superintendent of schools in St. Louis, Missouri, and later U.S. Commissioner of Education, was instrumental in implementing the idea on a broader scale. Kindergarten is now an established part of U.S. education. Many of Froebel's ideas of childhood experiences and methods of play have been incorporated into current theories of early childhood education and progressive schooling.

## Herbart: Moral and Intellectual Development

Johann Herbart (1776–1841) was a German philosopher known for his contributions to moral development in education and for his creation of a methodology of instruction designed to establish a highly structured mode of teaching. For Herbart, the chief aim of education was moral development, which he considered to be basic and necessary to all other educational goals or purposes. The chief objective of Herbartian education was to produce a good person who had many interests. Herbart argued that virtue is founded on knowledge and misconduct is the product of inadequate knowledge or of inferior education. Thus, he gave education a vital role in shaping moral character.

In elaborating on his work on moral education, Herbart specified five major kinds of ideas as the foundation of moral character: (1) the idea of *inner freedom,* which referred to action based on one's personal convictions; (2) the idea of *perfection,* which referred to the harmony and integration of behavior; (3) the idea of *benevolence,* by which a person was to be concerned with the social welfare of others; (4) the idea of *justice,* by which a person reconciled his or her individual behavior with that of the social group; and (5) the idea of *retribution,* which indicates that reward or punishment accrues to certain kinds of behavior.

Drawing from his ideas on moral education, Herbart also specified two major bodies of interests that should be included in education: knowledge interests and ethical interests. *Knowledge* interests involved empirical data, factual information, and speculative ideas, and *ethical* interests included sympathy for others, social relationships, and religious sentiments. Herbart's aim was to produce an educated individual who was also of good character and high morals. He believed that if a person's cognitive powers are properly exercised and his or her mind is stocked with proper ideas, then the person will use that knowledge to guide his or her behavior. The person who lives and acts according to knowledge will be a moral person.

In terms of organizing instruction, Herbart developed the concepts of curriculum *correlation.* These were to have a decided impact on education in the United States in the 1940s and 1950s. According to the doctrine of correlation, each subject should be taught in such a way that it refers to and relates to other subjects. Knowledge would then appear to the learner as an integrated system of ideas that form an apperceptive mass—the whole of a person's previous experience—into which new ideas could be related.

Herbart believed that the subjects of history, geography, and literature were ideally suited as core subjects. Herbart also developed four pedagogical principles that were accepted enthusiastically and transformed into five steps by his followers; these became known as the Herbartian method: (1) *preparation*, by which the teacher stimulates the readiness of the learner for the new lesson by referring to materials that were learned earlier; (2) *presentation,* in which the teacher presents the new lesson to the students; (3) *association*, in which the new lesson is deliberately related to the ideas or materials that students studied earlier; (4) *systemization,* which involves the use of examples to illustrate the principles or generalizations to be mastered by the students; and (5) *application*, which involves the testing of new ideas or the materials of the new lesson to determine if students have understood and mastered them.

Speaking of Herbart's contribution to the instruction of teaching, John Dewey said: "Few attempts have been made to formulate a method, resting on general principles, of conducting a recitation. One of these is of great importance and has probably had more influence upon the learning of lessons than all others put together; namely, the analysis by Herbart of a recitation into five successive steps."[32]

Herbart's formal steps of instruction were applied to teacher training as well as adopted by classroom teachers. In theory, the teacher would prepare carefully by thinking of the five steps and asking: What do my students know? What questions should I ask? What events should I relate? What conclusions should be reached? How can students apply what they have learned? To a large extent, these principles still serve as the guidelines for today's classroom lesson plan. His five steps also form the basis of what today's curriculum theorists would refer to as the *instructional* or *implementation* phase of curriculum planning, or what the authors call *curriculum development* (see Chapter 7).

## Spencer: Utilitarian and Scientific Education

Herbert Spencer (1820–1903) was an English social scientist who based his ideas of education on Charles Darwin's theory of biological evolution and subsequently introduced the notion of "survival of the fittest". Spencer maintained that simple societies evolve to more complex social systems, characterized by an increased variety of specialized professions and occupations.[33] Because of nature's laws, only intelligent and productive populations adapt to environmental changes. Less intelligent, weak, or lazy people slowly disappear. Spencer's notions of excellence, social-economic progress, and intellectual development based on heredity had immense implications for education and economic outcomes.

Spencer criticized religious doctrines and classical subject matter as unscientific and unrelated to contemporary society. He advocated a scientific and practical curriculum suited to industrialized society. Spencer believed that traditional schools were impractical and ornamental, a luxury for the upper class that failed to meet the needs of the people living in a modern society.

Spencer constructed a curriculum aimed at advancing human survival and progress. His curriculum included knowledge and activities (in order of importance) for sustaining life, earning a living, rearing children properly, maintaining effective citizenship, and enjoying leisure time.[34] These five purposes became the basis of the famous Principles of Secondary Education, published in 1918. The document proved to be a turning point by which progressive thought (focus on the whole child) trumped perennialist philosophy (focus on subject matter) in education.

Spencer maintained that students should be taught *how* to think, not what to think. His notion about discovery learning, an offshoot of scientific reasoning, also influenced 20th-century curricuralists, including Dewey and his 1916 publication of *How We Think* and, later, essentialist disciplinary educators such as Jerome Bruner and Phil Phenix.[35]

In his famous essay "What Knowledge Is of Most Worth?" Spencer argued that science was the most practical subject for the survival of the individual and society, yet it occupied minimal space in the curriculum. Spencer reasoned that a curriculum should be constructed on the basis of what is useful and essential for promoting progress. In effect, he was suggesting an educational program that would apply scientific knowledge and skills for an industrialized society (such as the one we live in today).

Both John Dewey and Charles Judd were later influenced by Spencer's thinking when they formulated a science of education 25 years later based on the methods of hypothesizing, finding facts, and making generalizations. Edward Thorndike, probably the best known behavioral psychologist of the early 20th century, was also influenced by Spencer's scientific theories—specifically, those involving Thorndike's principles of learning and organization of experiences.

Although many of Spencer's ideas about religion, evolution, and social progress created a furor (and still do among some religious and political observers), the ideas suited his era, which was characterized by industrial growth and territorial expansion by Europe and the United States.

## THE RISE OF UNIVERSAL EDUCATION: 1820–1900

During the early 1800s, the United States expanded westward. Life on the new frontier deepened America's faith in the common person who built the new nation. Equality and rugged individualism were important concepts, expressed in the Declaration of Independence and reaffirmed by Westerners, who believed all people of all classes were important. This kind of faith in the working person and in American civilization underscored to the frontier people the necessity of school.[36] In the urban East, the lower classes, particularly immigrants, also valued free schooling and linked it to social mobility and the American dream. The upper-class establishment may not have had faith in the masses, but they reluctantly accepted the argument (of Jefferson, Rush, and now Mann) that mass education was necessary for intelligent participation in a political democracy and for economic growth of the country.

### Monitorial Schools

The monitorial school was a European invention based on Joseph Lancaster's model of education. It spread quickly to the U.S. urban centers, where the immigrant population was increasing, and to the frontier, where there was need for a system of schools. It was attractive in the 1820s and the following decades due to its economy and efficiency. Bright student monitors served as instructors. The teacher taught the lesson to the monitors (high-achieving students), who presented the material to their classmates. The instruction was highly structured and based on rote learning and drilling the three R's

Proponents of monitorial teaching stressed that it was economical and kept all students busy while the teacher was occupied with a few students. The class was divided into smaller groups, with a monitor in charge of each group. The students were kept actively involved in practice and drill activities and moved at their own pace. Teachers were freed from some of their instructional chores. The monitorial system was considered "efficient."[37]

The monitorial system deemphasized classical education and religious theory, stressed the three R's and good citizenship, demonstrated the possibility of systematic instruction, acquainted many people with formal education, and made educational opportunities more widely available. Most important, it promoted mass education and tax-supported elementary schools.[38] At the peak of its popularity, in the 1840s, it was introduced in some high schools and suggested (by educators and state agencies) for colleges.

However, many people considered the monitorial system too mechanical. It also was criticized for using poorly informed students as instructors. By 1850, its popularity had waned.

### Common Schools

The common school was established in 1826 in Massachusetts, when the state passed a law requiring every town to choose a school board to be responsible for all local schools. Eleven years later, the state legislature created the first state board of education, and Massachusetts organized the public common schools under a single authority. Connecticut quickly followed its neighbor's example.[39] The common schools were devoted to elementary education, with an emphasis on the three R's. Horace Mann spearheaded the movement, which was rooted in progressive thought.

As a member of the Massachusetts legislature and later as Massachusetts' first Commissioner of Education, Mann rallied public support for the common school by appealing to various segments of the population. To enlist the business community, he argued that "education has a market value" with a yield similar to "common bullion." Industry's aim and the nation's wealth would be augmented "in proportion to the diffusion of knowledge."[40] Workers would be more diligent and productive. Mann also established a stewardship theory, aimed at the upper class, which stated that the public good would be enhanced by public education. Universal education would create a stable society in which people would obey the laws and increase the nation's political and economic well-being. Mann told workers and farmers that the common school would be a great equalizer and a means of social mobility for their children. To the Protestant community, he argued that the common school would assimilate ethnic and religious groups, promote a common culture, and help immigrant children learn English, U.S. customs, and U.S. laws.[41] Mann was convinced that the common school was crucial to equal opportunity and a national identity.

The pattern for establishing common schools and their quality varied among the states, but the foundation of the U.S. public school was being forged. Schools taught youngsters of all socioeconomic and religious backgrounds, from age 6 to 14 or 15. Because individual teachers taught a variety of subjects to children of all ages, they had to plan as many as 10 to 20 different lessons a day.[42] Teachers also had to try to keep their schoolrooms cool in the summer and warm in the winter (a responsibility shared by the older boys, who cut and fetched wood). Schoolhouses often needed major repairs, and teachers were paid miserably low salaries.

New England state legislatures encouraged the establishment of school districts, elected school boards, and enacted laws to govern the schools. Although the common school had problems and critics, it especially flourished on the frontier, where the local one-room schoolhouse embodied the pioneers' desire to provide free education for their children. The one-room schoolhouse eventually led to one of America's most lasting, sentimentalized pictures—the "Little Red Schoolhouse"—in almost every community. "It was a manifestation of the belief held by most of the frontier leaders that a school was necessary to raise the level of American civilization."[43]

This small school, meager in outlook and thwarted by inadequate funding and insufficient teachers, nevertheless fit with the conditions of the American frontier. It was a "blah" school, according to Abe Lincoln, but it was the kind of school in which the common person's children—even those born in log cabins—could begin their "readin," "writin," and "cipherin."[44] It was a school local citizens could use as a polling place, meeting hall, and site for dances and other community activities; it was here on the frontier that neighborhood schools, local control, and government support of schools took a firm hold.

## Elementary Schools

There was no consensus regarding an appropriate elementary school curriculum. Throughout the 1800s, the trend was to add courses to the essential subjects of reading, spelling, grammar, and arithmetic. Religious doctrine changed to "manners" and "moral" instruction by 1825. Textbook content was heavily moralistic and teachers provided extensive training in character building. By 1875, lessons in morality were replaced by lessons in "conduct," which remained part of the 20th-century curriculum. More and more subjects were added to the curriculum: geography and history by 1850; science, visual art, and physical education by 1875; and nature study (biology and zoology), music, homemaking (later called *home economics*), and manual training by 1900. Table 3.1 shows this evolution of the elementary school curriculum.

## Secondary Schools

The common school created the basis for tax-supported and locally controlled elementary school education. The U.S. high school was established on this base. By 1900, most children ages 6 to 13 were enrolled in public elementary school, but only 11.5 percent of children ages 14 to 17 were enrolled in public secondary schools (and only 6.5 percent graduated). As shown in Table 3.2, not until 1930 did the secondary school enrollment figure exceed 50 percent. By 1970, 98 percent of elementary-age children attended school, and 94 percent of secondary-age children did (with 77 percent graduating). The great enrollment boom occurred between 1850 and 1900 for elementary schools and between 1900 and 1970 for high schools. From the 1980s to 2010, enrollment percentages leveled off in the mid- to high 90s.

| Table 3.1 | Evolution of the Elementary School Curriculum, 1800–1900 | | | |
|---|---|---|---|---|
| **1800** | **1825** | **1850** | **1875** | **1900** |
| *Reading* | *Reading* | *Reading* | *Reading* | *Reading* |
| | Declamation | Declamation | Literary selections | *Literature* |
| *Spelling* | *Spelling* | *Spelling* | *Spelling* | Spelling |
| Writing | Writing | *Writing* | *Penmanship* | Writing |
| Catechism | Good behavior | Conduct | Conduct | Conduct |
| *Bible* | Manners and morals | Manners | | |
| Arithmetic | *Arithmetic* | *Mental arithmetic* | *Primary arithmetic* | *Arithmetic* |
| | | Ciphering | *Advanced arithmetic* | |
| | Bookkeeping | Bookkeeping | | |
| | *Grammar* | *Grammar* | *Grammar* | Grammar |
| | | Elementary language | Oral language | *Oral language* |
| | Geography | Geography | Home geography | Home geography |
| | | | *Text geography* | *Text geography* |
| | | U.S. history | U.S. history | History studies |
| | | | Constitution | |
| | | Object lessons | Object lessons | Nature study |
| | | | Elementary science | Elemenatary science |
| | | | Drawing | Drawing |
| | | | | Music |
| | | | Physical exercises | Physical training |
| | | | | Play |
| | Sewing | | | Sewing |
| | | | | Cooking |
| | | | Manual training | |

*Source:* E. P. Cubberley, *The History of Education* (Boston: Houghton Mifflin, 1920), p. 756.

*Note:* Italics indicate the most important subjects.

## Academies

In the early 1800s, the academy began to replace the Latin grammar school; by 1850, it dominated the school landscape. The academy offered a wide range of curricula; it was designed to provide a practical program for terminal students as well as a college-preparatory course of study. By 1855, more than 6,000 academies were teaching 263,000 students[45] (more than two thirds of the period's total secondary school enrollment).

According to Ellwood Cubberley, the academy taught "useful things, [and] subjects of modern nature," that prepared students for life, not just college.[46] By 1828, the academies of the state of New York offered as many as 50 different subjects. In rank order, the top 15 were Latin, Greek, English grammar, geography, arithmetic, algebra, composition and declamation, natural philosophy, rhetoric, philosophy, U.S. history, French, chemistry, logic, and astronomy. By 1837, the state Board of Regents reported 72 different subjects.[47]

Academies tended to offer a traditional curriculum that prepared students for college. Elmer Brown writes that in the best academies, "the college preparatory course was the backbone of the whole system of instruction." Although practical courses were offered, "it was the

| Table 3.2 | Percentage of Students Enrolled in Secondary School and College, 1900–2010 | | |
| --- | --- | --- | --- |
| | **14- to 17-Year-Olds Enrolled In Secondary School** | **17-Year-Olds Graduating High School** | **18- to 21-Year-Olds Enrolled In College** |
| 1900 | 11.5 | 6.5 | 3.9 |
| 1910 | 15.4 | 8.8 | 5.0 |
| 1920 | 32.3 | 16.8 | 7.9 |
| 1930 | 51.4 | 29.0 | 11.9 |
| 1940 | 73.3 | 50.8 | 14.5 |
| 1950 | 76.8 | 59.0 | 26.9 |
| 1960 | 86.1 | 65.1 | 31.3 |
| 1970 | 93.4 | 76.5 | 45.2 |
| 1980 | 93.7 | 74.4 | 46.3 |
| 1990 | 95.8 | 85.4 | 48.5 |
| 2000 | 97.9 | 87.5 | 53.7 |
| 2010 | 96.5 | 86.0 | 60.0 |

*Source:* Allan C. Ornstein. *Teaching and Schooling in America* (Boston: Allyn & Bacon, 2003); and Projections of Education. Statistics to 2015 (Washington, DC: U.S. Government Printing Office, 2011).

admission requirements of the colleges, more than anything else, that determined their standards of scholarship."[48] Paul Monroe concurs: "The core of academy education yet remained the old classical curriculum . . . just as the core of the student body in the more flourishing academies remained the group preparing for college."[49]

The era of the academies extended to the 1870s, when public high schools replaced academies. The academies then served as finishing schools for young ladies, providing courses in classical and modern languages, science, mathematics, art, music, and homemaking. They also offered the "normal" program for prospective school teachers, which combined courses in the arts and science with principles of pedagogy. A few private military and elite academic academies still exist today.

## High Schools

Although a few high schools existed in the early half of the 1800s (the first was founded in Boston in 1821), they did not become a major U.S. institution until after 1874, when the Michigan Supreme Court ruled, in the "Kalamazoo Case," that the public could establish and support high schools with tax funds. Thereafter, high schools rapidly spread, and state after state made attendance compulsory.

Students were permitted to attend private schools, but the states had the right to establish minimum standards for all. By 1890, the 2,525 public high schools in the United States had more than 200,000 students, compared to 1,600 private secondary schools, which had fewer than 95,000 students. By 1900, the number of high schools had soared to 6,000, whereas the number of academies had declined to 1,200.[50] The public high school system, contiguous with common schools, had evolved. As late as 1900, high schools were attended by only a small percentage of the total youth population. However, the presence of terminal and college-preparatory, rich and poor students under one roof showed that the U.S. public had rejected the European dual system of secondary education. Fifty years later, when the U.S. high school had fully evolved, James Conant argued for comprehensive high schools that served all types of learners and helped eliminate class distinctions. The comprehensive high school provided curriculum options for all students.

**Table 3.3**   Evolution of Secondary School Curriculum, 1800–1900

| 1800–1825 | 1825–1850 | 1850–1875 | 1875–1900 |
|---|---|---|---|
| **Latin Grammar School** | | | |
| Latin | Latin | | |
| Greek | Greek | | |
| Arithmetic | Arithmetic | | |
| Classical literature | Classical literature | | |
| | Ancient history | | |
| **Academy and High School** | | | |
| Latin | Latin | Latin | Latin |
| Greek | Greek | Greek | Greek[b] |
| Classical literature | Classical literature | English literature | English literature |
| Writing[a] | Writing[a] | Composition[a] | Composition[a] |
| Arithmetic[a] | Arithmetic[a] | Arithmetic[a] | Arithmetic[a] |
| | | Higher arithmetic | |
| Geometry | Geometry | Geometry | Geometry |
| Trigonometry | Trigonometry | Trigonometry | Trigonometry |
| | Algebra | Algebra | Algebra |
| Bookkeeping[a] | Bookkeeping[a] | Bookkeeping[a] | Bookkeeping[a,b] |
| English grammar | English grammar | English grammar | English |
| Rhetoric | Rhetoric | Rhetoric | Rhetoric[a] |
| Oratory | Oratory[b] | | |
| | Debating | Debating[b] | |
| Surveying[a] | Surveying[a] | | |
| Astronomy[a] | Astronomy[a] | Astronomy | Astronomy[a,b] |
| Navigation[a] | Navigation[a,b] | | |
| Geography | Geography | Physical geography | Physical geography[b] |
| | Natural philosophy | Natural philosophy[b] | |
| | | Meteorology | Meteorology[b] |
| | | Chemistry | Chemistry |
| | | Physiology | Physiology |
| | | | Health education |
| | | Botany | Botany[b] |
| | | Zoology | Zoology[b] |
| | | | Biology |
| | | | Physics |
| Foreign language[a] (French, Spanish, German) | Foreign language[a] (French, Spanish, German) | Foreign language (French, Spanish, German) | Foreign language (French, Spanish, German) |
| Philosophy | Philosophy | Mental philosophy | |
| | | Moral philosophy[b] | |
| | History | General history[b] | World history |
| | Greek history | Greek history[b] | Ancient history |
| | U.S. history | U.S. history | U.S. history |
| | | | Civil government |
| | | | Political economy |
| | | | Manual training[a] |

| 1800–1825 | 1825–1850 | 1850–1875 | 1875–1900 |
|-----------|-----------|-----------|-----------|
| | | | Home economics[a] |
| | | | Agriculture[a] |
| | | | Music |
| | | | Art |
| | | | Physical education |

*Source:* Information from Calvin Davis, *Our Evolving High School Curriculum* (New York: World Book, 1927), p. 38; Committee of Ten, *Report of the Committee of Ten on Secondary Studies* (Washington, DC: National Education Association, 1893), p. 4; Newton Edwards and Herman G. Richey, *The School in the American Social Order,* 2nd ed. (Boston: Houghton Mifflin, 1963), p. 250; and Gerald R. Firth and Richard D. Kimpston, *The Curricular Continuum in Perspective* (Itasca, IL: Peacock, 1973), pp. 102–104.

[a]Considered part of practical studies.

[b]All but disappeared; limited enrollments.

High schools stressed the college-preparatory program, but they also completed the formal education of terminal students. They offered a more diversified curriculum than the academies. Around 1900, high schools began to offer vocational, industrial, commercial, and clerical courses. Public high schools contributed to social and political reform. They produced a skilled workforce for an expanding industrial economy, and they assimilated and Americanized millions of immigrant children in U.S. cities.

Summing up, then, the curriculum of the Latin grammar school was virtually the same at the beginning and end of the colonial period. Table 3.3 lists the most popular courses. Latin, Greek, arithmetic, and the classics were stressed. Academies introduced greater variation (e.g., courses for practical studies) into the curriculum. By 1800, a typical academy offered about 25 different subjects (the table lists the 17 most popular). Between 1850 and 1875, the peak period for academies, some academies offered as many as 150 courses.[51] In rank order, the 15 most popular were (1) algebra, (2) higher arithmetic, (3) English grammar, (4) Latin, (5) geometry, (6) U.S. history, (7) physiology, (8) natural philosophy, (9) physical geography, (10) German, (11) general history, (12) rhetoric, (13) bookkeeping, (14) French, and (15) zoology.[52] These courses had no real philosophy or aim, except that most were college preparatory in nature, even though the original aim of the academy was to offer a practical program.

After 1875, the number of high schools rapidly grew, and the number of academies rapidly fell. The secondary courses listed in Table 3.3 for 1875–1900 were high school courses. The curriculum and the variety in course offerings continued to expand, presumably making it easier for students to determine their interests and capabilities.[53] (See Curriculum Tips 3.2.)

## CURRICULUM TIPS 3.2    Process of Historical Research

The following suggestions provide guidance for conducting historical research:

1. Define a problem or issue with roots in the past, or attempt to recreate a historical event and give it meaning.
2. Use primary-source writings from the time of a historical event that relate to an event and were part of the context in which it occurred.
3. Use secondary sources (literature written after the event occurred) in which historians have interpreted the event.
4. Based on an examination of primary and secondary sources, recreate an event, life, or situation from the past and interpret it so that it has meaning for people today.
5. Use history, especially case examples or case studies, to add a moral dimension to your teaching.
6. Explain and interpret, but do not rewrite, history.

*Source:* Information from Gerald Gutek, unpublished materials (January 1992).

## THE TRANSITIONAL PERIOD: 1893–1918

From the colonial period until the turn of the 20th century, the traditional curriculum, which emphasized classical studies for college-bound students, dominated at the elementary and secondary levels. The rationale for this emphasis was that the classics were difficult and thus were a good way to develop mental abilities.

More and more subjects were added to the curriculum. As a result, there was a growing need to bring some order and unity to curriculum, especially at the secondary level. According to two educators, the subjects taught, the time allotted to them, and their "grade placements" differed from school to school.[54]

As late as 1900, most children completed their formal education at the elementary level, and those who went on to secondary schools usually ended their formal education upon graduation. As of 1890, only 14.5 percent of high school students were preparing for college, and less than 3 percent went on to college.[55] Hence, high schools were catering to approximately 15 percent of the student population.

Reformers began to ask if elementary schools should offer two curriculum tracks: one for children bound for high school and one for children whose formal education would end at the elementary level. They also began to question high schools' focus on preparing students for college, on mental discipline, and on the classics.

### Reaffirming the Traditional Curriculum: Three Committees

With these unsettled questions as background, the National Education Association (NEA) organized three major committees between 1893 and 1895: the Committee of Fifteen on Elementary Education, the Committee of Ten on Secondary School Studies, and the Committee on College Entrance Requirements. These committees were to determine schools' curricula. Their reports "standardized" the curriculum for much of the 20th century. In Cubberley's words, "The committees were dominated by subject-matter specialists, possessed of a profound faith in mental discipline." No concern for student "abilities, social needs, interest, or capabilities . . . found a place in their . . . deliberations."[56]

**THE COMMITTEE OF FIFTEEN.**  The Committee of Fifteen was heavily influenced by Harvard University president Charles Eliot, who had initiated vigorous discussion on the need for school reform, and by William Harris, then the U.S. Commissioner of Education, who believed in strict teacher authority and discipline. Both Eliot and Harris wanted the traditional curriculum to remain intact. The committee adopted Eliot's plan to reduce the elementary grades from 10 to 8 and stressed the three R's, English grammar, literature, geography, and history. Hygiene, culture, vocal music, and drawing were each allotted 1 hour per week. Manual training, sewing cooking, algebra, and Latin were introduced in the seventh and eighth grades.

In general, the committee rejected the idea of newer subjects (see Table 3.1), the pedagogical principles that had characterized the reform movement of the European pioneers since the early 1800s, kindergarten, the idea that children's needs and interests should be considered when planning the curriculum,[57] and the notion of interdisciplinary subjects. They compartmentalized subject matter, and this compartmentalization has remained the norm.

**THE COMMITTEE OF TEN.**  Chaired by Eliot, the Committee of Ten was the most influential of the three committees. It identified nine academic subjects as central to the high school curriculum: (1) Latin, (2) Greek, (3) English, (4) other modern languages, (5) mathematics (algebra, geometry, trigonometry, and higher, or advanced, algebra), (6) physical sciences (physics, astronomy, and chemistry), (7) natural history or biological sciences (biology, botany, zoology, and physiology), (8) social sciences (history, civil government, and political economy), and (9) geography, geology, and meteorology. (See Table 3.4.)

The committee recommended four different tracks: (1) classical, (2) Latin scientific, (3) modern languages, and (4) English. The first two required four years of Latin. The first program

**Table 3.4** Secondary School Programs and Subjects Proposed by Committee of Ten, 1893

| First Year | | Second Year | | Third Year | | Fourth Year | |
|---|---|---|---|---|---|---|---|
| Latin | 5 p.* | Latin | 4 p. | Latin | 4 p. | Latin | 4 p. |
| English literature | 2 p. } | Greek | 5 p. | Greek | 4 p. | Greek | 4 p. |
| English composition | 2 p. } | English literature | 2 p. } | English literature | 2 p. } | English literature | 2 p. } |
| German (or French) | 5 p. | English composition | 2 p. } 4 p. | English composition | 1 p. } 4 p. | English composition | 1 p. } 4 p. |
| | | | | Rhetoric | 1 p. } | Grammar | 1 p. } |
| Algebra | 4 p. | German (continued) | 4 p. | German | 4 p. | German | 4 p. |
| History of Italy, Spain, and France | 3 p. | French (begun) | 5 p. | French | 4 p. | French | 4 p. |
| Applied geography (European political-continental and oceanic flora and fauna) | 4 p. | Algebra | 2 p. } | Algebra | 2 p. } | Trigonometry | |
| | | Geometry | 2 p. } | Geometry | 2 p. } 4 p. | Higher algebra | 2 p. |
| | | Botany or zoology | 4 p. | Physics | 4 p. | Chemistry | 4 p. |
| | | English history to 1688 | 3 p. | History, English and U.S. | 3 p. | History (intensive) and civil government | 3 p. |
| | | | | Astronomy, 1 1/2 p. 1st 1/2 yr | | Geology or physiography, 2 p. 1st 1/2 yr | |
| | | | | Meteorology, 1 1/2 p. 2nd 1/2 yr | 3 p. | Anatomy, physiology, and hygiene, 2 p. 2nd 1/2 yr | 4 p. |
| Total | 25 p. | Total | 33 p. | Total | 34 p. | Total | 33 p. |

*Source:* Committee of Ten, *Report of the Committee of Ten on Secondary School Studies* (Washington, DC: National Educational Association, 1893), p. 4.
*Note:* *p. = periods.

emphasized classic English literature and math; the second, math and science. The modern-language program required four years of French or German (Spanish was considered too easy and culturally and linguistically less important). The English program permitted four years of Latin, German, or French. The modern language and English programs also included literature, composition, and history. The Committee of Ten considered these two programs (which did not require Latin or emphasize literature, science, or mathematics) "in practice distinctly inferior to the other two."[58] In taking this position, the committee indirectly tracked college-bound students into the first two programs and non-college-bound students into the latter two programs. To some extent, this bias reflected the committee's composition: 8 of the 10 members represented college and private preparatory school interests.

The committee ignored art, music, physical education, and vocational education, maintaining that these subjects contributed little to mental discipline. Two curricularists write, "The choice of these subjects and the omission of others from consideration was enough to set the course for secondary education for many years" and indirectly set the tone at the elementary level as well. The committee suggested that each of the nine subjects except Latin and Greek be taught at the elementary school level.[59]

At the time, few students went to college. Nonetheless, this college preparatory program established a curriculum hierarchy, from elementary school to college, that promoted academics and ignored most students who were not college bound. Today, schools offer vocational, industrial, or technical programs, but the academic program is still considered superior to others.

**THE COMMITTEE ON COLLEGE ENTRANCE REQUIREMENTS.**   When the Committee on College Entrance Requirements met in 1895, it reaffirmed the dominance of college-preparatory curriculum in high schools, emphasizing college-admission requirements and classical subjects. Consisting mainly of college and university presidents, including Eliot, the committee recommended strengthening the college-preparatory aspect of the high school curriculum and made recommendations regarding the number of credits required in different subjects for college admission. The recommendations were reflected in the Carnegie Unit, a method of evaluating credits for college admission, imposed on high schools in 1909 and still used in most high schools.

## Harris and Eliot: Two Conservative Reformers

From 1878 (when the Kalamazoo court decision provided for free public high schools) to 1900, education questions revolved around curriculum: What should be taught in elementary and secondary schools? Should high school be considered an extension of elementary school? Should the curriculum differ at the two school levels or should it remain unbroken? Should the high schools be considered prepatory for college? If so, at what grade level should the secondary curriculum start college prepatory work? What curriculum provisions should be made for terminal students? If high schools offered two or more separate programs, would the result be a dual-track system? Should the same education be available to all students?

William Harris (1834–1926) and Charles Eliot (1835–1909) dominated the reform movement during this period: Harris, the former St. Louis Commissioner of Education (1868–1881) and U.S. Commissioner of Education (1889–1906), was a traditionalist who subscribed to McGuffey's moralism and Mann's faith in free public schools. Harris wrote in 1871, "If the rising generation does not grow up with democratic principles, the fault will lie in the system of popular education."[60] He thought that U.S. common schools should teach morality and citizenship, "lift all classes of people into a participation in civilized life," and instill "social order."[61] Whereas Mann saw the common school as a great equalizer and force for social mobility, Harris saw it as an instrument for preserving society's customs and norms. Mann saw schools as key to a child's growth and development, whereas Harris saw the school as one of many factors (e.g., family, playmates, church, community) in educating and socializing children. Harris saw schools as an extension of society, not as agents of change.

Harris advocated a traditional curriculum: a mix of essentialism (five core academic areas) and perennialism (emphasis on the classics and moral values). Harris's elementary curriculum was composed of mathematics, geography, history, grammar, literature, and art. (Mann also advocated music and art.) At the high school level, Harris emphasized the classics, Greek and Latin, and mathematics. His curriculum was rigorously academic. Harris resisted the idea of a vocational or practical curriculum, arguing that all children should follow the same curriculum. The ideal was for each student to work with his or her mind, not with his or her hands.

Education historian Lawrence Cremin states that Harris "consolidated the revolution Mann had wrought" but was "patently conservative." Harris's emphasis was "on order rather than freedom, on work rather than play, on effort rather than interest, on prescription rather than election, on regularity [and] silence," and on preserving "the civil order."[62] Harris stressed rules, scheduling, testing, and grading. Harris argued that the curriculum would give poor children the same opportunities as wealthy children. However, his focus on the classics discouraged working-class students from attending high school.

As president of Harvard University, Eliot played a prominent role in the shaping of higher education. He argued that, as late as the 1890s, 80 percent of U.S. colleges and universities had to organize their own preparatory high schools because public high schools were doing an inadequate job. Also, more than 80 percent of eligible youth did not attend high school. Eliot maintained that there was a huge discrepancy in purpose and quality "between the elementary schools and the colleges."[63] Although the elementary schools served a larger segment of the population, their curriculum was characterized by repetitive drill in grammar, spelling, and basic math at the expense of science, foreign languages, and advanced math.

The curriculum had to be revamped and pedagogical methods had to be changed from lock-step teaching, rote drill, and the memorization of facts to comprehension and problem solving. Eliot believed that elementary children were capable of pursuing subjects such as algebra, physics, and foreign languages. Sixty years later, in *The Process of Education,* Jerome Bruner similarly argued, "Any subject can be taught in some effectively honest form to any child at any stage of development."[64] Unlike most educators of his time, Bruner held that students can comprehend the fundamental principles and concepts of any subject at almost any age if they're taught properly.

Elliot called on pedagogical experts to establish goals and standards for every subject, "even though not all children would study the same subjects or move at the same pace while studying them."[65] To some extent, he allowed for different rates and ways of learning; this is now called *independent learning*, *continuous progress*, or *learning styles*.

Eliot saw "civilized society" as being composed of four layers: (1) the upper one, "thin" in numbers and consisting of "the managing, leading, guiding class—the intellectual discoverers, the inventors, the organizers, and the managers"; (2) a "much more numerous class, namely, the highly trained hand-workers" who function as "skilled manual labor"; (3) a populous "commercial class" consisting of those who engage in "buying, selling, and distributing"; and (4) a large class engaged in "household work, agriculture, mining, quarrying, and forestry." Schools, Eliot argued, must offer programs to all four classes.[66] The more progressive and democratic reformers saw Eliot's class system as elitist and biased.

Eliot argued for vocational and trade schools separate from high schools. He also maintained that elementary school teachers should sort children into tracks according to their abilities (as European dual-track schools do).[67] Later, Eliot somewhat retreated from that position, but measurement and school efficiency advocates picked up on the idea of "vocational guidance," based partly on testing,[68] and advocated tracking secondary students into academic and nonacademic programs.

## Vocational Education

In later years the NEA would support the concept of vocational education. A 1910 report by the NEA's Committee on the Place of Industries in Public Education advocated "manual activities" at the elementary level and "testing of children's aptitudes as a basis for subsequent choice of specific pursuits either in vocations or in higher schools" and "manual training" for some high school students."[69]

In 1917, the Smith-Hughes Act provided federal aid for vocational education related to agriculture, home economics, and the trades. Federal funds were to match state monies allocated to school curricula in these three vocations. Business, labor, and farm groups hailed the act as a reform.[70] They did not see the act as shunting lower-class children into second-rate, nonacademic programs. However, Jane Addams—and, to a lesser extent, Dewey and Kilpatrick— would see the promotion of vocational education as hindering the democratic common school movement. Addams was most concerned that immigrant children would be steered into such programs. Seventy-five years later, Michael Apple, Alfie Kohn, and Jeannie Oaks would similarly argue that working-class students were being placed in nonacademic vocational programs due to the class biases of middle-class educators.[71]

Within 2 years the enrollment in vocational programs doubled. By 1918, 164,000 students were enrolled in such programs, the vast majority (118,000) in trade and industrial programs. By 1944, the total enrollment was 2.5 million, evenly distributed in agriculture, home economics, and trade and industry. By 1970, some 9 million students (26 percent of secondary students) were enrolled in vocational programs.[72] By 2000, vocational education enrollment had declined to 20 percent,[73] reflecting growing criticism of tracking students.

The shift from classical and academic high school courses in 1900 to the comprehensive high school with substantial enrollments in vocational education (and a lowering of the academic bar) has had major consequences. For one thing, vocational programs tend to be outdated. They rarely are relevant to a high-tech/information society that communicates and operates through verbal and mathematical symbols, computers, and electronic media. Given the growth of electronic and health-related industries, vocational education needs major revamping.

## Pressure for a Modern Curriculum

Among other factors, immigration and industrial development led a growing number of educators to question the classical curriculum and its emphasis on mental discipline. The scientific movement in psychology and education in the late 19th and early 20th centuries also played a role—particularly the pragmatic theories of Charles Peirce and William James; the social theories of Darwin, Herbart, and Spencer; and the pedagogical views of Pestalozzi, Froebel, Maria Montessori, and others. This movement rejected the mental-discipline approach and classic curriculum and emphasized vocational, technical, and scientific subjects.

At the turn of the 20th century, education was strongly influenced by the ideas of Dewey and Francis Parker, the Gestalt psychology and child psychology movements, the learning theories of behaviorism and transfer learning, and the progressive movement in schools and society.

Educators increasingly argued that the classics had no greater mental value than other subjects and that mental discipline (which emphasized rote learning, drill, and memorization) was not conducive to the inductive method of science or compatible with contemporary educational theory. Edward Thorndike, the era's most influential learning psychologist, wrote, "The expectation of any large difference in general improvement of the mind from one study rather than another seems doomed to disappointment. The chief reason why good thinkers seem superficially to have been made such by having taken certain school studies is that good thinkers have taken such studies. . . . Now that good thinkers study Physics and Trigonometry, these seem to make good thinkers. If abler pupils should all study Physical Education and Dramatic Art, these subjects would seem to make good thinkers."[74]

**FLEXNER: A MODERN CURRICULUM.** By 1917, Eliot, a former advocate of Latin, was saying that Latin should no longer be compulsory for high school or college students.[75] Abraham Flexner (1866–1959), a former teacher of the classics, contended that Latin had "no purpose" in the curriculum and that the classics were out of step with scientific developments.[76] Flexner now argued that tradition was an inadequate criterion for justifying subject matter; society was changing and educators also had to make changes in the curriculum.

In his 1916 paper "A Modern School," Flexner rejected the traditional secondary curriculum and proposed a "modern" curriculum consisting of four basic areas: (1) science (the curriculum's major emphasis), (2) industry (occupations and trades of the industrial world), (3) civics (history, economics, and government), and (4) aesthetics (literature, languages, art, and music).[77] Modern languages would replace Latin and Greek. Flexner concluded that a subject had little value in the curriculum unless a utilitarian argument could be made for its inclusion.

Flexner's concept of utility and modern subjects tended to resemble Spencer's views on science and subject matter. The difference is that Flexner was attuned to the social and political climate of his time. Educators were willing to listen to his proposals. In 1917, the Lincoln School of Teachers College, Columbia University (while Dewey was teaching) adopted Flexner's proposed curriculum; the school combined the four core areas of study, with emphasis on scientific inquiry.

**DEWEY: PRAGMATIC AND SCIENTIFIC PRINCIPLES OF EDUCATION.** The same year that Flexner published "A Modern School," Dewey published *Democracy and Education,* one of his most influential (and cumbersome) books, which discussed all the elements of his philosophy.[78] In the book, Dewey set forth the relationship between education and democracy as well as the notion that democracy itself was a social process that could be enhanced through the school. Dewey considered schools as neutral institutions that could serve the ends of either freedom or repression and authority; thus, the aims of education went hand in hand with the particular type of society involved.

According to Dewey, subjects cannot be placed in a value hierarchy; study of any subject can promote a child's development. Any study or body of knowledge was capable of expanding the child's experiences and contributing to his or her social and cognitive growth. Traditional subjects such as Greek or Latin were no more valuable than music or art.

At the same time, Dewey prioritized science, which he saw as epitomizing rational inquiry. Science, for Dewey, was another name for knowledge, and it represented the perfect outcome of learning—its consummation, "what is known and settled." Dewey considered scientific inquiry to be the best form of knowledge for a society because it consisted of "special methods which the race worked out in order to conduct reflection under conditions whereby its procedures and results are tested."[79]

Dewey's emphasis on science was based partially in the work of Spencer, who believed science was the key to complete living, and to G. Stanley Hall, who started the child-study movement in the 1880s and 1890s and under whom Dewey studied when he was a doctoral student at Johns Hopkins University. With Hall, the child-study movement was both research based and systematic, whereby findings were supposed to be applied to the classroom. Although knowledge obtained from child-study research was rarely used by teachers, it formed the basis of the child development movement in the 1930s and 1940s that was spearheaded by Robert Thorndike and Arthur Jersild in the United States and Jean Piaget in Europe.

**JUDD: SYSTEMATIC STUDIES AND SOCIAL SCIENCES.** Charles Judd (1873–1946) was a colleague of Dewey. He headed the University of Chicago's Department of Education when Dewey directed the lab school. With Dewey and others, Judd constructed a science of education based on finding facts and constructing generalizations and then applying them in decision-making and problem-solving areas. Whereas Peirce and James referred to this method as *pragmatism,* Judd referred to it as *scientism in education.*

Judd was an evolutionist (who believed in Darwin's theories of adaption and Spencer's theories of survival) and believed the laws of nature should be used to educate the young. He used statistical research (which was then in its infancy) to determine the worth of curriculum content—that is, the extent to which particular content enhanced students' ability to promote thinking and solve problems. By preparing students to deal with problems, not acquire or recall endless knowledge, he argued that students would be prepared to deal with the changing world and the problems they would encounter as adults.

In *Introduction to the Scientific Study of Education,* Judd outlined "systematic studies . . . of the curriculum."[80] He emphasized reading, writing, and spelling based on words statistically shown to be used by successful adults. He also emphasized science and math problems applicable to everyday life. Utilitarian and pragmatic in philosophy, Judd urged that elementary students be exposed to "career education" to help prepare them for an occupation. At the secondary level, Judd recommended practical subjects with a vocational or technical orientation, not a "cultural" or elitist curriculum. For slower students he advocated English, business math, mechanics or stenography, and office management. For average and superior students, he recommended science, mathematics, modern languages, and the social sciences.

Judd influenced the next generation of theorists, who sought to apply scientific methods to curriculum development. This generation (sometimes called *technicians*) began with Franklin Bobbitt and Werrett Charters in the 1920s and reached its height of influence with Ralph Tyler and Hilda Taba in the 1950s.

**COMMISSION ON THE REORGANIZATION OF SECONDARY EDUCATION.**   In 1918, the NEA's Commission on the Reorganization of Secondary Education published the highly progressive *Cardinal Principles of Secondary Education.*[81] Influenced by Herbert's purposes, Flexner's "A Modern School," and Dewey's *Democracy and Education,* the commission stressed the whole child (not only cognitive development); education for all youth (not only college-bound youth); diversified areas of study (not just classical or traditional studies); and common culture, ideas, and principles for a democratic society (not religious, elitist, or mental-discipline learning).

The Commission noted the following:

1. Education should promote seven aims: health, command of the fundamentals, "worthy home membership" (e.g., preparation for marriage, raising children), vocation, citizenship, leisure, and ethical character.
2. High school should be a comprehensive institution having the nation's social and economic groups.
3. High school curricula should meet varied student needs—agricultural, business and commercial, vocational, and college preparatory.
4. Current educational psychology, psychological principles, and methods of measurement and evaluation should be applied to secondary curriculum and instruction.
5. U.S. educational institutions should function in conjunction with one another.

High schools were assuming their modern curricular patterns: combining academic programs with several nonacademic programs. English, math, science, social science, and modern languages were being emphasized. Classical languages and literature were losing ground. Aims and subjects were becoming interrelated. Utilitarianism was replacing the idea of mental discipline. Students' needs and interests were being considered. Schools were expected to serve all students, not only college-bound youth. The whole child was being emphasized, not just cognitive learning. Traditional education, which had long dominated U.S. education, was in decline.

## THE BIRTH OF THE FIELD OF CURRICULUM: 1918–1949

In the early 1900s, scientific methods of research, psychology, the child-study movement, industrial efficiency, and the progressive movement in society all influenced education. Curriculum now was viewed as a science, with principles and methodology, not simply as content or subject matter. The idea of planning a curriculum, rather than simply describing it in terms of subjects and the time allotted to them, appeared in the literature.

### Bobbitt and Charters: Behaviorism and Scientific Principles

The idea of efficiency, promoted by business and industry, influenced Franklin Bobbitt (1876–1956) and W. W. Charters (1875–1952). Frederick Taylor analyzed factory efficiency in time and motion studies and concluded that workers should be paid on the basis of their individual output, and his theories influenced Bobbitt and Charters.[82] Efficient operation of schools became a major goal in the 1920s. Efficiency often entailed eliminating small classes, increasing the student-teacher ratio, reducing teachers' salaries, and so on, and then preparing charts and graphs to show the cost reduction. Raymond Callahan later branded this approach the "cult of efficiency."[83] Curriculum making became more scientific; teaching and learning were reduced to measurable behaviors and outcomes.

Bobbitt's 1918 book *The Curriculum* was possibly the first book devoted solely to curriculum as a science and to all its phases. Bobbitt's principles of curriculum planning reflected an activities approach, "a series of things which children and youth must do and experience by way of developing abilities to do things well and make up the affairs of adult life."[84] To Bobbitt, curriculum should outline the knowledge important for each subject and then develop appropriate activities. Bobbitt set out to organize a course of studies for the elementary grades: "We need principles of curriculum making."[85]

Bobbitt further developed his activities approach in the early 1920s in *How to Make a Curriculum,* in which he outlined more than 800 objectives and related student activities. These activities ranged from personal health and hygiene to spelling and grammar and "to keeping home appliances in good working condition."[86]

Bobbitt's guidelines for selecting objectives can be applied today: (1) *Eliminate* objectives that are impractical or cannot be accomplished through normal living, (2) *emphasize* objectives that are important for success and adult living, (3) *avoid* objectives opposed by the community, (4) *involve* the community in selecting objectives, (5) *differentiate* between objectives for all students and objectives for only some students, and (6) *sequence* objectives by grade level. Taken out of context, Bobbitt's list of hundreds of objectives and activities, along with the machine, or factory, analogy that he advocated, was easy to criticize. Nevertheless, Bobbitt's insistence that curriculum making was a specialty based on scientific methods and procedures was important for elevating curriculum to a field of study, or what he called a *new specialization.*

Charters, too, advocated a behaviorist approach influenced by business notions of efficiency. He termed his approach *scientific.* Charters viewed the curriculum as a series of goals that students must reach. In *Curriculum Construction,* he discussed curriculum in terms of specific operations, such as those involved in running a machine.[87]

Charters argued that curriculum makers must apply clear principles in order to select materials that would lead to the achievement of specific and measurable objectives.[88] He believed the state of knowledge at that time did not permit scientific measurement that would specifically identify the outcome of the objectives, but he set out to develop a method for selecting objectives based on social consensus and for applying analysis and verification to subject matter and student activities. Although he did not use the term evaluation during this period, he was laying the groundwork for curriculum evaluation.

As initiators of the behavioral and scientific movements in curriculum, Bobbitt and Charters had a profound impact on curriculum. They (1) developed principles for curriculum making, involving aims, objectives, needs, and learning experiences (which they called *activities*); (2) highlighted the use of behavioral objectives; (3) introduced the ideas that objectives are derived from the study of needs (later called *needs assessment*) and that objectives and activities are subject to analysis and verification (later called *evaluation*); and (4) emphasized that curriculum making cuts across subject matter and that a curriculum specialist need not be a specialist in any *subject* but should be a professional in *method* or *process.*

Bobbitt and Charters taught at the University of Chicago when Ralph Tyler was a graduate student in the department of education (Tyler was a graduate assistant of Charters). Tyler was highly influenced by Bobbitt's and Charters's behaviorist ideas, particularly the ideas that (1) objectives derive from student needs and society, (2) learning experiences relate to objectives, (3) activities organized by the teacher should be integrated into the subject matter, and (4) instructional outcomes should be evaluated. Tyler's emphasis on evaluation as a component of curriculum derives from Charters, who helped Tyler get appointed head of testing and evaluation at the Ohio State Bureau of Educational Research in 1929. (Charters became the bureau's director in 1928.) Tyler's four major curriculum components (objectives, learning experiences, methods of organization, and evaluation) are rooted in Bobbitt's, and especially Charters's, ideas.

---

**CURRICULUM TIPS 3.3    Enriching the Curriculum**

The following suggestions combine Kilpatrick's activities curriculum and Rugg's child-centered curriculum. In general, the suggestions integrate elementary schooling with progressivist philosophy, which evolved during the first half of the 20th century. They are especially suited to schools and teachers who stress a student-centered curriculum.

1. Study each child's cumulative record.
2. Compare achievement scores with ability indices.
3. Examine a pupil's creative output for frequently used words, symbols, and topics.
4. Listen to pupils talk about themselves.
5. Provide a choice of activities.
6. If possible, visit each pupil's home.
7. Help individual pupils learn as much as possible about their values, attitudes, purposes, skills, interests, and abilities.
8. Allow pupils to say what they think.
9. Encourage students to reflect on their beliefs and values.
10. Together with pupils, analyze their interpretations of their in-class and out-of-class experiences.
11. Organize class activities around individual or group study of problems important to the individuals involved.
12. Help individual students state their immediate and long-term goals. Share with pupils the information available about their present situation.
13. Clarify a situation's limitations (in time, materials, and resources) with pupils.
14. Ask each pupil to formulate a plan of work.
15. Encourage each pupil to collect and share materials.
16. Arrange for students to collect information in out-of-class situations.
17. Use record keeping to help individual students organize their learning.

*Source:* Kimball Wiles, *Teaching for Better Schools* (Englewood Cliffs, NJ: Prentice Hall, 1952), p. 286.

---

### Kilpatrick: The Progressive Influence

The rise of progressive education and universal education led to a backlash against the classical curriculum's rigidity and rote memorization, the emphasis on tough subject matter, and a secondary curriculum standardized for preparation for college. Progressive curricularists emphasized the learner rather than subject matter and social processes rather than cognitive ones. The curriculum was organized around classroom and school social activities, group enterprises, and group projects. (See Curriculum Tips 3.3.)

Student self-expression and freedom were major goals. In the 1920s and 1930s, Dewey warned against teaching that lacks a plan and simply allows students to respond according to their interests.[89]

Kilpatrick, a colleague of Dewey at Teachers College, Columbia University, attempted to merge the behaviorist psychology of the day with Dewey's and Judd's progressive philosophy. The blend became known as the "Project Method"[90] (later called *purposeful activity*). Kilpatrick divided his methodology into four steps: purposing, planning, executing, and judging. His curriculum projects ranged from classroom projects to school and community projects.

Two of Kilpatrick's doctoral students applied his ideas in Missouri schools. One was Junius Merian, who called Kilpatrick's projects "subjects of study" and organized them into four areas: observation, play, stories, and hard work.[91] The second was Ellsworth Collings, who developed a curriculum around children's real-life experiences. He urged teachers and students to present organized experiences or activities that were related and developmental in nature; one activity should lead to another. "The curriculum was continuously revised 'on the spot' by the joint action of pupils and teachers." He believed that such a joint endeavor "would mean most for the children."[92] His projects resembled Merian's four study areas but included more field trips and community activities.

Kilpatrick's project method, which he presented in his book *Foundations of Method,* was implemented mainly at the elementary level. Kilpatrick advocated giving children considerable input in determining the curriculum. Kilpatrick's project method became part of the activity movement, but he argued that the difference was that his doctrine had "social purpose," whereas the activity-centered curriculum had only "child purpose." When forced to decide who should plan the curriculum, the child or teacher, Kilpatrick opted for the child, arguing that "if you want to educate the boy to think and plan for himself, then let him make his own plan."[93] In this respect, he differed from Dewey, who put more emphasis on the role of the teacher. In Kilpatrick's view, children had to learn to "search, . . . compare, . . . think why," and make their own decisions.[94] Teachers should guide rather than dispense knowledge. When Kilpatrick's project method was eventually introduced into the high school curriculum, it was blended with social studies and the core curriculum.[95]

Concerned with social issues and part of the radical progressive wing (later to be called *reconstructionism*), Kilpatrick saw traditional education as reactionary. Along with other progressives such as Boyd Bode, Hollis Caswell, George Counts, and Harold Rugg, he criticized the Committee of Ten, which he felt had legitimized traditional systems of education. The Committee of Ten urged a compartmentalized and academic curriculum emphasizing Latin, language, and science. Kilpatrick argued for integrated subject matter and a general education emphasizing values and social issues. Whereas the Committee of Ten saw school as a place where students go primarily to acquire knowledge, Kilpatrick and his progressive colleagues saw school as a "community" in which students practiced "cooperation, self-government . . . and application of intelligence . . . to problems as they may arise."[96]

The traditional practice of education focused on certain subjects, usually the three R's at the elementary level and basic academic subjects at the secondary level. The basic teaching method was rote practice. In contrast, Kilpatrick and his followers saw education's purpose as the child's growth along social lines, not the mastery of content.[97] The curriculum must derive from real-life experiences, not organized bodies of subject matter, and must take the form of purposeful activities. School was preparation for life; it had social purpose.

## The Twenty-Sixth Yearbook

In 1930, the National Society for the Study of Education (NSSE), an honor society headquartered at the University of Chicago, published its Twenty-Sixth Yearbook in two volumes: *Curriculum-Making: Past and Present* and *The Foundations of Curriculum Making.*[98] The committee that developed the two volumes consisted of 12 members, including Rugg (the chairperson) and Bagley, Bobbitt, Charters, Counts, Judd, and Kilpatrick. Most of the period's leaders of curriculum development were scientifically oriented and progressive. Many were affiliated with the University of Chicago, which emphasized this science of education.

The yearbook's first volume harshly criticized traditional education and its emphasis on subject matter, rote learning, drill, and mental discipline. It also offered a synthesis of progressive practices and programs in U.S. public and private schools. The second volume described the state of the art in curriculum making and outlined the ideal curriculum, which should do the following:

1. Focus on affairs of human life.
2. Deal with local, national, and international issues.
3. Enable students to think critically about various forms of government.
4. Foster open-mindedness.
5. Consider students' interests and needs and provide opportunities for discussion and debate.
6. Deal with the issues of modern life and society's cultural and historical aspects.
7. Consider problem-solving activities and practice in choosing alternatives such as role playing, independent learning, and cooperative learning.
8. Organize problems and exercises in a graded organization.
9. Deal with humanitarian themes in purposeful, constructive way.[99]

Harold Rugg maintained that educational committees or legislative groups should formulate the curriculum's goals, materials, and instructional methods. Trained curriculum specialists should plan the curriculum and include "(1) a statement of objectives, (2) a sequence of experiences [to achieve] the objectives, (3) subject matter found to be . . . the best means of engaging in the experiences, and (4) statements of immediate outcomes of achievements to be derived from the experiences."[100] These four planning principles were later to become the basis of Tyler's four organizing principles, as delienated in *Basic Principles of Curriculum and Instruction*. Rugg concluded that curriculum needed to adapt scientific methods that were needed "for specialization and for professional training."[101] Experienced teachers and curriculum specialists should work together to organize the content and materials within each subject area.

The NSSE yearbook greatly clarified problems that curriculum workers were encountering and significantly advanced curriculum making. It had major influence in many school districts (large and small, as well as city, suburban, and rural).

## Rugg and Caswell: The Development Period

From the late 1920s through the early 1940s, a number of important books were published on curriculum principles and processes. Trained as an engineer, Harold Rugg (1886–1960) shared Bobbitt's and Charters's faith in a "science of curriculum." In 1928, Rugg and Ann Shumaker coauthored *The Child-Centered School*. In an era that stressed student input in curriculum planning, the authors stressed the need for curriculum specialists to construct the curriculum.[102] They also stressed the teacher's role in implementing the curriculum and the need for preplanning. Rugg did not believe that a curriculum should be based on students' input, needs, or interests. He believed that a student-directed curriculum would lack direction and logic. Rugg advocated cooperation among educational professionals, including teachers, administrators, test experts, and curriculum specialists from various fields.

In the 1930s and 1940s, Rugg shifted his attention to the integration of history, geography, civics, and economics (often collectively referred to as *social studies*). Some of his ideas about labor history, unionism, and collectivism, compounded by his activities with the teachers' union, resulted in a great deal of criticism from established groups. Like Counts and Dewey, Rugg also had an FBI file.

During the mid-1920s and 1930s, most school districts and state education departments were developing curriculum guides. However, the selection of methods and activities was left to teachers. Hollis Caswell (1901–1989) wanted to shift emphasis from formulating a course of study to improving instruction. He envisioned curriculum making as a means of helping teachers coordinate their instructional activities with subject matter and students' needs and interests. Caswell regarded courses of study as guides that teachers should use in planning their daily lessons, not as plans they should follow in detail.

Caswell provided a step-by-step procedure for curriculum making. He and his colleagues presented seven questions that still have relevance:

1. What is a curriculum?
2. Why is there need for curriculum revision?
3. What is the function of subject matter?
4. How do we determine educational objectives?
5. How do we organize curriculum?
6. How do we select subject matter?
7. How do we measure the outcomes of instruction?[103]

Influenced by Bobbitt's definition of *curriculum* ("that series of things which children and youth must do and experience"), Caswell and Campbell maintained in their book *Curriculum Development* that the curriculum must consider "all elements in the experience of the learner."[104] They thought that the field of curriculum should incorporate philosophy, psychology, and sociology. Caswell saw curriculum as a process involving scientific steps of development, organization, instruction, and evaluation.

Caswell and Campbell believed that the curriculum must address children's interests, social functions, and organized knowledge. It should provide the proper scope and sequence of subject matter at every grade level. *Scope* was to represent broad themes such as conservation of natural resources, "worthy home membership," and democratic living. *Sequence* depended on children's interests and experiences. *Subject matter* should match the social functions and the learner's interests; knowledge obtained should be measured.

## Eight-Year Study

Although traditional subject matter and methods dominated most school curricula, the progressive movement was influential in certain parts of the United States, particularly Denver, St. Louis, and Winnetka (Illinois). Most high school teachers and principals were reluctant to implement progressive changes because the curriculum was (as it is today) test driven, textbook dominated, and directed by college-admission requirements.[105]

The Progressive Education Association launched the "Eight-Year Study" (1932–1940) to show that a new curriculum designed to meet students' needs and interests was just as effective as one designed around traditional tests and college-admission requirements. As many as 30 progressive or experimental high schools and 1,475 graduates were compared to schools and students following traditional college preparatory tracks. The experimental/progressive group did as well as or better on cognitive, social, and psychological measures.

The study led to several books—for example, by Wilford Aiken and Harry Giles.[106] Tyler, a colleague of Giles, was a major participant in the project. Many of his ideas, later published in *Basic Principles of Curriculum and Instruction,* stemmed from principles and ideas generated by the study (as well as the NSSE Twenty-six Yearbook).

Although the idea of stating objectives in behavioral terms had been introduced 20 years prior to the study, the curriculum specialists behind the study introduced it on a national level. These curricularists grouped objectives into related categories. (Tyler and Taba later grouped objectives into these categories: (1) knowledge acquisition, (2) intellectual skills, (3) attitudes and feelings, and (4) academic skills or study habits.[107]) (See Curriculum Tips 3.4.)

Members of the Eight-Year Study understood that evaluation must determine whether a curriculum's objectives had been achieved. The study confirmed the need for comprehensive evaluation, including data on (1) *student achievement,* such as initial levels of mastery, performance on standardized tests, social and psychological skills, and creativity; (2) *social factors,* such as social class, peer group, community patterns, and motivation; (3) *teaching-learning processes,* such as classroom management, homework assignments, and student-teacher interaction; and (4) *instructional methods,* such as discussions, demonstrations, problem solving, and discovery.

Taba and Tyler worked on the study's evaluation team. In the 1940s and 1950s, Taba developed the idea of comprehensive evaluation in her work as chair of the Association for Supervision and Curriculum Development's Commission on Evaluation. She further developed the idea in her 1962 book, *Curriculum Development: Theory and Practice.* Tyler elaborated his ideas on evaluation in his 1949 book, *Basic Principles of Curriculum and Instruction.*

The ideas on curriculum making that the study developed did not filter down to the schools because teachers were not deeply involved in curriculum. As Dewey had stated 25 years before the study, teachers often viewed "outside contacts and considerations" as "interferences."[108] Most of the study's curriculum committees failed to include teachers and restricted them to examining classroom textbooks and materials or modifying curriculum guides developed by central district offices. The exclusion of teachers from the clarification of school goals and program objectives, the organization of subject matter and learning activities, and the evaluation process perpetuated traditional top-down curriculum making.

## Tyler: Basic Principles

Although Ralph Tyler (1902–1994) published more than 700 articles and 16 books on curriculum, instruction, and evaluation, he is best known for his small 1949 book, *Basic Principles of Curriculum and Instruction.*[109] Originally written as a course syllabus for his students at the

### CURRICULUM TIPS 3.4    Classifying Objectives

Translating school goals into objectives entails (1) formulating objectives in terms of subject areas or grade levels and (2) grouping objectives into categories. The following example, derived from the South Bend school district, involves elementary social studies and was developed during the era of the Eight-Year Study. It includes three major categories later advocated by Tyler and Taba for grouping objectives. The objectives are still relevant today.

1. *Knowledge:* Children need to understand that
   a. all people are interdependent and must get along with one another;
   b. our world is constantly changing;
   c. events, discoveries, and inventions may improve life in some ways but also create problems;
   d. people have established communities and governments to meet their needs;
   e. groups develop traditions, values, and customs, and new generations learn these from their elders; and
   f. a place's geography affects the way people live.
2. *Skills:* Children need to learn how to
   a. seek information from many sources and judge its validity;
   b. organize facts and form generalizations based on facts;
   c. carry on a discussion based on facts, make generalizations, and draw conclusions;
   d. plan, carry out plans, and evaluate the work and the planning;
   e. accept responsibility; and
   f. develop values by which to judge actions as right or wrong.
3. *Attitudes:* Children need to be
   a. willing to undertake and complete a job;
   b. anxious to help others and work with others for desirable group goals; and
   c. appreciative of others like and unlike themselves.

*Source: For Our Time: A Handbook for Elementary Social Studies Teachers* (South Bend, IN: School City of South Bend, 1949), pp. 229–230.

University of Chicago, the book has gone through more than 35 printings. In 128 pages, Tyler covers the basic questions that he believes should be answered by anyone involved in planning or writing a curriculum for any subject or grade level:

1. What educational goals should a school seek to accomplish?
2. What educational experiences are likely to lead to these goals?
3. How can these educational experiences be effectively organized?
4. How can we determine whether a school's goals are being accomplished?[110]

Judd's and Dewey's progressive social theories and Thorndike's and Piaget's learning theories strongly influenced Tyler. He also drew from behaviorists such as Bobbitt and Charters, under whom he studied as a graduate student. Other contemporaries, such as Counts and Bode, also influenced Tyler's philosophy and principles of curriculum.

We might consider Tyler's curriculum model an elaboration of Rugg's four major curriculum tasks and a condensed version of the NSSE's Twenty-Sixth Yearbook. His model represents a rational, logical, and systematic approach to curriculum making. It emphasizes the learner's needs, its principles are applicable in varying situations, and it prioritizes objectives. Tyler's book has been highly influential because of its rational, no-nonsense, sequential approach. In just over 100 pages, he laid out a basic procedure, illustrated with easy-to-understand examples. Tyler provides students a series of concise steps by which to plan curriculum.

Although Tyler does not specify the role of the teacher, supervisor, or principal in curriculum planning or the differences between curriculum and instruction, he shows how any school or school district can formulate goals and organize its means and resources to shape curriculum and instruction in the desired direction. Tyler offers a thoughtful and easy-to-follow method. Although critics have charged that Tyler's model is lockstep, technocratic, and overly simplistic,[111] it still works for many. Because it is easy to grasp, it serves as a starting point for curriculum students.

A number of Tyler's influential colleagues—such as Paul Diederich, Harold Dunkel, Maurice Hartung, Virgil Herrick, and Joseph Schwab—accepted many of his ideas and also influenced curriculum. In addition, many of his graduate students became prominent in the field,[112] including Ned Flanders, David Krathwohl, Louis Rath, and Harold Shane. A number of his other students—Ben Bloom, Lee Cronbach, John Goodlad, and Herbert Thelen—were also his colleagues for many years. With the exception of Elliot Eisner, who is inclined toward qualitative and artistic factors in curriculum making, these colleagues continuously praised Tyler's work in the professional literature. See Table 3.5 for an overview of theorists, including Tyler.

## Goodlad: School Reform

John Goodlad (1920–) extended Dewey's ideas of democracy and social activism and Tyler's rational model of curriculum making. Like Dewey, Goodlad believes that philosophy is the starting point in curriculum and the basis for determining goals, means, and ends. In contrast, Tyler viewed philosophy solely as a filter for modifying the school's goals and subsequently developing education programs. Whereas Goodlad advocated teacher involvement in modifying education's goals and developing curriculum, Tyler was unclear about the teacher's role. In fact, Goodlad maintained that schools should allow teachers to teach half-time and spend the rest of their time interpreting and modifying state goals and planning curriculum activities. As part of a school-renewal program, Goodlad advocated that researchers and teachers collaborate in developing and testing new ideas related to curriculum and teaching.[113]

In Goodlad's view, schools should help individuals fulfill their potential but should also promote society's goals. He writes, "Developing individuals to their fullest potential often has been argued as the antithesis of educating the individual to serve the state . . . Whatever the schools may be able to accomplish in promoting [individual growth and enlightenment], they are simultaneously required to instill a sense of devotion to the nation-state."[114]

Dewey believed that education should socialize children and instill society's values and norms. In *Democracy and Education* (1916), he stressed schooling for civic and moral responsibility. In *In Praise of Education* (1997), Goodlad argued that education is an inalienable right in a democratic society and its main purpose is "to develop an individual and collective democratic character." Teachers must inculcate morals and foster "skills dispositions and knowledge necessary for effective participation in a social democracy."[115]

Early in his career, Goodlad launched a study of 260 kindergarten and first-grade classrooms in 100 schools in 13 states. In 1969, he reported his findings: Things were much the same as they had been 20 years before, when Tyler published his classic book on curriculum. "Teaching was predominantly telling and questioning by the teacher with children responding one by one or occasionally in chorus." Teacher talk and the textbook dominated classroom activities. "Rarely did we find small groups intensely in pursuit of knowledge; rarely did we find individual pupils at work in self-sustaining and inquiry. . . . We are forced to conclude much of the so-called educational reform movement has been blunted on the classroom door."[116] Goodlad pointed out that the curriculum reform movement of the 1950s and 1960s was led by university scholars with little practical experience in schools and little respect for teachers; researchers tended to ignore the realities of classrooms and schools.[117]

Fifteen years later in *A Place Called School,* Goodlad and his colleagues reported the results of their studies of more than 17,000 students. They described widespread patterns of passive and rote learning. The findings include the following:

1. The classroom is generally organized as a group that the teacher treats as a whole; individual or small-group instruction is rare.
2. The emphasis is on classroom control and order.

**Table 3.5** Overview of Curriculum Theorists, 1918–present

| Theorist | Purpose | Principles | Content | Major Book |
|---|---|---|---|---|
| Franklin Bobbitt (1876–1956) | Curriculum as a science<br>Emphasis on student needs<br>Prepare students for adult life<br>Clarify objectives<br>Cost-effective education | Grouping and sequencing objectives with corresponding activities<br>Clarifying instructional specifications and tasks | Basic three R's in elementary schools<br>Academic subjects in high school<br>Subject matter and related activities planned by teacher | *The Curriculum*, 1918<br>*How to Make a Curriculum*, 1924 |
| Werrett Charters (1875–1952) | Curriculum as a science<br>Emphasis on student needs (and needs assessment)<br>Bridging theory and practice in curriculum | Curriculum process, described as job analysis<br>Listing of objectives and corresponding activities<br>Verification of objectives through evaluation | Subject matter related to objectives<br>Subject matter and corresponding activities planned by teacher | *Curriculum Construction*, 1923 |
| William Kilpatrick (1871–1965) | School as a social and community experience<br>Curriculum identified as purposeful activities<br>Child-centered curriculum<br>Child development and growth | Project method, a blend of behaviorism and progressivism<br>Teacher and student planning, emphasis on the student<br>Emphasis on pedagogy or instructional activities: creative projects, social relationships, and small-group instruction | Educating a generalist, not a specialist<br>Integrated subject matter<br>Problem solving | *Foundations of Education*, 1926 |
| Harold Rugg (1886–1960) | Education in context with society<br>Child-centered curriculum<br>Whole child<br>Curriculum specialist as an engineer | Statement of objectives, related learning experiences, and outcomes<br>Teacher plans curriculum in advance | Emphasis on social studies | *The Child Centered Curriculum* (with Ann Shumaker), 1928 |

| Theorist | Purpose | Principles | Content | Major Book |
|---|---|---|---|---|
| Hollis Caswell (1901–1989) | Foundations of education (history, philosophy, and soon) influence curriculum development<br>Relationship of three major components: curriculum, instruction, and learning<br>Student needs and interests<br>Curriculum organized around social functions (themes), organized knowledge, and learners' interests | Curriculum as a set of experiences<br>Curriculum guides as a source of teacher planning<br>Teachers coordinate instructional activities to implement curriculum | Subject matter organized in relation to student needs and interests<br>Subject matter developed around social functions and learners' interests | *Curriculum Development* (with Doak Campbell), 1935 |
| Ralph W. Tyler (1902–1994) | Curriculum as a science and extension of school's philosophy<br>Clarify purposes (objectives) by studies of learners and contemporary life, suggestions from subject specialists, and use of philosophy and psychology<br>Student needs and interests<br>Relationship between curriculum and instruction | Curriculum as a rational process<br>Using objectives to select and organize learning experiences<br>Using evaluation to determine outcomes (whether objectives have been achieved)<br>Vertical and horizontal relationship of curriculum | Subject matter organized in terms of knowledge, skills, and values<br>Emphasis on problem solving<br>Educating a generalist, not a specialist | *Basic Principles of Curriculum and Instruction*, 1949 |
| John Goodlad (1920–) | Curriculum organized around needs of society and students<br>Wide range of purposes, including cognitive, social, civic, vocational, aesthetic, and moral<br>Realistic reform policies and programs | Reduce student conformity in classroom<br>Constant need for school improvement<br>School reforms frequently come and go and add costs to the system; teacher input is preferred<br>Standards and high-stakes tests currently drive school reform | Emphasis on active learning and critical thinking<br>Involvement of students in planning curriculum content and instructional activities<br>Need to align content with standards and high-stakes tests | *A Place Called School*, 1984<br>*What Are Schools For?* 1989 |

3. Teachers check enthusiasm and excitement; the educational tone is flat and neutral.
4. Students passively listen to teachers, write answers to questions, and take tests; they rarely interact or learn from one another.
5. Little use is made of media, guest speakers, or field trips.
6. Instruction rarely goes beyond knowledge acquisition; little effort is made to motivate students to reflect, solve problems, hypothesize, or think creatively.
7. When teachers prioritize order and students prefer to do as little work as possible, the result is often minimum standards and expectations.
8. Overwhelmingly, secondary school students say that "good looking students" and "athletes" are the most popular students. Only 10 percent of secondary school students say that "smart students are popular."[118]

Goodlad concluded that (1) the curriculum prescribed in most schools is ineffective because it has little relation to real events in society; (2) in most schools, there is a disparity between agreed-on goals and the actual program; and (3) students are treated as "passive recipients" of content, and teachers stress correct answers in their classroom instruction.

At the end of his professional career, Goodlad stated that, over the past hundred years, education has consistently embraced the seven Cardinal Principles of Secondary Education. As for school reform, he saw it reemerge in many national commission reports, such as *A Nation at Risk,* published in 1983, which employed "military language" in trying to link reform to the U.S. decline in the global economy. Goodlad contended that reformers have "tricked" the public by continually suggesting that "all schools are failing," even though most parents rate their local schools relatively highly. Today, school reform has been narrowed to standards, especially issues of testing and accurate assessment of student outcomes. Test scores have become "the bottom line."[119]

## CURRENT FOCUS

The Tyler model summed up the best principles of curriculum making for the first half of the 20th century. Many curricularists have used this model. In fact, many practitioners in schools consider Tyler's model the basic way to create curricula. Currently, however, all traditional and technical models are being challenged.

According to nontraditional and nontechnocratic scholars, we cannot reduce curriculum to a particular theory, plan, or definition, much less agree on what is acceptable or valid. Critics claim that "philosophies, theories, [and principles] are not determined only by static knowledge and empirical data. The world of subjectivity and art is considered just as valid as Aristotelian logic and Newtonian science."[120] Given the postmodern world of relativism, there is considerable controversy regarding what is and is not objective and true.

Some critics of the educational status quo argue that schools need to be "liberated from institutional and capitalistic, [as well as racist and gender] indoctrination. Learners [should] no longer have an obligatory curriculum imposed on them. Schools and society should no longer discriminate and foster a class society based on possession of certificates" and standardized tests. Just as there is "an unequal distribution of economic capital and political power in society," the schools provide "an unequal distribution of cultural/educational capital."[121] Current curricularists such as Michael Apple, Henry Giroux, Ivan Illich, Peter McLaren, and William Pinar hold such views. Others, such as William Doll, Eliot Eisner, Maxine Greene, and Herb Kliebard, are more moderate but still have rejected the scientific/rational model and most forms of traditional/technocratic thinking. The latter group, instead of weaving radical politics into their discussion, are more concerned with reformulating curriculum along aesthetic, linguistic, historical, humanistic, and existentialist lines.

The field of curriculum now involves numerous political and social interpretations. It is dynamic and ever changing, incorporating knowledge from other disciplines (e.g., philosophy, psychology, sociology, political science).

## Conclusion

From the colonial period to around World War I, curriculum was a matter of evolving subject matter. Some reform ideas concerned pedagogical principles of the mid- and late 1800s, mainly as a result of European influence and the emerging progressive reform movement of the early 20th century, but these ideas were limited to theoretical discussions and a few isolated, innovative schools. The perennialist curriculum, which emphasized the classics and timeless and absolute values based on religious and then moral doctrines, dominated for the first 150 years of our nation's history.

The idea of curriculum principles and processes began to take shape after 1900, and scientific principles and progressive philosophy were increasingly influential. Curriculum as a field of study—with its own methods, theories, and ways of solving problems—has made real advances since the 1920s. Most of the advances have taken place since Tyler wrote his basic text on curriculum.

---

## MyEdLeadershipLab™

Go to Topics 3 and 10: *Education in Revolutionary America* and *Textbook as Curriculum* on the MyEdLeadershipLab™ site (www.MyEdLeadershipLab.com) for *Curriculum: Foundations, Principles, and Issues,* Sixth Edition where you can:

- Find learning outcomes for *Education in Revolutionary America* and *Textbook as Curriculum*, along with the national standards that connect to these outcomes.
- Complete Assignments and Activities that can help you more deeply understand the chapter content.
- Apply and Practice your understanding of the core skills identified in the chapter with the Building Leadership Skills unit.
- Prepare yourself for professional certification with a Practice for Certification quiz.

---

## Endnotes

1. John D. Pulliam and James J. Van Patten, ed., *History of Education in Americas* (Columbus, OH: Merrill, 2007); and R. Freeman Butts and Lawrence A. Cremin, *A History of Education in American Culture* (New York: Holt, Rinehart and Winston, 1953).

2. Gerald Gutek, *Historical and Philosophical Foundations of Education,* 4th ed. (Columbus, OH: Merrill, 2005); and Butts and Cremin, *A History of Education in American Culture.*

3. George A. Beauchamp, *The Curriculum of the Elementary School* (Boston: Allyn & Bacon, 1964), p. 34.

4. Allan C. Ornstein and Daniel U. Levine, *Foundations of Education,* 10th ed. (Boston: Houghton Mifflin, 2008), p. 165. See also S. Alexander Rippa, *Education in a Free Society,* 7th ed. (New York: Longman, 1992).

5. Beauchamp, *The Curriculum of the Elementary School,* p. 36.

6. Marvin Lazerson and W. Norton Grubb, *The Education Gospel* (Cambridge, MA: Harvard University Press, 2004); Paul Monroe, *Founding of the American Public School System* (New York: Macmillan, 1940); and Samuel E. Morrison, *The Intellectual Life of Colonial New England* (New York: New York University Press, 1956).

7. Robert Middlekauff, *Ancients and Axioms: Secondary Education in the Eighteenth-Century New England* (New Haven, CT: Yale University Press, 1963).

8. Elmer E. Brown, *The Making of Our Middle Schools* (New York: Longman, 1926), p. 133.

9. Newton Edwards and Herman G. Richey, *The School in the American Social Order,* 2nd ed. (Boston: Houghton Mifflin, 1963), p. 102.

10. Morrison, *The Intellectual Life of Colonial New England;* and Joel Spring, *The American School: 1642–2000* (Boston: McGraw-Hill, 2001).

11. John H. Best, *Benjamin Franklin on Education* (New York: Teachers College Press, Columbia University, 1962); Bernard Cohen, *Benjamin Franklin's Science* (Cambridge: Harvard University Press, 1990); and Edmund S. Morgan, *Benjamin Franklin* (New Haven, CT: Yale University Press, 2002).

12. Ellwood P. Cubberley, *Public Education in the United States,* rev. ed. (Boston: Houghton Mifflin, 1947), p. 30.

13. R. Freeman Butts, *The American Tradition in Religion and Education* (Boston: Beacon Press, 1950); and Gerald R. Firth and Richard D. Kimpston, *The Curricular Continuum in Perspective* (Itasca, IL: Peacock, 1973).

14. Paul L. Ford, *The New England Primer: A History of Its Origins and Development,* rev. ed. (New York: Dodd, Mead, 1897), pp. 329–330.

15. Henry Barnard, *Educational Developments in the United States* (Hartford, CT: Connecticut Department of Education, 1867), p. 367.

16. Cubberley, *Public Education in the United States;* and Merle Curti, *The Social Ideas of American Educators* (New York: Littlefield, Adams, 1959).

17. Benjamin Rush, *A Plan for the Establishment of Public Schools* (Philadelphia: Thomas Dobson, 1786), pp. 29–30.

18. Thomas Jefferson, "A Bill for the More General Diffusion of Knowledge," in P. L. Ford, ed., *The Writings of Thomas Jefferson* (New York: Putnam, 1893), p. 221.

19. Merle Curti, *The Growth of American Thought,* rev. ed. (New York: Harper & Row, 1951).

20. Hans Kohn, *American Nationalism: An Interpretive Essay* (New York: Macmillan, 1957), p. 47.

21. Noah Webster, *Dissertations on the English Language* (Boston: Isaiah Thomas, 1789), p. 27.

22. Harvey R. Warfel, *Noah Webster: Schoolmaster to America* (New York: Macmillan, 1936).

23. Henry Steele Commager, ed., *Noah Webster's American Spelling Book* (New York: Teachers College Press, Columbia University, 1962).

24. Robert K. Leavitt, *Noah's Ark, New England Yankees and the Endless Quest* (Springfield, MA: Merriam, 1947); and Richard M. Rollins, "Words as Social Control: Noah Webster and the Creation of the American Dictionary," *American Quarterly* (Fall 1976), pp. 415–430.

25. William H. McGuffey, *New Fifth Eclectic Reader* (Cincinnati, OH: Winthrop Smith, 1857), p. 271.

26. William H. McGuffey, *Newly Revised Eclectic Fourth Reader* (Cincinnati, OH: Winthrop Smith, 1853), p. 313.

27. James M. Lower, "William Holmes McGuffey: A Book or a Man?" *Vitae Scholasticae* (Fall 1984), pp. 311–320; and John H. Westerhoff, *McGuffey and His Readers: Piety, Morality, and Education in Nineteenth Century America* (Nashville, TN: Abingdon, 1978). See also Joel Westheimer, *Pledging Allegiance* (New York: Teachers College Press, Columbia University, 2007).

28. William B. Ragan and Gene D. Shepherd, *Modern Elementary Curriculum,* 7th ed. (New York: Holt, Rinehart and Winston, 1992), p. 23. See also Forrest W. Parkway et al., *Curriculum Planning,* 8th ed. (Boston: Allyn & Bacon, 2006).

29. Edgar W. Knight, *Education in the United States,* 3rd ed. (Boston: Ginn, 1951), p. 512.

30. Henry Barnard, *Pestalozzi and Pestalozzianism* (New York: Brownell, 1862).

31. Friedrich Froebel, *The Education of Man,* trans. W. Hailman (New York: Appleton, 1889).

32. John Dewey, *How We Think* (Boston: Health, 1910), p. 202.

33. Andreas Kazamias, *Herbert Spencer on Education* (New York: Teachers College Press, Columbia University, 1966); and Valerie A. Haines, "Spencer's Philosophy of Science," *British Journal of Sociology* (June 1992), pp. 155–172.

34. Herbert Spencer, *Education: Intellectual, Moral and Physical* (New York: Appleton, 1860).

35. See Chapter 4 for a discussion on Dewey's *How We Think* and Jerome Bruner's *The Process of Education.*

36. See Everett Dick, *Vanguards of the Frontier* (New York: Appleton-Century, 1940); and William W. Folwell, *The Autobiography and Letters of a Pioneer Culture* (Minneapolis: University of Minnesota Press, 1923).

37. Glen H. Elder and Rand D. Conger, *Children of the Land: Adversity and Success in Rural America* (Chicago: University of Chicago Press, 2000).

38. L. Dean Webb, *The History of American Education* (Columbus, OH: Merrill, 2006); and Monroe, *Founding of the American Public School System.*

39. Frederick M. Binder, *The Age of the Common School: 1830–1865* (New York: Wiley, 1974); and Wayne E. Fuller, *One-Room Schools of the Middle West* (Lawrence: University Press of Kansas, 1994).

40. V. T. Thayer and Martin Levit, *The Role of the School in American Society,* 2nd ed. (New York: Dodd, Mead, 1966), p. 6.

41. Lawrence A. Cremin, *The Republic and the School: Horace Mann on the Education of Free Man* (New York: Teachers College Press, Columbia University Press, 1957); and Jonathan Messerlie, *Horace Mann: A Biography* (New York: Knopf, 1972).

42. Andrew Gulliford, *America's Country Schools* (Washington, DC: National Trust for Historic Preservation, 1985). See also Evans Clinchy, *Rescuing the Public Schools* (New York: Teachers College Press, Columbia University, 2007).

43. James H. Hughes, *Education in America,* 3rd ed. (New York: Harper & Row, 1970), p. 233.

44. Carl Sandburg, *Abraham Lincoln: The Prairie Years* (New York: Harcourt Brace, 1926), p. 19.

45. Theodore R. Sizer, *The Age of Academies* (New York: Teachers College Press, Columbia University, 1964).

46. E. P. Cubberley, *The History of Education* (Boston: Houghton Mifflin, 1920), p. 697.

47. Edwards and Richey, *The School in the American Social Order;* and Jergen Herbst, *The Once and Future School: Three Hundred and Fifty Years of American Secondary Education* (New York: Routledge, 1996).

48. Brown, *The Making of Our Middle Schools,* p. 230.

49. Monroe, *Founding of the American Public School System,* p. 404.

50. Edward A. Krug, *The Shaping of the American High School: 1880–1920* (New York: Harper & Row, 1964); and Daniel Tanner, *Secondary Education: Perspectives and Prospects* (New York: Macmillan, 1972).

51. Cubberley, *Public Education in the United States;* Edwards and Richey, *The School in the American Social Order;* and Allan C. Ornstein, *Teaching and Schooling in America: Pre- and Post-September 11* (Boston: Allyn & Bacon, 2003).

52. Calvin O. Davis, *Our Evolving High School Curriculum* (Yonkers-on-Hudson, NY: 1927); and David H. Kamens and Yun-Kyung Cha, "The Legitimation of New Subjects in Mass Schooling," *Journal of Curriculum Studies* (January–February 1992), pp. 43–60.

53. David T. Hansen et al., *A Life in Classrooms* (New York: Teachers College Press, Columbia University, 2007); and William A. Reid, "The Educational Situation as Concerns Secondary Education," *Journal of Curriculum and Supervision* (Winter 2002), pp. 130–143.

54. Thayer and Levit, *The Role of the School in American Society,* p. 382.

55. *Report of the Year 1889–90* (Washington, DC: U.S. Bureau of Education, 1893), pp. 1388–1389, Table 3.2. See also Ornstein, *Teaching and Schooling in America: Pre- and Post-September 11,* Table 5.1, p. 249.

56. Cubberley, *Public Education in the United States,* p. 543.

57. William G. Wraga, "Left Out: The Villainization of Progressive Education in the United States," *Educational Researcher* (October 2001), pp. 34–39.

58. *Report of the Committee of Ten on Secondary School Studies,* book ed. (New York: American Book, 1894), p. 48.

59. Daniel Tanner and Laurel Tanner, *Curriculum Development: Theory into Practice,* 2nd ed. (New York: Macmillan, 1980), p. 233. See also Milton Gaithers, *American Educational History Revisited* (New York: Teachers College Press, Columbia University, 2002).

60. *Sixteenth Annual Report of the Board of Education* (St. Louis, MO: Board of Education, 1871), p. 28.

61. William T. Harris, *Psychologic Foundations of Education* (New York: Appleton, 1898), p. 282.

62. Lawrence A. Cremin, *The Transformation of the School* (New York: Random House, 1961), p. 20.

63. Charles Eliot, cited in W. H. Heck, *Mental Discipline and Educational Values* (New York: Lane, 1909), p. 127.

64. Jerome S. Bruner, *The Process of Education* (Cambridge, MA: Harvard University Press, 1959), p. 33.

65. Diane Ravitch, *Left Behind: A Century of Failed School Reform* (New York: Simon & Schuster, 2000), p. 31.

66. Charles Eliot, cited in Robert H. Bremmer, ed., *Children and Youth in America: A Documentary History, 1866–1932* (Cambridge, MA: Harvard University Press, 1971), p. 114.

67. James B. Conant, *Slums and Suburbs* (New York: McGraw-Hill, 1961).

68. R. Freeman Butts, *Public Education in the United States: From Revolution to Reform* (New York: Holt, Rinehart and Winston, 1978), p. 217.

69. Marvin Lazeron and Norton W. Grubb, eds., *American Education and Vocationalism: A Documentary History, 1870–1970* (New York: Teachers College Press, 1974), pp. 83–84.

70. Butts, *Public Education in the United States;* and Isaac L. Kandel, *History of Secondary Education* (Boston: Houghton Mifflin, 1930).

71. Michael Apple, *Ideology and Curriculum,* 3rd ed. (Boston: Routledge & Kegan Paul, 2004), p. 19; Alfie Kohn *What to Look for in a Classroom* (San Francisco: Jossey-Bass, 2000); and Jeannie Oakes et al., *Becoming Good American Schools* (San Francisco: Jossey-Bass, 1999).

72. Decker Walker, *Fundamentals of Curriculum* (Orlando, FL: Harcourt Brace, 1990).

73. *Digest of Education Statistics 2003* (Washington DC: U.S. Government Printing Office, 2004), Table 98, p. 130.

74. Edward L. Thorndike, "Mental Discipline in High School Studies," *Journal of Educational Psychology* (February 1924), p. 98.

75. Charles W. Eliot, "The Case against Compulsory Latin," *Atlantic* (March 1917), pp. 356–359.

76. Abraham Flexner, "Parents and School," *Atlantic* (July 1916), p. 30.

77. Abraham Flexner, "A Modern School," *Occasional Papers,* No. 3 (New York: General Education Board, 1916); and Abraham Flexner, *A Modern College and a Modern School* (New York: Doubleday, 1923).

78. John Dewey, *Democracy and Education* (New York: Macmillan, 1916).

79. Ibid, p. 190.

80. Charles H. Judd, *Introduction to the Scientific Study of Education* (Boston: Ginn, 1918).

81. Commission on the Reorganization of Secondary Education, *Cardinal Principles of Secondary Education,* Bulletin No. 35 (Washington, DC: U.S. Government Printing Office, 1918).

82. Frederick W. Taylor, *The Principles of Scientific Management* (New York: Harper & Row, 1911).

83. Raymond E. Callahan, *Education and the Cult of Efficiency* (Chicago: University of Chicago Press, 1962).

84. Franklin Bobbitt, *The Curriculum* (Boston: Houghton Mifflin, 1918), p. 42.

85. Ibid., p. 283.

86. Franklin Bobbitt, *How to Make a Curriculum* (Boston: Houghton Mifflin, 1924), pp. 14, 28.

87. W. W. Charters, *Curriculum Construction* (New York: Macmillan, 1923).

88. Ibid, pp. 6–7. See also W. W. Charters, "Idea Men and Engineers in Education," *Educational Forum* (Spring 1986), pp. 263–272. Originally published in *Educational Forum* (May 1948), pp. 399–406.

89. John Dewey, "Individuality and Experience," in J. Dewey, ed., *Art and Education* (Marion, PA: Barnes Foundation, 1929), p. 180. See also Kathy Hytten, "The Resurgence of Dewey: Are His Educational Ideas Still Relevant?" *Journal of Curriculum Studies* (May–June 2000), pp. 453–466.

90. William H. Kilpatrick, "The Project Method," *Teachers College Record* (September 1918), pp. 319–335.

91. Junius L. Merian, *Child Life and the School Curriculum* (New York: World Book, 1920).

92. Ellsworth Collings, *An Experiment with a Project Curriculum* (New York: Macmillan, 1923).

93. William H. Kilpatrick, *Foundations of Education* (New York: Macmillan, 1926), p. 212.

94. Ibid., p. 213.

95. John McNeil, *Curriculum: A Comprehensive Introduction* (Glenview, IL: Scott, Foresman, 1990); and Tanner and Tanner, *Curriculum Development*.

96. William H. Kilpatrick, ed., *The Educational Frontier* (New York: Century, 1933), p. 19.

97. Ellsworth Collings, *Project Teaching in Elementary Schools* (New York: Century, 1928).

98. Guy M. Whipple, ed., *Curriculum-Making: Past and Present,* Twenty-sixth Yearbook of the National Society for the Study of Education, Part I (Bloomington, IL: Public School Publishing, 1930); and Guy M. Whipple, ed., *The Foundations of Curriculum-Making,* Twenty-sixth Yearbook of the National Society for the Study of Education, Part II (Bloomington, IL: Public School Publishing, 1930).

99. Harold Rugg, "The School Curriculum and the Drama of American Life," in Guy M. Whipple, ed., *Curriculum-Making: Past and Present* (Bloomington, IL: Public School Publishing, 1930), pp. 3–16.

100. Harold Rugg, "Three Decades of Mental Discipline: Curriculum-Making via National Committees," in Guy M. Whipple, ed., *Curriculum-Making: Past and Present* (Bloomington, IL: Public School Publishing, 1930), pp. 52–53.

101. Ibid.

102. Harold Rugg and Ann Shumaker, *The Child-Centered School* (New York: World Book, 1928), p. 118.

103. Sidney B. Hall, D. W. Peters, and Hollis L. Caswell, *Study Course for Virginia State Curriculum* (Richmond: Virginia State Board of Education, 1932), p. 363.

104. Hollis L. Caswell and Doak S. Campbell, *Curriculum Development* (New York: American Book, 1935), p. 69.

105. Ralph W. Tyler, "Curriculum Development in the Twenties and Thirties," in R. M. McClure, ed., *The Curriculum: Retrospect and Prospect,* Seventieth Yearbook of the National Society for the Study of Education, Part I (Chicago: University of Chicago Press, 1971), pp. 26–44; and Ralph W. Tyler, "The Five Most Significant Curriculum Events in the Twentieth Century," *Educational Leadership* (December–January 1987), pp. 36–38. See also Louis Rubin, "Educational Evaluation: Classic Works of Ralph W. Tyler," *Journal of Curriculum Studies* (March–April 1991), pp. 193–198.

106. Wilford Aiken, *The Story of the Eight Year Study* (New York: Harper & Row, 1942); and H. H. Giles, S. P. McCutchen, and A. N. Zechiel, *Exploring the Curriculum* (New York: Harper & Row, 1942).

107. Hilda Taba, "Evaluation in High Schools and Junior Colleges," in W. S. Gray, ed., *Reading in Relation to Experience and Language* (Chicago: University of Chicago Press, 1944), pp. 199–204; Hilda Taba, *Curriculum Development: Theory and Practice* (New York: Harcourt Brace, 1962); Ralph W. Tyler, *Basic Principles of Curriculum and Instruction* (Chicago: University of Chicago Press, 1949); and E. R. Smith and Ralph W. Tyler, eds., *Appraising and Recording Student Progress* (New York: Harper & Row, 1942).

108. John Dewey, "The Educational Situation," *Journal of Curriculum and Supervision* (Winter 2002), p. 108. Originally published in 1906 as "Contributions to Education, Number III."

109. Ralph W. Tyler, *Basic Principles of Curriculum and Instruction* (Chicago: University of Chicago Press, 1949).

110. Ibid., p. 1.

111. Henry Giroux, *Teachers as Intellectuals* (Westport, CT: Bergin & Garvey, 1988); Herbert M. Kliebard, "Reappraisal: The Tyler Rationale," in A. A. Bellack and H. M. Kliebard, eds., *Curriculum and Evaluation* (Berkeley, CA: McCutchan, 1977), pp. 34–69; and James T. Sears and J. Dan Marshall, eds., *Teaching and Thinking about Curriculum* (New York: Teachers College Press, Columbia University, 1990).

112. Marie K. Stone, *Principles of Curriculum, Instruction, and Evaluation: Past Influence and Present Effects,* Ph.D. dissertation, Loyola University of Chicago, January 1985. Also from conversations by one of the authors with John Beck, April 12, 1991.

113. John I. Goodlad, "Curriculum Development beyond 1980," *Education Evolution and Policy Analysis* (September 1980), pp. 49–54.

114. John I. Goodlad, *What Are Schools For?* (Bloomington, IN: Phi Delta Kappa Educational Foundation, 1989), p. 36.

115. John Goodlad, *In Praise of Education* (New York: McGraw-Hill, 1997).

116. John I. Goodlad, "The Schools vs. Education," *Saturday Review* (April 19, 1969), p. 60.

117. John I. Goodlad and Frances M. Klein, *Behind the Classroom Doors* (Worthington, OH: Charles A. Jones Publishers, 1970).

118. John I. Goodlad et al., *A Place Called School* (New York: McGraw-Hill, 1984).

119. John I. Goodlad, "Kudzu, Rabbits, and School Reform," in A. C. Ornstein, E. Pajak, and S. B. Ornstein, eds., *Contemporary Issues in Curriculum* (Boston: Allyn & Bacon, 2007), pp. 51–58.

120. Allan C. Ornstein, *Pushing the Envelope: Critical Issues in Education* (Columbus, OH: Merrill, 2003), p. 30.

121. Ibid., pp. 30–31.

# 4

■ ■ ■

# Psychological Foundations of Curriculum

## FOCUSING QUESTIONS

1. In what ways do psychological foundations enable curriculum workers (teachers, supervisors, and curriculum developers) to perform their educational responsibilities?

2. How would you compare the three major theoretical schools of learning?

3. How has the view of multiple intelligences influenced the field of curriculum? How might this concept of intelligence influence the field in the future?

4. How does constructivism incorporate the most recent views of learning?

5. How should the concept of learning styles influence the thinking of those responsible for curriculum development and delivery?

6. How should an educator use the information about various types of thinking?

7. How do you define *humanistic learning* in schools?

8. In what ways can addressing emotional intelligence be justified in the curriculum?

Psychology is concerned with the question of how people learn, and curriculum specialists ask how psychology can contribute to the design and delivery of curriculum. Put another way, how can curriculum specialists incorporate psychological knowledge to increase the probability that students will learn? Psychology provides a basis for understanding the teaching and learning process. Both processes are essential to curricularists because the curriculum has worth only when students learn and gain knowledge. Other questions of interest to psychologists and curriculum specialists are the following: Why do learners respond as they do to teachers' efforts? How do cultural experiences affect students' learning? How should curriculum be organized to enhance learning? What impact does the school culture have on students' learning? What is the optimal level of student participation in learning the curriculum's various contents?

No curriculum scholar or practitioner would deny the importance of this psychological foundation. All agree that teaching the curriculum and learning it are interrelated, and psychology cements the relationship. This disciplined field of inquiry furnishes theories and principles of learning that influence teacher-student behavior within the context of the curriculum. Of course, we are not the first to realize the importance of this foundation. John Dewey knew that psychology was the basis for understanding how the individual learner interacts with objects and persons.

The process continues throughout life, and the quality of interaction determines the amount and type of learning. Ralph Tyler considered psychology a "screen" for helping determine what our objectives are and how our learning takes place.[1] More recently, Jerome Bruner linked psychology with modes of thinking that underlie the methods used in specific disciplines. These methods can be used to formulate concepts, principles, and generalizations that form the structure of the disciplines.[2] In short, psychology is the unifying element of the learning process; it forms the basis for the methods, materials, and activities of learning, and it provides the impetus for many curriculum decisions.

Historically, the major theories of learning have been classified into three groups: (1) behaviorist or association theories, the oldest group, which deals with various aspects of stimulus–response (S-R) and reinforcers; (2) cognitive information–processing theories, which view the learner in relation to the total environment and consider the way the learner applies information; and (3) phenomenological and humanistic theories, which consider the whole child, including their social, psychological, and cognitive development. When behaviorist theories are discussed separately, learning tends to focus on conditioning, modifying, or shaping behavior through reinforcement and rewards. When cognitive information–processing theories are stressed, the learning process focuses on the student's developmental stages and multiple forms of intelligence, as well as problem solving, critical thinking, and creativity. The phenomenological aspects of learning deal with the learner's needs, attitudes, and feelings and entail more alternatives in learning.

## BEHAVIORISM

The behaviorists, who represent traditional psychology, are rooted in philosophical speculation about the nature of learning—the ideas of Aristotle, Descartes, Locke, and Rousseau. They emphasize conditioning behavior and altering the environment to elicit selected responses from the learner. Behaviorism dominated much of 20th-century psychology.

### Connectionism

Edward Thorndike, one of the first Americans to test the learning process experimentally, is considered the founder of behavioral psychology. At Harvard, Thorndike began his work with animals, a course of experimentation other behaviorists also adopted.[3] Thorndike focused on testing the relationship between a stimulus and a response (classical conditioning). He defined *learning* as habit formation, that is, as connecting more and more habits into a complex structure. Knowledge resulted from the accumulation of these stimulus–response associations within this complex structure. Elementary knowledge is composed of groupings of simple components of a skill or knowledge. As one acquired more complicated units of association, one attained a more sophisticated understanding.[4] Thorndike defined *teaching* as arranging the classroom to enhance desirable connections and associations.

Thorndike developed three major laws of learning: (1) the *Law of Readiness*—when a "conduction" unit is ready to conduct, conduction is satisfying and lack of conduction is annoying; (2) the *Law of Exercise*—a connection is strengthened in proportion to its frequency and its average intensity and duration; and (3) the *Law of Effect*—responses accompanied by satisfaction strengthen the connection; responses accompanied by discomfort weaken the connection.[5]

The Law of Readiness suggests that, when the nervous system is ready to conduct, it leads to a satisfying state of affairs; some educators misinterpret this as referring to educational readiness, such as readiness to read. The Law of Exercise provides justification for drill, repetition, and review and is best illustrated today by behavior modification and basic-skills instructional approaches. Although teachers used rewards and punishments for centuries prior to Thorndike's formulation of the Law of Effect, his theory made more explicit and justified what was being done. B. F. Skinner's operant model of behavior, direct instruction, and many current ideas based on providing satisfying experiences to the learner, as well as reinforcement in the form of feedback, are rooted in this law.

Thorndike maintained that (1) behavior was influenced by conditions of learning; (2) learners' attitudes and abilities could improve over time through proper stimuli; (3) instructional experiences could be designed and controlled; and (4) it was important to select stimuli and learning experiences that were integrated, consistent, and mutually reinforcing. For Thorndike, no one subject was more likely than another to improve the mind; rather, learning was a matter of relating new learning to previous learning. He attacked the "psychology" of mental discipline, asserting that there was no hierarchy of subject matter.

## Thorndike's Influence: Tyler, Taba, and Bruner

Coinciding with Thorndike's (1874–1949) theories, Tyler and Hilda Taba maintained that learning had application and thus could be transferred to other situations.[6] This meant that rote learning and memorization were unnecessary. The student could organize and classify information into existing mental schemata or patterns and use it in different situations. Many of Thorndike's theories of learning had an impact on the behaviorist and logical approach outlined by Tyler and Taba. However, Tyler and Taba disagreed with Thorndike's view of connections between specific stimuli and specific responses. They outlined a more generalized view of learning, one that more closely corresponds with a cognitive approach. Whereas Bobbitt and Charters opted for the more precise behavioral approach to learning, along Thorndike's lines, and viewed objectives in context with highly specific habits to be acquired, Tyler and Taba leaned toward Dewey's and Judd's approach: Learning was based on *generalizations* and the teaching of important *principles* (terms used by the latter four educators) to explain concrete phenomena.[7]

Tyler and Taba gave credit to Thorndike in their classic texts. Tyler's recognition of Thorndike was minimal; nevertheless, he spent considerable space discussing connectionism and organizing learning principles along Thorndike's transfer theories. Taba devoted an entire chapter to "the transfer of learning" and the influence that Thorndike and others had on her learning theory. Like Thorndike, Taba argued that practice alone does not necessarily strengthen memory or learning transfer, which served to free the curriculum from the rigid roteness and drill of the past. "Since no program, no matter how thorough, can teach everything, the task of all education is to cause a maximum amount of transfer."[8] The idea was to develop content or methods that led to generalizations and that had wide transfer value. Taba advocated problem-solving and inquiry-discovery techniques.

The notions of "learning how to learn" and "inquiry discovery," although popularized by Bruner, are rooted in Thorndike. Thorndike, and later Bruner, assumed that learning that involves meaningful organization of experiences can be transferred more readily than learning acquired by rote.[9] The more abstract the principles and generalizations, the greater the possibility of transfer. (This view corresponds with Dewey's idea of reflective thinking and the steps that he outlined for problem solving.)

For Bruner, a true discipline contains structure, which provides the basis for the specific transfer of learning. The abilities to learn and recall are directly related to the learner's having a structural pattern by which information can be transferred to new situations. Transfer of learning is much more frequent when learning is basic and general. However, whereas Thorndike found that no one subject was more important than another for meaningful learning, Bruner emphasized science and mathematics as the major disciplines for teaching structure. In this connection, Thorndike was more progressive than Bruner; he gave equal weight and equal importance to various subjects—and he broke from traditional thinking about the hierarchy of subject matter.

According to classical-conditioning theory, learning consists of eliciting a response by means of previously neutral or inadequate stimuli; some neutral stimulus associated with an unconditioned stimulus at the time of response gradually acquires the ability to elicit the response. In Ivan Pavlov's well-known classical-conditioning experiment, a dog learned to salivate at the sound of a bell. The bell, a biologically neutral, or inadequate, stimulus, was presented simultaneously with food, a biologically nonneutral, or adequate, stimulus. The dog associated the two stimuli so closely that the bell came to be substituted for the food, and the dog reacted to the bell as he originally had to the food.[10]

The implications for human learning were important. Some neutral stimulus (bell) associated with an unconditioned stimulus (food) at the time of the response gradually acquired the association to elicit the response (salivation). This theory has led to a wealth of laboratory investigations about learning and has become a focal point in social and political discussions—for example, Aldous Huxley's novel *Brave New World* and the movies *The Deer Hunter, Jacob's Ladder,* and *Silence of the Lambs.*

On the American scene, James Watson used Pavlov's research as a foundation for building a new science of psychology based on *behaviorism.* The new science emphasized that learning was based on the science of behaviorism—what was observable or measurable—not on cognitive processes. The laws of behavior were derived from animal and then human studies and were expected to have the objectivity of scientific laws.[11]

For John Watson, an early exponent of behaviorism, learning *was* conditioning, and conditioning was adequate to explain all manifestations of higher mutual learning processes. All such activity was nothing more that the reactions from simple, unconditional responses joined to form more sophisticated conditional responses.

For Watson and others, the key to learning was to condition the child in the early years of life, based on the method Pavlov had demonstrated for animals. Watson once boasted, "Give me a dozen healthy infants, well-formed, and my own specified world to bring them up and I'll guarantee to take anyone at random and train him to be any type of specialist I might select—a doctor, lawyer, artist . . . and yes, even into beggarman and thief, regardless of his talents, . . . abilities, vocations, and race."[12] That said, Watson bolstered the case for environmental influence in an era when the vast majority of psychologists argued the case for genetics.

## Behaviorist Reinforcement Theory

Many contemporary psychologists believe in the basic stimulus–response principles but reject the rigid mechanistic views of Thorndike and Watson. These contemporary associationists are called "neobehaviorists."

According to one neobehaviorist, Clark Hull, the connection between stimulus and response is determined by its relation to drive and reward.[13] A *drive* is a state of tension arising from a person's biological or psychological needs. A *reward* is the satisfaction of the need or reduction of the drive. *Conditioning* takes place by acting upon the individual while he or she is experiencing these drives and the stimuli that lead to certain drive-reduction responses. The idea is to strengthen the stimulus–response connections that reduce the drive. Redirection of drives leads to reward, or *reinforcement.* Reward (reinforcement) of these connections in accordance with reducing drive results in an organization of behavior called *habit.*

It is important for the person to reduce his or her primary drives or else face possible death or destruction. The stimulus or stimuli that help reduce these drives form a stimulus–response connection, so that if, on subsequent occasions, any of these stimuli recur in conjunction with the drive, the reaction tends to be evoked. This is called the Law of Reinforcement (somewhat similar to Thorndike's Law of Effect).

Both laws are consistent with common sense. If you want to condition someone, permit that person to associate something pleasant with the behavior you are trying to evoke. The implication for the classroom is to motivate the child when introducing subject matter. On a lighter note, if you want to increase summer attendance at symphonic orchestras among students, serve free ice cream. The students will become conditioned to the enjoyment of music.

The drive that functions for the survival of the individual takes precedence over all others, and a threat to normal body functioning reduces the level of activity in other drive areas. Teachers should understand, then, that children who are hungry or have not slept become restless or inattentive and are not concerned with secondary drive areas—such as satisfying curiosity or learning. Furthermore, teachers should space classroom exercises to minimize fatigue and maximize performance. Although Hull's theories have been modified by educators, the idea of establishing appropriate reward and reinforcement activities is, in part, derived from him.

## Operant Conditioning

Perhaps more than any other recent behaviorist, B. Frederick Skinner attempted to apply his theories to the classroom. Basing much of his theory on experiments with mice and pigeons, Skinner distinguished between two kinds of responses: *elicited,* a response identified with a definite stimulus, and *emitted,* a response apparently unrelated to an identifiable stimulus. When a response is elicited, the behavior is *respondent.* When it is emitted, the behavior is *operant*— no observable or measurable stimuli explain the response's appearance.[14] In operant conditioning, the role of stimuli is less definite; often, the emitted behavior cannot be connected to a specific stimulus.

Reinforcers can be classified, also, as primary, secondary, or generalized. A *primary* reinforcer applies to any stimulus that helps satisfy a basic drive, such as for food, water, or sex. (This reinforcer is also paramount in classical conditioning.) A *secondary* reinforcer, such as getting approval from friends or teachers, receiving money, or winning school awards, is important for people. Although secondary reinforcers do not satisfy primary drives, they can be converted into primary reinforcers. Because of the choice and range of secondary reinforcers, Skinner refers to them as *generalized* reinforcers. Classroom teachers have a variety of secondary reinforcers at their disposal, ranging from praise or smiles to admonishment or punishment.

Operant behavior discontinues when it is not followed by reinforcement. Skinner classifies reinforcers as positive or negative. A *positive* reinforcer is simply the presentation of a reinforcing stimulus. A student receives positive reinforcement when a test paper is returned with a grade of A or a note that says, "Keep up the good work." A *negative* reinforcement is the removal or withdrawal of a stimulus. When a teacher shouts "Keep quiet!" to the class and the students quiet down, the students' silence reinforces the teacher's shouting. Punishment, however, entails the presentation of unpleasant or harmful stimuli or the withdrawal of a (positive) reinforcer, but it is not always a negative reinforcer.[15] Although Skinner believes in both positive and negative reinforcement, he rejects punishment because he believes it inhibits learning.[16]

## Acquiring New Operants

Skinner's approach of selective reinforcement, whereby only desired responses are reinforced, has wide appeal to educators because he demonstrated its application to the instructional and learning processes. An essential principle in the reinforcement interpretation of learning is the variability of human behavior, which makes change possible. Individuals can acquire *new operants;* behavior can be shaped or modified and complex concepts can be taught. The individual's capacity for the desired response enables the shaping of behavior or the learning. Behavior and learning can be shaped through a series of successive approximations or a sequence of responses that increasingly approximate the desired one. Thus, through a combination of reinforcing and sequencing desired responses, new behavior is shaped; this is what some people today refer to as *behavior modification.*

Although behavior-modification approaches vary according to the student and the behavior being sought, they are widely used in conjunction with individualized instructional techniques, programmed learning, and classroom-management techniques. Student activities are specified, structured, paced, reinforced, rewarded, and frequently assessed in terms of desired learning outcomes or behaviors.

**OBSERVATIONAL LEARNING AND MODELING.**    Albert Bandura has greatly contributed to our understanding of learning through observation and modeling. In a classic study, he showed how aggressive behavior can be learned from seeing human adults act aggressively in real situations or in films and cartoons. The same children also learned nonaggressive behavior by observing humans of subdued temperaments.[17]

The repeated demonstration that people can learn and have their behavior shaped by observing another person or even film (obviously, the influence of TV is immense) has tremendous implications for modifying tastes and attitudes, how we learn and perform, and whether we want to develop soldiers or artists. For behaviorists, the findings suggest that cognitive factors are unnecessary in explaining learning; through modeling, students can learn to perform at sophisticated levels. Although recognizing the value of reinforcement and reward, the learner must primarily attend and acquire the necessary responses through observation and then model the behavior. (See Curriculum Tips 4.1.) Coaches in various sports and instructors in the military make use of this type of instruction; teachers who use coaching techniques find the modeling concept and specific tips useful.

**HIERARCHICAL LEARNING.**    Robert Gagné has presented a hierarchical arrangement of eight types of learning sets, or behaviors, that has become a classic model. The first five may be defined as behavioral operations, the next two, as both behavioral and cognitive, and the last (and highest form of thinking), as cognitive. The behaviors are based on prerequisite conditions, resulting in a cumulative process of learning. The eight types of learning and examples of each follow.

1. *Signal learning* (classical conditioning, a response to a given signal). Example: Fear response to a rat.
2. *Stimulus–response* (operant conditioning [S–R], a response to a given stimulus). Example: Student's response to the command, "Please sit."
3. *Motor chains* (linking together two or more S–R connections to form a more complex skill). Example: Dotting the *i* and crossing the *t* to write a word with an *i* and *t*.
4. *Verbal association* (linking two or more words or ideas). Example: Translating a foreign word.
5. *Multiple discriminations* (responding in different ways to different items of a particular set). Example: Discriminating between grass and trees.
6. *Concepts* (reacting to stimuli in an abstract way). Examples: animals, grammar, and so on.
7. *Rules* (chaining two or more stimulus situations or concepts). Examples: Animals have offspring. An adjective modifies a noun.
8. *Problem solving* (combining known rules or principles into new elements to solve a problem). Example: Finding the area of a triangle given the dimensions of two sides.[18]

Gagné's hierarchy of learning represents a transition between behaviorism and cognitive psychology; the first four behaviors are behaviorist and the last four are mainly cognitive. According to Gagné, learning is composed of a hierarchical sequence of instructional materials and methods, from simple to complex. The idea is that general theories, principles, or concepts (what Jerome Bruner termed a subject's *structure*) encompass specific ideas and knowledge that must be learned before advanced learning. Other learning theorists (including David Ausubel and Robert Marzano) maintain that by understanding general principles and concepts (Ausubel calls them *advance organizers*), people learn more efficiently because it is easier to assimilate new information into prior information. Whereas Gagné and Bruner represent a *bottom-up* theory of learning, Ausubel and Marzano represent a *top-down* theory. Dewey delineated a *middle* position that information is best learned and remembered when it is related to students' experiences and has direct application to their immediate environment. All three approaches to

## CURRICULUM TIPS 4.1    Behaviorism in Classroom Learning Situations

A wide range of behaviors can be used when applying behavioral theories in the classroom. These suggestions have meaning for behaviorist teaching and learning situations.

1. Consider that behavior is the result of particular conditions; alter conditions to achieve desired behaviors.
2. Use reinforcement and rewards to strengthen the behavior you wish to encourage.
3. Consider extinction or forgetting of undesirable behaviors by reducing their frequency.
4. Reduce undesirable behaviors as follows:
   a. Withhold reinforcement or ignore the behavior.
   b. Call attention to rewards that will follow the desired behavior.
   c. Take away a privilege or resort to punishment.
5. When students are learning factual material, provide frequent feedback; for abstract or complex material, provide delayed feedback.
6. Provide practice, drill, and review exercises; monitor learners' progress.
7. Consider workbooks, programmed materials, and computer programs that rely on sequenced approaches.
8. When students struggle with uninteresting material, use special reinforcers and rewards to motivate them:
   a. Select a variety of reinforcers students enjoy (toys, gum, baseball cards).
   b. Establish a contract for work to be performed to earn a particular reward or grade.
   c. Provide frequent, immediate rewards.
9. Make use of observational learning:
   a. Select the most appropriate model.
   b. Model the behavior clearly and accurately.
   c. Insist that learners attend to what is being modeled.
   d. Provide praise when the desired behavior is exhibited.
   e. Have the learner practice the observed behavior.
   f. Provide corrective feedback during practice.
   g. Repeat demonstrations when necessary.
   h. Reinforce desired behaviors.
   i. Model behavior in similar settings in which learners will use the new skills.
10. Assess changes in learning and behavior:
   a. Diagnose learning problems.
   b. Establish levels of competency or mastery.
   c. Provide feedback.
   d. Integrate old tasks or skills with new ones.
   e. Reteach when necessary.

learning are acceptable and used by teachers, depending on the students' abilities (and ages) and the subject content.

Gagné also describes five learning outcomes that can be observed and measured and, for him, encompass all learning domains: (1) *intellectual skills,* "knowing how" to categorize and use verbal and mathematical symbols, forming concepts through rules, and problem solving; (2) *information,* "knowing what," knowledge about facts, names, and dates; (3) *cognitive strategies,* skills needed to process and organize information, today called *learning strategies* or *learning skills*; (4) *motor skills,* the ability to coordinate movements, both simple and complex, which comes with practice and coaching; and (5) *attitudes,* feelings and emotions learned through positive and negative experiences.[19]

The five outcomes overlap with the three domains (cognitive, psychomotor, and affective) of the taxonomy of educational objectives (see Chapter 7). The first three capabilities fall mainly within the cognitive domain, motor skills correspond to the psychomotor domain, and attitudes correspond to the affective domain. The mental operations and conditions involved in each of the five outcomes differ. Gagné writes, "Learning intellectual skills requires a different design of instructional events from those required for learning verbal information or from those required for learning motor skills, and so on."[20]

**CONSCIOUSNESS, CHOICE, AND CONDITIONING.** According to the latest theory on conditioning, humans became conditioned by habit and routine and largely lose their individual consciousness. As children develop, their brains develop methods of identifying objects and responding to people, thus predicting how they move and respond to their environment. As stimuli flow from the external world to the brain, humans compare those stimuli to what they already know. If things are familiar or match up, there is little conscious awareness of the surrounding environment. If there is a surprise or a detour in our daily life experiences, the brain shifts to a new state, and we become more conscious of our behavior.

According to one recent estimate, 90 percent of what people do every day is a habitual response to predictable events, so we usually operate on "automatic." Like other animals, we use our brain circuits to determine what to attend to, what to react to, and what to ignore. We also make decisions about what to learn, what to eat, and other matters. For example, we assess rewards or lack of rewards. Our behavior is conditioned by a set of expectations and reward systems. According to this theory, people learn best when confronted with an unexpected event or reward, which produces a dopamine rush. Fluctuating levels of rewards make people do things outside their conscious awareness.[21]

For most people, money, food, and sex are rewarding. Cookies and candy give pleasure. Anything that people crave can be used to modify behavior. Some people crave winning in sports because of recognition or money and will engage in unethical behavior; others crave power and will steal or kill to maintain it; still others crave martyrdom and will commit suicide for a political or religious cause. Once people's minds are hijacked (conditioned) so that people lose conscious awareness, they become capable of mindless group behavior and easily become absorbed into an *ism*, where they often lose their individual thought and rationality.

Once the brain becomes conditioned to crave a stimulus, a person may become self-destructive or dangerous to others. Some people gamble regularly, even though they know they're likely to lose money. Others smoke, knowing that smoking can be deadly. Still others lose their individual identities and critical faculties and simply conform to prevailing behavior.

## Behaviorism and Curriculum

Behaviorism still has a major impact on education. Behaviorist educators in charge of curricula use many behaviorist principles in creating new programs. Curriculum specialists can adopt procedures to increase the likelihood that each student will find learning relevant and enjoyable. When new topics or activities are introduced, connections should be built on students' positive experiences. Things about which each student is likely to have negative feelings should be identified and modified, if possible, to produce positive results.

Like other curricularists, behaviorists believe that the curriculum should be organized so that students can master the subject matter. However, behaviorists are highly prescriptive and diagnostic; they rely on step-by-step, structured learning methods. For students who have difficulty learning, curriculum and instruction can be broken down into small units with appropriate sequencing of tasks and reinforcement of desired behavior.

Behaviorist theories have been criticized as describing learning too simply and mechanically and perhaps as reflecting overreliance on classical animal experimentation. Human learning involves complex thinking processes beyond respondent conditioning (or recall and habit) and operant conditioning (or emitted and reinforced behavior).

Many behaviorists today recognize cognitive processes much more than classical or S-R processes. Current theorists are flexible enough to hold that learning can occur without individuals having to act on the environment or exhibit overt behavior. They acknowledge that cognitive processes partially explain aspects of learning.

In general, combining behaviorism with learning includes careful analysis and sequencing of learners' needs and behaviors. Principles of testing, monitoring, drilling, and feedback are characteristic. The learning conditions needed for successful outcomes are carefully planned through small instructional steps and sequences of responses that increasingly approximate the desired behavior or learning. These basic principles tend to coincide with today's basic-skills training programs in reading and language development (such as DISTAR, SQ3R, and Continuous Progress), as well as methods of individualized instruction, direct instruction, mastery learning, instructional training (design), and competency-based education. The emphasis to these programs and methods involves remediation, skill acquisition, matching instructional materials to learners' abilities, step-by-step activities, repetition, practice, drill, reinforcement, and review. These steps and sequences are shown in Table 4.1. Although these procedures are predetermined and planned in advance, some observers might claim they have a cognitive flavor, too.

To a large extent, the procedures or steps coincide with the structural strategies developed by Robert Marzano in *Classroom Instruction That Works*: (1) identifying similarities and differences, (2) note taking, (3) reinforcing effort, (4) homework and practice, (5) nonlinguistic recommendations, (6) cooperative learning, (7) feedback, (8) testing hypotheses, and (9) cues and advances.[22] The instructional strategies developed by Marzano tend to have a positive effect on student achievement, especially for low- and average-achieving students, but not for all students.

Behaviorists have contributed a great deal to psychology and curriculum during the 20th century, and it is likely that behaviorism will continue to influence the curriculum field. However, most behaviorists know that we cannot adhere to rigid doctrines as we learn more about humans and their learning. Perspectives that allow for investigations of the mind have been incorporated into behaviorism.[23] Cognitive developmental theories are being integrated into some behaviorists' approaches to human learning.

## COGNITIVE PSYCHOLOGY

Whenever we categorize phenomena, we risk misinterpretation. Today, most psychologists classify human growth and development as cognitive, social, psychological, and physical. Although an individual grows and develops along all these fronts, most psychologists agree that learning in school is mainly cognitive.

Most, if not all, psychologists agree that learning results from humans' interactions with the world. However, there is no consensus regarding how to determine the extent to which an individual's characteristics (cognitive, social, psychological, and physical) result from inherited limitations or potential or harmful or favorable environments. Considerable controversy continues about heredity versus environment in determining cognitive outcomes (e.g., IQ and achievement scores) in school. As more educators view academic results as more than achievement scores, these debates are likely to intensify. It is essential that curriculum specialists be aware of these debates because the issue affects education and teaching theories in general.

### Cognitive Perspective

Cognitive psychologists are interested in generating theories that give insight into the nature of learning, specifically how individuals generate structures of knowledge and how they create or learn reasoning and problem-solving strategies. How do people organize knowledge? How do they store information? How do they retrieve data and generate conclusions? These are central questions for cognitive psychologists, who also are interested in how individuals use new information and understandings. Cognitive psychologists are interested not only in the amount of knowledge people possess but also in its type and its influence on further cognitive actions.[24] These psychologists focus on how individuals process information, how they monitor and manage their thinking, and the results of their thinking on their information-processing capabilities.

| Table 4.1 | Instructional Components by Current Authorities: A Behaviorist Approach to Teaching and Learning |
|---|---|

| **Direct Instruction: Rosenshine Model** | **Mastery Learning: Block and Anderson Model** |
|---|---|
| 1. *State learning objectives.* Begin lesson with a short statement of objectives. | 1. *Clarify.* Explain to students what they are expected to learn. |
| 2. *Review.* Introduce short review of previous or prerequisite learning. | 2. *Inform.* Teach the lesson, relying on whole-group instruction. |
| 3. *Present new materials.* Present new materials in small, sequenced steps. | 3. *Pretest.* Give a *formative* quiz on a no-fault basis; students can check their own papers. |
| 4. *Explain.* Give clear and detailed instructions and explanations. | 4. *Group.* Based on results, divide the class into mastery and nonmastery groups (80 percent is considered mastery). |
| 5. *Practice.* Provide active practice for all students. | 5. *Enrich and correct.* Give enrichment instruction to mastery group; give corrective (practice/drill) to nonmastery group. |
| 6. *Guide.* Guide students during initial practice; provide seatwork activities. | 6. *Monitor.* Monitor student progress; vary amount of teacher time and support for each group based on group size and performance. |
| 7. *Check* for *understanding.* Ask several questions; assess student comprehension. | 7. *Posttest.* Give a *summative* quiz to nonmastery group. |
| 8. *Provide feedback.* Provide systematic feedback and corrections. | 8. *Assess performance.* At least 75 percent of students should achieve mastery by the summative test. |
| 9. *Assess performance.* Obtain student success rate of 80 percent or more during practice session. | 9. *Reteach.* If not, repeat procedures, starting with corrective instruction (small study groups, individual tutoring, alternative instructional materials, extra homework, reading materials practice and drill). |
| 10. *Review and test.* Provide for spaced review and testing. | |

| **Guided Instruction: Hunter Model** | **Systematic Instruction: Good and Brophy Model** |
|---|---|
| 1. *Review.* Focus on previous lesson; ask students to summarize main points. | 1. *Review.* Review concepts and skills related to homework; provide review exercises. |
| 2. *Anticipatory set.* Focus students' attention on new lesson; stimulate interest in new materials. | 2. *Development.* Promote student understanding; provide examples, explanations, demonstrations. |
| 3. *Objective.* State explicitly what is to be learned; state rationale or how it will be useful. | 3. *Assess comprehension.* Ask questions; provide controlled practice. |
| 4. *Input.* Identify needed knowledge and skills for learning new lesson; present material in sequenced steps. | 4. *Seatwork.* Provide uninterrupted seatwork; get everyone involved; sustain momentum. |
| 5. *Modeling.* Provide several examples or demonstrations throughout the lesson. | 5. *Accountability.* Check the students' work. |
| 6. *Check for understanding.* Monitor students' work before they become involved in lesson activities; check to see they understand directions or tasks. | 6. *Homework.* Assign homework regularly; provide review problems. |
| 7. *Guided practice.* Periodically ask students questions and check their answers. Again monitor for understanding. | 7. *Special reviews.* Provide weekly reviews to check and enhance learning; provide monthly reviews to further maintain and enhance learning. |
| 8. *Independent practice.* Assign independent work or practice when it is reasonably sure that students can work on their own with understanding and minimal frustration. | |

Cognitive psychologists essentially are interested in the mind's architecture. They believe there are two types of memory: short term and long term. Some educators have divided short-term memory into immediate memory and working memory.[25] Immediate memory operates consciously or subconsciously, holding inputs for approximately 30 seconds, during which a person decides whether perceived data are important. If not, they are discarded. If the data are important, they are placed in working memory, where only conscious processing occurs. The key point with regard to working memory is that the individual is acting on immediately present information or situations. Working memory has a definite focus and can process only a limited amount of information. However, the limits are flexible, influenced by how the information is organized. Individuals can increase the capacity of their working memories by grouping bits of information in chunks that are meaningful to them.[26]

Long-term memory deals with two types of information: semantic ("the way the world is") and procedural ("the way we do things"). This memory stores and retrieves information. In contrast to working memory, long-term memory has infinite capacity. Effective learners transfer information from working memory into long-term memory as quickly as possible.

## The Montessori Method

Maria Montessori (1870–1952), a great pedagogist of the early 20th century, directed the Psychiatric Clinic at the University of Rome. There she encountered children with mental and physical disabilities who had been placed in insane asylums. She soon concluded that the root of the problem in many cases was not medical (the prevailing opinion), but educational and psychological.

Montessori's contemporaries were astonished when she taught these "difficult" children to read and write at a normal level. Her public response was that her instructional methods were based on a *rational, scientific* approach that considered children's developmental stages. She became "convinced that similar methods applied to normal children"; instead of being forced to memorize facts and sit quietly in their seats, they could "develop or set free their personality in a marvelous and surprising way."[27]

In 1906, after 5 years of advanced study in psychology and pedagogy, Montessori was asked to develop a new, progressive school for slum children in Rome. The school, Casa dei Bambini (The Children's House), became the model for the kindergarten at the famous Henry Street Settlement House in New York City. To a lesser extent, some Montessori practices were adopted by William Kilpatrick at the Lincoln Lab School, affiliated with Teachers College, Columbia University. For this reason, and because she was influenced by the child-oriented pedagogy of Rousseau and Pestalozzi (see Chapter 3), the vast majority of education authors place her in the progressive and child-centered movements. However, Montessori was much more concerned with cognitive development and the use of appropriate learning experiences built around a structured classroom environment (not necessarily free play or child centered), where students' interests came first, than around an environment that the teacher planned.

Rejecting the dominant behaviorist theories based on stimulus–response, Montessori emphasized looking and listening, which she viewed as sensory input channels of learning and as the first phases of intellectual development. Whereas "the behaviorists believed that it is the motor side, rather than the sensory side, that is important in learning," she believed that the more things a child listens to and looks at, the better for mental development. "Dewey [also] gave emphasis to the motor side . . . in his belief that the child learns chiefly by doing."[28] Montessori emphasized a rich variety of visual and auditory inputs (often absent in low-income families). Therefore, it can be argued that she was a cognitive developmentalist first and a progressive educator second.

Montessori maintained that children develop at different rates. Some are more coordinated than others and more mature in their thinking and social relationships. Except in extreme cases, such differences are normal. Some children need additional encouragement and support in certain areas of growth; others need it in other areas. (Piaget would later refer to this as *positive environment.*) Montessori also recognized that certain cognitive and social abilities develop before others: children sit before they walk, grab objects before they manipulate them, and babble before they talk.

Montessori also noted that poor children were unprepared for school and that they increasingly lagged behind middle-class children as they progressed through grade levels. She concluded, "The down-trodden of society are also down-trodden in the school."[29] Her goal was threefold:

enrich children's school environment, provide children with success in performing tasks to bolster their self-confidence, and provide structural play to teach basic skills. In short, she compensated for the deficiencies of the children's homes and slum conditions. Thus, the seeds of compensatory education were planted. Sixty years would pass before compensatory education would be fully accepted in the United States, as part of President Johnson's War on Poverty.

Montessori recognized that the homes of poor children lacked intellectual stimulation such as books, as well as private, quiet places to learn. It was impractical to give lower-class children books to take home to study. Many of these children didn't even have "light by which to read." Montessori observed that her students lived "in the misery of human poverty" and that some kind of environmental "nourishment" was needed to foster intellectual development.[30] She set the stage for cognitive developmental and environmental theorists to oppose behaviorist and hereditarian theories, which were entrenched at the turn of the 20th century. Most importantly, Montessori had the compassion and understanding to believe that poor children could learn despite their test scores and environmental disadvantages. Her efforts represented the beginning of an ongoing argument over the best ways to educate lower-class children.

Montessori's school environment was antidotal. She provided *sensory* impressions (Piaget and others would later call these *sensory stimuli*) to enhance the children's visual and auditory discrimination. Her approach, rooted in Pestalozzi's pedagogy, was based on sensory experiences with objects of the environment and a belief that learning proceeds mostly in an atmosphere of emotional security. Pestalozzi also worked with poor children and orphans. Montessori's sensory approach originated with Rousseau and Pestalozzi and was adopted in the 1960s by Martin and Cynthia Deutsch, J. McViker Hunt, and Lev Vygotsky as they developed a "new" theory of experience (visual and auditory), language development, and intelligence.[31] Most social scientists now shifted to an emphasis on environment rather than heredity and cognitive development rather than behaviorism. Montessori was a psychological pioneer in cognition.

## Jean Piaget's Theories

Swiss psychologist Jean Piaget (1896–1980) presented the most comprehensive theory of cognitive development stages. After 25 years of research in European settings, Piaget's work came to the attention of American educators during the 1950s and 1960s as cognitive developmental psychology, environmentalist theories, and the compensatory education movement increased in influence.

Like many of today's investigators, Piaget described cognitive development in terms of stages from birth to maturity. The stages can be summarized as follows.[32]

1. *Sensorimotor stage* (birth to age 2). The child progresses from reflex operations and undifferentiated surroundings to complex sensorimotor actions in relation to environmental patterns, comes to realize that objects have permanence (they can be found again), and begins to establish simple relations between similar objects.
2. *Preoperational stage* (ages 2 to 7). Objects and events begin to take on symbolic meaning. For example, a chair is for sitting; clothing is for wearing. The child shows an ability to learn more complex concepts from experience, as long as familiar examples of the concepts are provided. (For example, oranges, apples, and bananas are fruit; the child must have the chance to touch and eat them.)
3. *Concrete operations stage* (ages 7 to 11). The child begins to organize data into logical relationships and gains facility in manipulating data in problem-solving situations. However, this learning situation occurs only if concrete objects are available or the child can draw on past experience. The child is able to make judgments in terms of reversibility and reciprocal relations (for example, left and right are relative to spatial relations) and conservation (a long, narrow glass may hold the same amount of water as a short, wide one).
4. *Formal operations stage* (ages 11 and up). The individual can grasp formal and abstract operations, analyze ideas, comprehend spatial and temporal relationships, think logically

about abstract data, evaluate data according to acceptable criteria, formulate hypotheses, deduce possible consequences, and construct theories and reach conclusions without direct experience in the subject. At this stage there are few or no limitations on the content of learning. Learning depends on the individual's intellectual potential and environmental experiences.

Piaget's cognitive stages presuppose a *maturation:* mental operations are sequential. The stages are hierarchical, the mental operations are increasingly sophisticated and integrated. Although the succession of stages is constant, levels of attainment vary due to heredity and environment.

Like Dewey's learning principles, Piaget's cognitive theories focus on environmental experiences. The educator's role involves "the shaping of actual experience by environing conditions" and knowing "what surroundings are conducive to having experiences that lead to growth."[33] Three basic cognitive processes form the basis of Dewey's and Piaget's environmental and experiential theories.

For Piaget, *assimilation* is the incorporation of new experiences into existing ones. However, handling new situations and problems requires more than assimilation. The child must also develop new cognitive structures. This process is *accommodation;* child's existing cognitive structures are modified and adapted in response to the environment. *Equilibration* is the process of balancing what is already understood with what has yet to be understood, the dual process of assimilating and accommodating of one's environment.[34]

This coincides with Dewey's "conceptions of situation and interaction [which] are inseparable" and which form the basis of continuity.[35] For Dewey, a *situation* represents the environment's effects on the child and is similar to Piaget's assimilation. Similar to Piaget's accommodation, *interaction* entails current interactions between the child and the environment, including the child's capacities to establish meaning. Similar to Piaget's equilibration, *continuity* refers to situations and interactions that follow.

## Piaget's Influence: Tyler, Taba, Bruner, and Kohlberg

Piaget's three cognitive processes (and Dewey's educational experiences) also serve as a basis for Tyler's three methods of organizing learning experiences: (1) *continuity*—skills and concepts should be repeated within the curriculum; there should be "continuing opportunity for these skills to be practiced"; (2) *sequence*—the curriculum should progressively develop understanding; "each successive experience builds upon the preceding one" and goes "more broadly and deeply into matters involved"; (3) *integration*—the curriculum's elements should be "unified"; subjects "should not be isolated . . . or taught as a single course."[36]

Taba extensively reviews Piaget's four stages of cognitive development and their implications for mental development. She concludes that learning experiences must be "designed to match assessment of age levels at which certain processes of thought can occur." The idea is to transform complex concepts and subject matter into mental operations appropriate to the learner and to develop a curriculum that provides for "increasingly deeper and more formal levels" of thinking. "Building such a curriculum would naturally also involve a better understanding of the hierarchies [Piaget's stages] of concept formation and mental operations [and] a better understanding of the sequences in the development of thought."[37]

Similarly, Taba notes Piaget's cognitive processes—assimilation, accommodation, and equilibration—in her discussion of generalizations and abstract thinking. She is concerned with organizing curricula and teaching new experiences so they are compatible with existing experiences (assimilation), moving from concrete experiences to concepts and principles (accommodation), and classifying and understanding new relationships (equilibration). Taba's "curriculum strategies for productive learning" are rooted in Piaget's synthesis of experiences into more complex forms and levels.

For Bruner, learning how things are related means learning the structure of knowledge. Such learning is based on Piagetian assimilation and accommodation.[38] The student who grasps how bits of information within a subject area are related can continually and independently relate additional information to a field of study. Learning something should not be an end of learning. Instead, as Piaget and Dewey suggest, what is learned should be related to other aspects of the subject and be general enough to apply in other situations. The structure of knowledge provides the basis for this kind of specific transfer of learning.

Piaget's equilibration forms the basis of Bruner's notion of a "spiral curriculum": previous learning is the basis of subsequent learning, learning should be continuous, and subject matter is built on a foundation (from grade to grade). Bruner is also influenced by Dewey, who uses the term *continuity* and explains that what a person has already learned "becomes an instrument of understanding and dealing effectively with the situations that follow."[39] Like Dewey and Piaget, Bruner also uses the term *continuity* to describe how subject matter and mental operations can be "continually deepened by using them in a progressively more complex form."[40]

To Bruner, learning consists of three related processes, similar to Piaget's cognitive processes:

1. *Acquisition,* which mainly corresponds to assimilation, is the grasping of new information. Such information may be "new" to one's store of data, may replace previously acquired information, or may merely refine or qualify previous information.
2. *Transformation* is processing new information in a transformative way—for example, through extrapolation, interpolation, or translation into another form. This process mainly overlaps with accommodation.
3. *Evaluation* is determining whether information is appropriate for dealing with a particular task or problem. It closely corresponds to equilibration.

Piaget was also concerned with children's moral development, which Lawrence Kohlberg investigated in some detail. Kohlberg studied the development of children's moral standards and concluded that our thinking about moral issues reflects not only our society, but also our stages of growth or age. Kohlberg outlined six types of moral judgment grouped into three moral levels, or stages, corresponding to Piaget's cognitive stages of development:

1. **Preconventional level.** Children at this level have not yet developed a sense of right or wrong. They do as they are told because they fear punishment or realize that certain actions bring rewards.
2. **Conventional level.** Children at this level are concerned about what other people think of them. Their behavior is largely other directed. These children seek their parents' approval by being "nice" and think in terms of rules.
3. **Postconventional level.** At this level, morality is based on what other people feel or on their precepts of authority. Children at this level view morality in terms of contractual obligations and democratically accepted laws or in terms of individual principles of conscience.

Kohlberg and Piaget hold the cognitive developmental view of morality: moral judgments entail a considerable amount of reasoning. However, whereas Piaget stresses differences in the way children think about morality at different ages, Kohlberg finds considerable overlap at various ages. Both believe that social arrangements and society play a major role. However, Piaget emphasizes maturation. Kohlberg says, "As opposed to Piaget's view, the data suggest that the 'natural' aspects of moral development are continuous and a reaction to the whole social world rather than a product of a certain stage, a certain concept . . . or a certain type of social regulations."[41]

Teachers (in conjunction with learning psychologists and curriculum specialists) should determine the appropriate emphasis to give each of Piaget's stages of cognitive development. Piaget's stages overlap with Tyler's methods, Taba's strategies, Bruner's processes, and Kohlberg's moral stages. Educators should regard Piaget's stages as suggestive rather than proven facts.

## Developmental Theories: Beyond Piaget

Prior to the 1960s, the hereditarian school of thought dominated social science thinking regarding human growth and development, including cognitive development and intelligence. Piaget was not widely accepted in the United States, although every major psychologist since the 1940s and 1950s was aware of his research on the influence of environment and the stages of cognitive and moral development. Gradually, developmental theorists gained a foothold in psychology, but it was Ben Bloom's longitudinal research on human characteristics that shifted majority opinion to accept the importance of early childhood environment; in turn, this formed the rationale behind the compensatory education movement and Head Start program in the 1960s and infant education today.

Developmental theory basically asserts that inadequate or adequate development in one area affects the other areas of human development. For example, if an individual is unable to develop fully a cognitive characteristic at a particular stage in life, he or she usually cannot fully develop that particular characteristic (or the characteristics that are dependent on the prior one) in later stages of life. The idea is well established in animal and infant behavior.

Although there is danger in extrapolating from animals to humans or from infants to adults, this reasoning has been extended to hypothesize that there is a tendency for deficits in cognitive development to occur if the child is deprived of necessary stimulation during critical periods. The corollary of this hypothesis is that individuals who fail to acquire these skills at appropriate times are forever handicapped in attaining them. The reason is that the deficits become irreversible and cumulative in nature (known as the *cumulative intellectual deficit*), because current and future rates of intellectual growth are always based on or limited by the attained level of development. (New growth, in other words, proceeds from existing growth.) This helps explain the increasing academic gap of slow readers or nonreaders as they proceed through school.

## Bloom: Early Environment

Developmental theory also holds that the early years are more important than successive years. Although not all human characteristics reveal the same patterns of development, the most rapid period of development of human characteristics, including cognitive skills, is during the preschool years. For example, Benjamin Bloom presents longitudinal data (extending over a period of several years) that strongly suggests that from birth to 4 years of age an individual develops 50 percent of his or her potential intelligence; from ages 4 to 8, the child develops another 30 percent, and between ages 8 and 17, he or she develops the remaining 20 percent.[42] Supplementary evidence suggests 33 percent of learning potential takes place by the time the child is 6 years old—before he or she enters first grade; another 17 percent takes place between ages 6 and 9. The potential for learning is cumulative. As much as 50 percent is developed by the age of 9, 75 percent by the age of 13, and 100 percent by the age of 17. (This tends to correspond with Piaget's data that by age 15½, a person's formal reasoning ability is fully developed.)

Based on the preceding estimates for intelligence and learning, home environment is crucial, according to Bloom, because of the large amount of cognitive development that has already taken place before the child enters the first grade. These estimates also suggest the very rapid cognitive growth in the early years and the great influence of the early environment (largely home environment) on cognitive development and that *all* subsequent learning "is affected and a large part determined by what the child has [previously] learned."[43] Furthermore, what the child learns in the early and most important years is shaped by what the child has experienced at home. (Even the prenatal stages affect the child's intellectual development—that is, the mother's general habits and biochemical changes related to stress, food, and other emotional factors. And, in this regard, substantially more lower-income mothers than the middle- and upper-income mothers and more Black mothers than White mothers suffer from poor physical and mental health as well as from poor diet.)

This does not mean that once a learning deficit occurs, remediation is impossible; however, it does clearly imply that it is more difficult to effect changes for older children and that a more powerful environment is needed to effect these changes. Thus, 2-year deficits in reading or math for a ninth-grade student is more difficult to overcome than 2-year deficits for a third-grade student. Bloom reports, however, that learning differences can be reduced over time with appropriate environmental and training conditions, thus contradicting the cumulative intellectual deficit theory.[44] In short, our information on the extent to which intellectual deficits of one's maturation period or age can be made up in another is limited and contradictory. We cannot now precisely equate differences in difficulty in reversing deficits at different stages of cognitive development. However, the older the person, the more powerful the stimuli needed to affect positive changes.

As noted earlier, the theory of development also coincides with the research findings that a child of low-income status often suffers from a deprived environment or limited stimuli, which, in turn, negatively affects the child's opportunities for adequate cognitive development. Conversely, a child of middle- or upper-socioeconomic status usually has an enriched environment (or a sufficient quantity of high-quality stimuli), which affects positively his or her opportunities for adequate cognitive development. Thus, the child's social class is related to his or her environment experiences, which subsequently influence the child's learning capabilities and academic experiences.

Because the relationships are group patterns, there is room for individual differences among children in both deprived and enriched environments. It cannot be emphasized too strongly, for example, that a lower-class child may have an enriched home environment and his or her middle-class counterpart may have a deprived home environment. Similarly, all children from deprived environments do not necessarily have limited school abilities, whereas all children from enriched environments do not have academic success: rather, social class and home environment handicap or assist children in developing their mental capabilities.

## Lev Vygotsky's Theories

Lev Vygotsky developed his theories in the early 20th century. However, the West discovered his work only in the latter part of that century. In 1987, Jerome Bruner stated, "When I remarked a quarter century ago that Vygotsky's view of development was also a theory of education, I did not realize the half of it. In fact, his educational theory is a theory of cultural transmission as well as a theory of development, for education implies for Vygotsky not only the development of the individual's potential, but the historical expression and growth of the human culture from which Man springs."[45] Vygotsky developed not only a cognitive theory but also a general theory of sociocultural development.

He primarily addressed the social origins and cultural bases of individual development. In his view, children developed their potential via enculturation into society's mores and norms. Whereas Piaget believed that children had to enter certain stages to accomplish particular cognitive tasks, Vygotsky believed that children could begin to gain command of language prior to arriving at a particular stage of development.

According to Vygotsky, child development is a sociogenetic process shaped by the individual's interactions, "dialogue," and "play" with the culture. Individuals exist within environments that the actions of previous generations have transformed. These generations produced artifacts that enable people to interact with their physical and social worlds. Individuals exist within two worlds, one natural and one made by humans. The human-made world, a creation of culture, has fundamentally shaped the structure of human growth and development.

For Vygotsky, cultural and psychological functions must be considered in historical context. People's thoughts, language, and methods of solving problems must be considered within the historical context of the person's lifetime. People's behavior is unique to the institutions of their time. Culture and human action evolve over time. As the mind changes, so does cognitive processing. Such modifications influence people's practical activities and tools, which have an impact on thinking.

Vygotsky argued that culture (and thinking) required skilled tool use. He identified several types of human tools: language, counting systems, works of art, mechanical drawings, and mnemonic techniques. To him, language was a primary tool invented by humans that enabled the organization of thinking.[46] Without language, humans would have no thought as we know it. If we consider language to be the attachment of meaning to symbols, we conclude that language is human culture's main tool. Mathematics employs symbols to which meaning has been subscribed; therefore, it is a language. Visual art employs symbols through various media, so it is a language. Via written and auditory symbols, music carries meaning; it too is a language. Language enables and elicits thought. When dealing with psychological foundations, we are essentially trying to understand language both within and outside of schools.

Many inner cities are not conducive to the formal "language learning" implicit in Vygotsky's theory of learning. Whereas effective education enables students to develop intellectual skills, students require contexts within which they can practice their newly learned competencies. If these formal contexts are unavailable, such skills "rust" from lack of use.[47] Changing a school and its curriculum but not the home or community in which the school exists is fodder for failure.

Vygotsky was an educator first and a psychologist second. He believed that children's higher mental functions result primarily from enculturation and that the key institution for this enculturation is formal education. He did not discount informal education, but he considered formal education the optimal laboratory for human improvement. Within such an environment, the child, under an educator's guidance, had opportunities to receive and perfect psychological tools that assisted in organizing and reorganizing mental functions.[48]

As mentioned earlier, Piaget and others believed that biological maturity had to be experienced before certain types of learning could occur. One had to go through various developmental stages in order to learn certain facts and master certain skills. Vygotsky took exception to this view, arguing that the learning process preceded the developmental process. "Pedagogy creates learning processes that lead [to] development."[49] In other words, children at a particular developmental level could, via instruction, be "pulled" to a higher level. Effective teaching or peer engagement can raise a student's level. This certainly has relevance today to meaningful instruction. Although students interacting with effective teachers may perform or think "better" than before, what about students interacting with less effective teachers? Will students always move beyond their developmental levels when working with more capable peers? What happens to the development of more capable peers when they work with less capable classmates? All these questions have serious implications as educators attempt to implement school reform and improve learning of low-performing students.

## Focus on Thinking and Learning

Many, if not most, psychologists are concerned with the cognitive structures that individuals invent and use. These cognitive scientists focus on thought processes—what is happening inside a person's head. The brain is complex, as is the process of thinking.[50] We have developed various ways to classify thinking and the structure of human intellect.

**IQ AND BIRTH ORDER.**   The latest IQ research by Northwestern psychologist Dan McAdams indicates that the eldest children in families tend to develop higher IQs than their siblings—averaging about 3 points higher than second-born children and 4 points higher than third-born children. Similarly, among families in which the firstborn dies in infancy, the IQs of second-born children tend to be 3 points higher than those of third-born children.[51] The reason is not biological or genetic but a matter of family dynamics: how children are treated. Three or 4 points on a scale of 100± may not sound like much, but it can be the difference between an A or A– average in school; that, in turn, can affect college admission to an Ivy League school or less exclusive college. The study included 241,000 subjects between 18 and 19 years old, born between 1967 and 1976 and controlled by several class, family, educational, and other environmental factors. The explanation for the difference is that firstborn children have their parents' undivided attention as infants (infancy is a critical time for cognitive development), and this adult attention enriches language and reasoning potential.

The firstborn child is often expected to assume a responsible or tutoring role with siblings. Responsibility encourages organization, self-discipline, and other characteristics of high achievers. Younger siblings tend to develop social and artistic skills (e.g., dramatic or musical) as alternative ways of coping with their environment and not directly competing with the older sibling. Hence, younger siblings develop diverse interests and coping skills that IQ tests do not measure. In general, they also live more adventurous lives than their older siblings and tend to be less conventional and more creative.

Firstborns have won more Nobel Prizes in science and math than younger siblings—but often by advancing current ideas rather than overturning them. According to one psychologist, "It's the difference between every year or every-decade creativity and every-century creativity, between innovation and radical innovation."[52] Most importantly, the idea of birth order and IQ differences is relatively easy to accept because it relates to nurture, not nature; moreover, it does not compare differences among gender, race, or ethnicity.

**MULTIPLE INTELLIGENCES.**   Howard Gardner postulated multiple intelligences. He contends that there are different mental operations associated with intelligence, and there are many different types of intelligence. Too often our society overemphasizes verbal ability. Gardner outlines eight types of intelligence: (1) verbal/linguistic, (2) logical/mathematic, (3) visual/spatial, (4) bodily/kinesthetic, (5) musical/rhythmic, (6) interpersonal, (7) intrapersonal, and (8) naturalistic.[53]

Gardner's ideas provide a place in the school curriculum not only for cognitive excellence, but also for music, art, dance, sports, and social skills (winning friends and influencing people). Noncognitive types of intelligence have a place in our "other-directed" society (which considers the importance of people working in groups) and fosters success in adulthood, including corporate America. Academic merit is not the only avenue for social and economic mobility. Highly important in a democratic society is fostering excellence in many endeavors and providing multiple chances for people to succeed.

Gardner's ideas encompass different kinds of mastery, from dancing to playing baseball. If encouraged and given a chance, many of our school dropouts' potential would not be wasted. Those in charge of planning and implementing curricula must expand their vision beyond intellectual and academic pursuits, without creating "soft" subjects or a "watered-down curriculum." We must nurture all types of intelligence and all types of excellence that contribute to the worth of the individual and society. We must consider the versatility of children and youth, their multiple abilities and ways of thinking and learning. In an age of tolerance, pluralism, and diversity, Gardner's views are welcomed by school people.

**GUILFORD'S INFLUENCE ON GARDNER.**   What Gardner has to say is not new but is rooted in the work of J. P. Guilford. In the 1950s and 1960s, Guilford formulated a theory of intelligence around a three-dimensional model called the *structure of intellect*. It consisted of six *products* (units, classes, relations, systems, transformations, and implications), five *operations* (knowledge, memory, divergent thinking, convergent thinking, and evaluation), and four *contents* (figured, symbolic, semantic, and behavioral).[54] Therefore, the model was composed of 120 cells of distinct mental abilities. By 1985, Guilford and his doctoral students recognized and separated nearly 100 abilities by factor analysis of standardized achievement and aptitude tests. Guilford concluded that the remaining cells indicated uncovered mental abilities. It is possible that cognitive tests do not measure other mental operations or that such abilities do not exist.

The Guilford model is highly abstract and theoretical and involves administering and grading extra tests. Instead of using the single index of IQ (or aptitude), we are required to recognize and report several scores. Thus, the theoretical issues surrounding intelligence and cognitive operations take on much more complexity than in Gardner's theory of intelligence or Binet's and Weschler's idea of reporting one IQ score.

As previously noted, the idea of multiple intelligences stems from the work of Guilford, who, in turn, formulated his theory to challenge Charles Spearman's *factor of intelligence*—the idea that intelligence consists of a general factor *g* underlying all mental functions and a multitude of *s* factors, each related to a specific task.[55] According to Spearman, to be smart was to have lots of *g,* an umbrella factor permeating all mental operations. Whereas Gardner feels that the search for empirically grounded components of intelligence may be misleading and delineates fewer components (8 in broad areas of life), Guilford maintains that the criteria for intelligence can be quantified and that intelligence consists of many (120) mental operations, or *cognitive processes.* Rather than a single index of IQ (or of aptitude), the idea of 120 different mental operations confounds teachers and thus remains a theoretical construct. Gardner is more popular with school people because his discussion avoids statistics and is more positive and democratic. Gardner stretches the notion of human growth and development by focusing on more than cognition. He accommodates the progressive ideas of teaching the whole child, developing his or her full potential, opening academic and nonacademic career doors, and encouraging low achievers whom schools might otherwise shunt aside.

**LEARNING STYLES.**   If we reasonably assume that people possess multiple intelligences and have at their disposal various ways of thinking, it is also appropriate to think that people prefer certain ways of thinking and learning methods.[56] Some people learn better by *reading* than by *hearing* material; others are the opposite. Still others learn best through *visual* experiences. We know that many students learn more effectively from *physical* activities than from verbal explanations. There is much discussion about the value of *kinesthetic,* or hands-on, activities.

Defined as preferred ways to learn, learning styles have received attention since the 1970s. However, educators still do not have conclusive evidence that it is beneficial to address learning styles. Some individuals suggest that learning styles are preferences that operate consciously and unconsciously; still others view learning styles as only myths.[57]

Two researchers have developed a set of categories by which we can get a sense of learning styles. The set deals with (1) how information is best perceived (visually or auditorially); (2) the type of information preferred (sensory, intuitive); (3) how a person prefers information to be organized (inductively, deductively); (4) how information is processed (actively, reflectively); and (5) how a person progresses to understanding (sequentially, globally).[58] People who deal with information visually prefer pictures, diagrams, and demonstrations, whereas those who favor an auditory mode enjoy receiving and interacting with information via words and sounds. People with a sensory preference for information attend to sights, sounds, and physical sensations. Intuitive people process information via insights and hunches—what Bruner might call *intuitive leaps.* Inductive and deductive approaches are well known; they need no explanation. Active learners like physical activity in their learning. They want to engage people in discussion. Reflective people prefer introspection. People who learn sequentially do so in steps. Their global counterparts, synthesizers, process information in leaps, absorbing information more holistically.

Although we should not overinterpret differences in learning styles, bearing them in mind can be helpful in preparing curricula. We should not simply cater to a preferred style of thinking or learning. Individuals should be encouraged to apply a range of strategies. If we teach only to students' strengths, we may actually limit their learning.

## Emotional Intelligence

Most people, psychologists included, think of humans as highly rational. For most educators, attention to student learning has centered on the rational mind. When we think of intelligence, we tend to think of intellect, or IQ. However, as Daniel Goleman notes, ignoring humans' emotional side is shortsighted.[59]

Educators often urge students to "stick to the facts" and "be logical." However, it is more important to remember that students' feelings color their view of a topic, including their willingness to consider evidence. Emotions strongly influence how we treat information and even construct meaning.

Goleman notes that the root of the word *emotion* is *motere,* Latin for "to move." Emotions can drive action, as is especially clear in young children. As adults, we tend to prize reason over emotion and think of the latter as negative or dysfunctional. However, as more individuals recognize the impossibility of reason completely divorced from emotion, there is increasing focus on emotions, or what some call emotional intelligence.

In his 1985 book *Frames of Mind,* Gardner suggested that people possess a wide spectrum of intelligence. He noted that people possess a personal–social intelligence and spoke of inter- and intrapersonal intelligence. *Interpersonal intelligence* refers to the ability to understand other people: what makes them tick, how they work, and how we can work with them. *Intrapersonal intelligence* is a correlative ability. Individuals with this ability possess or develop an accurate sense of self and can use that understanding to operate effectively in life.[60]

Yale psychologist Peter Salovey outlined the ways in which individuals can bring intelligence into their emotional realm. Salovey has taken Gardner's personal intelligences and generated five main domains that expand these abilities. The first domain is *self-awareness.* Here the focus is on a person's recognizing an emotional response as it happens and realizing how it affects his or her functioning. The second domain is *managing emotions.* This relates to learning beneficial ways to handle emotions. People skilled in this domain experience less stress and can process life's ups and downs with skill. The third domain is *motivating oneself,* realizing that a person must have the energy and will to act. The fourth domain is *recognizing emotions in others.* Many people act as if they are the only ones with feelings. People need to possess empathy, to be attuned to others' emotions, for effective social relations. The fifth domain, *handling relationships,* relates to those understandings and skills that enable us to respond to and manage emotions in others. Those skilled in this domain possess interpersonal effectiveness.[61]

Certainly, these five domains are not absolute, nor are they really separate from rational abilities. However, we must recognize that people differ in their emotional abilities, which are flexible. We can educate people and people can educate themselves in ways that address their emotional intelligence. Developing this intelligence is essential: the challenges to our society seem to be in social interactions as well as in technology.[62]

## Constructivism

Constructivism addresses the nature of *knowledge* and the nature of *learning.* Individuals who fail to distinguish between these two realms leave themselves and others open to confusion.

Concerned with how individuals learn, constructivism treats the individual as actively involved in the process of thinking and learning. The central question for the cognitive psychologist is how individuals engage themselves in the cognitive process. This differs from the behaviorist's driving question: What can an external force (a teacher) do to elicit a response from a student? This focus on the active student is not new; constructivist learning theory harks back to the work of Vygotsky and Piaget. Much of what Dewey discussed in the 20th century also places him within the constructivist camp.[63]

In constructivism the learner is the key player; learners participate in generating meaning or understanding. The learner cannot passively accept information by mimicking others' wordings or conclusions. Rather, the learner must internalize and reshape or transform the information.[64] The student connects new learning with already-existing knowledge. Learning is optimized when students are aware of the processes that they are structuring, inventing, and employing. Such awareness of our cognitive processes is *metacognition.* Metacognition with regard to constructivist processes means that students are aware of the process whereby they are obtaining and using knowledge.[65]

As learners construct knowledge and understanding, they question themselves and their views and interpret and interact with their world. Students must bring their "world knowledge" into their cognitive processes. They must draw on their perceptions of context, past, and present.[66] By reflecting on contexts relevant to their learning, they come to understand concepts and ideas.

## Brain Research and Learning

The human brain possesses about "100 billion nerve cells wired together with 100 billion inter-connections."[67] There are about a thousand types of *connections,* each with a special subset of instructions that make us individually prone to love or hate, obedience or rebellion, intelligence or lack of intelligence.

Recent controversies explored in brain research include (1) the ages at which *synaptic densities* and *brain connections* peak (ranging from age 3 to puberty); (2) whether early visual and auditory experiences increase synaptic densities during or after puberty; (3) the effects of language use and type of language (formal, informal, oral, written, televised, digital, and so on), training, and education on the efficiency of connections; (4) whether there is a critical period during which synapses influence how the brain will be wired and whether synaptic densities are more susceptible to deterioration after puberty; (5) what kinds of synapses are pruned when pruning begins, at what rate they are pruned, and the extent to which pruning affects behavior and memory; and (6) whether people with greater synaptic densities or connections are more intelligent.[68]

No doubt, we will soon have drugs to enhance cognition, to complement the many psycho-active and mood-changing drugs already on the market. We already have drug treatments for depression, schizophrenia, and hyperactivity. For example, Ritalin makes it easier for teachers and counselors to modify behavior and control students. We are on the verge of treating Alzheimer's disease and enhancing memory. Soon we will be shaping and expanding intelligence, repairing and improving brain networks, and possibly using computers for complete brain overhauls. The availability of all these new chemicals (and computer chips) will pose difficult ethical questions concerning their use.

We might argue that there is nothing wrong in increasing the intelligence of kids who have trouble learning or eliminating from their memory a painful or emotional experience such as rape or a parent's death. However, people must come to terms with loss and emotional injury as part of growth and development. The best we can all agree on is the basic need for brains, what the Scarecrow in *The Wizard of Oz* wanted. We can all agree on some form of memory improvement through conventional methods such as a 2-hour course or reading 10 tips on brain exercises in a magazine or book. We also can agree that there are different forms of brain development, types of intelligence, and learning styles.

## Problem Solving and Creative Thinking

Since the Sputnik era, many curriculum theorists have renewed their examination of problem solving and creative thinking. Some curricularists, especially those who talk about the structure of disciplines, feel that problem solving and creative thinking are complementary: Students must be given supportive conditions in which they can develop creativity, but they must be held responsible for confirming or disproving the value or correctness of their assumptions. Problem-solving procedures do not lead to creative discovery but establish discoveries' validity. In this view, problem solving and creative thinking are considered methods of inquiry conducive to scholarship and science.[69]

An opposing view is that problem solving (previously referred to as *reflective thinking* and today called *critical thinking*) is based on inductive thinking, analytical procedures, and *convergent* processes. Creative thinking, which includes intuition and discovery, is based on deductive thinking, originality, and *divergent* processes. Problem solving, in this second view, is condu-cive to rational and scientific thinking and is the *method* of arriving at a solution or correct answer, whereas creativity is conducive to artistic and literary thinking and is a *quality* of thought. There is no right solution or answer when creativity is the goal.

Actually, problem solving and creativity may or may not go hand in hand. Some people perform well on problems without being creative, and others can be highly creative but do poorly in problem solving. However, the two thinking processes are not necessarily independent of each other. Research does reveal a correlation between the two.[70]

Complex cognitive tasks should be taught as generic skills and principles, relevant for all subject matter. The idea is to develop metacognitive strategies that students can transfer to many curriculum areas and content materials. We must develop strategies of reflective, critical, creative, intuitive, and discovery thinking that fit a wide variety of course and content situations.

**REFLECTIVE THINKING.**   Problem solving played a major role in Dewey's concept of education. Dewey believed not only that problem-solving activities in school developed intelligence and social growth, but also that the skills developed in problem solving could be transferred to resolving society's everyday problems. Dewey's concept of problem solving is rooted in his idea of the scientific method and has become a classic model:

1. Become aware of a difficulty (or a perceived difficulty).
2. Identify the problem.
3. Assemble and classify data and formulate hypotheses.
4. Accept or reject the tentative hypotheses.
5. Formulate conclusions and evaluate them.[71]

Dewey's problem-solving method encourages systemic interpretation of everyday experiences through reasoning. This method coincides with his strong belief in a science of education (see Chapter 2). Because Dewey believed that the school's chief function is to improve reasoning, he recommended adapting this problem-solving method to other subjects at all levels. Problems selected for study should derive from student interests because an unmotivated student does not perceive a problem.

Others, however, criticize the problem-solving method as producing the misconception that scientists have a be-all and end-all formula for solving practical problems. James Conant, for example, defines the problem-solving approach as a series of six steps that can be used both by experimental scientists in the laboratory and by laypersons confronted with everyday problems:

1. Recognize a problem and formulate objectives.
2. Collect relevant information.
3. Formulate a hypothesis.
4. Deduce from the hypothesis.
5. Use tests by actual trial.
6. Depending on the outcome, accept, modify, or discard the hypothesis.[72]

Conant believes that science does not enhance problem solving. The scientific method is not readily applied to everyday problems, he claims; science has simply borrowed the method of testing hypotheses from the practical person. Whereas Dewey's model, developed for all disciplines, involved social problem solving, advocates of science and math (not social thinking) used Conant's model during the Sputnik era. The predominant notion then was that each discipline had its own method of problem solving.

Some researchers consider both models and their derivatives incomplete. First, the analysis occurs after the person has solved the problem. Second, the models ignore intuition, insight, and ideas that are nonlogical and perhaps even personal—in short, procedures that cannot be easily observed or tested but that are sometimes used successfully in problem solving. Present theories of cognitive processes suggest that logical and observable steps are not always used in problem solving, nor are the steps always related or sequential. Finally, different problem-solving techniques are used for different subjects or disciplines and different grade levels. Presumably, they share features, but they also involve variance.

**CRITICAL THINKING.**   *Critical thinking* and *thinking skills* are terms used to connote problem solving and related behaviors. Critical thinking is a form of intelligence that can be taught (it is not a fixed entity). The leading proponents of this school are Robert Ennis, Matthew Lipman, and Robert Sternberg.

Ennis identifies 13 attributes of critical thinkers. They tend to (1) be open-minded, (2) take or change a position based on evidence, (3) take the entire situation into account, (4) seek information, (5) seek precision in information, (6) deal in an orderly manner with parts of a complex whole, (7) look for options, (8) search for reasons, (9) seek a clear statement of the issue, (10) keep the original problem in mind, (11) use credible sources, (12) stick to the point, and (13) exhibit sensitivity to others' feelings and knowledge level.[73]

Lipman distinguishes between *ordinary thinking* and *critical thinking*. Ordinary thinking is simple and lacks standards; critical thinking is more complex and is based on standards of objectivity, utility, or consistency. He wants teachers to help students change (1) from guessing to estimating, (2) from preferring to evaluating, (3) from grouping to classifying, (4) from believing to assuming, (5) from inferring to inferring logically, (6) from associating concepts to grasping principles, (7) from noting relationships to noting relationships among relationships, (8) from supposing to hypothesizing, (9) from offering opinions without reasons to offering opinions with reasons, and (10) from making judgments without criteria to making judgments with criteria.[74] (See Curriculum Tips 4.2.)

---

## CURRICULUM TIPS 4.2   Teaching Critical Thinking

Teachers must understand the cognitive processes that constitute critical thinking, be familiar with the tasks, skills, and situations to which these processes can be applied, and employ varied classroom activities that develop these processes. Robert Ennis provides a framework for such instruction. He divides critical thinking into four components, each consisting of several specific skills that can be taught to students.

1. Defining and clarifying
   a. Identifying conclusions
   b. Identifying stated reasons
   c. Identifying assumptions
   d. Seeing similarities and differences
   e. Determining relevant data
2. Asking appropriate questions to clarify or challenge
   a. Why?
   b. What is the main point?
   c. What does this mean?
   d. What is an example?
   e. How does this apply to the case?
   f. What are the facts?
3. Judging the credibility of a source
   a. Expertise
   b. Lack of conflict of interest
   c. Reputation
   d. Use of appropriate methods
4. Solving problems and drawing conclusions
   a. Deducing and judging validity
   b. Inducing and judging conclusions
   c. Predicting probable consequences

*Source:* Based on Robert H. Ennis, "A Logical Basis for Measuring Critical Thinking," *Educational Leadership* (October 1985), p. 46.

Sternberg seeks to foster many of the same intellectual skills, albeit in a very different way. He points out three mental processes that enhance critical thinking: (1) *meta components*—higher-order mental processes used to plan, monitor, and evaluate action; (2) *performance components*—the actual steps or strategies taken; and (3) *knowledge-acquisition components*—processes used to relate old material to new material and to apply and use new material.[75] Sternberg does not outline "how" as Lipman does; rather, he provides general guidelines for developing or selecting a program.

Some educators, including most phenomenologists and humanistic theorists, contend that teaching a person to think is like teaching someone to swing a golf club; it involves a holistic approach, not a piecemeal effort, as implied by Ennis, Lipman, and Sternberg. According to two critics, "Trying to break thinking skills into discrete units may be helpful for diagnostic proposals, but it does not seem to be the right way to move in the teaching of such skills." Critical thinking is too complex a mental operation to divide into small processes; the approach depends on "a student's total intellectual functioning, not on a set of narrowly defined skills."[76]

The method's own proponent has voiced the major criticism. Sternberg cautions that the kinds of critical-thinking skills we stress in schools and the way we teach them fail to prepare students "for the kinds of problems they will face in everyday life."[77] Furthermore, critical-skills programs that stress "right" answers based on "objectively scorable" test items are removed from real-world relevance. Most problems in real life have social, economic, and psychological implications. They involve interpersonal relations and judgments about people, personal stress and crisis, and dilemmas involving choice, responsibility, and survival. How we deal with illness, aging, or death—or with simple things like starting new jobs or meeting new people—has little to do with the way we think in class or on critical-thinking tests. But they are important matters. By stressing cognitive skills in classrooms and schools, we ignore life's realities.

**CREATIVE THINKING.** Standardized tests do not always accurately measure creativity; in fact, we have difficulty agreeing on what creativity is. There are many types of creativity—visual, musical, scientific, manual, and so on—yet we tend to talk about creativity as one thing. Creative students often puzzle teachers. They are difficult to characterize; their novel answers frequently seem threatening to teachers, and their behavior often deviates from what is considered normal. Sometimes teachers discourage creativity and punish creative students. Curriculum specialists also tend to ignore them in their curriculum plans (subject matter or course descriptions, subject guides, and subject materials and activities) because they represent only a small proportion (about 2 to 5 percent, depending on the definition of *creativity*) of the student population. Also, curriculum specialists have little money earmarked for special programs and for personnel for creative students. Frequently, educators lump creative children with highly intelligent or gifted children, even though high intelligence and high creativity are not necessarily related, and there are many types of creative children.

There is agreement that creativity represents a quality of mind: It is composed of both a cognitive and a humanistic component in learning; although no one agrees on the exact mix, creativity is probably more cognitive than humanistic. Its essence is its novelty; hence, we have no standard by which to judge it. The individual creates primarily because creating is satisfying and because the behavior or product is self-actualizing. (This is creativity's humanistic side, even though the process and intellect involved in creating are cognitive.) Eric Fromm defines the *creative attitude* as (1) the willingness to be puzzled—to orient oneself to something new without frustration, (2) the ability to concentrate, (3) the ability to experience oneself as a true originator of one's acts, and (4) the willingness to accept conflict and tension caused by the climate of opinion or intolerance of creative ideas.[78]

What are the effects of school and classroom climates on creativity? A number of pioneering studies have been made that have implications for teachers. The best known cross-cultural study, by E. P. Torrance, investigated the ratings of elementary and secondary teachers using 62 statements to describe their concept of the "ideal" creative personality.[79] From 95 to 375 teachers

**Table 4.2**  Selected Characteristics of an "Ideal" Creative Personality as Rated by Teachers in Different Cultures

| United States | Germany | India | Greece | Philippines |
|---|---|---|---|---|
| Independent thinking | Sincerity | Curiosity | Energetic | Industriousness |
| Curiosity | Sense of humor | Obedience | Strives for distant goals | Obedience |
| Sense of humor | Industriousness | Does work on time | Thoroughness | Courtesy |
| Consideration of others | Independent thinking | Courtesy | Sincerity | Health |
| Industriousness | Willingness to attempt difficult tasks | Health | Nonconforming | Consideration of others |
| Receptivity to others' ideas | Independent judgment | Self-confidence | Remembers well | Does work on time |
| Determination | Curiosity | Self-starting | Health | Self-confidence |
| Self-starting | Self-confidence | Industriousness | Altruism | Remembering well |
| Sincerity | Health | Affectionateness | Self-confidence | Willingness to accept difficult tasks |
| Thoroughness | Adventurousness | Determination | Courtesy | Affectionateness |

*Source:* E. Paul Torrance, *Rewarding Creative Behavior* (Englewood Cliffs, N.J.: Prentice Hall, 1965) p. 228.

of each of the following countries were sampled: United States, Germany, India, Greece, and the Philippines. Each statement was ranked on a 4-point scale, and the 10 most favored statements of each of the 5 groups appear in Table 4.2.

An examination of Table 4.2 indicates some of the cultural values that encourage and discourage creativity. Although the data are more than 50 years old, the results are still considered relevant today—with implications for technology, innovation, and globalization. For example, the United States and Germany (technologically developed countries) both encourage independent thinking, industriousness, and curiosity. India lists curiosity and the Philippines list industriousness; otherwise, these traits do not appear important in the less developed countries. Greece and the Philippines reward remembering, which connotes convergent thinking, but for many American researchers this type of thinking is considered anticreative. All the countries, or at least their teachers, put great stress on being well liked, considerate of others, and obedient. This is especially true of the less developed nations.

Robert Sternberg identifies 6 attributes associated with creativity from a list of 131 mentioned by U.S. laypeople and professors in the arts, science, and business: (1) lack of conventionality, (2) integration of ideas or things, (3) aesthetic taste and imagination, (4) decision-making skills and flexibility, (5) perspicacity (in questioning social norms), and (6) drive for accomplishment and recognition.[80] He also makes important distinctions among creativity, intelligence, and wisdom. Creativity overlaps more with intelligence ($r = 0.55$) than with wisdom ($r = 0.27$); creativity emphasizes imagination and unconventional methods, whereas intelligence deals with logical and analytical absolutes. Wisdom and intelligence are most closely related ($r = 0.68$) but differ in emphasis on mature judgment and use of experience with different situations.

All three types of people—creative, intelligent, and wise—can solve problems, but they do so in different ways. Creative people tend to be divergent thinkers, and teachers must understand that creative students go beyond the ordinary limitations of classrooms and schools and think and act in unconventional and even imaginary ways. Intelligent people rely on logic and have good vocabularies and stores of information. Such students tend to be convergent thinkers and score high on conventional tests. Few students exhibit wisdom because this comes with age and experience. Nonetheless, mature students show good judgment, make expedient use of information, and profit from the advice of others and their own experiences. They "read between the lines" and have a good understanding of peers and adults (including their teachers). They usually exhibit cognitive intelligence, what we might call "traditional intelligence," and social intelligence, what we might call "people skills."

For teachers, the definition of creativity comes down to how new ideas originate. We are dealing with logical, observable processes and with unconscious, unrecognizable processes. The latter processes give teachers trouble in the classroom and sometimes lead to misunderstandings between teachers and creative students. For some students, the methods of Edison and Einstein seem appropriate—theoretical, deductive, and developmental. For others, creativity may correspond more closely to the insights and originality of Kafka, Picasso, or Bob Dylan.

Creative thinking is not a one-dimensional process; instead it is an aspect of the total personality of someone who relishes new ways of observing the world. This type of thinking encourages imagination, which encourages more creative thinking. Imagination, as Maxine Greene notes, stimulates a "wide-awakeness," an awareness of what it means to be present in the world.[81] Such awareness fosters playfulness in which students manipulate objects and thoughts in "fun" ways. This manipulation triggers a curiosity in students as creative thinkers. Having fun with new or differently considered ideas, thoughts, and objectives brings out humor—the ability to be amused by a situation. Being playful with "things" in actual or imagined environments stimulates flexibility of thought and process. Very creative thinkers can shift from reality to fantasy, from the serious to the sublime, from the immediate to the distant, and from fact to metaphor.[82] Others are adept at making large mental leaps that the average person cannot follow or fully fathom.

**INTUITIVE THINKING.** Intuitive thinking is not new, but it was either overlooked because teaching practices have relied on facts and rote learning or ignored because it was difficult to define and measure. Bruner long ago popularized the idea of intuition in his book *Process of Education.* The good thinker has not only knowledge, but also an intuitive grasp of the subject. Intuitive thinking is part of a discovery process that is similar to the scholar–specialist's engaging in hunches, playing with ideas, and understanding relationships so that they can make discoveries or add to the storehouse of knowledge.

The following explanation by Bruner describes how some people work with intuitive thinking:

> Intuitive thinking characteristically does not advance in careful, well-defined steps. Indeed, it tends to involve maneuvers based seemingly on implicit perception of the total problem. The thinker arrives at an answer, which may be right or wrong, with little, if any, awareness of the process by which he reached it. He rarely can provide an adequate account of how he obtained his answer, and he may be unaware of just what aspects of the problem situation he was responding to. Usually intuitive thinking rests on familiarity with the domain of knowledge involved and with its structure, which makes it possible for the thinker to leap about skipping steps and employing shortcuts in a manner that requires later rechecking of conclusions by more analytical means.[83]

The preceding process has very little to do with a convergent, or step-by-step, approach. It speaks of the revelation of discovery coupled with the ability to use knowledge and find new ways to fit things together. According to this interpretation, problem solving and free discovery come together; knowledge is dynamic, built around the process of discovery, without precise steps or rules to follow.

**DISCOVERY LEARNING.** Since the Sputnik era, the inquiry–discovery method has been examined in conjunction with the discipline-centered curriculum—as a unifying element related to the knowledge and methodology of a domain of study. Taba, Bruner, Phil Phenix, and Gail Inlow were products of this era.[84] Taba was influenced by Bruner, Phenix was to a lesser extent influenced by both of them, and Inlow was influenced by all three. All four educators were more concerned with *how* we think than with *what* we think or what knowledge we possess.

Although Bruner went to great lengths to fuse the inquiry-discovery methods in the sciences and mathematics, Phenix, Taba, and Inlow claimed that the discovery method was separate from inquiry and that both methods of thinking cut across all subjects (not just science and math). Phenix, for example, proposed that discovery was a form of inquiry that dealt with new knowledge, hypotheses, and hunches. Most of his efforts focused on defining inquiry, which he claimed was the method of deriving, organizing, analyzing, and evaluating knowledge (like problem solving). He believed that inquiry binds all aspects of knowledge into a coherent discipline and considered inquiry more important than discovery.

Taba and Inlow contrasted discovery learning with verbal and concrete learning. Most of traditional learning was described as a process of *transmitting* verbal and concrete information to the learner; it was authority centered, subject centered, highly organized, and flexible and open. Discovery, however, involved extensive exploration of the concrete at the elementary level. For older students, according to Inlow, it involved "problem identification, data organization and application, postulation, . . . evaluation and generalization."[85] For Taba, it meant "abstracting, deducing, comparing, contrasting, inferring, and contemplating."[86] All these discovery processes are rational and logical and thus entail a problem-solving, or convergent, component. Inlow and Taba, however, were quick to point out that discovery also included divergent thinking and intuitiveness. Taba added creativity and limitless learning to help define discovery; the inference here is that discovery means to go beyond existing knowledge to synthesize or make something new.

Bruner, who is well known for elaborating the idea of discovery, defined *discovery* as the learning that occurs when students are not presented with subject matter in its final form, when students rather than teachers organize subject matter. Discovery is the formation of a coding system whereby students discover relationships among presented data. Successful discovery experiences make the learner more capable of discovering new experiences and more willing to learn.

## Cognition and Curriculum

Most curriculum specialists, and learning theorists and teachers, are cognitive oriented because (1) the cognitive approach constitutes a logical method for organizing and interpreting learning, (2) the approach is rooted in the tradition of subject matter, and (3) educators have been trained in cognitive approaches and understand them. As previously mentioned, even many contemporary behaviorists incorporate cognitive processes into their theories of learning. Because learning in school involves cognitive processes and because schools emphasize learning's cognitive domain, it follows that most educators equate learning with cognitive developmental theory.

The teacher who has a structured style of teaching would prefer the problem-solving method, based on reflective thinking or the scientific method. Most curricularists are cognitive oriented in their approach to learning, but we believe that this learning model is incomplete and that something gets lost in its translation to the classroom. For example, we believe that many schools are not pleasant places for all learners and that the "quality of life" in classrooms can be improved.

Much of the current teaching–learning process still has teachers predominantly talking and students mostly responding to the teachers. The workbook and textbook continue as the main sources of instruction.

Curriculum specialists must understand that school should be a place where students are not afraid to ask questions, be wrong, take cognitive risks, and play with ideas. With all our cognitive theory, we might expect students to want to learn and know how to learn, but we observe, both in the literature and in schools, that after a few years of school most students have to be cajoled to learn and have learned how not to learn. So-called successful students become cunning strategists in a game of beating the system and figuring out the teacher. Schools should be places where students can fulfill their potential, "play" with ideas, and not always be right in order to be rewarded by the teacher.

## PHENOMENOLOGY AND HUMANISTIC PSYCHOLOGY

Traditional psychologists do not recognize phenomenology or humanistic psychology as a school of psychology, much less a wing or form of psychology. They contend that most psychologists are humanistic because they are concerned with people and with bettering society. Moreover, they claim that the label *humanism* should not be used to mask generalizations based on little knowledge and "soft" research. Nonetheless, some observers have viewed phenomenology, sometimes called *humanistic psychology,* as a "third force" learning theory—after behaviorism and cognitive development. Phenomenology is sometimes considered a cognitive theory because it emphasizes the total person. However, the differences between learning cognitive and affective aspects have led us to separate these domains.

The most obvious contrast with behaviorism's mechanistic, deterministic view is the phenomenological version of learning, illustrated by individual self-awareness of an "I" who has feelings and attitudes, experiences stimuli, and acts on the environment. We possess some sense of control and freedom to produce certain conditions in our environment. When we speak of this awareness of control, we are speaking of the self. The study of immediate experiences as one's reality is called *phenomenology* and is influenced by, and perhaps even based on, an existentialist philosophy. Most phenomenological ideas derive from clinical settings; nevertheless, educators are becoming aware that they have implications for the classroom.

Phenomenologists point out that the way we look at ourselves is basic for understanding our behavior. Our self-concept determines what we do, even to what extent we learn.[87] If people think they are dull or stupid, that self-concept influences their cognitive performance.

### Gestalt Theory

Phenomenologist ideas are rooted in early field theories and field–ground ideas, which view the total person in relationship to his or her environment, or "field," and his or her perception of this environment. Learning is explained in terms of the *whole* problem. People do not respond to isolated stimuli but to a pattern of stimuli.

Field theories derive from Gestalt psychology of the 1930s and 1940s. The German word *Gestalt* means shape, form, and configuration. In the context of Gestalt theory, stimuli are perceived in relation to other stimuli within a field. What people perceive determines the meaning they give to the field; likewise, their solutions to other problems depend on their recognition of the relationship between individual stimuli and the whole.[88] This relationship is considered the *field–ground* relationship, and how the individual perceives this relationship determines behavior. Perception alone is not crucial to learning; rather, the crucial factor is structuring and restructuring field relationships to form evolving patterns.

On this basis, learning is complex and abstract. When confronted with a learning situation, the learner analyzes the problem, discriminates between essential and nonessential data, and perceives relationships. The environment continuously changes, and the learner continuously reorganizes his or her perceptions. In terms of teaching, learning is conceived as a process of selection by the student. Curriculum specialists must understand that learners perceive something in relation to the whole; what they perceive and how they perceive it is related to their previous experiences.

### Maslow: Self-Actualizing Individuals

Abraham Maslow, a well-known phenomenologist, set forth a classic theory of human needs. Based on a hierarchy, and in order of importance, the needs are as follows.

1. *Survival needs.* Those necessary to maintain life: needs for food, water, oxygen, and rest.
2. *Safety needs.* Those necessary for routine and the avoidance of danger.
3. *Love and belonging needs.* Those related to affectionate relations with people in general and to a place in the group.

4. ***Esteem needs.*** Those related to receiving recognition as a worthwhile person.
5. ***Knowing and understanding needs.*** Those more evident in people of high intelligence than those of limited intelligence, a desire to learn and organize intellectual and social relationships.
6. ***Self-actualization needs.*** Those related to becoming the best person one can be, to developing one's fullest potential.[89]

These needs have obvious implications for teaching and learning. A child whose basic needs— say, love or esteem—are not filled will not be interested in acquiring knowledge of the world. The child's goal of satisfying the need for love or esteem takes precedence over learning and directs his or her behavior. To some extent, Maslow's ideas with classroom implications are based on Pestalozzi and Froebel, who believed in the importance of human emotions and a methodology based on love and trust.

Maslow coined the term *humanistic psychology,* which stresses three major principles: (1) centering attention on the experiencing person, thus focusing on experience as the primary phenomenon in learning; (2) emphasizing human qualities, such as choice, creativity, values, and self-realization, as opposed to thinking about people in mechanistic (or behavioristic) terms and learning in cognitive terms; and (3) showing ultimate concern for people's dignity and worth and an interest in learners' psychological development and human potential.[90]

The teacher's and curriculum maker's role in this scheme is to view the student as a whole person. The student is to be positive, purposeful, active, and involved in life experiences (not S-R or only cognitive experiences). Learning is to be a lifelong educational process. Learning is experimental, its essence being freedom and its outcome full human potential and reform of society.

For Maslow, the goal of education is to produce a healthy, happy learner who can accomplish, grow, and self-actualize. Learners should strive for, and teachers should stress, student self-actualization and its attendant sense of fulfillment. Self-actualizing people are psychologically healthy and mature. Maslow characterized them as (1) having an efficient perception of reality; (2) being comfortable with themselves and others; (3) not being overwhelmed with guilt, shame, or anxiety; (4) relatively spontaneous and natural; and (5) problem- rather than ego-centered.[91]

## Rogers: Nondirective and Therapeutic Learning

Carl Rogers, perhaps the most noted phenomenologist, established counseling procedures and methods for facilitating learning. His ideas are based on those of early field theorists and field–ground theories. According to Rogers, reality is based on what the individual learner perceives: "Man lives by a perceptual 'map' which is not reality itself."[92]

This concept of reality should make the teacher aware that children differ in their level and kind of response to a particular experience. Children's perceptions, which are highly individualistic, influence their learning and behavior in class, for example, whether they see meaning or confusion in what is being taught.

Rogers views therapy as a learning method to be used by the curriculum worker and teacher. He believes that positive human relationships enable people to grow; therefore, interpersonal relationships among learners are as important as cognitive scores.[93] The teacher's role in nondirective teaching is that of a facilitator who has close professional relationships with students and guides their growth and development. The teacher helps students explore new ideas about their lives, their schoolwork, their relationships, and their interaction with society. The counseling method assumes that students are willing to be responsible for their own behavior and learning, that they can make intelligent choices, and that they can share ideas with the teacher and communicate honestly as people who are confronted with decisions about themselves and about life in general.

The curriculum is concerned with process, not products; personal needs, not subject matter; psychological meaning, not cognitive scores; and changing environments (in terms of space and time), not predetermined environments. Indeed, there must be freedom to learn, not restrictions or preplanned activities. The environment's psychological and social conditions limit or enhance a person's field or life space. A psychological field or life space is a necessary consideration in the curriculum, and everything that is taking place in relation to a specific learner at a given time gives meaning to the field and eventually to learning. See Table 4.3.

## Phenomenology and Curriculum

Phenomenologists view individuals in relation to the fields in which they operate. In this, phenomenologists have much in common with constructivists. But what determines behavior and learning is mainly psychological. The individual's experiences are accessible to others only through inferences; thus, such data are questionable scientific evidence. But to the phenomenologist, the raw data of personal experiences are vital to understanding learning. Perhaps the data cannot be measured accurately and perhaps they are vague, but they are "out there." The definitions and the processes are also subjective and evaluative rather than precise and substantive. Besides the concept of humanistic psychology, the subject matter of phenomenology can be used synonymously with many other concepts, including existentialist psychology, neoprogressivism, creativity, love, higher consciousness, valuing, transcendentalism, psychological health, ego identity, psychoanalysis—almost anything that suggests maximum self-fulfillment, self-actualization, and self-realization.[94]

Although this umbrella aspect of phenomenology makes it difficult to provide a clear, agreed-on definition of the term, the same broadness makes the concept acceptable to educational reformers of various psychological orientations. The fact that phenomenology means different things to different people is one reason for its easy acceptance, but it is also a basis for criticism. Nonetheless, phenomenologists attempt to rescue learning theory from the narrow and rigid behaviorists and from overstress on cognitive processes.

**MOTIVATION AND ACHIEVEMENT.**   As previously mentioned, phenomenologists seek to understand what goes on inside us—our desires, feelings, and ways of perceiving and understanding. Although cognitive functions are recognized by theorists, teachers and schools must first commit to dealing with the learners' social and psychological factors. Frustrated or upset students learn very little; they resist, withdraw, or act out their problems. Students' needs must be satisfied. Similarly, self-esteem and self-concept must be recognized as essential factors in learning. Without good feelings about themselves and without curiosity or motivation, there is little chance for continual cognitive (or even psychomotor) learning. Learners must feel confident about performing the skill or task required, be eager to learn, and feel that what they are being asked to perform is psychologically satisfying. This applies to learning the ABCs or to simple or complex problems.

We must reform schools not by changing the length of the school day or year, changing the amount of homework, or beefing up the curriculum, but by making school more satisfying to students and more consistent with their interests so that they gain a sense of power, fulfillment, and importance in the classroom. When we learn to deal with learners' psychological requirements and when we become sensitive to what makes them want to learn, we can then focus on what they must learn. *Affective needs are more important than cognitive needs.* Similarly, solutions to the problems of discipline and achievement are based primarily on making students feel someone listens to them, thinks about them, cares about them, and feels that they are important.

The humanistic approach to learning involves a certain amount of warmth, genuineness, maturity, and concern for people, in our case children and youth. The focus is not on academic achievement but on the whole child—on his or her social, psychological, physical, and cognitive needs. Progressive educators are likely to adopt many of the phenomenologists' theories, without even knowing that they are, because many of these ideas coincide with classic progressive thinking from Pestalozzi and Froebel to Parker and Washburne.

**Table 4.3** Overview of Major Learning Theories and Principles

| Psychologist | Major Theory or Principle | Definition or Explanation |
|---|---|---|
| **Behaviorist** | | |
| Thorndike | Law of Effect | When a connection between a situation and a response is made and it is accompanied by a satisfying state of affairs, that connection is strengthened; when accompanied by an annoying state of affairs, the connection is weakened. |
| Pavlov–Watson | Classical conditioning | Whenever a response is closely followed by the reduction of a drive, the tendency is for the stimulus to evoke that reaction on subsequent occasions; association strength of the stimulus–response bond depends on the conditioning of the response and the stimulus. |
| Skinner | Operant conditioning | In contrast to classical conditioning, no specific or identifiable stimulus consistently elicits operant behavior. If an operant response is followed by a reinforcing stimulus, the strength of the response is increased. |
| Bandura | Observational learning | Behavior is best learned through observing and modeling. Emphasis is placed on vicarious, symbolic, and self-regulatory processes. |
| Gagné | Hierarchical learning | Eight behaviors or categories are based on prerequisite conditions and cumulative stages of learning. |
| **Cognitive** | | |
| Montessori | Structured play | Instructional emphasis of visual and auditory activities; children learn at different rates. |
| Piaget | Cognitive stages of development | Four cognitive stages form a sequence of progressive mental operations; the stages are hierarchical and increasingly more complex. |
| | Assimilation, accommodation, and equilibration | The incorporation of new experiences, the method of modifying new experiences to derive meaning, and the process of blending new experiences into a systematic whole. |
| Vygotsky | Theory of language and cultural transmission | Learning involves human development (and potential) as well as cultural development (or environments shaped by beliefs and behaviors of previous generations). |
| Bruner–Phenix | Structure of a subject | The knowledge, concepts, and principles of a subject; learning how things are related is learning the structure of a subject; inquiry-discovery methods of learning are essential. |
| Gardner | Eight multiple intelligences | This is a cross-cultural, expanded concept of what is intelligence—such areas as linguistics, music, logical-mathematical, spatial, body-kinesthetic, and personal. |
| Guilford | 120 potential cognitive processes | This involves three-dimensional model (6 5 4) of intelligence called the *structure of intellect.* |
| Ennis-Lipman-Sternberg | Critical thinking | This involves teaching students how to think, including forming concepts, generalizations, cause–effect relationships, inferences, consistencies and contradictions, assumptions, analogies, and the like. |
| **Humanistic** | | |
| Maslow | Human needs | Six human needs are related to survival and psychological well-being; the needs are hierarchical and serve to direct behavior. |
| Rogers | Freedom to learn | Becoming a full person requires freedom to learn; the learner is encouraged to be open, self-trusting, and self-accepting. |

*Source:* Information from Allan C. Ornstein and Richard C. Sinatra, *K–8 Instructional Methods* (Boston: Allyn & Bacon, 2005), pp. 31–32.

In the final analysis, learning in school occurs in groups with a formalized curriculum (although some might argue that there is also an informal or hidden curriculum). The child is but one learner among as many as 30 students, all needing some attention and following a text that usually promotes passivity, not activity. Everything in and around us competes for our attention. When we pay attention to something, it usually means we are not paying attention to something else. All of us, including our students, must choose how we dispense our attention and time. When attention wanders or when students cannot focus on their tasks, this means that the tasks are too complex or that there is some kind of sociopsychological problem.

The question that arises, then, is how curriculum workers, especially teachers, can motivate students to pay attention to long division problems or Shakespearean sonnets when youngsters are being bombarded by a host of needs, interests, and feelings that compete for their attention and time. How can we better incorporate students' needs, interests, and feelings into the teaching–learning process?

As educators, we must support and nurture various learning opportunities; recognize several different domains of learning (not only cognitive domains); and provide rewards, or at least recognition, for various forms and levels of achievement, including effort, improvement, imagination, intuition, individuality, vitality, enthusiasm, and maturity—all of which have little to do with standard achievement scores but are important for enhancing personal wholeness and society.

**THE CONCEPT OF FREEDOM.**   Personal freedom is another important issue in phenomenology or humanistic psychology. One of the early humanistic psychologists put it this way: "I think people have a great deal more freedom than they ever use, simply because they operate out of habits, prejudices, and stereotypes. . . . [T]hey have a lot more self-determinism than is reflected in the traditional . . . view of humans as reactive beings. . . . [W]e have more freedom than most of today's psychology admits."[95]

The idea of freedom is at the center of Rogers's learning theory. The more children and youth are aware of their freedom, the more they can discover themselves and develop fully.[96] Freedom permits learners to probe, explore, and deepen their understanding of what they are studying. It permits them latitude to accomplish goals, find the fit between goals and achievements and past learning and new learning, and find the direction for additional learning. Freedom broadens the learners' knowledge of alternative ways of perceiving themselves and the environment.

Freedom was the watchword of the radical school, free school, and alternative school movements of the 1960s and 1970s, and it was part of the educational choice, charter, and private school movements of the 1980s and 1990s. These movements increase possibilities for learning and schooling and for enhancing school environments to match the diversity of learners' needs, feelings, attitudes, and abilities. The free school, alternative school, and radical school movements overlap; they were fueled by child-centered education and humanistic psychology. Even though their proponents protested against established teaching and school practices, they never were able to develop a detailed plan for reform.

Unquestionably, curricularists must enhance students' opportunities and alternatives for learning without lessening teachers' authority. They must strive for the "golden mean": student freedom without license and teacher authority without control. The idea is to design a curriculum that helps learners realize their full potential in a behavioral, cognitive, and humanistic sphere of learning.

**IN SEARCH OF A CURRICULUM.**   Because each individual has specific needs and interests related to self-fulfillment and realization, there is no generally prescribed humanistic curriculum. Rather, the learners draw on those experiences, subject matter, and intellectual skills necessary to attain full potential. The humanities and arts, especially philosophy, psychology, and aesthetics, are appropriate content because they further introspection, reflection, and creativity. A curriculum of affect, one that stresses attitudes and feelings, is also acceptable. Appropriate labels might be *relevant curriculum, humanistic curriculum, value-laden curriculum,* or *existentialist curriculum.*

According to phenomenologists, the student has a right to reject the teacher's interpretation of subject matter. In their view, it is important that the student–teacher relationship be based on trust and honesty so that the student knows when the teacher's ideas of a subject are wise and deserve respect. To phenomenologists, student choice is crucial—the power to decide what to do and how to do it, a sense of control over his or her ideas and work. School routine and rules should be minimal; learners should be left alone to do what they want to do, as long as it does not harm or endanger anyone. Frequent evaluation, criticism, and competition are not conducive to learning. The essence of many recent instructional trends, such as academic time, direct instruction, and mastery learning (which stress prescribed behaviors and tasks, well-defined procedures and outcomes, and constant drill and testing), are rejected as narrow, rigid, and high pressure.

Most reconceptualists accept the phenomenologist–humanistic interpretation of learning because both these curricularists and learning theorists value the uniqueness of human personality. Both groups prefer classrooms characterized by freedom, an existential educational experience, and subjects in the humanities and arts, not the hard sciences. Reconceptualists tend to approve this learning theory because it rejects the rational means-ends approach, the processes that the traditional, or hard, curricularists follow. Instead of presenting empirical data to justify the means, phenomenologists and reconceptualists rely on psychological and philosophical positions for validating proposed ends.

When asked to judge the effectiveness of their curriculum, both phenomenologists and humanists (like reconceptualists) rely on testimonials and subjective assessments by students and teachers. They may also present such materials as students' paintings, poems, interviews, reports, biographies, and projects or talk about improvement in student behavior and attitudes.[97] However, they present very little empirical evidence or few student-achievement scores to support their stance. Moreover, phenomenologists do not agree about how to teach self-actualization, self-determination, human striving, and so on. Nor do they agree about how to determine what subject matter is worthwhile; how to mesh the paintings, poems, and personal biographies with learning outcomes; and how to test or confirm many of their ideas.

There is great need to examine and construct a relevant, humanistic curriculum and to enhance the self-actualizing, self-determining learning processes. However, until the previously described issues are resolved, we will continue to flounder in the phenomenologist area of learning. Those who trust the behavioral, or cognitive–developmental, process in teaching and learning or the traditional, or scientific, spirit in curriculum making will continue to distrust the "third force" in psychology and the "soft" approach to curriculum.

## Conclusion

In general, learning can be examined in terms of three major theories: behaviorism, cognitive development, and phenomenology. We believe that change is occurring within the three major camps in psychology. Behaviorism is the oldest theory of learning and is being transformed into several current teaching–learning models, such as individualized learning, direct instruction, and mastery learning. We also explored the difference between classical and operant conditioning: traditional behavior is related to elicited responses (a well-defined stimulus–response association) and operant behavior is related to emitted response (no well-defined stimulus–response association).

Cognitive–developmental theory represents the second theory of learning, which has developed rapidly since the 1950s. This corresponds with the increasing influence of Piaget and Vygotsky and the growing explanation of environment (as opposed to heredity) as an explanation of cognitive growth and development. Cognitive learning theory is conducive to thinking among humans, including critical thinking, creative thinking, and intuitive thinking. Phenomenology, or humanistic, psychology can be considered the third and most recent learning theory. Its emphasis is on attitudes and feelings, self-actualization, motivation, and freedom to learn.

The authors believe that each theory of learning is incomplete by itself, but all three theories have something to contribute to explain various aspects of behavior and learning in classrooms and schools. Readers should come to their own conclusions about what aspects of each theory they can use for their own teaching and curriculum development. Table 4.2 (p. 115) should help in this activity.

---

**MyEdLeadershipLab™**

Go to Topics 3, 7, and 10: *Education in Revolutionary America, A Culture of Data,* and *Textbook as Curriculum* on the **My**EdLeadership**Lab**™ site (www.MyEdLeadershipLab.com) for *Curriculum: Foundations, Principles, and Issues,* Sixth Edition where you can:

- Find learning outcomes for *Education in Revolutionary America, A Culture of Data,* and *Textbook as Curriculum,* along with the national standards that connect to these outcomes.
- Complete Assignments and Activities that can help you more deeply understand the chapter content.
- Apply and practice your understanding of the core skills identified in the chapter with the Building Leadership Skills unit.
- Prepare yourself for professional certification with a Practice for Certification quiz.

---

## Endnotes

1. Ralph W. Tyler, *Basic Principles of Curriculum and Instruction* (Chicago: University of Chicago Press, 1949).
2. Jerome S. Bruner, *The Process of Education* (Cambridge, MA: Harvard University Press, 1959).
3. Edward L. Thorndike, *Animal Intelligence* (New York: Macmillan, 1911).
4. James W. Pelegrino, Naomi Chudowsky, and Robert Glaser, eds., *Knowing What Students Know: The Science and Design of Educational Assessment* (Washington, DC: National Academy Press, 2001).
5. Edward L. Thorndike, *Psychology of Learning,* 3 vols. (New York: Teachers College Press, Columbia University, 1913); and Edward L. Thorndike, *The Fundamentals of Learning* (New York: Teachers College Press, Columbia University, 1932).
6. Tyler, *Basic Principles of Curriculum and Instruction;* and Hilda Taba, *Curriculum Development: Theory and Practice* (New York: Harcourt Brace, 1962).
7. John Dewey, *How We Think* (Boston: D. C. Heath, 1910); John Dewey, *My Pedalogic Creed* (Washington, DC: National Education Association, 1929); and Charles H. Judd, *Education and Social Progress* (New York: Harcourt Brace, 1934).
8. Taba, *Curriculum Development: Theory and Practice,* p. 121.
9. Bruner, *The Process of Education.*
10. Ivan P. Pavlov, *Conditioned Reflexes,* trans. G. V. Anrep (London: Oxford University Press, 1927). The experiment was conducted in 1903 and 1904.
11. .John B. Watson, *Behaviorism* (New York: Norton, 1939).
12. .John B. Watson, "What the Nursery Has to Say about Instincts," in C. A. Murchison, ed., *Psychologies of 1925* (Worcester, MA: Clark University Press, 1926), p. 10.
13. Clark L. Hull, *Principles of Behavior* (New York: Appleton, 1943); and Clark L, Hull, *A Behavior System* (New Haven, Conn.: Yale University Press, 1951).
14. B. F. Skinner, *Science and Human Behavior* (New York: Macmillan, 1953).
15. Ibid.; and B. F. Skinner, *Reflections on Behaviorism and Society* (Englewood Cliffs, NJ: Prentice Hall, 1978).
16. B. F. Skinner, "The Science of Learning and the Art of Teaching," *Harvard Educational Review* (Spring 1954), pp. 86–97.
17. Albert Bandura, *Social Learning Theory* (Englewood Cliffs, NJ: Prentice Hall, 1977).
18. Robert M. Gagné, *The Conditions of Learning,* 4th ed. (New York: Holt, Rinehart and Winston, 1987).
19. Robert M. Gagné, Leslie J. Briggs, and Walter W. Wager, *Principles of Instructional Design,* 3rd ed. (New York: Holt, Rinehart and Winston, 1988).
20. Gagné, *The Conditions of Learning,* p. 245.
21. Sandra Blakeslee, "Hijacking the Brain Circuits," *New York Times* (February 19, 2002), Sec. F, p. 1.
22. Robert Marzano, *Classroom Instruction That Works* (Alexandria, VA: ASCD, 2001); and Marzano "Setting the Record Straight on 'High-Yield' Strategies," *Phi Delta Kappan* (September 2009), pp. 30–27.
23. Linda Darling-Hammond and Jon Snyder, "Curriculum Studies and the Traditions of Inquiry: The Scientific Tradition," in P. W. Jackson, ed., *Handbook of Research on Curriculum* (New York: Macmillan, 1992), pp. 41–78.
24. Pellegrino et al., *Knowing What Students Know;* and Rick Stiggins and Rick DeFour, "Maximizing the Power of Formative Assessments," *Phi Delta Kappan* (May 2009), pp. 640–644.
25. David A. Sousa, *How the Brain Learns,* 2nd ed. (Thousand Oaks, CA: Corwin Press, 2001).

26. Pellegrino et al., *Knowing What Students Know.*
27. Maria Montessori, *The Montessori Method: Scientific Pedagogy as Applied to Child Education in the Children's Houses,* trans. Anne George (New York: Fredrick Stokes, 1912), p. 33.
28. J. McVicker Hunt, "Environment, Development and Scholastic Achievement" in M. Deutsch, I. Katz, and A. R. Jensen, eds., *Social Class, Race and Psychological Development* (New York: Holt, Rinehart and Winston, 1968), p. 311. See also Dewey, *The Child and the Curriculum.*
29. Maria Montessori, *Pedagogical Anthropology,* trans. Frederick Cooper (New York: Frederick Stockes, 1913), p. 19.
30. Montessori, *The Montessori Method,* pp. 48–49.
31. Martin Deutsch, "The Role of Social Class in Language Development and Cognition" in A. H. Passow, M. L. Goldberg, and A. J. Tannenbaum, eds., *The Education of the Disadvantaged* (New York: Holt, Rinehart and Winston, 1967), pp. 214–224; Martin Deutch et al., *The Disadvantaged Child* (New York: Basic Books, 1967); J. McVicker Hunt, *Intelligence and Experience* (New York: Ronald Press, 1961); and Les S. Vygotsky, *Thought and Language* (Boston: MIT Press, 1962).
32. Jean Piaget, *Judgment and Reasoning in the Child* (New York: Harcourt Brace, 1948); and Jean Piaget, *The Psychology of Intelligence,* rev. ed. (London: Broadway, 1950). See also Hans Furth and Harry Wachs, *Thinking Goes to School: Piaget's Theory in Practice* (New York: Oxford University Press, 1974).
33. John Dewey, *Experience and Education* (New York: Macmillan, 1938), p. 40.
34. Jean Piaget, *The Child's Conception of Physical Causality* (New York: Harcourt, 1932). See also Piaget, *The Equilibrium of Cognitive Structures,* trans. T. Brown and K. J. Thampy (Chicago: University of Chicago Press, 1985).
35. Dewey, *Experience and Education,* p. 43.
36. Tyler, *Basic Principles of Curriculum and Instruction,* pp. 84–86.
37. Taba, *Curriculum Development: Theory and Practice,* pp. 118–119.
38. Bruner, *The Process of Education.*
39. Dewey, *Experience and Education,* p. 44.
40. Bruner, *The Process of Education,* p. 13.
41. Lawrence Kohlberg, "Moral Development and Identification," in N. B. Henry and H. G. Richey, eds., *Child Psychology,* Sixty-Second Yearbook of the National Society for the Study of Education, Part 1 (Chicago: University of Chicago Press, 1963), pp. 322–323.
42. Benjamin S. Bloom, *Stability and Change in Human Characteristics* (New York: Wiley, 1964). p. 88.
43. Ibid, p. 110.
44. Benjamin S. Bloom, *Human Characteristics and School Learning (*New York: McGraw-Hill, 1976).
45. Jerome Bruner, cited in Luis C. Moll, ed., *Vygotsky and Education* (New York: Cambridge University Press, 1990), pp. 1–2.
46. Luis C. Moll, ed., *Vygotsky and Education* (New York: Cambridge University Press, 1990).
47. Ibid.
48. Guillermo Blanck, "Vygotsky: The Man and His Cause," in Luis Moll, ed., *Vygotsky and Education* (New York: Cambridge University Press, 1990), pp. 31–58.
49. Ibid.
50. Carl Bereiter and Marlene Scardamalia, "Cognition and Curriculum," in Philip W. Jackson, ed., *Handbook of Research on Curriculum* (New York: Macmillan, 1992), pp. 517–542.
51. Benedict Carey, "Research Finds Firstborn Gain the Higher IQ," *New York Times* (June 22, 2007), pp. 1, 16; and Benedict Carey, "Birth Order," *New York Times* (July 1, 2007), Sec. 4, pp. 1, 4.
52. Carey, "Research Finds Firstborns Gain the Higher IQ," p. 16.
53. Howard Gardner, *Frames of Mind: The Theory of Multiple Intelligences* (New York: Basic Books, 1983).
54. J. P. Guilford, *The Nature of Human Intelligence* (New York: McGraw-Hill, 1967).
55. Charles E. Spearman, *The Abilities of Man* (New York: Macmillan, 1927).
56. Jerrold E. Kemp, Gary R. Morrison, and Steven M. Ross, *Designing Effective Instruction* (Columbus, OH: Merrill, 1994).
57. Kenneth W. Howell and Victor Nolet, *Curriculum Based Evaluation: Teaching and Decision Making,* 3rd ed. (Belmont, CA: Wadsworth, 2000); and Elinor Perry Ross, *Pathways to Thinking: Strategies for Developing Independent Learners K–8* (Norwood, MA: Christopher-Gordon, 1998).
58. Robert Reiser and John V. Dempsey, *Trends and Issues in Instructional Design,* 2nd ed. (Columbus, OH: Merrill, 2007).
59. Daniel Goleman, *Emotional Intelligence* (New York: Bantam Books, 1995).
60. Howard Gardner, *Frames of Mind* (New York: Bantam Books, 1985).
61. Peter Salovey, as referred to in Goleman, *Emotional Intelligence.*
62. Goleman, *Emotional Intelligence.*
63. Kenneth R. Howe and Jason Berv, "Constructing Constructivism, Epistemological and Pedagogical," in D. C. Phillips, ed., *Constructivism in Education,* Ninety-Ninth Yearbook of the National Society for the Study of Education, Part I (Chicago: The University of Chicago Press, 2000), pp. 19–40.
64. Jacqueline G. Brooks and Martin G. Brooks, *The Case for Constructivist Classrooms* (Alexandria, VA: Association for Supervision and Curriculum Development, 1993).
65. Thomas M. Duffy and David H. Jonassen, "Constructivism: Implications for Instructional Technology," in T. M. Duffy and D. H. Jonassen, eds., *Constructivism and the Technology of Instruction: A Conversation* (Hillsdale, NJ: Lawrence Erlbaum, 1992), pp. 1–16.
66. Ibid.

67. Nicholas Wade, "The Four Letter Alphabet That Spells Life," *New York Times* (July 2, 2000), p. 4.

68. John T. Bruer, *The Myth of the First Three Years* (New York: Free Press, 1999); Peter R. Huttenlocher and A.S. Dabholkar, "Regional Differences in Synaptogenesis in Human Cerebral Cortex," *Journal of Comparative Neurology* (March 1997), pp. 167–178; and Rima Shore, *Rethinking the Brain: New Insights into Early Development* (New York: Families & Work Institute, 1997).

69. Bruner, *The Process of Education;* Philip H. Phenix, *Realms of Meaning* (New York: McGraw-Hill, 1964); and Joseph J. Schwab, "The Concept of the Structure of a Discipline," *Educational Record* (July 1962), pp. 197–205.

70. See Jacob W. Getzels and Philip D. Jackson, *Creativity and Intelligence: Explorations with Gifted Students* (New York: Wiley, 1962); Robert J. Sternberg, ed., *Handbook for Human Intelligence* (New York: Cambridge University Press, 1982); and Michael A. Wallach and Nathan Kogan, *Modes of Thinking in Young Children: A Study of the Creativity-Intelligence Distinction* (New York: Holt, Rinehart and Winston, 1965).

71. Dewey, *How We Think.*

72. James B. Conant, *Science and Common Sense* (New Haven: Yale University Press, 1951).

73. Robert H. Ennis, "Logical Basis for Measuring Critical Thinking Skills," *Educational Leadership* (October 1985), pp. 44–48; and Robert H. Ennis, "Critical Thinking and Subject Specificity," *Educational Researcher* (April 1989), pp. 4–10.

74. Matthew Lipman, "Critical Thinking—What Can It Be?" *Educational Leadership* (September 1988), pp. 38–43.

75. Robert J. Sternberg, "How Can We Teach Intelligence?" *Educational Leadership* (September 1984), pp. 38–48; Robert J. Sternberg, "Thinking Styles: Keys to Understanding Performance," *Phi Delta Kappan* (January 1990), pp. 366–371; and Robert J. Sternberg. "Who Are the Bright Children?" *Educational Researcher* (April 2007), pp. 148–155.

76. William A. Sadler and Arthur Whimbey, "A Holistic Approach to Improving Thinking Skills," *Phi Delta Kappan* (November 1985), p. 200. See also John Barell, *Teaching for Thoughtfulness* (New York: Longman, 1991).

77. Robert J. Sternberg, "Teaching Critical Thinking: Possible Solutions," *Phi Delta Kappan* (December 1985), p. 277. Also see Robert J. Sternberg, "The Rainbow Project: Enhancing the SAT through Assessments of Analytical, Practical and Creative Skills." *Intelligence* (April 2006), pp. 321–350.

78. Eric Fromm, "The Creative Attitude," in H. H. Anderson, ed., *Creativity and Its Cultivation* (New York: Harper & Row, 1959), pp. 44–54.

79. E. Paul Torrance, *Rewarding Creative Behavior* (Englewood Cliffs, N.J.: Prentice Hall, 1965).

80. Robert J. Sternberg, "Intelligence, Wisdom, and Creativity: Three Is Better Than One," *Educational Psychologist* (Summer 1986), pp. 175–190; and Robert J. Sternberg, "Practical Intelligence for Success in School," *Educational Leadership* (September 1990), pp. 35–39.

81. Maxine Greene, *Releasing the Imagination, Essays on Education, the Arts, and Social Change* (San Francisco: Jossey-Bass, 2002).

82. Thomas Armstrong, *Awakening Genius in the Classroom* (Alexandria, VA: Association for Supervision and Curriculum Development, 1998); and Jessica Hoffmann Davis, *Ordinary Gifted Children* (New York: Teachers College Press, Columbia University, 2010).

83. Bruner, *The Process of Education,* pp. 56–57.

84. Bruner, *The Process of Education;* Gall M. Inlow, *Maturity in High School Teaching* (Englewood Cliffs, NJ: Prentice Hall, 1964); Philip H. Phenix, *Realms of Meaning* (New York: McGraw-Hill, 1964); and Taba, *Curriculum Development: Theory and Practice.*

85. Inlow, *Maturity in High School,* p. 78.

86. Taba, *Curriculum Development: Theory and Practice,* p. 156.

87. Arthur W. Combs, *A Personal Approach to Teaching* (Boston: Allyn & Bacon, 1982).

88. Kurt Koffka, *Principles of Gestalt Psychology* (New York: Harcourt, 1935); Wolfgang Kohler, *Gestalt Psychology,* 2nd ed. (New York: Liveright, 1947); and Max Wertheimer, *Productive Thinking* (New York: Harper & Row, 1945).

89. Abraham H. Maslow, *Toward a Psychology of Being,* 2nd ed. (New York: Van Nostrand Reinhold, 1968); and Abraham H. Maslow, *Motivation and Personality,* 2nd ed. (New York: Harper & Row, 1970).

90. Ibid.

91. Abraham Maslow, *The Farther Reaches of Human Nature* (New York: Viking Press, 1971); and Maslow, *Motivation and Personality.*

92. Carl Rogers, *Client-Centered Therapy* (Boston: Houghton Mifflin, 1951), p. 485.

93. Carl Rogers, *A Way of Being* (Boston: Houghton Mifflin, 1981); and Carl Rogers, *Freedom to Learn for the 1980s,* 2nd ed. (Columbus, OH: Merrill, 1983).

94. Edmund V. Sullivan, *Critical Psychology and Pedagogy: Interpretation of the Personal World* (Westport, CT: Bergin & Garvey, 1990).

95. Gordon Allport, "A Conversation," *Psychology Today* (April 1971), p. 59.

96. Rogers, *Freedom to Learn.*

97. William H. Schubert, "Reconceptualizing and the Matter of Paradigms," *Journal of Teacher Education* (January–February 1989), pp. 27–32; J. Smyth, "A Critical Pedagogy of Classroom Practice," *Journal of Curriculum Studies* (November–December 1989), pp. 483–502; and Sean A. Walmsley and Trudy P. Walp, "Integrating Literature and Composing into the Language Arts," *Elementary School Journal* (January 1990), pp. 251–274.

# 5

■ ■ ■

# Social Foundations
of Curriculum

## FOCUSING QUESTIONS

1. What is the difference between *education* and *schooling*?
2. How do you define *developmental tasks*? Why is it important for children and youths to learn these tasks for successful growth in our society?
3. How does gender influence teaching and schooling? Are schools feminized institutions? Why or why not?
4. What content is essential for moral teaching? What should be the teacher's role in promoting moral education?
5. How do family conditions and social class affect learning?
6. In what ways does the peer group replace potential authority during adolescence? How do you describe the power of the peer group?

Any discussion of curriculum should consider the social setting, especially the relationship between schools and society and how that relationship influences curriculum decisions. Social astuteness is essential for curriculum planners and developers. Curriculum decisions take place in complex social settings, through demands that society imposes and that filter down to schools. Indeed, curriculum workers must consider and use social foundations to plan and develop curricula.

## SOCIETY, EDUCATION, AND SCHOOLING

Education can be used for constructive or destructive ends, to promote one type of political institution, or *ism*, or another. The kind of education our young receive determines the extent of freedom and equality within our society. The transmission of culture is the primary task of society's educational system. Society's values, beliefs, and norms are maintained and passed to the next generation not merely by teaching about them, but also by embodying them in the educational system's very operation.

For Dewey, education perpetuates and improves society by properly organizing learners' experiences. It is "a primary responsibility of educators . . . [to] be aware of the general principle of the shaping of actual experiences by environing conditions" and to understand "what surroundings are conducive to having experiences that lead to growth." For Dewey, experience must be channeled properly, "for it influences the formation of attitudes of desire and purpose."[1] It is up to educators, particularly those in charge of subject matter, to judge which content and activities (what Dewey calls *experiences*) enhance individual personal and social growth and improve society and which do not (those he calls *miseducative*).

Most of us regard education as synonymous with schooling. Even a society without schools educates its young through the family or special ritual and training. "Schooling plays a major role in education in modern industrial [societies]"; it becomes more important as societies become "more complex and as the frontiers of knowledge expand. In simple, nontechnological societies, almost everyone becomes proficient over the whole range of knowledge necessary for survival." In technological societies, "people acquire different proficiencies and abilities; no individual can range over the entire body of complex knowledge or expect to be proficient in all areas of learning."[2]

In traditional and illiterate societies, education is processed through ceremonies, rituals, stories, observation and emulation of older children and adults, and strictly enforced codes of conduct and behavior. In modern and technological societies, the educational process starts at home but "school takes on greater importance as the child becomes older." The school is a vital institution "for helping the young acquire systematic knowledge," inculcating them with the proper attitudes and values, and "bonding the gap between generations." In contemporary society, the mass media also play a major role in processing knowledge and "redefining values and ideas."[3]

Schools serve a modern society by educating its children and youth. The curriculum worker who helps determine education's content, activities, and environment plays a major role in shaping and indirectly socializing students.

## Society and Modal Personality

When social scientists speak of *modal personality,* they do not mean that all members of a particular society are exactly alike. As Ruth Benedict wrote, "No culture yet observed has been able to eradicate the differences in temperament of the persons who composed it."[4] However, members of a society do have much in common; they are nursed or fed on schedule, toilet trained a certain way, and educated in similar fashion. They marry one or several spouses; live by labor or perform common economic tasks; and believe in one God, many deities, or no deities. These shared experiences temper individual differences so that individuals behave in similar ways. According to Benedict, society's norms govern interpersonal relations and produce a modal personality—the attitudes, feelings, and behavior patterns most members of a society share. In a study of the U.S. modal personality, anthropologist Margaret Mead stressed that the United States offers unlimited opportunity. Whether or not this is true, the belief that anyone can become president, which is reinforced by our notion of equal opportunity, places a heavy burden on most U.S. residents. By implication, those who do not become president (or a doctor, lawyer, engineer, or corporate executive) have shirked their "moral responsibility to succeed."[5] Most other people in the world blame poverty, fate, or the government for personal failure. Most Americans tend to blame themselves.

Whereas European parents usually raise their children to carry on family traditions, first- and second-generation American parents want their children to leave home for better lives. U.S. residents tend to evaluate their self-worth according to how high they have climbed above their parents' status and how they compare with their friends and neighbors. At no point do Americans feel they have truly "arrived"; the climb is endless but within reach, and it is very much a part of the American value system and the nature of our schools and the traditional curriculum.

## Social and Developmental Theories

A number of theories focus on global aspects of human growth and development. Because they emphasize the study of behavior as a totality, starting with infancy, they combine Gestalt psychology with socialization. Developmental theories address the cumulative effects of change that occur as a consequence of learning or failing to learn appropriate tasks during the critical stages of life. Failure to learn a task at a given stage of development tends to have detrimental effects on the developmental sequence that follows.

Development proceeds through a rather fixed sequence of relatively continuous stages, and it is assumed that maturation and appropriate societal experiences are necessary to move the individual from stage to stage. Shifts from one stage to the next are based not only on age but also on variations in the amount and quality of social experiences an individual accumulates over long periods.

Robert Havighust identified six periods in human development: (1) infancy and early childhood, (2) middle childhood, (3) adolescence, (4) early adulthood, (5) middle age, and (6) late maturity. Developmental tasks are defined as "the tasks the individual must learn" for purposes of "healthy and satisfactory growth in our society." A person must learn them to be reasonably happy and successful. "A developmental task is a task that occurs at a certain stage or period in the life of that individual. Successful achievement . . . leads to happiness and to success with later tasks, while failure leads to unhappiness, disapproval by the society, and difficulty with later tasks."[6]

A youngster's schooling is concerned with the developmental tasks of early childhood and the next two periods of life. The tasks are as follows:

1. Early childhood
   a. Forming concepts and learning language to describe social and physical reality
   b. Getting ready to read
   c. Learning to distinguish right from wrong and beginning to develop a conscience
2. Middle childhood
   a. Learning physical skills necessary for ordinary games
   b. Building wholesome attitudes about self
   c. Learning to get along with peers
   d. Learning appropriate male and female roles
   e. Developing fundamental skills in reading, writing, and mathematics
   f. Developing concepts for everyday living
   g. Developing morality and a set of values
   h. Achieving personal independence
   i. Developing (democratic) attitudes toward social groups and institutions
3. Adolescence
   a. Achieving new and more mature relations with peers of both sexes
   b. Achieving a masculine or feminine social role
   c. Accepting one's physique and using the body effectively
   d. Achieving emotional independence from parents and other adults
   e. Preparing for marriage and family life
   f. Preparing for a career
   g. Acquiring a set of values and an ethical system to guide behavior
   h. Achieving socially responsible behavior[7]

Although the Havighurst model is the best known, other models have been proposed to deal with student or adolescent needs. Havighurst uses the term *human* instead of *adolescent* to connote a wider range of ages and the term *tasks* instead of *needs* to suggest a solution, but the other models are just as comprehensive and balanced as Havighurst's. For example, Harry Giles outlined 4 "basic needs"—personal, social, civic, and economic—each of which has three to four subdivisions.[8] Florence Stratemeyer and her colleagues categorized 10 "areas of living" into three "life situations."[9] B. Othanel Smith and his colleagues classified 29 "adolescent needs" into 6 major social–personal classifications,[10] and Henry Harap outlined 30 "life activities" needed for successful human development.[11] The aforementioned authors were major curriculum theorists of the mid-20th century who recognized the need for a developmental approach to teaching, learning, planning, and implementing the curriculum.

Different as these classification schemes are, they clearly show that many common topics of concern tend to be social in nature and include environmental, moral, civic, psychological, physical, and productive (or economic) dimensions of learning. This degree of agreement may be the best we can aim for in developing a student-needs approach to curriculum and teaching. All the models consider the *whole child,* as opposed to only cognitive learning; tend to stress *achievement* categories, that is, tasks or needs; recognize the concept of *readiness;* and focus on the *individual,* even though they refer to a person's social circumstances. Whereas the Havighurst model professes to be developmental and consists of a hierarchy of human needs called *tasks,* with no one curriculum emphasis, the other models tend to be organized around equally important student or adolescent needs and developed in context with a core curriculum and a social-issues curriculum. This does not mean that these models cannot be used for *all* curricula. All the models can be used as a framework for a needs-assessment plan, discussed in greater detail in Chapter 7.

The *needs-assessment* plan is rooted in the *student-needs* or *adolescent-needs* approach of the 1940s and 1950s. This plan evolved during the mid-1970s, when the federal government required such a plan before providing funding. This requirement has filtered down to state and local guidelines, and many curriculum workers have adopted the idea. Whereas the student-needs approach focuses on the learner, a needs assessment may not. A needs assessment can also include the needs of professional staff, school, parents, and community. The intent is to clarify a school district's aims and goals; the assessment is conducted because school officials believe there is room for improvement.

## Changing American Society

David Riesman's *The Lonely Crowd* appeared 60 years ago; its central thesis coincided with the most important change shaping American culture: moving from a society governed by the imperative of production and savings to a society governed by technology and consumption. The character of the middle class was shifting, and Riesman conceptualized and described its change and new habits—from *inner-directed* people, who, as children, formed behaviors and goals (influenced by adult authority) that would guide them later in life, to *other-directed* people, who became sensitized to expectations and preferences of others (peer and mass media).[12]

The book was expected to sell a few thousand copies in college social science courses but wound up selling more than 1.5 million copies by 1995—making Riesman the best-selling sociologist in U.S. history.[13] For the next 25 years, *inner-directed* and *other-directed* ideas surfaced as popular conversation topics on college campuses and at cocktail parties in the West Villages, Harvard Squares, and Hyde Parks of the country. The ideas helped explain "flower power," Woodstock, and a new generation of middle-age men and woman like Willy Loman (*Death of a Salesman*), Mrs. Robinson (*The Graduate*), and Beth Jarrid (*Ordinary People*).

Riesman formulated three major classifications of society in terms of how people think and behave: traditional, inner, and other directed. The *traditional-directed* character prevailed in a folk, rural, agrarian society. Primitive tribes, feudal-era Europe, and present-day third-world countries, especially isolated villages in Asia, Africa, and Latin America are examples—although the Internet is likely to break down their isolation in terms of ideas and issues. Although these societies varied, they were and still are dominated by centuries-old tradition. Little energy was directed toward finding new solutions to age-old problems. Most tasks, occupations, and roles were substantially the same as they had been for countless generations past, and each was so explicit and obvious that it was understood by all. Each person knew his or her station in life (women were generally in second place, or worse, in terms of education and power), and each was obedient to tradition. In most cases, the individual was not encouraged to use initiative beyond the limits and defined position of society. Formal education was minimal and socialization was reduced to rituals, storytelling, and preservation of old customs, beliefs, and norms.

The Renaissance, the Reformation, the Age of Enlightenment, and the commercial and industrial revolutions ushered in discovery, innovation, change—and a new dynamism characterized by the landing of the pilgrims and America's Declaration of Independence (and the French Revolution), followed by America's 19th-century westward expansion, Darwinist thinking, the

Robber Barons, and early 20th-century colonial expansion. Conformity to the past no longer dominated intellectual thinking or predetermined the behavior of men and women. Experimentation and progress (including American pragmatism and progressive educational thought) became important patterns of conduct and behavior. Within this shift came an *inner-directed society*, characterized by increased personal mobility, population shifts, growth and expansion, accumulation of wealth, exploration, and colonization. Tradition gave way to individual initiative; the strong survived and even conquered the weaker or more traditional societies.

The prevailing values of an *inner-directed* society also highlighted Puritan morality, the work ethic, individualism, achievement and merit, savings and future orientation, with the nuclear family and other adults (teachers, police officers, clergy, and so on) knowing best and influencing the behavior of children and youths. On a negative note, however, minorities were "invisible," out of sight and segregated; women were expected to be subservient to men and had few professional opportunities; and society was unaccepting of gays and lesbians.

Finally, *other-directedness* is the emergent character of U.S. society, evolving since the post–World War II period. It is the product of a social and cultural climate that has come to support and encourage teamwork, group integration, gregariousness, organizational behavior, and homogenized suburbs—and to disparage the individualism and independence of inner-directed virtues.

In the other-directed society, parents and other adults have less influence over children than they did in the inner-directed society, and adult knowledge is diminished relative to the child's knowledge. First television, and now the Internet and iPod, provide young people with access to information that was in the past mainly limited to adults; the information barrier between children and adults is increasingly shattered, or at least made porous, and in some cases the children know more about certain subjects than adults.

## Postmodern Society

Today, we live in a society where diversity and pluralism dominate discourse and challenge conventional norms and values transmitted by larger society, including the concepts of traditional family, church, and national sentiments. In *postmodern* society, according to David Elkind, language is used to "challenge universal and regular laws that govern the physical and social worlds" with which we are familiar.[14] For the past 400 years, universal principles (such as Newtonian physics) and rational thought (such as Descartes' reasoning) have guided and transformed our scientific and social thinking. Now, all these fundamental concepts are labeled as technological rationality and viewed as machine theory.

In technological and scientific societies, according to critics, schools become distributors of cultural capital; they play a major role in distributing various forms of knowledge, which, in turn, leads to discrimination by one group over others as well as power and control over others.[15] Under the guise of objectivity and generalizable situations, it is argued by postmodernist thinkers that artistry, drama, poetry, and qualitative research have been disparaged. The world is evolving—and uncertainty, irregularity, and even chaos assume new importance for reinterpreting our physical and social worlds.

In the new world we live in, there is no one language common to all. Language is used to convey political and social messages; it contains cultural meaning that is used to address specific issues dealing with class, gender, and race; moreover, the three terms become fused with "liberation" politics—all of which become part of the folklore and heart of postmodern theory. The idea is to be relevant, not necessarily objective, and to reconceptualize, reinterpret, and rewrite contemporary social science and education theory and then link this new theory to liberation causes.

## Postindustrial Society: Bits and Bytes

Postmodern society includes what Daniel Bell called *postindustrial* society, which is produced by information and technology.[16] The singular feature of this new society is the importance of knowledge (including the transmission, storage, and retrieval of it) as the source of production, innovation, career advancement, and policy information. Knowledge becomes a form of power, and those individuals or nations with more knowledge have more power.

Emerging from the old industrial society, driven by the motor and how much horsepower could be produced, postindustrialism was (and still is) a knowledge-based society, driven by the production of information and the preeminence of professionals and technicians. In a society based on "brain power" rather than "muscle power," meritocracy and mobility tend to be equalized among men and women. (This assumes equal educational opportunities and minimal job bias.) The stratification structure of this new society produces a highly trained research elite, supported by a large scientific, technical, and computer-proficient staff—all retrieving, manipulating, and producing knowledge. Given the computer and the Internet, brain power can be marketed on a global basis, and people in China or India can compete for knowledge-based jobs in the United States without ever having to step on U.S. soil. In short, the world is "flat," a term recently used by *The New York Times* writer Thomas Friedman, inferring that knowledge-based jobs have become globalized and the playing field has been leveled by the Internet.

Although Daniel Bell gets much of the credit for developing the original concept of the postindustrial society, his ideas are rooted in articles that appeared in the 1948 *Bell System Technical Journal* and in the 1952 *Scientific American* magazine, in which Claude Shannon (certainly not a household name) described his mathematical theory of communication.[17] Shannon proposed the term *bits* to represent *binary digits*. A bit was a choice: on or off, yes or no, stop or continue, one or zero. Whereas some information was continuous and based on sound waves (such as phonograph records, radio, and television), other information was not continuous but discrete (such as smoke signals, telegraph, and teletype). On or off and yes or no suggested that circuits could transmit bits of information based on logic. Eventually, bits led to bytes for storage capacity and, subsequently, to kilobytes, megabytes, and gigabytes.[18]

Information, in a true sense, is neutral, just like education is neutral by itself. Although information systems and random numbers are meaningless by themselves, they are packed full of information when strung together and lead to new fields of information and power based on information. The medium is not really the message, as the cliché goes; rather, it's bytes of information that count—provided by Google and Yahoo. (Originally, it was bits of information, but like the wheel in discussing the history of horsepower, bits are now passé when it comes to the storage of information.)

## Postnuclear Family

The 2010 census showed that the nuclear family (mom and dad and the children living under one roof) now makes up fewer than 25 percent of the households in the United States.

Divorce rates continue to hover at more than 50 percent, but most former spouses remarry for a second or even third time. Within these new blended families, we have a growth of stepsisters and stepbrothers, and former spouses and family members who 20 years ago would have had nothing to do with the other are now finding it practical to stay connected, especially during holidays. American divorce culture has traveled far beyond *The War of the Roses* or *Kramer vs. Kramer*. Although postdivorce life may not be as cozy as depicted on the *Brady Bunch*, former spouses seem to be in closer contact with one another, exhibiting a new tolerance because of the children. Indeed, it is not surprising in some households to find "Dad and wife no. 2 [sitting] down with mom and her new beau" and all the stepchildren from the blended marriages at the holiday dinner table.

Today, there are about 6.4 million unwed couples living together, a 100 percent increase over the previous decade.[19] The figures include gay and lesbian couples, although the increase is mainly due to couples of the opposite sex, and some of these couples have children. Profamily and church groups obviously view this trend as evidence of moral and social decline.

Given the nuclear family of the post–World War II period up to the Eisenhower years, Mom stayed at home and displayed her maternal and caring instincts by raising children and cooking and cleaning, as exhibited by June Cleaver in *Leave it to Beaver*. Dad "brought home the bacon" and was considered rational, knowledgeable, hardworking, and head of the family—best represented by Robert Young in *Father Knows Best* and by James Stewart in *It's a Wonderful Life*.

Dr. Spock was once popular with moms and dads alike. He told parents they could use common sense to discipline and help children grow and develop. He saw children as innocent and immature and, just as Norman Rockwell and Andy Griffith did, in need of parental guidance and support, which the nuclear family was expected to provide. Spock's "how-to" book outlined for parents (and other adult authorities) methods for protecting and supervising children—and children fell in line and embraced the parental and adult authority.

### New Family Types

Historically, U.S. society and schools have drawn support from the nuclear family (two parents living with the family), which grew to prominence in Western society throughout the 19th and 20th centuries. The nuclear family has been described as highly child centered, devoting its resources to preparing children for success in school and a better life in adulthood than that of the parents. But the recession of 2008–2010 has lead many middle-class baby boomers to question whether their children or grandchildren will have a better life, that is, be as mobile as they were when growing up in the last half of the 20th century, when America was at its economic zenith and power.

Today, the notion of family is very different. Given the popularity of diversity, pluralism, and irregularity, the nuclear family is an anomaly. Overall, about half the youth under age 18 have been in a single-parent family for some part of their childhood.[20] The nuclear family has been replaced by many different family forms.

Given today's alternative communicative and cultural contexts, the claim is that the traditional nuclear family is far from ideal, often loveless and dysfunctional, whereas the modern, postnuclear family provides love and support for children. The fact is, however, parent–child interaction has declined 40 percent since the early 1990s, 71.3 percent of women with children were working in 2000 compared to 18 percent in 1950, and the number of latchkey children, ages 6–14, soared to 77 percent by 2008.[21]

## MORAL EDUCATION

It is possible to give instruction in *moral knowledge* and ethics. We can discuss philosophers such as Socrates, Plato, and Aristotle, who examined the good society and good person; the more controversial philosophers Immanuel Kant and Jean-Paul Sartre; religious leaders such as Moses, Jesus, and Confucius; and political leaders such as Abraham Lincoln, Mohandas Gandhi, and Martin Luther King, Jr. By studying the writings and principles of these moral people, students can learn about moral knowledge. The idea is to encourage good reading at an early age, reading that teaches self-respect, tolerance, and social good.

The teaching of morality can start with folktales such as "Aesop's Fables," "Jack and the Beanstalk," "Guinea Fowl and Rabbit Get Justice," and the stories and fables of the Grimm Brothers, Robert Louis Stevenson, and Langston Hughes. For older children, there are *Sadako and the Thousand Paper Cranes, Up from Slavery,* and *Anne Frank: Diary of a Young Girl.* And for adolescents, there are *Of Mice and Men, A Man for All Seasons, Lord of the Flies, Death of a Salesman,* and *The Adventures of Huckleberry Finn.* By the eighth grade, assuming average or above-average reading ability, students should be able to read the books listed in Table 5.1. This list of 25 recommended titles exemplifies literature rich in social and moral messages.

As students move up the grade levels and their reading improves, a greater range of authors is available to them. No doubt, community mores will influence book selection. Virtues such as hard work, honesty, integrity, civility, and caring are widespread. Educators must find such common values.

### Moral Conduct and Controversy

Is Mark Twain's *The Adventures of Huckleberry Finn* a racist book that should be banned or a masterpiece that should be read, discussed, and analyzed? Huck is a backwoods kid, not too

| Table 5.1 | Twenty-five Recommended Works to be Read by Eighth Grade |
|---|---|

1. Maya Angelou, *The Graduation*
2. Pearl Buck, *The Good Earth*
3. Truman Capote, *Miriam*
4. James Fenimore Cooper, *The Last of the Mohicans*
5. Charles Dickens, *Great Expectations*
6. William Faulkner, *Brer Tiger and the Big Wind*
7. Anne Frank, *The Diary of a Young Girl*
8. William Golding, *Lord of the Flies*
9. John Kennedy, *Profiles in Courage*
10. Martin Luther King, Jr., *Why We Can't Wait*
11. Rudyard Kipling, *Letting in the Jungle*
12. Harper Lee, *To Kill a Mockingbird*
13. Jack London, *The Call of the Wild*
14. Herman Melville, *Billy Budd*
15. George Orwell, *Animal Farm*
16. Tomas Rivera, *Zoo Island*
17. William Saroyan, *The Summer of the Beautiful White Horse*
18. John Steinbeck, *Of Mice and Men*
19. Robert Louis Stevenson, *Dr. Jekyll and Mr. Hyde*
20. William Still, *The Underground Railroad*
21. Ivan Turgenev, *The Watch*
22. Mark Twain, *The Adventures of Huckleberry Finn*
23. John Updike, *The Alligators*
24. H. G. Wells, *The Time Machine*
25. Elie Wiesel, *Night*

bright, the precursor of the modern juvenile delinquent, and a rebel who finds a moral cause without giving up his pranks or surrendering his identity. Jim is a runaway slave and a clown and companion, living in a White-dominated world in a servile role. Because of his place in society and his cleverness, he neither says all that he means nor means all that he says. Acting the clown with poetic imagination and humor, he can get along in his troubled world. The reader learns to respect his wit, jokes, and other compensatory devices.

Schools should be sensitive to students of all racial, ethnic, and religious groups. Similarly, people's genders, sexual preferences, or disabilities should not elicit discrimination. At the same time, sensitivity should not be at the expense of truth. Sadly, schools can select a biology textbook that doesn't mention evolution or a history book that excludes the Holocaust. They also can electronically alter literary classics (e.g., Homer's *Odyssey*, Shakespeare's *Merchant of Venice*, Chekhov's *Rothschild's Fiddle*), removing passages that some people might find offensive. Rather than expecting students to question and analyze such texts, schools too often use revisionary and doctored versions. Do we really create a purer school environment or purer society by such omission?

Instead of asking moral questions and requiring students to grapple with them, schools teach prescribed content and skills. As John Goodlad has commented for 15 years, across the curriculum at all grade levels, students are expected to memorize information, answer mundane questions in workbooks and textbooks, and pass multiple-choice and true–false tests.[22] The point is, Huck and Jim need to be heard and then analyzed and discussed, along with Homer, Shakespeare, and Chekhov.

According to Philip Phenix, the most important sources of moral knowledge are society's laws and customs, which can be taught in courses dealing with law, ethics, and sociology. However, *moral conduct* cannot be taught; rather, it is learned by "participating in everyday life of society according to recognized standards of society" (such as the Ten Commandments or the Golden Rule).[23] Although laws and customs are not always morally right, accepted standards do provide guidance for behavior. In the final analysis, individuals' behavior reflects their view of right and wrong. Existentialist educators such as Maxine Greene and Van Cleve Morris view morality as beyond cognitive processes, akin to social–psychological processes such as personal sensitivity, feelings, openness to others, and aesthetic awareness.[24] One is free, but *freedom* is essentially an inner matter involving *responsibility* and *choice*. Freedom, responsibility, and choice involve moral judgments and are related to social standards and personal beliefs.

Curriculum specialists, who must view moral development in conjunction with cognitive development, probably feel more comfortable with Piaget's perspective (see Chapter 3) or Dewey's position. Dewey points out that the social and moral worth of subject matter should be integrated "under conditions where their social significance is realized, [and] they feed moral interests and develop moral insight."[25] However, according to Dewey, the actual decisions and behaviors related to morality involve social growth and social experiences, which schools can help shape. He uses such descriptors as *character, conditions,* and *environment* to describe morality and the organization of subject matter.[26]

## Moral Teaching

The works suggested in Table 5.1 can be read in traditional history and English courses or in an integrated course such as Junior Great Books,[27] World Studies, or American Studies. Harry Broudy refers to this type of content as a *broad fields approach* to curriculum; he organizes the high school curriculum into five social and moral issues.[28] Florence Stratemeyer and her coauthors developed a curriculum based on 10 "life situations," made up of the ability to deal with social, political, and economic forces.[29] Mortimer Adler divided the curriculum into organized knowledge, intellectual skills, and ideas and values. The last deals with discussion of *good books* (his term), not textbooks, and the Socratic method of questioning.[30] Ted Sizer has organized the high school curriculum into four broad areas, including "History and Philosophy" and "Literature and the Arts."[31]

According to Philip Phenix, the content of moral knowledge covers five main areas: (1) *human rights,* involving conditions of life that ought to prevail; (2) *ethics,* concerning family relations and sex; (3) *social relationships,* dealing with class, racial, ethnic, and religious groups; (4) *economic life,* involving wealth and poverty; and (5) *political life,* involving justice, equity, and power.[32] The way we translate moral content into moral conduct defines the kind of people we are. It is not our moral knowledge that counts, but our moral behavior in everyday affairs. This distinction between knowledge and behavior should be taught to all students as a basis for envisioning the kind of people and society we are now and wish to become.

The aforementioned different moral approaches and courses of study represent a way of organizing and combining history and English into an interdisciplinary area. Great books can be added to this approach. In general, the courses' content deals with moral and social issues; ideas regarding how to live; elegant, witty, and weighty thoughts; and dilemmas that help us understand ourselves, our society, our universe, and our realities. By engaging in purposeful discussion, agreeing and disagreeing with the ideas expressed, synthesizing and building on ideas through conversation and consensus, questioning and testing arguments, and using evidence to bolster opinions, students can gain insight into making personal choices. The readings and discussions should also help students accept responsibility for their behavior and appreciate the religious and political freedom and economic opportunities that exist in the United States. Ultimately, the idea is to respect and promote human rights and social justice among all people and nations, as well as to attain a global perspective and appreciation of different people, cultures, and nations.

As teachers, we must involve all students in great ideas and books. However, we should not overemphasize the written word because there are other methods for transmitting our culture—the values and virtues we wish to teach. If we rely only on good literature, we lose more than half our students—those who are disadvantaged, learning disabled, semiliterate, non–English speaking, or limited in English speaking. Unintentionally, schools have increased the divide between concrete and abstract thinkers by tracking students and because so many students are unable to read and understand good literature.

We can make the same kind of lists as in Table 5.1 for great works of poetry (e.g., by Robert Frost, Carl Sandburg, Emily Dickinson), songs (by Irving Berlin, George Gershwin, Bob Dylan), art (by Rivera, Picasso, Goya), drama (*Les Miserables, A Doll's House, An Enemy of the People*), and film (*Gallipoli, The Grapes of Wrath, A Man for All Seasons*). The vast majority of "nonreaders" and "slow" learners can learn through audio and visual materials. Film is probably the most powerful medium for these learners, and there are great films, just as there are great books. Often, teachers believe that films use up precious class time. They fail to recognize that even the poorest households have DVDs or other access to movies. Just as schools distribute textbooks to students, teachers should distribute videos for home use or should show selected movies at the school after 3:00 p.m. or on Saturdays—movies that deal with larger social/moral ideas and issues.

Public television offers another option for nonreaders and readers. In particular, the Public Broadcasting Service (PBS) produces a host of interesting video stories. There are more than a thousand topics to choose from, including 350 award-winning documentaries (ranging from 90 minutes to 17 hours). In addition, there is an online directory of some 40,000 video segments, cross-referenced and linked to national and state standards.[33]

## Moral Character

A person can have moral knowledge and obey secular and religious laws but still lack moral character. *Moral character* is difficult to teach because it involves attitudes and behavior that result from stages of growth, distinctive qualities of personality, and experiences. It involves a coherent philosophy. Moral character entails helping people; accepting their weaknesses without exploiting them; seeing the best in people and building on their strengths; acting civilly and courteously toward classmates, friends, or colleagues; and acting as a responsible individual even if doing so means being different from the crowd.

Perhaps the real tests of moral character are to cope with crisis or setbacks, to deal with adversity, and to be willing to take risks (e.g., possible job loss) because of our convictions. Courage, conviction, and compassion are characters' ingredients. What kind of person do we want to emerge as a result of our efforts as teachers or principals? We can engage in moral education and teach moral knowledge, but can we teach moral character? In general, the morally mature person understands moral principles and applies these principles in real life.

The world is full of people who understand the notions of morality but take the expedient way out or follow the crowd. Who among us possesses moral character? Moral character cannot be taught by one teacher; rather, it involves the leadership of the principal and takes a concerted effort by the entire school, cooperation among a critical mass of supervisors and teachers within the school, and the nurturing of children and youths over many years. Ted and Nancy Sizer ask teachers to confront students with moral questions and moral issues about their own actions or inactions in ways that may be unsettling or difficult; teachers must address things that threaten students' self-concept and self-esteem. We must deal with issues of inequity and social injustice while promoting cooperative behaviors and intergroup relations among children and youths.[34]

The Sizers want teachers to "grapple" with ideas; "dig deep"; ask why things are so, what evidence there is, what thoughts and actions mean. They hope that teachers will stop "bluffing," that is, taking short cuts in their preparation, homework, testing, or other evaluation practices.

They hope that schools will reduce the "sorting" practice in ways that sometimes correspond with social (class or caste) groupings. Although some sorting of students is necessary, it should be flexible enough to respect students' and parents' wishes and to avoid stereotyping. In the end, the Sizers argue, students should not experience hypocrisy in classrooms and schools that claim all students are equal or free to be themselves while discriminating against students on the basis of class or low ability.

The authors believe that school leaders and teachers should adopt moral character as a matter of priority or policy. By themselves, one or two teachers cannot have real, long-term impact. It takes the principal's leadership, as well as a school community, to implement a program cultivating moral character, a program in which students are taught responsibility for their actions and the worth of values such as honesty, respect, tolerance, compassion, and justice.

As education leaders, we have an obligation to promote character development while still recognizing that there is a broad range of opinion on what this means or whether it is even possible. Amy Gutman represents one extreme in her belief that moral issues are inappropriate in public schools because of students' diverse backgrounds and biases. At the other extreme is Nel Noddings's notion that caring for strangers is more important than shaping students' minds and attitudes.[35]

Despite the controversy, school leaders must not be afraid to take moral positions. Much human behavior is horrific. Students who laugh at pictures of the rape of Nanking, the Holocaust, the Killing Fields, or the incineration of the World Trade Center should not be excused because of their ignorance or their religious, racial, or ethnic backgrounds. Nor should they be encouraged to spew racist, sexist, or otherwise hate-centered views. Schools are not being asked to impose Western or Christian values on the nation's students. Rather, they can help teach fundamental principles such as fairness, compassion, tolerance, and justice.

## Binary Bits and Reading Habits

Who invented the computer? (a) John Atanasoff, (b) Daniel Bell, (c) Thomas Edison, (d) Steve Jobs, or (e) James Zogby? Hint, it's the guy from Iowa State University, the physicist who in the 1930s was frustrated with the time-consuming task of calculating differential equations and was looking for an easier way to solve the answers.[36] For the answer, check endnote 36. The information seems especially suited to surprise most readers. Indeed, the majority of techies from Silicon Valley and East Coast elites give IBM's John Watson credit for inventing the computer. But that thinking reflects part of the "fly-over" mentality of people living on the U.S. coasts as well as the ignorance of the heartland and the unfounded "intellectual" belief that most worthwhile epic tales unfold on the two U.S. coasts.

And now that you know this "bit" of information about Professor Atanasoff, you may better appreciate *Los Angeles Times* book editor David Ulin's *The Lost Art of Reading.* In an overly connected digital world, reading books has become a chore for most of us, especially for children and youths. It is much easier, and more fashionable to blog, twitter, or text—free from contemplation, analysis, or logic.[37] Has the ability to read lengthy prose, to think and integrate ideas, or even to read for pleasure been lost by the new generation that is wired, networked, and distracted by the Internet?

The habit of reading and simply sitting down and engaging a good book may become a lost art. In a world where we instantly click a link while searching for a name or place or even an item to purchase, it is difficult to picture people seriously reading a collection of poems or a novel. In an age of immediate gratification and instant connection, reading a book can be considered a burden. For many children and youths, reading is considered an "uncool act" committed by "uncool kids" who are nonsocial or fat and flabby. The result is that an endless number of good books go unread because the habit of reading is in decline. The long-term effect on the knowledge base and thinking process of American high school and college students is serious, although somewhat difficult to measure and agree upon. It is partially reflected by the fact that only

38 percent of the 12th-graders tested by the National Education Assessment Program (NEAP) were considered "proficient" readers in 2009.

Some of the achievement problems in reading can also be contributed to what researchers call *summer setback*. During those 10 weeks, middle-class children usually read, prompted by their parents and school, and low-class children usually do not. Gains made in the school year

---

## CURRICULUM TIPS 5.1    Principles for Improving Schools

A number of important principles result in school effectiveness and excellence. Based on recent efforts to improve schools and reform education, school leaders and teachers can adapt many of the following principles for improving their own schools and the education of students.

1. The school has a clearly stated mission or set of goals.
2. School achievement is closely monitored.
3. Provisions are made for *all* students, including tutoring for low achievers and enrichment programs for the gifted.
4. Teachers and administrators agree on what is good teaching and learning; a general and agreed-upon psychology of learning prevails.
5. Emphasis on cognition is balanced with concerns for students' personal, social, and moral growth; students are taught to be responsible for their behavior.
6. Teachers and administrators expect students to learn, and they convey these expectations to students and parents.
7. The school day and school year are increased approximately 10 percent (or about 35 to 40 minutes per day and 15 to 20 days per year). This amounts to 1½ to 1¾ additional years of schooling over a 12-year period.
8. Additional remedial reading and math classes, with reduced teacher–student ratios, are provided for all students in the lowest 50th percentile on state or national tests. These additional classes replace physical education, study hall, foreign language, and elective courses—or, if extra money is provided, they are part of an after-school program or weekend program.
9. Teachers are expected to make significant school improvement; they are paid extra for staying after school and planning curriculum.
10. Administrators provide ample support and information, time for teacher enrichment, and time for teachers to work together. Individual lunch breaks and preparation periods are discouraged; the focus is on socialization and collegial planning.
11. A sense of teamwork prevails; there is interdisciplinary and interdepartmental communication. The emphasis is on group activities, group cooperation, and group morale.
12. Incentives, recognition, and rewards are conveyed to teachers and administrators for their efforts on behalf of the team effort and school mission.
13. The interests and needs of the individual staff members are matched with the expectations and norms of the institution (school/school district).
14. The staff has the opportunity to be challenged and creative; there is a sense of professional enrichment and renewal.
15. Staff development is planned by teachers and administrators to provide opportunities for continuous professional growth.
16. The school environment is safe and healthy; there is a sense of order (and safety) in class Rooms and hallways.
17. There is a agreement that standards are needed, but they are not imposed by outside "authorities" or "experts"; rather, they are implemented (or at least modified) by teachers and administrators at the local level.
18. Teachers are treated with respect and as professionals. They are trusted to make important decisions that deal with standards and involve teacher evaluation and accountability.
19. Parents and community members are supportive of the school and are involved in school activities.
20. The school is a learning center for the larger community; it reflects the norms and values of the community; and the community sees the school as an extension of the community.

slip away over the summer.[38] Not only do low-income (and single-parent families) get less adult attention, there is also a discrepancy in the number of books in the home between poor and middle-class families. Poor parents also speak fewer words, shorter sentences, and a restricted language in communicating to their children. Hence, there is a need to require summer school for *all* low-achieving students, starting in the first grade, and to make more books available through the mail or a library pick-up system during the summer to target children.[39] The purpose is to close the reading gap between proficient and nonproficient readers, because the ability to read is tied to academic success.

## THE CULTURE OF THE SCHOOL

Although each school in the United States reflects the culture of the larger society (namely, middle-class values, beliefs, and norms), it also has its own culture—its own ethos or way of thinking and behaving that it reinforces and rewards. Some schools emphasize highly traditional goals and "essential" subjects, and other schools may be more progressive and emphasize student participation and encourage music and art. In many rural and suburban schools, sports dominate student activities and, in part, define pride and spirit of the community; the Friday night basketball game or Sunday afternoon football game attracts a large portion of local residents. In another school, however, the emphasis may be on community service and intramural sports; fine arts may have a definite place on the curriculum. In creative and innovative areas of the country, the school may be organized around the Internet or WiFi usage. "Geeks," "dorks" and "nerds" may be considered part of the "in" crowd and even have comparable status to the jocks and students involved in student government and school newspaper.

Education in school, compared with that in the family or peer group, is carried on in relatively formal ways. Groupings are formed not by voluntary choice, but in terms of age, aptitudes, and sometimes gender and ethnicity (graphically illustrated by voluntary seating arrangements in the student cafeteria). Students are evaluated and often labeled—and sometimes mislabeled. Indeed, one third of a teacher's professional time in school (not counting time outside of school) is devoted to preparing and administering tests, grading papers, and evaluating students.[40] Interestingly, teachers rarely, if ever, enroll in a course on testing and evaluation.

### Conformity in Class

Students are told when and where to sit, when to stand, how to walk through hallways, when they can have lunch in the cafeteria, and when and how to line up and exit the school at the end of the day. The emphasis is on the teacher controlling the behavior of students. It is the teacher who decides in class who speaks and when, who goes to the front of the line and the back of the line, and who receives what grade. To be sure, grades can be used as an instrument for controlling behavior in class—at least for students who are grade oriented.

Getting through school for many students, then, means subordinating their own interests and needs to those of the teachers. In a classic text on sociology of teaching, originally published in 1932, Willard Waller described it as a contest between adult and youth cultures in which the teacher, in order to protect his or her own authority, had to win.[41] Charles Silberman, in a best-selling book 30 years later, described it as a useful learning experience for students— "a necessary aspect of learning to live in society." But he warned that teachers and schools sometimes translate this "virtue into a fault by . . . excluding the child's interest altogether."[42] One way students cope is they live in two worlds—one with peers and the other with adults. In this connection, Dewey observed, "Children acquire great dexterity in exhibiting conventional and expected ways the *form* of attention to school work . . . while reserving the inner play of their own thoughts, images, and emotions for subjects that are more important to them, but quite irrelevant" to adults.[43]

Just as teachers learn to cope with and control their students, students learn similar strategies for dealing with their teachers. By adolescence, children are very adept at observing and manipulating adults, and they do an excellent job in classrooms, sometimes without their teacher's knowledge. Don't ever think that the 25 or 30 students in your classroom are not sizing you up and judging your weaknesses and strengths—assessing what they can get away with and how much they can outwit you. It's a classroom game involving the one who is not only smarter, but who is also in control. In many inner-city schools, students are in control and teachers experience frustration and even symptoms of battle fatigue, one reason for the large turnover of beginning teachers in these types of schools (nearly 50 percent in the first 5 years).[44]

## Coping and Caring

Some students, however, survive in classrooms and schools by turning off or withdrawing into apathy. One way for students to avoid the pain of failure or the lower expectations of teachers is to persuade themselves that they don't care. Thus, threatening some students with lower grades has no effect. Sadly, most students who claim they don't care initially did care. The point is, repeated failure coupled with receiving unfavorable remarks and grades in a public arena (say, the classroom) takes its toll on all people. The effects are worse for young children because they have fewer defense mechanisms against adults and less ability to ward off learned low expectations for themselves.

Unquestionably, negative stimuli have a much greater impact than positive stimuli on all people. You can turn a person into a vegetable in a few days, but it take many years to make a doctor, lawyer, or CEO. Ineffective or hostile teachers can change a child's behavior in a matter of weeks through comments, gestures, and other body language, turning a young, motivated student into an unmotivated and self-doubting student who exhibits frustration, bites his or her nails, has temper tantrums at home, and no longer likes going to school. The younger the child, the easier it is for a teacher's negativism to influence his or her behavior.

The idea is to encourage different intellectual abilities and other skills and aptitudes of all students in class, not to make one group feel "smart" and the other "dumb." The best thing, observe Oakes and Lipton, is that "teachers can assure students that, although no one in class will be 'good' on all [problems or tasks], each student will be good on at least one."[45] Other researchers have found that when teachers stop publicly judging students, students begin identifying each other and themselves as "smart" in some areas, weakening previous negative expectations. However, when evaluation of tasks distinguishes between successful and unsuccessful student performance or when students are organized into ability groups, classmates begin to make the same distinctions.[46] The goal is for all students to assume that everyone in the class is competent in one or more areas and that everyone has something to contribute. (The notion of "multiple intelligences"—see Chapter 4—coincides with this positive interpretation of aptitude and talent, one reason for its popularity among school people.)

In this connection, a few progressive schools have eliminated all elementary school grades in order to reduce labeling of students and academic expectations of themselves. Grades basically create "winners" and "losers"—usually the same winners and losers. Over time, students get the message; it's called *dropping out*. Robert Slavin puts it in a slightly different, more moderate way: "In the usual, competitive reward structure, the probability of one student receiving a reward (good grade) is negatively related to the probability of another student receiving a reward."[47]

For this reason, one educator urges a school progress or mastery report card without grades, on which a list of descriptors or categories are given and the teacher describes what the student can do or how he or she is performing by writing a narrative describing the student's progress and problems.[48] Imagine, no grades, no labels; every school year, no one always plays right field or bats last every time and no one finishes last or next to last in every school yard race until he or she gets the message and says "I don't like this game. I don't want to play any-more"—and drops out. This nongrading approach could continue until students enter junior high school, until seventh or eighth grade.[49] Then, grades, percentages, and rankings must be used to prepare students for high school; likewise, high schools want to have knowledge of the students' abilities so they can track them and devise programs relative to their needs.

Oh, the wonders of tracking—who is "fit" and "unfit," who is "bright" and "slow." The schools have been labeling kids for the past 200 years, much more so since Binet devised his original IQ test in 1905. Kids who usually win the race, or get good grades, don't really know what it feels like to be judged "less than average," "inadequate," or "slow" by their peers and teachers. Given the academic success of most teachers (i.e., they have graduated from college), the authors wonder if teachers fully understand how much their judgments and evaluations affect lower-achieving students.

## CULTURE OF THE CLASSROOM

In his study of the elementary schools, Philip Jackson found a diversity of specific subjects but few different types of classroom activities. The terms *seatwork, group discussion, teacher dem-onstration,* and *question-and-answer period* described most of what happened in the classroom. Further, these activities were performed according to well-defined rules, such as "No loud talk-ing during seatwork" and "Raise your hand if you have a question." The teacher served as a "combination traffic cop, judge, supply sergeant, and time-keeper." In this cultural system, the classroom often becomes a place where things happen, not because students want them to, but because it is "time for them to occur."[50] Life in classrooms, according to Jackson, is dull. It is a place "in which yawns are stifled and initials scratched on desktops, where milk money is col-lected and recess lines are formed."[51]

Similarly, in John Goodlad's study of schools, he and his colleagues describe the following widespread patterns: The classroom is generally organized as a group that the teacher treats as a whole. The teacher is the dominant figure in the classroom and makes virtually all the decisions regarding instructional activities. "Enthusiasm and joy and anger are kept under control." As a result, the general emotional tone is "flat" or "neutral." Most student work involves "listening to teachers, answering the teacher, or writing answers to questions and taking tests and quizzes." Stu-dents rarely learn from one another. Instruction seldom goes beyond "mere possession of informa-tion." Little effort is made to arouse students' curiosity or to emphasize problem solving.[52]

Such systematic emphasis on passive learning by rote is in opposition to most contempo-rary ideas of what education should accomplish. You might ask: Why, then do so many class-rooms often function in this way? Think about it in terms of your own teacher preparation, student preference for passive learning, and the bargains and compromises between students and teachers—in short, taking the easy way out. Passive learning requires no extra teacher time for planning creative classroom activities. Often, there is a tacit conspiracy to avoid active learning and rigorous standards because this involves extra work by teachers and potential conflict with students. All teachers make compromises, take shortcuts, or avoid certain tasks that we know should be performed, simply because there are not enough hours in the day, as Ted Sizer notes in his appropriately titled book, *Horace's Compromise.*[53]

Thus, classroom patterns suggest boring and repetitive interactions between the teacher and students—instructional activities divorced of human feelings and emotions. It suggests a place where students must restrict their feelings and emotions, learn what behavior pleases the teacher, and learn what strategies and methods to use to get through the day, often with the least amount of work. In this connection, John Holt talks about how students adopt strategies of fear and failure. For most students, it means pleasing the teacher; for others, it means outwitting the teacher; for still others, it means doing the work as quickly as possible, like taking medicine and getting it over with.[54]

Given all these negative attributes of how classrooms operate, it is little wonder that many teachers often lose their students' interest after 10 or 15 minutes of instruction: "Students doze off, stare out of the window, or just stare past the teacher, while others doodle, pass notes, or throw 'spitballs'—or just pass time in classrooms."[55] What remedy or behavior do you as a student exhibit in class when you are bored? What percentage of your classmates in college open up their laptops under the guise of taking notes—and are actually shopping at J. Crew or text-messaging their friends? As a teacher, do you expect your students to be different? Can you look squarely in the looking glass and ask: What changes am I going to make to improve my instruction? How am I going to motivate my class?

Because much of this section has focused on negative aspects of school culture, we should emphasize that many positive statements can be made about schools in the United States. Most schools provide an orderly learning environment, and most students learn to read and compute at a level required to function in society. Relationships among teachers, students, and parents are generally positive. Almost all students become better persons and productive members of society as a result of schooling, despite all the criticism. The vast majority of students receive a high school diploma, and most proceed to some form of postsecondary education. (See Curriculum Tips 5.1.)

## The Peer Group

Whereas family relationships constitute a child's first experience of social life, peer group interactions soon begin to make their powerful socializing effects felt. From play group to teenage clique, the peer group affords young people many important learning experiences: how to interact with others and how to achieve status in a circle of friends. Peers are equals in a way that parents and their children (or teachers and their students) are not. A parent or teacher can pressure and sometimes force young children to conform to rules they neither understand nor like, but peers do not have formal authority to do this; thus, the true meaning of fairness, cooperation, and equality can be learned more easily in a peer setting.

A major tenet of cooperative learning is based on peers learning together, communicating and helping each other, and working as a group to achieve specific (in this case, academic) goals. David Johnson and Roger Johnson, the major authorities on the subject, envision cooperative learning as a means of increasing cooperation and socialization and reducing competition and individualization.[56] Actually, the idea is rooted in John Dewey's notion of education and democracy. Peer groups increase in importance as the child grows up and reaches maximum influence in adolescence, by which time they sometimes dictate much of a young person's behavior both in and out of school. Some researchers believe that peer groups are more important now than in earlier periods, partly because many children have little close contact with their parents and other adults and few strong linkages with the larger society.[57]

Other researchers note the influence of the peer group as early as first grade and the need to introduce rules and behavioral expectations early in the primary grade levels that create "a respectful, caring, learning community." The idea is for the children in a class to feel safe, valued, and respected by building a sense of peer respect, responsible behavior, and self-control within the classroom and school.[58] This is an issue involving not only socialization, but also moral character—attitudes and behaviors that must be introduced and modeled as early as possible by the teacher and infused through the school. Teachers should not underestimate the power of the young mind and heart to understand social and moral choices.

To foster peer relationships that support rather than impede learning, teachers must conduct activities that encourage students to learn cooperatively. In addition, teachers should promote children's interaction with peers, teach interpersonal and small-group skills, assign children responsibility for the welfare of their peers, and encourage older children to interact with and assist younger children. They must encourage their students to care for each other, to expect helping others learn, and to do what is right, rather than rely on rewards or punishment—in short, to build a sense of community in the classroom and school. Such steps promote character development and may even help counteract peer pressure for antisocial behavior.

Teachers must introduce age-appropriate and nonlitigious solutions to limit bullying and sexual-harassment practices (which were once ignored or considered "cute" by some educators). Teachers must also respond to the growing religious and ethnic diversity in classrooms and schools. As of 2012, minority students will constitute more than 40 percent of all public school students in grades K through 12 and more than 50 percent in grades K through 8.[59] Teachers must be prepared to meet the unique needs of growing and diverse student populations. Even teachers of single-culture classrooms must help their students understand, appreciate, and interact with other cultures, unless they expect these children to live in cocoons for their entire lives.

## Peer Culture and the School

Regardless of the type of school or grade level, the classroom is an "accidental group" as far as its participants are concerned. Students are brought together by an accident of birth, residence, and academic (or reading) ability, rather than by choice. The students of different classrooms are participants in a miniature society because they happen to have been born about the same time, live in the same area, and are assigned by the school to a particular room. The teacher may not be in this particular classroom entirely by choice; however, he or she had the opportunity to choose his or her profession and school district. The students have no choice in their assigned classroom or whether they participate; they are compelled to attend school. Student dorks and nerds have to interface with jocks and good-looking, personable boys and girls; immature kids have to mingle with mature kids; and various ethnicities must learn to respect and get along with each other. The classroom lacks the characteristics of a voluntary group—far different from the school yard or cafeteria, which is more than likely to exhibit certain cliques or groups held together by free choice of association and mutual interests, goals, or even ethnicity.

Of course, it is a nightmare for most students to sit alone in the cafeteria, have no one to eat with, or be ignored and left out in school activities. As Philip Cusick points out, "The single most important thing in school is to have friends," to be part of a group. Not to have friends, or to be repeatedly shunned by the peer group, results in many students disliking school. (Students who were interviewed by Cusick referred to "hating school.")[60] One can see the task of the teacher in a better perspective by remembering the accidental and mandatory nature of the classroom and the power of the peer group.

The classroom is the place where children and youths must learn to get along with peers and learn the rudiments of socialization and democracy. A student learns his or her own needs are not the only needs that must be met, and his or her own views are one of many. Compromise, tolerance toward others, and positive peer relationships are conducive to learning, and future social living must be introduced and modeled by the teacher. The influence of peer consensus and teacher (adult) approval are subtle but constantly in the background. Over time, these influences shape the students' attitudes and behaviors toward each other—and how they respect and work with other.

Willard Waller discussed the authority given to the teacher by both law and custom. However, because of the shift from an inner-directed to an other-directed society—most notably, a decline in all forms of adult authority—a teacher's word is less authoritative and respected today. In describing the teacher's role, Waller maintained that "conflict is in the role, for the wishes of the teacher and the student are necessarily divergent, and will conflict because the teacher must protect himself from the possible destruction of his authority that might arise from his divergence of motives." Waller analyzed the teacher–student relationship as a "special form of dominance and subordination," an unstable relationship that was "supported by sanction and the arm of the authority."[61] The teacher was forced into this role to limit the students' impulses and to preserve order in the classroom. This is a harsh analysis of what teaching is about, and Waller's thoughts must be put into perspective; he wrote during an era of growing child psychology and progressive thought, which he opposed. Today, a good teacher affirms the child's identity, nurtures the child's needs, and gives students a say in shaping their environment, but Waller thought that if the children in the classroom weren't controlled by the teacher, they would consort against him or her. He maintained that the teacher "not adapt to the demands of the childish group . . . but must force the group to adapt to him."[62]

Of course, as we all know, "The times are a-changing." When Cusick, Jackson, and Waller described classroom and social dynamics, students were categorized as the jocks, student government, newspaper groups, or academic achievers. The geeks and dorks are now the first generation of students growing up with computer gadgets. Now we have a growing digital world, where students are wired for distraction and instant gratification.[63] While sitting in the seats of the classroom, in doing homework, or even when they are supposed to be sleeping, there are children and youths texting or clicking onto to YouTube or Facebook.

"You get the entire story on YouTube in 5 minutes, whereas reading a book takes forever", "I prefer to text message than to talk on the phone", "I need instant gratification", "I have hundreds of texts to reply to", and "I forget to do my homework" are typical remarks of today's high school students. Young minds are becoming distracted in schools and at home, conducting multiple digital tasks and seeking immediate gratification but not focusing on homework or integrating what they read for school. Students engage YouTube or Facebook, listen to music, play video games, or text message, switching their brains from one task to another, sometime not leaving their chairs at home for hours.

Across the nation, schools are connecting to the Internet and using mobile devices so they can teach students in this electronic world. But in this new age, teachers must fight to keep students on task in class and not to text message or surf the Internet. Young students perceive this new computerized world in terms of socialization and entertainment, not for academic work. Unchecked use of tech devices has resulted in students becoming addicted in the digital world—and lost in it. The use of new technology by students sorts them into three loosely defined groups based on their personalities: *social butterflies*, that is, heavy texters (250+ a day) or those addicted to Facebook; *gamers,* or less social students who escape into video games (characterized by violence or sex), and *potatoheads,* or procrastinators who surf the Web or escape into YouTube or iPods.

### Peer and Racial Groups

Demographics are changing quickly, and White populations are expected to drop—from 16 percent in 2010 to 9 percent in 2050—so here is a need to understand, respect, and get along with people of color.[64] The fertility rate in North Africa and Southeast Asian is more than 5.5 children per female, whereas the average fertility rate of Whites is 1.7 children per female. A declining White population is most pronounced in Europe, which had a 2000 White population of 727 million and is projected ("medium rate") by 2050 to have 603 million.

White populations in Western and industrialized countries continue to shrink, and populations of color in poor countries continue to accelerate (the fastest growing is in Africa). For example, the Congo will increase from 49.1 million in 1998 to 160.3 million in 2050 (226 percent change); Ethiopia, from 59.7 million to 169.5 million (184 percent change); Ghana, from 19.1 million to 51.8 million (170 percent change); and Uganda, from 20.6 million to 64.9 million (216 percent change).[65] All the old legacies of "separate" and "unequal" in the United States and "colonization" and "White supremacy" abroad are viewed as self-destructive in nature. Although the health and vitality of America depend on technology and efficiency, they also assume a good political and economic relationship with Africa, Asia, and Latin America—the non-Western, people of color of the world—as well as people of all races and ethnic groups getting along in our own country.

Although the United States is the only Western country (along with Australia), expected to grow in population in the next several decades, by 2050 the majority (White) populace in the United States will be in the minority, and the minority population (Blacks, Hispanic Americans, and Asian Americans) will be in the majority.[66] Put in different terms, about 65 percent of the U.S. population growth in the next 40 years will be "minority," particularly Hispanic and Asian, because of immigration trends and fertility rates. In fact, from 2000 to 2010, the Hispanic population increased three times as fast as the Black population because of the Hispanic immigration trends (whereas Blacks have no comparable immigration pool). Thus, by 2010 there were more Hispanic students than Black students in U.S. schools.[67]

In fact, the Hispanic population represented 16 percent (48 million) of the U.S. population, and by 2050 they are projected to be 130 million strong and make up 20 percent of the U.S. population.[68] Most of this population growth has taken place in 10 states (with the main shift in California, Texas, Florida, and the New York–New Jersey metropolitan area).

The dominant norm and behaviors of the peer group put pressure on others to reject White behavior and act Black—even if it is self-destructive. This preference, or attitude, is referred to as *cultural inversion*—a tendency for minorities who feel at odds with the larger society to regard certain attitudes, norms, and events as inappropriate for them because these are representative of the dominant culture of White Americans.[69] Thus, what is appropriate or rational behavior for the in-group (Black) members in a particular community may be defined in opposition to out-group (White) members' practices.

## Conclusion

*Understanding* social foundations of curriculum is essential because such foundations have always had major influences on schools and curriculum decisions. Comprehending those forces in society at large and locally enables educators to determine what aspects of society to transmit to current and future students and what dimensions of society require reinvention. Curricularists must be social historians, current social analysts, and social futurists. Current and future consideration of society, education, and schooling are challenging in light of the diversity of our local, state, national, and international societies.

Educators involved with the creation, implementation, evaluation, and management of curricula must possess competence regarding our various societies and our national personality. Curriculum specialists, teachers, and administrators must keep up to date on social and developmental theories, understand both the modern and the postmodern family, and process the challenges of moral and character education.

Analyzing the social foundations of curriculum allows educators to determine the myriad roles schools and educators play. Dealing with these foundations directs educators in processing questions as to how or even if schools make a difference in knowledge and procedures

learned, and whether schools and their curricula affect society and its challenges.

Now consider these summary points: (1) The purposes of education are influenced by changing social forces, but there tends to be a balancing act between developing the potential of the individual and improving society. (2) Another balancing act or duality is the need to stress intellectual and moral matters. Most schools, however, emphasize learning in the cognitive domain and deemphasize the moral domain. (3) Since the early 1960s, American society has changed from an inner-directed society to an other-directed society and now to a postmodern society. (4) The American family is changing from households headed by two adults to households headed by one adult. In an age of diversity and pluralism, the nuclear family is being replaced by many different family forms. (5) The peer group becomes increasingly important as children proceed through adolescence; it has an important influence on social behavior and academic achievement. (6) The culture of the classroom and school tends to stress passive and conforming behaviors; students adapt to the environment by exhibiting various strategies, ranging from manipulative and pleasing to withdrawing and hostility.

**MyEdLeadershipLab™**

Go to Topics 1, 4, 6, 7, 8, and 12: *Defining Curriculum, Democratic Principles, Accountability, A Culture of Data, Focus on Testing,* and *Changing School Leadership* on the MyEdLeadershipLab™ site (www.MyEdLeadershipLab.com) for *Curriculum: Foundations, Principles, and Issues,* Sixth Edition where you can:

- Find learning outcomes for *Defining Curriculum, Democratic Principles, Accountability, A Culture of Data, Focus on Testing,* and *Changing School Leadership,* along with the national standards that connect to these outcomes.
- Complete Assignments and Activities that can help you more deeply understand the chapter content.
- Apply and practice your understanding of the core skills identified in the chapter with the Building Leadership Skills unit.
- Prepare yourself for professional certification with a Practice for Certification quiz.

## Endnotes

1. John Dewey, *Experience and Education* (New York: Macmillan, 1938), pp. 39–40.
2. Allan C. Ornstein and Daniel U. Levine, *Foundations of Education,* 10th ed. (Boston: Houghton Mifflin, 2008), p. 325.
3. Ibid.
4. Ruth Benedict, *Patterns of Culture* (Boston: Houghton Mifflin, 1934), p. 253.
5. Margaret Mead, *And Keep Your Powder Dry* (New York: William Morrow, 1941).
6. Robert J. Havighurst, *Human Development and Education* (New York: Longman, 1953), p. 2.
7. Robert J. Havighurst, *Developmental Tasks and Education,* 3rd ed. (New York: Longman, 1972), pp. 14–35, 43–82.
8. H. H. Giles, S. P. McCutchen, and A. N. Zechiel, *Exploring the Curriculum* (New York: Harper & Row, 1942).
9. Florence B. Stratemeyer, Hamden L. Forkner, Margaret G. McKim, and A. Harry Passow, *Developing a Curriculum for Modern Living,* 2nd ed. (New York: Teachers College Press, Columbia University, 1957).
10. B. Othanel Smith, William O. Stanley, and J. Harlan Shores, *Fundamental Curriculum Development,* rev. ed. (New York: World Book, 1957).
11. Henry Harap, *The Changing Curriculum* (New York: Appleton-Century-Crofts, 1937).
12. David Riesman (with Nathan Glazer and Ruel Denny), *The Lonely Crowd* (Garden City, NY: Doubleday, 1953).
13. Todd Gitlin, "How Our Crowd Got Lonely," *New York Times Book Review* (January 9, 2000), p. 35.
14. David Elkind, "School and Family in the Post Modern World," *Phi Delta Kappan* (September 1995), p. 10.
15. Michael Apple, *Ideology and Curriculum* (Boston: Routledge & Kegan Paul, 1979); Paulo Friere, *Pedagogy of the Oppressed*; Friere, *The Politics of Education* (Westport, CT: Bergin and Garvy, 1985); and Ivan Illich, *Deschooling Society* (New York: Harper & Row, 1971).
16. Daniel Bell, *The Coming of Post Industrial Society* (New York: Basic Books, 1973).
17. Bell gave credit to Shannon.
18. James Gleick, "Bit Player," *New York Times Magazine* (December 30, 2001), p. 48.
19. Sharon Jayson, "Census Reports More Unmarried Couples Living Together," *USA Today* (July 28, 2008).
20. Stephanie Coontz, "The American Family and the Nostalgia Trap," *Phi Delta Kappan* (March 1995), pp. K1–K10; and Lynn Smith, "Giving Context to Issues '90's Family's Face," *Los Angeles Times* (November 12, 1997), p. 3.
21. David Blankenhorn, *Fatherless America* (New York: Basic, Books, 1955); Peter Brimelow, "Marriage Rings and Nose Rings," *Forbes* (February 10, 1997), pp. 140–141; Allan Ornstein and Daniel Levine, *Foundations of Education,* 11th ed. (Boston: Houghton Mifflin, 2010); Jareb Collins, "Latchkey Kids: An American Epidemic," *Associated Content* (October 23 2006); and U.S. Department of Labor, Bureau of Labor Statistics. *Women in the Labor Force: A Databook* (September 2008).
22. John I. Goodlad, *A Place Called School* (New York: McGraw-Hill, 1984); and John I. Goodlad, *Educational Renewal* (San Francisco: Jossey-Bass, 1994).
23. Phillip H. Phenix, *Realms of Meaning* (New York: McGraw-Hill, 1964), pp. 220–221.
24. Maxine Greene, *Teachers as Strangers* (Belmont, CA: Wadsworth, 1973); Maxine Greene, *Variation on a Blue Guitar* (New York: Teachers College Press, Columbia University, 2001); and Van Cleve Morris, *Existentialism in Education* (New York: Harper & Row, 1990).
25. John Dewey, *Democracy and Education* (New York: Macmillan, 1916), p. 414.

26. Ibid., pp. 411, 415–416.

27. The Junior Great Books Program is headquartered in Chicago. It organizes workshops on a regular basis to train selected teachers to train colleagues in the principles and methods of teaching students in grades K–12 great ideas by emphasizing social and moral issues.

28. Harry S. Broudy, B. O. Smith, and Joe R. Bunnett, *Democracy and Excellence in American Secondary Education* (Chicago: Rand McNally), p. 19.

29. Florence B. Stratemeyer et al., *Developing a Curriculum for Modern Living* (New York: Teachers College Press, Columbia University, 1947).

30. Mortimer J. Adler, *The Paideia Program* (New York: Macmillan, 1984).

31. Theodore Sizer, *Horace's Compromise* (Boston: Houghton Mifflin, 1987).

32. Phenix, *Realms of Meaning*.

33. PBS Video: Catalog of Educational Resources (Spring 2006).

34. Theodore R. Sizer and Nancy Faust Sizer, *The Students Are Watching: Schools and the Moral Context* (Boston: Beacon Press, 1999).

35. Amy Gutman, *Democratic Education*, rev. ed. (Princeton: Princeton University Press, 1999); and Nel Noddings, *Educating Moral People: A Caring Alternative to Character Education* (New York: Teachers College Press, Columbia University, 2002).

36. Jane Smiley, *The Man Who Invented the Computer* (Garden City, NY: Doubleday 2010). The answer is (a) John Atanasoff.

37. David L. Ulin, *The Lost Art of Reading* (New York: Basic Books, 2010).

38. Richard Arlington and Anne McGill-Franzen. "Got Books?" *Educational Leadership* (April 2008), pp. 20–23.

39. Donna Celano, and Susan B. Neuman, "Schools Close, the Knowledge Gap Grows," *Phi Delta Kappan* (December 2008), pp. 256–262.

40. Peter W. Airasian and Michael Russell, *Classroom Assessment: Concepts and Application,* 6th ed. (Boston: McGraw-Hill, 2007); Lorin Anderson, *Increasing Teacher Effectiveness*, 2nd ed. (Paris: UNESCO International Institute for Educational Planning, 2004); Allan C. Ornstein and Thomas J. Lasley, *Strategies for Effective Teaching,* 3rd ed. (Boston: McGraw-Hill, 2000).

41. Willard Waller, *Sociology of Teaching,* rev. ed. (New York: Wiley, 1965).

42. Charles E. Silberman, *Crisis in the Classroom,* (New York: Random House, 1971), p. 151.

43. John Dewey, *The Child and the Curriculum* (Chicago: University of Chicago Press, 1902).

44. Selma Wasserman, "Growing Teachers: Some Important Principles for Professional Development," *Phi Delta Kappan* (March 2009), pp. 465–489.

45. Jeannie Oakes and Martin Lipton, *Teaching Change the World* (Boston: McGraw-Hill, 1999), p. 204.

46. Elizabeth Cohen and Rachel Lotan, *Working for Equality in Heterogenous Classrooms.* (New York: Teacher's College Press, 1977); and Lisa Delpet, *Other People's Children,* (New York: Teachers College Press 1995).

47. Robert E. Slavin, "Classroom Reward Structure: An Analytical and Practical Review," *Review of Education Research* (Fall 1977), pp. 650–663.

48. Allan C. Ornstein, *Secondary and Middle School Teaching Methods* (New York: Harper-Collins, 1992); Allan Ornstein and Richard Sapaci, *The Practice of Teaching* (Glencoe, IL: Waveland Press, 2012).

49. In lieu of grades, the authors would recommend a report of children's abilities, needs, and interests, coupled with strengths and recommendations; the report would be in narrative form and would not grade or rank the student. Also see Heather Deddeh et al., "Eight Steps to Meaningful Grading," *Phi Delta Kappan* (April 2010), pp. 59–63; and Richard Rothstein, *Grading Education* (New York: Teachers College Press, Columbia University, 2009).

50. Phillip W. Jackson, *Life in Classrooms,* (New York: Hoet, 1968).

51. Ibid., p. 4.

52. John I. Goodlad, *A Place Called School* (New York: McGraw-Hill, 1984); and John I. Goodlad, *Educational Renewal* (San Francisco: Jossey-Bass, 1998).

53. Theodore R. Sizer, *Horace's Compromise* (Boston: Houghton Mifflin, 1987).

54. John Holt, *How Children Fail* (New York: Putnam, 1964).

55. Allan C. Ornstein, *Secondary and Middle School Teaching Methods* (New Jersey: Prentice Hall), p. 20.

56. David W. Johnson and Roger T. Johnson, *Joining Together,* 10th ed.(Boston: Allyn & Bacon, 2008); and David W. Johnson and Roger T. Johnson, *Learning Together and Alone* 5th ed. (Boston: Allyn & Bacon, 1999).

57. Janis B. Kupersmidt et al, "Childhood Aggression and Peer Relations in the Context of Family and Neighborhood Factors," *Childhood Development* (April 1995), pp. 361–375; and Malcolm Gladwell, "Do Parents Matter?" *New Yorker* (August 17, 1998), pp. 56–65.

58. Elizabeth Meyer, *Gender, Bullying and Harrassment* (New York: Teachers College Press, Columbia University, 2009); and Allan R. Odden and Sarah J. Archibald, *Doubling Student Performance* (Thousand Oaks, CA: Corwin Press, 2009).

59. Based on extrapolating 2007 enrollment data from the *Digest of Education Statistics 2010*, Table 41.

60. Philip A. Cusick, *Inside High School* (New York: Holt, Rinehart, 1973), p. 66. Also see Philip A. Cusick, *The Educational Ideal and the American High School* (New York: Longman, 1983).

61. Waller, *The Sociology of Teaching*

62. Ibid., p.384

63. Matt Richitel, "Growing Up Digital." *New York Times* (November 21, 2010), pp. 1, 26–27.

64. "Global White Population to Plummet to Single Digit—Black Population to Double," *National Policy Institute* (April 18, 2008).

65. Ornstein, *Class Counts: Education, Inequality, and the Shrinking Middle Class.*

66. "Fastest Growing Countries," *New York Times* (January 1, 2000), p. 8.

67. Between 2000 and 2010, the Hispanic population increased by 11 million, compared to the Black population increase of 3 million. Also see *Digest of Education Statistics 2009*, Table 41, p. 75.

68. The McLaughlin Report, CBS (October 24, 2010).

69. John N. Ogbum "Understanding Cultural Diversity and Learning," in A. C. Ornstein and L. S. Behar, eds., *Contemporary Issues in Curriculum* (Boston: Allyn & Bacon, 1995), pp. 349–367; and Debra Viadero, "Even in Well-off Suburbs, Minority Achievement Lags," *Education Week* (March 15, 2000), pp. 22–23.

# 6

■ ■ ■

# Curriculum Design

## FOCUSING QUESTIONS

1. What "myths" about education's purposes do many educators and the general public seem to believe?
2. What three main, or "big," ideas influence our thinking about education?
3. What are the main sources of curriculum design?
4. What are major components of curriculum design?
5. In what ways has current brain research had an influence on curriculum design?
6. What are the major curriculum design dimensions?
7. Which curriculum design is most common in U.S. schools? Is having such a dominant curriculum design positive or negative? Explain.
8. Why is it essential to consider shadows within curricula?
9. Which design do you think is most likely to change in the future?
10. Which curriculum design would you most like to see become dominant in the future? Why?

Anyone charged with developing and delivering curriculum has a conception of curriculum and its components.

Opinions differ regarding how to design curriculum. David Orr discussed four myths about education that educators and the general public embrace and curriculum's proper aims.[1] They are still relevant. The first myth is that education—the right curriculum and curriculum design—can eliminate ignorance. The second myth is that education and well-designed curricula can supply all the knowledge needed to manage society and the Earth. The third myth is that educational curricula are increasing human goodness: Well-designed curricula instill wisdom. The fourth myth is that education's primary purpose is to enable students to be upwardly mobile and economically successful.[2] This myth is evident in much discussion about standards.

In response to Orr's discussion of myths, some people might argue that education can *reduce* ignorance, *help* people manage society and the Earth, *increase* wisdom, and *foster* upward mobility.

Implicit in these myths is a key question: What is education for?[3] Can we actually agree upon its purpose? You would think that after all the discussion on reforming education, creating curricula to make us competitive in the world, solving our and the world's social, economic, and health problems, we would be close to an answer.

Several years ago, Ron Ritchhart informed us that we educate, create, and teach curricula to create intelligence.[4] But, does intelligence guarantee eliminating ignorance? Does it foster human goodness? Is teaching for intelligence making students smarter? And what does *smart* mean?

Ritchhart noted in 2002, and these authors concur, that schools, even with all the discussions about reforms and revised curricula, still teach to fill students with knowledge and skills rather than making them competent thinkers. One reason is because it is easier to measure attainment of knowledge and skills and much more challenging to assess heightened intelligence.[5]

Kieran Egan asks, Why are educational considerations so challenging and contentious?[6] Can we make them less so? Egan notes that the difficulty lies in the fact that "our minds are both a part of the world while also being our means of viewing the world." Ideas and concepts focus what we see and do not see. We assume the validity of these "idea-lenses" and accept that we "observe reality directly."[7]

Egan postulates that most individuals think about education and its purposes drawing upon three main ideas, consciously considered or not. One reason for people, and educators in particular, to reflect on curriculum design in general and on selecting or employing a curriculum design is to become cognizant of the base ideas of socialization, Plato's academic idea, and Rousseau's developmental idea. These three ideas orchestrate "all players" in selecting curricular design and bringing it into reality through curriculum development. Attending to these three ideas makes a case for knowing something about curriculum foundations in the philosophical, historical, social, and psychological realms.

These three big ideas do not work in synergistic fashion. Rather, they tend to interact at cross purposes, seeming to create different "educational realities."[8] Most accept that education serves to socialize students to be functioning members of society, or good citizens. But to *socialize* means to foster conformity. Socialization stressed too much leads to indoctrination. To varying degrees, we all educate/indoctrinate our students so they have allegiance to complex sets of beliefs and particular patterns of behavior, the validity of which will never be challenged.[9]

When thinking of socialization, are we too tied to a current static situation or to an anticipated and future created social situation? Do we create or select a design that addresses current needs and behaviors, or design templates that allow for imagined possible and quickly forming futures?

The second big idea, Plato's academic idea, centrally deals with what knowledge is of most worth. The curriculum design we select influences how we select and organize knowledge and content in curriculum development. The major challenge is this: Out of all "collected" and stored knowledge, what should be selected to foster students becoming literate and thinking individuals? Some suggest a banquet of knowledge so that all stakeholders are pleased and represented.

Egan notes that there is no knowledge stored in literacy in libraries and computer data bases. What is stored are symbols that trigger awareness of knowledge. Therefore, in contemplating curriculum design, we need careful reflection of how our selected design and related educational materials facilitate symbol processes in knowledge developed. Currently, some schools are "playing" with the symbols they are putting in schools via textbooks. Mastering codes is not synonymous with knowledge.[10]

The third base idea, Rousseau's development idea, brings into consideration the basic maturing of the individual, specifically the growth of mind. Egan notes that Plato correctly asserted that academic knowledge was important to education, but to complete a total read on knowledge, Plato needed to recognize the various stages at which individuals—young, mature, and senior—are at optimal stages for learning or experiencing diverse realms of knowledge. Also central to consideration are the variety of ways in which individuals process knowledge to gain literacy.[11] Thus it is central, when considering curriculum design, to include learner development in the curriculum algorithm.

These three base ideas have been woven into our educational fabric and have influenced our perceptions as to the nature and purpose of education. They certainly have shaped the basic curriculum designs to be discussed later. These three base ideas exist, all have contributions to give, and all have significant flaws that must be recognized. However, the strengths of each idea can offset the flaws of each idea. Thus, we can aim for socialization, but we must avoid stressing indoctrination. We also undercut indoctrination by emphasizing the uniqueness of each individual and his or her right to unique knowledge. And while we incorporate the base idea of academics, we put in place stops to intellectual elitism by celebrating the innate equality of all individuals. We accentuate "being your own person, developing your individuality," while also emphasizing the need to participate in a society of equals.[12]

## CONNECTING CONCEPTIONS

The previous discussion reveals that how we contemplate education, curriculum, and curriculum design is influenced by myriad realms of knowing and feeling. Individuals draw from their experiences, their lived histories, their values, their belief systems, their social interactions, and their imaginations.

How do we choose from among diverse views? How do we process the three base questions? How do we deal with the central question: What is the purpose of education and thus the curriculum? There is no simple answer. Educational thinkers of all stripes and educational doers must ponder multiplicity.[13]

## COMPONENTS OF DESIGN

To design a curriculum, we must consider how its parts interrelate. Thinking about a curriculum plan's "shape," or "gestalt," and the arrangement of its parts addresses the essence of curriculum design. A curriculum's parts should promote the whole.

In designing a curriculum, we should consider philosophical and learning theories to determine if our design decisions are in consonance with our basic beliefs concerning people, what and how they should learn, and how they should use their acquired knowledge. In designing curriculum, we should give serious attention to the three base ideas discussed by Egan.[14]

Curriculum design is concerned with the nature and arrangement of four basic parts: objectives, content, learning experiences, and evaluation. These parts are rooted in Harry Giles's "The Eight-Year Study." Giles used the term *components* to show the relationship among the basic parts, but included learning experiences under "method and organization."[15] Curriculum design's four components suggest these questions: What should be done? What subject matter should be included? What instructional strategies, resources, and activities should be employed? What methods and instruments should be used to appraise the results of the curriculum?

Curriculum design involves philosophical and theoretical—as well as practical—issues. Our philosophy certainly influences our dealings with the three base ideas. These three base ideas influence our interpretation and selection of objectives, selection and organization of content, decisions about how to teach or deliver the curriculum content, and judgment about how to evaluate the success of the developed curriculum.

Some people argue that objectives suggest an undesirable willingness to control individuals and unwarranted certainty regarding outcomes. However, all curriculum makers must reflect on the curriculum's content.

Much current talk centers on engaging students in the construction, deconstruction, and reconstruction of knowledge. This refers to the components of method and organization. The component of evaluation also is widely discussed. Even if we argue that final measurement is impossible, we engage in some sort of assessment.[16]

In Ronald Doll's view, curriculum design is the parent of instructional design.[17] Curriculum arranges objectives, content, instruction, and evaluation. In contrast, instructional design maps out pedagogically and technologically defensible teaching methods, teaching materials, and educational activities that engage students in learning the curriculum's content. What resources are appropriate for a particular lesson indicated in the curriculum plan? Which students should be involved in particular activities? Curriculum design draws from curriculum theory, knowledge theory, social theory, political theory, and learning theory. Essentially, a curriculum results from a blend of curriculum design and instructional design.

## Sources of Curriculum Design

Curriculum designers must clarify their philosophical, social, and political views of society and the individual learner—views commonly called *curriculum's sources*. As David Ferrero notes, educational action (in this case, curricular design) begins with recognizing one's beliefs and values, which influence what one considers worth knowing and teaching.[18] If we neglect philosophical, social, and political questions, we design curriculum with limited or confused rationales.

Doll describes four foundations of curriculum design: science, society, eternal truths, and divine will.[19] These sources partially overlap with curriculum sources identified by Dewey and Bode and popularized by Tyler: knowledge, society, and the learner.[20]

**SCIENCE AS A SOURCE.**   Some curriculum workers rely on the scientific method when designing curriculum. Their design contains only observable and quantifiable elements. Problem solving is prioritized. The design emphasizes learning how to learn.

Much discussion of thinking processes is based on cognitive psychology. Advocated problem-solving procedures reflect our understanding of science and organization of knowledge. Some educators think the curriculum should prioritize the teaching of thinking strategies. With knowledge increasing so rapidly, the only constant seems to be the procedures by which we process knowledge.

**SOCIETY AS A SOURCE.**   Curriculum designers who stress society as a curriculum source believe that school is an agent of society and should draw its curriculum ideas from analysis of the social situation. Individuals with this orientation believe heavily in the socialization function of schooling.

Schools must realize that they are part of and are designed to serve to some extent the interests of their local communities and larger society. But, as indicated earlier, school members must be mindful of the other two base ideas: academics and development. Further, curriculum designers must consider current and future society at the local, national, and global levels.

In considering society as a source, educators must realize that schools function with not only social communities, but political ones as well. Political pressure on schools continues at the local, state, and national level. No Child Left Behind is still on the books and is being revised. Race to the Top, offering federal incentive money, aims at stimulating innovative programs in local schools. These federal governmental programs aim at all three ideas identified by Egan.[21]

But the political realm of society is contentious. We have political drama with conservative, liberal, and radical players.[22] And no one considers that schools and their curricula are measuring up; students, so it appears and assessments seem to confirm, are not succeeding in their learning. In general, conservatives believe that the basics are being ignored and that schools are failing to instill traditional U.S. virtues and values. Here we see demands that schools socialize in particular ways that could touch on indoctrination. We also see the academic big idea being narrowly interpreted: a curriculum focusing on significant Western and American history, basic mathematics, specific Americans who have contributed to the United States, and basic language skills. In May 2010, the Texas State Board of Education voted to have a revised K–12 social studies curriculum that would contribute to the education of Texas students for a 10-year period. Those in favor of this decision believed that the revised social studies curriculum would put balance back in that curriculum. Opponents feared that the decision would result in social studies content losing its validity and actually leading to indoctrination.[23]

Adding to the political drama are critiques of schools and their curricula voiced by liberal and radical players. Liberals have criticized schools for failing to make students effective professionals or workers. Students in the United States must be more competitive in the world. Education should give students the means for upward mobility and success.[24] Here we see a reference to the fourth myth of education offered by Orr.[25]

Radical education players are dissatisfied with schools and school curricula because they center on the privileged members of our population and dismiss or deny the interests and cultural knowledge of underrepresented groups, such as indigenous people, people of color, women, and homosexuals. They often critique the curriculum from a Marxist or feminist perspective. They tend to think in terms of oppressors and oppressed, empowered and victimized, privileged and disadvantaged. Radical educators want U.S. schools to provide the educational and social opportunities necessary for all students to succeed.

It does seem that all three groups—conservative, liberal, and radical—value the individual. They call for balancing our uniqueness as individuals with our responsibilities as community members. Here we see the big idea of socialization attempting to avoid the danger of indoctrination.

Effective curriculum designers realize the need for collaboration among diverse individuals and groups. People from disparate backgrounds and cultures are demanding a voice regarding how education is organized and experienced. Society currently is a powerful influence on curriculum design. As Arthur Ellis notes, no curriculum or curriculum design can be considered or created apart from the people who make up our evolving society.[26]

**MORAL DOCTRINE AS A SOURCE.**   Some curriculum designers look to the past for guidance regarding appropriate content. These persons emphasize what they view as lasting truths advanced by the great thinkers of the past. Their designs stress content and rank some subjects as more important than others.

Some people believe that curriculum design should be guided by the Bible or other religious texts. Although this view was common in the schools of colonial America, it has had little influence in public schools for more than a century, primarily because of the mandated separation of church and state. However, many private and parochial schools still subscribe to this now, including a growing number of Islamic schools.

In this century, public schools are increasingly considering the relationship between knowledge and people's spirituality. Many people are criticizing Western society's emphases on science, rationality, and material wealth.

Dwayne Huebner argued that education can address spirituality without bringing in religion. For him, to have spirit is to be in touch with life's forces, or energies.[27] Being in touch with spirit allows us to see the essences of reality and to generate new ways of viewing knowledge, new relationships among people, and new ways of perceiving our existence.

According to James Moffett, spirituality fosters mindfulness, attentiveness, awareness of the outside world, and self-awareness.[28] Spiritual individuals develop empathy and insight. Curriculum designers who draw on spirituality reach a fuller understanding than those who rely only on science. Spiritual individuals develop empathy and compassion. They consider and promote the welfare of others. They welcome differing viewpoints.[29] Spiritual curriculum designers ask questions about the nature of the world, the purpose of life, and what it means to be human and knowledgeable.

William Pinar comments that viewing curriculum as religious text may allow for a blending of truth, faith, knowledge, ethics, thought, and action. He believes that faith, ethics, and action need more emphasis.[30]

**KNOWLEDGE AS A SOURCE.**    Knowledge, according to some, is the primary source of curriculum. This view dates back to Plato, who communicated that when the most prized and useful knowledge is coded in writing, it can then be taught to students. Teaching such valued knowledge stimulates and develops the minds of learners. The result of such learning enables students to apprehend the world closer to the real reality.[31]

This view celebrates Plato's academic idea. Herbert Spencer placed knowledge within the framework of curriculum when he asked, "What knowledge is of most worth?"

Those who place knowledge at the center of curriculum design realize that knowledge may be a discipline, having a particular structure and a particular method or methods by which scholars extend its boundaries. Undisciplined knowledge does not have unique content; instead, its content is shaped according to an investigation's focus. For example, physics as a discipline has a unique conceptual structure and entails a unique process. In contrast, environmental education is undisciplined in that its content is drawn from various disciplines and adapted to a special focus.

The challenge to those who accept knowledge as the primary source of curricular design is that knowledge is exploding exponentially. But the time for engaging students with curriculum is not increasing. Most schools still require 180-school-day sessions. Spencer's question is now even more daunting. Not only must we rethink "What knowledge is of most worth?" but we must also posit the following inquiries: For whom is this knowledge of value? Is there any knowledge that must be possessed by the majority? What intellectual skills must be taught to enable common and uncommon knowledge to be utilized for individual and social good?

**THE LEARNER AS A SOURCE.**    Some believe that the curriculum should derive from our knowledge of students: how they learn, form attitudes, generate interests, and develop values. For progressive curricularists, humanistic educators, and many curricularists engaged in postmodern dialogue, the learner should be the primary source of curriculum design. Here we have the third big idea: Rousseau's theory of development.

Such curricularists tend to draw heavily on psychological foundations, especially how minds create meaning. Much cognitive research has provided curriculum designers with ways to develop educational activities that facilitate perceiving, thinking, and learning. Since the final years of the 1900s, microbiological research on the brain has had much significance for educators. We are learning that the educational environment can influence the anatomy of a child's brain. Quantity and quality of experiences physically affect brain development.[32]

Much of this new knowledge about the brain has resulted from neuroimaging technologies that have been perfected since the early 1980s. It is now possible to map areas where the brain is active during various cognitive functions by measuring specific changes in cerebral blood supply.[33]

Instead of surmising what a person's brain is doing when he or she is engaged in specific types of thinking, as was done in most—if not all—cognitive research for the first seven decades of the last century, we now can view the human brain when it thinks.[34] We can photograph such brain activity; we can observe brain networks changing before our eyes and observe brain networks altering themselves to learning information and skills. In essence, we are gaining the ability to map more precisely the parts of the human brain involved in learning language, developing perceptions, and even reading and learning arithmetic.[35] As Michael Posner and Mary Rothbart note, new brain research findings will allow the general public and educators unparalleled access to new levels of understanding human brain development. This design source has the greatest possibility of being the most powerful new fount of data for reconceptualizing curriculum design.[36]

We are actually "seeing" individuals construct and change brain neural pathways rather than simply acquiring knowledge, and they do so in unique ways with specific conclusions. They may use the same words to answer a question, but research indicates that their deep comprehension of the material is quite distinct.[37] Although technology is giving us clearer vision of what is occurring in the anatomy of particular sections of the brain, we still have questions to answer and new avenues of inquiry to pursue. Indeed, neuroimaging of the brain still has not settled questions regarding whether the brain comes to school already preprogrammed (selectionism) or whether the brain attends school in a most malleable state ready to develop new skills and learnings (constructivism).[38]

Even with all the new advances in brain research, educators must realize that this source of curriculum design overlaps with approaches that focus on knowledge or science in that the science-based approach emphasizes strategies for processing knowledge, and the knowledge-based approach emphasizes how individuals process information. Your authors counsel readers to realize the value of melding these primary sources of curriculum design.

## Conceptual Framework: Horizontal and Vertical Organization

Curriculum design, the organization of curriculum's components, exists along two basic organizational dimensions: horizontal and vertical. *Horizontal* organization blends curriculum elements—for example, by combining history, anthropology, and sociology content to create a contemporary studies course or by combining math and science content.

*Vertical* organization refers to the sequencing of curriculum elements. Placing "the family" in first-grade social studies and "the community" in second-grade social studies is an example of vertical organization. Frequently, curricula are organized so that the same topics are addressed in different grades, but in increasing detail and at increasingly higher levels of difficulty. For instance, the mathematical concept of *set* is introduced in first grade and revisited each succeeding year in the elementary curriculum. See Curriculum Tips 6.1 for ways to create a broad curriculum design.

Although design decisions are essential, in most school districts overall, curricular designs receive little attention. The primary reason for this is that in most schools the district curriculum or textbook committee selects "the curriculum." In Texas, the State Board of Education determines the textbook or textbook series that may be considered for school district adoption. Even district curriculum/textbook committees do not give in-depth consideration to curriculum design. Most attention at district or state levels seems to go to design dimensions of scope, sequence, continuity, integration, articulation, and balance, which are discussed in the next section.

However, curricularists at the state and district levels and teachers at the classroom level should do more than just recommend content that reflects their philosophical and political views, which are frequently not carefully formulated. When considering how to design a curriculum beyond that suggested by the sequence of textbook chapters, we must contemplate carefully the socio-economic, political, and cultural factors that influence their choices about horizontal and vertical organization.[39] Curricular designs should reflect diverse voices, meanings, and points of view.[40]

---

**CURRICULUM TIPS 6.1    Points to Consider When Contemplating Curriculum Design**

Curriculum design reflects the curriculum's architecture. Here are some useful points to consider in building an effective curriculum design.

1. Reflect on your philosophical, educational, and curriculum assumptions with regard to the goals of the school (or school district).
2. Consider your students' needs and aspirations.
3. Consider the various design components and their organization.
4. Sketch out the various design components to be implemented.
5. Cross-check your selected design components (objectives, content, learning experiences, and evaluation approaches) against the school's mission.
6. Share your curriculum design with a colleague.

## DESIGN DIMENSION CONSIDERATIONS

Curriculum design addresses relationships among curriculum's components. It should achieve scope, sequence, continuity, integration, articulation, and balance.

### Scope

Curriculum designers must consider a curriculum's breadth and depth of content—that is, its *scope*. In *Basic Principles of Curriculum Instruction,* Ralph Tyler referred to *scope* as consisting of all the content, topics, learning experiences, and organizing threads comprising the educational plan.[41] John Goodlad and Zhixin Su reiterated this definition, pointing out that it refers to the curriculum's horizontal organization.[42] *Scope* includes all the types of educational experiences created to engage students in learning. It includes both cognitive and affective learning (and some might add spiritual learning).[43] Sometimes a curriculum's scope is limited to a simple listing of key topics and activities.

A curriculum's full scope can extend over a year or more. A curriculum whose scope covers only months or weeks usually is organized in units. Units are divided into lesson plans, which usually organize the information and activities into periods of hours or minutes.[44]

When teachers and other educators are deciding on curriculum content and its degree of detail, they are considering the curriculum's scope. In many ways, the current knowledge explosion has made dealing with scope almost overwhelming. Also, student diversity places increasing demands on teachers regarding which content and activities to include. Some teachers respond to content overload by ignoring certain content areas or excluding new content topics. Others attempt to interrelate certain topics to create curriculum themes.

When considering scope, we must consider learning's cognitive, affective, and psychomotor domains. (We might add the moral or spiritual domain.) We must determine what will be covered and in what detail within each domain. We must decide also which domain should be the most emphasized. Traditionally, the cognitive domain, drawing on the realm of knowledge, has been most emphasized. At the secondary level of schooling, we frequently draw on disciplines of knowledge and their main concepts to determine the curriculum's scope. However, the affective domain (dealing with values and attitudes) and the psychomotor domain (dealing with motor skills and coordination) are receiving growing attention.

### Sequence

When considering sequence, curricularists seek a curriculum that fosters cumulative and continuous learning. Specifically, curricularists must decide how content and experiences can build on what came before.[45]

There is a long-standing controversy over whether the sequence of content and experiences should be based on the logic of the subject matter or the way individuals process knowledge. Those arguing for sequence based on psychological principles draw on research on human growth, development, and learning–essentially the third big idea: Rousseau's developmental theory. Piaget's research provided a framework for sequencing content and experiences (or activities) and for relating expectations to students' cognitive levels.[46] Most school districts consider students' stages of thinking in formulating curriculum objectives, content, and experiences by grade levels. The curriculum is thus sequenced according to Piaget's theory of cognitive development.

Curriculum designers are also influenced by current research on brain development. With increasing work in neuroscience, specifically developmental neurobiology, scientists are gaining understanding leading to ways to create educational agendas to enable educators to create educational environments that contain experiences that will greatly affect the individual's brain. Ideally, curricular experiences should maximize brain development.[47]

Neuroscientists know that in the first year of life, cells that have only sparsely populated the upper layers of the cortex migrate to these layers. This migration allows for increased mental activity. An infant's brain has more synaptic connections, or links between neurons, than an adult's brain. From ages 2 to 12, these connections strengthen. They were thought to decrease in number at puberty, but recent research seems to indicate that the opportunity for creating new brain circuits continues into adulthood. During this period, the brain appears to be creating and maintaining only the hardiest dendrites (the parts of the nerve cell that accept messages) to be incorporated into the adult brain.[48] With current brain research, educators must give careful thought to the contents and experiences sequenced in the educational program.

Curricularists faced with sequencing content have drawn on some fairly well accepted learning principles. In 1957, B. Othanel Smith, William Stanley, and Harlan Shores introduced four such principles: simple-to-complex learning, prerequisite learning, whole-to-part learning, and chronological learning.

**1.** *Simple-to-complex learning* indicates that content is optimally organized in a sequence proceeding from simple subordinate components to complex components, highlighting interrelationships among components. Optimal learning results when individuals are presented with easy (often concrete) content and then with more difficult (often abstract) content.

**2.** *Prerequisite learning* is similar to part-to-whole learning. It works on the assumption that bits of information must be grasped before other bits can be comprehended.

**3.** *Whole-to-part learning* receives support from cognitive psychologists. They have urged that the curriculum be arranged so that the content or experience is first presented in an overview that provides students with a general idea of the information or situation.

**4.** *Chronological learning* refers to content whose sequence reflects the times of real-world occurrences.[49] History, political science, and world events frequently are organized chronologically.

In 1976, Gerald Posner and Kenneth Strike furnished the field of curriculum with four other types of sequencing: concept related, inquiry related, learning related, and utilization related.[50] The *concept-related* method draws heavily on the structure of knowledge. It focuses on concepts' interrelationships rather than on knowledge of the concrete. In the *inquiry-related* sequence, topics are sequenced to reflect the steps of scholarly investigation.

Instructional designers have incorporated the inquiry-related sequence into what they call *case-based reasoning,* which was developed to maximize computers' capabilities.[51] The computer applies previous learning to new situations. Similarly, people advance their knowledge by processing and organizing new experiences for later use. According to the inquiry-related model, if people fail to use acquired information, they must recognize a failure in reasoning or a deficiency in knowledge. In essence, this is how scholars advance inquiries. In the *learner-related* sequence, individuals learn through experiencing content and activities. *Utilization-related* learning focuses on how people who use knowledge or engage in a particular activity in the world actually proceed through the activity.

## Continuity

*Continuity* is vertical repetition of curriculum components. For example, if reading skills are an important objective, then, in Tyler's words, "it is necessary to see that there is recurring and continuing opportunity for these skills to be practiced and developed. This means that over time the same kinds of skills will be brought into continuing operation."[52]

Ideas and skills that educators believe students should develop over time reappear over the length of the curriculum. This continuity ensures that students revisit crucial concepts and skills. For instance, becoming a skilled reader requires numerous encounters over time with various types of reading materials. Similarly, we do not learn how to conduct experiments unless we engage in such activities at various points in the curriculum; each subsequent experiment provides the opportunity to become more sophisticated in the processes. We learn to think deeply by having myriad experiences in which thinking and questioning are enriched.

It appears that the design dimension of continuity is being supported by recent brain research to supplement research in cognitive psychology. Brain research suggests that the amount of brain employed in performing a process may explain somewhat how well an individual performs particular tasks. The research has been done with both animals and humans.[53] Tyler, as pointed out earlier, stated that if reading skills are important, then they must be experienced repeatedly to be further developed. Studies by Elbert et al., as reported in Posner and Rothbart, of long practice playing the violin seem to nurture an increase in brain tissue related to such playing.[54] This research appears to support Herbert Simon's argument that we all can become masters of something if we devote sufficient time and effort, an example of a constructivist approach to learning.

Continuity is most evident in Jerome Bruner's notion of the *spiral curriculum*. Bruner noted that the curriculum should be organized according to the interrelationships among the basic ideas and structures of each major discipline. For students to grasp these ideas and structures, "they should be developed and redeveloped in a spiral fashion," in increasing depth and breadth as pupils advance through the school program.[55]

## Integration

*Integration* refers to linking all types of knowledge and experiences contained within the curriculum plan. Essentially, it links all the curriculum's pieces so that students comprehend knowledge as unified rather than atomized.[56] Integration emphasizes horizontal relationships among topics and themes from all knowledge domains.

Curriculum theorists and practitioners tend to disproportionately emphasize integration, advocating an interdisciplinary curriculum, which is essentially a curriculum that would not be characterized as standard curriculum content. In some ways, curriculum integration is not simply a design dimension, but also a way of thinking about schools' purposes, curriculum's sources, and the nature and uses of knowledge.[57]

Advocates of curriculum integration do not advocate a multidisciplinary curriculum. In their view, such a curriculum still artificially compartmentalizes knowledge.[58] These advocates argue that the curriculum should be organized around world themes derived from real-life concerns; lines between the subject content of different disciplines should be erased.

Certainly, some integration is necessary. In the 1960s, Hilda Taba pointed out that the curriculum was disjointed, fragmented, segmented, and detached from reality. She noted that a curriculum that presents information only in bits and pieces prevents students from seeing knowledge as unified.[59]

Postmodernism, constructionism, and poststructuralism nurture continued discussion of curriculum integration, as does continued brain research. These movements advance the idea that knowledge cannot be separated from its reality, people cannot disconnect themselves from their inquiries, and the curriculum cannot exist as separate bits.

## Articulation

*Articulation* refers to the vertical and horizontal interrelatedness of various aspects of the curriculum, that is, to the ways in which curriculum components occurring later in a program's sequence relate to those occurring earlier. For instance, a teacher might design an algebra course so that it relates algebra concepts to key concepts presented in a geometry course. *Vertical articulation* usually refers to the sequencing of content from one grade level to another. Such articulation ensures that students receive necessary preparation for coursework. *Horizontal articulation* (sometimes called *correlation*) refers to the association among simultaneous elements, as when curriculum designers develop relationships between eighth-grade social studies and eighth-grade English.

When they engage in horizontal articulation, curriculum makers seek to blend contents in one part of the educational program with contents similar in logic or subject matter. For example, curricularists might link mathematical and scientific thinking. Much of the current emphasis on integrating the curriculum is an effort at horizontal articulation.

---

**CURRICULUM TIPS 6.2     Guidelines for Curriculum Design**

The following statements identify some steps that can be taken in designing a curriculum. These statements, drawn from observations of school practice, are applicable to whatever design is selected.

1. Create a curriculum design committee composed of teachers, parents, community members, administrators, and, if appropriate, students.
2. Create a schedule for meetings to make curriculum-design decisions.
3. Gather data about educational issues and suggested solutions.
4. Process data on available curriculum designs, and compare designs with regard to advantages and disadvantages such as cost, scheduling, class size, student population characteristics, students' academic strengths, adequacy of learning environments, and match with existing curricula. Also, assess whether the community is likely to accept the design.
5. Schedule time for reflection on the design.
6. Schedule time for revision of the design.
7. Explain the design to educational colleagues, community members, and, if appropriate, students.

---

Articulation is difficult to achieve, and few school districts have developed procedures by which the interrelationships among subjects are clearly defined.

Also, within school districts it is sometimes difficult to achieve articulation from one school to another. Similarly, there is a need for greater articulation among school districts. Often, students new to a school district are retaught material they learned in their former school at a lower grade level, or they miss a particular concept or topic because it was addressed in a lower grade at their new school.

## Balance

When designing a curriculum, educators strive to give appropriate weight to each aspect of the design. In a balanced curriculum, students can acquire and use knowledge in ways that advance their personal, social, and intellectual goals.

Doll points out that achieving balance is difficult because we are striving to localize and individualize the curriculum while trying to maintain a common content.[60] Keeping the curriculum balanced requires continuous fine-tuning as well as balance in our philosophy and psychology of learning. (See Curriculum Tips 6.2.)

## REPRESENTATIVE CURRICULUM DESIGNS

Curriculum components can be organized in numerous ways. However, despite all the discussion about postmodern views of knowledge and creating curricula for social awareness and emancipation, most curriculum designs are modifications or interpretations of three basic designs: (1) subject-centered designs, (2) learner-centered designs, and (3) problem-centered designs. Each of these designs attend in different degrees of emphasis to the three central ideas noted by Egan: "socialization, Plato's academic idea, and Rousseau's developmental idea."[61] Each category is composed of several examples. Subject-centered designs include subject designs, discipline designs, broad field designs, correlation designs, and process designs. Learner-centered designs are those identified as child-centered designs, experience-centered designs, romantic/radical designs, and humanistic designs. Problem-centered designs consider life situations, core designs, or social problem/reconstructionist designs.

## Subject-Centered Designs

Subject-centered designs are by far the most popular and widely used. Knowledge and content are well accepted as integral parts of the curriculum. This design draws heavily on Plato's academic idea. Schools have a strong history of academic rationalism; also, the materials available for school use reflect content organization.

Among designs, subject-centered designs have the most classifications. Concepts central to a culture are more highly elaborated than peripheral ones. In our culture, content is central to schooling; therefore, we have many concepts to interpret our diverse organizations.

**SUBJECT DESIGN.**    The subject design is both the oldest and best known school design to both teachers and laypeople. Teachers and laypersons usually are educated or trained in schools employing it. The subject design corresponds to textbook treatment and teachers' training as subject specialists. It is also emphasized because of the continued stress on school standards and accountability.

An early spokesperson for the subject curriculum was Henry Morrison, who was New Hampshire's superintendent of public instruction before he joined the University of Chicago. Morrison argued that the subject matter curriculum contributed most to literacy, which should be the focus of the elementary curriculum. He also believed that such a design allowed secondary students to develop interests and competencies in particular subject areas. However, he believed that a variety of courses should be offered to meet students' diverse needs.[62]

William Harris, superintendent of the St. Louis schools in the 1870s, also fostered subject-based curriculum design. Under his guidance, St. Louis schools established a subject-oriented curriculum. One educator notes that most Americans would recognize this curriculum design (which he classifies as the conservative liberal arts design) as the type they experienced in school. In the mid-1930s, Robert Hutchins indicated which subjects such a curriculum design were made of (1) language and its uses (reading, writing, grammar, literature), (2) mathematics, (3) sciences, (4) history, and (5) foreign languages.[63]

In subject-matter design, the curriculum is organized according to how essential knowledge has developed in various subject areas. With the explosion of knowledge and the resulting specializations in various knowledge fields, subject divisions have increased in number and sophistication. For instance, history is now divided into cultural, economic, and geographic history. English can be divided into literature, writing, speech, reading, linguistics, and grammar.

Such subject design rests on the assumption that subjects are best outlined in textbooks. In many schools the curriculum selected is in reality a textbook series. For this reason, some educators say that teachers do not need to know much about curriculum design or curriculum development. However, your authors counter that just because many "curricula" selected in schools are primarily influenced by the textbooks, educators at all levels must know about curricular design in order to make informed selections of textbooks and intelligent selections regarding organizing textbook content. Teachers still have to assume an active role in lecturing, direct instruction, recitation, and large-group discussion. Teachers have to determine avenues by which discussion proceeds from simple to complex ideas. Logic is emphasized.

Advocates of this design defend the emphasis on verbal activities, arguing that knowledge and ideas are best communicated and stored in verbal form. They also note that the subject design introduces students to essential knowledge of society. This essential knowledge of society addresses the big idea of socialization. Also, this design is easy to deliver because complementary textbooks and support materials are commercially available.

Critics, however, contend that the subject design prevents program individualization and deemphasizes the learner. Some argue that this design disempowers students by not allowing them to choose the content most meaningful to them.[64] Curricular content is presented without consideration of context. Other critics contend that stressing subject matter fails to foster social, psychological, and physical development and, to some extent, promotes a scholarly elite. Another drawback of the subject design is that learning tends to be compartmentalized and mnemonic skills tend to be stressed. The subject design stresses content and neglects students' needs, interests, and experiences. Also, in delivering such a curriculum, teachers tend to foster student passivity.

Dewey was concerned about divorcing knowledge from the learner's experiences and essentially transmitting secondhand knowledge and others' ideas.[65] For Dewey, the curriculum should emphasize both subject matter and the learner.

**DISCIPLINE DESIGN.** The discipline design, which appeared after World War II, evolved from the separate-subject design. This new design gained popularity during the 1950s and reached its zenith during the mid-1960s. As is the case of the separate-subject design, the basis of the discipline design is with content's inherent organization. However, whereas the subject design does not make clear the foundational basis on which it is organized or established, the discipline design's orientation does specify its focus on the academic disciplines.

Arthur King and John Brownell, proponents of the discipline design, long ago indicated that a *discipline* is specific knowledge that has the following essential characteristics: a community of persons, an expression of human imagination, a domain, a tradition, a mode of inquiry, a conceptual structure, a specialized language, a heritage of literature, a network of communications, a valuative and affective stance, and an instructive community.[66]

This stress on disciplined knowledge emphasizes science, mathematics, English, history, and certain other disciplines. Advocates view the school as a microcosm of the world of intellect, reflected by such disciplines. The methods by which scholars study the content of their fields suggest the ways in which students learn that content. In other words, students approach history as a historian would, and students investigate biological topics by following procedures used by biologists.

Proponents of the discipline design stress understanding the conceptual structures and processes of the disciplines. This is perhaps the essential difference between the discipline design and the subject-matter design. With the discipline design, students experience the disciplines so that they can comprehend and conceptualize; with the subject-matter design, students are considered to have learned if they simply acquire information. Sometimes it is difficult to determine whether a classroom has a subject-matter or discipline design. The key distinguishing characteristic seems to be whether students actually use some of the discipline's methods to process information. Stated differently, the subject matter design emphasizes "filling" students with knowledge, whereas the discipline design aims to foster student thinkers who can utilize information to generate knowledge and understandings. Discipline design fosters teachers teaching for intelligence.[67]

Bruner notes, "Getting to know something is an adventure in how to account for a great many things that you encounter in as simple and elegant a way as possible."[68] This "getting to know" relies on students engaging with a discipline's content and methods. So engaged, students analyze the components of the disciplined content and draw conclusions (albeit incomplete ones).

The discipline design encourages students to see each discipline's basic logic or structure—the key relationships, concepts, and principles, what Joseph Schwab called the "substantive structure"[69] and Philip Phenix called the "realms of meaning."[70] Considering structure or meaning allows a deep understanding of the content and a knowledge of how it can be applied. Harry Broudy called such knowledge (e.g., problem-solving procedures) "applicative knowledge."[71]

Students who become fluent in a discipline's modes of inquiry master the content area and are able to independently continue their learning in the field. Such students do not need the teacher to continually present information. Supporters of this design want students to function as little scholars in the school curriculum's respective fields. When learning mathematics, students are neophyte mathematicians. When studying history, they use the methods of historiography.

The emphasis on disciplines and structure led to Bruner's classic book *Process of Education.* The very title suggests that learning should emphasize process or procedural knowledge. Bruner states that a subject's curriculum "should be determined by . . . the underlying principles that give structure to that subject."[72] Organizing the curriculum according to the discipline's structure elucidates relationships, indicates how elementary knowledge is related to advanced knowledge, allows individuals to reconstruct meaning within the content area, and furnishes the means for advancing through the content area.

Bruner believed that "any subject can be taught in some effectively honest form to any child at any stage of development."[73] He argued that students can comprehend any subject's fundamental principles at almost any age. Bruner's view has been criticized as romantic. Developmentalists disagree with his thesis that "intellectual activity anywhere is the same."[74] They point out that the thinking processes of young children differ in kind and degree from those of adolescents and adults. Young boys and girls also differ in how they process information.

Many individuals both within and outside the educational community believe that the discipline design is appropriate for all students, college bound or not. The discipline design gives students opportunities to learn knowledge essential for effective living. An academic course of study meets all students' needs. Our society requires literate individuals with the skills necessary to function in an information age. The curriculum should educate students, not train them for a job (as vocational education does). In a crowded curriculum, there is neither time nor room for courses in the various trades or even for environmental studies.[75]

Many have criticized the discipline design for assuming that students must adapt to the curriculum rather than the other way around. Some also argue that the view that curriculum knowledge should mirror disciplined knowledge sustains the biases and assumptions of those who wish to maintain the status quo.[76] The discipline design is also criticized for its underlying assumption that all students have a common or a similar learning style.

Perhaps this design's greatest shortcoming is that it causes schools to ignore the vast amount of information that cannot be classified as disciplined knowledge. Such knowledge—dealing with aesthetics, humanism, personal–social living, and vocational education—is difficult to categorize as a discipline.

**BROAD-FIELDS DESIGN.** The broad-fields design (often called the *interdisciplinary design*) is another variation of the subject-centered design. It appeared as an effort to correct what many educators considered the fragmentation and compartmentalization caused by the subject design. Broad-fields designers strove to give students a sweeping understanding of all content areas.[77] They attempted to integrate content that fit together logically. Geography, economics, political science, anthropology, sociology, and history were fused into social studies. Linguistics, grammar, literature, composition, and spelling were collapsed into language arts. Biology, chemistry, and physics were integrated into general science.

The idea for the broad-fields design was both bold and simple. Essentially, educators could simply meld two or more related subjects, already well known in the schools, into a single broader field of study. However, this design was a change from traditional subject patterns. Although it first appeared at the college level in the 1910s, it became most popular at the elementary and secondary levels. This continues to be the case. Today the broad-fields design is seen at the college level only in introductory courses, but it is widespread within the K–12 curriculum.

Harry Broudy and colleagues offered a unique broad-fields design during the Sputnik era. They suggested that the entire curriculum be organized into these categories: (1) symbolics of information (English, foreign languages, and mathematics), (2) basic sciences (general science, biology, physics, and chemistry), (3) developmental studies (evolution of the cosmos, of social institutions, and of human culture), (4) exemplars (modes of aesthetic experience, including art, music, drama, and literature), and (5) "molar problems," which address typical social problems.[78] This last category entails an annual variety of courses, depending on current social problems.

The broad-fields design still brings together well-accepted content fields. Some curricularists prefer that broad fields consist of related conceptual clusters rather than subjects or disciplines combined in interdisciplinary organization. These clusters can be connected by themes.

Some educators are calling for the organization of curriculum as integrated thematic units. Others are using the term *holistic curriculum.*[79]

The broad-fields design can be interpreted as saying that the separate subject is dead. Rather, we should have a design that draws on emergent clusters of problems and questions that engages students in constructing and reconstructing information.[80]

Much of broad-fields design focuses on *curriculum webs,* connections among related themes or concepts. Many years ago, Taba discussed the concept of webs when urging teachers to create cognitive maps in constructing curriculum.[81]

The broad-fields design may be the most active in the future, allowing for hybrid forms of content and knowledge in the curriculum and for student participation in constructing knowledge.

Like other designs, this design has its problems. One is breadth at the expense of depth. A year of social studies teaches students a greater range of social science concepts than a year of history. But, is the resulting knowledge of social sciences superficial? Certainly, a year of history builds more historical knowledge than a year of social studies. Is it necessary to have great depth at the elementary level? Is it not the purpose of the curriculum to acquaint students with the complete field of social science?

The issue of depth is even more central when we expand the broad-fields design to an integrated curriculum design. Just how much depth will students get following or constructing webs of related concepts? How much depth can one attain in science by following the theme of dinosaurs or machines? In whole language, will students attain a sufficiently deep appreciation of reading, writing, and listening? The philosophies of schools and educators influence their responses.

**CORRELATION DESIGN.**  Correlation designers do not wish to create a broad-fields design but realize there are times when separate subjects require linkage to avoid fragmentation of curricular content. Midway between separate subjects and total content integration, the correlation design attempts to identify ways in which subjects can be related, yet maintain their separate identities.

Perhaps the most frequently correlated subjects are English literature and history at the secondary level and language arts and social studies at the elementary level. While studying a historical period, students read novels related to the same period in their English class. Science and mathematics courses are also frequently correlated. Students in a chemistry course may have a unit in math that deals with the mathematics required to conduct an experiment. However, the content areas remain distinct, and the teachers of these courses retain their subject-matter specialties.

In the 1950s and 1960s, many found the notion of correlation design attractive. Harold and Elsie Alberty discussed correlated curriculum at the secondary level. They presented a correlation design with an "overarching theme." This thematic organizer retained subjects' basic content, but it was selected and organized with reference to broad themes, problems, or units.[82] It required that classes be scheduled within a block of time. Teachers of the various content areas to be correlated could then work together and have students work on assignments drawing from the correlated content areas. Subjects can be combined in innovative ways. For example, it is possible to relate literature and art that depict similar content. Science can be taught through literature. Courses in computer science might be correlated with courses in art, music, or economics.

Currently, few teachers use correlation design, possibly because it requires that they plan their lessons cooperatively. This is somewhat difficult to accomplish because teachers have self-contained classes at the elementary level and often do not have time for such collaboration. At the secondary level, teachers are organized into separate departments that tend to encourage isolation. Teachers must also meet time schedules dictated by specific classes and so may have little time to work with other teachers on team teaching. Also, most class schedules do not allow a block of time sufficient for students to meaningfully study correlated subjects. Modular scheduling and flexible scheduling, which allow for this, have not been widely accepted.

**PROCESS DESIGNS.**   As previously discussed, attention is often given to the procedures and processes by which individuals obtain knowledge. Students studying biology learn methods for dealing with biological knowledge, students in history classes learn the ways of historiography, and students investigating anthropology learn ethnographic procedures appropriate for studying culture and society.

Although advocates of the disciplines design urge students to learn process, other educators are suggesting curricular designs that stress the learning of general procedures applicable to all disciplines. Curricula for teaching critical thinking exemplify this procedural design.

Educators always have suggested that students be taught to think. Curricular designs must address how learners learn and the application of process to subject matter. "The good thinker, possessing attributes enabling him or her to create and use meaning . . . possesses a spirit of inquiry, a desire to pose questions central to the world. The good thinker ponders the world, actual and desired, querying things valued and desired."[83] Process designs focus on the student as meaning maker.

Process designs focus on teaching for intelligence and on the development of intellectual character. Ron Ritchhart borrowed this term from Tishman[84] to cluster particular dispositions requisite for effective and productive thinking. Intellectual character goes beyond a listing of abilities and the speed of enactment of those abilities, or the retrieval of detailed information. In Ritchhart's thinking, *intellectual character* "recognizes the role of attitude and affect in everyday cognition and the importance of developed patterns of behavior."[85] Intellectual character encompasses sets of dispositions that actually shape and activate intellectual behavior.

Process designs emphasize those procedures that enable students to analyze reality and create frameworks by which to arrange derived knowledge. Often the organizational frameworks differ from the way the world appears to the casual observer.[86] There is much dialogue about involving students in their learning and empowering them to be the central players in the classroom. However, there is much debate regarding the nature of the process to be stressed. Some postmodernists criticize process designs that privilege the scientific method and imply the existence of a fully objective reality. Students must realize that methods of inquiry result in a world that, to some extent, they construct.[87]

In process designs that reflect a modern orientation, students learn the process of knowledge acquisition in order to reach some degree of consensus. However, people such as Jean-François Lyotard argue that we engage in process not to reach consensus but to search for instabilities. Postmodern process design stresses statements and ideas that are open to challenge; designs are organized so that students can continually revise their understandings.[88]

Bruner and others call this continual revision *hermeneutic composition*. The challenge of a process curriculum is to analyze the validity of our conclusions and to determine the "rightness" of our interpretation of a text or content realm by reference not to observed reality but to other interpretations by scholars.[89] The authors of this text believe that we could engage in hermeneutic analysis and determine the rightness of conclusions based on the observation of actual phenomena.

A postmodern process-design curriculum has students do more than simply analyze their conclusions. It encourages them to unravel the processes by which they investigate and reach conclusions. Students are to study their information-processing methods in order to gain insights into how knowledge is generated.[90] Postmodern process design emphasizes the role of language in constructing as well as representing reality. Process designs may be the most dynamic in the future. It is quite likely that they will increasingly meld with designs identified as learner centered.

### Learner-Centered Designs

All curricularists wish to create curricula valuable to students. In response to educational planners who valued subject matter, educators in the early 1900s asserted that students were the program's focus. Progressives advocated what have come to be called *learner-centered designs*.

These designs are found more frequently at the elementary than the secondary school level. In elementary schools, teachers tend to stress the whole child. At the secondary level, the emphasis is more on subject-centered designs, largely because of the influence of textbooks and the colleges and universities at which the discipline is a major organizer for the curriculum. Learner-centered designs essentially stress two of the three big ideas regarding thinking about education: socialization and Rousseau's developmental ideas.[91]

**CHILD-CENTERED DESIGN.**    Advocates of child- or student-centered design believe that students must be active in their learning environments and that learning should not be separated from students' lives, as is often the case with subject-centered designs. Instead, the design should be based on students' lives, needs, and interests.

Attending to students' needs and interests requires careful observation of students and faith that they can articulate those needs and interests. Also, young students' interests must have educational value.[92]

People with this view consider knowledge as an outgrowth of personal experience. People use knowledge to advance their goals and construct it from their interactions with their world. Learners actively construct their own understandings. Learning is not the passive reception of information from an authority. Students must have classroom opportunities to explore, firsthand, physical, social, emotional, and logical knowledge.[93] This view has a long history. John Locke noted that individuals construct bodies of knowledge from a foundation of simple ideas derived from their experiences. Immanuel Kant postulated that aspects of our knowledge result from our cognitive actions; we construct our universe to have certain properties.[94] The shift in emphasis from subject matter to children's needs and interests was part of Rousseau's educational philosophy, as expressed in his 1762 book, *Emile*. Rousseau believed that children should be taught within the context of their natural environment, not in an artificial one like a classroom.[95] Teaching must suit a child's developmental level.

Proponents of child-centered design draw on the thinking of some other pedagogical giants. Heinrich Pestalozzi and Friedrich Froebel argued that children attain self-realization through social participation; they voiced the principle of learning by doing. Their social approach to education furnished a foundation for much of Francis Parker's work.

Child-centered design, often attributed to Dewey, was actually conceived by Parker, who laid its foundations. Parker had studied pedagogy in Germany, and he knew the work of Pestalozzi and Froebel. Like Rousseau, Parker believed that effective education did not require strict discipline. Rather, the instructional approach should be somewhat free, drawing on the child's innate tendency to become engaged in interesting things. Teachers who involved children in conversations would find that they could effectively participate in their own learning. Parker put his views of teaching into practice in developing science and geography curricula. He urged geography teachers to have children experience the content as a geographer out in the field would, by making observations, recording them in sketchbooks, and analyzing them. Parker was superintendent of schools in Quincy, Massachusetts, and his approach to curriculum was called the Quincy system.[96]

Dewey's early thinking entailed similar notions. In 1896, he put some of his ideas into action in his laboratory school at the University of Chicago. The curriculum was organized around human impulses: the impulses to socialize, construct, inquire, question, experiment, and express or create artistically.[97]

The emphasis on the child displaced the emphasis on subject matter. Also, when subject matter was presented, it no longer was separated into narrow divisions but was integrated around units of experience or social problems. The idea that solving a problem required methods and materials from several subject fields was inherent in the child-centered, experience-centered curriculum. This new emphasis on the learner also led to "life needs," "life-adjustment education," "persistent life situations," "common learnings," and "core" methods of organizing bodies of knowledge and subject matter.[98] The idea was to integrate subject matter from various fields to understand and solve social problems and to meet students' developmental needs.

Child-centered curriculum design flourished in the 1920s and 1930s, primarily though the work of the progressives such as Ellsworth Collings (who introduced the child-centered curriculum into the public schools of McDonald County, Missouri) and William Kilpatrick (who created the *project method,* which engaged children in their learning at the Lincoln School in New York City).[99] Although the project method was written up and extensively discussed in the literature, it gained only limited acceptance.

Today some schools employ child-centered designs. However, as John Goodlad and Zhixin Su point out, such designs are often found to contradict a view of curriculum as primarily content driven.[100] There are attempts by some curricularists to have more educators accept child-centered design by way of negotiated curriculum, which involves student–teacher negotiations regarding which content addresses what interests. Teachers and students participate in planning the unit, its purposes, the content focuses, the activities, and even the materials to be used.[101]

Having students negotiate the curriculum empowers them. It gives them opportunities to construct their own curricula and learning.[102]

**EXPERIENCE-CENTERED DESIGN.** Experience-centered curriculum designs closely resemble child-centered designs in that children's concerns are the basis for organizing children's school world. However, they differ from child-centered designs in that children's needs and interests cannot be anticipated; therefore, a curriculum framework cannot be planned for all children.

The notion that a curriculum cannot be preplanned, that everything must be done "on the spot" as a teacher reacts to each child, makes experienced-center design almost impossible to implement. It also ignores the vast amount of information available about children's growth and development—cognitive, affective, emotional, and social.

Those favoring a child or experience-centered curriculum heavily emphasize the learners' interests, creativity, and self-direction. The teacher's task is to create a stimulating learning environment in which students can explore, come into direct contact with knowledge, and observe others' learning and actions. Learning is a social activity. Students essentially design their own learning; they construct and revise their knowledge through direct participation and active observation.[103]

At the beginning of the 1900s, Dewey noted that children's spontaneous power—their demand for self-expression—cannot be suppressed. For Dewey, interest was purposeful. In *Experience and Education,* he noted that education should commence with the experience learners already possessed when they entered school. Experience was essentially the starting point for all further learning.[104] Dewey further noted that children exist in a personal world of experiences. Their interests are personal concerns rather than bodies of knowledge and their attendant facts, concepts, generalizations, and theories.

Even so, Dewey never advocated making children's interests the curriculum or placing children in the role of curriculum makers. He commented, "The easy thing is to seize upon something in the nature of the child, or upon something in the developed consciousness of the adult, and insist upon that as the key to the whole problem."[105]

Dewey wanted educators to analyze children's experiences and see how these experiences shaped children's knowledge. One searched for starting points, places where the child's natural interests could be linked to formalized knowledge. Dewey wanted educators to think of the child's experience as fluid and dynamic. Thus, the curriculum would continually change to address students' needs.[106]

Dewey contended that the subjects studied in the curriculum are formalized learnings derived from children's experiences. The content is systematically organized as a result of careful reflection.

Those who subscribe to experience-centered curriculum design have faith in each student's uniqueness and ability. They believe that an open and free school environment stimulates all students to excel. Students in optimal school environments are self-motivated; the educator's role is to provide opportunities, not to mandate certain actions. Thomas Armstrong speaks of creating a genial classroom environment, one that exudes a festive atmosphere and capitalizes on students' natural disposition to learn. Such an environment celebrates students' freedom to choose. It does not demand that they think and study in particular ways in order to succeed. This does not mean that students are left to drift in their academic efforts. The teacher who has designed an experience-centered curriculum has designed potential experiences for students to consider. Students are empowered to shape their own learning within the context furnished by the teacher.[107]

**ROMANTIC (RADICAL) DESIGN.**    More recently, reformers who advocate radical school modi-fication have stressed learner-centered design. These individuals essentially adhere to Rous-seau's posture on the value of attending to the nature of individuals and Pestalozzi's thinking that individuals can find their true selves by looking to their own nature. Although their thinking appears progressive, they draw primarily on the views of more recent philosophers: Jurgen Habermas, a German philosopher, and Paulo Freire, a radical Brazilian educator.

Individuals in the radical camp believe that schools have organized themselves, their cur-riculum, and their students in stratifications that are not benign. The ways schools are, the curricu-lar designs selected or stressed, and the content selected and organized result from people's careful planning and intent. And the intent is to continue the dominant social segments of the nation so that advantages these segments enjoy will continue without challenge from those people deemed subordinate.[108] School curricular designs, school curricula, and the administration of schools' programs are planned and manipulated to reflect and address the desires of those in power. Educa-tors in the radical camp work to alter this dividing of students into haves and have nots.

Radicals consider that presently schools are using their curricula to control students and indoctrinate rather than educate and emancipate. Students in "have" societies are manipulated to believe that what they have and will learn is good and just, whereas students in the "have-not" societies are shaped to gladly accept their subordinate positions. Curricula are organized to foster in students a belief in and desire for a common culture that does not actually exist and to promote intolerance of difference.[109]

Freire's *Pedagogy of the Oppressed* influenced the thinking of some present-day radicals. Freire believed that education should enlighten the masses about their oppression, prompt them to feel dissatisfied with their condition, and give them the competencies necessary for correcting the identified inequities.[110]

Many radicals draw on the theory of Jurgen Habermas, who emphasizes that education's goal is emancipation of the awarenesses, competencies, and attitudes that people need to take control of their lives. In this view, educated people do not follow social conventions without reflection. In writing about Habermas and his critical theory of education, Robert Young notes that the theme of emancipation dates back to Roman times and was also expressed by many Enlightenment philosophers. Students must accept responsibility for educating themselves and demand freedom.[111]

Radical curricularists believe that individuals must learn to critique knowledge. Learning is reflective; it is not externally imposed by someone in power. William Ayers posits that stu-dents should be invited by the teacher not to just "learn" the curricula, but to travel and to experi-ence the curricula as coadventures and, perhaps at times, coconspirators. To Ayers, "curriculum is an ongoing engagement with the problem of determining what knowledge and experiences are the most worthwhile."[112] Teachers function as "awareness makers." They are present within the curricular arena to "expose, offer, encourage, stimulate,"[113] and your authors would add to chal-lenge, create awe and wonder, and nurture inquisitiveness.

Curricula in the radical camp are characterized by teacher and students' actions that break barriers, challenge and unpack preconceptions, critically analyze theories, and discover new ways to process significant questions. And, curricula are perceived essentially as all the materi-als offered and implied and all the experiences planned and unplanned that happen both inside and outside the school.[114]

Curricula are not just endpoints or waypoints on a predetermined school journey. Curricula are a universe of possibilities and of limitless avenues of inquiry, a plethora of experiences that engage the minds, the bodies, and the spirits of teachers and students. Such curricula are exploding galaxies of intended and unintended consequences.

Although your authors do not characterize themselves as radical curricularists, they do believe that many, if not most, of the features of the radical curricular design should be incorporated into more traditional designs. Students should be challenged in their learning; students should have adventures in total learning in cognitive, physical, emotional, and spiritual realms. Education is an adventure!

Perhaps the biggest difference between mainstream educators and radicals is that radicals view society as deeply flawed and believe that education indoctrinates students to serve controlling groups. Many radicals view the Western intellectual tradition, and its standard curricula, as imperialistic and oppressive. Curricula with a radical design address social and economic inequality and injustice. Radical educators are overtly political.

**HUMANISTIC DESIGN.**   Humanistic designs gained prominence in the 1960s and 1970s, partly in response to the excessive emphasis on the disciplines during the 1950s and early 1960s. Humanistic education appeared in the 1920s and 1930s as part of progressive philosophy and the whole-child movement in psychology. After World War II, humanistic designs connected to existentialism in educational philosophy.

Humanistic psychology developed in the 1950s in opposition to the then-dominant psychological school of behaviorism. This new psychological orientation emphasized that human action was much more than a response to a stimulus, that meaning was more important than methods, that the focus of attention should be on the subjective rather than objective nature of human existence, and that there is a relationship between learning and feeling.

Within this context, the Association for Supervision and Curriculum Development (ASCD) published its 1962 yearbook, *Perceiving, Behaving, Becoming.*[115] This book represented a new focus for education—an approach to curricular design and instructional delivery that would allow individuals to become fully functioning persons. Arthur Combs, the yearbook's chairperson, posed some key questions: What kind of person achieves self-realization? What goes into making such a person?[116] The emphasis was on empowering individuals by actively involving them in their own growth.

The ASCD's 1977 yearbook, *Feeling, Valuing, and the Art of Growing,* also stressed the affective dimensions of humanistic educational designs and emphasized human potential. It suggested that educators must permit students to feel, value, and grow.[117]

Abraham Maslow's concept of self-actualization heavily influenced humanistic design. Maslow listed the characteristics of a self-actualized person: (1) accepting of self, others, and nature; (2) spontaneous, simple, and natural; (3) problem oriented; (4) open to experiences beyond the ordinary; (5) empathetic and sympathetic toward the less fortunate; (6) sophisticated in interpersonal relations; (7) favoring democratic decision making; and (8) possessing a philosophical sense of humor.[118] Maslow emphasized that people do not self-actualize until they are 40 or older, but the process begins when they are students. Some educators miss this point and think that their humanistic designs will have students attain self-actualization as an end product.

Carl Rogers's work has been another major humanistic force. Rogers advocates self-directed learning, in which students draw on their own resources to improve self-understanding and guide their own behavior. Educators should provide an environment that encourages genuineness, empathy, and respect for self and others.[119] Students in such an environment naturally develop into what Rogers called fully functioning people. Individuals able to initiate action and take responsibility are capable of intelligent choice and self-direction. Rogers stressed knowledge relevant to problem solving. Classroom questions foster learning and deep thinking. The quest is collaborative and the inquiries are multidisciplinary. There is no need to "stay within discipline lines." Mistakes are accepted as part of the learning process. Conclusions are regarded as temporary. Students approach problems with flexibility and intelligence; they work coopera-tively but do not need others' approval.[120]

In the 1970s, humanistic education absorbed the notion of *confluence*. Confluence educa-tion blends the affective domain (feelings, attitudes, values) with the cognitive domain (intel-lectual knowledge and problem-solving abilities). It adds the affective component to the conventional subject-matter curriculum.[121]

Confluent education stresses participation; it emphasizes power sharing, negotiation, and joint responsibility. It also stresses the whole person and the integration of thinking, feeling, and acting. It centers on subject matter's relevance to students' needs and lives.

Humanistic educators realize that the cognitive, affective, and psychomotor domains are interconnected and that curricula should address these dimensions. Some humanistic educators would add the social and spiritual domains as well.[122]

Some humanistic designs stress intuition, creative thinking, and a holistic perception of reality. They produce curricula that prioritize the uniqueness of the human personality but also transcendence of individuality. As Phenix notes, such a curriculum presents reality as a "single interconnected whole, such that a complete description of any entity would require the compre-hension of every other entity."[123]

James Moffett suggests that a curriculum that emphasizes spirituality enables students to enter "on a personal spiritual path unique to each that nevertheless entails joining increasingly expansive memberships of humanity and nature."[124] He cautions that society must foster moral-ity and spirituality, not just knowledge and power. Transcendent education is hope, creativity, awareness, doubt and faith, wonder, awe, and reverence.[125] (See Curriculum Tips 6.3.)

For humanists, education should address pleasure and desire such as aesthetic pleasure. Emphasizing natural and human-created beauty, humanistic curriculum designs allow students to experience learning with emotion, imagination, and wonder. Curricular content should elicit emotion as well as thought. It should address not only the conceptual structures of knowledge but also its implications. The curriculum design should allow students to formulate a perceived individual and social good, and encourage them to participate in a community.[126]

---

## CURRICULUM TIPS 6.3   The Curriculum Matrix

In designing a curriculum, keep in mind the various levels at which we can consider the curriculum's con-tent components. The following list of curriculum dimensions should assist in considering content in depth.

1. Consider the content's intellectual dimension. This is perhaps curriculum's most commonly thought of dimension. The content selected should stimulate students' intellectual development.
2. Consider the content's emotional dimension. We know much less about this dimension, but we are obtaining a better understanding of it as the affective domain of knowledge.
3. Consider the content's social dimension. The content selected should contribute to students' social development and stress human relations.
4. Consider the content's physical dimension, commonly referred to as the *psychomotor domain of knowledge*. Content should be selected to develop physical skills and allow students to become more physically self-aware.
5. Consider the content's aesthetic dimension. People have an aesthetic dimension, yet we currently have little knowledge of aesthetics' place in education.
6. Consider the content's transcendent or spiritual dimension, which most public schools almost totally exclude from consideration. We tend to confuse this dimension with formal religion. This content dimension does not directly relate to the rational. However, we must have content that causes students to reflect on the nature of their humanness and helps them transcend their current levels of knowledge and action.

*Source:* Information from Arthur W. Foshay, "The Curriculum Matrix: Transcendence and Mathematics," *Curricu-lum* (Autumn 1990), pp. 36–46.

Although humanistic curricular designs have great potential, they have many of the same weaknesses as learner-centered designs. They require that teachers have great skill and competence in dealing with individuals. For many teachers, they also require almost a complete change of mindset because they value the social, emotional, and spiritual realms above the intellectual realm. Also, available educational materials often are not appropriate.

One criticism of humanistic design is that it fails to adequately consider the consequences for learners. Another criticism is that its emphasis on human uniqueness conflicts with its emphasis on activities that all students experience. Yet another criticism is that humanistic design overemphasizes the individual, ignoring society's needs. Finally, some critics charge that humanistic design does not incorporate insight from behaviorism and cognitive developmental theory.

## Problem-Centered Designs

The third major type of curriculum design, problem-centered design, focuses on real-life problems of individuals and society. Problem-centered curriculum designs are intended to reinforce cultural traditions and address unmet needs of the community and society. They are based on social issues.[127]

Problem-centered designs place the individual within a social setting, but they differ from learner-centered designs in that they are planned before the students' arrival (although they can then be adjusted to students' concerns and situations).

With problem-centered design, a curricular organization depends in large part on the nature of the problems to be studied. The content often extends beyond subject boundaries. It must also address students' needs, concerns, and abilities. This dual emphasis on both content and learners' development distinguishes problem-centered design from the other major types of curriculum design.

Some problem-centered designs focus on persistent life situations. Others center on contemporary social problems. Still others address areas of living. Some are even concerned with reconstructing society. The various types of problem-centered design differ in the degrees to which they emphasize social needs, as opposed to individual needs.[128]

**LIFE-SITUATIONS DESIGN.** Life-situations curriculum design can be traced back to the 19th century and Herbert Spencer's writings on a curriculum for complete living. Spencer's curriculum emphasized activities that (1) sustain life, (2) enhance life, (3) aid in rearing children, (4) maintain the individual's social and political relations, and (5) enhance leisure, tasks, and feelings.[129] The Commission on the Reorganization of Secondary Education, sponsored by the National Education Association, recommended this design in 1918. The commission outlined a curriculum that would deal with health, command of fundamentals, "worthy home membership," vocation, citizenship, leisure, and ethical character.

Three assumptions are fundamental to life-situations design: (1) dealing with persistent life situations is crucial to a society's successful functioning, and it makes educational sense to organize a curriculum around them; (2) students see the relevance of content if it is organized around aspects of community life; and (3) having students study social or life situations will directly involve them in improving society.

One strength of life-situations design is its focus on problem-solving procedures. Process and content are effectively integrated into curricular experience. Some critics contend that the students do not learn much subject matter. However, proponents counter that life-situations design draws heavily from traditional content. What makes the design unique is that the content is organized in ways that allow students to clearly view problem areas.

Another strong feature of life-situations design is that it uses learners' past and present experiences to get them to analyze the basic aspects of living. In this respect, the design significantly differs from experience-centered design, in which the felt needs and interests of learners are the sole basis for content and experience selection. The life-situations design takes students' existing concerns, as well as society's pressing problems, as a starting point.

Life-situations design integrates subject matter, cutting across separate subjects and centering on related categories of social life. It encourages students to learn and apply problem-solving procedures. Linking subject matter to real situations increases the curriculum's relevance.

However, it is challenging to determine the scope and sequence of living's essential aspects. Are major activities of today going to be essential activities in the future?

Some critics believe that life-situations design does not adequately expose students to their cultural heritage; moreover, it tends to indoctrinate youth to accept existing conditions and thus perpetuates the social status quo. However, if students are educated to be critical of their social situations, they will intelligently assess, rather than blindly adhere to, the status quo.

Some critics contend that teachers lack adequate preparation to mount life-situations curriculum. Others argue that textbooks and other teaching materials inhibit the implementation of such a curriculum. Further, many teachers are uncomfortable with life-situations design because it departs too much from their training. Finally, life-situations organization departs from the traditional curriculum promoted by secondary schools, colleges, and universities.

**RECONSTRUCTIONIST DESIGN.**    Educators who favor reconstructionist design believe that the curriculum should foster social action aimed at reconstructing society; it should promote society's social, political, and economic development. These educators want curricula to advance social justice.

Aspects of reconstructionism first appeared in the 1920s and 1930s. George Counts believed that society must be totally reorganized to promote the common good. The times demanded a new social order, and schools should play a major role in such redesign. Counts presented some of his thinking in a speech entitled, "Dare Progressive Education Be Progressive?"[130] He challenged the Progressive Education Association to broaden its thinking beyond the current social structure and accused its members of advocating only curricula that perpetuated middle-class dominance and privilege. Counts expanded on his call for a reconstructed society in *Dare the Schools Build a New Social Order?* He argued that curricula should involve students in creating a more equitable society.[131]

Harold Rugg also believed that schools should engage children in critical analysis of society in order to improve it. Rugg criticized child-centered schools, contending that their laissez-faire approach to curriculum development produced a chaos of disjointed curriculum and rarely involved a careful review of a child's educational program.[132] In the 1940s, he observed that the Progressive Education Association still overemphasized the child. The association's seven stated purposes all referred to the child; not one took "crucial social conditions and problems" into consideration.[133]

Theodore Brameld, who advocated reconstructionism well into the 1950s, argued that reconstructionists were committed to facilitating the emergence of a new culture. The times demanded a new social order; existing society displayed decay, poverty, crime, racial conflict, unemployment, political oppression, and the destruction of the environment.[134] Such an argument certainly remains relevant. Brameld believed that schools should help students develop into social beings dedicated to the common good.

The primary purpose of the social reconstructionist curriculum is to engage students in critical analysis of the local, national, and international community in order to address humanity's problems. Attention is given to the political practices of business and government groups and their impact on the workforce. The curriculum encourages industrial and political changes.

Today, educators who believe that curricula should address social inequality and injustice tend to call themselves reconceptualists rather than reconstructionists. However, like reconstructionists, they believe that the curriculum should provide students with the learning requisite for altering social, economic, and political realities. We could classify reconceptualists as a variation of curricular radicals, the difference being that reconceptualists may not deem as given that the Western intellectual tradition and its standard curricula are imperialistic and oppressive. Rather, reconceptualists accept that the world is dynamic and ever changing, requiring that curricula must present myriad possibilities of learning and reacting.

## The Shadows Within Curricula

Most people, educators included, think of the curriculum as a plan with identified materials, contents, and experiences. As Ayers indicates, this plan deals with two questions: Are the materials, contents, and experiences of educational worth? By what means can educators get students to optimize their utilization of the materials, content, and experiences so that a more complete understanding is attained rather than a mere knowing?[135]

But, the planned and visible curriculum, including contents, materials, and planned experiences, is also accompanied by "shadow curricula." Such shadow curricula are briefly discussed in Chapter 1: the operational curriculum, the hidden curriculum, the implicit curriculum, and the null curriculum. All curricula, regardless of design, have these shadow curricula.

The operational curriculum is the curriculum that actually gets taught or that emerges as a result of the teachers selecting particular aspects of the planned curriculum. Teachers decide what aspects of the content to stress, what materials to use, what experiences to provide students, and what motivational prompts to employ. The teacher's decisions are influenced by his or her "read" of the community's and the school's political, social, and philosophical views and beliefs. Also impacting the teacher's instructional choices are his or her own educational, political, social, and even economic histories. A teacher's curricular choices also are influenced by experiences brought into the classroom and the teacher's personality.

The hidden curriculum, as previously indicated, arises from the interactions among students and between students and teachers. Essentially, the hidden curriculum presents content and understandings that are implicit in the operational curriculum. And, the hidden curriculum can be influenced by the sequencing and emphases of the operational curriculum content and engaged experiences.[136] Even teachers' instructional strategies, and particularly their questions, influence the hidden curriculum either positively or negatively. A skillful or devious teacher can use the hidden curriculum for propaganda or indoctrination purposes. We might not think teachers of this stripe exist in schools, but many teachers fearful about their job security do, in fact, engage in such action, partly in response to community political dispositions and mores. Intangible aspects of community life do have an impact on the formal, the operational, and the hidden curriculum, as well as the null curriculum, discussed next.

The *null curriculum,* as discussed by Eisner, refers to curriculum content, values, and experiences that are omitted by the teacher but recognized as being ignored by students, community, or both. They often are controversial topics.[137] Also, the null curriculum can relate to ways of learning. Some schools, even though they might deny it, do not want students taught to challenge authority, or, as Ayers notes, be coconspirators in modifying the curriculum.[138]

Shadow curricula exist because curricula are the products of humans. Educators make decisions about what content to teach and what experiences contribute to a student's total development. Teachers make some decisions without comprehending all the consequences of those decisions. Students make decisions also: whether to accept or reject content presented or experiences provided. Students are influenced in myriad ways by their home environment, their family's culture, and their prior educational experiences. There are a multitude of factors that influence the actions of all the players in the educational drama. For students of curriculum, it is important to study the "shadows" of curriculum within the focus of curriculum design. A tree exists on a hillside, and it casts its shadow. We must study the tree, but perhaps more can be learned if we focus on the shadow. What impact does the shadow have on the plants within it? How might we learn about the effectiveness of a particular design by looking at its shadow?

# Conclusion

Curriculum design, especially currently, is a complex activity both conceptually and in its implementation. Designing a curriculum requires a vision of education's meaning and purpose. But the complexity of curriculum designs is largely fueled by myriad educational visions. These visions play into the dynamics of educational dialogue, increasingly challenging and often contentious. Not surprisingly, as we reflect more deeply on why we educate, and as we gain new insights from research, especially brain research, we often become overwhelmed regarding just how to structure a curriculum so as to optimize student learning and satisfy a cacophony of community voices, from local to national. Despite this expanding universe of voices regarding the purpose or purposes of schools, we cannot avoid our responsibilities as educators. Curriculum design, more than

ever, must be carefully considered so that the curriculum imparts essential understandings, attitudes, and skills.

Educators do not have to start from scratch when considering curriculum design. They can choose from subject-, learner-, and problem-centered design, each of which has a history and is associated with a particular philosophy. However, while these designs are familiar to us all, we must realize that current research and philosophical inquiry are furnishing us with new supports for these various designs. We must also be cognizant of the diverse communities that designs attract. Additionally, we must welcome hybrid and entirely new designs that meld new technologies. Lest we feel completely overwhelmed, remember that new designs contain the same basic design components. Table 6.1 presents an overview of the major designs currently in use.

**Table 6.1** Overview of Major Curriculum Designs

| Design | Curricular Emphasis | Underlying Philosophy | Source | Spokespeople |
|---|---|---|---|---|
| **Subject Centered** | | | | |
| Subject design | Separate subjects | Essentialism, perennialism | Science, knowledge | Harris, Hutchins |
| Discipline design | Scholarly disciplines (mathematics, biology, psychology, etc.) | Essentialism, perennialism | Knowledge, science | Bruner, Phenix, Schwab, Taba |
| Broad-fields design | Interdisciplinary subjects and scholarly disciplines | Essentialism, progressivism | Knowledge, society | Broudy, Dewey |
| Correlation design | Separate subjects, disciplines linked but their separate identities maintained | Progressivism, essentialism | Knowledge | Alberty, Alberty |
| Process design | Procedural knowledge of various disciplines; generic ways of information processing, thinking | Progressivism | Psychology, knowledge | Adams, Dewey, Papert |
| **Learner Centered** | | | | |
| Child-centered design | Child's interests and needs | Progressivism | Child | Dewey, Kilpatrick, Parker |
| Experience-centered design | Child's experiences and interests | Progressivism | Child | Dewey, Rugg, Shumaker |
| Radical design | Child's experiences and interests | Reconstructionism | Child, society | Freire, Habermas, Holt, Illich |
| Humanistic design | Experiences, interests, needs of person and group | Reconstructionism, existentialism | Psychology, child, society | Combs, Fantini, Maslow, Rogers |
| **Problem Centered** | | | | |
| Life-situations design | Life (social) problems | Reconstructionism | Society | Spencer |
| Reconstructionist design | Focus on society and its problems | Reconstructionism | Society, eternal truths | Apple, Brameld, Counts, Rugg |

## Endnotes

1. David W. Orr, *Earth in Mind: On Education, Environment, and the Human Prospect* (Washington, DC: Island Press, 2004).
2. Ibid.
3. Ron Ritchhart, *Intellectual Character* (San Francisco, CA: Jossey-Bass, 2002).
4. Ibid.
5. Ibid.
6. Kieran Egan, *The Future of Education* (New Haven: Yale University Press, 2008).
7. Ibid, p. 9.
8. Ibid.
9. Ibid.
10. Ibid.
11. Ibid.
12. Ibid., p. 28.
13. Deborah Meier, "Racing through Childhood," in Brenda S. Engel with Ann C. Martin, eds., *Holding Values: What We Mean by Progressive Education* (Portsmouth, NH: Heinemann, 2005), pp. 122–128.
14. Egan, *The Future of Education.*
15. H. H. Giles, S. P. McCutchen, and A. N. Zechiel, *Exploring the Curriculum* (New York: Harper, 1942), p. 2.
16. William F. Pinar, William M. Reynolds, Patrick Slattery, and Peter M. Taubman, *Understanding Curriculum* (New York: Peter Lang, 1995).
17. Ronald C. Doll, *Curriculum Improvement: Decision Making and Process,* 9th ed. (Boston: Allyn & Bacon, 1996).
18. David J. Ferrero, "Pathways to Reform: Start with Values," *Educational Leadership* (February 2005), pp. 8–14.
19. Doll, *Curriculum Improvement.*
20. Ralph W. Tyler, *Basic Principles of Curriculum and Instruction* (Chicago: University of Chicago Press, 1949).
21. Egan, *The Future of Education.*
22. Timothy A. Hacsi. *Children as Pawns: The Politics of Educational Renewal* (Cambridge, MA: Harvard University Press, 2002).
23. Andrew Thurston, "The Texas Textbook Showdown," at SED, Boston University School of Education (Fall 2010), pp. 6–9.
24. James Moffett, *The Universal School House* (San Francisco, Jossey-Bass, 1994).
25. Orr, *Earth in Mind: On Education, Environment, and the Human Prospect.*
26. Arthur K. Ellis, *Exemplars of Curriculum Theory* (Larchmont, NY: Eye on Education, 2004).
27. Dwayne E. Huebner, "Spirituality and Knowing," in E. W. Eisner, ed., *Learning and Teaching the Ways of Knowing,* Eighty-fourth Yearbook of the National Society for the Study of Education, Part II (Chicago: University of Chicago Press, 1985), p. 163.
28. James Moffett, *The Universal Schoolhouse* (San Francisco: Jossey-Bass, 1994).
29. James M. Banner Jr. and Harold C. Cannon, *The Elements of Teaching* (New Haven, CT: Yale University Press, 1997).
30. Pinar et al., *Understanding Curriculum.*
31. Egan, *The Future of Education.*
32. Thomas Armstrong, *Awakening Genius in the Classroom* (Alexandria, VA: Association for Supervision and Curriculum Development, 1998).
33. Michael L. Posner and Mary K. Rothbart, *Educating the Human Brain* (Washington, DC: American Psychological Association, 2007).
34. Ibid.
35. Ibid.
36. Ibid.
37. D. C. Phillips, "An Opinionated Account of the Constructivist Landscape," in D. C. Phillips, ed., *Constructivism in Education: Opinions and Second Opinions on Controversial Issues,* Ninety-ninth Yearbook of the National Society for the Study of Education, Part I (Chicago: University of Chicago Press, 2000), pp. 1–16.
38. Posner and Rothbart, *Educating the Human Brain,* p. 10.
39. Richard A. Brosio, *Philosophical Scaffolding for the Construction of Critical Democratic Education* (New York: Peter Lang, 2000).
40. Forrest W. Parkay and Glen Hass, *Curriculum Planning: A Contemporary Approach,* 7th ed. (Boston: Allyn & Bacon, 2000).
41. Tyler, *Basic Principles of Curriculum and Instruction.*
42. John I. Goodlad and Zhixin Su, "Organization and the Curriculum," in Philip W. Jackson, ed., *Handbook of Research on Curriculum* (New York: Macmillan, 1992), pp. 327–344.
43. Ibid.
44. Abbie Brown and Timothy D. Green, *The Essentials of Instructional Design* (Upper Saddle River, NJ: Pearson, 2006).
45. Goodlad and Su, "Organization and the Curriculum."
46. Jean Piaget, *The Psychology of Intelligence* (Paterson, NJ: Littlefield, Adams, 1960).
47. Posner and Rothbart, *Educating the Human Brain.*
48. Ibid.
49. B. Othanel Smith, William O. Stanley, and Harlan J. Shores, *Fundamentals of Curriculum Development,* rev. ed. (New York: Harcourt Brace, 1957).
50. Gerald J. Posner and Kenneth A. Strike, "A Categorization Scheme for Principles of Sequencing Content," *Review of Educational Research* (Fall 1976), pp. 401–406.
51. Janet L. Kolodner et al., "Promoting Deep Science Learning through Case-Based Reasoning: Rituals, and Practices in Learning by Design Classrooms," in Norbert

M. Seel and Sanne Dijkstra, eds., *Curriculum Plans and Processes in Instructional Design: International Perspectives* (Mahwah, NJ: Lawrence Erlbaum Association, 2004), pp. 89–114.

52. Tyler, *Basic Principles of Curriculum and Instruction,* p. 86.

53. M. M. Merzenich and W. M. Jenkins, "Cortical Plasticity, Learning, and Learning Dysfunction"; and T. Elbert, C. Pantev, C. Rockstroh, C. Wienbruch, and E. Taub, "Increased Cortical Representation of the Fingers of the Left Hand in String Players," *Science* (October 1995), pp. 270, 305–307, cited in Posner and Rothbart, p. 45.

54. Ibid.

55. Jerome Bruner, *The Process of Education* (Cambridge, MA: Harvard University Press, 1959), p. 52.

56. Goodlad and Su, "Organization and the Curriculum."

57. James A. Beane, "Curriculum Integration and the Disciplines of Knowledge," in Forrest W. Parkay and Glen Hass, *Curriculum Planning: A Contemporary Approach,* 7th ed. (Boston: Allyn and Bacon, 2000), pp. 228–237.

58. Ibid.

59. Hilda Taba, *Curriculum Development: Theory and Practice* (New York: Harcourt Brace, 1962).

60. Doll, *Curriculum Improvement.*

61. Egan, *The Future of Education,* p. 9.

62. Henry C. Morrison, *The Curriculum of the Common School* (Chicago: University of Chicago Press, 1940).

63. Robert M. Hutchins, *The Higher Learning in America* (New Haven, CT: Yale University Press, 1936).

64. James Moffett, *The Universal Schoolhouse* (San Francisco: Jossey-Bass, 1994).

65. John Dewey, *Experience and Education* (New York: Macmillan, 1938).

66. Arthur R. King and John A. Brownell, *The Curriculum and the Disciplines of Knowledge* (New York: Wiley, 1966).

67. Ron Ritchhart, *Intellectual Character.*

68. Jerome Bruner, *The Culture of Education* (Cambridge, MA: Harvard University Press, 2001), p. 115.

69. Joseph L. Schwab, *The Practical: A Language for Curriculum* (Washington, DC: National Education Association, 1970).

70. Philip Phenix, "Realm of Meaning," in *Education and the Structure of Knowledge* (Chicago: Rand McNally, 1964), pp. 4–43.

71. Harry S. Broudy, "Becoming Educated in Contemporary Society," in K. D. Benne and S. Tozer, eds., *Society as Educator in an Age of Transition,* Eighty-sixth Yearbook of the National Society for the Study of Education, Part II (Chicago: University of Chicago Press, 1987), pp. 247–268.

72. Bruner, *The Process of Education,* p. 8.

73. Ibid., p. 33.

74. Ibid., p. 33.

75. Ellis, *Exemplars of Curriculum Theory.*

76. Broudy, "Becoming Educated in Contemporary Society."

77. Kenneth T. Henson, *Curriculum Planning: Integrating Multiculturalism, Constructivism, and Educational Reform,* 3rd ed. (New York: McGraw-Hill, 2001).

78. Harry S. Broudy, B. O. Smith, and Joe R. Burnett, *Democracy and Excellence in American Secondary Education* (Chicago: Rand McNally, 1964).

79. Linda Crafton, *Challenges of Holistic Teaching: Answering the Tough Questions* (Norwood, MA: Christopher-Gordon, 1994).

80. Jacqueline Grennon Brooks and Martin G. Brooks, *The Case for Constructivist Classrooms* (Alexandria, VA: Association for Supervision and Curriculum Development, 1993).

81. Hilda Taba, *A Teacher's Handbook to Elementary Social Studies* (Reading, MA: Addison-Wesley, 1971).

82. Harold B. Alberty and Elsie J. Alberty, *Reorganizing the High School Curriculum,* 3rd ed. (New York: Macmillan, 1962).

83. Francis P. Hunkins, *Teaching Thinking through Effective Questioning,* 2nd ed. (Norwood, MA: Christopher Gordon, 1995), p. 18.

84. S. Tishman, D. N. Perkinds, and E. Jav, "The Thinking Classroom," in *Learning and Teaching in a Culture of Thinking* (Needham Heights, MA: Allyn & Bacon, 1995), referred to in Ron Ritchhart, *Intellectual Character.*

85. Ritchhart, *Intellectual Character,* p. 18.

86. William Bain, "The Loss of Innocence: Lyotard, Foucault, and the Challenge of Postmodern Education," in Michael Peters, ed., *Education and the Postmodern Condition* (Westport, CT: Bergin & Garvey, 1995), pp. 1–20.

87. Ibid.

88. Michael Peters, "Legitimation Problems: Knowledge and Education in the Postmodern Condition," in Michael Peters, ed., *Education and the Postmodern Condition,* (Westport, CT: Bergin & Garvey, 1995), pp. 21–39.

89. Bruner, *The Culture of Education.*

90. Joseph D. Novak and D. Bob Corwin, *Learning How to Learn* (Cambridge, England: Cambridge University Press, 1984).

91. Egan, *The Future of Education.*

92. Ibid.

93. Ibid.

94. D. C. Phillips, "An Opinionated Account of the Constructivist Landscape," pp. 1–16.

95. J. Rousseau, *Emile,* trans. by B. Foxley (New York: Dutton, 1955).

96. Francis W. Parker, *Talks on Pedagogics* (New York: E. L. Kellogg, 1894).

97. John Dewey, *The Child and the Curriculum* (Chicago: University of Chicago Press, 1902).

98. Frederick G. Bonser, *Life Needs and Education* (New York: Teachers College Press, Columbia University, 1932); Charles Prosser, *Life Adjustment Education for Every Youth* (Washington, DC: U.S. Government Printing Office, 1951); and Florence B. Stratemeyer et al., *Developing a Curriculum for Modern Living* (New York: Teachers College Press, Columbia University, 1947).

99. William H. Kilpatrick, "The Project Method," *Teachers College Record* (September 1918), pp. 319–335; and William Kilpatrick, *Foundations of Method* (New York: Macmillan, 1925).

100. Goodlad and Su, "Organization and the Curriculum."

101. Garth Boomer, "Negotiating the Curriculum," in Garth Boomer, Nancy Lester, Cynthia Onore, and Jon Cook, *Negotiating the Curriculum: Educating for the 21st Century* (Washington, DC: Falmer Press, 1992), pp. 4–14.

102. Jacqueline Grennon Brooks and Martin G. Brooks, *The Case for Constructivist Classrooms* (Alexandria, VA: Association for Supervision and Curriculum Development, 1993).

103. Norbert M. Seel, "Model-Centered Learning Environments: Theory, Instructional Design, and Effects," in Norbert M. Seel and Sanne Dijkstra, eds., *Curriculum Plans and Processes in Instructional Design: International Perspectives* (Mahwah, NJ: Lawrence Erlbaum Associates, 2004), pp. 49–73.

104. John Dewey, *Experience and Education* (New York: Macmillan, 1938).

105. Reginald D. Archambault, ed., *John Dewey on Education* (Chicago: University of Chicago Press, 1964).

106. Daniel Tanner and Laurel Tanner, *Curriculum Development: Theory into Practice,* 5th ed. (New York: Macmillan, 2004).

107. Armstrong, *Awakening Genius in the Classroom.*

108. Ellen Brantlinger, *Dividing Classes* (New York: Routledge, 2003).

109. Peter McLaren, "Education as a Political Issue: What's Missing in the Public Conversation about Education?" in Joe L. Kincheloe and Shirley R. Steinberg, eds., *Thirteen Questions,* 2nd ed. (New York: Peter Lang, 1995), pp. 267–280.

110. Paulo Freire, *Pedagogy of the Oppressed* (New York: Herder and Herder, 1970); and Paolo Freire, *The Politics of Education* (South Hadley, MA: Bergin & Garvey, 1985).

111. Robert Young, *A Critical Theory of Education* (New York: Teachers College Press, Columbia University, 1990).

112. William Ayers, *To Teach: The Journey of a Teacher,* 3rd ed. (New York: Teachers College Press, 2010), p. 98.

113. Ibid., p. 100.

114. Ibid.

115. Arthur W. Combs, ed., *Perceiving, Behaving, Becoming* (Washington, DC: Association for Supervision and Curriculum Development, 1962).

116. Arthur W. Combs, "What Can Man Become?" in Arthur W. Combs, ed., *Perceiving, Behaving, Becoming* (Washington, DC: Association for Supervision and Curriculum Development, 1962), pp. 1–8.

117. Louise M. Berman and Jessie A. Roderick, eds., *Feeling, Valuing, and the Art of Growing: Insights into the Affective* (Washington, DC: Association for Supervision and Curriculum Development, 1977). See also Louise M. Berman et al., *Toward Curriculum for Being* (New York: State University of New York Press, 1992).

118. Abraham H. Maslow, *Toward a Psychology of Being* (New York: D. Van Nostrand, 1962).

119. Carl Rogers, "Toward Becoming a Fully Functioning Person," in Arthur W. Combs, ed., *Perceiving, Behaving, Becoming* (Washington, DC: Association for Supervision and Curriculum Development, 1962), pp. 21–33.

120. Alfie Kohn, *The Schools Our Children Deserve* (Boston: Houghton Mifflin, 1999).

121. Gloria A. Castillo, *Left-Handed Teaching: Lessons in Affective Teaching,* 2nd ed. (New York: Holt, Rinehart and Winston, 1970); and Gerald Weinstein and Mario D. Fantini, *Toward Humanistic Education: A Curriculum of Affect* (New York: Praeger, 1970).

122. Ibid.

123. Philip H. Phenix, "Transcendence and the Curriculum," in Eisner and Vallance, eds., *Conflicting Conceptions of Curriculum* (Berkeley, CA: McCutchen, 1974), p. 123.

124. Moffett, *The Universal Schoolhouse,* p. 36.

125. Francis P. Hunkins, "Sailing: Celebrating and Educating Self," *Educational Forum* (Summer 1992), pp. 1–9.

126. Kerry T. Burch, *Eros as the Educational Principles of Democracy* (New York: Peter Lang, 2000).

127. Ellis, *Exemplars of Curriculum Theory.*

128. Jacqueline C. Mancall, Erica K. Lodish, and Judith Springer, "Searching Across the Curriculum," *Phi Delta Kappan* (March 1992), pp. 526–528.

129. Herbert Spencer, *Education: Intellectual, Moral, and Physical* (New York: Appleton, 1860).

130. George S. Counts, "Dare Progressive Education Be Progressive?," *Progressive Education* (April 1932).

131. George S. Counts, *Dare the Schools Build a New Social Order?* (Yonkers, NY: World Book, 1932).

132. Harold Rugg, *Culture and Education in America* (New York: Harcourt, 1931).

133. Harold Rugg, *Foundations for American Education* (New York: Harcourt, 1947), p. 745.

134. Theodore Brameld, *Toward a Reconstructed Philosophy of Education* (New York: Holt, Rinehart and Winston, 1956).

135. Ayers, *To Teach: The Journey of a Teacher.*

136. Elliot W. Eisner, *The Educational Imagination,* 3rd ed. (Columbus, OH: Merrill, 2002).

137. Ibid.

138. Ayers, *To Teach: The Journey of a Teacher.*

# 7

■■■

# Curriculum Development

## FOCUSING QUESTIONS

1. How does *education* differ from *schooling*?
2. Why is it useful to think of curriculum development as a variety of games?
3. How would you describe the technical–scientific approach to curriculum development?
4. What are the major hallmarks in the nontechnical–nonscientific approaches to curriculum development?
5. Which curriculum model—technical–scientific or nontechnical–nonscientific—do you believe has greater relevance in the 21st century? Explain.
6. What influences is current brain research having on curriculum development?
7. How can *teacher communities* assist in curriculum development?
8. What are the major sources of educational aims?
9. What dangers are there in equating goals and standards?
10. What guidelines are helpful in formulating educational objectives?
11. Why is agreeing upon standards so contentious?
12. What are some major challenges to educators in determining and selecting curricular content?
13. What are the central criteria to consider when selecting curriculum content? Curriculum experiences?
14. Why is it necessary to consider carefully educational environments?

Education and schooling have a troubled relationship, making it necessary that educators, teachers especially, reflect on just what each concept represents. Hidden within these concepts are knowing and understanding. Also, there is this question: Does school contribute or hinder students' education? This question has a long history. Ever since compulsory public school began in the 19th century, groups have queried whether schools possessed the capacity to educate.[1] We are not going to answer this question definitively. However, we do believe that the school's function is to educate, not to mold students who just regurgitate information or perform mindless skills.

As Ken Osborne asserts, in a democracy, students must realize that dialogue is central to democratic participation. Students need deep knowledge to debate myriad viewpoints; students must relish interacting with individuals with opposing views; students must attain capacities to process opinion into action.[2]

Education, in contrast to schooling, enables students to become individuals with intellectual character. As Ron Ritchhart queries, Why would we be teaching a curriculum if not for intelligence?[3] Schooling tends to indoctrinate. Education strives to liberate. Schooling tends to stress efficiency and standardization. Education endeavors to be messy and spontaneous. Schooling attempts to fill students with knowledge. Education tries to make students utilize knowledge in thinking and to become intelligent utilizers of information. Education fosters intellectual character in students.[4]

To educate, educators must engage in serious curriculum development. A curriculum is more than a school board–approved textbook series. Although many textbook series are excellent educational materials, curricularists—and this includes teachers—must realize that educating students demands more than just following a teacher's textbook guide.

We are not suggesting that teachers disregard textbooks and other educational materials. However textbooks and related materials provide only a suggested curriculum. Teachers must still make informed decisions about the purposes of learning certain information, what content to stress, what materials to emphasize, and how to sequence such materials. Further, teachers must decide what instructional strategies to use and what student activities are essential and appropriate for diverse class members. Also, teachers must select various assessment instruments and processes to support their teaching and students' learnings.

Curriculum development is not static. It draws on emerging views of modernism and postmodernism, new understandings of cognitive theories, new understandings of the anatomy and physiology of the brain, and new formulations of instructional design and systems theory. The melding of thought regarding the various world and educational philosophies is also having an impact on curriculum development.

There are various ways to define curriculum development. Also, different curriculum designs take subject matter, students, and society into account to differing degrees. Curriculum development consists of various processes (technical, humanistic, and artistic) that allow schools and schoolpeople to realize certain educational goals. Ideally, everyone affected by a curriculum is involved in its development.

A useful way to reflect on curriculum development is to think of it as a variety of games with myriad rules. Allan Garrett makes a case for the ecology of games metaphor when he states that it "provides an elegant and useful framework for the consideration of the various parties that seek to influence American public education."[5] Garrett notes that Norton E. Long first introduced studying local communities as ecologies of games.[6]

Looking at curriculum development as a series of games engaged in by various educators, teachers, curricularists, administrators, and even, at times, groups from the general public assists us in realizing that people have varied goals for playing the game or games. Employing the game mentality, there are winners and losers, although we should strive for the curriculum game as win–win.

In the curriculum-development game, there are players who collaborate for diverse and particular ends. Many teachers may share particular ends—that is, to have students "win" the game of really learning the curriculum developed and implemented—whereas some teachers, especially in districts advocating merit pay for "successful" teaching, might aim at advancing themselves on the pay scale. Administrators might play the game to have their schools attain state and national standards. School board members might strive to get reelected. Legislators might engage in the curriculum game to define themselves as "educational" leaders. We can analyze not only how the "many" play the game, but deduce their rationales for playing and the criteria they use for success. And some players might be participating in related and parallel games. Individuals might use others for their own benefits. Garrett posits that legislators might argue for better schools and curricula solely to win public support for their particular agendas.

Some players are engaged in Race to the Top to gain funding for novel ideas regarding education in general and curriculum in particular. Some play for pride, for praise, or for attainment; but all play for a purpose. They play for success! Currently, *success* has a plethora of meanings, however: attaining standards, liberating minds, indoctrinating, opening intellectual horizons, scoring high on tests, knowing the mores of particular cultures, and so on.

Although many players are multitasking in their games, most center their play on a particular game—in our discussion, on playing curriculum development. And most curriculum players play the game from a technical, nontechnical, or holistic model.

Many social and educational critics believe that society has been moving from modernism (which stresses the technical, precise, and certain) to postmodernism (which stresses the nontechnical, emergent, and uncertain). Because postmodernism is relatively new, we have more technical than nontechnical curriculum models on which to draw. People who believe in a curriculum design that stresses subject matter usually favor technical approaches to curriculum development. People who focus on the learner often prefer a nontechnical approach. People who consider the curriculum a vehicle for addressing social problems can favor either approach. Also, in reality curricula result from some blend of technical and nontechnical approaches.

## TECHNICAL–SCIENTIFIC APPROACH

The technical–scientific approach to education and curriculum stresses students learning specific subject matter with specific outputs. Curriculum development is a plan for structuring the learning environment and coordinating personnel, materials, and equipment. The approach applies scientific principles and involves detailed monitoring of the components of curriculum design.[7] Curriculum is viewed as a complex unity of parts organized to foster learning.

Educators who use a technical–scientific approach attempt to systematically outline those procedures that facilitate curriculum development. The various models use a means–end paradigm that suggests that the more rigorous the means, the more likely the desired ends will be attained. Followers of this approach indicate that such a systematically designed program can be evaluated. However, others question just how precise the evaluation can be.

The various technical–scientific models exhibit what James Macdonald called a "technological" rationality, as opposed to an "aesthetic rationality."[8] People who favor technical–scientific models prioritize knowledge acquisition and an educational system that is maximally efficient.

Technical–scientific curriculum development began around 1900, when educators sought to apply empirical methods (surveys and analysis of human conduct) to the question of curriculum content. The push for a science of curriculum making accompanied the rise of biology, physics, and chemistry as well as the use of the "machine theory" evolving in business and industry.

### The Models of Bobbitt and Charters

Franklin Bobbitt compared creating a curriculum to constructing a railroad: Once the general route is planned, the builder engages in surveying and then the laying of track. Developing a curriculum is like planning a person's route to growth, culture, and that individual's special abilities.[9] Like a railroad engineer, an educator must "take a broad over-view of the entire field [and see] the major factors in perspective and in relation." A general plan for the educational program can then be formulated, followed by "determining content and experiences necessary for the [learner]."[10]

Even today, many educators believe that curriculum development must include some means of monitoring and managing learning, that is, students' interactions with specific contents. Such monitoring enables an effective structure of curriculum and instruction.[11]

For Bobbitt, the first task of curriculum development is to "discover the activities which ought to make up the lives of students and along with these, the abilities and personal qualities necessary for proper performance."[12] Educational objectives are derived from this activity analysis. Bobbitt insisted that the analysis address humans' actual activities and consider the broad range of human experiences. This approach continues in various types of task analysis.[13] It shares features of what some educators call *backward design*.[14]

Bobbitt's contemporary Werrett Charters also believed in activity analysis. However, Charters noted that "changes in the curriculum are always preceded by modifications in our conception of the aim of education."[15] Our aims (ideals) influence the selection of school content and experiences.

Charters wanted educators to connect aims with activities that individuals performed. He advocated four steps of curriculum construction: "(1) selecting objectives, (2) dividing them into ideals and activities, (3) analyzing them to the limits of working units, and (4) collecting methods of achievement."[16]

For Charters, philosophy supplied the ideals that were to serve as objectives and standards. He noted that the curriculum could contain both primary and derived subjects. *Primary subjects* were those directly required by a particular occupation. For example, a meteorologist must fill out various types of reports. Therefore, report writing is a primary subject for all students to experience in English classes. Meteorology requires a knowledge of physics and mathematics, which are *derived subjects,* "service subjects which are important not because they are directly useful in the performance of activities, but because they are derived from material which has practical service value."[17]

Bobbitt and Charters firmly established scientific curriculum making. They saw effective curriculum development as a process that results in a meaningful program. Bobbitt and Charters initiated a concern for the relationships among goals, objectives, and activities. They regarded goal selection as a normative process and the selection of objectives and activities as empirical and scientific. Bobbitt and Charters indicated that curricular activity can be planned and systematically studied and evaluated.

The field of curriculum achieved independent status with the 1932 establishment of the Society for Curriculum Study. In 1938, Teachers College at Columbia University established a department of curriculum and teaching. For the next 20 years, Teachers College dominated the field of curriculum; its influence even surpassed the earlier influence of the University of Chicago.

## The Tyler Model: Four Basic Principles

Tyler's technical–scientific model is one of the best known. In 1949, Tyler published *Basic Principles of Curriculum and Instruction,* in which he outlined an approach to curriculum and instruction.[18] Those involved in curriculum inquiry must try to (1) determine the school's purposes, (2) identify educational experiences related to those purposes, (3) ascertain how the experiences are organized, and (4) evaluate the purposes.

By *purposes,* Tyler meant general objectives. He indicated that curriculum planners should identify these objectives by gathering data from the subject matter, the learners, and the society. After identifying numerous general objectives, the curriculum planners were to refine them by filtering them through the school's philosophy and the psychology of learning. Specific instructional objectives would result.

Tyler discussed how to select educational experiences that allow the attainment of objectives. Learning experiences had to take into account learners' perceptions and previous experience. Also, they were to be selected in light of knowledge about learning and human development.

Tyler addressed the organization and sequencing of these experiences. He believed that the sequencing had to be somewhat systematic to produce a maximum cumulative effect. He thought that ideas, concepts, values, and skills should be woven into the curriculum fabric. These key elements could link different subjects and learning experiences.

Tyler's last principle deals with evaluating plans and actions. Tyler believed that evaluation was important in determining whether a program was effective.

Although Tyler did not display his model of curriculum development graphically, several other people have. The authors' diagram of this model appears in Figure 7.1.

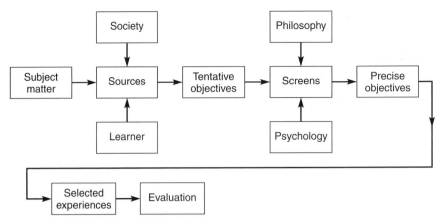

**FIGURE 7.1** Tyler's Curriculum Development Model

Some people have criticized Tyler's approach as too linear, too reliant on objectivity, and somewhat based on assumptions about cause and effect; it allows all educational experiences to be justified by the objectives that they address. Nevertheless, Tyler's approach to curriculum development remains popular with school district personnel and still influences universities. Its reasonableness and workability appeal to many people. Tyler's approach works regardless of context or one's philosophical orientation.[19]

## The Taba Model: Grassroots Rationale

Hilda Taba was an influential colleague of Tyler's. In *Curriculum Development: Theory and Practice* (1962), she argued that there was a definite order to creating a thoughtful, dynamic curriculum.[20] Unlike Tyler, Taba believed that teachers should participate in developing curricula. She advocated what has been called the *grassroots approach*,[21] a model whose steps resemble Tyler's. Although Tyler did not advocate that his model be used only by people in the central office, educators during the early days of curriculum making thought that the central authorities had the knowledge to create curricula. They subscribed to a top-down (administrative) model. Frequently, administrators gave teachers ideas from curriculum experts and then supervised the teachers to ensure that the ideas were implemented. In contrast, Taba believed that a curriculum should be designed by its users. Teachers should begin by creating specific teaching–learning units for their students and then build to a general design. Taba advocated an inductive approach rather than the more traditional deductive approach of starting with a general design and working toward specifics.

Taba's grassroots model entails seven major steps:

1. ***Diagnosis of needs.*** The teacher (curriculum designer) identifies the needs of the students for whom the curriculum is being planned. (See Curriculum Tips 7.1.)
2. ***Formulation of objectives.*** The teacher specifies objectives.
3. ***Selection of content.*** The objectives suggest the curriculum's content. The objectives and content should match. The content's validity and significance also are determined.
4. ***Organization of content.*** The teacher organizes the content into a sequence, taking into consideration learners' maturity, academic achievement, and interests.
5. ***Selection of learning experiences.*** The teacher selects instructional methods that engage the students with the content.
6. ***Organization of learning activities.*** The teacher organizes the learning activities into a sequence, often determined by the content. The teacher must bear in mind the particular students who will be taught.
7. ***Evaluation and means of evaluation.*** The curriculum planner determines which objectives have been accomplished. Students and teachers must consider evaluation procedures.

---

**CURRICULUM TIPS 7.1    Conducting a Needs Analysis**

1. Set aside time and designate people who will conduct the needs analysis.
2. Create or obtain data gathering instruments and schedule time to gather data (for example, through surveys, town meetings, questionnaires, tests, and interviews).
3. List the curriculum's aims and goals.
4. Match the aims and goals.
5. Identify gaps between desired and actual results.
6. Decide which gaps require immediate curricular attention.
7. Suggest ways to address the identified gaps.

---

*Source:* Information from Abbie Brown and Timothy D. Green, *The Essentials of Instructional Design* (Upper Saddle River, NJ: Pearson, 2006), p. 97.

---

Taba was far ahead of her time. Most of today's curriculum designers still follow steps 1, 2, 5, 6, and 7. They first examine the extant situation, analyzing the learners and their needs (Taba's step 1). They then develop instructional goals and objectives (Taba's step 2). Third, they organize instruction and create learning environments (Taba's steps 5 and 6), selecting learning experiences and organizing learning activities. Finally, they evaluate the learners and the instructional program's overall success (Taba's step 7).

## The Backward-Design Model

Another popular model of curriculum development is the "backward design" advocated by Grant Wiggins and Jay McTighe.[22] Essentially, this model is a variation of task analysis. Its roots can be traced back to Bobbitt and Charters. It also draws from the fields of architecture and engineering.

*Backward design* (we prefer to call it *backward development*) begins with a statement of desired results. Just what do you want to accomplish? What should students know and be able to do? What values and attitudes should they have? What skills should they possess and be able to demonstrate? Essentially, this first stage involves identifying the school program's goals.

Wiggins and McTighe specify three levels of decision making in this first stage. At the first and most general level, an educator considers goals and checks on national, state, and local content standards. At the second level of decision making, curriculum developers (including classroom teachers) select content—valuable information and skills that might lead students to the desired results. What basic understandings and skills do students need in light of stated standards, community expectations, and research results? What generalizations, concepts, and facts must students master in order to achieve? What procedures, methods of analysis, and thinking strategies must students experience to become self-learners?

The final level of decision making in this first general stage involves narrowing the content possibilities. What specific courses will be taught, and what particular content (both declarative and procedural)? Wiggins and McTighe refer to this final level of decision making as identifying enduring understanding that anchors the unit or course. "The term enduring refers to the big ideas, the important understandings, that we want students to 'get inside of' and retain after they've forgotten many of the details."[23]

Stage 2 of the backward-design model involves determining how the curriculum will be evaluated once it is in place. How will we know whether students have met the set standards? What evidence will be collected to assess the curriculum's effectiveness? According to Wiggins and McTighe, the backward-design model gets teachers thinking like assessors before they develop curriculum units and lessons. Wiggins and McTighe suggest various assessment methods that can be considered at this stage, including informal checks, observations of students, dialogue with students, quizzes and tests, and performance tasks and projects.[24]

Identify expected endpoints ➔ Determine evidence ➔ Plan learning experiences

- Consider possible contents
- Narrow choices to important contents
- Select the final enduring contents

**FIGURE 7.2** Backward-Design Model

When educators have clearly identified the curriculum's goals and determined how to assess the extent to which those goals have been reached, they are ready to plan instructional activities. Wiggins and McTighe list several key questions that curriculum developers and teachers must raise at this stage:

What knowledge and skills do students need to succeed in the course?

What activities enable students to master the requisite knowledge and skills?

What should be taught, and how should it be taught, for students to become knowledgeable and skillful in the identified content realm?

What materials foster student success in the curriculum?

Does the overall design of the course or unit fulfill the principles of curriculum development?

Figure 7.2 shows a variation of Wiggins and McTighe's backward-design model.

### The Task-Analysis Model

Task-analysis models differ widely. However, they all share a focus on identifying essential content and skills, which are determined by analyzing the tasks necessary for school learning or some real-world task.[25]

Basically, there are two types of task analysis: subject-matter analysis and learning analysis.

**SUBJECT-MATTER ANALYSIS.** *Subject matter,* or *content,* is the starting point in subject-matter analysis. The key question is, What knowledge is most important for students? We usually ask this question of subject-matter experts. Ideally, these experts are the educators responsible for creating and teaching the curriculum. However, we can draw on the expertise of scholars in various disciplines. When the curriculum is intended to prepare people for certain professions, then the question is, What subject matter enables students to perform the tasks of particular jobs within those professions?[26]

Subject matter must be broken into parts. Consider the subject of government. Students must understand the general concepts *government* and *citizen,* but also the narrower concepts of *representative government* and *citizen responsibility*. They must also know certain facts, such as the number of branches of government and the dates when amendments to the U.S. Constitution were passed. Breaking down knowledge of government requires giving that knowledge realm some structure. One way to do this is to use a master design chart.

A master design chart uses information gained from experts in the subject matter. This information covers important facts, concepts, rules, laws, generalizations, theories, and so on. Essentially, the master design chart contains the topics and related information to be learned in a certain course or a total curriculum. One way to design the chart is to create a row for each crucial topic and a column for the degrees of emphasis that topics will receive. One also could indicate the various learning behaviors that students must exhibit regarding each topic: concepts, generalizations, and so on. Figure 7.3 provides a sample master design chart.

| Content | | KNOW | | | ANALYZE | | APPLY | EVALUATE | |
|---|---|---|---|---|---|---|---|---|---|
| | | State Facts | Explain Concepts | Present Generalizations | Deconstruct Concepts | Determine Relationships | Do Fieldwork to Gather Data | Determine Accuracy of Field Data | Judge Validity of Conclusion |
| Land Forms | Mountains | 3 | 2 | 2 | 2 | 2 | 0 | 0 | 0 |
| | Hills | 3 | 2 | 2 | 2 | 2 | 1 | 1 | 1 |
| | Plateaus | 3 | 2 | 2 | 2 | 1 | 0 | 0 | 0 |
| | Plains | 3 | 2 | 2 | 2 | 1 | 1 | 1 | 1 |
| Water Bodies | Oceans | 3 | 2 | 2 | 2 | 2 | 1 | 0 | 0 |
| | Lakes | 3 | 1 | 1 | 0 | 0 | 0 | 0 | 0 |
| | Rivers | 3 | 2 | 2 | 2 | 1 | 0 | 0 | 0 |
| | Seas | 3 | 1 | 1 | 0 | 0 | 0 | 0 | 0 |

Numbers show level of emphasis given to content and activities.
3   Heavy emphasis
2   Major emphasis
1   Minor emphasis
0   Mention but no emphasis
—   No mention

**FIGURE 7.3**   Master Design Chart (for Geography)

Someone reading about a master design chart might think that it is the same as a curriculum map. There are similarities. However, curriculum maps deal with content topics to be covered, but not how they are to be experienced. Also, curriculum maps are generated primarily by teachers scheduled to teach the curriculum.[27]

Once the chart has been completed, it is necessary to identify the relationships among the content topics, concepts, generalizations, and so on. In determining the relationships, we reflect on how to construct the curriculum unit so that the content has a meaningful organization. The content can be organized chronologically, according to the specific content's knowledge structure, in the order in which it might be used, or according to the manner in which psychologists indicate students might best learn it.

**LEARNING ANALYSIS.**   Ideally, learning analysis begins when content is being organized. It encompasses activity analysis and addresses which learning processes are required for students to learn the selected content. What activities might students engage in to learn the content and master some problem-solving process? It is helpful to consult experts in instructional design and psychology, especially cognitive psychology and brain research.

Learning analysis addresses the sequence of the learning activities. Is there an optimal time line for learning certain content and skills? What should the learner do to gain competence in the skill or content? At this stage, the learning analyst selects instructional approaches that moves students toward the curriculum's goals.

Until recently, curricularists had to rely on the research results of cognitive psychology to accomplish learning analysis. The brain was essentially a "black box," about which we inferred how the brain developed and processed learning. Now, with recent brain research, learning analysis can be more precise. Recent discoveries about brain functioning and networking enable us to determine with greater precision those curricular contents and experiences that foster learning.[28]

| OBJECTIVES | CONTENT/SUBJECT MATTER | LEARNING/ACTIVITY/ INSTRUCTIONAL APPROACH | MATERIALS/ EVALUATION METHODS |
|---|---|---|---|
| | | | |

**FIGURE 7.4**  Master Plan Format

In the next stage of learning analysis, the curriculum developer creates a master curriculum plan that synthesizes the information obtained and organized through the selection of subject content and learning approaches. Those who have been involved in the task analysis determine the plan's format.

The curriculum team studies the selected content and determines specific objectives with regard to that content. The objectives deal with the cognitive, affective, and (sometimes) psychomotor domains. The sequence of the objectives is linked to the sequence of the selected content and learning activities. The master plan also can indicate educational materials and evaluation methods. Figure 7.4 illustrates the format for a master plan.

Other technical-scientific models exist. These other models are more likely to be used by subject-centered designers, who tend to be in the traditional philosophical and technological camps. However, people of any design orientation can use the models when developing a curriculum. Curricularists can be systematic in creating subject-, child-, or problem-centered curricula.

## NONTECHNICAL–NONSCIENTIFIC APPROACH

### The Approach in General

The technical–scientific approach to curriculum development suggests that the process of curriculum development is highly objective, universal, and logical. It rests on an assumption that reality can be defined and represented in symbolic form. Knowledge can exist as a matter of fact, unaffected by the process of creating and learning it. The aims of education can be specified and addressed in linear fashion. The technical–scientific approach to curriculum development is modernist; it rests on a belief in rationality, objectivity, and certainty.

In contrast, nontechnical curriculum developers stress the subjective, personal, aesthetic, heuristic, and transactional. They stress the learner rather than the learner's output, emphasizing activity-oriented approaches to teaching and learning. Students are always evolving. They are active participants in the learning process, not passive recipients of knowledge. Those favoring a nontechnical–nonscientific approach note that not all educational goals can be known. The curriculum should evolve rather than be precisely planned.

Nontechnical curriculum developers also assert that much of what a curriculum accomplishes is immeasurable (e.g., not fully reflected by test scores). They are postmodern, viewing the world as a living organism, not a machine. They note that curriculum development is somewhat subjective, inseparable from the people involved.

Nontechnical curriculum developers prioritize learners over subject matter. Tentatively selected subject matter has importance only to the degree that students find it meaningful. It should provide opportunities for reflection and critique and should engage students in the creation of meaning.[29]

To nontechnical curriculum developers, learning is holistic; it cannot be broken into discrete parts or steps. Instead of developing curricula prior to students' arrival in school, teachers are students' colearners. Teachers and students engage in an educational conversation about topics of mutual interest and concern. In many nontechnical models, the curriculum evolves from teacher–pupil interaction.

Nontechnical–nonscientific curriculum developers are likely to favor child-centered and, to a lesser extent, problem–centered designs. However, they can still take a somewhat systematic approach.

## The Deliberation Model

In the deliberation model of nontechnical curriculum development, educators communicate their views to their colleagues and sometimes to students regarding education's goals and what should be taught. However, curriculum development is nonlinear. A blend of modernism and postmodernism, the deliberation approach draws on systems thinking and on feedback and adjustments but also takes into account that reality is somewhat subjective.

Dillon notes that deliberation essentially proceeds from problem to proposals to solution.[30] This process occurs within a recognized socially constructed context. People are aware of the participants in the process and of their views, ideas, and agendas.

Curriculum development through deliberation occurs within cultural contexts. Currently, this is one of the challenges confronting curriculum creators. How can one generate solid curricula while taking diverse cultures, customs, and values into account?

The deliberation model has six stages, as suggested by Noye: (1) public sharing, (2) highlighting agreement and disagreement, (3) explaining positions, (4) highlighting changes in position, (5) negotiating points of agreement, and (6) adopting a decision.[31]

In the first stage, public sharing, people come together to share ideas related to curriculum development. The participants advocate various agendas, which may be in conflict. They express their views regarding the curriculum's nature and purpose, make suggestions and demands, propose particular contents and pedagogies, and identify information that they consider relevant to creating curricula. People discuss their visions of students' roles, optimal learning environments, and teachers' proper functions. At the conclusion of this stage, to which the group can return at any time, the group should record a summary of its thoughts expressed throughout this stage on the common places of content, student, teacher, and school and the challenges confronting the group. The group is now ready for stage 2, highlighting agreements and disagreements.

In stage 2, the group identifies agreements and disagreements regarding educational goals, curriculum content, and instructional approach. All views should be respectfully considered.

In stage 3, group members explain their positions. Why do I think this is a problem? What data support my view? Is a particular group of students failing? What is the curricular solution? To arrive at a consensus, group members must appreciate one another as professionals and not consider their colleagues to be adversaries.[32] The group leader must have considerable skill in guiding groups.

Stage 4 of deliberation evolves from the activity of explaining positions. Group members change their opinions in response to presented data and arguments. When people change their minds, they inform other group members.

In stage 5 of the deliberative process, participants work toward agreement regarding curriculum content, instructional approaches, and educational goals. In other words, they negotiate and persuade (or become persuaded). Roger Soder argues that persuasion is a critical function of leadership. It relies on appeals to reason and emotion.[33] In stage 5, the group seeks to identify possible curricular solutions to educational needs.

In stage 6, the group achieves consensus regarding the curriculum's nature and purpose. It specifies curricular topics, pedagogy, educational material, school environment, methods of implementation, and assessment methods. The agreed-on curriculum reflects the group's social, political, and philosophical composition. Of course, some uncertainty remains.

Table 7.1 provides an overview of technical and nontechnical approaches to curriculum development.

| Table 7.1 | Overview of Curriculum Development Approaches | | |
|---|---|---|---|
| **Approach** | **Major Assumptions** | **View of Curriculum** | **Major Models** |
| Technical–scientific | Major steps can be identified and managed. | Curriculum is viewed as knowable components selected and organized. | Bobbitt, Charters: Curriculum activities; Tyler: Four basic principles |
| | Curriculum development has a high degree of objectivity, logic. | Curriculum is viewed as a compendium of parts. | Taba: Grassroots rationale |
| | Curriculum development involves task analysis and draws on separating key points of curriculum from major endpoint to starting point. | Curriculum is viewed as the delivery of mapped-out content and experiences. | Wiggins, McTighe: Backward design |
| | Curriculum can be broken into distinct parts or tasks. | Curriculum is viewed as engaging students in distinct and meaningful tasks. | Jonassen, Tessmer, Hannum: Task-analysis approach |
| Nontechnical–nonscientific | Curriculum development is subjective, personal, aesthetic, transactional. | Curriculum is viewed as quality activities. | — |
| | Curriculum development is "specialized talk." | Curriculum is viewed as conversation. | The deliberation model |
| | Curriculum development is a dynamic process fraught with uncertainty. | Curriculum is viewed as an emerging phenomenon with which humans interact; it is viewed as a dynamic and uncertain system. | — |

## ENACTING CURRICULUM DEVELOPMENT

Curriculum development essentially draws on two realms of knowledge: curriculum design and instructional design. Especially at the K–12 level, most educators know more about the former than the latter. As Richard Elmore notes, schools continually modify their curricula, but instructional practice seems to change little.[34]

Researchers at Pennsylvania State University's Applied Research Laboratory defined instructional design as "the systematic development of instructional specifications using learning and instructional theory to ensure the quality of instruction."[35] Programs must give more than cursory attention to how new content will be taught and how classroom and school environments will be organized. In many cases, those charged with curriculum development must draw on the expertise of instructional design specialists.

### Establishing Curriculum Teams

The highest-level curriculum teams are those at the federal or state level. These committee members generate programs, policies, and laws, such as No Child Left Behind and Race to the Top. This chapter primarily addresses curriculum teams at the local level, the level at which the curricular specifics are mapped out and aligned with state or federal mandates and standards.

Most curricular team members are teachers. This makes sense, because teachers implement the curriculum and can draw on their classroom experiences when developing curricula. They are likely to be familiar with effective subject content and instructional strategies.

In some school districts, teachers are more involved in adapting textbook series to classroom lesson plans than in creating new curricula writ large. However, creating lesson plans is curriculum development. In such districts, textbooks and related materials are selected by curriculum boards. In Texas, as previously mentioned, various textbook series are selected by the Texas State Board of Education. The schools then select the series they prefer from a list of acceptable materials.

Although the ideal is for teachers to be the key players on curriculum teams, there are teachers who resist involvement. "There is not just time for me to collaborate with fellow teachers. I already have too many demands on me," is a frequent response. We realize that schools often are organized so that teachers exist as if in solitary confinement in their classrooms. However, such "teacher separation" need not be the norm. Indeed, it has been found that schools with effective and innovative curricula have high teacher commitment to both the latest educational thinking and to collaborative engagement with colleagues.[36]

Successful curriculum development requires the involvement of school principals. In previous editions, we noted that the principal should be supportive but not dominate the process.[37] With such advice, the principal, as Fullan notes, was often sidelined in reform efforts, and especially in curricular change efforts. More recent research supports the idea that school principals should be key players in directing change initiatives.[38] And although this research is centered mostly on administrative and policy issues and changing school cultures, we argue that it also applies to curriculum development.

Effective principals, we are finding, foster the creation of teacher communities, which often result in a "critical mass of distributive leadership" essential for continued educational renewal.[39] Effective principals, and we include vice principals as well, are characterized by being *relationship centered*.[40] These principals have faith in powerful professionals who participate in collegial relationships. Thus, there is a symbolic relationship among all players: administrators, teachers, and support staff. All participate in curriculum teams as well as teams focused on other educational matters.[41]

Sometimes schools hire outside curriculum experts to be members of the development team. Often, these individuals can provide background information on development procedures, share details about curriculum design, and illuminate the complexities of instruction design.

In general, an elementary teacher teaches most subjects. Therefore, at the elementary level, it is especially important that teachers from various grades be involved in curriculum development. That way the created curricula fit into the overall program. In middle and high schools, there is more emphasis on particular subject areas, so the amount of teacher involvement partly depends on whether a new curriculum is being created for a particular subject or an entirely new program of studies. In general, at least some individuals who will be teaching the new or revised curriculum should be on the development team.

Teachers selected for the development team should want to be involved. "Forced labor" does not make for a good development team, as implied previously. Some teachers prefer just to teach. Others relish opportunities to create educational programs.

## Generating Aims, Goals, and Objectives

Curriculum development begins with a realization of the major challenges involved. People agree that school curricula should enable students to attain knowledge, skills, and attitudes. However, many people also want curricula to reproduce the culture within which the school exists and to further that society's economic, political, social, and cultural interests.[42]

Some people favor curricula that cultivate a global perspective; others think that local concerns should be prioritized. Our focus influences our response to questions such as these: What does it mean to know at a particular level? Whose knowledge is of value? Whose history? Whose literature? Orr laments that the globalization of knowledge is resulting in a neglect of local knowledge.[43]

In most cases, a school's curricular aims and goals come from local citizens, state organizations, national groups, or the federal government. Schools have much greater input with regard to objectives.

Educators' first step in curriculum development should be analysis of needs and tasks. Educators must determine what students must learn for success in school, on the job, and in life. During this phase, curriculum developers gather data that inform their decisions regarding what content is necessary, appropriate sequencing of the content, appropriate instructional strategies, and how the various curricular components should be tailored to students.[44] Analysis of needs and tasks often includes school and classroom observations. Focus groups may also define the rationales for such observations. Those charged with these initial analyses may also talk to principals, teachers, and students.[45]

By analyzing needs and tasks, educators determine what the curriculum should include. Data analysis can reveal gaps in students' learning, thereby indicating needed objectives and content. Educators start to sense what content, student activities, means of implementation, and means of evaluation the curriculum should include.

**GENERATING AIMS.**   People involved in curriculum development must identify their aims, which provide direction and reflect value judgments. Ralph Tyler summarized the aims of U.S. schooling as (1) developing self-realization, (2) making individuals literate, (3) encouraging social mobility, (4) providing the skills and understanding necessary for productive employment, (5) furnishing tools requisite for making effective choices regarding material and nonmaterial things and services, and (6) furnishing the tools necessary for continued learning.[46] These aims reflect a progressive philosophy.

Ronald Doll notes that educational aims should address the intellectual (or cognitive), the social–personal (or affective), and the productive.[47]

1. *Intellectual* aims focus on the acquisition and comprehension of knowledge, problem-solving skills, and methods of thinking.
2. *Social-personal* aims are concerned with the ways in which people relate to other individuals and society and how individuals view themselves. These aims address individual psychology and how people fit into their families and communities.
3. *Productive* aims center on educating students to function within the home, on the job, and as a citizen.

We add four other types of aims: (1) *physical,* dealing with the development and maintenance of strong, healthy bodies; (2) *aesthetic,* dealing with values and appreciation of the arts; (3) *moral,* dealing with values and appropriate conduct; and (4) *spiritual,* dealing with transcendence of self.

How curriculum development committees determine aims vary. Sometimes they adopt aims stated in educational documents. For instance, in 1918, the National Education Association's Commission on the Reorganization of Secondary Education listed education's general aims:

1. Health
2. Command of fundamental processes
3. Worthy home membership
4. Vocational education
5. Civic education
6. Worthy use of leisure
7. Ethical character[48]

Curriculum development committees can also base their aims on current social issues. For example, the issue of immigration might suggest an emphasis on language skills. The issues of race and gender equality might suggest an aim of increased representation of women and minorities in curricula such as history, literature, and political science.

Aims deal with the general process of education, such as building worldmindedness or creating technical literacy. No particular school program will accomplish these aims. Instead, many aspects of the curriculum will address them.

**GENERATING GOALS.** The next step in curriculum development is creating goals. According to Evelyn Sowell, goals answer the question: "What destination do you have in mind for learners as far as a particular curriculum or subject is concerned?"[49] Goals might include the following: Students think critically, students are diverse people, and students assume responsibility for their own learning.

Goals and standards seem to have melded together in educational dialogue. In 1995, Diane Ravitch posited that a *standard* is a goal as to what should be accomplished and also a measure of progress in attaining that goal. It is both part of curriculum development and also curriculum evaluation. One could also include discussion of goals and standards with consideration of instructional strategies, specifically how a method of instruction might or motivates students to attain a particular standard or group of standards in a particular curricular area.[50]

We take exception to equating a standard to a goal. A goal does indicate what could or should be learned, but it is much more general than a standard. *Standards,* as Ravitch and others define the term, are more akin to educational objectives that define in quite specific terms what students are to learn and what behavior or behaviors they are to demonstrate. What students are to learn, Ravitch defines as *content standards*. What behaviors students are to master, she defines as *performance standards*. Explicit in these two types of standards are the content teachers are to teach and what behaviors their students are to demonstrate. Also, performance standards regulate what teaching strategies teachers are to use.

To make our point, consider the first goal that the Phi Delta Kappa honor society has listed for students: Learn how to be a good citizen. This is a general endpoint of educational experiences. However, one would not state that learning how to be a good citizen is or has a standard. We must create various educational objectives using a variety of standards in order to determine what content must be learned and what performances must be mastered for us to state with some precision that students have attained the knowledge, skills, and attitudes indicative of being a good citizen. The same can be argued for the remaining goals suggested by Phi Delta Kappa.

By analyzing a school's goals, we can determine the scope of its educational program. Unlike aims, goals are more specific. Curriculum developers can use them as guidelines to achieve particular purposes.

Aims become goals when they become more specific and refer to a particular school, school system, or subject area.

The Phi Delta Kappa honor society has listed these goals for students:

1. Learn how to be a good citizen.
2. Learn how to respect and get along with people who think, dress, and act differently.
3. Learn about, and try to understand, the changes that take place in the world.
4. Develop skills in reading, writing, speaking, and listening.
5. Understand and practice democratic values.
6. Learn how to examine and use information.
7. Develop skills needed to enter a specific field of work.
8. Develop a desire to learn now and in the future.
9. Understand and practice health and safety.
10. Appreciate culture and beauty.[51]

In 1990, President George H. W. Bush and U.S. governors generated a list of six goals for U.S. schools to reach by 2000, and the National Goals Panel was established to determine the nation's progress in meeting these goals.

1. All U.S. children will start school ready to learn.
2. The high school graduation rate will increase to at least 90 percent.

3. U.S. students will leave grades 4, 8, and 12 having demonstrated competency in challenging subject matter (English, mathematics, science, history, and geography).

4. U.S. students will rank first in the world in science and mathematics achievement.

5. Every adult American will be literate and possess the knowledge and skills necessary to compete in a global economy and to exercise citizenship's rights and responsibilities.

6. Every U.S. school will be free of drugs and violence and will offer a disciplined environment conducive to learning.[52]

Like aims, goals should address the current times but also be relevant for the future. Creating educational goals is an ongoing activity. The needs of students, society, and a particular community give rise to initial statements of curriculum goals.

The goals are sometimes rank-ordered in terms of importance, feasibility, or both. People involved in goal development—teachers, community members, and even students—are asked if these are appropriate goals. If they answer yes, the goals are accepted by those who are creating and delivering the curriculum. (See Curriculum Tips 7.2.)

**GENERATING OBJECTIVES.** Within the context of educational aims and goals, it is necessary to formulate more specific objectives. Whereas aims and goals are long term, objectives are short term.

For a particular science program or project, curriculum developers may state a goal such as "improving students' skill in information processing when dealing with science material." This goal may then be approached through a series of objectives.

**Guidelines for Formulating Objectives.** When creating objectives, educators should consider how well they match the stated goals and aims. For example, an objective stating that students understand certain science concepts does not match a goal that students be able to use particular information-processing approaches to scientific understanding. A standard must relate more specifically to an objective; to fine-tune this objective, educators must identify the content standard—that is, define the procedural knowledge that must be demonstrated and then indicate the performance or skill level or levels that must be attained.

Objectives must also have worth and be nontrivial. For example, the objective "The student knows that the Mississippi River empties into the Gulf of Mexico" is overly narrow. An objective should have value to the student in both the present and the future. In other words, the content and performance standards must have worth for the students. It makes little sense to say that a certain content must be learned to a high level and a certain performance must be demonstrated at a high level if the content really has no value or relevance in the general society. To know what a slide rule is and how it functions and to be able to use it skillfully most likely has little value in the 21st century.

---

**CURRICULUM TIPS 7.2**    **Developing Goals at the School District or School Level**

When creating curriculum goals, individuals need to know the following:

1. Federal and state mandates regarding education
2. The specific students who are to receive the planned curriculum
3. The expected competencies and understandings expected of the learners
4. Educational environments and situations that will enable the goals to be attained
5. The standards of performance and comprehension that are expected from students who have experienced the newly created curriculum

*Source:* Information from Abbie Brown and Timothy D. Green, *The Essentials of Instructional Design* (Upper Saddle River, NJ: Pearson, 2006), pp. 146–147.

The guideline that objectives have worth and be nontrivial is challenging if you consider that what has worth to one student may, in fact, be worthless to another. That is a major challenge in employing standards in curricular decision making. As Taubman notes, most discussions of standards seem to have them exist with a false sense of precision and without a consideration of context. Standards are presented as independent of circumstance. We have a dilemma. Standards, to be standards, Taubman informs us, must serve as "'immutable mobiles,' which can move across contexts and cross local, state, and national borders, can move from one community of practice to another, transforming as they go, but not being transformed in the process."[53]

Standards, and particularly national standards, assume that all students, all communities, all teachers, and all school districts are alike and that they face the same challenges, possess the same values, and have students of the same intellectual abilities, the same intellectual interests, the same behavioral dispositions, and the same cultural and ethnic backgrounds. Standards imply that all school districts define the worth of a particular objective with the same metric. This is not reality. However, many voices advocating standards declare that all schools should strive for the same or at least similar interpretations of worth. Standards imply the standardization of curriculum, instruction, educational experiences, and learning. "Same" standards are requisite for us to compare educational successes among our schools.

Another guideline is that objectives should be clearly expressed—easy to understand and agree on. Likewise, the standards within the objective should be clearly expressed and agreed on. Lisa Carter criticized some published state standards as vague. So written, teachers must translate them in their classrooms. Thus, there would be no "standardization" of teaching, curriculum, or learning and no ways to measure attainment of valuable content and skills.[54]

Although making objectives and the explicit and implicit standards comprehensible may be easily accomplished, getting everyone to agree to the objectives, even goals, and certainly standards is a daunting task. The next guideline for generating objectives is even more problematic. To determine appropriateness, educators must consider students' needs and the content to be covered. Some objectives might be inappropriate because they demand behavior that students are incapable of attaining or because they do not consider students' interests. Some objectives might be better suited to students in a particular subject who have unique aspirations than to students with other motivations.

However, as Taubman discusses, although teachers may realize that students arrive with various abilities, capabilities, interests, cultural and ethnic backgrounds, different life experiences, and myriad dreams about their presents and futures, teachers are commanded not to apply different standards to each student, lest we lose what "standard" means.[55] The curricula cannot vary in objective or standard and cannot digress in intent; all variables must be kept constant in emphasis and support. The curriculum must be standardized.

This is not the reality of schooling and not the reality of the community, the regions, or the state nor of the nation or the world community. Yet, standards still hold center stage in educational and, specifically, curricular and instructional conversations. We certainly are not advocating eliminating standards. We need standards, but not for generating standard curriculum, one size fits all. We should not concede to other authorities, often outside of education, the task of determining the standards for our objectives, our curricula, our instruction, or our educational materials. Certainly, selecting educational objectives and selecting standards for content and procedures is not the sole domain of educators. However, it seems that today, much activity within the standards theater has left out educators. National political boards determine standards for children in New Hampshire and in Arizona. They set the bars for success for students in Washington State and Georgia. They inform educators how far to jump, suggesting that their salaries will be calibrated as to whether they fall at or over the bar.

Who are these people, these power groups, active in determining educational objectives and standards? We have mentioned national groups, some governmental and some professional. No Child Left Behind was generated at the national level. The Race to the Top contest is a national effort. The Gates Foundation, giving millions to various schools, is influencing objectives and standards. Certainly, state boards of education are key players.

A fourth guideline for formulating objectives is that they should be grouped logically so as to make sense when units of instruction and evaluations are being determined. Even standards should be grouped logically, which may mean that the standards implicit in objectives must be personalized to the diversities of particular students. Objectives frequently lack coherence. For example, objectives at different levels of specificity are grouped together, as when understanding how to process information is grouped with knowing how to write complete sentences. The standard implicit in understanding how to engage procedural knowledge has more complexity than the standard implicit in knowing how to write a complete sentence.

The fifth guideline is that objectives require periodic revision. Students change, society changes, knowledge changes, instructional strategies change, and competencies required for functioning in particular aspects of society change. This guideline suggests that contrary to popular thinking, standards must change. If standards are targets, as some suggest, we must realize that they are moving targets, propelled by time.[56] Educators must occasionally analyze their objectives and reconsider particular standards to determine if they still possess value.

The sixth guideline is that useful objectives enable students to proceed to the next part of a unit plan or lesson plan. Useful standards address those contents and skills requisite to continuing the educational journey. Useful objectives and enabling standards assist students in participating in the world outside of school.

The last factor to consider is an objective's legality. Regarding legality, there is—there must be—a standardization of the standard so that there is compliance with federal and state mandates. Some mandates require that all students be taught certain material, such as state history or basic mathematics. Here, your authors have little difficulty in accepting standards. However, we must still make a case that with standards, we are talking minimal levels of content knowledge and skills attainment. Of course, there are some mandates that prohibit certain content. Still other mandates address the needs of particular student populations, such as those in special education.[57]

**Types of Objectives.**   Educational objectives range from objectives for specific curriculum areas (often subjects or courses) at particular grade levels to specific outcomes of classroom instruction. Abbie Brown and Timothy Green note that an instructional objective should clearly indicate some observable or quantifiable student behavior. In other words, these instructional objectives must be explicit about standards.[58]

Outcome-based education is popular in most states. Washington State established a commission to develop a list of learning outcomes essential for all students. Such outcomes are *standards*.

***Behavioral Objectives.***   Most educators (and the general public) believe that educational objectives should be couched in terms of observable or measurable achievement. That is, the objective is behavioral. Students can demonstrate that they have acquired particular skills or knowledge—that is, attained standards.

Mager contends that an educational objective must describe (1) the *behavior* that indicates a learner has achieved the objective, (2) the *condition* or situation imposed on the learner when he or she demonstrates achievement, and (3) the minimum standard *proficiency* level acceptable.[59] A behavioral objective in science that satisfies Mager's criteria might read as follows:

> After studying the unit on energy, the student must complete a 100-question, 1-hour, multiple-choice test on the subject. The student must answer 75 questions correctly.

A behavioral objective for mathematics might read:

> Given a multiplication worksheet, the pupil will be able to multiply 10 sets of 3-digit numbers at the rate of one problem per minute, with 80 percent accuracy.

Some educators subscribe to behavioral objectives but do not believe that these objectives must address the condition or situation in which the behavior is performed or its proficiency. Also, unlike Mager, they consider it essential that behavioral objectives state what the student will do (e.g., write a paragraph, compare data) in terms of subject content. Such objectives might state, "The student will write a paragraph in English composition dealing with late 20th-century literature," or "The student in an economics class will compare a chart's data on gross national product for two different years."

It is not always necessary to include level of achievement and conditions of performance. However, it is necessary to include level of achievement (how well, how much, or how accurate) when dealing with minimum requirements, that is, standards, for some aspect of a course. Conditions of performance are necessary when it is important to know where and how the knowledge was demonstrated or the skill was performed. What was the nature of the environment? Did the conditions of performance resemble real-life conditions? The following objective includes both essential and optional parts: "The student in a geography field-study exercise will arrange field notes so that they meet the guidelines in the manual on geography field study."

"In a geography field-study exercise" refers to the condition; "will arrange" refers to the required student action, and "in a way that meets the suggested guidelines" refers to the level, or standard, of achievement.[60]

***Nonbehavioral General Objectives.*** Advocates of nonbehavioral objectives use words such as *appreciate, know,* and *understand*. They believe stating objectives too specifically restricts learning to measurable achievements. Objectives that address higher-order learning (e.g., analytical thinking, appreciation of literature) are likely to be neglected.

Postmodern educators reject behavioral objectives as too narrow and rigid. Some believe educators have no right to stipulate what students must know, how they must behave, or what skills they must possess.[61] Learning is not about performance level but about inquiry.

When making curricular decisions, especially when generating objectives, educators ideally consider all domains of learning: cognitive, affective, and psychomotor. Depending on which domain they address, objectives focus on different skills, competencies, and understandings. Within each domain, objectives are listed in an order that reflects increasing complexity.

***Cognitive Objectives.*** In 1956, Benjamin Bloom introduced us to the Taxonomy of Educational Objectives, Cognitive Domain. In his taxonomy, he divided cognitive learning into (1) knowledge, (2) comprehension, (3) application, (4) analysis, (5) synthesis, and (6) evaluation.[62] For many years, teachers used this classification as a guide for creating cognitive objectives. In 2001, a revision of Bloom's taxonomy was published. The revision created a grid for generating objectives that addressed the knowledge and cognitive process dimensions. The knowledge dimension subsumed factual knowledge, conceptual knowledge, procedural knowledge, and metacognitive knowledge. The cognitive process dimension addressed remember, understand, apply, analyze, evaluate, and create.[63] Attending to these two dimensions, knowledge and process, allows educators to formulate objectives that consider not only the type of content to be taught, but also the cognitive strategies intended.

*Factual knowledge objectives* address knowledge of specifics, such as facts and terminology. These objectives identify those basic elements that students must grasp to indicate they know a discipline or content area.

*Conceptual knowledge objectives* indicate that students comprehend how basic bits and clusters of facts relate to each other and to the discipline writ large. Stress is on knowledge of classifications and categories; principles and generalizations; and theories, models, and organizational structures.

*Procedural knowledge objectives* address those processes and methods that enable students to "work" with factual and conceptual knowledge. These objectives also include the knowledge of criteria in order to determine what procedures are most productive in processing information.

*Metacognitive knowledge objectives* address what has been a neglected aspect of school learning: knowledge of cognition in general, knowledge of how the brain functions in general, and knowledge of an individual's own specific cognition. Awareness of strategic knowledge and how to utilize heuristics and algorithms to engage students in the learning process receive attention with these objectives. Metacognitive knowledge objectives direct students to focus on the development of their intelligence.

***The Cognitive Processes.***    Although the knowledge dimension focuses on the content to be learned, the noun of the objective, we must provide the verb of the objective, the action. What is the student to do; what actions are to be demonstrated?

There are six cognitive processes that the four types of knowledge objectives can incorporate: remember, understand, apply, analyze, evaluate, and create. The cognitive processes advance in complexity and intellectual value. The first process, remember, is the least complex. Remember is essentially recognizing and recalling information. It is the knowing of something, whereas the next cognitive process, understanding, refers to making sense of what is recalled and can be utilized in other cognitive processes. In the revision of the taxonomy, understanding subsumes the cognitive activities of interpreting, exemplifying, classifying, summarizing, inferring, comparing, and explaining.[64]

Students require more than understanding: They must utilize that which they understand. Students must activate their procedural knowledge and apply it to both familiar and unfamiliar tasks and situations.

The fourth cognitive process dimension is analyze. At this juncture, students must break a whole into parts and distinguish elements, relationships, and organizational principles. Students must uncover the structures inherent in subject matter. They must deconstruct and reconstruct what they remember and understand.

The fifth cognitive process of cognitive objectives is most crucial to the intelligent use of knowledge, the evaluative cognitive process. Here students and teacher must judge conclusions based on criteria and standards. Here emphasis is on making judgments, engaging in critiques, and utilizing internal evidence or logical consistency and external evidence or consistency with data produced elsewhere.

The sixth, and last, cognitive process dimension is generating methods of creating. At this stage, the synthesis stage in Bloom's first taxonomy, students generate hypotheses, design future strategies for learning, and construct products or environments that indicate students' creative competence regarding content.[65]

***The Multipurpose Objective.***    Certainly, we can have cognitive objectives of various degrees of complexity. We could simply have an objective that focused on remembering, the cognitive process of factual knowledge. Such an objective might read: "The student will name the highest mountain range in Asia." However, most teachers would like cognitive objectives to address high knowledge dimensions and engage students in more sophisticated cognitive processes. For instance, a teacher might create the following objective for a unit on global warming: "Students will utilize weather data to make forecasts about likely future weather consequences on various geographic areas." This objective addresses three knowledge dimensions: factual, conceptual, and procedural knowledge. The objective requires students to learn specific geography and meteorology facts. Students also must know reliable sources of information. Students must comprehend conceptual knowledge such as weather patterns, trend analyses, and knowledge of various weather models and structures. They must also possess knowledge of specific forecasting procedures and even algorithms related to weather analysis.

This particular objective also requires that students engage in various cognitive processes, the "verb" of the objective. Certainly, for students to utilize weather data to generate forecasts about the consequences of global warming, they must remember and apprehend a quantity of data to interpret map data and global imaging. They must implement a procedure of analysis. To do this, students must engage in analysis of gathered data and determine what data contribute to a position on global warming. Students must judge, critique, their forecast or conclusion. Upon attainment of this objective, students might be asked to produce their own forecast.

It is evident from this example that what at first appeared as a straightforward objective really possessed many dimensions of knowledge and cognitive processes. The revised taxonomy is a most useful tool in reflecting upon and creating cognitive objectives.

*Affective Objectives.*    David Krathwohl and others have broken affective objectives into five levels of achievement. Each level depends on attainment of the previous level. For example, to express a value preference, a student must be able to receive information and respond to situations.[66]

**1.** *Receiving* objectives refer to the learner's sensitivity to stimuli. This sensitivity includes (1) awareness, (2) willingness to receive, and (3) selected attention. Example: From studying various Eastern cultures, the student develops an awareness of aesthetic factors in Eastern dress, furnishings, and architecture.

**2.** *Responding* objectives refer to the learner's active attention to stimuli such as (1) acquiescence, (2) willing responses, and (3) feelings of satisfaction. Example: The student displays an interest in the topic of conversation by actively participating in a research project.

**3.** *Valuing* objectives refer to the learner's beliefs and attitudes of worth, which manifest as (1) acceptance, (2) preference, and (3) commitment. Example: The student takes a stance regarding the advantages or disadvantages of nuclear power.

**4.** *Organization* objectives refer to internalization of values and beliefs, which involves (1) conceptualization of values and (2) organization of a value system. Example: The student forms judgments about his or her responsibilities for conserving natural resources.

**5.** *Characterization.* This is the highest level of internalization. Objectives at this level relate to behavior that reflects (1) a generalized set of values and (2) philosophy of life. Example: The student regulates his or her personal and civic life in accordance with ethical principles.

Considering affective objectives requires a realization that we are pushing boundaries of the knowledge dimension, the cognitive process dimension, and the emotional dimension. Here we have a messy fusion. If, as Anderson and Krathwohl suggest, the dimension of metacognitive knowledge includes knowledge about our own cognition, we must then realize that it relates to students' affect and to students' emotional awareness and intellectual awareness. The affective domain dominates metacognitive self-knowledge.

Flavell articulated many years ago that self-knowledge is a crucial component of metacognition.[67] Reflecting on self-knowledge, students record their strengths and weakness as they relate to their educational adventures. Students, possessing self-awareness of the depth and breadth of their own learning, have valuable information to guide future learning.[68]

Self-knowledge also relates to individuals' apprehension of their temperament. Research has shown that temperament is biologically based, with an additional impact by genes, environment, and experience. Individuals have no "voice" regarding their genes, but they do have voice regarding their environment and, certainly, their experience. Realizing this, students have more control over self-regulation of intensity and duration of interest and emotion in response to particular situations.[69] Teachers must schedule time for students to engage in metacognitive thought and build self-knowledge. Attention to affective objectives addresses more than the brain; it nurtures the emotional self, the knowledgeable self, and the intellectual self.

*Psychomotor Objectives.*    The psychomotor domain has received much less emphasis than the cognitive and affective domains. Anita Harrow divided objectives into six levels. As with cognitive and affective levels, psychomotor levels require attainment of previous levels. For example, to meet perceptual objectives, a child must have mastered fundamental movements.[70]

**1.** *Reflex movements.* Objectives at this level include (1) segmental reflexes (involving one spinal segment) and (2) intersegmental reflexes (involving more than one spinal segment).

Example: After engaging in this activity, the student will respond automatically to a physical stimulus.

**2. *Fundamental movements.*** Objectives at this level address behaviors related to (1) walking, (2) running, (3) jumping, (4) pushing, (5) pulling, and (6) manipulating. Example: The student will jump over a 2-foot hurdle.

**3. *Perceptual abilities.*** Objectives at this level address (1) kinesthetic, (2) visual, (3) auditory, (4) tactile, and (5) coordination abilities. Example: The student will categorize building blocks by shape.

**4. *Physical abilities.*** Objectives at this level relate to (1) endurance, (2) strength, (3) flexibility, (4) agility, (5) reaction time, and (6) dexterity. Example: By the end of the year, the student will be able to do at least five more pushups.

**5. *Skilled movements.*** Objectives at this level are concerned with (1) games, (2) sports, (3) dances, and (4) the arts. Example: The student can perform a series of somersaults.

**6. *Nondiscursive communication.*** Objectives at this level relate to expressive movement through (1) posture, (2) gestures, (3) facial expressions, and (4) creative movements. Example: The student will create a movement sequence and perform it to music.

Although these taxonomies are useful in developing and grouping objectives and curricular emphases, there is overlap among the taxonomies and within the taxonomic levels. This is true because in reality, knowledge, skills, emotions, and attitudes (and even ethics, morals, and spiritual dimensions) make up the complexity of human learning and action.

**Table 7.2** Overview of Aims, Goals, and Objectives

| Educational Statement | Features | Source | Samples | Curriculum Implications |
|---|---|---|---|---|
| Aims | General statements provide direction or intent to educational action. | From national commissions, task forces, and panels | *Cardinal Principles of Secondary Education; The Purpose of Education in American Democracy; A Nation at Risk* | Identifies the curriculum's overall direction. |
| Goals | Statements of purpose given, which are more specific than aims. | From professional associations, government agencies, state departments of education, and school districts | ASCD, Measuring and Maintaining the Goals of Education; PDK, Phase III of the Educational Planning Model; National Goals for Education | Identifies specific content areas of the curriculum. |
| Objectives | Specific statements indicate either general or specific outcomes; behavioral objectives indicate the specific behavior the student is to demonstrate to indicate learning. Nonbehavioral objectives use more general words to denote the learning desired, such as to *know* or *understand*. | From school districts, schools, and individual writers | Taxonomy of Educational Objectives; Posner, Gronlund, Mager | Behavioral objectives tend to make curriculum more sequenced, precise, and compartmentalized. Nonbehavioral objectives allow for a more open-ended curriculum and integration of subject matter |

## Selecting Curriculum Content

Curricularists must determine what knowledge students need in order to succeed. This is the same question that Spencer raised; "What knowledge is of most worth?" However, today, the question must be rephrased to, What knowledge is of most worth in the global and digital world?[71] A related question is, To what degree should students 'master' the determined, selected knowledge? This query brings the issue of standards. Those who believe that the knowledge selected for the curriculum should have standards and that the curriculum should be standardized are ignoring two obvious truths; useful knowledge is both culturally and historically specific,[72] and the skill level for using selected knowledge varies with individuals' interests and needs.

As societies change, what is useful and essential to know changes. As Yong Zhao posits, the knowledge considered valuable and necessary in one society may be of little value or totally valueless in another.[73] Information essential in an agricultural society has little value in an urban global society. And certainly, knowledge of agriculture to a city dweller requires a different mind and skill set than for someone in agribusiness.

What is so challenging to curricularists in determining and selecting curricular content, both declarative and procedural, is that schools are responsible for creating programs of study not just for a local community, not just for a state or national society, but for a global, world society, or, specifically, world *societies*. And all these societies are in flux. Educators are selecting content for anticipated, imagined, emerging, expanding, and contracting societies. Adding to the challenges of content selection is that we have to select content from two worlds: real and virtual. As Yong Zhao notes, educators and other professionals must apprehend that the virtual world is something different from the physical world. He states that the virtual world is fundamentally different, thus requiring different knowledge and skills. Curricularists and communities might ask why we have to consider the virtual world. We must, because many of our current students live in both.

Zhao describes a 3-D virtual world called Second Life, created and run by Linden Lab, a software company in San Francisco. Although existing for only a few years, it currently involves many players worldwide who are very active as "residents" in a virtual world. In this cyber world, the residents engage in activities similar to the physical world: building houses, constructing buildings, purchasing cars, buying food, and engaging in business activities in which they actually make real, physical world money.

Second Life is more than a game just played for enjoyment. It can serve as a vehicle for formal education. If a student is interested in art, he or she can travel to virtual representations of particular art museums. If travel is an interest, the student can, via his or her online persona, travel to many European cities.[74]

Several years ago, Christine Sleeter noted that schools tend to stress content that benefited the dominant culture and excluded content central to groups that have been historically marginalized, such as Blacks, Hispanics, and Native Americans. The knowledge and learning styles of the dominant culture were deemed most important.[75] Although this view still has relevance, curricularists must recognize that in our global worldview, there are many dominant cultures that are constantly interacting. Numerous learning styles and knowledge realms are being morphed as technology has made distance irrelevant in many cases. In the global and digital world, U.S. schools must select content that serves students well as both U.S. and world citizens.

**CONCEPTIONS OF CONTENT.** Groups charged with curriculum planning must select content that enables students to learn the most—whatever curriculum design or developmental model they implement. The curriculum must supply information that relates to students' concerns. Contents should be organized so that students find the information useful and meaningful. When selecting content, the curriculum planner must take into account how well it addresses students' cognitive, social, and psychological dimensions.

| KNOWLEDGE $\longrightarrow$ | Content $\longrightarrow$ | Knowledge |
|---|---|---|
| (information formally organized) | (knowledge selected for educational purposes) | (school content at levels sufficient for use) |

**FIGURE 7.5** World Knowledge to School Knowledge

Content (subject matter) is a compendium of facts, concepts, generalizations, principles, and theories. It also incorporates methods of processing information. Curricular content provides students with opportunities for discovering knowledge. Content is selected from knowledge domains. (See Figure 7.5.)

**ORGANIZATION OF CONTENT.** Paul Hirst has noted that different knowledge domains have unique types of concepts in specialized relationships. For instance, mathematics has the concepts of number, integer, and matrix. Physics has the concepts of matter and energy. Within any knowledge domain, concepts are organized into specialized networks. Different types of tests and processes are tailored to different knowledge domains.[76]

Program planners can organize content in philosophical/logical, psychological, political, or practical terms. Curriculum makers who use logical orientation organize content according to certain rules and concepts. In economics, for example, the concepts of supply and demand are major organizers, without which the ideas of capital, labor, and marketplace cannot be understood. Arranging economics content in this manner makes sense, but it really does not denote the way an individual might actually learn economics.

Curricularists who use a psychological organization focus on how students learn or process information. Behaviorists think that content should be selected and organized so that correct responses are reinforced. Cognitivists think that content should prompt students to analyze, hypothesize, investigate, identify patterns, critique, and draw conclusions.[77] Most educators believe that content should be organized so that students move from the concrete to the abstract. This is a key principle of sequencing content.

Political organization is increasingly popular. According to those who favor this approach, content should be sequenced so that adequate emphasis is given to topics and people important to various pressure groups. Often politically driven content selection results from political or legal action.[78] For example, history curricula must now include the views and deeds of Blacks, Native Americans, Hispanics, and women. The goal is to include "concepts, paradigms, themes, and explanations that challenge mainstream academic knowledge and that expand the historical and literary canon."[79]

The last content organizer is practicality, which deals with cost-effectiveness, such as the expense of structuring the content in a particular way. Practicality includes questions such as these: Which organization of curriculum content optimizes learning? Can one find textbooks, technology, and other educational materials that support this content organization? Will teachers, students, parents, and the general public readily accept this organization?[80]

**CRITERIA FOR SELECTING CONTENT.** Regardless of their curriculum design preferences or their philosophical orientations, curriculum planners must apply criteria in choosing curriculum content. Although the criteria are common to most curricular orientations, educators in the various philosophical camps might place greater emphasis on particular criteria.

**Self-Sufficiency.** Israel Scheffler argues that the prime guiding principle for content selection is helping the learners to attain maximum self-sufficiency in the most economical manner. He elaborates three types of economy: economy of teaching effort and educational resources, economy of students' efforts, and economy of subject matter's extent of generalizability.[81] This criterion—helping learners to attain maximum self-sufficiency—is also supported by many humanists, radicals, and reconceptualists as a means by which learners can actualize their potential and crystallize their identities.

The criterion of self-sufficiency must be considered in ample depth. It does not mean just learning knowledge and skills that allow one to function independently in society. It means furnishing content that enables learners to connect their intellectual, emotional, and spiritual selves. It means content that nurtures connections of intellectual and emotional selves to the selves of others. Content chosen should address self-sufficiency so that individual learners commence transforming themselves into more complete individual and social beings, moving toward being in a state of communion with others.[82]

**Significance.**    Content to be learned is significant only to the degree to which it contributes to the basic ideas, concepts, principles, generalizations, and so on, of the overall aims of the curriculum. Content should also consider the development of particular learning abilities, skills, processes, and attitude formation.

**Validity.**    *Validity* is the authenticity of the content selected. In this time of information explosion and the rapid technological means of delivering information, such as Facebook, YouTube, and Wikipedia, knowledge selected for school content can quickly become obsolete and even incorrect. It seems that anyone can post information and not identify its source. It appears that an assumption or conclusion can travel digitally around the world several times before anyone even bothers to check its accuracy. As new knowledge is discovered, content assumed valid may become misleading or even false. Validity must be verified at the initial selection of curriculum content, but it must also be checked at regular intervals through the duration of the curricular program to determine if content originally valid continues to be so.

Validity seems to be a rather straightforward criterion. Something is either accurate or inaccurate; something either happened or it did not. Nevertheless, the ideological stance and attendant metaphors that any individual brings to a situation vastly influence what he or she perceives as valid. Metaphors influence how we think about different situations and different phenomena. For instance, labeling a society patriarchal or oppressive is valid only if one uses a metaphor of gender hierarchy or a dynamic of competing physical forces. Because of the use of metaphors, some can state that certain information in school content is valid or truthful, whereas others can consider the same information invalid. Revisionists, radical school critics, reconstructionists, and postpositivists state that much of the curriculum offered to students is invalid.[83]

**Interest.**    Another criterion is *interest*. To those who favor the learner-centered design, this is a key criterion. These persons note that knowledge exists in the learner when it is meaningful to his or her life. When it fails to be meaningful, it dehumanizes education. The interest criterion has been with us since the times of the child-centered school in the 1920s. Advocates of this movement urged that the child should be the source of the curriculum; in other words, the children's interest should determine the curriculum.

Those currently advocating a learner-centered curriculum point out that the content of the curriculum must be selected with students' interests in mind; however, the school experience should create and broaden interests as well as address them. A key question is, Are students' current interests of long-lasting educational value for both the students and society? Dealing with this question is difficult because it assumes educators possess some degree of perception regarding future society and students' places in that future.

The criterion of students' interests should be weighted and adjusted to allow for students' maturity, their prior experiences, the educational and social value of their interests, and the way they are expected to interact within society. Attending to this criterion of interest means that, in selecting content or arranging for content to be experienced or constructed, the educator must be sure that the content does engage the individual. The content must contribute to the welfare of the student.

**Utility.**    *Utility* concerns the usefulness of the content. Again, how a person defines usefulness is influenced by his or her philosophical view and favored curriculum design. Usefulness to those favoring the subject-centered design is often judged in terms of how the content learned enables students to use that knowledge in job situations and other adult activities. Usefulness to those in the learner-centered camp is related to how the content enables the individual to gain an accurate perception of his or her self-identity and to attain meaning in his or her life. Is the content useful for the learner developing his or her human potential? Proponents of the problem-centered mode think of content as having utility if it has direct application to ongoing life and to social and political issues.

A challenge in dealing with the criterion of utility is that educational decision makers must consider two kinds of utility: current utility and future utility. There are certain contents and processes that students must learn for immediate application to be successful in their current lives. Some of these contents and processes have utility for all students, regardless of the students' desires or life ambitions. However, there are some contents that have immediate utility only for students who have very specialized needs, desires, or ambitions. Thus, utility must be considered with the student audience in mind. In addition to content that has current utility or immediate application, there are contents that have current utility for preparing students to deal with the future, not the immediate present. These contents have utility in getting students to think in particular ways that will be useful in the future. These contents have utility in getting students to be futurists themselves, to engage in futures planning, to forecast events, and to assess future consequences of current and emerging trends.

In the global and digital world, educators must rethink the criterion of utility. Some content might have limited utility, perhaps even be useless, in particular students' immediate environment. However, those charged with selecting content must recognize that in today's shrinking world, what might be of little value in the immediate community may have great worth in a distant community. Some might argue this point by asserting that their students are unlikely to travel to distant places. However, a student might indeed be able to market his or her knowledge or skills in a distant place without actually leaving his or her home office. We do not need to travel to India to work there.[84]

Zhao presents an interesting idea, "Nothing is too strange to be useful." Phrased differently, nothing is too strange to have utility. No content, no knowledge, if presented on a world scale, lacks utility to some audience, however small. Companies like Amazon and Netflix function with this concept. They focus on what may appeal to only a small number of individuals, but they announce to the world community that they have this "narrow-focus" material. Because they announce this fact worldwide, they always have enough people interested in the material, this bit of knowledge. Small numbers of people interested in strange and unusual materials generate major sales. Millions of small orders spell success for companies using this business model. If educators "toy" with the idea of putting specific curricula online that might only have limited local interest but, globally, might entice profitable numbers, they might be motivated to create such a curriculum. Zhao indicates that with Second Life, Michigan State University's Confucius Center has created for Second Life a virtual Chinese Island designed so players can learn Mandarin Chinese. The Island allows players to visit a Chinese museum, markets, even restaurants. Zhao notes that other universities are exploring courses to be offered in this cyber universe.[85] School districts, especially those offering the international baccalaureate degree, might create curricula that have utility for students from around the world as well as from their home district. There is no knowledge, no content, that does not have utility to someone.

**Learnability.**    Could anyone select content without considering this obvious criterion? Some critics of the schools say yes. Certain contents are selected that are out of the range of experiences of particular students and are thus difficult, if not impossible, to learn. Furthermore, selected contents are sometimes arranged and presented in ways that make their learning difficult for some students. Critics often say that content selected reflects a middle-class bias and that it is organized to favor those who have convergent (and right-answer) learning styles. The learnability criterion relates to the optimal placement and appropriate organization and sequencing of content. Furthermore, it addresses the issue of appropriateness for the intended student audience.

**Feasibility.**    *Feasibility,* the last criterion, forces curriculum planners to consider content in light of the time allowed, the resources available, the expertise of current staff, the nature of the political climate, the existing legislation, and the amount of public monies available. Although educators may think that they have an entire world of content from which to choose, they do have limitations on their actions. Even the number of days in the school calendar, for example, limits what can be taught. So do the size of the classroom and the personnel of the school. Content selection must be considered within the context of the existing reality, which usually boils down to economics and politics.

## Selecting Curriculum Experiences

Curriculum developers must consider not only content, but also how students experience that content. They must consider instructional strategies and educational activities. Possible instructional strategies include inquiry strategies, lecture, discussion, and demonstration. Educational activities include viewing films or videos, conducting experiments, interacting with computer programs, taking field trips, and listening to speakers.

Curricularists select and sequence pedagogical approaches and manipulate experiences and materials in the hope not only of imparting knowledge, but also of enhancing students' values and attitudes, abilities to think critically and creatively, and desire to learn individually and collaboratively.

Curriculum experiences should nurture the enhancement of intellectual activities in both hemispheres of the brain. The focus in the 20th century tended to be on left-brain-directed thinking skills. Such skills stressed the "sequential, literal, functional, textual, and analytic."[86] The 21st century requires more right-hemisphere thinking skills. These skills are simultaneous, metaphorical, aesthetic, contextual, and synthetic.[87]

Curriculum experiences that stimulate student excitement in adapting to and managing complexity, celebrating uncertainty, and rewarding intellectual risk taking will serve students of this century well. Also, educational experiences that foster in students a playfulness in their learning and a joyfulness in interacting with ideas, materials, technology, and people of various cultural, ethnic, and knowledge views will be valuable.

Curriculum experiences of this century should go from didactic teacher presentation to teacher–student, student–student, and student–outside expert interactions. And, these interactions need not be just interactions with local community members. Remember, technology has eliminated distance. Students might collaborate on a project with a student or knowledge expert in another country. Field studies can roam the world seeking answers to particular questions. Interaction strategies alter the educational metric from answers and certainty to questions and uncertainty. Puzzlement is rewarded in new 21st century pedagogies. This does not mean that educators ignore strategies that stimulate the left-brain hemisphere. Rather, it means that we are attempting to maximize the total brain—both hemispheres, the serious logical and the playful inventive.[88] With such balancing, educational experiences mirror ways in which knowledge and skills are actually applied in out-of-school situations. With such balancing, students attain a greater understanding of themselves as individual students and persons as well as members of groups, both local and worldwide.

Of course, various pedagogies and educational activities must be feasible in terms of time, staff expertise, facilities available within and outside of the school, and community expectations. However, as pointed out previously, technology has and continues to introduce the world community to students. We no longer need a yellow school bus for field trips to a farm or museum. Students can visit art museums in London by being "residents" in the metaverse of Second Life.[89]

We realize that many who read the preceding paragraphs may take exception to the points advanced. Certainly, with the stress on meeting standards, to suggest that school work should be reclassified as school play will raise eyebrows. What is the standard for playfulness? How is it measured? And how would one measure whether a standard was attained in a school project conducted with various players engaged in Second Life? And, where are teachers going to get all the time for such actions? And what about teacher expertise?

However, teachers are professionals, and most community members think that the school their child attends is really quite good. The sorry state of public schools applies only to schools in other communities. In the Seattle area, four high schools in one school district were ranked in the top 25 nationally. However, we recognize that all schools are not equal regarding curriculum, teachers, funding, and student preparedness for academic study. Even so, we should strive for "best" practice in selecting curriculum experiences.

Educators striving for best practice and attempting to attain high standards must realize that in reality, content and experiences are inseparable. Students reading a book or playing Second Life are combining content (what they are reading) with experience (the act of reading or the actual processing of what is learned in the cyber game).

## Selecting Educational Environments

Just as we cannot separate content from experiences in the actual delivery of a curriculum, neither can we divorce the experiencing of content, the learning of content, and the attainment of knowledge from the space or spaces within which experience occurs. At least, this has been the case until recently. Neither, until recently, could we divorce the experiencing of the curriculum from the realm of time. The space and time in which individuals place themselves or are placed affects their inner experiences, their learnings, their knowledge, and their understandings. As William Ayers notes, "The learning environment is a complex, living reflection of a teacher's values."[90] We add that the learning or educational environment is more than a reflection of a teacher's values. An educational environment is a representation of values from communities of persons, seen and unseen.

An educational environment represents a milieu in which teachers and students engage in mutual communication about content and mutually participate with educational materials and technological programs to attain meaningful educational experience.[91] Children who experience a creative environment are much more likely to be stimulated, to realize their potential, and to be excited about learning. As William Ayers indicates, such an environment must be arranged both physically and conceptually so as to challenge the breadth and depth of students' abilities and interests.[92] However, as Deborah L. Voltz, Michele Jean Sims, and Betty Nelson articulate, an educational environment must be created and orchestrated so that students feel intellectually safe. Students should be encouraged to investigate content realms in ways that appeal to them and in ways that celebrate their cultural orientations to learning, topics, and people.[93]

Educational environments often are ignored by curricularists and teachers. One tends to just accept the classroom to which one is assigned. Certainly, one has to function in the given classroom space, but teachers have an obligation to question the educational, the curricular, and the instructional attributes of the classroom space. What is obvious about the classroom space? Will it allow for teacher–student and student–student interactions? What are the hidden curriculum messages? What are the obvious messages? Will the environment make students feel comfortable and appreciated? Will I as teacher feel at home in this environment?[94] Educators must consider a classroom as a biosphere—as an ecosystem. Is the space and what grows within it healthful regarding nurturing curiosities, intellectual risk taking, dispositions to explore, experiment, concern and empathy for fellow students? Will it foster intellectual character and technological competencies?[95]

Certainly, educational environments should be planned so that purposeful student activity is stimulated. However, today's environments must also allow for nonpurposeful student activities—just playing around with information to see what happens when one mixes ideas and actions. Computer games can foster such nonpurposeful actions. Having playfulness as part of the hidden curriculum can arouse in students a wish to engage in serendipitous learnings and to take pleasure in the excitement of uncertainty. The hidden curriculum should also shout out that all students' learnings and results of learning are valued and encouraged. Another hidden curriculum message is that students have responsibilities for selecting contents they wish to learn. This hidden message might be nothing more than scheduling time for students to suggest ideas for lessons.

Only purposeful learnings exist. What we classify as nonpurposeful are activities or contents that we do not find of use to us. However, these contents and activities have utility, even if not articulated, to someone. As Ayers posits, and we tend to agree, individuals learn what they deem important without much outside intervention. After all, babies learn to speak a language without direct instruction. They learn to walk, to play ball, and to dress themselves. They develop a number sense prior to experiencing a structured school curriculum. Young individuals learn these things on their own because we structure, or create, environments in which they can practice actions and learnings. We try to make the environment appealing in order to tempt the individual to try some learning and some action. We offer encouragement at any sign of success. We make the environment safe. Individuals, starting with babies, can read the hidden curriculum messages that cheer "try this, hold on to that, take this step, throw the ball." An effective educational environment encourages learning, cheers human effort, celebrates social interaction, and encourages forming a learning community.[96]

As mentioned previously, the educational environment is an ecosystem, or biosphere. Further consideration is whether the ecosystem is completely natural; if so, we are called to manage the flora and fauna in ways that keep them vibrant. Our first reaction to educational environments is that they are humanmade. However, the curriculum in today's school does not just take place in human constructions.

According to Ursula M. Franklin, education is not just happening in natural and human biospheres, it is happening in numerous bitspheres.[97] Bitspheres exist within the *space,* the inner environments of the various technologies that we are placing in our schools' educational environments and the technologies we utilize in our out-of-school lives. Our technologies are enabling us to expand *school space,* or educational environments, to limits known and unknown. Franklin asserts that our house—in our case, our schoolhouse—is being expanded and remodeled. And with the remodel, more and more of human life is being lived in the bitspheres. Building within bitspheres is altering how people interact with others and with nature.[98]

Much of the transformation of our lives by our increasing use of technologies is occurring without our awareness. Students, we know, spend a particular amount of time in the educational spaces in schools. We, as educators, have some control over what occurs within the space and time zones. However, increasing numbers of students are engaged with technologies in bitsphere worlds over which we have little or no control. In these bitspheres, there are no time or space constraints. Students can text a message on their iPhone, no matter the hour of the day. There is no day or no night, just "now." And messages can be texts or tweets sent to people whom we have never met in a place where we have never visited. The new technologies are contributing, Franklin asserts, to the destruction or a major alteration of time, space, human community, and the relationship of actual community. Facebook has altered how many interact with others. Students with thousands of "friends" are not going to interact to standard educational school environments. They may be less willing to engage in face-to-face interactions, preferring instead to dialogue in cyberspace.

And students given a science assignment may feel more comfortable going on their own time frame to visit various libraries on the Internet. They may read the great books on their e-readers. They may document their research reports with electronic articles and reports. They even may be able to interview, in cyberspace, various authorities from around the world. And this drifting to unpatterned structures from patterned social and community structures is occurring while many are arguing that we need smaller and more personalized schools.

John Goodlad suggested attention to this dynamic shift several years ago when he argued that schools must develop an ecocentric ethic.[99] An *ecocentric ethic* defines a school's particular culture—the relationships among all the people within the school and outside the school. In an ecocentric school, students interact with institutions and social practices. However, Goodlad could not have known, as your authors did not, that technologies would allow students to expand their interactions from the various biospheres to the bitspheres, that students would be interacting in cyberspace with individuals not really known and never met, or that students would, in some cases, be engaging with avatars.

Franklin offers a caution. With our technologies, students can quickly access massive amounts of information from anywhere in the world. However, she notes, delivering and experiencing curriculum is not just to supply information. Education, writ large, enables students to attain knowledge and understanding. The educational environment, the specifically human sphere, should be considered and developed so that students acquire knowledge and understanding at deep conceptual levels. But in acquiring knowledge and understanding are two levels of learning: explicit and implicit learning. We can perhaps gain explicit learning with ever increasing engagement with the bitsphere, but implicit learning is diminished or even stifled with such bitsphere emersion.[100]

Students engage in explicit learning in gaining knowledge of historical events, learning the construction of correct sentences, learning algorithms to solve problems. And such learning is essential in knowledge acquisition. However, for students to be complete, they must address the affective and psychomotor domains as well as the cognitive. Implicit learning results from individuals interacting together and engaging in social dynamics whether in school or community. Educators must design educational environments that foster in students connections not only with other humans but with all Earth, living and nonliving. Educators must consciously create social situations so that students implicitly develop empathy, tolerance, patience, trust, humility, self-confidence, love, reverence, wonder, and awe. Further learnings should foster respect, concern, inquisitiveness, joy, responsibility, and spirituality. Franklin states that often educators assume that such implicit learnings accompany explicit learnings. Such double learnings cannot be taken for granted. She also asserts that some explicit learnings may become less useful in rapidly evolving futures, whereas the implicit learnings may become truly central to our future welfare.[101]

Decisions about the educational environment may be even more crucial and complex than decisions about selecting content and instructional strategies. We can select a particular science concept and select an instructional strategy, but if we are not careful in designing the educational environment, the science concept experienced may actually "blow up" in the teacher's and students' faces. As Ron Ritchhart articulates, "when the implicit message contradicts the explicit message, the implicit message is likely to win out."[102] Emotion usually trumps reason. When considering educational environments, we must look at the implicit messages hidden within the educational arrangement of space as well as the explicit locations of furniture and educational materials. What educators think important is placed in a power position so that students will notice it more or have more opportunities to employ it in their learning. If students do not pick up on our placements, we often explicitly point them to correct encounters.

Attention to selecting educational environments, while certainly not a major focus of educators when contemplating curricular design and development, has not been totally ignored. In 1987, Brian Castaldi suggested that curriculum planners must consider educational environments in which curricula are experienced. He suggested four criteria that educators should employ when designing educational environments: adequacy, suitability, efficiency, and economy.[103] *Adequacy* refers to the planned spaces. He was referring to the actual classroom space. Are classrooms large enough, well lit, and sufficiently temperature controlled? Today, the adequacy criterion must also be engaged when thinking of cyberspace. Can the cyberspace allow for a few or many participants? Is the visual space of the real classroom large enough to engage all students? With regard to virtual books, there is no need to raise the question about the condition of educational materials. Materials on e-readers never wear out, but, of course, they can become irrelevant.

*Suitability* relates to planned activities. This criterion may be even more crucial to consider in that the virtual worlds opened by technologies can present an ocean of materials and activities that may or may not be appropriate for students. In dealing with suitability, teachers must consider both the chronological and developmental ages of their students. Educators must think about the cultural backgrounds of their students. Concepts such as cultural views of personal space must be incorporated into decision making.

*Efficiency* refers to operational and instructional effectiveness. Does the environment maximize learning while minimizing the efforts required of teachers and students? With technology becoming a central part of the educational environment, the efficiency criterion has taken on new meaning. Students assigned a research activity can engage in conducting virtual experiments or interviewing experts in another country without leaving the classroom. Students can skim through documents provided by the World Wide Web or the Internet in a matter of minutes instead of hours. Students can instantly develop personal connections with multiple learning communities.[104]

Efficiency addresses more than the operational and instructional effectiveness in the explicit realm. This criterion also must guide the effectiveness of the educational environment in stimulating implicit and emotional learnings and dispositions. What is placed in the educational environment must engage, challenge, mystify, excite, and encourage students to book their educational travels. And the environment must allow for such travels, such mind trips, such emotional adventures. It should foster students raising questions that have answers to be known but, perhaps more importantly, questions that are unanswerable. Such questions are: What is my mind? How do emotions work? Who am I? What is space? Are there parallel universes? From whence did time come? What was here before the big bang?[105]

The final criterion, *economy,* refers to cost-effectiveness. As Brian Castaldi first presented it, economy dealt with the specific cost of teaching some part of the curriculum in the environment provided. Just how much money is required for the purchase of textbooks and materials? How much do we need to supply computers to some or all students? How much do we need for salaries for teachers competent in the particular curriculum in this particular educational environment? What do computer programs cost? What expenses are necessary to connect to the Internet or World Wide Web?

As Castaldi developed this criterion, it appears that the economy criterion was influenced by "Time is money." However, economy is not simply related to the cost of doing something or of teaching some subject. Today, we believe that the economy criterion must also consider the cost of not teaching something, or not designing an educational environment that encourages interactions with real persons as well as individuals visited through technologies. Contemplating this criterion, educators must realize that what is done quickly and at the lowest monetary cost today may in future realities be the most ineffective and costly of programs. This concept of what it costs not to do something now in terms of future consequences adds complexity to this final criterion. Although we cannot be certain about future costs of nonaction—not teaching some subject or not allowing students to access certain technologies—we at least must be vigilant in constantly revisiting our educational environments as well as our curricula and instructional methods performed in these environments to make sure that everything educational is still adequate, suitable, efficient, and economical.

## The Final Synthesis

The stages of curriculum development should result in a document that addresses content, educational experiences, and educational environments in keeping with the school's aims, goals, and objectives. Whether educators are creating master curriculum designs, curriculum guides for particular courses of study, or lesson plans for a particular day, they essentially engage in all the stages discussed in this chapter.

## PARTICIPANTS IN CURRICULUM DEVELOPMENT

Developing a curriculum involves many people from both the school and the community. It also involves planning at the classroom, school, district, state, and national levels. Sometimes curriculum planners are at odds with one another. This is especially likely when different political interest groups are competing for resources and influence. Macdonald long ago advocated that all parties affected by the curriculum should be involved in deciding its nature and purpose. The key players should be scholar–experts, professional educators (consultants, administrators, supervisors, and so on), teachers, and students. Parents and community members (including businesspeople and politicians) should play lesser roles.[106]

### Teachers

Teachers occupy the central position in curriculum decision making. They decide which aspects of the curriculum, newly developed or ongoing, to implement or stress in a particular class. Teachers decide how much time to spend on developing basic or critical-thinking skills.

In addition to being curriculum participants at the classroom level, teachers are involved with curriculum committees. These committees may be organized by grade level (e.g., fifth grade), subject area (e.g., biology), or the type of student under consideration (e.g., gifted or learning disabled).

The committees reflect either site-based management (SBM) or school-based curriculum development (SBCD).[107] In either case, the committees' procedures and organization are the same. However, the focus of SBM committees differs from that of SBCD committees. In school-based management, teachers collaborate with school administrators and community members in managing the school: its curriculum, funding, personnel, community relations, and so on. With school-based curriculum development, the focus is on creating and implementing a curriculum. Other matters, such as personnel, are discussed only as they relate to the new curriculum.

Teachers should be involved in every phase of curriculum development. As Michael Fullan and his colleagues remarked, teachers function not only as codesigners of expert curricular and instructional systems, but also as co-researchers into the effectiveness of implemented curricula.[108] Many schools are beginning to allow teachers to choose or develop the program or programs for which they are responsible. Many schools are beginning to follow Fullan's advice that teachers need opportunities to work together as professionals. "There is no getting around the primacy of personal contact."[109] With collaboration, teachers can create quality programs and also modify external programs to personalize them to the specific needs of their students.

### Students

Students should have a voice in curriculum development. It is surprising that teachers, although they think in terms of what students will learn, largely ignore them as individuals who could collaborate in creating or modifying curricula. Curricular change is a people-related phenomenon.[110] Student input into the contents and experiences of the curriculum is important, and the actual involvement in curricular decision making can be, in itself, a learning experience. Students involved to some degree in creating their curriculum are motivated to learn that explicit content and also learn implicitly that their opinions and choices matter. Students involved in creating their own curriculum are empowered and encouraged to assume responsibility for matters that concern them.

### Principals

For curriculum planning to succeed in a school or school system, the principal(s) must be involved.[111] Fullan asserts that where schools have been successful in creating quality education, the principals were leaders of instruction. We interpret instruction as synonymous with curriculum. When principals had accepted an instructional leadership role, they spent less time on administrative, financial, and logistical tasks.[112] Principals did not become the instructional leaders, but they worked closely with those individuals who were.

Yet to be a curriculum and instruction leader requires specialized knowledge. However, many principals are sorely lacking in curricular and instructional expertise. When principals give attention to curricular activities, they often do so from a largely managerial perspective.[113] Even today, most college programs for principals devote little time to curriculum. Some colleges of education have even eliminated the area of curriculum studies. Most administration programs stress personnel matters, education law, financial planning, organizational models, and change strategies to the detriment of curriculum and instruction.

Certainly, no new curriculum will be introduced or created for schools or school systems without the moral and psychological support of principals. Principals, effective in leading any type of innovation—in our case, curricular innovation—must possess the skills requisite for maintaining the relationship between teachers and the larger community, whether local, state, or national.[114]

Principals, especially those involved in SBM, realize that schools must function as learning communities with close ties to the outside neighborhood. Ideally, they believe that curriculum committees should involve community members along with students in decision making. This is no small task, especially at this time of myriad voices expressing divergent demands on the school. Fullan notes that "the principal is the gatekeeper of change."[115] We would submit that the 21st-century principal is the gatekeeper of numerous gates of multiple diverse changes occurring at exponential rates.

## Curriculum Specialists

Curriculum specialists play a major role in curriculum development and implementation. Those who are called curriculum coordinators or directors usually are curriculum generalists. They have a broad knowledge of curriculum and are experts in creating and implementing curricula. They usually do not have a major in specific content. Other generalists in a school district are known as directors of elementary or secondary education. Usually, these people have expertise in administration as well as curriculum, but their focus is either elementary or secondary education.

People with specific content specialties are often called supervisors, chairs, or heads of a particular subject area (e.g., "supervisor of science"). They have some background in curriculum, but they possess a major in a content discipline and are often more concerned with supervising instruction.[116]

Curriculum specialists are responsible for ensuring that programs are conceptualized, designed, and implemented. This requires considerable understanding of curriculum and skill in managing people. Curriculum specialists must know how to design and develop curriculum and how to supervise and evaluate instruction.

School districts, especially small ones, sometimes ask outsiders to assist in curriculum development. These outside facilitators may be subject-matter experts who assist in selecting and organizing content, experts in instructional design who provide guidance on choosing pedagogical approaches or integrating media systems into the curriculum, or experts in needs analysis.[117]

## Assistant (Associate) Superintendents

In many school districts, the assistant, or associate, superintendent is most responsible for curriculum development. This person reports directly to the superintendent. In large school districts, curriculum directors report to the assistant, or associate, superintendent. Ideally, this person (1) chairs or advises the general curriculum advisory committee; (2) informs the superintendent of major trends in the field of curriculum and how these trends are affecting the school system; (3) works with elementary and secondary directors regarding curricular activity; (4) is in charge of the budget for curricular activity; (5) provides input into the statement of philosophy, aims, and goals; (6) guides evaluation relevant to aims and goals; and (7) manages long- and short-term activities designed to strengthen programs.[118] The assistant (associate) superintendent also helps formulate policies concerning curriculum innovation.

## Superintendents

The superintendent is the school system's chief administrator. The superintendent responds to matters before the school board, initiates curriculum activity, starts programs for in-service training of teachers, informs all district personnel of changes occurring in other schools, and processes demands from outside the system for change or maintenance of educational offerings.

Good superintendents inspire change and enable curricula to respond to changing demands. They are directly responsible to the school board for the district's total educational action. They must establish the means for curricular action, interpret all aspects of the school's program to the board, and set up communication networks to inform and involve the public with regard to curriculum process.

## Boards of Education

Boards of education are the schools' legal agents. They are composed of laypeople, usually elected as representatives of the general public. Board members are responsible for the schools' overall management. They must ensure that the curriculum advances the school system's goals. School boards have the final say as to whether a new program is funded or implemented districtwide. They enact district policies that facilitate the development and implementation of new curricula.

School boards and central administrative staffs seem to be losing some control over school districts. In some cases, legislated definitions of basic education have removed some control. In other cases, special-interest groups have gone to court to alter board policies that they found unacceptable. In some communities, angry community members have recalled board members. In many school districts, the school board plays only a secondary role in determining curriculum and policy; federal, state, and local professionals create new curricula.

## Lay Citizens

The relationship between communities and schools reveals much confusion and seeming contradictions regarding what roles lay persons should play in determining goals, programs, instructional strategies, and standards of pupil success. Just how involved should lay persons be in curriculum development? How included do community members wish to be? In most school districts, lay citizens' role is minimal.

Many reasons exist for the lack of engagement. Perhaps the major reason is that noneducators realize they possess little knowledge about course content, course designs, or models of curriculum development. Another is that they believe that educators should be the ones engaged; it is the educators' job, after all. In some communities, there are diverse social classes and differences in real and assumed power to influence the schools. Fullan, citing Bryk and Schneider, notes that often poor parents are frequently unconfident in their relationship with schools.[119]

Many poor parents did not do well in their own schooling and so view school as a place where they had little success. This is not the case with community members in the middle and upper classes. These people realize that they possess power to influence education. However, their participation in educational or curricular matters appears to be reactive. They make their voices heard when the schools do not measure up. Often these parents appear at school board meetings to argue for or against a certain program of study or their child's school assignment.

Presently, with the emphasis on standards, more community members are striving to have their voices heard. However, because of increasing diversity throughout the nation, the ideas of trying to influence education standards are becoming increasingly complex. Many parents are recent immigrants, bringing with them radically different views of what education should be. Some immigrants come from countries in which people did not advance beyond primary school.

How to involve lay citizens with these backgrounds in contributing to the education of their children is increasingly challenging. Increasing diversity regarding ethnicity and levels of affluence offer new problems. Many children come from single homes. Many are living in poverty. The gap between the haves and the have nots is increasing, and has an impact on when and how lay citizens furnish input into the school systems.

In general, parental involvement in school affairs drops off considerably as students enter middle and high school. Communities that are poor often do not even have any involvement at the elementary school level. Educators must recognize that parents and other community members can be resources for creating dynamic curricula. Principals and teachers must realize that they must, in many cases, initiate the contacts with the various communities. As Fullan posits, educators must be sensitive to the cultural mores in order to create opportunities to participate that are not threatening.[120]

## The Federal Government

For much of the 20th century, the federal government left curricular matters to the states and local districts. However, beginning in the 1960s, the federal government became a powerful force in determining educational materials and their uses. Federal dollars established and maintained regional laboratories and centers, first centering on science and mathematics and later focusing on programs for disadvantaged and minority groups.

Fullan delineates that government should and can push for accountability, should and can provide incentives, and should and can foster capacity building. He notes that if only the first two are addressed, any change in education will not last.[121] It appears that with the passage of No Child Left Behind in 2002, only the push for accountability was stressed. Perhaps the incentives push was there if we consider the threats made that if schools failed to get their students at 100 percent proficiency in 2 years time, they would be classified for all to see as "in need of improvement." If the schools were still not attaining success after 5 years, they were cautioned they would be classified as in need of "restructuring," with the possibilities of being taken over by the state, turned over to private management, or redesigned as a charter school.[122] However, No Child Left Behind came with no money for making educational changes and no money for capacity building and maintenance of the curricular innovation.

Presently, it seems that the federal government, in its passage of Race to the Top, included accountability, incentives, and capacity building in encouraging school districts to apply for federal dollars for educational innovations. Time will tell if schools can race to the top. Also at issue is that various schools and school districts have varying levels of personnel and resources to create educational proposals.

## State Agencies

States have increased their role in educational policy making, to some extent at the expense of local school districts. Many state boards of education have made formal recommendations and issued guidelines regarding what the curriculum should contain and how it should be organized. Growing state involvement is partly based on the position that managing education is a state function, a position supported by the decrease in federal funding of education.[123]

States affect the curriculum in many ways. State legislatures frequently publish guidelines on what will be taught. They also mandate courses such as driver education and drug education. Associations and other special-interest groups often lobby state legislatures to mandate that curricula include particular content or address the needs of particular students. Nationwide, state agencies have initiated minimum-competency and gate-keeping tests aimed at upgrading academic content and standards.

State boards of education continue to play roles in determining competency and certification requirements for teachers, supervisors, and administrators. In some states, people who wish to become supervisors or administrators must take specific courses on curriculum to obtain certification. State legislators' more active role in financing education indirectly affects both old and new programs. Finally, some governors have assumed the role of educational innovators within the context of the national reform movement in education.

## Regional Organizations

Regional educational laboratories funded by the federal government influence school curricula by providing guidance in the production of educational materials and by furnishing consultants who serve on planning teams. Research and development (R and D) centers, both federally and privately funded, investigate curricular problems; the research results can be of value to curriculum planners. R and D centers also aid curriculum specialists by documenting the effectiveness of particular programs or approaches.

Intermediate school districts (also called *educational service districts* and *educational service agencies*) are offices or agencies that occupy a position between state departments of education and local school districts. About 40 states have some form of intermediate school district. The average intermediate district is made of 20 to 30 school districts within an area of about 50 square miles.[124]

In recent years intermediate districts have provided school districts with resource personnel in such general areas of education as curriculum, instruction, and evaluation; in specialized areas, such as education of students who are disabled, gifted and talented, or bilingual; and in more specific areas, such as prekindergarten education, vocational education, data processing, and computer education.

## Other Participants

In large part, educational publishers have given the United States an unofficial national curriculum. In most schools, the textbooks used largely determine the curriculum. Students spend most of their classroom time, and nearly all their homework time, engaged with instructional materials.

Testing organizations, such as the Educational Testing Service and Psychological Corporation, have also contributed to a national curriculum. By standardizing the content tested, these organizations have affected what content the curriculum covers and how much emphasis is given to particular topics.

Many state departments of education have become involved in testing, thereby influencing the specifics of curricula and the time spent on the specifics. Washington State has created the Washington Assessment of Student Learning Test, which assesses reading and mathematics achievement in grades 3, 7, and 10. Since 2008, high school students in Washington State must pass language and mathematics exams in order to graduate. A comparable science-exam requirement is developed but not yet implemented.

Professional organizations such as the Association for Supervision and Curriculum Development (ASCD), the National Council of Teachers of English, the National Council for the Social Studies, the National Association of Teachers of Mathematics, and the American Educational Research Association have directly and indirectly influenced the curriculum. Their members bring goals set forth at state and national conferences to their home school districts. Increasingly, such professional organizations are formalizing networks of schools (and school districts) to communicate curricular concerns, mount curriculum studies, and publish reports that set curricular guidelines and standards.

Although the previously mentioned professional organizations are large and well established, the American Association for Teaching and Curriculum (AATC) is small and rather recently organized. Its focus, as its name implies, centers on the areas of teaching and curriculum. As indicated before, the field of curriculum seems to be increasingly neglected, with areas of curriculum studies being eliminated in colleges of education. The AATC organization has as its primary goal to assure that the field of curriculum studies as well as the field of instruction continue to be addressed by educational schools and practitioners.

Many other people and groups outside of the schools also influence the curriculum. Colleges and universities directly and indirectly influence curriculum development. Many educational consultants to the schools come from the colleges. Business and private industry are building closer connections to schools by providing special personnel, donating equipment and materials, and funding programs of special interest. Minority groups often organize to affect the curriculum. Individual educators and lay critics attempt, mostly through their writings, to give direction to curriculum development.

Various foundations also have influenced curriculum formulation, largely by supplying funds. The Ford, Rockefeller, Carnegie, Kettering, and Gates foundations have modified the curriculum through pilot and experimental programs. International in scope, the Gates Foundation is unique in the amount of money that it allocates to educational matters.

## Conclusion

Prior to engaging in curriculum development, educators must determine whether they are responsible for educating students or schooling students. As mentioned at the beginning of this chapter, education and schooling have had a troubled relationship. Although the general public most often fails to distinguish between the two, educators must ascertain to what camp they have allegiance. Certainly, we can develop a curriculum for educating students and we can create a curriculum for schooling students. Both postures result in programs that get results. Both even utilize the same or similar processes in generating curricula. We do not characterize one position as right and the other as wrong. Reflection is required just to determine for what purposes curricula are being developed.

Educators' choice of purpose is influenced by their philosophical orientation, their perceptions of the social and political forces impacting the school, their access to educational and technical support for the program being contemplated, and, certainly, their conception of the student as learner. Regardless of whether we are in the "educating students" or "schooling students" camp, it is useful to apprehend curriculum development as a variety of games with myriad rules. These games can be enacted within a technical–scientific or nontechnical–nonscientific arena. All game plans seek to develop educational content, experiences, and environments that meet the schools' objectives, goals, and aims. Today, much debate revolves around how standards relate to objectives, goals, and aims. Educators' responses are influenced by whether they view themselves as educating students or schooling them. Also, educators are affected by how the local, state, and national communities look at these two camps.

## Endnotes

1. Ken Osborne, "Education and Schooling: A Relationship That Can Never Be Taken for Granted," in David L. Coulter and John R. Weins, eds., *Why Do We Educate? Renewing the Conversation,* 107th Yearbook of the National Society for the Study of Education, Vol. 1 (Malden, MA: Distributed by Blackwell Publishing, 2008), pp. 21–41.
2. Ibid.
3. Ron Ritchhart, *Intellectual Character* (San Francisco, CA: Jossey-Bass, 2002).
4. Ibid.
5. Allan W. Garrett, "The Games People Play: Educational Scholarship and School Practice," in Barbara Slater Stern, ed., *Curriculum and Teaching Dialogue,* Vol. 10, Nos. 1 and 2, American Association for Teaching and Curriculum (Charlotte, NC: published by Information Age Publishing, 2008), pp. 3–11.
6. N. E. Long, "Local Community as an Ecology of Games," *American Journal of Sociology,* 64, pp. 251–261, cited in Allan W. Garrett, "The Games People Play: Educational Scholarship and School Practice," p. 4.
7. Michael Fullan, Peter Hill, and Carmel Crevola, *Breakthrough* (Thousand Oaks, CA: Corwin Press, 2006).
8. James B. Macdonald, "The Quality of Everyday Life in School," in J. B. Macdonald and E. Zaret, eds., *Schools in Search of Meaning* (Washington, DC: Association for Supervision and Curriculum Development, 1975), pp. 76–94.
9. Franklin Bobbitt, *How to Make a Curriculum* (Boston: Houghton Mifflin, 1924), p. 2.
10. Ibid., p. 9.
11. Fullan, Hill, and Crevola, *Breakthrough.*
12. Franklin Bobbitt, *The Supervision of City Schools: Some General Principles of Management Applied to the Problems of City School Systems,* Twelfth Yearbook of the National Society for the Study of Education, Part I (Bloomington, IL: 1913), p. 11.

13. David H. Jonassen, Martin Tessmer, and Wallace H. Hannum, *Task Analysis Methods for Instructional Design* (Mahwah, NJ: Lawrence Erlbaum Associates, 1999).

14. Grant Wiggins and Jay McTighe, *Understanding by Design* (Alexandria, VA: Association for Supervision and Curriculum Development, 1998).

15. W. W. Charters, *Curriculum Construction* (New York: Macmillan, 1923), p. 5.

16. Ibid., p. 101.

17. Ibid., p. 105.

18. Ralph Tyler, *Basic Principles of Curriculum and Instruction* (Chicago: University of Chicago Press, 1949).

19. Francis P. Hunkins and Patricia A. Hammill, "Beyond Tyler and Taba: Reconceptualizing the Curriculum Process," *Peabody Journal of Education* (Spring 1994), pp. 4–18.

20. Ibid.

21. Hilda Taba, *Curriculum Development: Theory and Practice* (New York: Harcourt Brace, 1962).

22. Wiggins and McTighe, *Understanding by Design.*

23. Ibid., p. 12.

24. Ibid.

25. Abbie Brown and Timothy D. Green, *The Essentials of Instructional Design* (Upper Saddle River, NJ: Pearson, 2006).

26. Jonassen, Tessmer, and Hannum, *Task Analysis Methods for Instructional Design.*

27. Heidi Hayes Jacobs, ed., *Getting Results with Curriculum Mapping* (Alexandria, VA: Association for Supervision and Curriculum Development, 2004).

28. Michael I. Posner and Mary K. Rothbart, *Educating the Human Brain* (Washington, DC: American Psychological Association, 2007).

29. M. Frances Klein, "Approaches to Curriculum Theory and Practice," in J. T. Sears and J. D. Marshall, eds., *Teaching and Thinking about the Curriculum* (New York: Teachers College Press, Columbia University, 1990), pp. 3–14; and Robert Young, *A Critical Theory of Education* (New York: Teachers College Press, Columbia University, 1990).

30. J. T. Dillon, "The Questions of Deliberation," in J. T. Dillon, ed., *Deliberation in Education and Society* (Norwood, NJ: Ablex, 1994), pp. 3–24.

31. Didier Noye, "Guidelines for Conducting Deliberations," in J. T. Dillon, ed., *Deliberation in Education and Society* (Norwood, NJ: Ablex, 1994), pp. 239–248.

32. Noye, "Guidelines for Conducting Deliberations."

33. Roger Soder, *The Language of Leadership* (San Francisco: Jossey-Bass, 2001).

34. Richard F. Elmore, *School Reform from the Inside Out* (Cambridge, MA: Harvard Education Press, 2006).

35. Brown and Green, *The Essentials of Instructional Design,* p. 7.

36. Michael Fullan, "The Principal and Change," in Michael Fullan, ed., *The Challenge of Change*, 2nd ed. (Thousand Oaks, CA: Corwin, 2009), pp. 55–69.

37. Collin M. J. Marsh and George Willis, *Curriculum: Alternative Approaches, Ongoing Issues,* 4th ed. (Upper Saddle River, NJ: Pearson, 2007).

38. Fullan, "The Principal and Change."

39. M. McLaughlin and J. Talbert, *Building School-based Teacher Learning Communities* (New York: Teachers College Press, 2006), cited in Michael Fullan, *The Challenge of Change,* p. 62.

40. Fullan, "The Principal and Change."

41. Ibid.

42. Jerome Bruner, *The Culture of Education* (Cambridge, MA: Harvard University Press, 2001).

43. David W. Orr, *Earth in Mind: On Education, Environment, and the Human Prospect* (Washington, DC: Island Press, 2004).

44. Norbert M. Seel and Sanne Dijkstra, eds., *Curriculum, Plans, and Processes in Instructional Design: International Perspectives* (Mahwah, NJ: Lawrence Erlbaum Associates, 2004).

45. Barbara L. Grabowski, "Needs Assessment—Informing Instructional Decision Making in a Large Technology-Based Project," in Norbert M. Seel and Sanne Dijkstra, eds., *Curriculum, Plans, and Processes in Instructional Design: International Perspectives* (Mahwah, NJ: Lawrence Erlbaum Associates, 2004).

46. Ralph W. Tyler, "Purposes of Our Schools," *NASSP Bulletin* (May 1968), pp. 1–12.

47. Ronald C. Doll, *Curriculum Improvement: Decision Making and Process,* 9th ed. (Boston: Allyn and Bacon, 1996).

48. Commission on the Reorganization of Secondary Education, *Cardinal Principles of Secondary Education,* Bulletin 35 (Washington, DC: U.S. Office of Education, 1918), pp. 11–16.

49. Evelyn J. Sowell, *Curriculum: An Integrative Introduction* (Upper Saddle River, NJ: Merrill, 1996), p. 20.

50. D. Ravitch, *National Standards in American Education: A Citizen's Guide* (Washington, DC, The Orrkings Institution, 1995), cited in Peter M. Taubman, *Teaching by Numbers* (New York: Routledge, 2009), pp. 108–109.

51. *Phase III of the Educational Planning Model* (Bloomington, IN: Phi Delta Kappa Educational Foundation, 1976).

52. *National Goals for Education* (Washington, DC: U.S. Department of Education, 1990).

53. B. Latour, *We Have Never Been Modern* (Cambridge, MA: Harvard University Press, 1993), cited in Peter N. Taubman, *Teaching by Numbers*, p. 114.

54. Lisa Carter, *Total Instructional Alignment: From Standards to Student Success* (Blooming, IN: Solution Tree Press, 2007).

55. Taubman, *Teaching by Numbers.*

56. Ibid.

57. Kenneth W. Howell and Victor Nolet, *Curriculum-Based Evaluation: Teaching and Decision Making,* 3rd ed. (Belmont, CA: Wadsworth, 2000).

58. Brown and Green, *The Essentials of Instructional Design.*

59. Robert F. Mager, *Preparing Instructional Objectives,* 2nd ed. (Belmont, CA: Fearon, 1984).

60. Jerrold E. Kemp, Gary R. Morrison, and Steven M. Ross, *Designing Effective Instruction* (New York: Merrill, Macmillan, 1994).

61. William E. Doll, Jr., *A Post Modern Perspective on Curriculum* (New York: Teachers College Press, Columbia University, 1993).

62. Benjamin S. Bloom, ed., *Taxonomy of Educational Objectives, Handbook 1*: Cognitive Domain (New York: McKay, 1956).

63. Lorin W. Anderson and David R. Krathwohl, eds., *A Taxonomy for Learning, Teaching, and Assessing* (New York: Routledge, 2003).

64. Ibid.

65. Ibid.

66. David R. Krathwohl, ed., *Taxonomy of Educational Objectives, Handbook II: Affective Domain* (New York: McKay, 1964).

67. J. Flavell, "Metacognition and Cognitive Monitoring, A New Area of Cognitive Developmental Inquiry," *American Psychologist* (1979), pp. 906–911, cited in Lorin W. Anderson and David R. Krathwohl, eds., *A Taxonomy for Learning, Teaching, and Assessing*, p. 59.

68. Anderson and Krathwohl, eds., *A Taxonomy for Learning, Teaching, and Assessing*.

69. Posner and Rothbart, *Educating the Human Brain*.

70. Anita J. Harrow, *A Taxonomy of the Psychomotor Domain* (New York: McKay, 1972).

71. Yong Zhao, *Catching Up or Leading the Way* (Alexandria, VA: Association for Supervision and Curriculum Development, 2009).

72. Ibid.

73. Ibid.

74. Ibid.

75. Christine E. Sleeter, *Un-Standardizing Curriculum: Multicultural Teaching in the Standards-Based Classroom* (New York: Teachers College Press, 2005).

76. Paul Hirst, *Knowledge and the Curriculum* (Boston: Routledge & Kegan Paul, 1974).

77. John D. McNeil, *Curriculum: A Comprehensive Introduction,* 6th ed. (New York: HarperCollins, 2000).

78. Ibid.

79. James A. Banks, "The Canon Debate, Knowledge Construction, and Multicultural Education," *Educational Researcher* (1993), p. 9, cited in Christine E. Sleeter, *Un-Standardizing Curriculum: Multicultural Teaching in the Standards-Based Classroom.*

80. McNeil, *Curriculum: A Comprehensive Introduction.*

81. Israel Scheffler, "Justifying Curriculum Divisions," in J. Martin, ed., *Readings in the Philosophy of Education: A Study of Curriculum* (Boston: Allyn & Bacon, 1970), pp. 27–31.

82. John P. Miller, *Educating for Wisdom and Compassion* (Thousand Oaks, CA: Corwin Press, 2006), pp. 4–10.

83. Henry A. Giroux, *Postmodernism, Feminism and Cultural Politics* (Albany: State University of New York Press, 1991).

84. Zhao, *Catching Up or Leading the Way.*

85. Ibid.

86. Daniel Pink, *A Whole New Mind: Moving from the Information Age to the Conceptual Age* (New York: Riverhead Books, 2005), cited in Zhao, *Catching Up or Leading the Way,* p. 148.

87. Ibid.

88. Ibid.

89. Zhao, *Catching Up or Leading the Way.*

90. William Ayers, *To Teach: The Journey of a Teacher,* 3rd ed. (New York: Teachers College Press, 2010), p. 61.

91. Brown and Green, *The Essentials of Instructional Design.*

92. Ayers, *To Teach: The Journey of a Teacher.*

93. Deborah L. Voltz, Michele Jean Sims, and Betty Nelson, *Connecting Teachers Students and Standards* (Alexandria, VA: Association for Supervision and Curriculum Development, 2010).

94. Ayers, *To Teach: The Journey of a Teacher.*

95. Ibid., p. 65; and Ritchhart, *Intellectual Character.*

96. Ayers, *To Teach: The Journey of a Teacher.*

97. Ursula M. Franklin, "Educating at the Interface of Biosphere and Bitsphere," in David L. Coulter and John R. Wiens, eds., *Why Do We Educate? Renewing the Conversation,* pp. 242–255.

98. Ibid.

99. John I. Goodlad, *In Praise of Education* (New York: Teachers College Press, 1997).

100. Franklin, "Educating at the Interface of Biosphere and Bitsphere."

101. Ibid.

102. Ritchhart, *Intellectual Character,* p. 47.

103. Brian Castaldi, *Educational Facilities: Planning, Modernization, and Management,* 3rd ed. (Boston: Allyn & Bacon, 1987).

104. Allan Collins and Richard Halverson, *Rethinking Education in the Age of Technology* (New York: Teachers College Press, 2009).

105. Ritchhart, *Intellectual Character,* p. 155.

106. James B. Macdonald, "The Quality of Every Day Life in School," in J. B. Macdonald and E. Zaret, eds., *Schools in Search of Meaning* (Berkeley, CA: McCutchan, 1978).

107. Marsh and Willis, *Curriculum: Alternative Approaches, Ongoing Issues.*

108. Fullan, Hill, and Crevola, *Breakthrough.*

109. Michael Fullan, *The New Meaning of Educational Change,* 4th ed. (New York: Teachers College Press, 2007), p. 139.

110. Ibid.

111. Ibid.

112. L. Hubbard, H. Mehan, and M. K. Stein, *Reform as Learning* (London: Routledge, 2006), p. 75, cited in Michael Fullan, *The New Meaning of Educational Change,* p. 167.

113. Jon Wiles and Joseph Bondi, *Curriculum Development: A Guide to Practice,* 7th ed. (Upper Saddle River, NJ: Pearson, 2007).

114. Fullan, *The New Meaning of Educational Change.*

115. Ibid., p. 156.

116. Carl D. Glickman, ed., *Supervision in Transition* (Alexandria, VA: Association for Supervision and Curriculum Development, 1992).

117. Ibid.

118. Thomas J. Sergiovanni et al., *Educational Governance and Administration,* 3rd ed. (Boston: Allyn & Bacon, 1992).

119. A. Bryk and B. Schneider, *Trust in Schools* (New York: Russell Sage, 2002), cited in Michael Fullan, *The New Meaning of Educational Change,* p. 193.

120. Fullan, *The New Meaning of Educational Change.*

121. Ibid.

122. Ibid.

123. Ibid.

124. Allan C. Ornstein and Daniel U. Levine, *Foundations of Education,* 10th ed. (Boston: Houghton Mifflin, 2008).

# 8

■ ■ ■

# Curriculum Implementation

## FOCUSING QUESTIONS

1. How does planning curriculum relate to implementation?
2. In what ways does the implementation process reflect a power mentality?
3. How can "capacity building" facilitate curriculum implementation?
4. Why do people tend to resist change?
5. What impact do learning communities have on implementation?
6. Considering the complexities of the current century, which implementation models do you think the most effective?
7. In what ways is the systems implementation model like an evolving solar system? Does such consideration have any value to one engaged in implementation?
8. Who are or should be the major curriculum implementation players?

**M**any planned and developed curricula are not implemented because a plan to incorporate them into the school's educational program does not exist. Jon Wiles and Joseph Bondi note that more than 90 percent of new curricula fail to be implemented; in their view, educators lack the managerial skills and knowledge necessary to deliver a new curriculum.[1]

## THE NATURE OF IMPLEMENTATION

Leslie Bishop stated many years ago that implementation requires restructuring and replacement.[2] It requires adjusting personal habits, ways of behaving, program emphases, learning spaces, and existing curricula and schedules. The readiness with which teachers and others accept a new curriculum depends partly on the quality of the initial planning and the precision with which the steps of curriculum development have been carried out.[3]

Implementation became a major educational concern beginning around 1980. Millions of dollars were being spent to develop curriculum projects, especially for reading and mathematics, yet many of the projects did not succeed. Seymour Sarason suggests that much educational reform has failed because those in charge of the efforts had little or a distorted understanding of the culture of schools.[4]

Sarason notes two kinds of basic understanding essential to implementation. The first is an understanding of organizational change and how information and ideas fit into a real-world context. The second is an understanding of the relationship between curricula and the social–institutional contexts into which they are to be introduced. Educators must comprehend the structure of the school, its traditions, and its power relationships as well as how members see themselves and their roles.[5] Successful implementers of curriculum realize that implementation must appeal to participants not only logically, but also emotionally and morally. Indeed, Fullan notes that most teachers are motivated to action primarily by moral considerations.[6]

Our view of the social–institutional context is influenced by whether one perceives the world of education as technical or nontechnical. Those with a technical view believe that implementation can be planned down to specifics; those with a nontechnical view hold that implementation is fluid and emergent. Many people, of course, view implementation as a combination of technical and nontechnical aspects.

How might we persuade educators to accept and implement a curriculum? First, we could assure them that implementing the new curriculum will bring some reward. Second, we could indicate the negative consequences of inaction—for example, the school will not be in compliance with state mandates or students will fail to pass a standardized test. Third, we could point out ways in which the particular curriculum you wish to have implemented is similar to the one already in place. However, we might wish to tout the new program as nothing like—and even superior to—the existing one.[7]

Successful curriculum implementation results from careful planning, which focuses on three factors: people, programs, and processes. To implement a curriculum change, educators must get people to change some of their habits and, possibly, views. Many school districts failed to implement their programs because they ignored the people factor and spent time and money modifying only the program or process. However, focusing on the new program provides people with new ways to meet the objectives of the school's programs. Organizational processes, too, are important. Reorganizing departments can move people in the directions necessary for successful implementation. Many curriculum projects fail partly because the curriculum innovators, especially from universities, paid minimal attention to school organization.[8]

Implementation of a new curriculum must be tailored to the school. Each school is unique, with its own culture.[9]

## Incrementalism

Many educators, as well as members of the general public, think primarily of change when contemplating implementation. They view implementation as procedures for managing change. Yet as Richard E. Elmore advises, implementers must query themselves as to the actual purposes of the change being considered. Focusing just on changing the curriculum and the school culture gives emphasis to the management of change. Just introducing a new curriculum or even a new textbook series can be documented when all teachers are using the educational program or material. In addition, if educators do not use the material, it is rather easy to indicate noncompliance. However, in both the curriculum development and implementation stages, the central question is, What is the value of the change for teachers and students?[10]

Although we consider implementation to be a change process, we are constantly querying: Does the change have purpose and value? Will it improve teachers' pedagogical and curricular actions and students' learnings? Simply put, change must result in improvement, and improvement in students' learnings and teachers' actions requires time. As Elmore notes, "Improvement equals increased quality and performance over time."[11]

Implementation of a curriculum designed to improve and not just change students' accomplishments requires some agreement regarding what constitutes improvement. How do we define *quality*? In the various efforts at school reform writ large and the purchasing of textbooks to support curricular change, many assume that the latest program, the newest textbooks, or the latest computer programs signal improvement. Yet this is false simplification.

Whether some new program will spell improvement depends on our personal and educational philosophies. Also added to the equation is the social class of the major players in the community. With cultural and ethnic diversity increasing in a larger number of communities, it becomes more challenging to define improvement.

The implementation process exhibits a control mentality.[12] Various power groups strive to direct various avenues of change to serve their particular purposes. Power groups range from political, to parents', and to educators' power groups. Supposedly, there is cooperation among these various communities; they all want curricula that benefit students. However, the policies these various groups create or try to introduce, in reality, often generate controversy and flux to educational dialogue and program implementation.[13]

Impacting curricula implementation is often "gaming the system."[14] Politicians game the system when they advocate policy changes to make schools accountable, knowing full well they do not have any idea of how to measure accountability of a new curriculum. They have played the game to please their constituents, raise standards, and make the tests more difficult; then they threaten to withdraw financial support for the schools. Educators often play the game of advocating a new curriculum program that addresses the policy of higher standards. However, often the public has not given the schools the funding capacity to implement the recommended curricula or to use pedagogical approaches based on the latest brain research.

Improvement takes time, but improvement is in the eye of the beholder. What we might consider improvement designed to foster school creativity and inquisitiveness, others might view as a negative, fostering students questioning authority or challenging their place in society. Although it appears everyone is into the latest in technological gadgets, many "modern" 21st century people are fearful of rapid change, especially if they believe they have little control over it or if the change occurring is challenging their values and world views—their power positions.

## Communication

To ensure adequate communication, a curriculum specialist must understand a school's (or school system's) communication channels. Communication channels are vertical (between people at different levels of the school hierarchy) or horizontal (between people at the same level of the hierarchy). For example, communication between a principal and a teacher is vertical; communication between two teachers is horizontal.

Horizontal networking among peers is being encouraged in many school restructuring efforts. Communication flows more easily among persons who consider themselves equals and who are equally involved in some curriculum change. Many curricular activities that combine subject areas or integrate major segments of the curriculum presuppose effective horizontal communication.

Although formal channels of horizontal communication may exist in schools, much horizontal communication is informal. Effective curriculum leaders encourage an abundance of communication channels. They work to establish cohesive school communities composed of teachers, administrators, and students.[15]

Communication these days is spoken, written, and seen. The World Wide Web enables collaboration among educators regardless of distance. Time disappears with computers, BlackBerry devices, and smartphones. Educators may in the near future, if not now, communicate with "colleagues" in the virtual world. Ideally, such facilitation of communication should modify the cultures of schools. Teachers really do not need to work in isolation. In fact, if educational change is going to bring educational improvement in all realms of human growth, we must communicate effectively and more frequently. Technology is not going to be the death knell of face-to-face communication. Technology will likely serve to alter the educational environment in which teachers and students work.

## Support

To facilitate implementation, curriculum designers must provide the necessary support for their recommended curricular innovations or modifications. They and the entire school community must facilitate capacity or capability. Elmore defines *capacity* or *capability* as those resources, knowledge, and skills brought by both teacher and students to the instructional core and the skilled actions of the total school organization to support and maximize the delivery and engagement of teachers and students with the implemented curriculum.[16]

If the new curriculum is to enable improvement in students' learnings, it must be maintained and supported over time. As Michael Fullan and others note, building a cadre of competent implementers requires the school district's sustained support.[17] Teachers must become highly knowledgeable about the new curriculum content; they must perfect new instructional approaches; they must know how to manipulate the educational environment taking into consideration the backgrounds and learning styles of their students. Such support often takes the form of in-service training or staff development.[18]

In-service training or staff development is necessary for teachers who lack a deep understanding of curriculum and its creation. Even many educational administrators lack "curriculum literacy."[19] People who take teacher-education programs primarily take courses that focus on instructional methods in various subject areas. These courses lead many teachers to assume that the curriculum will be handed to them and their only responsibility will be to teach it. Teachers must have knowledge of curriculum development, even if they opt out of active involvement in it.

Research has revealed the characteristics of effective professional in-service programs. Such programs must fit into the schools that provide them. Effective in-service programs result from collaborative efforts and address the needs of those who will be affected by the new curricula. They are flexible enough to respond to the staff's changing needs. They spread knowledge of the new curriculum and increase people's commitment to it. For example, teachers in one school might learn about the curriculum from teachers at other schools or even schools in other countries. The Internet can help.[20] In-service programs should be scheduled at convenient times for curriculum implementers. Open discussions on new curricula should be scheduled throughout the implementation process. Such discussions allow implementers to express objections or concerns and consequently to reduce opposition. Effective in-service programs must also evaluate whether curricula are achieving their objectives and whether they are in harmony with the school district's philosophy and approach.

Without adequate financial support, new curricula fail. When federal funds were flowing, many school districts adopted innovations but failed to allocate funding to these innovations in their regular school budgets. When the federal funds (essentially intended as start-up funding) ran out, the districts discontinued their new curricula, citing lack of necessary funds. If school districts implement new curricula using federal or state grant money, they must devise ways to support these curricula with money allocated in the school budget.

Money is required for new materials and equipment and to pay people who help implement a new curriculum. At the local level, five steps are involved in budgeting for new programs: preparation, submission, adoption, execution, and evaluation. When a new program is adopted, the school board allocates funds for specific educational materials. The other four budgeting steps involve the superintendent at the district level and the principal (or chair) at the school level.[21]

A trusting relationship must exist among all parties in the school, especially between administrators and teachers. Effective implementation can and should utilize the services of lead teachers who are released from classroom teaching so that they can serve as salespeople for the new curricular program and as mentors or coaches so that teachers gain the knowledge and competency requisite for enacting the created curriculum.[22]

## IMPLEMENTATION AS A CHANGE PROCESS

The purpose of curriculum development, regardless of level, is to make a difference—to enable students to attain the school's, the society's, and, perhaps most importantly, their own aims and goals. Implementation, an essential part of curriculum development, brings into reality anticipated changes. Simply put, curriculum activity is change activity.

Yet what happens when change occurs? And of greater importance, what are the value and role of change? What is the source of change? What really motivates people to change? Can people predict the consequences of change? Are all the consequences of change beneficial to students and the general society? Can educators control changes that directly affect them? Do different educators—for instance, administrators and teachers—engage in change for the same or similar reasons? Do schools that make the most major changes actually become the most innovative and effective?

Indeed, people can exert control, to varying degrees, over the process of change, but to do so requires they understand change. Comprehending the concept of change and the various types of change allows individuals to determine sources of change. It also assists them in determining whether demands for change have educational value or just political expediency.

Even if we do have our values in place regarding educational change, we must appreciate that when all is said and done, we cannot predict, even with limited precision, how successful the change activities will be for those involved and for those who experience the changed curriculum—the students.

There is no denying that change can occur in several ways. The two most obvious ways are slow change (as when minor adjustments are made in the course schedule, when some books are added to the library, or when the unit or lesson plan is updated by the teacher) and rapid change (say, as the result of new knowledge or social trends affecting schools, such as computers being introduced into classrooms).

Currently, schools are being affected more by rapid change than slow change. We are experiencing rapid change not only in our knowledge bases of how the brain functions and how learning occurs, but also in changes in the demography of the country and the increasing diversity of groups within the general society. Rapid change is occurring in family backgrounds and structure, subcultures, and community groups. Cultural pluralism is exploding and competing voices are gaining agency. Additionally, educational technology also is exploding, having a greater impact on curricula and their implementations.

According to the research, for curriculum change to be successfully implemented, five guidelines should be followed:

1. *Innovations designed to improve student achievement must be technically sound.* Changes should reflect research findings regarding what does and does not work, not designs that simply are popular.
2. *Successful innovation requires change in the structure of a traditional school.* The way students and teachers are assigned to classes and interact with one another must be significantly modified.
3. *Innovation must be manageable and feasible for the average teacher.* For example, one cannot innovate ideas concerning critical thinking or problem solving when students cannot read or write basic English.
4. *Implementation of successful change efforts must be organic rather than bureaucratic.* A bureaucratic approach of strict rules and monitoring is not conducive to change. Such an approach should be replaced with an organic and adaptive approach that permits some deviation from the original plan and recognizes grassroots problems and the school's conditions.
5. *Avoid the "do something, anything" syndrome.* A definite curriculum plan is needed to focus efforts, time, and money on sound, rational content and activities.[23]

The data indicate that the guidelines "are systematically interrelated, and that with the possible exception of the guideline regarding structural change, they apply equally well to all levels of education." Curricularists benefit by "considering their applicability in the particular context of their own schools and school districts."[24]

## Types of Change

Curriculum implementers who do not understand the complexities of change are likely to initiate actions that will result in discord within the school, school district, or both. In the late 1960s, Warren Bennis identified three types of change. His categories remain useful:

1. *Planned change.* Those involved have equal power; they identify and follow precise procedures for dealing with the activity at hand. Planned change is the ideal.
2. *Coercion.* One group determines the goals, retains control, and excludes other people from participating.
3. *Interaction change.* There is a fairly equal distribution of power among groups who mutually set goals. However, few procedures are carefully developed. Also, those involved may lack deliberateness and be uncertain as to how they should implement the desired changes.[25]

We would add a fourth type of change to the list: random change. Such change occurs with no apparent thought and no goal setting. Random change is common in schools, as when curricula are modified in response to unanticipated events such as new legislation or pressure from special-interest groups.

We can also consider change in terms of its complexity. John McNeil listed increasingly complex types of change:

1. *Substitution.* This depicts alteration in which one element may be substituted for another. A teacher can, for example, substitute one textbook for another. By far, this is the easiest and most common type of change.
2. *Alteration.* This type of change exists when someone introduces, into existing materials and programs, new content, items, materials, or procedures that appear to be only minor and thus are likely to be adopted readily.
3. *Perturbations.* These changes could at first disrupt a program but can then be adjusted purposefully by the curriculum leader to the ongoing program within a short time span. An example of a perturbation is the principal's adjusting class schedules, which would affect the time allowed for teaching a particular subject.
4. *Restructuring.* These changes lead to modification of the system itself, that is, of the school or school district. New concepts of teaching roles, such as differentiated staffing or team teaching, would be a restructuring type of change.
5. *Value-orientation changes.* These are shifts in the participants' fundamental philosophies or curriculum orientations. Major power brokers of the school or participants in the curriculum must accept and strive for this level of change for it to occur. However, if teachers do not adjust their value domains, any changes enacted are most likely going to be short-lived.[26]

Although change that occurs in the schools cannot be fit into precise categories, curricularists must realize that types do exist and that planned change is the ideal. However, change is not synonymous with improvement.[27] Education is a normative activity. A person's advocating and then managing change means, in effect, making a statement about what he or she thinks is valuable.

## Resistance to Change

"When an institution of great complexity and importance, such as the school, becomes intricately bound up with nearly all other social institutions, attempting to bring about significant changes will meet a multitude of resistances. Some initial reforms may be allowed and even encouraged, but if they expand and threaten to cause deep and wide-scale changes, the institution will then inexorably, link by link, tighten into an adamantine obstacle preventing any major reforms."[28]

"I commend the hundreds of schools nationwide that are beginning to embrace extended school hours and academic calendars. But if they don't account for some of the potential pitfalls, I fear the plan could be discarded like so many other quick fixes. No cure, particularly when it comes to education, is quite so simple."[29]

A curriculum leader who accepts that people are the key to successful curriculum activity is cognizant of the barriers people place between themselves and efforts to change. In today's diverse society, groups react differently to suggested change, primarily because they do not perceive the change as leading to improvement. We live in a hierarchical society containing many social classes. Yet, to many educational change agents, the school and its curriculum are to contain content and be taught so that all children have an equal chance at success. However, many argue that in reality, schools do not furnish curricula that provide all students an equal chance at success.

Certainly schools should offer students opportunities to gain the competence and knowledge requisite for success in life. Yet the challenge is that students come to school with different backgrounds, capabilities, interests, and talents. Thus, the curricula introduced must cater to a multilayered student body. However, to do this, we must engage the total community to get them on board. This is the challenge in this century. For parents whose children are successful, there may be resistance to change. As Ellen Brantlinger notes, if influential people's desires are being met by the existing structures, curricula, and practices, there is no perceived need to alter them. Rather there is a desire to retain and even strengthen them.[30]

Even parents whose children are not attaining success in schools may not wish to have the curricula dramatically changed. Often these parents are quite conservative and wish their children to experience the traditional curricula that has enabled the more privileged children to succeed. Give my children basic mathematics so they can take advanced mathematics like they do in "affluent" schools. Direct teaching makes sense. Let us not bring in a program that engages students in inquiry, in creative problem solving. They will not pass the standardized tests, required for successful school advancement. These parents demand their students experience the standard curriculum to attain their personal interests.[31]

With regard to education, some educators strive for a classless society in which all attain that which they desire. However, in reality we do have classes. We do have communities that mold the curricula. Often these communities want only changes that work to their advantages. Communities with less power seek to gain power to influence the schools to serve their interests. Educators are ethically responsible for attempting to address all interests and aspirations of diverse communities. Yet, as noted in the first quote in this section, when an institution of great complexity and importance becomes intricately bound up with nearly all other social institutions, attempting to bring about change will meet with great resistance. Major change may eventually help all, but it initially pleases few.

Educators are being pulled in many directions. Everyone, including educators, possesses diverse thoughts. People's ruminations about education are complex, ever changing, and at times contradictory. Some want progressive, brain-friendly curricula and pedagogies. Others want more direct teaching and more conservative curricula addressing "standard" contents.

Faced with such diverse and ever-changing demands, educators often stall regarding implementing a new curriculum. Inertia shackles the staff, the administration, and even the community. Individuals are not even aware that they are resisting change. Their cognitive systems are overloaded. They have lost their ability to recognize a problem that requires attention. Even if they do recognize a problem or an unacceptable situation, they choose to ignore it for various reasons. Perhaps they realize that the problem demands efforts they are unwilling to make. Other times, people acknowledge problems that require educational change but explain the problem by blaming the community or a particular culture. There are times—especially when people attack the schools and insist on change—that educators become defensive, counterattacking those requesting the change rather than attempting to address what may well be legitimate demands.[32]

Perhaps the key reason for people's inertia is that they believe that it is simply easier to keep things as they are. It is more comfortable to stay with what is known than to attempt change and trigger the unknown. We like maintaining steady states, adhering to our cherished traditions and institutions. As humans, we tend to evade those problems and processes of change that we consider too complex.

The status quo is supported in schools when there is not a clear mission stated for a new program. At the phase of implementation, however, we must return to the mission—to the intent of the curriculum—to sell it to others in the educational organization. However, many schools phrase their mission statements as essentially bland general proclamations that do not really distinguish one new curriculum from another.

Often, teachers have not been able or willing to keep up with scholarly developments. They have not stayed abreast of the knowledge explosion, which would allow them to feel committed to curriculum change and the implementation of new programs. Teachers frequently view change as simply signaling more work—something else to add on to an already overloaded schedule for which little or no time is allotted. As Elmore denotes, "turning a school around" requires that teachers increase their knowledge base of the new curricular content, develop new expertise in pedagogical approaches, improve their knowledge of instructional design and theory, and become expert in the latest theories of how students learn. In other words, they must increase their capacities to deliver the new programs. Increasing teachers' and administrators' capacities, essentially the schools' capacities, requires not only extra effort but, usually, extra monies. Currently, many educators are overwhelmed by changes being proposed and their implications.

Despite teachers having tremendous demands on their time, many do a remarkable job of keeping up with the literature. Even so, many of these teachers tend to disregard available evidence regarding new curricular or pedagogical practice if it challenges their current understandings and outlook. They reject altering their programs and instructional strategies if this requires a change in outlook or practice.

Can educators cope with the demands for more change for new roles? Uncertainty fosters insecurity. Often, educators who feel comfortable with the present are reluctant to change for a future they cannot comprehend or see clearly. People often prefer to stay with certain known deficiencies than to venture forth to uncertain futures, even if the changes would most likely be improvements. Bringing new students or parents or content into the curriculum realm or organizing the program in new ways makes many teachers uneasy. However, this may change as we bring new people into education who consider education as a second career. Many of these people are coming from professions in industry and especially from high-tech fields, where change is embraced and recognized as essential for the continued well being of any institution. These people come into education with résumés noting high involvement in reconceptualizing the business organizations they have left. Another effort to bring in people who might otherwise not consider a career in education is the Teach for America program. This program recruits individuals with content-degree specialties such as mathematics, chemistry, or languages to become teachers after taking a 4- to 6-week educational program. Individuals accepting the offer must commit to at least 3 years in the classroom. This program maintains that a great change in education can come from individuals who posses more in-depth knowledge of a content area. Although this is change, it remains to be seen if the program translates into improvement. Many professors of education take umbrage at the notion that a person can become a competent teacher with only minimal education content.

Another factor that causes people to resist change is the rapidity of change. Many people believe that if something is implemented this year, it will most likely be abandoned when another innovation appears and will thus make all their efforts useless. Teachers are unwilling to support changes perceived as short lived. They will not commit energies to curricular changes or school reorganizations with little chance of lasting. Certainly, there have been enough "bandwagons" in education to make educators shy away from innovation.

Another key reason why some teachers resist getting involved in curricular change is that, although they may know about the planned school innovation, they do not know about the latest research, or if they know about it, they refuse to use it in guiding their actions.[33] An explanation for not knowing about the latest research is that teachers lack opportunities within their regular school day or week to read research studies. Few schools possess complete research libraries. Also, in most schools, teachers are classroom-bound and, therefore, lack opportunities to discuss the latest research with colleagues.

Even if teachers do have time to discuss research with fellow teachers, they frequently find that the research often furnishes contradictory results or does not really apply to the local school community in which the teachers work. Educational researchers often wish to obtain results that are generalizable. Teachers usually want research that essentially addresses their situations. As Shazia Miller, Karen Drill, and Ellen Behrstock submit, teachers utilize different criteria for judging quality research. Teachers classify high-quality research as that which has high potential to lead to change in curricula or instruction. If not, teachers tend to consider the research not worth their time or attention.[34]

One might think that if teachers really are knowledgeable about current research, they would engage in change, implementing new curriculum or pedagogical approaches. However, it appears that teachers tend to discount research that does not support what they are already doing. Research that supports their current practices actually increases teachers' resistance to change.[35]

People often resist change, too, if no financial or time support is given to the effort. A project for which no monies are budgeted is rarely destined to be implemented. Often, school districts budget monies for materials but fail to allocate funds for the creation of the curriculum plan, its delivery within the classroom, or necessary in-service training.

Several years ago Thomas Harvey, writing on the nature of change, provided an analysis of the obstacles to getting people involved in change—and why they resist it. The list is still useful.

1. *Lack of ownership.* Individuals may not accept change if they think it is coming from outside their organization; interestingly, much of the current demand for school reform and restructuring is coming from national commissions or state legislatures.
2. *Lack of benefits.* Teachers are likely to resist a new program if they are unconvinced that it will benefit students (in terms of learning) or themselves (e.g., by bringing them greater recognition and respect).
3. *Increased burdens.* Often, change means more work. Many teachers are hostile to changes that will add work to their already heavy schedules.
4. *Lack of administrative support.* People will not embrace change unless those officially responsible for the program have shown their support for the change.
5. *Loneliness.* Few people desire to innovate alone. Collaborative action is necessary to implement new programs successfully.
6. *Insecurity.* People resist what appears to threaten their security. Few will venture into programs with obvious threat to either job or reputation.
7. *Norm incongruence.* The assumptions underlying a new program must accord with those of the staff. Sometimes new programs represent philosophical orientations to education that are at odds with the staff's.
8. *Boredom.* Successful innovations must be presented as interesting, enjoyable, and thought-provoking.
9. *Chaos.* If a change is perceived as lessening control and order, it is likely to be opposed. We desire changes that make things more manageable and enable us to function more effectively.
10. *Differential knowledge.* If we perceive those who advocate change as considerably better informed than we are, we may see them as having excessive power.
11. *Sudden wholesale change.* People tend to resist major changes, especially changes requiring complete redirection.

12. ***Unique points of resistance.*** Unexpected circumstances and events can retard change. Not everything can be planned in advance; people or events outside the organization can impede our innovative spirit.[36]

Consideration of the points in the preceding list and sensitivity to the needs of people involved in curriculum change ease implementation. Also, resistance to change can benefit change agents by requiring them to think carefully about proposed innovations, consider the human dynamics involved in implementing programs, and avoid advocating change for its own sake or in order to allow some educational fad.

Leaders of curriculum activities must give primary attention to what Thomas Sergiovanni describes as a *lifeworld*. The lifeworld of a school refers to the culture of the school with its attendant meanings that hold significance to the key players in that lifeworld—the teachers and the students.[37]

Sensitive curriculum leaders realize that for successful implementation to occur, they must promote in teachers and in students their voice, their agency. They must foster in these key players opportunities to participate in and identify with the curriculum being implemented from cognitive, emotional, and spiritual orientations.[38] Essentially, for there to be successful implementation of the curriculum, there must be established, at least unofficially, a curriculum for the teacher implementers so they can develop their human agency. Teachers must have opportunities to mediate their behaviors through meditations that allow them to self-fashion their identities.

They must have quiet time and sharing time to give dimension and description about whom they are. In a very real way, teachers—and, we hope, students later—have opportunities to actually develop several identities with various and particular voices. Teachers nurtured to be receptive to change take on identities of curriculum implementer, innovative teacher, nurturer of creative and reflective students, and spokesperson of educational change. The list of persons and the variety of voices are limited only by the imaginations, dedications, and deep personalities of the individuals involved.

Those who have gained some degree of expertise over their varied persons and resultant voices have attained agency to some degree. They are major players in school worlds. They have come to truly work cooperatively to create and strengthen community.[39]

Individuals must understand how the curriculum change will affect them personally. They must clearly grasp the platform on which they are to build the curriculum. They must possess a clear sense of mission and confidence that the curriculum envisioned has the potential to enrich students and teachers.

## Stages of Change

Curriculum change has essentially three stages: initiation, implementation, and maintenance. *Initiation* of change sets the stage for implementation. It gets the school receptive to the planned innovation. Planners raise essential questions about who will be involved, what level of support is expected, and how ready people are for the innovation. Ideally, these questions relating to the initiation phase were asked when the parties were involved in curriculum development.

*Implementation* of change involves presenting innovation and getting people to try it out in their classrooms or other appropriate educational spaces. It means accepting the new curricular content and adapting the suggested educational activities to a particular classroom. Implementation does not mean accepting without question what the new program presents. Teachers must put their own stamp on the innovation; they must personalize the suggested curriculum so that they can optimize the learning experiences for their unique students. This adaptation actually must be done every year to cater to the newly entered class.

Mike Schmoker stresses that for effective school programs to be implemented, schools must establish learning communities. Such communities furnish teachers with support staff and with scheduled opportunities to discuss issues that arise as a result of innovation.[40] Successful implementation requires teamwork. Fullan notes that in successful implementation, teacher–collegial relationships are central to the activity. Interaction "flavors" the relationships and teachers' thinking regarding the innovation. Implementation requires teacher collaboration; it demands teachers exchange ideas, support new actions, rearrange thinking, and assess feelings about the new program. Fullan asserts that "collegiality, open communication, trust, support and help, learning on the job, getting results and job satisfaction and morale are closely interrelated."[41] Implementation strives to make schools "learning enriched" for all the players: administrators, teachers, and students.

*Maintenance* is the monitoring of the innovation after it has been introduced. *Maintenance* refers to those actions required for the continuation of the innovation. Unless maintenance is planned for, innovations often fade or are altered to such a degree that they cease to exist. As Fullan articulates, the problem of maintenance—or, as he states it, continuation—shadows all forms of educational innovation. This challenge to continue a new educational program is endemic regardless of whether the push for the new program was external or internal.[42]

Maintenance must be planned for, but such planning is not just solving technical problems or introducing flow charts. To maintain an innovation, we must address or even ignite the affective domain of teachers and others. We must excite the senses. We must spark passion. Commitment requires emotional attachment to the innovation adventure. The positive emotional response to a change of curriculum is what fosters success. Teachers must experience positive emotional attachment to all dimensions of the curriculum. They must be excited by its aims and goals. They must respond affectively to the contents and pedagogies to be implemented. Educators must see the morality of the curricular innovation. Also, of course, students should have their emotional and moral selves activated for the innovation to take root.[43]

## CURRICULUM IMPLEMENTATION MODELS

In today's world, choice—including choice regarding curricular change—can be overwhelming. Educators, especially in this new century, function within the construct of diversity in approaches to curricular innovation, purposes of education, organizations of school spaces, creation of diverse curricula, means of engaging students in such curricula, and approaches to measure successes of student learnings.

There also appears to be a tension between those who believe in a "precise" approach to implementing new curricula and those who advocate a serendipitous approach that takes into consideration the emergence of unanticipated goals as they unfold from planned and unplanned student encounters. Those moved to action by the adherence to standards appear to discount the planned surprises in the development and implementation processes. People who religiously follow the various states of curriculum change and implementation devolve teacher intuition, which can have an impact on the evolution of the educational experience. In truth, educators responsible for curricular change should embrace the notion that the "personal and tangential can stimulate a routine venture to a novel educative venture."[44]

As noted previously by Leslie Bishop, implementation requires restructuring and replacement. Primary in this restructuring is fostering and molding changes in people. Implementation, to be successful, actually requires the shaping of the school culture, that is, shaping the norms and behaviors extant in the school or school district.[45] However, enabling change in people's beliefs and behaviors is not easily or quickly accomplished.[46] Also, those engaged in new curricula or educational procedures must realize that the program being implemented deals with numerous changes: new curricular contents, new pedagogical approaches, new educational materials, new technologies, and perhaps even new educational environments. Of course, the major challenge is having an implementation procedure that allows educators time to try on different beliefs or to sample novel understandings about the innovation.

Although the models of implementation to be discussed appear to have distinct steps and stages, we must remember that implementation occurs in specific and individual settings with varying histories, unique competencies among staff, particular expectations among community members, and various capacities with regard to materials and monetary resources. Even though learning the various steps of implementation strategies appears easy, actually carrying them out is highly complex.[47] As Fullan contends, a person skilled in implementing an innovation juggles and fuses various factors that at first might appear at odds with each other: "simultaneous simplicity–complexity, looseness–tightness, strong leadership–user participation, bottom-up/top-down, fidelity–adaptivity, and evaluation–non-evaluation."[48] As Fullan submits, effective implementation—actually, any strategy for improvement—requires a nuanced apprehension of the process, a way of thinking that does not become apparent in a rigid following of a list of steps or phases to be enacted.[49]

We encourage our readers to read and consider the following implementation models with this mindset.

## Overcoming-Resistance-to-Change Model

The *overcoming-resistance-to-change (ORC) model* of curriculum implementation has been employed for many years. According to Neal Gross, it rests in the assumption that the success or failure of planned organizational change basically depends on leaders' ability to overcome staff resistance to change.[50] To implement a new program, we must gain advocates for it by addressing people's fears and doubts. We must convince individuals involved that the new program takes their values and perspective into account.[51]

One strategy for overcoming resistance to change is to give school administrators and teachers equal power. Subordinates should be involved in discussions and decisions about program change. When leaders adopt this strategy, staff members tend to view the innovation as self-created and, therefore, feel committed to it.

Curriculum leaders using the ORC model identify and deal with staff's concerns. They understand that individuals must change before organizations can be altered. Also, change must allow for the individuality and personal needs of those involved. Based on their research on curriculum innovations in schools and colleges, Gene Hall and Susan Loucks divided implementation into four stages:

> *Stage 1: Unrelated concerns.* At this stage, teachers do not see a relationship between themselves and the suggested change, which they therefore do not resist. For example, a teacher might be aware of the school's efforts to create a new science program but not feel personally or professionally affected.
>
> *Stage 2: Personal concerns.* At this stage, individuals react to the innovation in terms of their personal situation. They are concerned with how the new program will affect what they are doing. For example, biology teachers consider their involvement in a new science program and its effects on their teaching.
>
> *Stage 3: Task-related concerns.* These concerns relate to the actual use of the innovation in the classroom. For example, an English teacher would be concerned about how to implement a new language arts program. How much time will be required to teach this new program? Will adequate materials be provided? What are the best strategies for teaching the new program?
>
> *Stage 4: Impact-related concerns.* At this stage, a teacher is concerned with how the innovation will affect students, colleagues, and the community. The teacher might also want to determine the program's impact on his or her own subject area. For example, will a new mathematics program influence a teacher's teaching methods and content topics in ways that help students better understand mathematics?[52]

Educators who employ the ORC model must deal with people's personal, task-related, and impact-related concerns. Otherwise, people will not accept the innovation or will deal with it in unintended ways. Curriculum leaders must keep all staff informed of the innovation and involve those people who will be directly affected in the early decisions regarding the innovation. Often, faculty can be called together to share concerns and map strategies to deal with those concerns. Sometimes information can be gathered from questionnaires. Teachers may find that they have to change their strategies and teach different content. By sharing concerns, they can gain confidence that they can make the necessary changes.

## Organizational-Development Model

In the 1970s, Richard Schmuck and Matthew Miles developed the position that many approaches to educational improvement fail because the leaders assume that adoption is a rational process and rely too heavily on innovation's technical aspects. Such leaders assume that systematic properties (e.g., class size, school organization) of local school districts are constants.[53] Schmuck and Miles' views are postmodern to the extent that they suggest doubts about individual rationality, objective measures, universal truths, and the scientific method.[54]

Schmuck and Miles suggested an approach called *organizational development (OD)*. It is a long-range effort to improve an organization's problem-solving and renewal processes, particularly through collaborative diagnosis and management. The emphasis is on teamwork and organizational culture.

Wendell French and Cecil Bell list seven characteristics that separate OD from more traditional ways of intervening in organizations:

1. Emphasis on teamwork for addressing issues
2. Emphasis on group and intergroup processes
3. Use of action research
4. Emphasis on collaboration within the organization
5. Realization that the organization's culture must be perceived as part of the total system
6. Realization that those in charge of the organization serve as consultants/facilitators
7. Appreciation of the organization's ongoing dynamics within a continually changing environment[55]

OD treats implementation as an ongoing, interactive process. The approach rests on the assumption that individuals care about the future and desire to be actively engaged in designing, developing, implementing, and evaluating the educational system.[56]

OD treats implementation as never finished. There are always new ideas to bring to the new program, new materials and methods to try out, and new students to excite. Enacting the curriculum continually engages teachers and students in growth by providing enriched learning that benefits the total person.

## Concerns-Based Adoption Model

The *concerns-based adoption (CBA) model* is related to the OD model. However, those who use a CBA approach believe that all change originates with individuals. Individuals change, and, through their changed behaviors, institutions change. Change occurs when individuals' concerns are made known. For individuals to favor change, they must view the change as at least partly of their own making. They must also view it as directly relevant to their personal and professional lives. Because the change process involves so many individuals, it needs time to take shape. Individuals need time to learn new skills and formulate new attitudes.[57]

Also, unlike the OD model of change, the CBA model addresses only adoption (implementation) of curriculum, not development and design. It assumes that teachers and other educational workers have already analyzed the needs of the school and have created or selected a curriculum for the school or school district that meets those needs. It certainly functions with the belief that in addition to the needs of the students, the innovation also addresses the teachers' concerns. Because we are discussing curriculum implementation, this model of implementation

1. Awareness of innovation

2. Awareness of information level

3. Concern for self

4. Concern for teaching

5. Concern for students

**FIGURE 8.1** Concern Stages Relating to Implementing an Innovation

*Source:* Modified from Collin J. Marsh and George Willis, *Curriculum: Alternative Approaches, Ongoing Issues,* 4th ed. (Upper Saddle River, NJ: Pearson, 2007).

addresses teachers' concerns regarding content, materials, pedagogies, technologies, and educational experiences. These factors should be thought about in their varying relationships; they exist as an educational universe of variables that hopefully interact to furnish students a rich and productive learning experience.[58]

F. F. Fuller's research regarding the way in which preservice teachers evolve into experienced teachers provided the model's conceptual underpinnings. Fuller found that preservice teachers generally moved from concerns about self, to concerns about teaching, and then to concerns about students.[59] Ann Lieberman and Lyon Miller found a similar sequence of teachers' concerns.[60] Others have reported two stages of concern before concern for self: (1) awareness of the innovation and (2) interest in learning about the innovation, but no realization that the innovation may directly affect them. At stage 3, teachers wonder whether they have the skills and knowledge to implement the innovation. At stage 4, they have reservations about how to manage their time and resources to implement the program successfully, and how to actually teach it. At stage 5, teachers focus on how the new curriculum influences students' learning. Figure 8.1 depicts the concerns.

In the CBA model, the curriculum is implemented once teachers' concerns have been adequately addressed. Teachers are expected to be creative with the curriculum, modify it where necessary, and tailor it to their students. Additionally, teachers should work with their colleagues in fine-tuning the curriculum for the benefit of the total school program.

## Systems Model

The OD and CBA models draw on systems thinking. Both consider people's actions as performed within an organization defined by a system of relations among people and structures. People in schools and school districts have overlapping responsibilities. Also, the work of higher-level administrative or curricular teams affects that of lower-level professional teams. If people responsible for a major portion of an innovation respect, support, and trust one another, they are also likely to interact in a positive way with others throughout the organization.

The school is an organization of loosely coupled units: departments, classrooms, and individuals. These parts have flexible rather than rigidly defined relationships. Although a central administration is defined, most schools have little centralized control, especially over what occurs in the classroom. For this reason, it is difficult for curricular change to be implemented as an edict from the central office.

Planned change within the school should be perceived as "win–win." Also, we must recognize that the process never finishes: Every aspect of the implemented curriculum is unique, requiring that educators realize that even when some aspect of the program is implemented, it is not static. The implemented curriculum essentially has a life of its own. It interacts continually with the people teaching and learning it. Every encounter that students have with the new curriculum is unique; every learning is personalized. And educators must realize that even when a curriculum is fully introduced, it is taught and experienced differently each year. Although the teacher may be the same, his or her behaviors in engaging students with the implemented curriculum is unique. Different students, different times, and different demands on all the players in the educational theater is unique. Great teaching is always striving for better teaching and better curricula; each year is a new beginning.[61]

Accepting the systems model to curriculum implementation means realizing that curriculum change resembles an evolving solar system. Although it has rules, there is variation. Like the solar system, competing forces do enable order. Planets do stay in their orbits. Likewise, in implementation, conflict must be managed so that everyone can win: students, teachers, chairs, and principals. However, successful implementation requires energy, time, and patience. It demands recognizing that implementation is more than a set of techniques or disconnected approaches. In a systems approach, there must be engagement; there must be the drawing of energy among the participants; there must be the formulation of rationales for the innovation suggested. However, there must be the recognition that there is no complete attainment of final results. Curriculum implementation, regardless of approach, is like sailing to the horizon. We can direct our craft to the horizon, but it can never be attained. Thus with curriculum implementation, we realize we can never complete the task of introducing the new program. Curriculum innovators must be cognizant that their task is not to arrive at the perfect curriculum, but to comprehend that innovative curriculum development and implementation are continual pursuits of the next engagement of students in their learning. Implementation of novel curricula can never be finalized. Educators can never rest on their laurels. Time does not stand still; neither do the demands on curriculum developers and implementers. Educators are always called to consider something new, something that enables students to participate competently in an evolving world dynamic.

## Factors Affecting Implementation

Fullan discusses key factors that affect implementation.[62] People who wish to implement a new curriculum must understand the characteristics of the change being considered. Often people resist an innovation if they don't see the need for the change. When change acts with people's values, people are more willing to accept it.

People must know the purpose of an innovation and what the innovation involves. *Clarity* about goals and means is important. Often, people are not clear as to how a particular innovation differs from what they are already doing. *Complexity* refers to the difficulty of change. For staff experienced in curriculum development, extensive change can be rather easy. For inexperienced staff, the same change can be quite challenging. Implementers must recognize the level of difficulty and take adequate measures.[63] However, if the curriculum is totally different from the one being replaced, even experienced teachers need time to learn about the innovation and to experiment with varying ways of engaging students. Geoffrey Canada, president and chief executive officer of the Harlem Children's Zone Promise Academy charter schools in New York, indicates that successful schools are those where teachers are enabled to experiment. To gain new knowledge and skills, teachers are afforded opportunities for professional development.[64] Often, in regular schools, teachers receive only a 2-day workshop to "get up to speed" regarding a new curriculum.

To accept an innovation, people need to perceive its *quality, worth,* and *practicality.* Often, teachers simply do not have the time to carry out the suggestions. Sometimes curricula are haphazardly implemented that could have been well implemented if those in charge had ensured that the necessary materials were available for teachers. Often teachers in new programs soon realize that technical or support staff are unavailable to answer questions.

Table 8.1 provides an overview of curriculum implementation models.

**Table 8.1** Overview of Curriculum Implementation Models

| Model | Author–Originator | Assumptions | Key Players | Type of Change Process Engaged |
|---|---|---|---|---|
| Overcoming resistance to change (ORC) | Neal Gross | Resistance to change is natural. Need to overcome resistance at outset of innovation activities. Must address concerns of staff. | Administrators, directors, teachers, supervisors | Empirical change strategy Planned change strategy |
| Organizational development (OD) | Richard Schmuck and Matthew Miles | Top-down approach (vertical organization). Stress on organizational culture. Implementation is an ongoing interactive process. | Administrators, directors, supervisors | Empirical, rational change strategy Planned change strategy |
| Concerns-based adoption (CBA) | F. F. Fuller | Change is personal. Stress on school culture. | Teachers | Empirical change strategy Planned change strategy |
| Systems model | Rensis Likert and Chris Argyris | The organization is composed of parts, units, and departments. Linkages between people and groups. Implementations consist of corrective actions. | Administrators, directors, teachers, supervisors | Normative, rational change strategies Planned change strategy |
| Educational change | Michael Fullan | Successful change involves need, clarity, some complexity, and quality of programs. | Administrators, teachers, students, school board, community members, and government | Rational change strategies |

## KEY PLAYERS

People involved in curriculum implementation can include students, teachers, administrators, consultants, state employees, university professors, parents, lay citizens, and political officials interested in education. Depending on their skills, such people may play different roles at different times in the change process. Often, the same people are involved in both development and implementation of a new curriculum. At other times, the individuals differ, but the roles of the players remain the same. Certainly, principals and curriculum directors are involved in both development and implementation. However, implementation requires different knowledge and strategies than development.

Almost anyone in the educational community can initiate the change process. However, initiatives usually begin in the administrative hierarchy. Sometimes school districts pay one or more people to be internal initiators of change. These people are charged with discerning problems, demands, or deficiencies that require attention. They may get others to consider change by writing papers, forming ad hoc committees to analyze particular issues, submitting proposals, or simply sending memos to staff recommending concern for some action.

In some cases, an initiator participates in the entire change process. This is especially likely when the initiator is an insider. In other cases, an initiator can just serve as a catalyst but not be actively involved in any stage of curriculum change.

## Students

Before the late 1980s and 1990s, educators rarely thought of students as agents of change. However, since then, more and more educators have realized that students, even elementary students, can contribute to meaningful education change. The degree of student involvement depends on students' maturity and on the complexity and scope of the change being considered. As Dennis Thiessen notes, "student voice" has become the clarion call for change in the way we understand, respond to, and work with students in elementary and secondary schools.[65]

Increasingly, educational practitioners and researchers realize that students possess unique perspectives on their own learning and on the nature and purpose of their schooling.[66] As Alison Cook-Sather suggests, students "should be afforded opportunities to actively shape their education."[67] Students must be included in discussions about the organization of curricular programs. Educators must form partnerships with students in designing and implementing the curriculum.[68] That way students claim some ownership of the new curriculum. They also learn valuable approaches for organizing their own learning inside and outside of school.

For students to become involved in implementation, they must see the relevance of the new program and feel they truly have influence. As active participants, they are likely to greet the implemented curriculum with interest and enthusiasm.

## Teachers

Teachers must be central to any curricular improvement. Henry Giroux has posited that teachers are integral to the thinking that drives program creation and implementation. Teachers are directly involved with the implementation in the classroom. They possess clinical expertise.[69] As Elizabeth Campbell indicates, curriculum expectations emerge from teachers' capacities to enact curricular and pedagogic actions "with discretion, judgment, and proficiency."[70] Teachers modify and fine-tune the design work of their colleagues and outside professionals.

The key to getting teachers committed to an innovation is involvement. In addition to being members of the curriculum advisory committee, teachers should have opportunities to participate in curriculum learning communities in which they can develop identities as curriculum innovators.

Teachers need more than 1- or 2-day skill-training workshops. They need time to make sense of new curricula slated for implementation, time to gain competence in new instructional practices that engages students,[71] and time for frequent dialogue on the curriculum's educational purposes and the conditions necessary to implement and maintain the curriculum.[72]

Teachers must adhere to the essence of the innovation while adapting it to their students. Teachers must be viewed as full participants in curriculum implementation, not passive recipients of the curriculum. As Corey Drake and Miriam Gamoran Sherin note, teachers put their own spin on the new curriculum. Teachers bring their own knowledge, experiences, and dispositions to the curriculum and modify it to fit.[73]

## Supervisors

Curriculum implementation must be supervised and monitored. Both the manner of teaching and the content being addressed need oversight. The supervisor provides direction and guidance and makes sure teachers have the skills to carry out the change.

Effective supervisors realize that they must adjust their tactics to the situation and participants. Supervisors can give experienced teachers much responsibility. However, they might have to give beginning teachers more structure; they might need to schedule more supervisor–teacher conferences and more in-service training for such staff members to deliver the new curriculum.

Supervisors can carry out their responsibilities in numerous ways. A few popular ways are classroom observation, demonstration teaching, supervisor–teacher conferences, staff-development meetings, and grant funding. If supervisors are effective, teachers are likely to commit to, and feel comfortable with, the new program being implemented.

### Principals

The principal's leadership is critical to the success of curriculum implementation. Principals determine organizational climate and support the people involved in change. If a principal creates an atmosphere in which good working relationships exist among teachers and between teachers and support staff, it is more likely that program changes will be implemented. Effective principals foster enthusiasm for the new program.

Today, principals must not only be administrators with an in-depth understanding of curriculum and implementation, but also what Catherine Marshall and Maricela Oliva have called *boundary crossers*.[74] In addition to being a school leader, a principal must be a community activist. Principals must speak and act for teachers, students, *and* the community. Principals must listen to what these individuals have to say. Principals must facilitate meaningful action among all parties involved in curriculum implementation.[75]

### Curriculum Directors

Curriculum directors concentrate on the overall process of curriculum development, including implementation and evaluation. Large school districts have full-time directors who oversee curriculum activities. In some school districts, directors oversee the entire K–12 program; other districts have a director of elementary education and a separate director of secondary education. In small school districts, the superintendent or associate (assistant) superintendent assumes responsibility over curriculum matters.

Ideally, the curriculum director or assistant superintendent in charge of curriculum inspires trust and confidence and is knowledgeable, articulate, and charismatic.[76] The curriculum director or assistant superintendent in charge of curriculum should help teachers and principals gain the pedagogic and curricular knowledge requisite for curriculum implementation. They should be familiar with the latest research and theorizing about innovation and have the skills to communicate their knowledge to the school's staff.

### Curriculum Consultants

At times, a school district may wish to bring in an external facilitator or coordinator. Often, small school districts have no internal experts to consult regarding innovation. Even large districts may find they need an outside facilitator. School districts do not usually employ curriculum consultants over extended periods. Rather, schools bring in consultants to do 1- or 2-day workshops. However, such workshops are ineffective because curriculum implementation requires a much longer time frame. Consultants also help schools analyze programs, assess them, and obtain grant funding. Most such consultants are based at colleges and universities.

Many educational consultants are employed by state departments of education and sent to various schools and school districts to assist in curriculum development and implementation. Many consultants are on the staff of intermediate school districts and work closely with school districts served by such organizations. Private national consultants also assist in curricular activities.

Successful consultants cooperate with teachers in addressing some development or implementation issue. They assist rather than judge. Sometimes, but not usually, consultants are hired to work with teachers throughout the curriculum development and implementation process. Consultants can provide guidance, analysis, and critique without being in a district on a daily or weekly basis. Consultants can establish peer support systems, peer coaching, and networks for working with internal facilitators. They also can guide teachers to information that helps them become comfortable with, and knowledgeable about, the innovation.

### Parents and Community Members

Schools exist within communities, frequently in increasingly diverse communities. Educators must realize that students actually spend more time in their communities than in school.

Educators must also apprehend that curricula exist outside school walls; student learning does occur when students exit the school. In the development and implementation of curricula, educators must strive to focus on communities and develop means of engaging parents and community members in school activities, including implementation.

The work of Geoffrey Canada with the Harlem Children's Zone Academy charter schools has shown what academic success can be achieved by considering the communities within which students live and schools exist. He engaged the community block by block. Today, that community is almost 100 blocks in area. Children who lacked many resources and were underachieving are now achieving academic success. Canada's accomplishments have impressed President Barack Obama; he has urged the creation of 20 "Promise Neighborhoods" nationwide.[77]

Canada views community with a wide lens. He views innovation as requiring educators and community members not only to make the school innovative, but also work to make the community innovative. Canada posits, "We need to improve schools at the same time we address the barriers to academic success outside of schools from health problems to misguided parenting practices to lack of physical safety."[78] He urges us to broaden our definition of education and to realize that the educational experience commences at birth and continues in all environments within which students interact.

Although communities differ with regard to specific issues, the community should participate in varying degrees with the creation, implementation, and maintenance of curricula. This does not mean that parents and community members are going to do the teachers' jobs. But, a partnership should exist. As Fullan communicates, "The closer the parent is to the education of the children, the greater the impact on child development and educational achievement."[79]

Educators must take the lead in engaging the community in educational actions. Fullan suggests that while both educators and community members want only the best for children, they often differ in what they consider the best. In many communities, parents do not trust teachers. Community members often believe that teachers, especially those who do not actually live in their communities, frequently "don't get it" when it comes to understanding their children and the environment in which they live. Teachers, and certainly the principal, must extend a welcoming hand to parents and community members.

However, building trust in schools, as Bryk and Schneider point out, is a major challenge.[80] It requires modifying a community culture or cultures with school or school cultures. It requires teachers actually leaving their classrooms and entering the community. Teachers can no longer stay in the comfort of their schools; professors of education must leave their "towers" and mix with the "people." It means that educators must realize that what is occurring or should be occurring in the communities and schools is a rearrangement of power and influence. Educators should view community members as partners. Teachers cannot educate students alone in the isolation of the classroom.[81] Even with home schooling gaining in popularity, parents cannot educate their children alone. Adding to the complexity of working with parents and community members is the realization that although school and homes do have visible and measurable curricula, schools, homes, and the larger communities all possess various hidden curricula that can serve to advance or retard students' total academic learning. And we do not mean just the learning of disciplined knowledge; rather, we also consider the impact the community and community members have on students' attitudes, values, and belief systems. And what of the null curricula, that curricula that students know exists but to which we attempt to deny them access, the taboo topics we do not teach or from which we tend to shield their eyes?

Bringing in the total community to work with educators in developing and implementing curricula is not going to always be smooth. As Michelle Rhee, former chancellor of the Washington, DC, public school system, articulates, there will be conflict, but we should not shy away from it. Rearranging power and influence, shaking up the politics of the special interests, will ruffle feathers. However, as Rhee notes, we must mount various fights, but we can do it respectfully: "[T]his is the time to stand up and say what you believe, not sweep the issues under the rug so that we can feel good about getting along."[82] However, in dealing with the community, we must strive for a win–win result. We are not striving for anyone to lose. And educators must realize that this dynamic with parents and community members will be an ongoing drama. Educators and community members cannot wait for Superman; we must realize that challenges will be addressed by our efforts, cooperatively taken. We are superman and superwoman!

## Conclusion

Curriculum implementation is much more than handing out new materials and courses of study. For implementation to succeed, those involved must understand the program's purpose, the roles people play within the system, and the types of individuals who are to be affected by interaction with the new curriculum. For successful implementation, schools essentially must establish learning communities. A major emphasis is to make the school, as a result of curriculum implementation, learning enriched for everyone involved, certainly for teachers and students.

Effective implementation does not occur without serious planning. The change process demands planning, but planning with flexibility so as to address unintended circumstances and events. As events arise, procedures must be fine-tuned.

People who create a new curriculum or course are eager to see the school or school district enthusiastically implement it. Yet implementation does not demand that educators accept the curriculum without question. School players need time to "try on" the new curriculum or course and to put their own stamp on it. Teachers need opportunities to engage their colleagues in conversations about the curriculum or course being presented. Interaction "flavors" teachers' relationships regarding the curriculum to be implemented.

Curricularists can bring various perspectives to implementation and employ numerous strategies. Successful implementation requires a community of trust. Those in charge of change strategies must understand the relationship of change to planning and the dynamics of group processes.

## Endnotes

1. Jon Wiles and Joseph Bondi, *Curriculum Development: A Guide to Practice,* 7th ed. (Upper Saddle River, NJ: Pearson, 2007).
2. Leslie J. Bishop, *Staff Development and Instructional Improvement: Plans and Procedures* (Boston: Allyn & Bacon, 1976).
3. Michael Fullan, Peter Hill, and Carmel Crevola, *Breakthrough* (Thousand Oaks, CA: Corwin Press, 2006).
4. Seymour B. Sarason, *The Predictable Failure of Educational Reform* (San Francisco: Jossey-Bass, 1990).
5. Ibid.
6. Fullan, Hill, and Crevola, *Breakthrough.*
7. Roger Soder, *The Language of Leadership* (San Francisco: Jossey-Bass, 2001).
8. Michael Fullan, *The New Meaning of Educational Change,* 4th ed. (New York: Teachers College Press, 2007).
9. John I. Goodlad, *In Praise of Education* (New York: Teachers College Press, 1997).
10. Richard E. Elmore, *School Reform from the Inside Out* (Cambridge, MA: Harvard Education Press, Fourth Printing, 2007).
11. Ibid., p. 211.
12. Ellen Brantlinger, *Dividing Classes* (New York: Routledge, 2003).
13. Elmore, *School Reform from the Inside Out.*
14. Ibid., p. 223.
15. Valerie Truesdale, Claire Thompson, and Michael Lucas, "Use of Curriculum Mapping to Build a Learning Community," in Heidi Hayes Jacobs, ed., *Getting Results with Curriculum Mapping* (Alexandria, VA, Association for Supervision and Curriculum Development, 2004). pp. 10–24.
16. Elmore, *School Reform from the Inside Out.*
17. Fullan, *The New Meaning of Educational Change*; and Elmore, *School Reform from the Inside Out.*
18. Fullan, Hill, and Crevola, *Breakthrough.*
19. Colin M. J. Marsh and George Willis, *Curriculum: Alternative Approaches, Ongoing Issues,* 4th ed. (Upper Saddle River, NJ: Pearson, 2007).
20. Fullan, Hill, and Crevola, *Breakthrough.*
21. Harry J. Hartley, "Budgeting," in R. A. Gorton, ed., *Encyclopedia of School Administration and Supervision* (New York: Oryx Press, 1988), pp. 40–41.
22. Fullan, Hill, and Crevola, *Breakthrough.*
23. Daniel U. Levine, Rayna F. Levine, and Allan C. Ornstein, "Guidelines for Change and Innovation in the Secondary School Curriculum," *NASSP Bulletin* (May 1985), pp. 9–14.
24. Ibid., p. 14.
25. Warren Bennis, *Changing Organizations* (New York: McGraw-Hill, 1966); and Warren Bennis, *On Becoming a Leader* (Reading, MA: Addison Wesley, 1989).

26. John D. McNeil, *Curriculum: A Comprehensive Introduction,* 6th ed. (Glenview, IL: Scott Foresman, 2000).

27. Elmore, *School Reform from the Inside Out.*

28. Kieran Egan, *The Future of Education* (New Haven: Yale University Press, 2008), p. 88.

29. Sehba Ali, "Class Action," *Newsweek* (November 8, 2010), p. 10.

30. Brantlinger, *Dividing Classes.*

31. Ibid.

32. Soder, *The Language of Leadership.*

33. Kenneth T. Henson, *Curriculum Planning: Integrating Multiculturalism, Constructivism, and Educational Reform,* 2nd ed. (New York: McGraw-Hill, 2001); and Elmore, *School Reform from the Inside Out.*

34. Shazia Rafiullah Miller, Karen Drill, and Ellen Behrstock, "Meeting Teachers Half Way: Making Educational Research Relevant to Teachers," *Phi Delta Kappan* (April 2010), pp. 31–34.

35. Ibid.

36. Thomas R. Harvey, *Checklist for Change* (Boston: Allyn & Bacon, 1990).

37. Thomas Sergiovanni et al., *Educational Governance and Administration,* 3rd ed. (Boston: Allyn & Bacon, 1992).

38. Kris Sloan, "Teacher Identity and Agency in School Worlds: Beyond the All-Good/All-Bad Discourse on Accountability-Explicit Curriculum Policies," *Curriculum Inquiry* (Summer 2006), pp. 119–152.

39. Ibid.

40. Mike Schmoker, *Results Now* (Alexandria, VA: Association for Supervision and Curriculum Development, 2006).

41. Fullan, *The New Meaning of Educational Change,* p. 97.

42. Ibid.

43. Ibid.

44. Peter Hlebowitsh, "Centripetal Thinking in Curriculum Studies," *Curriculum Inquiry* (September 2010), pp. 503–513.

45. Stacey Childress, Richard E. Elmore, Allen Grossman, and Susan Moore Johnson, "The PELP Coherence Framework," in Michael Fullan, ed., *The Challenge of Change,* 2nd ed. (Thousand Oaks, CA: Corwin, 2009), pp. 179–184.

46. Ibid.

47. Fullan, *The New Meaning of Educational Change.*

48. Ibid., p. 86.

49. Ibid.

50. Neal Gross, "Basic Issues in the Management of Educational Change Efforts," in R. E. Herriott and N. Gross, eds., *The Dynamics of Planned Educational Change* (Berkeley, CA: McCutchan, 1979), pp. 20–46.

51. Parker J. Palmer, *The Courage to Teach: Exploring the Inner Landscape of a Teacher's Life* (San Francisco: Jossey-Bass, 1998).

52. Gene E. Hall and Susan Loucks, "Teacher Concerns as a Basis for Facilitating and Personalizing Staff Development," *Teachers College Record* (September 1978), pp. 36–53; and Gene E. Hall and Susan Loucks, "The Concept of Innovation Configurations: An Approach to Addressing Program Adaptation." Paper presented at the annual meeting of the American Educational Research Association, Los Angeles, April 1981.

53. Richard S. Schmuck and Matthew Miles, eds., *Organizational Development in Schools* (Palo Alto, CA: National Press Books, 1971); and Richard S. Schmuck et al., *The Second Handbook of Organizational Development in Schools* (Palo Alto, CA: Mayfield, 1977).

54. M. Jayne Fleener, "Introduction: Chaos, Complexity, Curriculum and Cultures: Setting Up the Conversation," in William C. Doll Jr., M. Jayne Fleener, Donna Trueit, and John S. Julien, eds., *Chaos, Complexity, Curriculum, and Culture* (New York: Peter Lang, 2005), pp. 1–17.

55. Wendell L. French and Cecil H. Bell, *Organization Development,* 4th ed. (Englewood Cliffs, NJ: Prentice Hall, 1990).

56. Roger Kaufman and L. W. Harrell, "Types of Functional Educational Planning Models," *Performance Improvement Quarterly, 2*(1), 1989, pp. 4–13, cited in Robert V. Carlson and Gary Awkerman, eds., *Educational Planning* (New York: Longman, 1991).

57. Marsh and Willis, *Curriculum: Alternative Approaches, Ongoing Issues.*

58. Fullan, *The New Meaning of Educational Change.*

59. F. F. Fuller, "Concerns of Teachers: A Developmental Conceptulation," *American Educational Research Journal, 6,* 2 (1969), pp. 207–226, cited in Colin M. J. Marsh and George Willis, *Curriculum: Alternative Approaches, Ongoing Issues,* 4th ed. (Upper Saddle River, NJ: Pearson, 2007).

60. Ann Lieberman and Lynn Miller, *Teachers—Their World and Their Work* (New York: Teachers College Press, Columbia University, 1991).

61. William Ayers, *To Teach: The Journey of a Teacher,* 3rd ed. (New York: Teachers College Press, 2010).

62. Fullan, *The New Meaning of Educational Change.*

63. French and Bell, *Organizational Development.*

64. Geoffrey Canada, "Bringing Change to Scale: The Next Big Reform Challenge," in Karl Weber, ed., *Waiting for "Superman"* (New York: Public Affairs, A Member of the Perseus Books Group, 2010), pp. 189–200.

65. Dennis Thiessen, "Student Knowledge, Engagement, and Voice in Educational Reform," *Curriculum Inquiry* (Winter 2006), pp. 345–358.

66. Alison Cook-Sather, "Sound, Presence, and Power: 'Student Voice' in Educational Research and Reform," *Curriculum Inquiry* (Winter 2006), pp. 359–390.

67. Ibid., p. 359.

68. Ibid.

69. Henry A. Giroux, *Schooling and the Struggle for Public Life,* 2nd ed. (Boulder, CO: Paradigm Publishers, 2005).

70. Elizabeth Campbell, "Curricular and Professional Authority in Schools," *Curriculum Inquiry* (Summer 2006), pp. 111–118.

71. Corey Drake and Miriam Gamoran Sherin, "Practicing Change: Curriculum Adaptation and Teacher Narrative in the Context of Mathematics Education Reform," *Curriculum Inquiry* (Summer 2006), pp. 153–187.

72. John R. Wiens, "Educational Leadership as Civic Humanism," in Paul Kelleher and Rebecca Van Der Bogert, *Voices for Democracy: Struggles and Celebrations of Transformational Leaders, 105th Yearbook, Part I* (Malden, MA: National Society for the Study of Education/Blackwell, 2006), pp. 199–225.

73. Drake and Sherin, "Practicing Change: Curriculum Adaptation and Teacher Narrative in the Context of Mathematics Education Reform."

74. Catherine Marshall and Maricela Oliva, *Leadership for Social Justice* (Boston: Pearson, 2006).

75. Soder, *The Language of Leadership.*

76. Paul Kelleher and Rebecca Van Der Bogert, "Introduction: The Landscape of the Superintendency: From Despair to Hope," in Paul Kelleher and Rebecca Van Der Bogert, eds., *Voice for Democracy: Struggles and Celebrations of Transformational Leaders,* (Malden, MA: National Society for the Study of Education/Blackwell, 2006), pp. 10–28.

77. Canada, "Bringing Change to Scale: The Next Big Reform Challenge."

78. Ibid., p. 196.

79. Fullan, *The New Meaning of Educational Change,* p. 189.

80. A. Bryk and B. Schneider. *Trust in Schools* (New York: Russell Sage, 2002), cited in Fullan, *The New Meaning of Educational Change,* p. 193.

81. Fullan, *The New Meaning of Educational Change.*

82. Michelle Rhee, "What I've Learned," *Newsweek* (December 13, 2010), pp. 36–41.

# 9

■ ■ ■

# Curriculum Evaluation

## FOCUSING QUESTIONS

1. Why is curriculum evaluation today more challenging to define and enact than in the past?
2. What challenges do educators face with meeting the three standards stated in the legislation of No Child Left Behind?
3. What myths follow the discussions regarding rewarding teacher pay for student performance?
4. What are the nature and purpose of evaluation?
5. How does evaluation focus on the domains of the teacher and the student?
6. What important questions should be considered with regard to evaluation?
7. What are the various definitions of *evaluation*? How are they helpful in your consideration of evaluation?
8. How do scientific and humanistic approaches to evaluation differ in their assumptions?
9. How do formative and summative evaluation differ? Why is it important to utilize both forms?
10. Data-driven decision making (DDDM) is influenced by two conditions. What are those two conditions, and how do they influence the processing of evaluative data?
11. How do an accountability culture and an organization learning culture differ? How do they influence evaluation?
12. What are the major differences between scientific and humanistic models of evaluation? Which do you prefer? Explain.
13. What are the pluses and minuses of high-stakes testing?
14. In what ways have standards controlled the education of students and teachers' actions?
15. What are the differences between norm-referenced tests and criterion-referenced tests?
16. Why is it essential for educators to utilize alternative assessment in judging student learning and curriculum effectiveness?
17. What human issues must be considered when dealing with curricular/educational evaluation?

People agree that curriculum evaluation is essential to curriculum development, implementation, and maintenance. However, they disagree regarding evaluation's meaning and purposes, how to approach evaluation, and how to employ its results. Ideally, evaluation determines the value of some action or program, the degree to which it helps students meet standards, and its importance.

Implicitly and explicitly, evaluation reflects value judgments about previous curricula and instructional designs. Evaluation critiques previous documents, plans, and actions.

We define *evaluation* as synonymous with *assessment.* We believe that assessment (evaluation) involves value judgments as to merit and worth. These judgments affect which data we gather and how we view those data. Evaluation requires of educators actions to judge the appropriateness of both their and students' actions. In evaluating students' learning, educators often give tests that assess what educators consider important. Teachers critique the quality of their teaching often by viewing videotapes of an instructional session.

In curriculum evaluation, attention focuses on both teachers' and students' actions that result in students' learning specific contents and skills. Today, curriculum evaluation is more challenging than in the past. Currently, education in general, and schools in particular, exist in a dynamic complex in which social, economic, political, and technological changes generate diverse views as to the school's purposes and the intellectual competencies and skills that will serve students well. As Peter M. Taubman asserts, we are living in a transformative time under the "twin banners of 'standards' and 'accountability.'"[1] Standards and accountability are battle cries often uttered by noneducators, particularly politicians and business leaders, with no idea as to the nature of curriculum and instruction. Most members of the public lack backgrounds in psychometrics and are especially unaware that holding educators accountable for attaining standards and also addressing diversity of students and the need for creativity in schools are often at cross-purposes.[2]

Certainly, educators should have standards and be accountable. But what does that mean? Taubman articulates that we are being consumed by an "audit culture" in which educational programs and practices, educational discourses are being encapsulated, standardized, and reduced to sterile quantifications. We seem to be functioning under a cloud of doom. To avert this doom, many are urging an enactment of a one-size-fits-all program and performance. All students must learn particular subject matter and must demonstrate identical proficiency.

Driving the chaos regarding curriculum evaluation is the No Child Left Behind Act, signed into law in January 2002 by President George W. Bush. This law is a directive that all educational agencies, schools included, at national, state, and local levels will work to create and then evaluate educational programs. It articulates that states will determine academic standards at three levels of achievement: basic, proficient, and advanced. However, it notes that 100 percent of students must be proficient on state and reading standards as determined by state-created examinations in reading and mathematics. Proficiency must be attained in science. Such must be accomplished if the United States is to be competitive in the world.[3]

Proficiency suggests high standards, but we must ask, "How high and for whom?"[4] What about just achieving the standard at the basic level? How do we report standards attained at the advanced levels? And must everyone engage in the same behavior? And must this all be evaluated by high-stakes exams administered at specific times? Also, can we say with certainty that a high score on a mathematics exam translates into student success 10 years later? Will achieving a high standard of history knowledge mean that a student will be an effectively contributing citizen 15 years hence? What about the uniqueness of individual students? And can everything that we wish to accomplish be measured by an exam? How does one measure empathy and tolerance? What is basic empathy? How does one measure proficiency in empathy?

Certainly, there are ways to measure students' attainments in knowledge and action other than employing high-stakes texts. However, No Child Left Behind (NCLB) seems to celebrate standardized tests as the primary means of gathering data to determine schools' accountability. Every state must build an accountability system that utilizes tests that validly measure student learnings, levels of achievement, and teacher effectiveness. Results from these tests must be disaggregated to take into account "socio-economic status, gender, race, ethnicity, disabilities, and levels of English language proficiency."[5] This directive seems to contradict that 100 percent of students will be proficient. And if we take into consideration students with limited English-speaking skills or students with learning disabilities, then we cannot simultaneously have 100 percent student proficiency.

Although schools have been ordered to develop curricula and evaluation means to document that no child is being left behind, the order does not indicate how the states are to develop such tests. There is no nationwide testing policy. Also, there does not seem to be much guidance from the federal Department of Education as to how to address the unique cultures and subcultures within their states. New York state, which has had the New York State Regents exam in place long before NCLB, is certainly culturally different from New Hampshire or New Mexico.

Further complicating curriculum evaluation are the explosions of knowledge regarding how the brain functions, how people learn, how the political realm affects schooling, how new pedagogies can address the needs of diverse student populations, how curricula can be created using various modern and postmodern approaches, and how assessment devices can be created and modified to get at the essences of learning. Educators should use evaluation methods and approaches that draw on the latest thinking. Yet, in some ways, the tests we currently use are based on 19th-century psychology.

James Pellegrino, Naomi Chudowsky, and Robert Glaser note that our current approaches to evaluation do not adequately take into account the increase in knowledge about how the brain functions. We already measure students' learning processes and knowledge of basic facts, and we derive estimates of students' command of particular curriculum areas, but we fail to get an accurate picture of the depth and breadth of students' knowledge and cognition. Current evaluation approaches do not provide views of the complex knowledge and skills required for learning.[6] They do not adequately address student creativity, compassion, commitment to action, and enthusiasm.[7]

Current evaluation takes snapshots of student achievement with regards to knowledge and process at particular points in time. Washington State obtains data on students' achievement at grades 4, 7, and 10, but not a view of how, for example, students' understandings and skills evolve. Testing students three times a year shows that scores are going up, going down, or remaining level, but it does not necessarily indicate the amount of learning.[8]

Adding to the difficulty of evaluating the curriculum is the increasingly voiced demand that assessment be fair and appropriate for diverse students. Certain segments of society express concerns that tests, especially standardized ones, favor certain student populations. Others argue that standardized tests are not fair because they focus on subjects, topics, and processes that have not been taught in their schools. Also, some claim that the standards set for passing these tests harm less advantaged students.

Today, with regard to curriculum evaluation, we are not only judging whether students are learning effectively the curriculum, but we are also charting teachers' instructional competence. We assume that the curriculum developed and implemented is of value and is worth knowing. Doubting this, we would not teach it. The value of the curriculum developed and presented is a given. However, in the current evaluation climate, some are suggesting that teachers' pay be connected to how well they teach the curriculum. Effective teaching translates into high test scores. Effective teachers will receive higher salaries. Some even have suggested that competent teachers of high-status subjects such as mathematics and science receive more salary because their subjects are more crucial to the nation's welfare. Such a notion would violate a rule of merit pay: Create a program that encourages collaboration.[9] It likely will foster a deleterious competition among school faculty.

There is much dialogue centered on evaluating and rewarding teacher performance with merit pay. There are several myths regarding merit pay, as articulated by Chris Hulleman and Kenneth Barron.[10]

The first myth is that performance pay systems improve performance. Performance pay enhancement may increase performance quantity, but that does not necessarily equate with quality. Students might learn more, but their understanding may not be increased essentially.

A second myth advanced by Hulleman and Barron is that performance pay systems will heighten teacher motivation. They cite research that indicates the opposite; expected rewards based on performing a task at a specific level actually undermine intrinsic motivation for performing the task. Most teachers do not engage a particular instructional strategy to gain a pay raise. The authors also point out the danger of applying motivational business strategies to the educational arena. Additionally, although a business person can document an increase in sales to request a bonus, it is far more difficult to quantify quality learning by students.[11] Results of quality teaching may not appear for decades. Should we give delayed bonuses if students in later years create a new business or win a Nobel prize? How can we make an evaluation of a teacher's impact on a student? The challenge is to make a direct causal connection from a teacher's action and a student's future accomplishment. It cannot be done.

Despite our protest, the idea of teacher pay tied to performance is not going to disappear. Quite likely, it will increase as a clarion call for improving schools. We are not going to separate curriculum evaluation from teacher effectiveness in "teaching" the curriculum that is delivered. As Matthew Springer and Catherine Gardner note, we are entering a perfect storm: Teacher compensation is being battered by performance and market-oriented pay policies.[12]

Although we assert that we cannot make a direct causal connection between a teacher's action and student's knowledge or skills, this argument, according to Springer and Gardner, may be losing validity. They note that many states and school districts have created sophisticated longitudinal data systems that enable determining links between individual student performances and teachers' instructional strategies. They note that with such data systems, one can more precisely estimate teachers' contributions to students' learnings. Additionally, they note that there is increasing research that aims to develop and validate sophisticated measures of effective teaching.[13]

It does appear that curriculum evaluation, or assessment, will continue to focus on teachers' competencies to deliver optimal student learning. And educators' competencies will continue to gain more attention than teachers' seniority, as is currently the case.

Pay for performance is likely to become more reality than dialogue and argument. But, presently, the research results of performance pay and students' learnings are inconclusive. We even have little agreement on what questions to raise. Should teacher effectiveness be judged on students' test scores? Should the principals' evaluations of teachers be part of the metric? And what weight should we give to various measures? Do we consider teacher dramatics and enthusiasm? How does that weigh with teacher's knowledge of subject? What about teacher creativity regarding developing students' learning experiences?

Evaluation is essential to the continual usage of a meaningful curriculum. If teachers and the community are to support the curriculum, educators must conceive and carry out effective evaluation and reporting processes. They must apprehend evaluation's nature and purpose.

## THE NATURE AND PURPOSE OF EVALUATION

Evaluators gather and interpret data to determine whether to accept, change, or eliminate aspects of the curriculum, such as particular textbooks. Curriculum evaluation is necessary not only at the end of a program or school year but also at various points throughout the program's development and implementation.

At the beginning of curriculum development, the very concept of the program must be evaluated. Does the program have worth and merit? Throughout the process, educators must evaluate the worth and merit of the curriculum's content and experiences. Curriculum evaluation focuses on whether the curriculum is producing the desired results. For example, does it get students to perform at the level of standards indicated for student success? Evaluation identifies the curriculum's strengths and weaknesses before and after implementation. Evaluation also enables educators to compare different programs in terms of effectiveness. People want to know how their students measure up against other students at the local, state, national, and international levels.

Pellegrino, Chudowsky, and Glaser view assessment as a process of reasoning from evidence.[14] The first question in this process is, "Evidence about what?"[15] Data interpretation is possible only when we understand what we are attempting to do and know what standards we want students to meet.

The process of reasoning from evidence in curriculum evaluation can be conceptualized as an hourglass. This schema is an expansion of the reasoning assessment triangle of Pellegrino, Chudowsky, and Glaser's, which had the following features: cognition at the top of the triangle and observation and interpretation at the corners of the triangle base.[16] Your authors have added to their model, placing curriculum at one corner of the top of the hourglass with cognition at the other corner (Figure 9.1). The neck of the hourglass represents the observation stage of reasoning. The base of the hourglass represents interpretation.

The curriculum organizes subject matter in terms of scope and sequence. In curriculum development, educators must make evaluative judgments regarding the worth of the subject matter being considered and organized as well as the political and social climates within which the curriculum will exist. Educators consider this question: What evidence suggests that the curriculum contemplated, planned, and then delivered has value, meets students' and society's needs and is consistent with curriculum theory?

Cognitive theories inform us in our data gathering. How do students acquire knowledge, construct meaning, and develop competence? Cognitive models of teaching can assist teachers in shaping their instructional approaches and evaluating students' learning.

*Observation* includes all the means by which data are gathered. It may involve written tests, reviews of students' work (e.g., their portfolios), and viewing students as they engage in particular educational actions. Observation includes questionnaires, checklists, inventories, interview schedules, and video performances. It also includes data on teachers—for example, from observations of teachers, viewing of videotaped lessons, analyses of lesson plans, and interviews.

In the interpretation stage of curriculum evaluation, educators draw on their assumptions about curriculum and cognition. They process data into evidence regarding the curriculum's success. At the classroom level, interpretation tends to be informal and qualitative, including interpretation regarding teachers' instructional approaches. At the district level, interpretation tends to be more formal, but it still can be qualitative rather than quantitative (employing a statistical model).[17] Often, district-level interpretation is both qualitative and quantitative. Interpretation implicitly draws on theories of testing, statistical models of data analysis, and theories of decision making.

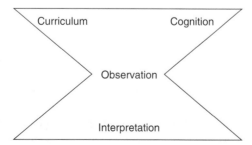

**FIGURE 9.1**  Process of Reasoning from Evidence in Curriculum Evaluation

*Source:* Modified from James W. Pellegrino, Naomi Chudowsky, and Robert Glaser, eds., *Knowing What Students Know: The Science and Design of Educational Assessment* (Washington, DC: National Academy Press, 2001).

*Evaluation* must remain connected to the totality of curricular activities. Evaluators first must ask themselves what aspect(s) of the curriculum they wish to evaluate and what types of learning will receive focus. They then must determine which means of data gathering best suit one or more particular goals of the curriculum. Which questions will furnish the data desired for interpretation?[18]

Often, evaluators investigate the appropriateness of a particular assessment procedure or form of assessment. Frequently, evaluation centers on how to modify the staff's in-service education. Sometimes evaluation focuses on just how educators can communicate with and educate the community. Sometimes, evaluation focuses on the effectiveness of a school environment. However, most evaluation focuses on curriculum or instruction.

We assert that evaluation, or assessment, essentially focuses on two domains of activity: teacher instructional strategies and students' learning strategies. Catherine Taylor and Susan Nolen note that teachers first engage in assessment to gather information about students' understandings and skills.[19] Such information is gathered via various procedures so that teachers can decide what to teach and the manner of teaching and student engagement. Essentially, this is the view that assessment is a process of reasoning from evidence. They must determine the individuals' degrees of success in processing particular content and concepts. This assessment is used primarily at the commencement of a lesson or unit of study. At or toward the end of a lesson or unit, teachers map out assessment procedures to record students' mastery of some content or expertise in some skill or intellectual process. Here teachers primarily engage in observation and interpretation phases of evidence gathering. Common methods employed are tests, with teachers often assigning grades. Taylor and Nolen suggest that the final purpose of assessment is to make comparisons of their students with others, that is, to measure their students' standings compared with other students. More is said about this last purpose later in this chapter.

It does seem that evaluation, or assessment, can and does have two purposes. Lisa Carter suggests that one view is that evaluation is activated so educators can sort and select not only curricular content and instructional strategies, but also which students experience various curricula and instructional experiences. Heavy emphasis is on employing test scores to sort and track students, that is, to place them in similar groups according to abilities, interests, and accomplishments. The second purpose of evaluation, Carter indicates, is to gather information, or evidence, in order to make educational, curricular, and instructional decisions that enhance students' learning of the curriculum being taught. Here evaluation aims to adapt the curriculum to the students rather than to mold the student to fit the curriculum.[20]

To be successful in carrying out evaluation, with emphasis on the second purpose, there are key questions to be raised. These questions, developed by Harriet Talmage in the mid-1980s, are still relevant today.

## Evaluation Questions

Talmage posed five types of questions that educators can consider when evaluating curricula: questions of intrinsic, instrumental, comparative, idealization, and decision value.[21]

The question of intrinsic value addresses the curriculum's goodness and appropriateness. It deals with both the planned curriculum and the finished (delivered) curriculum. For example, a school would ask if a new language arts curriculum incorporates the best thinking to date on language arts content and that content's arrangement and presentation. Would specialists in linguistics, composition, grammar, and communication give the planned curriculum high marks?

Raising such questions is not a simple matter of getting experts to analyze the curriculum document. People bring their philosophical and psychological views to the question of intrinsic value. They perceive the curriculum in light of the purpose of education that they see as paramount. (Should we stress critical thinking, citizenship, or preparation for employment?) They also see curriculum in terms of their preferred learning theory. (Behaviorists, cognitivists, and humanists have different views about content and presentation methods.)

The question of instrumental value asks, What is the curriculum good for, and who is its intended audience? Educators deal with the first part of this question by attempting to link the planned curriculum with the program's stated goals and objectives. The question of instrumental value also addresses which students accomplish what is planned in the curriculum and to what extent. The level of attainment relates to standards that reflect value preferences. Evaluation efforts should identify the types of students who are likely to benefit the most from the planned curriculum.

People faced with possible new programs often ask the question of comparative value. Is the proposed new program better than the one it is supposed to replace? Usually, new programs are created because people feel that the existing program is inadequate. When comparing programs, remember that different programs may have different goals. Is a program that stresses skills better than one that stresses contemporary world issues? Certainly, the two are different. Whether one is better than the other relates to educators' values and priorities. However, if a suggested program is of the same type as the existing program, evaluators should consider comparative value not only in terms of student achievement but also in terms of the two programs' ease of delivery, cost, demand on resources, role in the existing school organization, and responsiveness to the community expectations.

The question of comparative value is often raised when comparing the achievement of students in various countries, if not the curricula of the countries. Currently, voices in our national educational discussion suggest that when tested, American students do not compare favorably with students in other countries. It is often noted that the standings of American students, especially in mathematics and science, do not compare well. Usually, in such comparisons we essentially are not interested in what these various students actually know. We are more attentive to just how our students compare with others. We employ such data to rank students and to determine differences between students.[22] Basing the quality of our students' achievement in mathematics or science solely on a test number provides us with scant evaluative information. It denies us evidence essential for making evaluative decisions.

The question of idealization value addresses ways to improve a curriculum. Evaluators should not be concerned only with determining whether what was planned actually happened; they should also view data in terms of ways to create and maintain the best possible programs. They consider information on how the program is working and ask themselves if there are alternative ways to make the program even better—for example, to heighten student achievement or involve students more fully in their learning. The question of idealization value should be asked throughout the delivery of the new program. Educators must continually reconsider how they might fine-tune the program's content, materials, methods, and so on, so that students will optimally benefit.

The idealization question currently is reshaped into the question of curricular and instructional improvement. This question, newly redefined, requires "finer-grained measures for detecting improvement."[23] Assessing improvements in students' performances or even changes in teacher's strategies is much like measuring the movement of a glacier. Spend the day observing a glacier, and it appears stationary. However, if you take monthly observations, you can observe whether it is advancing or retreating. Certainly, a yearly observation schedule would document movement.

In raising the idealization question, the improvement question, one should remember Fullan's comment that "changes in student performance lag behind changes in the quality of instructional practice."[24] He suggests that we need more refined assessment instruments to detect changes in students' classroom learnings and behaviors. If we neglect field studies and employ only yearend tests, we will be able to report only students' particular level of learning. We will have violated the "evidence factor" because we will be unable to articulate the little daily learnings that assisted or sabotaged student progress. The idealization question requires frequent measurement of teacher and student action, employing a variety of evaluation procedures and materials.[25]

The question of decision value deals with the vital role that the previous four questions play in the evaluation process. If those four questions have been addressed, the decisions made should be quality decisions. The evaluator and the curriculum decision maker should now have evidence documented in such a manner that they can decide whether to retain, modify, or discard the new program. However, the question of decision value is ongoing. The value of the decisions made to date must be assessed as the curriculum is delivered in classrooms.

That the decision value question is ongoing essentially means that the previous four questions are constantly considered. Evaluation is never completed. Evaluation is challenging work. We suggest that the results we obtain and the evidences we gather are more like impressionistic paintings rather than designs generated by algorithms in a computer program. Individuals viewing an impressionistic painting draw a multitude of learnings and insights and ever-differing emotions; we must consider students more as paintings than computer programs.

## Definitions of Evaluation

*Evaluation* is a process whereby people gather data in order to make decisions. Apart from that generality, however, definitions of evaluation vary. Blaine Worthen and James Sanders define evaluation as "the formal determination of the quality, effectiveness, or value of a program, product, project, process, objective, or curriculum." Evaluation includes inquiry and judgment methods: "(1) determining standards for judging quality and deciding whether those standards should be relative or absolute, (2) collecting relevant information, and (3) applying the standards to determine quality."[26]

Abbie Brown and Timothy Green define evaluation as the process of judging, based on gathered data, the success level of an individual's learning or a product's effectiveness.[27] According to Norbert Seel and Sanne Dijkstra, evaluation furnishes data that enable us to compare worth or value of two or more programs. It provides a basis or bases for selecting programs or determining whether they should be continued.[28]

Daniel Stufflebeam has defined evaluation as "the process of delineating, obtaining, and providing useful information for judging decision alternatives."[29] Collin Marsh and George Willis indicate that evaluation permeates all human activity. It deals with questions such as these: Is something worth doing? How well is it being done? Do I like doing it? Should I spend my time doing something else?[30]

Many view evaluation as critical inquiry, studying phenomena in order to make informed judgments. Kenneth Sirotnik and Jeannie Oakes expand on this concept of evaluation. They argue that we should inquire into the assumptions underlying the values that we hold, the positions that we advocate, and the actions that we undertake.[31] Most evaluators maintain that although the presence and importance of values cannot be ignored, they can be considered only within a particular context. We judge whether a program reflects its values and if those in charge of a curriculum have made their values explicit. Then we evaluate whether these goals have been attained. Sirotnik and Oakes advocate a type of critical inquiry that some have called *hermeneutics*. The dictionary defines *hermeneutics* as "the study of the methodological principles of interpretation."[32]

In taking a hermeneutic approach to evaluating curricula and their effects, an evaluator raises "deep" questions as to the educational program's value, worth, and merit. Certainly, we pose obvious questions as to what students learn. However, we also recognize that what students have learned is decided by people both inside and outside the immediate community. We judge the value of the opinions of those who decide what students are to learn and who determines levels of success. Evaluators who take a hermeneutic approach consider how well the educational program fits into the current climate.[33]

## Measurement versus Evaluation

Sometimes educators confuse measurement with evaluation. Fred Kerlinger defined *measurement* as assigning numerals to objects or events according to rules.[34] *Evaluation* assigns value and meaning to measurement. For example, an evaluator might decide that a score of 70 percent correct answers means "passing" or "successful performance."

Measurement describes a situation or behavior in numerical terms. We make observations and then assign numbers to aspects of the observed phenomena.[35] For instance, a gym teacher can note the number of pushups a student does; or a reading teacher can record the number of pages per hour a student reads.

Measurement enables educators to record students' degrees of competency. However, educators must do something with the gathered data. They must decide how many pushups are enough to be good and the extent to which reading *speed* equates to reading *ability*. They must decide whether a student who spells 18 of 20 words correctly should get an A, an A–, or some other grade. Measurement always precedes evaluation. The value judgments made in evaluation are always influenced by the educators' understandings of a program's—and education's—purposes.

## APPROACHES TO EVALUATION

Evaluation is not content specific. The same procedures can be used to evaluate the effectiveness of any curriculum. Essentially, evaluation consists of gathering data and relating them to goals. In determining the value of a curriculum plan, educators must ask whether the expected results are worth the likely cost of delivering them.[36]

How people process data is influenced by their philosophy and psychology. Those who take a behavioristic, prescriptive, or sequenced approach to evaluation tend to specify specific behaviors or content learned as a result of curriculum and instruction. They like clearly stated objectives, precise indicators of whether their students have achieved the program's intended outcomes. Those who take a humanistic approach are more interested in whether the planned situations have enabled students to improve their self-concepts. They may not pay as much attention to students' specific achievements as indicated by objective tests.

In general, evaluation enables educators to (1) decide whether to maintain, revise, or replace the existing curriculum; (2) assess individuals (primarily teachers and students) in terms of instruction and learning; and (3) decide whether the existing managerial organization of the school and its program should be maintained or reformed. Also, part of evaluation focuses on the school environment and the community environment within which the school exists.

Evaluation occurs at different levels. At the broadest levels, evaluation focuses on an entire school district, state educational system, or even national system (e.g., with regard to No Child Left Behind legislation).

Narrower evaluation focuses on particular institutions, either individually (e.g., a particular high school) or a group (e.g., all the high schools within a particular district).

At the most specific level, evaluation attends to a particular program for a particular course at a particular grade level. What is valued at a broader level should also be valued at a narrower level. It makes no sense to indicate that U.S. schools will be judged according to particular criteria if schools at the local level reject or cannot feasibly apply those criteria.[37] In 2002, No Child Left Behind mandated that all students, even those with learning disabilities or limited English-language competency, be held to the same standards as the regular school population. They had to pass tests in reading and mathematics. Educators and others noted then and continued to protest that it was unrealistic to expect students with limited or no ability to speak English to pass a test written in English. It was also not realistic to assume that children with limited intellectual capacities could achieve at levels comparable to average children.

The U.S. Department of Education began to listen. In 2004, the Department altered the rule, enabling first-year immigrants to opt out of taking the reading test. However, they still had to take the state's mathematics test. Their reasoning appears based on the fact that many students, especially Asian students, with limited English skills still do quite well in mathematics. In 2007, the Department of Education admitted that there would always exist a small number of students whose abilities are such that it is not possible to assess them meaningfully. School districts are allowed in certain cases to use alternative standards of assessment or developmentally appropriate versions of the state assessment.[38]

## Scientific versus Humanistic Approach

Lee Cronbach places scientific and humanistic approaches at opposite ends of the evaluation continuum. Scientific evaluators favor an experimental approach: "(1) Two or more conditions are in place, at least one of them being the consequence of deliberative intervention. (2) Persons or institutions are assigned to conditions in a way that creates equivalent groups. (3) All participants are assessed on the same outcome measures."[39]

Scientific evaluators tend to concentrate on the learners. They use data, frequently in the form of test scores, to compare students' achievement in different situations. Data are quantitative, so they can be analyzed statistically. Program decisions are based on the comparative information gathered.

Most scientific approaches to evaluation draw on methods used by physical scientists. Objective tests, a hallmark of traditional approaches, are still major vehicles by which educators gather data. Of course, with further research on evaluation, essay exams and other forms of gathering data are being employed within the scientific camp. Data tend to be quantitative, but this is changing. Often program decisions are based on the comparative information gathered, but evaluators are beginning to realize the shortcomings of just using data to compare students' achievement levels. This has been noticed previously.

Catherine Taylor and Susan Nolen mention that within the scientific camp, people make four assumptions that are, in reality, problematic: (1) Students are randomly assigned to schools, teachers, and curricula; (2) instruction is identical for all students in the "treatment" condition; (3) some students will have positive learning experiences from the treatment and other students will not; and (4) objective tests are accurate and impartial judges of students' learnings and skills.[40]

Taylor and Nolen note that educators cannot blindly accept these assumptions for the following reasons: (1) Students are not randomly assigned to districts, schools, programs, or teachers; (2) rarely is instruction identical for all students, even in the same school or classroom; (3) treatments in classrooms do not remain constant; and (4) tests are not impartial.[41]

These authors expand on why these assumptions must be challenged. The geography of school districts and the policies of school placements are not driven by a desire to create random groups of students. Schools serve most often the students within an attendance region. Teachers realize that they individualize their instructional strategies and educational activities, even when teaching the same curriculum. A creative classroom has much diversity of teacher and students' actions. Also, effective teachers strive to be an educator of many "notes," not just a "Johnny-one-note." And teachers know that tests as they are designed address various students' academic strengths and even cultural backgrounds. Students who do well on multiple-choice tests are often highly skilled in memorization and recognition. Students have various learning styles, and tests usually do not stress several learning styles.[42]

It certainly appears that the high-stakes accountability environment in which we find ourselves does favor some version of the scientific approach to evaluation. The No Child Left Behind legislation seems to be forcing educators to hold supreme objective exams, and even subjective exams in some instances, to document that educational programs developed and delivered are attaining desired results. Gina Schuyler Ikemoto and Julie Marsh note that schools and educators are realizing that data-driven decision making (DDDM) is central to proving accountability and the meeting of standards. However, Ikemoto and Marsh caution that we must not assume that DDDM is a rather straightforward process. They point out, and support it with their research, that there is variety in the ways in which educators at school levels use and interpret data.[43]

They assert that DDDM in evaluation can be influenced by two conditions: the type of data gathered and the approach or approaches to data analysis and decision making. In the DDDM process, educators can process a plethora of various types of data that can go from simple to complex. Simple data are less complicated and inclusive, usually focusing on only one specific aspect of a particular subject. Usually, evaluators dealing with a less complicated evaluative focus bring only one perspective to the analysis. Those dealing with complex data tend to view the evaluation situation as multidimensional. In such situations, evaluators draw on both quantitative and qualitative data. Here we see a blurring of scientific and humanistic approaches to evaluation. We submit that perhaps centering on these two camps of evaluation really does not serve us well. We should not worry about classifications of evaluation, but rather focus on those strategies that enable us to gather evidence that answer the question, Is what we are doing in delivering this curriculum successful in attaining our goals?

Ikemoto and Marsh note that the evaluative process, as mentioned previously, is also influenced by the type of decision making regarding the data gathered. They assert that the types of decision making also follow a continuum from simple to complex along several dimensions: "basis of interpretation (use of assumptions versus empirical evidence); reliance on knowledge (basic versus expert …); type of analysis (straightforward techniques, such as descriptive analyses, versus sophisticated analyses, such as value-added modeling); extent of participation (individual versus collection); and frequency (one time versus interactive)."[44]

"All the money we spend on research, training, equipment, instructional programs, and the like will give us too small a return on our investment until we help the adults working together in a building learn to create a culture in which they can collaborate with each other in a way that will support the development of students."[45]

"As districts grow beyond a certain size, they take on certain staff functions related to curriculum and the support of teaching, so they house experts who use evidence about student achievement to make decisions. Finally, their staff roles often extend to collecting, analyzing, interpreting, and distributing data, especially student assessment or test data."[46]

Rather than trying to classify in which approach to evaluation they are, it might better serve educators to realize that they function in an evaluative culture that they must nurture. In order to be an effective educator, educators must assess the effectiveness of the curriculum and its delivery. Evaluative data, whether gathered in a scientific or humanistic frame, provides guidance for the continuation or the cessation of action regarding the curriculum. School cultures must foster not only creativity in creating curricula, but also creativity in evaluating the curricula and the instructional strategies embraced. Teachers must embrace the collaborative model of teaching. Teaching is not a solitary series of actions performed behind closed doors. We advise that schools foster a culture that enables the sharing of data, instructional ideas, evaluative data, so that school curricula are determined successful in stimulating total student growth.

Having said that it might be more useful for educators to realize that they exist in an evaluative culture rather than trying to classify themselves as either scientific or humanistic, it behooves educators to realize that their approach to their school cultures is colored by whether they view data gathered on the effectiveness of curricula from an accountability culture or an organization learning culture. If educators subscribe to the first view, they gather data to assert that the curricula offered raise test scores. Higher scores define curricular and instructional success. Those who embrace the organization learning culture view test results not as an endpoint, but a way point, to indicate that the curriculum is contributing to the students' educational advancement.

Educators who adhere to the accountability culture value a polishing of student understanding, efficiency of instruction and learning, and an immediate identification of learning. Those in the organizational learning culture consider education as a dance, or a movement in motion between teacher and students. This posture celebrates adventure, "discovery, risk-taking, and long term development."[47]

Of course, we need not take sides. We can have allegiance to both accountability and to organization learning. However, as William Firestone and Raymond Gonzalez point out, districts tend to be drawn to one or the other philosophical orientations.[48] The camp to which people are drawn has intended and unintended consequences that influence how they view students and their learning, how they view themselves as educators, how they use data gathered, how they reflect on how time is processed within the evaluation process, and how teachers and administrators view their interactions in curricular activity, specifically evaluation.[49]

As previously mentioned, a school culture that stresses an accountability culture primarily centers on test scores as the ultimate indicator of student learning. What do the students know? A school culture tending toward an organizational approach to evaluation is more interested in utilizing data that furnish information that enables an improvement in student learning.

In an accountability culture, teachers employ data to determine how well they are teaching and how well students are learning. Do data indicate that teachers are in compliance with district, state, or national edicts? Schools stressing organizational learning are more concerned with improving learning and curricular experiences. The stress is on way points, not endpoints. Rather than just reporting that data indicate that students have learned, a school with the organizational learning culture wants to know not only if students are learning, but why they are learning, and if not learning, why not. In this latter camp, data are employed in diagnostic manners.

Educators stressing accountability consider the time frame to be essentially short term. Educators within the organizational camp realize that student success takes time. The accountability emphasis in evaluation favors a top-down organization. Data are directed to the central office or the office of evaluation or research, where they are processed. After analysis, information and guidance are issued down the chain of command. Organizational cultures are horizontal. Colleagues behave more like learning communities mutually analyzing data and suggesting educational approaches or curricular content that might improve student learning.[50]

The organizational school culture tends toward utilizing humanistic approaches to evaluation. Students and teachers are not test-taking or test-giving machines. Students are not one-dimensional individuals. Educational colleagues likewise are not one-dimensional. And although important, tests and their scores do not reveal the entire story. And, where tests are used to compare and rank students, the tests might not provide any information of value. It appears that people are increasingly interested in more humanistic approaches. People are realizing that nontraditional evaluational procedures may furnish more complete pictures of curricula. The humanistic approach, although not completely rejecting objective tests, stresses that educators can gather more useful data employing more naturalistic approaches such as case studies and participant observations. Educators of this stripe prefer to study programs already in place, rather than programs imposed by groups outside of the school district.

Humanistic evaluators primarily analyze qualitative data, such as impressions of what they observe. They describe actual incidents. They gain data by interviews and discussions with participants, students and teachers included. Analysis seeks to uncover patterns among many observations.

Those advocating the humanistic approach to evaluation argue that this approach is necessary at a time of multiple voices and multiple realities. We must make judgments about the complexities we find within the educational system and within the general society. And these judgments must be tentative; we cannot arrive at judgments and conclusions with abstract and generalized certainties, as advocates of the scientific approaches would have us believe.[51]

Although various models are employed in the traditional quantitative camp, most seem not to have particular names. Such is not the case with approaches to qualitative evaluation and research. Five major humanistic approaches have been identified: interpretive, artistic, systematic, theory driven, and critical–emancipatory.[52]

In the *interpretive approach,* the evaluator considers the educational scene and interprets the meaning and significance of people's actions. Attention to social context is essential. The evaluators are people directly involved with the curriculum, especially teachers and students.

In the *artistic approach,* the evaluator engages in aesthetic inquiry, observing classes and other enactments of curricula, and then publicly announcing what is good and bad about the curriculum. This approach relies on individual intuition honed by experience.[53] The evaluator focuses on the quality of the relationships between teacher and students. The key advocate of this approach is Elliot Eisner, professor emeritus of art and curriculum at Stanford University.

Among humanistic approaches to evaluation, the *systematic approach* is most familiar. Evaluators try to be as objective as possible in their descriptions, employ logical analysis and base their judgments on fact. However, they do not rely primarily on statistical techniques, the hallmark of the scientific approach.

Many evaluators take a *theory-driven* approach. These calculators apply philosophical, political, or social theories when judging the quality of curricula.

*Critical–emancipatory* evaluators tend to be the most radical. They judge a curriculum's quality and effectiveness according to how well the curriculum counters social forces that impede individual development and fulfillment. These evaluators draw heavily on Jurgen Habermas's work on the construction of knowledge and meaning. They also draw on critical theory, especially Marxist theory.[54]

Educators need not be tied to any one of these five major approaches. Indeed, there are several other ways to identify the approaches to evaluation.

## Utilitarian versus Intuitionist Approach

Evaluation can be classified as either utilitarian or intuitionist. The utilitarian approach is closely linked to the scientific approach, whereas the intuitionist approach is tied to the humanistic approach. *Utilitarian evaluation* operates according to the premise that the greatest good is that which benefits the greatest number of individuals.[55] Utilitarian evaluators look at large groups, such as an entire school or school district. Attention is on total group performances. Programs are judged by how they affect the school's overall student population. Programs that allow the most students to attain the objectives are judged worthy of continuation.

*Intuitionist evaluators* gather data to judge the program's impact on individuals or small groups. There is no one criterion regarding worth. Numerous criteria are employed to assess a program's worth. Program participants, not outside evaluators, consider the program's quality. Everyone affected by the program can make judgments about it.[56]

## Intrinsic versus Payoff Approach

In addition to viewing evaluation in terms of scientific versus humanistic or utilitarian versus intuitionist, we can view it in terms of what Michael Scriven has called intrinsic versus payoff.

*Intrinsic evaluators* study the curriculum plan separately. Their evaluation criteria are not usually operationally defined. Instead, the evaluators are merely trying to answer the question, "How good is the curriculum?"[57] Intrinsic evaluators study the particular content included, the way it is sequenced, its accuracy, the types of experiences suggested for dealing with the content, and the types of materials to be employed. They assume that if a curriculum plan has accurate content and a firm basis for its particular organization, it will effectively stimulate student learning.

All evaluators must engage in intrinsic evaluation—that is, they must determine if the curriculum has value. Evaluators must consider not only how well a course or curriculum achieves its goals and objectives, but whether those goals and objectives are worthwhile.

Once a curriculum's basic worth has been assessed, evaluators must examine the effects of the delivered curriculum. This is *payoff evaluation*. Often, the outcomes are operationally defined. Evaluators can consider the curriculum's effects on students, teachers, parents, and, perhaps, administrators. This evaluation approach may involve judgments regarding the differences between pre- and posttests and between experimental-group and control-group tests on one or more criteria parameters. Payoff evaluation receives the most attention from educators because it indicates curriculum's effects on learners in terms of stated objectives.

Supporters of the intrinsic approach agree that important values cannot be assessed via the payoff approach because of deficiencies in present test instruments and scoring procedures. Also, the results reported in payoff evaluation studies are usually short-term results of a curriculum.

Little attention is given to a program's long-term outcomes. If educators want to have an idea of a curriculum's relevance and perhaps elegance, they would do better to look at the curriculum's materials directly rather than at students' test scores.

## Formative and Summative Evaluation

Another way to view evaluation is in terms of formative and summative evaluation. *Formative evaluation* encompasses activities undertaken to improve an intended program—that is, optimize student learning. Formative evaluation (sometimes called *rapid-prototype evaluation* by instruction designers) is carried out during program development and implementation.[58] In the curriculum-development phase, formative evaluation furnishes evidence that directs decisions about how to revise a program while it is being developed. Formative evaluators look at specific sub-units of the curriculum being developed and test them in brief trial situations. They gather data, often in classrooms, that inform their decisions about how to modify these program elements before they are fully implemented. During a curriculum's developmental and early piloting stages, formative evaluation provides frequent, detailed, specific information. Formative evaluation takes place at a number of specific points in the curriculum-development process. It is essential, especially during the initial stages of the development process.[59] Formative evaluation allows educators to modify, reject, or accept the program as it is evolving.

How educators conduct formative evaluation varies widely. If they are evaluating only one unit plan, their manner of evaluation may be very informal, perhaps involving only the people teaching the unit. However, if they are engaged in creating a new program for an entire school district, formative evaluation may be more formal and systematic.

Formative evaluation also occurs during the teaching of a new or existing curriculum, focusing on teachers as well as students. Teachers can use formative evaluation to judge the effectiveness of their pedagogical approaches. Teachers must realize that formative evaluation is not a sometime activity. It is a grand composite of ways to gather and utilize data in order to make those instructional adjustments necessary for optimal student learning. Such evaluation furnishes feedback to the teacher as to how a lesson is going and how it might be fine-tuned.

Frederick Erickson notes that for formative evaluation to really occur, teachers must know how to interpret the data gathered. Lacking interpretative understanding prevents the teacher from making instructional adjustments. Erickson asserts that often teachers are not skilled in analyzing and comprehending data. Thus, no formative evaluation occurs. Even if teachers do know how to apprehend the data, they often lack the time for analysis. It seems that perhaps a majority of teachers feel the need to "cover the book" in a certain time period. It takes time to self-critique and make pedagogical adjustments. Teachers often report that they do not have time to reteach a lesson. That objective test must be administered on time. There is so much content to teach; so much content is on the test.[60]

Erickson argues that we cannot just mandate that teachers employ formative evaluation; we must schedule time for them, working alone and with colleagues, to raise questions about what the data are telling them. He points out that teachers must really possess pedagogical content knowledge at a deep level. Skilled teaching is complicated, and often it represents improvisational theater in which teachers have to pick up on classroom dialogue from the questions and statements of students. Pedagogical content knowledge, we declare, is not solely in the domain of educational methods or instructional strategies. Pedagogical content knowledge is essentially drawn from procedural knowledge associated with the declarative knowledge of a discipline of study. Essentially, pedagogical content knowledge draws and adapts its techniques from the ways that scholars actually advance their understandings within their specific fields. Biologists use specific methods to advance biology. These methods differ from how historians advance their understandings of some historical period or event. Mathematicians engage in processes of solving problems unique to their fields of expertise. For example, a biologist who seeks to prove the validity of some experiment does not argue the case in point as would a historian or a mathematician. A biological investigation is greatly different from an historical inquiry. If we wish students to learn biology, history, or mathematics, our instructional methods must mimic the ways that experts in these fields also go about their learning.

Of course, experts in various disciplined fields often engage in interdisciplinary activities. Thus the biologists often utilize mathematics in experiments. Understanding this and the range of fields of study makes it even more challenging for teachers to teach, or more accurately, to get students to learn these subjects.

*Formative evaluation* also refers to procedures employed by students to assess their learning tactics as well as their levels of knowledge.[61] Students must know what they know and how well they employ particular learning strategies. The level of student involvement in formative assessment depends, of course, on their maturity levels. However, even students in primary school have some idea as to whether they understand something. They certainly need the teacher's guidance to determine ways to approach learning. We want our students to become independent learners. As students gain more expertise in learning and greater knowledge, they can assume more management and refining of their learning adjustments. As James Popham indicates, teachers take on a more supporting role in suggesting ways to learn more effectively.[62]

Today, as more and more schools are establishing computer-based learning environments, they are actually employing formative evaluation or assessment. As Allan Collins and Richard Halverson indicate, these computer programs embedded formative assessment into the actual lessons. As students proceed through the computer curriculum, the computer furnishes feedback indicating either progress or where an error has occurred. If an error is indicated, the computer program maps out a strategy or strategies to correct the error or arrive at a correct answer. Essentially, the computer can be assessing the cumulative results of particular learnings of knowledge and strategies. In interacting with the computer program in this way, students realize that making a mistake actually provides an opportunity for immediate learning. With such feedback and really no grade on the line, students avoid taking misinformation or misunderstandings into their further learning.

We point out here that the computer is not replacing the teacher as instructor or evaluator. It is merely enabling the teacher at times to reach more students.[63] As classrooms become more like "learning laboratories," teachers and students become highly involved in the learning and evaluation processes, more engaged in dynamic interactions with each other and evolving "technological assistants." Technology will, we believe, actually humanize the teaching–learning process. Also, technology means that teachers, students, and even expert evaluators need not always be in the same physical spaces.

Of course, one need not abandon relatively mundane means of gathering formative evaluative data. Taylor and Nolen list various assessment tools that are not high tech: anecdotal records, checklists, rating scales, conferences, journals, even homework.[64] They also note that teachers can engage in formative assessment just by walking around the classroom and observing and listening to students. Much data can be obtained when teachers listen in on brainstorming. Even wish lists regarding topics to be covered can be employed. Having students enumerate what they like to do when away from school can furnish much evaluative data useful in planning future lessons.

Summative evaluation is aimed at assessing the overall quality of a produced and then taught curriculum. As Wilhelmina Savenye notes, data are gathered to ascertain the new program's worth and effectiveness.[65] If formative evaluation has been implemented carefully, summative evaluation should indicate that the program has enabled students to attain the curriculum goals. Such summative evaluation informs educators that students have met the school's or state's educational standards. It also indicates that teachers have met the minimum accountability standards.

Overall, summative evaluation poses the question, Has the curriculum worked? As its name implies, summative evaluation gathers evidence about the summed effects of a particular curriculum's components or units.

Brown and Green discuss an approach to summative evaluation that D. L. Kirkpatrick developed in the mid-1990s. Although Brown and Green are discussing summative evaluation in terms of instructional design, Kirkpatrick's approach can be applied to curriculum evaluation. Kirkpatrick delineates four levels of summative evaluation: (1) reactions, (2) learning, (3) transfer, and (4) results.[66]

Level 1, reactions, focuses on gathering data about how students reacted to the new program. The data indicate not only the amount of new knowledge acquired, but also whether what was provided to students was relevant to them. Did the new curriculum and attendant experiences meet students' social, emotional, and intellectual needs? Did the students react in anticipated ways? At level 1, evaluators might interview students or have them respond to attitude surveys (rather than tests).

At level 2, evaluators gather data on whether students have gained new knowledge, skills, and techniques implicit in the new program's goals and objectives. To collect such data, evaluators usually administer a series of pretests and posttests at various junctures of the implemented curriculum.

At level 3, evaluators pose questions about whether the individuals who experienced the new program can effectively employ newly acquired skills and knowledge and whether their attitudes have changed for the better. Using various types of tests, evaluators determine if students show evidence in everyday life, job situations, or further schooling that they are applying their new knowledge, skills, and attitudes.[67]

Level 4, results, is a major challenge for evaluators. The results of a newly developed curriculum may not be evident immediately, if ever. Some schools assess results partly through exit interviews of students, which indicate how the new curriculum has changed their knowledge, skill, or attitudes. Evaluation at this final level might also be conducted via focus-group activities. Surveys given to graduates of new curricula can also furnish summative data.[68]

The results of summative evaluation presents not just a major challenge for evaluators, but a multitude of challenges for all concerned with the total educational "theater." Many educators and the general public are not even aware of these challenges, largely because most of us rarely question our conceptions of world realities. We educators take for granted that we truly comprehend the essential natures of teaching and learning. Accepting that, we neglect to reflect deeply on just what they are. Can we really know their nature?

In summative evaluation, it is assumed, usually without challenge, that teaching is an activity that can be accomplished in a specific time frame. Likewise, learning also exists in time. We can finish teaching a unit. Students can finish learning a particular lesson. We can, in our evaluative roles, create summative tests given at a specific time that can accurately document a level of understanding or accomplishment. And we can make, from analyzing the test data or score, that "'what is learned' by students is … an entity that comes to exist after instruction has taken place, and thus, can be measured as a whole thing of the past. This ontological presupposition is the foundation for the entire enterprise of summative evaluation."[69]

Some, if not most, advocates of summative evaluation also assume that formal psychometric procedures are essentially the best way to gather reliable and valid documentation of student learning. Essentially, we cannot trust that teachers in the classroom using observational and other formative measures will furnish us with results that can inform us as to what educators are doing.[70]

Teaching is never completed, nor is it performed only by the teacher. Also, teaching at times occurs outside the classroom or school environment. Time is fluid with teaching. Likewise, complete learning, sometimes called *mastery learning,* in reality is never attained. Learning is ongoing, never ceasing to enrich understanding. Certainly learning exists, just as a horizon on an ocean exists. However, most of us know that we can only advance toward the horizon; it can never be reached.

And if we could somehow magically reach that horizon, our voyage would be over. Likewise, if we could really attain mastery, then our education, our journey of learning, would cease.

Learning is the result of ongoing interactions with numerous peoples in a multitude of environments. Erickson notes that learning is "the process of acquisition itself, as continual change within an ongoing course of activity."[71] In this view, learning to know and comprehend the content of the curriculum represents beginnings and waypoints, not endpoints that can be precisely noted and statistically analyzed.

In summative evaluation, attention is on demonstrated results—on acceptance of an audit culture.[72] Summative evaluation essentially ignores the subjective aspects of learning, the emotional valences students possess. It is difficult to have a summative test for thrills or infatuation.

As Taubman notes, the learning sciences have and continue to strive for objectively measuring learning, writ large. Essentially, learning sciences are not concerned with intrinsic evaluation of the worth of curricular content or curricular experiences. Learning sciences seem enamored only of getting students to learn and urging teachers to teach.[73] After all, we hear often that if we just had good teachers and good schools, students would learn and would be prepared to compete in the world marketplace. Few question that if we just had a quality curriculum, if we just had highly emotional experiences, students would truly be changed. It is hard to measure that summatively.

The preceding discussion is not to discount summative evaluation procedures, but rather to enlighten us that even if we could create the perfect summative test with reliability and validity, we will still have only an incomplete portrait of what students have learned and teachers have taught. Much of learning and teaching will never be known, and the mysteries around these human interactions are to be celebrated. All evaluations, both formative and summative, are to be enacted with an awareness of their pluses and minuses. Education is not engineering; it is far more complex. We know when a building is complete. In education, we never know what it means for a person to be complete. Humans never attain completeness.

We hope that you, the reader, realize that the next section, evaluation models, is to be processed essentially as descriptions of evaluative procedures. It is to be hoped that the models contain within them explanatory elements.[74] Also, keep in mind that although the models may present a clean procedural pathway to gather data and make decisions, in actuality, the models can and do get messy when actually employed.

## EVALUATION MODELS

### Scientific Models

The first large-scale formal evaluation in the United States was reported in Joseph Rice's 1897–1898 comparative study of the spelling performance of more than 30,000 students in an urban school system. Soon after, Robert Thorndike was instrumental in getting educators to measure human change.[75] Finally, the Eight-Year Study (1933–1941) was a turning point in educational evaluation, ushering in the modern era of program evaluation.[76] The Eight-Year Study's evaluation plan was organized in seven sequential steps: focusing on the program's goals and objectives, classifying objectives, defining objectives in behavioral terms, finding situations in which achievement can be demonstrated, developing or selecting measurement techniques, collecting student performance data, and comparing data against objectives.

**STAKE'S CONGRUENCE–CONTINGENCY MODEL.**    Robert Stake distinguishes between formal and informal evaluation procedures. Although recognizing that educational evaluation continues to depend on casual observation, implicit goals, intuitive norms, and subjective judgment, he notes that educators should strive to establish formal evaluation procedures. Formal procedures are objective and supply data that enable descriptions and judgments regarding the program being evaluated.

Evaluators seem to be increasing their emphasis on providing full objective descriptions and on collecting and reporting hard data. Stake asks that evaluators collect and process more extensive types of data, consider the dynamics among people involved in the curriculum process, assess the roles various people play, allow those people greater participation in judging programs, and take positions regarding a program's worth.

Stake delineates three data categories: antecedents, transactions, and results. Applying this organization to modern-day evaluating processes yields three new categories: prerequisites, curriculum, and results. Prerequisites refer to any condition that exists prior to teaching and learning that may influence outcomes. *Prerequisites* include the status or characteristics of students prior to their lessons: their aptitudes, previous achievement scores, psychological profile scores, grades, discipline, and attendance. Prerequisites also include teacher characteristics such as years of experience, type of education, and teacher–behavior ratings.

*Curriculum* in the model refers to the planned or potentially considered interactions among students and teachers, students and students, and students and resource people. Curriculum also addresses students' potential interactions with curriculum materials and classroom environments. At this stage, educators attend to how the planned curriculum is affected by time allocation, space arrangements, and communication flow. Attention essentially is directed at the teaching process. In the curriculum planning stage, educators contemplate how the engagements considered actually play out when the curriculum is applied and evaluated.

*Results* are the program's anticipated and then acquired outcomes, including student achievement and, sometimes, attitudes and motor skills; impact on teachers' perceptions of their competence; and influence on administrators' actions. Evaluators must also consider long-range results and other outcomes not evident when a program concludes. According to Stake, educational outcomes are immediate and long-range, cognitive and affective, personal and communitywide.

Stake's evaluation model encompasses curriculum design, development, and implementation. Data elucidate disparities between what was planned and what has actually occurred.

Figure 9.2 shows the deliberate connection of the prerequisites, curricula, and results in the planning stage. The evaluator looks for empirical information in the implemented curriculum. Do the data reveal that transactions are supported empirically in the implemented curriculum? Do data make the case that the results attained are really the consequence of the procedures employed during instruction? Effective evaluation links prerequisites, curriculum, and results in both the planning and evaluation stages.

Stake's model also depicts the relationships between what is planned and what is enacted and then evaluated. For complete congruence between plans and results, all observed prerequisites, curricula, and results must be the same as the intended ones. Although Stake's model is

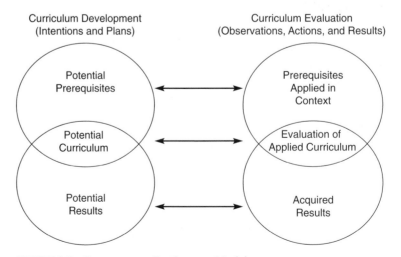

**FIGURE 9.2**   Consequence–Contingency Model

*Source:* Based on Robert E. Stake, "The Countenance of Educational Evolution," *Teachers College Record* (1967), p. 7.

very useful, complete congruence is impossible. There is no exact correspondence between some action and student learning. Outside of school, students encounter material that affects their thinking about a particular lesson. Such an unintended transaction can result in learning noted as an attained outcome.[77]

**STUFFLEBEAM'S MODEL: CONTEXT, INPUT, PROCESS, AND PRODUCT.**   Daniel Stufflebeam provides a comprehensive evaluation model that is an important contribution to a decision-management approach. According to Stufflebeam, information is provided to management for decision making. Evaluation must include the following: *delineating* what information must be collected, *obtaining* the information, and *providing* the information to interested parties. Stufflebeam delineates four types of evaluation: context, input, process, and product.[78]

*Context evaluation* involves studying the program's environment. Its purpose is to define the relevant environment, portray the desired and actual conditions pertaining to that environment, focus on unmet needs and missed opportunities, and diagnose the reason for unmet needs. Context evaluation is not a one-time activity. It continues to furnish information on the total system's operations and accomplishments. (See Curriculum Tips 9.1.)

*Input evaluation* provides information regarding resource use. It focuses on feasibility. Evaluators assess the school's ability to carry out evaluation. They consider the suggested strategies for achieving program goals, and they identify the means by which a selected strategy will be implemented. They might consider alternative designs that lead to the objectives while requiring fewer resources, less time, and less money.

Evaluators assess specific aspects or components of the curriculum plan. Input evaluation addresses these questions: Are the objectives stated appropriately? Are they congruent with the school's goals? Is the content congruent with the program's goals and objectives? Are the instructional strategies appropriate? Do other strategies exist that could achieve the objectives? What is the basis for believing that these contents and instructional strategies will result in attainment of the objectives?

*Process evaluation* addresses implementation decisions that control and manage the program. It is used to determine the congruency between the planned and actual activities. It includes three strategies: "The first is to detect or predict defects in the procedural design or its implementation stage, the second is to provide information for decisions, and the third is to maintain a

---

## CURRICULUM TIPS 9.1   Assessing the Curriculum Context

Most curricular actions occur within a socialized context and most of their delivery or enactment processes take place within a socialized context. Those in charge of the overall program must evaluate the process by which they create and deliver curriculum. The following tips can assist in assessing the context of curricular action:

1. Determine the values, goals, and beliefs that drive the curriculum.
2. Obtain a reading of the community, noting the key players.
3. Determine the history of past curricular activity in the school district.
4. Get some indication of the physical facilities available and necessary for enactment of the curriculum.
5. Judge the pressures for and against actions generated from within and from without the community and school district.
6. Determine the budget needed and the budget allocated.
7. Determine what performance outcomes are important for the school and community.
8. Get a fix on the perceptions, expectations, and judgments of teachers and administrators and what they expect out of the evaluation and how they intend to use it.

*Source:* Personal paper, F. P. Hunkins, 2005.

record of procedures as they occur."[79] To deal with program defects, educators must identify and continually monitor potential sources of project failure. They must attend to the logistics of the entire operation and maintain communication channels among all affected parties. The second strategy involves decisions to be made by project managers during project implementation. For example, managers may decide that certain in-service activities are needed before program implementation. The third strategy addresses the main feature of the project design—for example, the particular content selected, new instructional strategies, or innovative student–teacher planning sessions. Process evaluation occurs during implementation. It is a piloting process conducted to debug the program before district-wide implementation. It enables evaluators to anticipate and overcome procedural difficulties.

Product evaluation has evaluators gathering data to determine whether the final curriculum product now in use is accomplishing what they had hoped. To what extent are the objectives being met? Product evaluation provides information that enables evaluators to decide whether to continue, terminate, or modify the new curriculum. For example, a product evaluation might furnish data showing that a science program planned for talented science students has allowed students to achieve the program's objectives. The program is then ready to be implemented in other schools within the system.

## Humanistic Models

Stake's and Stufflebeam's evaluation models draw heavily on the quantitative–technical approach to evaluation. Their models are most useful for addressing the standards and accountability demands of this century. They certainly find acceptance within the camps of cognitive science, educational psychology, computer science, and now neuroscience.[80] Also, their scientific models mesh with the thinking of those managers of the marketplace as well as most politicians.

However, there seems to be a constant, but small, number of educators who believe that evaluators have bought excessively into the "education as a business within the marketplace" paradigm. Some educators have become mesmerized by observing or measuring the attainment of specific "learnings." They have spent excessive amounts of time generating elaborate evaluative schemes to measure program success.

Challenging this business posture, some educators are advocating more humanistic (naturalistic) methods of evaluative inquiry. These humanistic evaluators realize that actual learning is messy. Students and teachers are unpredictable actors in educational theater.[81] Individuals have different values, abilities, interests, dispositions, histories, cultures, and even different perceptions of reality. There are no standardized students. Thus, these evaluators argue for a more holistic approach to evaluation, one that provides detailed portraits of the situations being evaluated.

Evaluation reports are less lists of numbers than written descriptions of findings or occurrences. The approach focuses more on human interactions than on outcomes and more on the quality than the quantity of classroom or school life. Humanistic evaluators delve into the *why* behind the *what* of performance. The stress is on interpretative understanding rather than objective explanation.[82]

Whereas scientific evaluators might simply ask what students learned, humanistic evaluators query the value of the knowledge learned. These evaluators generate questions that cannot be answered with any finality.[83] Such a question is anathema to scientific evaluators. Often, humanistic evaluators raise questions in their approaches that may not even relate to the aims of education. They realize, in assessing the curriculum, that it exists within political, social, and moral realms. Data must be processed as to its significance. Humanistic evaluators are cognizant that inquiry is not value-free. Even objective data exist within a sphere of subjectivity.[84] This acceptance of subjectivity allows focus on the true, the good, the beautiful, the just, the right, the spontaneous, the awesome, the amazed, the unexpected, the imaginative, the unique, and the emotional.[85]

**EISNER'S CONNOISSEURSHIP AND CRITICISM MODELS.**   Elliot Eisner has recommended two humanistic evaluation models—connoisseurship and criticism—that draw heavily from the arts. Both models are designed to produce a rich description of educational life as a consequence of new programs.

Eisner describes *connoisseurship* as a private act engaged in to personally "appreciate the qualities that constitute some objects, situation, or event."[86] Connoisseurship has essentially five dimensions: (1) intentional, (2) structural, (3) curricular, (4) pedagogical, and (5) evaluative.[87]

These dimensions reflect different aspects of curriculum and evaluation. *Intentional evaluation* refers to a personal assessment of a curriculum's value, merit, and worth. *Structural evaluation* assesses the curriculum's design and the school's organization. (According to Eisner, the spaces within which educators and students function influence the quality of the curricular experience.) *Curricular evaluation* assesses a curriculum's specific contents and how they are organized and sequenced. *Pedagogical evaluation* assesses instructional design and teaching strategies. (Does the instructional approach suit the curriculum's aims and content?) *Evaluative evaluation* assesses evaluation itself. How are evaluative data obtained? How is the curriculum assessed? Are tests and other evaluation methods giving a full and accurate picture of student progress?

The data sources for connoisseurship evaluation are many.[88] Evaluators observe teachers in the classroom and note how they interact with students. Evaluators might also interview students. Other data sources include the particular instructional materials used, student products, and teacher-made tests.[89]

Unlike connoisseurship evaluators, criticism evaluators share their critique of a new curriculum with the public. They interpret and explain the results of the new program.

*Criticism evaluation* entails (1) description, (2) interpretation, (3) evaluation, and (4) thematics. Evaluators (1) write reports in which they describe the curriculum and educational environment; (2) interpret their findings for audiences—for example, by answering questions as to the reasons for the new curriculum; (3) attempt to determine and communicate the new program's educational value; and (4) ascertain from looking at the curriculum what theme or themes emerge.

In considering specific curricular situations, criticism evaluators seek to extrapolate general themes about learning and meaningful knowledge—themes that can guide curriculum development and execution.

By definition, connoisseurs possess expert knowledge. Educational connoisseurs must have knowledge of curriculum and instruction to determine what to observe, how to see, and how to value or appreciate. Good critics are aware of and appreciate a situation's subtleties; they can write about nuances in ways that help others become more aware of the phenomenon under consideration.

Eisner would have evaluators engage in qualitative activities—for example, participate in the classes they observe and ask many questions about the quality of the school and the curriculum. Evaluators following Eisner's model engage in detailed analyses of pupils' work. They use films, videotapes, photographs, and audiotapes of teachers and students in action. They note what is said and done but also what is *not* said or done. They strive to describe the *tone* of the curriculum in action.

Eisner makes the point that evaluation should include reporting to the public (parents, school boards, local or state agencies, and so on). Evaluators must communicate the educational scene.

**ILLUMINATIVE EVALUATION MODEL.**   Another humanistic approach to evaluation is illuminative evaluation, sometimes called *explication*. Originally developed by Malcolm Parlett and David Hamilton, this approach illuminates an educational program's specific problems and unique features. To determine these problems and features, we must focus on the educational environment within which a curriculum is developed and delivered. Curricula rarely (if ever) are implemented and maintained as originally conceptualized and created.

Illuminative evaluation allows evaluators to discern the total program as it exists and functions and to gather data about its particular workings. The evaluator determines the results of the taught curriculum and identifies assumptions evident in its delivery; the attitudes and dispositions of teachers, students, and the public; and the personal and material factors that facilitate or impede the program.

Illuminative evaluation has three steps: observation, further inquiry, and explanation.[90]

**1.** *Observation.* Evaluators get an overview of the program and describe the context within which the curriculum is being delivered, considering all factors that might influence the program. They can gather data on the arrangement of school subjects, teaching and learning styles evident, the materials being used, and the evaluation methods employed by the teacher.

**2.** *Further inquiry.* Evaluators separate the significant from the trivial and seek to determine whether the program works and why or why not. They gain a sharper focus from continually examining the program in action, spending extended time in the field. They also gather data by examining school documents and portfolios of students' work and by interviewing or giving questionnaires to staff and parents.

**3.** *Explanation.* Evaluators who use this model are not attempting to pass judgment on the program but to furnish data on what is happening with the program and why. Evaluators' explanations are presented to the people affected by the program, who then make decisions.

The illuminative approach is holistic and subjective. Observed interactions are not broken down into discrete categories for measurement, but considered within the context of their environment.

## Action-Research Model

Action research is an evaluative approach that blends the scientific and humanistic. It is concerned with continual modification of the educational experience so that every educational event is fresh.[91]

*Action-research evaluation* is distinguished by direct participation in the curriculum. Parker Palmer states that the only way to evaluate teaching and learning is to be present within the learning environment.[92] Teachers are the key players in action-research evaluation. They evaluate both the curriculum and the teaching of the curriculum. They are willing to take chances and learn partly by trial and error.

When the action-research approach is weighted toward research, evaluators investigate quantifiable results of particular classroom actions—results that they hope will allow them to generalize to similar groups of students in similar classrooms. The data suggest general approaches to creating and delivering curricula. They also encourage self-evaluation by teachers and provide insights into the effects on teachers of conducting research within their classrooms and schools. Such data illuminate how teachers' attitudes and prejudices affect student learning.

When action-research evaluation is weighted toward assessment, it is not concerned with education in general but with the unique classrooms of individual teachers. It does not focus on gathering data from which to generalize to other teachers, students, and classrooms. It is concerned with engaging a specific teacher in problem solving to optimize the learning of specific students at a particular time. Gathered data are used to determine whether to continue or modify a particular curriculum or particular instructional approach. The teacher continuously adjusts content, teaching, and educational experiences.

The first step in this fine-tuning is for the teacher to identify what he or she wants to accomplish with a particular aspect of the curriculum or a particular pedagogy and what students wish to accomplish from their engagement with the curriculum. The next step is to determine how to monitor the implemented curriculum. The third step is to interpret the data gathered during monitoring. The fourth step is to continue the process of action research. This step can be accomplished only by teachers who gather data during the actual teaching of the curriculum. Teachers may videotape their teaching, have colleagues observe their teaching, take time from their teaching to record actions and their results in journals, interview students after a particular educational activity, and, of course, administer tests.

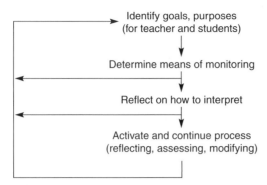

**FIGURE 9.3** General Sequence/Feedback: Action Research

*Source:* Model influenced from comments by Collin J. Marsh and George Willis, *Curriculum: Alternative Approaches, Ongoing Issues,* 4th ed. (Upper Saddle River, NJ: Pearson, 2007).

Figure 9.3 depicts the general sequence and feedback of action research. Table 9.1 provides an overview of evaluation models.

## TESTING

### High-Stakes Tests

"Why has the test—throughout history, and perhaps most pervasively today—come to define our relationship to questions of trust, knowledge and even reality?"[93]

"[H]igh-stakes testing is taken as an a priori assumption in educational policy. An educational system without high-stakes testing is nearly unthinkable, unimaginable, . . . the tests are 'here to stay.'"[94]

"Teaching and assessment play critical roles in helping students develop an understanding of why they study different subjects in school. . . . The purpose of learning" is "to do well on tests."[95]

Education is expensive. The public is increasingly concerned with getting the most for their money. The public demands that schools maintain high academic standards. National associations of content and discipline specialists have created standards that give consideration to

| Table 9.1 | Overview of Evaluation Models | | | | |
|---|---|---|---|---|---|
| **Model** | **Author** | **Approach** | **View of Reality** | **Possibility of Generalization** | **Role of Values** |
| Congruence–contingency | Stake | Scientific | Reality is tangible, single. | Yes | Value free |
| Context, input, process, product | Stufflebeam | Scientific | Reality is tangible, single. | Yes | Value free |
| Connoisseurship/criticism | Eisner | Humanistic | Realities are multiple, holistic. | No | Value bound |
| Illuminative | Parlett and Hamilton | Humanistic | Realities are multiple, holistic. | No | Value bound |
| Action research | Wolf | Humanistic, Scientific | Realities are multiple, holistic. | No<br>Yes | Value bound<br>Value free |

student knowledge of specific content, skills, and procedures. The standards of the National Council of Teachers of Mathematics, National Research Council (which sets science standards), National Council for the Social Studies, and National Council of Teachers of English have significantly influenced assessment. State departments of education, as well as most U.S. school districts, have taken note of these standards and the public's demand that they be met. These standards are provided to guide teachers' curricular and instructional actions and influence the performance levels that students must demonstrate.

However, are standards to be used as guides? Increasing numbers of educators are perceiving standards not as guides to teachers' and students' actions, but as controls and regulations of what occurs regarding curricula and instructional strategies. High-stakes standardized tests are being used as instruments to determine how close educators and students adhere to the standards most frequently set from afar. If students and teachers miss their marks, they are penalized. Students may not be advanced or get diplomas or teachers may not have contracts renewed. Schools can even be shut down.

Wayne Au notes that with the emphasis on high-stakes testing, there is a narrowing of curriculum content. Content is selected to match what is on the test. Essential subjects are only those that are tested. Subjects considered nonessential receive less emphasis or are eliminated. Many schools have reduced or eliminated subject areas such as art and music. Some schools have even eliminated recess—it's not on the test. Physical education usually is not part of the high-stakes testing picture.

Au suggests that high-stakes testing controls not only the content, but also the manner in which content is experienced. Teaching to the test shapes curriculum form—"the organization of meaning and action, including the order in which [students] are introduced to content and the very form that knowledge itself takes, in the curriculum."[96] The flow of knowledge organization suffers as the content knowledge is dissected so that it meshes with how the high-stakes test will measure students' mastery of it.

Not only is the content being molded and organized to mirror that contained in the high-stakes test, but teachers are having to relinquish their instructional strategies and accept those pedagogies that correlate "to the forms of knowledge and content contained on the high-stakes tests."[97] Some assert that teachers are abandoning what they consider best practice in order to be in compliance with standards-based education and to be judged accountable.[98]

Standards from professional and other organizations, both public and private, have certainly increased testing in public schools. Currently, there is considerable controversy regarding the soundness and consequences of testing to address particular standards. Do we want to narrow the curriculum? Do we desire to shape how the curricular content is organized? Do we wish to limit the creativity of teachers in the way that they orchestrate their instruction? Finally, do we want various outside sources at local, state, and even federal levels essentially to determine school policies with regard to curricula, instruction, and approaches to evaluation?

It appears that we do, or at least educators are not able to counter the demand for being accountable and efficient. Of course, educators do wish to be accountable; they wish to be effective in educating their students. However, are the key criteria for evaluating education efficiency to be the maximum amount of content knowledge learned in the least amount of time and the speed in which skills are demonstrated at high rates of accomplishment? As Taubman asserts, it does seem that testing, especially high-stakes testing, is now defining not only our approach to education, but just what we mean by student and teacher "knowing" and competencies.[99]

Today, all states have statewide testing programs. Vast numbers of school districts have their own district-wide testing programs. Testing, it seems, is almost the school's major educational activity. Often, as suggested before, whether students advance to the next grade or graduate depends on whether they pass or fail a particular test.[100]

Teachers whose students pass such exams tend to be evaluated more favorably than teachers whose students fail. Some people, as indicated earlier, recommend that teacher pay should be determined by the performance of their students on these high-stakes tests. Pay for performance has been in the news for more than a decade. Matthew Springer and Catherine Gardner note that Google News reported in 2010 that an average of 4,558 news stories per year dealt with teacher pay being determined by student performance on tests.[101] States such as Texas, Florida, and Minnesota have allocated more than a half billion dollars to incentive pay programs that aim at rewarding teachers for "effective" teaching. The funding of the federal Teacher Incentive Fund was quadrupled in 2010. The Race to the Top federal program emphasizes performance pay. This program has allocated more than $4 billion to this effort.

It does appear, as Springer and Gardner assert, that pay for performance is poised to become a reality factor when evaluating educational effectiveness.[102] This being the case, educators and those advocating for increased effectiveness of education must query themselves about how we are to define teacher and student performance. Certainly, one score on a high-stakes test cannot be the sole deciding indictor. As Taubman cautions, "in reducing everyone and everything to quantifiable data from test scores and attendance records to performance on behavioral check sheets, all historical, personal, idiosyncratic, and context-specific details about the person or event are erased, creating, as the anthropologist Geoffrey C. Bowker states, 'the least possible information that can be shared about events, objects, and people while still maintaining a viable discourse around them.'"[103]

We mentioned in a previous chapter that when standards are emphasized at the time of creating aims, goals, and objectives, there is a tendency to engage in activities that standardize the educational experience of both teachers and students. We cited some cautions. Taubman states that in enforcing standards and a standardization of curricula and instruction, we endanger individuals' idiosyncrasy. In using the same metric to measure "attainment of the standard," we break down human spirits and behaviors into a sameness that crosses boundaries, both geographic and intellectual.[104] Employing the same metric ignores that students are diverse, unique, and differing in abilities, interests, values, beliefs, anxieties, dispositions, and often language.[105]

High-stakes testing has caused many teachers to game the system—not only teaching to the test, but coaching students with sample test questions or even excusing those students who might not do well on the test to have a "day off." Although gaming the system might boost test scores, are such scores evidence of high-quality learning? Indeed, that is the key question with regard to all tests, either teacher-made or standardized. What do the resulting scores actually tell you? According to Alfie Kohn, tests, especially standardized tests, provide scant information about what students actually know and can do. Tests can indicate that some students are more proficient than others, but we still do not know how proficient each student is regarding specific subject matter.[106] Likewise, tests can indicate that one teacher's students attained higher scores than another teacher's, but the scores do not note with any precision whether one teacher was more effective than the other.

It appears that most tests administered by U.S. schools measure knowledge in an unsophisticated way. Various studies have indicated these tests require of students only relatively shallow thinking.[107] Essentially, they test superficial knowledge, not understanding.

## Norm-Referenced Tests

Norm-referenced tests (NRTs) are the most commonly used. A student's performance on a particular test is compared with that of other students who are his or her peers. The items in an NRT usually address a wide area of content. The students, as a group, establish a norm. Students can be grouped by age, grade level, ethnicity, sex, geographic location, or any other easy-to-categorize factor. In order to make comparisons among the students, these tests must be administered to the students in similar fashion and formats and at basically the same time. The manner of scoring the tests must also be the same to furnish meaningful comparison data.[108]

Standardized achievement tests are probably the best-known NRTs. They provide information useful in ranking individual students or groups of students. Specifically, these tests identify which students are successful in their learning and which students might require remediation.

Are the students who took this test progressing at a rate comparable to their peers? If groups of students are tested only once, the test results have questionable value for measuring the quality of a curriculum or instruction. However, when such tests are administered each year at the same time, then the test data can furnish information that depicts patterns revealing both the quality and shortcomings of the curriculum and instructional strategies.[109] However, teachers must realize that NRTs do not specifically relate to a particular curriculum. Neither do they effectively measure what has been taught. They do not indicate what a student can or cannot do, nor do they provide evidence that a student knows or does not know specific content.[110] In addition, many educators fail to realize that different standardized achievement tests are not interchangeable.[111] When educators use a particular test to rank their students with regard to other students who have taken a different standardized achievement test, the rankings cannot be accepted with any confidence. When states employ such tests to compare their students with students in other states, they cannot reach meaningful conclusions regarding the relative worth of their curricula.

James Popham faults the educational community and general public for ignoring the nature of standardized tests used in curriculum comparisons or various other educational research attempts. He states that "inadequate scrutiny of the tests used in key investigations is particularly galling whenever a study's results indicate that there is 'no significant difference' between the achievement of students from one group to that of another group."[112] He indicates that reporting no significant difference deprives us of any useful conclusion. Standardized achievement tests cannot detect the "differences between students taught effectively and students taught ineffectively."[113]

Research indicates that standardized achievement tests highly correlate with students' socioeconomic status. This high positive correlation obscures the impact of educational efforts such as new curriculum. Despite these limitations, educators continue to employ standardized tests to determine the curriculum's success and evaluate teachers' effectiveness. Educators continue to use such tests to rank students in various schools and to determine which students should advance or graduate.

## Criterion-Referenced Tests

The most common alternative to the NRT is the criterion-referenced test (CRT). The CRT is designed to indicate how a student performs a skill or task, or understands a concept, with respect to a fixed criterion or standard. The performing of a skill or task is measured against what are defined as proficiency or achievement standards. The depth of understanding of a concept or certain content is measured by a content standard.[114]

Currently, many of these standards are created by groups outside of school districts (state education agencies or state legislatures). Often, the standards are broken down into specific objectives, frequently stated in behavioral terms. For example, a CRT might require a learner to identify longitude and latitude lines on a map or multiply two-digit numbers. Well-delineated descriptions of the learning are the key features of such tests. This specificity enables educators to determine precisely what a student does or does not know—or can or cannot do—in relation to a particular curriculum. The score on each item interests the evaluator. The teacher wants the student to master the content, skills, or attitudes addressed in each item. Teacher and student will persevere until the student gets the test item right.[115]

CRTs indicate changes in learning over time (in contrast, NRTs measure learning at a specific time). As Taylor and Nolen indicate, teacher-made tests most often are CRTs administered to determine the proficiency of a student's learning in relation to a standard or goal.[116] For CRTs to indicate student mastery, the criterion must be appropriate. Most educators consider 80 percent correct as indicative of mastery. Why? We don't know exactly, but 80 percent does seem to indicate a high level of performance. However, we must consider a test item's age-appropriateness. Otherwise, a test item might be so easy that everyone scores 80 percent or higher, or so difficult that no one does.[117] We must also ask ourselves if a standard of 80 percent is appropriate for all learners in all realms of the curriculum. A level of 80 percent mastery might suffice with regard to understanding a book but not suffice with regard to conducting a science experiment. Likewise, 80 percent is inadequate with regard to accounting exercises (which require 100 percent accuracy) or knowing the rules of the road.

The primary value of CRTs is that they are curriculum specific. They enable curriculum evaluators to assess a new curriculum in their school districts. Evaluators also can determine the instructional realm's effectiveness and whether certain content and skills have been taught. The tests are good tools for assessing student learning and teachers' pedagogical approaches.

The specificity of CRTs can be a disadvantage. Because such tests address specific objectives, as many as 10 to 15 tests are necessary to get a thorough picture of the curriculum. Also, as previously noted, it is not easy to determine the standards for acceptable performance. Just what is the cutoff score for mastery of an objective? Educators usually set the passing score somewhat arbitrarily. Perhaps the most serious criticism of CRTs is that most lack information regarding their reliability. In fact, most are constructed without any attention to reliability.

However, CRTs have curricular validity: the items usually coincide with the curriculum's objectives.[118] Table 9.2 presents a comparison of NRTs and CRTs.

## Subjective Tests

NRTs and CRTs are both categorized as objective tests. This essentially means that the test questions have one correct answer. However, curriculum evaluators also have access to subjective (constructed-response) tests. These tests have many correct responses to each question. For this reason, they are much more challenging to score than objective tests. Often, it is the depth or creativity of the response that determines the evaluative ranking. Essay tests are subjective. Style, insight, originality, use of accurate information, strength of argument, and knowledge of the topic are criteria by which an essay is judged. If educators wish to use essay questions to compare students or programs, the essay questions presented must be the same for all students.[119]

## ALTERNATIVE ASSESSMENT

Since the early 1900s, student data have been gathered by means of teacher-made or standardized tests. Today there is an increasing call for alternative forms of assessment.

States and school districts are engaged in efforts to better align tests and other evaluation efforts with state and district standards and to create means of assessment that truly capture students' knowledge and skills.[120] Many new forms of assessment involve open-ended tasks; students are required to use their knowledge and skills to create a product or solve a problem. Such evaluation events are called *performance assessments.*

Many educators consider performance assessment to be synonymous with authentic assessment. Certainly, they both are examples of alternative assessment, because they employ methods other than multiple-choice or like-developed objective tests. However, in 1992, Carol Meyer argued that performance assessment and authentic assessment are not the same. For an alternative (performance) assessment to be authentic, it must engage students in tasks and activities that resemble actions in the real world. The tests cannot be contrived by the teacher.[121]

A writing exercise is an example of a performance assessment, but it may not be authentic. For instance, here is an example of an inauthentic assessment of students' writing skills. The teacher presents the students with a precise formula for preparing to write and actually writing a short story. On the first day, the students have 50 minutes to generate the story's topic; on the second day, they have 50 minutes in which to create a rough draft; and on the third day, they

**Table 9.2**  Comparison of Norm-Referenced Tests (NRTs) and Criterion-Referenced Tests (CRTs)

| Characteristic | NRT | CRT |
| --- | --- | --- |
| 1. Comparisons made | Score to group average | Score to minimum standard |
| 2. Purpose | Survey or achievement test | Mastery or performance test |
| 3. Validity | Content, criterion, or construct | Content *and* curricular validity |
| 4. Degree of validity | Dependent on instruction | Usually high |
| 5. Reliability | Usually high | Usually unknown |
| 6. Importance of reliability to test model | Important | Unimportant |
| 7. Traits measured | Exist in varying degrees | Present or not present |
| 8. Usability | | |
| Diagnoses | Low general ability | Specific problems |
| Estimation of performance | Broad area | Specific area |
| Basis for decision making | How much was learned | What has been learned |
| 9. Item difficulty | Medium | Easy items |
| 10. Administration | Standardized | Variable |
| 11. Size of group tested | Large | Small |
| 12. Content covered | Broad | Narrow |
| 13. Skills tested | Integrated | Isolated |
| 14. Control of content | Publisher | Instructor or school |
| 15. Limitations | Inability of school personnel to interpret tests on local level | Difficulty of constructing quality tests |
| 16. Versatility | Extensive | Limited |
| 17. Comparison of results between schools | Readily available | Not yet developed |
| 18. Distribution of scores | Normal (one) | Rectangular (two) |
| 19. Range of scores | High | Low |
| 20. Repetition of test if test is failed | No, one test | Until mastery occurs |
| 21. Basis for content | Expert opinion | Local curriculum |
| 22. Quality of items | High | Varies, depending on ability of test constructor |
| 23. Pilot testing | Yes | No |
| 24. Basis of item quality | High discrimination | Content of items |
| 25. Student preparation | Studying for test does not help much | Studying for test should help |
| 26. Teaching to test | Difficult to do | Encouraged |
| 27. Standards | Averages | Performance levels |
| 28. Scores | Ranking, standard score, or number correct | Pass or fail |
| 29. Type of measure | Relative | Absolute |
| 30. Purpose | Ranking students | Improving instruction |
| 31. Revision of test | Not possible | Often necessary |
| 32. Student Information about test content | Little available | Known in advance |
| 33. Motivation of students | Avoidance of failure | Likelihood of success |
| 34. Competition | Student to student | Student to criterion |
| 35. Domain of instruction | Cognitive | Cognitive or psychomotor |

*Source:* Information from Allan C. Ornstein and David A. Gilman, "The Striking Contrasts between Norm-Referenced and Criterion-Referenced Tests," *Contemporary Education* (Summer 1991), p. 293.

have 50 minutes in which to revise and prepare the final draft.[122] Certainly, the students have been engaged in the writing process. However, actual writers do not follow such a restricted process in their writing of short stories. Thus, the contrived activity is not authentic. To make this writing of a short story more authentic, teachers might indicate that students should engage in creative writing throughout the year when the spirit moves them and then file such writing in portfolios. Students select the time for their writing and decide when to share their drafts with the teacher and other students. They revise their drafts according to their own schedules. In this case, students are engaged in an authentic writing assessment, writing in a way that resembles the way that professional writers actually work.

Authentic assessment includes real problem solving, designing and conducting experiments on real problems, engaging in debates, constructing models, creating videotapes of performances, doing fieldwork, creating exhibits, developing demonstrations, writing in journals, creating new products, formulating computer simulations, and creating portfolios. Authentic assessment employs strategies and approaches that present students with real-life situations and conditions.[123]

Authentic assessment is more than the gathering of students' products. It involves teachers' observations and inventories of students' work with accompanying commentary regarding the judgments made. Authentic assessment reports on individuals and groups within the classroom.

Table 9.3 presents some comparisons between alternative, authentic assessment and traditional paper-and-pencil test assessment.

We believe that both alternative and traditional assessment should be used. Educators sometimes accept new practice too readily. Dennis Wolf and Sean Reardon caution, "If new forms of assessment are to work, they require serious gestation."[124] Educators must reconceptualize intelligence, rethink what it means to know something, redefine excellence, and rethink their measurement habits. At the same time, educators must be careful not to interpret the new means of evaluation with traditional mindsets.

William Glasser has proposed seven features of optimal assessment. First, assessment itself should foster student growth. Second, it should allow us to see the consequences of instructional effects. Third, assessment should illuminate the processes and products of learning.

**Table 9.3** Alternative Assessment versus Traditional Assessment

| Alternative Assessment | Traditional Assessment |
|---|---|
| *Samples:* student experiments, debates, portfolios, student products | *Samples:* multiple-choice tests, matching tests, true-false tests, completion tests |
| Evaluation judgment based on observation and subjective, yet professional, judgment | Evaluation judgment based on objective recording and interpretation of scores |
| Focus on individual students in light of their learning | Focus more on score of student as it compares with scores of other students |
| Evaluator able to create an evaluation story regarding an individual or group | Evaluator able to present student knowledge as a score only |
| Evaluation that tends to be idiosyncratic | Evaluation that tends to be generalizable |
| Furnishes data in ways that allow curricular action | Furnishes data in ways that inhibit curricular or instructional action |
| Allows students to participate in their assessment | Tends to place evaluation under the aegis of the teacher or external force |

*Source:* Information from Dennie Palmer Wolf and Sean F. Reardon, "Access to Excellence through New Forms of Student Assessment," in Joan Boykoff Baron and Dennie Palmer. Wolf, eds., *Performance-Based Student Assessment: Challenges and Possibilities,* Ninety-fifth Yearbook of the National Society for the Study of Education (Chicago: University of Chicago Press, 1966), pp. 52–83.

Fourth, it should involve student self-assessment; that is, students should be active participants in judging their achievement. Fifth, assessment should be an integral part of group activity. Assessment data should inform the educator not only about what a student knows, but also about how well the student works with others and adapts to group dynamics. Sixth, assessment should entail meaningful tasks that tie in to overall learning and the curriculum's knowledge goals. Seventh, assessment should be comprehensive, addressing a broad range of information and skills rather than centering on narrow understanding of a particular content.[125]

Alternative assessment should be an ongoing activity integral to curriculum enactment, not an activity engaged in only at particular times of the year to obtain information on student progress. Teachers and students should continually question how well things are being taught and learned. A paper trail should elucidate the quality of student learning.

New assessment methods require new assessment criteria. George Hein would include a moral standard among indicators of effective schooling. A school curriculum that meets a moral standard provides students with skills and knowledge requisite for contributing to the general social good. As Hein indicates, moral purpose was central to the progressive education philosophy.[126]

The portfolio is perhaps the most popular method of alternative assessment. Because it is a sampling of student work over time, a portfolio provides evidence of a student's understandings, skills, and behavioral dispositions. It often records a student's degree of effort and participation in learning. Taylor and Nolen identify several different kinds of portfolios, each one having a different purpose: showcase portfolios, growth portfolios, process portfolios, and cumulative portfolios.[127]

Showcase portfolios, truthful to their name, use concrete examples to emphasize what students have attained in a particular time capsule and at a particular level of accomplishment. Such a portfolio might show a student's art for a given year or samples of a student's essays. With regard to a science showcase, the portfolio might present write-ups of experiments done or notes on field studies.

Growth portfolios provide a visual mapping of a student's increased skills or competencies or understandings over time. A student, often assisted by a teacher, plots out waypoints denoting progress in both declarative and procedural knowledge. Such a portfolio serves to both guide and inspire students in their learning journeys. For example, a portfolio can include a composition that a student wrote at the beginning of the school year and another composition written at year's end. The student and teacher can critique the two papers to determine writing progress. As Taylor and Nolen denote, growth portfolios enable students to assess their increased competencies regarding learning a completely new subject or skill. Such a portfolio is most informative to students and teachers in activities such as learning a new language.[128]

A useful device for documenting students' process or enactment of procedural knowledge is the process portfolio. Here materials included denote how successful students have been in accomplishing authentic performance. These authors define *authenticity in work* as that which has relevance and authenticity in the out-of-school world.[129]

The fourth type of portfolio is the cumulative portfolio. This portfolio is part of the summative evaluative data story. This portfolio contains a student's entries of all his or her work for a year or even longer. The works presented are considered by both student and teacher to be the best examples of work done and tasks attained. Taylor and Nolen posit that these cumulative portfolios become part of students' cumulative records, denoting their progress during their total school experience. Teachers at the start of each year can use cumulative portfolios from the previous years to personalize the curriculum for the incoming students.[130]

For students to create each type of portfolio at a quality level, they must determine, with the teacher's assistance, what criteria are to be employed in judging what should be included. Of course, as students progress through the year or years, they can delete material that, upon later reflection, does not exemplify quality work. Specifically, students working with teachers must engage in critical analysis of their work and their learning strategies.

One of the greatest benefits of portfolios is that students are major players in their own evaluation. Students must reflect on their work; they must critique their level of understanding;

they must judge their study and analytic skills. Portfolios enable, even demand, that students continually self-evaluate, not for a grade, but to increase the quality of their learning procedures, the depth of their understandings, and the significance of their resultant works. Additionally, students can utilize this alternative evaluative instrument to personalize their curricular experiences.

Portfolios essentially allow students to present themselves as whole individuals. Portfolios enable students to become their own scholars and to define their works in regard to value and significance. In using portfolios, students use their voice to add evidence regarding their progress. Students have more than a list of scores or letter grades. Portfolios furnish students, teachers, and parents with material for conversation.

## HUMAN ISSUES OF EVALUATION

We are not widgets. Wayne Au counters that the way we engage in evaluation assumes we are.[131] Yet despite our evaluative actions, deep down we realize that we are individuals with diverse personalities, talents, dispositions, interests, values, emotional stabilities, and intellectual capacities. This section deals with human issues of evaluation, yet the human dimension seems absent in our evaluative deliberations and actions.

Students have been quantified, objectified, made into commodities to be molded, assembled, inspected, and then compared in the world marketplace.[132] We have standardized them and embraced the assumption that all students are essentially alike. We have touted that our tests are indeed objective and that factors such as local cultures, ethnicity, languages spoken, racial group, and socioeconomic status are essentially meaningless.[133] We need not really consider the environments of the "factories" in which the widgets are manufactured. All we must do is measure and judge the quality and quantity of the widgets.

However, ignoring the environments within which evaluation occurs means that it often is destined to fail, despite being valid in all technical details. Evaluation must be sensitive to ethnic or racial bias. Evaluation must be enacted with sophisticated consideration of the evaluative process and the social milieu. Evaluation is shaped by the stakeholders to whom it is reported. Evaluation neglecting the manner of presentation risks having evaluation results being misused, misinterpreted, or simply ignored.

Today, there exists a hidden dimension in evaluation activities: control. This control is over the teachers, the students, the curriculum. A central question is, Who is behind this control? We know that evaluation entails value judgments. The key question is, Whose value judgments are they, and are they worthwhile? Who is deciding the purposes of education and the standards by which education is judged?

There is no definitive answer. It depends on the sociological nature of various communities. However, it is apparent that evaluation is part of the political process. Often, schools release test results not to improve programs, but to please various power groups within the community or demonstrate to legislators that an educational program is effective. Sometimes test results are broadcast to convince various minority groups that their children are experiencing equity within the school system.

Not only that, students are being tested, via standardized testing, with fairness and equality. All students are being measured with the same metric. The tests put everyone on a level playing field. However, we assert that although the standardized tests may put students on a level evaluative playing field, they certainly ignore a level playing field when it comes to instruction and the curriculum. We must consider, when evaluating students, their social, economic, ethnic, and, certainly, educational backgrounds. Not all students come to school with equal backgrounds for assuring school success.

We agree that our students function in a society that celebrates meritocracy. Accepting this, most citizens believe that "regardless of social position, economic class, gender, or culture (or any other form of difference), based on merit and hard work, any individual competes freely and equally with other individuals in order to become 'successful.'"[134]

Yet such a belief is challenged by reality. Clearly, some students come to schools more likely to succeed in our schools and to master the curriculum. We do have inequalities in our society that place many students at a disadvantage regarding school success. And there is considerable debate if we should use our schools to reproduce our current society. Certainly, we must consider multiple interests when designing curricula and creating evaluative measures to determine student success. However, many educators and evaluators are reluctant to confront issues such as social justice within the educational system.[135] Educators are eager not to polarize communities and stir up controversy. However, fairness is crucial to consider when dealing with evaluation.

According to James Pellegrino, Naomi Chudowsky, and Robert Glaser, the idea of comparable validity is at the core of fairness. A fair test furnishes data from which we can draw valid inferences across individuals and groups.[136] Many people believe that tests tend to be biased in favor of students who belong to the dominant culture. Tests use language and terms more familiar to the mainstream majority than to minority cultures. Students bring their cultural backgrounds and world knowledge to test situations. Deborah Meier states that "any choice of subject matter, vocabulary, syntax, metaphors, word associations, and values presupposes a certain social and personal history. We may have equally big vocabularies, but different ones. We may be speaking a grammar that is consistent and accepted, but not the standardized one used in academia."[137]

Evaluators and test designers realize that certain test items produce different results among students from different groups, even when all students have been matched in ability regarding the attribute or knowledge being assessed. For example, students responding to a test question about the discovery of the Americas might well respond differently depending on whether their cultural group sees the actions of Europeans as discovery or conquest. Students raised on farms are more likely than inner-city students to answer a question about agriculture correctly.

Also, is it fair to hold students with disabilities to the same standards as other students? Obviously, wheelchair-bound students cannot be held to physical education standards. Should students with reading and writing disabilities have to meet school standards in order to advance to the next grade or graduate?[138] Should we furnish computer systems to students with reading disabilities to help them with their reading?

The issue of fairness also affects evaluation of students classified as gifted. How do we judge the performance of such students? Many secondary students in advanced-placement and college-level classes complain that their A's look no different on their transcripts than the A's of students in the regular curriculum. Is this fair?

Evaluators are attempting to address the issue of fairness in evaluation by looking at a variety of means of evaluation. Certainly, the alternative methods of evaluation are useful here. Also, we can have grading that is based on multiple criteria. Several evaluators and assessment experts suggest that to really address the issue of fairness, we must consider students' backgrounds when we engage in evaluation. If we do this, we will be able to make conditional inferences from the data analyzed.

Students experienced with particular tasks find them easier than inexperienced students of similar innate ability. Confronted with a new aspect of the curriculum or a new problem, students first determine whether they have background information on which to draw. Those who do are likely to deal successfully with the content or problem. Those who don't may find the content or problem beyond them. We cannot simply say that some students succeeded and others failed. We must consider students' background when we make an evaluative judgment.[139]

Evaluation should encourage, not intimidate, students. It should foster cooperation and a sense of community among students rather than feelings of tense or aggressive competition. Teachers should present tests as learning experiences, not as means of reward and punishment.

Much evaluation, especially standardized testing, produces fear among both students and teachers. Deborah Landry investigated the behavior of 1,058 K–5 students during a standardized reading test by asking teachers to report on their observations of these students. Landry conducted an online survey of 63 teachers and interviewed 4 others. The teachers reported that the standardized testing produced anxiety in the students, who commonly sighed, moaned, and even cried. Teachers reported that 49 percent of the students fidgeted during the testing; 33 percent were worried about how hard the test was; and 21 percent said they were nervous. Landry concluded that the students' behavior indicated strong feelings of helplessness, fear, abandonment, and self-doubt.[140] Other studies of standardized testing have yielded similar results.

Must we test all things? It seems so. As Landry reported, we seem to be not only assessing our students, but also creating psychological problems in students that we are not assessing. In some cities, infants are being assessed as to whether they will fit in to particular preschools or kindergartens. In 2006, Peg Tyre wrote an article querying whether, in the first grade, we are doing too much too soon.[141] Must first graders be tested for everything? Must we score their play? Must students measure up right from the beginning of school? Where is the emphasis on the uniqueness of individuals?

It does appear that we are evaluating with such frequency and intensity that we are smothering students' joy of learning. With our push for standardizing, students are becoming widgets to be shaped and polished. Even students who are precocious are not always ready to be evaluated and sorted by psychometric devices. Tyre noted in 2006 that it appears that early schooling has become "less like a trip to Mr. Rogers' Neighborhood and more like SAT prep."[142]

It does appear that we are excessive in our evaluation of students during their schooling. We probe, poke, measure, assess, judge, sort, encourage, discourage students so we can inform them as to how they measure up with regard to others. Educators should not make evaluation like a gauntlet that students must somehow survive. The educational experience should not be a series of pressured encounters for grasping a brass ring.

## Conclusion

Evaluation addresses the value and effectiveness of curricular matters and activities. It centers on both teachers' and students' actions within the educational arena, primarily the classroom. Today, there is much debate regarding evaluation, primarily with demands that we must assess more effectively the actions of teachers and the learnings of students. There are clarion calls for teachers to be more effective in their pedagogical approaches and students to achieve more and to attain higher standards to be competitive in the world community. These calls exist under twin banners of *standards* and *accountability*.

Much talk about evaluation and, particularly, testing reveals a "buy in" by many people that education is a "business within the marketplace" and that its effectiveness should be judged with the same metric by which we judge workers and businesses. Productivity, attaining business goals, meeting quotas, and meeting market expectations are all ways to determine whether a business is meeting what it has set out to do. Schools should do the same.

This argument essentially reflects a scientific approach to evaluation. However, educators primarily in the humanistic camp of evaluation counter that schools are not making cars, processing mortgages, raising corn, or producing televisions or other electronics. You can count cars produced in a certain time period and make a judgment

as to efficiency of production. Not so, many educators argue, with students' learnings. Certainly, you can compare test scores, and this seems to be the major metric for determining the effectiveness of teachers and the amount of student learnings. However, many in the evaluation debate this query: What do test scores really say other than someone attained a 95 percent or is at the ninth stanine, and someone else got an 85 percent and is at the eighth stanine? And what do such comparisons really mean?

The current dialogue does indicate that evaluation addresses complex activities within complex contexts. There are myriad voices within these contexts, all driven by particular agendas. It behooves us to be knowledgeable about the clusters of procedures that deal with people as well as programs. Much dialogue regarding evaluation seems to exist within clouds of fear, confusion, ignorance, myopic thinking, and, of course, enlightened ruminations. And these dialogues involve individuals and groups of all stripes: educational, social, business, political, and even religious. And within these stripes we have stratifications of views, beliefs, aspirations, and attitudes. And within the stratifications we have degrees of certainties, uncertainties, stubbornness, and tolerance. This being the current state of affairs regarding educational evaluation, we should be mindful that evaluation not only assesses learning, it promotes and nourishes it.

# Endnotes

1. Peter Taubman, *Teaching by Numbers* (New York: Routledge, 2009), p. 12.
2. Ibid.
3. Ibid.
4. James W. Pellegrino, Naomi Chudowsky, and Robert Glaser, eds., *Knowing What Students Know: The Science and Design of Educational Assessment* (Washington, DC: National Academy Press, 2001).
5. Taubman, *Teaching by Numbers*, p. 29.
6. Pellegrino et al., *Knowing What Students Know: The Science and Design of Educational Assessment*.
7. Maxine Greene, *Releasing the Imagination: Essays on Education, the Arts, and Social Change* (San Francisco: Jossey-Bass, 1995).
8. Pellegrino et al., *Knowing What Students Know: The Science and Design of Educational Assessment*.
9. Gary W. Ritter and Nathan C. Jensen, "The Delicate Task of Developing an Attractive Merit Pay Plan for Teachers," *Phi Delta Kappan* (May 2010), pp. 32–37.
10. Chris S. Hulleman and Kenneth E. Barron, "Performance Pay and Teacher Motivation: Separating Myth from Reality," *Phi Delta Kappan* (May 2010), pp. 27–31.
11. Ibid.
12. Matthew C. Springer and Catherine P. Gardner, "Teacher Pay for Performance: Context, Status, and Direction," *Phi Delta Kappan* (May 2010), pp. 8–15.
13. Ibid.
14. Pellegrino et al., *Knowing What Students Know: The Science and Design of Educational Assessment*.
15. Ibid., p. 43.
16. Ibid.
17. Ibid.
18. David E. Tanner, *Assessing Academic Achievement* (Boston: Allyn & Bacon, 2001).
19. Catherine S. Taylor and Susan Bobbitt Nolen, *Classroom Assessment*, 2nd ed. (Upper Saddle River, NJ: Pearson, 2008).
20. Lisa Carter, *Total Instructional Alignment: From Standards to Student Success* (Blooming, IN: Solution Tree Press, 2007).
21. Harriet Talmage, "Evaluating the Curriculum: What, Why and How," *National Association for Secondary School Principals* (May 1985), pp. 1–8.
22. Taylor and Nolen, *Classroom Assessment*.
23. Michael Fullan, ed., *The Challenge of Change*, 2nd ed. (Thousand Oaks, CA: Corwin, 2009), p. 25.
24. Ibid.
25. L. Lezotte and K. McKee, *Assembly Required: A Continuous School Improvement System* (Okemos, MI: Effective Schools Product, LTD, 2002), cited in Carter, *Total Instructional Alignment: From Standards to Student Success,* p. 55.
26. Blaine R. Worthen and James R. Sanders, *Educational Evaluation: Alternative Approaches and Practical Guidelines,* 2nd ed. (New York: Longman, 1987), pp. 22–23.
27. Abbie Brown and Timothy D. Green, *The Essentials of Instructional Design* (Upper Saddle River, NJ: Pearson, 2006).
28. Wilhelmina Savenye, "Evaluating Web-based Learning Systems and Software," in Norbert M. Seel and Sanne Dijkstra, eds., *Curriculum, Plans, and Processes in Instructional Design: International Perspectives* (Mahwah, NJ: Lawrence Erlbaum Associates, 2004), pp. 309–330.
29. Daniel L. Stufflebeam, *Educational Evaluation and Decision Making* (Itasca, IL: Peacock, 1971), p. 25.
30. Collin J. Marsh and George Willis, *Curriculum: Alternative Approaches, Ongoing Issues,* 4th ed. (Upper Saddle River, NJ: Pearson, 2007), p. 266.
31. Kenneth A. Sirotnik and Jeannie Oakes, "Evaluation as Critical Inquiry: School Improvement as a Case in Point," in K. A. Sirotnik, ed., *Evaluation and Social Justice: Issues in Public Education* (San Francisco: Jossey-Bass, 1990), pp. 37–60.
32. *Merriam-Webster's Collegiate Dictionary,* 11th ed. (Springfield, MA: Merriam-Webster, 2004), p. 582.
33. Donald Blumenfeld-Jones, "Dance Curricula Then and Now: A Critical Historical-Hermeneutic Evaluation," in William M. Reynolds and Julie A. Webber, *Expanding Curriculum Theory: Dis/Positions and Lines of Flight* (Mahwah, NJ: Lawrence Erlbaum Associates, 2004), pp. 125–153.
34. Fred N. Kerlinger, *Behavioral Research: A Conceptual Approach* (New York: Holt, Rinehart and Winston, 1979).
35. Brown and Green, *The Essentials of Instructional Design*.
36. Michael Scriven, "The Methodology of Evaluation," in J. R. Gress and D. E. Purpel, eds., *Curriculum: An Introduction to the Field,* 2nd ed. (Berkeley, CA: McCutchan, 1988), pp. 340–412; and Blaine R. Worthen and Vicki Spandel, "Putting the Standardized Test Debate in Perspective," *Educational Leadership* (February 1991), pp. 65–69.
37. Savenye, "Evaluating Web-based Learning Systems and Software."
38. Taylor and Nolen, *Classroom Assessment*.
39. Lee J. Cronbach, *Designing Evaluations of Educational and Social Programs* (San Francisco: Jossey-Bass, 1982), p. 24.
40. Taylor and Nolen, *Classroom Assessment*.
41. Ibid.
42. Ibid.
43. Gina Schuyler Ikemoto and Julie A. Marsh, "Cutting Through the 'Data-Driven' Mantra: Different Conceptions of Data-Driven Decision Making," in Pamela A. Moss, ed., *Evidence and Decision Making,* 106th Yearbook of the National Society for the Study of Education, Part 1 (Malden, MA: Distributed by Blackwell Publishing, 2007), pp. 105–131.
44. Ibid., p. 111.
45. James P. Comer, *What I Learned in School* (San Francisco, CA: Jossey-Bass, 2009), p. 137.

46. William A. Firestone and Raymond A. Gonzalez, "Culture and Processes Affecting Data Use in School," in Pamela A. Moss, ed., *Evidence and Decision Making,* pp. 132–154.

47. Ibid., p. 141.

48. Ibid., p. 49.

49. Ibid.

50. Ibid.

51. Greene, *Releasing the Imagination, Essays on Education, the Arts, and Social Change.*

52. George F. Madaus and Thomas Kellaghan, "Curriculum Evaluation and Assessment," in Philip W. Jackson, ed., *Handbook of Research on Curriculum* (New York: MacMillan, 1992), pp. 119–154.

53. Ibid.

54. Pepi Leistyna, Arlie Woodrum, and Stephen A. Sherblom, *Breaking Free: The Transformative Power of Critical Pedagogy* (Cambridge, MA: Harvard Educational Review, 1999).

55. Ernest R. House, "Assumptions Underlying Evaluation Models," in G. F. Madaus, ed., *Evaluation Models: Viewpoints on Educational and Human Services* (Hingham, MA: Kluwer, 1983), pp. 45–64.

56. Worthen and Sanders, *Educational Evaluation: Alternative Approaches and Practical Guidelines.*

57. Scriven, "The Methodology of Evaluation."

58. Savenye, "Evaluating Web-based Learning Systems and Software."

59. Brown and Green, *The Essentials of Instructional Design.*

60. Frederick Erickson, "Some Thoughts on 'Proximal' Formative Assessment in Student Learning," in Pamela A. Moss, ed., *Evidence and Decision Making,* pp. 186–216.

61. W. James Popham, *Transformative Assessment* (Alexandria, VA: Association for Supervision and Curriculum Development, 2008).

62. Ibid.

63. Allan Collins and Richard Halverson, *Rethinking Education in the Age of Technology* (New York: Teachers College Press, 2009).

64. Taylor and Nolen, *Classroom Assessment.*

65. Savenye, "Evaluating Web-based Learning Systems and Software."

66. D. L. Kirkpatrick, *Evaluating Training Programs: The Four Levels* (San Francisco: Berrett-Koehler, 1994), cited in Abbie Brown and Timothy D. Green, *The Essentials of Instructional Design* (Upper Saddle River, NJ: Pearson, 2006).

67. Ibid., pp. 249–250.

68. Ibid., p. 250.

69. Erickson, "Some Thoughts on 'Proximal' Formative Assessment in Student Learning," p. 190.

70. Ibid., p. 191.

71. Ibid., p. 191.

72. Taubman, *Teaching by Numbers.*

73. Ibid.

74. Ibid.

75. Robert L. Thorndike, *Applied Psychometrics* (Boston: Houghton Mifflin, 1982).

76. H. H. Giles, S. P. McCutchen, and A. N. Zechiel, *Exploring the Curriculum* (New York: Harper & Row, 1942); and R. E. Smith and Ralph W. Tyler, *Appraising and Recording Student Progress* (New York: Harper & Row, 1942).

77. Robert E. Stake, "The Countenance of Educational Evaluation," *Teachers College Record* (April 1967), pp. 523–540.

78. Stufflebeam, *Educational Evaluation and Decision Making.*

79. Ibid., p. 229.

80. Taubman, *Teaching by Numbers.*

81. Ibid.

82. Sirotnik and Oakes, "Evaluation as Critical Inquiry: School Improvement as a Case in Point."

83. Taubman, *Teaching by Numbers.*

84. Ibid.

85. J. F. Lyotard, *The Postmodern Condition: A Report on Knowledge* (Minneapolis, MN: University of Minnesota Press, 1989), cited in Taubman, *Teaching by Numbers.*

86. Elliot W. Eisner, *The Enlightened Eye* (Upper Saddle River, NJ: Merrill, 1998).

87. Ibid.

88. Ibid., p. 80.

89. Ibid.

90. M. Parlett and D. Hamilton, "Evaluation as Illumination: A New Approach to the Study of Innovative Programs," in G. V. Glass, ed., *Evaluation Studies Review Annual* (Beverly Hills, CA: Sage, 1976).

91. Greene, *Releasing the Imagination: Essays on Education, the Arts, and Social Change.*

92. Parker J. Palmer, *The Courage to Teach: Exploring the Inner Landscape of a Teacher's Life* (San Francisco: Jossey-Bass, 1998).

93. A. Ronnell, *The Test* (Urbana, IL: University of Illinois Press, 2005), cited in Taubman, *Teaching by Numbers*, p. 17.

94. Wayne Au, *Unequal by Design* (New York: Routledge, 2009), pp, 122–123.

95. Taylor and Nolen, *Classroom Assessment,* p. 203.

96. Au, *Unequal by Design,* p. 87.

97. Ibid., p. 88.

98. Ibid., p. 89.

99. Taubman, *Teaching by Numbers.*

100. Brown and Green, *The Essentials of Instructional Design.*

101. Springer and Gardner, "Teacher Pay for Performance: Context, Status, and Direction."

102. Ibid.

103. G. Bowker, "Time, Money, and Biodiversity," in A. Ong and S. Collier, eds., *Global Assemblages: Technology, Politics and Ethics as Anthropological Problems* (Malden, MA: Blackwell, 2005), p. 109, cited in Taubman, *Teaching by Numbers,* p. 117.

104. Taubman, *Teaching by Numbers.*

105. Taylor and Nolen, *Classroom Assessment.*

106. Alfie Kohn, *The Schools Our Children Deserve* (Boston: Houghton Mifflin Company, 1999).

107. Ibid.

108. Taylor and Nolen, *Classroom Assessment.*
109. Ibid.
110. Marsh and Willis, *Curriculum: Alternative Approaches, Ongoing Issues.*
111. W. James Popham, "A Test Is a Test Is a Test—Not!" *Educational Leadership* (December 2006–January 2007), pp. 88–89.
112. Ibid., p. 88.
113. Ibid.
114. Taylor and Nolen, *Classroom Assessment.*
115. Marsh and Willis, *Curriculum: Alternative Approaches, Ongoing Issues.*
116. Taylor and Nolen, *Classroom Assessment.*
117. Tanner, *Assessing Academic Achievement.*
118. Allan C. Ornstein, "Comparing and Constructing Norm-Referenced and Criterion-Referenced Tests," *NASSP Bulletin* (1993).
119. Brown and Green, *The Essentials of Instructional Design.*
120. Pellegrino et al., *Knowing What Students Know: The Science and Design of Educational Assessment.*
121. Carol A. Meyer, "What's the Difference between 'Authentic' and 'Performance' Assessment?" *Educational Leadership* (May 1992), pp. 39–40.
122. Ibid.
123. Bruce Frazee and Rose Ann Rudnitski, *Integrated Teaching Methods* (Albany, NY: Delmar, 1995).
124. Dennie Palmer Wolf and Sean F. Reardon, "Access to Excellence through New Forms of Student Assessment," in Joan Boykoff Baron and Dennie Palmer Wolf, eds., *Performance-Based Student Assessment: Challenges and Possibilities,* Ninety-fifth Yearbook of the National Society for the Study of Education, Part 1 (Chicago: University of Chicago Press, 1996).
125. Linda Darling-Hammond and Jacqueline Ancess, "Authentic Assessment and School Development," in Joan Boykoff Baron and Dennie Palmer Wolf, eds., *Performance-based*

*Student Assessment: Challenges and Possibilities* (Chicago: University of Chicago Press, 1996).
126. George E. Hein, "A Progressive Education Perspective on Evaluation," in Brenda S. Engel with Anne C. Martin, *Holding Values: What We Mean by Progressive Education* (Portsmouth, NH: Heinemann, 2005), pp. 176–185.
127. Taylor and Nolen, *Classroom Assessment.*
128. Ibid.
129. Ibid.
130. Ibid.
131. Au, *Unequal by Design.*
132. Ibid.
133. Ibid.
134. N. Lemann, *The Big Test: The Secret History of the American Meritocracy* (New York: Farrar, Straus, and Giroux, 1999); and P. Sacks, *Standardized Minds: The High Price of America's Testing Culture and What We Can Do to Change It* (Cambridge, MA: Perseus Books, 1999), cited in Au, *Unequal by Design,* pp. 45–46.
135. David P. Ericson, "Social Justice, Evaluation and the Educational System," in K. A. Sirotnik, ed., *Evaluation and Social Justice: Issues in Public Education,* pp. 5–22.
136. Pellegrino et al., *Knowing What Students Know: The Science and Design of Educational Assessment.*
137. Deborah Meier, *In Schools We Trust* (Boston: Beacon Press, 2002), p. 109.
138. Pellegrino et al., *Knowing What Students Know: The Science and Design of Educational Assessment.*
139. Ibid.
140. Deborah Landry, "Teachers' (K–5) Perceptions of Student Behaviors during Standardized Testing," in Barbara Slater Stern, ed., *Curriculum and Teaching Dialogue* (Greenwich, CT: Information Age Publishing, 2006), pp. 29–40.
141. Peg Tyre, "The New First Grade: Too Much Too Soon," *Newsweek* (September 11, 2006), pp. 34–44.
142. Ibid., p. 36.

# 10

### ▪ ▪ ▪

# International Scenes
# in Education

## FOCUSING QUESTIONS

1. What assumptions come into play when Americans compare U.S. students' academic achievements with students' achievements in other countries?

2. How do you judge the claims enunciated in the various U.S. governmental educational reports and programs such as No Child Left Behind and Race to the Top? Explain your judgments.

3. What foci should educators and members of the general public bring to their thinking about education in general and U.S. education in particular?

4. How do you define the purposes of education in general and American education in particular? Are you in agreement or disagreement with educational purposes discussed in this chapter? Defend your positions.

5. What are your affective responses to the educational systems of the six countries discussed in this chapter? Explain your responses.

6. What are your reactions to Finnish education? How you might utilize your reactions for the improvement of American education?

7. What, if anything, surprised you about education in Turkey?

8. How successful have the educational systems discussed in this chapter been in dealing with the issue of equity, especially ethnic and gender equity? How do American schools compare?

9. Considering the background of Australia, how have Australians differed from Americans in dealing with their educational challenges? What lessons might American educators learn from their Australian counterparts?

10. How does teacher education differ in the six countries discussed? Are there any lessons for American teacher education?

11. How does China's history influence its current educational activities?

12. What major challenges does China face in this century? How do these challenges compare to those confronting American education?

13. How does Brazilian primary and secondary education compare with American education?

14. How do you interpret the statement, "As Brazil goes, so goes the U.S. relationship with the Western Hemisphere"? How valid do you think your interpretation is?

15. What are the major educational challenges of South Africa?

16. Does South Africa's current educational system provide any insights for Americans and American educators?

We live in the 21st century. However, the question of how we should live in the 21st century generates no precise answer or answers. Even more challenging is the question of how we should educate our students in and for the 21st century. This question generates myriad answers but also fear and intense concerns. Before addressing this question, there exists the prior question: What are the purposes of education in this century?

Accompanying these questions is, How do we compare with other educational systems? Some proclaim we are not showing equal or superior competencies. "It's a given that America's once-great schools are slipping, sliding behind the rest of the world. The big fight, then, is over what to do about it?"[1] The present situation seems unchanged from when the Nation at Risk report was published in 1983. The same lamentation was echoed when the No Child Left Behind legislation appeared in 2006. American educators are failing American children. The Race to the Top federal program adds credibility to this view. We have lost our educational lead in the world. Our students are not measuring up to students in other developed and even developing countries. Test scores document our failure to educate our students to high standards. Our students are not being equipped to compete—actually, to dominate—global communities.

"But, what if the first part (American schools are slipping behind the rest of the world) isn't true?"[2] What if it is suspect that we are losing the brain race compared to current and emerging world competitors? What if "We have to face the brutal truth that we're being out-educated" is exaggerated?[3] What if educators, accompanied by politicians, business leaders, and the general public, are handicapped by a psychological immune system?[4] Psychologists note that individuals are most comfortable cogitating about the future when they utilize assumptions currently accepted to solve future situations. Rarely do they question whether current assumptions are applicable in evolving futures. As Martinez posits, "Essentially, our brain is hard-wired to look for confirmation of our existing hypotheses."[5] We must challenge present assumptions about American education and how we as a nation stack up compared to other nations. We might well be responding to the current dynamic times in ways that are essentially self-defeating.

Martinez states that the legislation No Child Left Behind is arguably a result of activation of our psychological immune system, an autoimmune response. Such a response, while enabling decisions to be made and ideas to be constructed under the aegis of rational action, actually contributed to weakening the system further.[6] The reasoning went that our schools were not measuring up to expectations. We needed to raise educational attainments by demanding that schools be more responsible for student performance. Standards needed to be written. Weak teachers had to be weeded out, and competent teachers had to be rewarded with higher pay. These demands reflect a business-market view of education, employing assumptions that essentially applied to times long past. No Child Left Behind, instead of improving the system, actually hindered real reform by mandating rigid and narrow measures that corralled the types of learning truly essential for functioning in this century.[7]

The reader may wish to argue this point, but the Race to the Top legislation currently being encouraged suggests that No Child Left Behind failed. However, look at the test results of U.S. students, especially in mathematics and science, compared with students in other countries. Finland is the current exemplary statistic. U.S. students are not number 1. You cannot brush that statistic under the rug. Yet, what does that factoid tell you? Have U.S. students ever been the top scorers on these international standardized tests?

Danny Westneat reports that Tom Loveless, a researcher at the Brookings Institution, has noted that the United States never has led the world with regard to objective test scores. U.S.

students have never even been close. However, we are doing better now than in the early 1960s. Now, we are about average but still behind some Asian counties. In fact, U.S. students' latest scores in both mathematics and science reveal our greatest gains. Our students now rank 22nd out of a pool of 67 countries or territories.[8]

Some educational critics might assert that the preceding paragraphs support their contention that American schools are not effective. Twenty-second out of a pool of 67 countries or territories is still TWENTY-SECOND! Our students should be first. We must seize the future. Being second is unacceptable. Such comments provide evidence of autoimmune response—dealing with future educational challenges employing present-centered, comfortable assumptions. We must realize that we all suffer from this cultural, psychological, metacognitive "ailment." We are "in" our cultural context so deeply that we are unaware of it, much as a fish is unaware of the water in which it swims.

However, current times demand that we focus our inquiries inward as we reflect on the current state of education. Past metrics such as content covered, facts cited, grades passed, tests taken, scores attained, goals reached, and standards attained to determine educational success and student achievement mislead us in our quest for excellence in 21st-century education. This is not to advocate scrapping these metrics. Rather, it is to encourage new metrics to accompany these well-accepted metrics. Certainly, we want content covered to be considered in judging schools' successes. Yet what does content covered mean? And does content covered precisely indicate student knowledge and understanding? And is knowledge as defined in the 20th century adequate for judging educational quality in the 21st century?

As R. Hanvey noted in 1976, educators and those who would offer advice regarding education must possess mindsets that provide insight into what education should be in this century. Hanvey remarked that truly modern educators must embrace five dimensions of focus for thinking about education.[9] The first dimension involves perspective consciousness. Just what are our views regarding local, state, national, and global realities? How do these views influence our thinking and our problem solving regarding educational challenges? Are our perspectives, what we think of our situational environments, enabling us to develop new insights or are our perspectives hindering our views of current and evolving situations? Perspective consciousnesses influence the second dimension of focus, the state-of-the-planet awareness. Most of us possess some awareness of local and, perhaps, national scenes, but few of us are really aware of the state of the planet. This second dimension requires identifying global issues and examining their impacts on students' lives. This second dimension requires a mapping of cultural, economic, and physical dimensions on this globe and the current and potential impacts on people.

Attending to the second dimension leads to a third dimension—awareness of global dynamics. Just being aware of the planet and its specific aspects is insufficient to make informed determinations, in our case, educational judgments. We must be cognizant of the dynamics of the myriad planet–world dynamics. Peoples and nation–states are no longer islands unto themselves. Global dynamics have been occurring since the 17th century. Today, these world interactions are occurring not in centuries or decades, but in years and days.

This third dimension of the world's dynamics writ large feeds into the fourth dimension—cross-cultural awareness. Here, attention centers on gaining in-depth understanding of the various cultural and political groups. This fourth dimension directs our efforts to analyze other nations—in our case, their schools—to gain information to enable us to adjust or maintain our school activities.

The fifth and last dimension is awareness of human choices. When all is said and done, what happens in our world is up to what people choose to do or not do. If we have an enemy regarding quality education, it is we, the people. The weapons we, the enemy, employ are outdated thinking, false aims, rigid ideologies, lack of compassion, lack of comfort in our beliefs, fear of uncertainty, and outdated views of the world and the world community.[10] A prime reason for having a chapter focusing on certain nations in the world community is to deduce lessons about how to educate our students, not for educational victory over others, but to free human potential.

Activating the five dimensions of focus to direct our thinking about education in this century requires us to comprehend present and evolving scenes, remaining cognizant of the pasts through which we have traveled. Most modern educational systems have evolved within a rather precisely defined product—the nation–state.[11] Our schools and schools in other countries have been designed primarily for national purposes—economic, political, and social.[12] Schools are the primary arenas where young people "learn what it is to be 'x'—either formally, through what is explicitly taught, or informally, through adapting to the practices that structure daily life." Curricula are selected to shape students into various social, cultural, economic, and political behaviors requisite for effective national and global citizenship. Pedagogies are orchestrated to configure students to be acceptable x's, to think and approach knowledge and national citizenship in particular ways.[13] A danger of educating students to become successful x's is that they will learn their lessons too well. They become x's who can function effectively within their nation, but they develop myopic views of the world.[14]

Readers, as they consider education in the countries selected for this chapter, should be cognizant of the forces of globalization that have an impact on established bonds between nation–states and educational systems. National boundaries are becoming more porous, figuratively and literally.

Although we can strive to tighten our boundaries in attempts to keep out certain groups, we must realize that our borders are porous to ideas, ideals, and desires of various world groups. With technologies such as Facebook, YouTube, and Twitter, the world is essentially an open book.

Nation–states have always been products of interaction. The United States did not self-generate in isolation. Our country evolved not only from interaction with Great Britain, but also from relations with other European countries. Our conception of nation resulted from centuries of idea distillations by myriad peoples and cultures. Our present political, social, economic, and educational behaviors are driven by our interchanges with the current world—thus the need for this chapter.[15]

## EDUCATION IN PARTICULAR COUNTRIES

No nation is an island unto itself. We are living at "warp-speed" globalization. We are challenged not to retreat, but to embrace our evolving world for the benefit of all. Some people are enthusiastically welcoming opportunities for new human relations. Others seem to ignore the world as a global community.

As we consider the six countries (Finland, Turkey, Australia, China, Brazil, and South Africa) in this chapter, we must do so with a mindset of expansive global consciousness. We must wean ourselves from overreliance on standards, testing, and test scores. We must purge ourselves of classifying individuals, conformity, privileging certain groups, and overcontrolling students and teachers. We must reject those curricular and pedagogical approaches designed to train students for slots in the marketplace. Einstein observed, "Imagination is more important than knowledge."[16]

## FINLAND

"The aim [of Finish education policy] is a coherent policy geared to educational equity and a high level of education among the population as a whole. The principle of life-long learning entails that everyone has sufficient learning skills and opportunities to develop their knowledge and skills in different learning environments throughout their lifespan."[17]

"The objective of basic education is to support pupils' growth toward humanity and ethical responsible membership of society, and to provide them with the knowledge and skills necessary in life. The instruction shall promote equality in society and the pupils' abilities to participate in education and to otherwise develop themselves during their lives."[18]

## Background

The Republic of Finland exemplifies a country that has progressed from an agrarian society in the 1950s and lagging behind its northern European neighbors in educational attainments to an information society whose economy was judged the most competitive in the world from 2001 to 2005.[19] Just prior to its stellar economic achievements, the world spotlighted Finland in 2000 for its 15-year-old students excelling in the Organization for Economic Co-operation and Development's Program for International Student Assessments (PISA). These Finnish students surpassed their peers from 32 countries in reading, literacy, mathematical literacy, and scientific literacy.[20]

However impressive, these test scores really provide little information useful to educators and others. As Ari Antikainen suggests, a more useful and valid way to consider these results is to investigate what, specifically, those individuals involved in Finnish education actually did to have their students attain such results. Inquiring into the "why" of such results—investigating in detail what actions and what procedures were engaged, what curricula were employed, what pedagogies were utilized, what educational policies were implemented, and what organizational strategies were implemented—can furnish other educators from around the world with new knowledge and new motivation to innovate within the educational arena.[21]

Although answers to these queries can prove useful, we must remember when looking at Finland and other countries that we are not striving just to raise students' test scores. Quality education is not defined by high marks on international standardized tests. As Keith Baker reminds us, "There is no association between test scores and national success, and, contrary to one of the major beliefs driving U.S. education policy for nearly half a century, international test scores are nothing to be concerned about."[22] Baker further argues that policy makers and politicians, when they hold up other nations' test scores as evidence that U.S. schools are falling behind, are committing a logical error identified as the *ecological correlation fallacy.* There is evidence, usually unknown to many and ignored by some, that the actions and the effects of those actions in education with nations "does not transfer to differences among nations."[23] Thus, when individuals in the United States state that the data drawn from other countries' students' performances lead us to conclude that our schools are failing, we must recognize such conclusions not as proven generalizations, but rather as hypotheses, requiring further study and research.[24]

The preceding comments are not intended to diminish Finland's educational accomplishment nor to suggest that American citizens, and particularly educators, cannot learn from Finnish educational actions. The statements are to remind us that while Finland and the United States share the same globe, we are not Finland and Finland is not the United States. Recognizing this, we can view Finland and its educational system as offering potential lessons for Americans and American educators.

## The Uniqueness of Finland

On December 6, 1917, Finland declared its independence from Russia. Until that time, Finland had been claimed at times by Sweden and at other times by Russia. Lenin recognized Finnish independence in the final week of December 1917. Sweden, Germany, and France followed suit. However, Finland's independence was threatened during the Bolshevik revolution and again during World War II. In the winter of 1939–1940, the Soviet Union invaded Finland. The Finns strongly resisted. In the summer of 1944, Finland and the Soviet Union signed a peace agreement.

Because Finland shares an eastern border with Russia, it has been ever mindful of its geographically large neighbor. National leaders realized the wisdom of balancing their actions between the East (the Russians) and the West (the United States and its European allies). Since 1995, it has been a member of the European Union.[25]

Woven into the uniqueness of Finland has been the Finnish people's struggles for survival and to maintain their Finnish identity. Developing, maintaining, and shaping their Finnishness has been challenging. Sweden ruled the area from the 100s to the 1800s. Russia controlled Finland from 1809 to 1917.[26]

Geographically, Finland is a Nordic country and shares many parallels throughout its history with the other Nordic countries (Denmark, Norway, and Sweden), but, essentially, it is not Nordic. Neither is Finland Scandinavian. Its culture and language differ greatly from the Scandinavian peoples.

As indicated previously, Finland evolved from an agrarian state into an industrial, capitalist welfare state and, since the 1980s, into a postindustrial, or informational, society. Today, Finland has transformed itself into a competitive state within the global community. Although competitive, it still is a *welfare state,* meaning that the government has formed a productive relationship between labor and capital.[27] Social welfare shapes much government action and activities of societal groups. Specifically, this means that minimum levels of the following services are nonnegotiable: education, health, social security, employment, and housing. These services are provided as rights of citizenship.

Finland's successes as an information society and knowledge-based economy essentially provide the financial bases for the health of Finland's welfare state. Electronics leads the information society. Some have indentified Finland as the Silicon Valley of Europe, a key member of network societies. Network societies shape a new social dynamic. "Networking logic substantially modifies the operation and outcomes in processes of production, experience, power, and culture."[28] Finland's networking has strengthened its long-standing commitment to education as a basic citizen right. Schools, colleges, and universities network with each other. Likewise, these educational institutions generate functioning links with companies, their employees, and even citizen groups, all cognizant of education's centrality to working life and civic participation. Additionally, Finns realize that working communities and civic associations also have an impact on education.

## Finnish Education: Cultural Linchpin

Finland can be defined as a learning society. Torsten Husen has four criteria with which to define such a society: (1) people are afforded opportunities for lifelong learning, (2) formal education is available to all ages in the society, (3) informal learning is prized and independent studies are urged, and (4) other institutions are invited into the educational enterprise.[29]

## Ministry of Education

The Ministry of Education in Finland has a broad range of responsibilities relating to educational, scientific, and cultural matters. The Ministry is accountable not only for promoting education in schools, colleges, and universities, but for science, culture, sports, and youth work. It also has responsibilities relating to the civil education of all Finns so that they recognize their responsibilities as it benefits their personal goals as well as society's goals.[30]

Within the Ministry of Education are two ministers: the Minister of Education and Science, responsible for education and research relevant to educational issues, and the Minister of Culture, who manages matters relating to "culture, sports, youth copyright, student financial aid, and church affairs."[31] Finland has a long history of including religious instruction in its curriculum. Its religious curricula deal with the teachings of the Evangelican Lutheran Church of Finland or the Orthodox Church of Finland. However, the Finnish government is neutral with regard to religion and churches in curricular content and experiences. Nevertheless, it does fund the education of clergy in university schools of theology. Also, it funds denominational instruction in elementary and secondary school. For students not affiliated with any denomination, the Ministry of Education supports ethics education at primary and secondary levels.

## The Finnish Educational System

**THE COMPREHENSIVE SCHOOL.**   Presently, the Finnish educational system is divided into preprimary education, 9-year comprehensive schools, postcomprehensive general and vocational education, and higher education and adult education. The 9-year comprehensive and the upper secondary school consists of two divisions: primary school and lower secondary school. Instead of grades, the primary school has forms 1 through 6. Students enter the primary school in the year they turn 7.

The forms, or age-based classes, are very similar to how U.S. elementary schools are organized. However, there is a major difference regarding primary teacher placement. In most schools, teachers are kept with the same group of students for several years in a process called *looping*. Essentially, teachers determine how long they remain with a particular group of students. If a teacher so desires, he or she can remain with the same group of students for the entire primary school experience—6 years. This practice allows teachers to know their students at a deeper level.[32]

The lower secondary school division of the comprehensive school engages students for three additional years. In this division, comparable to grades 7 to 9 in U.S. schools, the students are organized into subject-area classrooms. Those students who wish to complete their compulsory education have to complete a 10th year of schooling. Completion of this curriculum is requisite for gaining entry into upper secondary postcomprehensive education, enrolling students 16 to 19 years old. All students attending comprehensive school have an academic year of 190 school days.[33]

Although the Finnish government formulates broad national objectives and the time allotments for teaching various subjects at particular school levels, it is the National Board of Education that specifies the global objectives and core curricular content. Local educational professionals and individual teachers create the basic and specific curriculum for the local community's students. The basic curriculum addresses the mother tongue and literature (Finnish or other national languages, either Swedish or Lapp [Sami]), foreign language (commencing at the third form), environmental studies, civics, religion or ethics, history, social studies, mathematics, physics, chemistry, biology, geography, physical education, music, visual arts, crafts, and home economics.

Upon completion of the curriculum, students receive a certificate indicating acceptable completion of the curriculum of the comprehensive school. The standards for completing the certificate qualifications are determined at the local school level by administrators, teachers, and other support staff. As students travel through the curriculum of the comprehensive school, they never are tracked or placed in special groups, nor are they subjected to various tests at specific levels to determine whether they advance to the next school level or form.[34]

**THE POSTCOMPREHENSIVE EDUCATION (UPPER SECONDARY EDUCATION).**    The postcomprehensive curriculum has three track offerings: compulsory, specialized, and applied. The total curriculum contains 38 lessons focused on specific subjects: "mother tongue and literature (Finnish or other national language), foreign language, a second foreign language, environmental studies, civics, religion or ethics, history, social studies, mathematics, physics, chemistry, biology, geography, physical education, music, visual arts, crafts, and home economics." The National Board of Education is charged with generating the core objectives and the content foci of the complete curriculum; the detailed curriculum is generated by educators at the local level.[35]

Although there are no exams for students to attain their certificate for completing the comprehensive and postcomprehensive schools, there is a matriculation exam that students must take if they wish to be accepted for college or university study. This exam is scheduled in the spring and autumn and is administered in all upper secondary schools. This exam contains four tests: a test in the mother tongue, a test in the second official language, a test in a foreign language, and a test in either mathematics or general studies. All these tests are open ended, stressing critical thinking, problem solving, and writing mastery. Each test is created at two levels of difficulty, reflecting the curriculum that a student has taken in school. Students are free to choose the exam's level of difficulty. However, they must take one exam at the upper level and pass it. They must pass all tests, regardless of level.[36]

## Lessons from Finland

Just what did Finland do to make it an educational envy of the world? Certainly, it was not the Finnish school year of 190 school days. The curriculum subjects did not seem out of the ordinary. Your authors suggest the following novelties that the Finnish Ministry of Educational introduced: going from an agency that was highly centralized managing education with curriculum guides exceeding 700 pages to an organization working more as a catalyst to get educators at the local level to assume responsibility for creating curricula and assessments; going from a central authority prone to issue edicts as to what teachers should do in schools and classrooms to an organization that expressed confidence that teachers, with excellent preparatory programs, could be trusted with creating curricula and innovative pedagogical strategies; and a stress on local and idiosyncratic assessment generated by teachers.[37]

Perhaps the most significant novelty embraced by Finnish authorities at the national level was their exhibiting trust in educational professionals, particularly teachers. They also trusted educators at the college and university levels to create educational programs that would graduate competent, creative, and committed educators. In Finland, universities are responsible for teacher education. Individuals wishing to teach at the lower levels of comprehensive schools must earn a master's degree in education. The degree requires a total of 160 credits and 5 years of study, including practice teaching. The education of persons focused on being subject-matter or discipline teachers is offered at the university level in the respective discipline faculties. Again, teachers in these programs must earn a master's degree in their respective fields. This program also requires 5 years of study (160–180 credits), including a teaching internship. Teachers with this degree can teach at the lower elementary schools and also at the secondary and upper secondary school levels.[38]

However, not everyone wishing to be a teacher is admitted into teacher education. Prospective teacher education students must compete with others with this academic and professional goal. As Linda Darling-Hammond notes, of those who apply, only the top 15 percent are accepted. Of those approved for the program, the college or university offers them a free 3-year graduate program and also a living stipend.[39]

A hallmark of the student teacher's experience is working a full year with an experienced teacher in a model school frequently associated with a university. Not only does the novice teacher learn how to teach, but he or she learns how to draw on educational research that supports pedagogical approaches. Novices are encouraged to experiment with varied instructional approaches. In Finland, teachers and students engage in inquiry directed not only at learning content, but also at polishing methods of teaching and learning. Student teachers are presented with visions of classrooms as laboratories where teachers and students collaborate in varied investigations. They also are presented with notions that the classroom is an arena where views, conclusions, and hypotheses can be challenged. A major purpose for these experimental classrooms is to cultivate independent and active learning in students.[40]

Additionally, students having clinical experiences in model classrooms have opportunities to learn how to develop innovative and challenging curricula. They also acquire skill in creating appropriate assessment instruments (tests and alternative means) for communicating to students their learning strengths and areas needing improvement. In Finland, there are no external standardized tests administered to students. Students are not ranked as a result of any assessment. The primary means of teacher feedback to students is delivered in narrative form, noting not only knowledge gained or needed to be gained, but also the effectiveness of the student learning process employed.[41]

Finally, education students come to realize that teaching and related activities such as developing curricula and assessment are not solitary activities. In many Finnish classrooms, the teacher has a cadre of fellow educators to assist in teaching, collaboration with students, and individual remedial work with students. Many schools have a teacher's assistant available to work with various teachers in a school. This person may not have a master's degree in education, but rather may be a postcomprehensive graduate with some specialized education in how to work with students needing special academic assistance. In many schools, there are special-needs teachers who have appropriate degrees to allow them to teach at various levels. Often, these individuals are special education teachers who not only help with instruction but assist teachers with designing and creating curricula that address particular student needs.[42]

> Overall, the Finnish approach to . . . schooling relies on building the capacity of schools—the competencies of teachers, the availability of support personnel like school assistants and special-needs teachers, the creation of conditions that enhance the ability of teachers to work effectively (such as small scale and teacher participation in decision making)—as well as the capacity of social programs to back up schools. It does not rely on excessive amounts of low-level testing or on draconian accountability systems.[43]

## TURKEY

### Background

Turkey is both geographically and culturally unique. The Republic is an independent country located in both Europe and Asia. It is both Muslim and secular. Granted, its European area occupies only 3 percent of Turkey, in a region called Thrace. The remaining 97 percent of Turkey, identified as Anatolia, is in Asia Minor. Muslims make up almost 99 percent of the population; most are Sunni. The remaining 1 percent are Christians and Jews. Regarding the total population, 80 percent are Turkish, the remaining 20 percent being Kurdish. Essentially, there are no Arabs. The Turkish people speak Turkish, which is the nation's official language. The Kurdish people speak Kurdish. However, Arabic, Armenian, and Greek are also spoken.[44]

It appears that Turkish citizens wish to be included in both the Middle East and in Europe. For several years, the Turkish government has attempted to join the European Union. Some member countries of the European Union favor Turkey joining; others do not.

Although the European area of Turkey, Thrace, has been occupied by humans for more than 20 centuries, modern Turkey is a more recent political organization. It rose from the ashes of the Ottoman Empire, which officially ended in 1922. A Turkish nationalist, Mustafa Kemal, successfully led Turkish forces against Western military forces for control of the region. In November 1922, the National Assembly assumed governmental control of Turkey. The following year, in October 1923, the people proclaimed the Republic of Turkey. The people elected Mustafa Kemal president. Later, Kemal was celebrated as Atatürk, meaning Father of Turkey.

Kemal was not only the president, he was the key force in transforming Turkey into a modern, Westernized nation. He removed the sultanate as the chief form of national leadership. He enabled a new political and legal system to be established. Perhaps more importantly, he made the government and education secular. After 1924, all schools were secular, and elementary school attendance was both coeducational and compulsory. Besides opening up schools to women, Kemal also granted them equal rights. A major innovation Kemal introduced was the Roman alphabet and number system to replace Arabic script. To bring Turkey into the family of modern nations, he also urged the government to pass policies that nurtured the nation's industries, agriculture, arts, and sciences.[45] Perhaps Mustafa Kemal's greatest gift to his country was his insistence that the new nation stress education. Through education, the nation would attain modernity.

The new nation had political challenges, but the "hand" of Atatürk provided guidance. The nation went through several governments. In 1960, a coup ousted the ruling Democratic Party. A new constitution was written in 1961. However, political instability existed in the latter third of the 20th century. In November 1982, the government wrote a new constitution. Education was deemed essential for the nation.

### Turkish Educational System

The Turkish national education system has two main divisions: formal education and nonformal education. Under formal education are preprimary education, primary education, secondary education, and higher education. Nonformal education contains specific programs and activities designed especially for students who did not have success in formal education or who, for various reasons, did not attend such programs. There are private schools at all levels of education, many of which are Islamic. Both private and public schools must follow the directives of the Ministry of National Education.

## The Ministry of National Education

Compared to Finland, where the Ministry of Education serves as a catalyst for the local control and development of educational programs, Turkey seems to be at the opposite extreme. The Ministry of National Education has total responsibility for the appropriateness of all educational materials. All curricula developed at the ministerial level are approved by that body before distribution to the various schools. Additionally, the Ministry prepares or purchases all students' textbooks and related materials. The Ministry even prepares teachers' resource materials, with pedagogical suggestions. Because Turkey is a secular nation, the Ministry monitors the students' clothing in both public and private schools. Clothing suggesting a religious nature is not allowed in any school. This ban has been somewhat controversial for Muslims who send their children to Islamic private schools.

**PRIMARY EDUCATION.** Children from ages 6 to 14 are required to attend primary schools, which are provided free of charge. However, parents must purchase school uniforms, books, and other school supplies. The major primary school aim is to engage students with knowledge and skills requisite for further education or job training. Curricula and educational experiences also nurture student behaviors and dispositions needed to become effective Turkish and global citizens. Primary students commence their learning journeys to more fully comprehend multiple perspectives and give evidence of increasing knowledge of different world cultures; to develop capacities to process the complexities of global dynamics; and to formulate complex processes of thinking, employing a world view.[46] The primary school also recognizes that students live in a technological world. Thus goals stress students not only becoming knowledgeable about information technologies, but also becoming increasingly competent in utilizing new technologies.

The majority of Turkish people live in the northern part of the Anatolian Plateau and along the coastal plains. The rest of Turkey is sparsely populated, providing a challenge for the Ministry of National Education to furnish high-quality education for students in these isolated rural areas. Some areas do not have primary schools at all. For students from 6 to 14 years of age living in such areas, as well as poor students, the Turkish government manages Regional Primary Education Boarding schools and regular primary schools. These students and their parents receive a pension that covers all school expenses.[47]

**SECONDARY EDUCATION.** Secondary education is not compulsory in Turkey, but it is an option. Increasing numbers of students, both males and females, are taking advantage of this option.

Even though the Turkish Constitution and various national laws promote gender equality, females have traditionally been provided fewer opportunities for formal education at all educational levels. This inequity finds its roots in Turkey's patriarchal society and Muslim beliefs. Turkey's government has been addressing this issue of women's rights since the founding of the modern Turkish republic.[48] Turkey's stance regarding equity for girls' and women's education and job opportunities remains somewhat fluid and disputed among its citizens. However, Turkey's emphasis on maintaining a secular nation is enabling greater strides in gender equity.

In this century, Turkey is aligning itself increasingly with international agencies who assert that furnishing females with access to education is a prerequisite to attaining social progress. However, Turkey, as well as other nation states in the region and around the world, must be cognizant that progress in attaining gender equity in education and in other areas cannot be assessed with uncritical reliance on current measurement methods that narrowly focus on numbers of females in schools or in various jobs; neither can indicators of progress be based solely on longevity of girls and women in schools. Attention must be given to defining and redefining the concept of gender equity in the 21st century.[49]

The overall goal of Turkish secondary education is to furnish students with a general core of knowledge that will prepare them for a profession and for higher education. The various curricula offered are either 3 to 4 years, emphasizing general, vocational, or technical education. These curricular pathways are offered in either general high schools or vocational–technical high schools. The general secondary school is divided into six categorical types: General High School, Foreign Language High School, Anatolian High School, Science High School, Anatolian Fine Arts High School, and Anatolian Teacher Preparatory High School.[50]

The General High School offers a 3-year program that serves as a foundation for higher education. The Foreign Language High School has a 4-year curriculum especially created for students who demonstrate high academic achievement. The curriculum also provides a strong foundation for further education work in higher education. The Ministry of Higher Education created these high schools in the 1992–1993 school year as a way to accommodate the needs of high academic achievers. The Anatolian High School also was created to challenge gifted students. These schools differ from the Foreign Language High School in that instruction uses a foreign language. Often, instruction is in English. Another difference of the Anatolian High School from the Foreign Language High School is that students are admitted on the basis of passing a competitive placement examination. Both schools have curricula that require 4 years of study.

Also addressing gifted students, the Ministry of National Education created the Science High School in 1982. This school was designed specifically for students who demonstrate exceptional giftedness in mathematics and science. These schools are all boarding schools. Instruction is in Turkish. The educational experiences stress conducting research and engaging in laboratory activities. The Anatolian Fine Arts High School, established in 1989, also caters to gifted students, in this case in the various fine arts. This high school has a 4-year program, the first year being devoted to intense foreign language learning.

The sixth high school type is the Anatolian Teacher Preparatory High School. These schools have a 4-year curriculum geared to preparing students to enter the university specializing in teacher education. Students take a broad base of basic knowledge and liberal arts courses as well as courses in educational theory, various methods of instruction, and the history of education.

Regardless of the type of secondary school, all offer the same core curriculum: "Turkish language and literature, religious culture and ethics, history, geography, mathematics, physics, chemistry, biology, health, foreign language, physical education, military science, history of the Turkish revolution and the reforms of Atatürk, and philosophy." Besides these core subjects, students attending the General High Schools, the Anatolian High Schools, and the Foreign Language High Schools have a choice of a subject concentration in six disciplines: science, social studies, Turkish language and literature and mathematics, foreign language, fine arts, or sports. Students enrolled in Science High Schools have only one choice: concentration in science. Those students attending the Anatolian Fine Arts High Schools can either major in art or music.[51]

## Teacher Education

As noted previously, education has been deemed essential to the successful development of Turkey. Embracing the centrality of education stimulated the establishment of the Anatolian Teacher Preparatory High School. Individuals wishing to become teachers must enroll in this high school and complete the program. After graduation, they must meet the entrance requirements established by a university faculty of education. Those wishing to be primary education teachers focusing on the first 5 grades must successfully complete a 4-year bachelor's degree program. Additionally, they must successfully exhibit mastery of teaching competencies to receive the Primary Education Teachers Certificate. If students desire to teach in grades 6, 7, and 8, additional and more specialized subject matter courses are required. Those teachers are hired for a 1-year probationary period before gaining employment as regular teachers.

Completion of a 4-year bachelor's program is required for those who wish to teach at the secondary school level. For teacher graduates aiming to teach in certain secondary schools, such as the Foreign Language or Science High School, a competitive examination must be passed in the specialty stressed at the particular high school. Teachers at all levels have opportunities to advance beyond receiving bachelor's degrees. Master's and even doctorate degrees are available.

## Lessons from Turkey

For Americans, a key lesson is that similar terms are often used to define various educational organization, but these terms differ, sometimes radically, from U.S. understandings. It is important to realize this especially when comparing the performances of U.S. students with students in various countries who are classified as "high school students." Comparing the mathematics scores of U.S. high school students with scores attained by gifted mathematics students in the Science High Schools is misleading. Few U.S. students take competitive placement exams to enter U.S. high schools.

One useful lesson to consider is that Turkish high schools, in general, have a very broad offering of disciplined content compared to U.S. high schools. We know of no U.S. schools that offer curricula focusing on religious cultures. Few U.S. high schools offer courses in ethics. Few U.S. schools have extensive health curricula. Most U.S. schools do not require students other than college-track students to take courses in physics, chemistry, and biology. Few U.S. schools offer philosophy. All these courses mentioned are part of the Turkish secondary school curriculum. U.S. educators might be wise to create a core curriculum for all students that has extensive discipline coverage.

## AUSTRALIA

### Background

Australia and the United States share some similarities in their histories as well as currently. Both were claimed by the British through the actions of explorers. In Australia's case, it was Captain James Cook who, in 1770, sailed northward along the eastern shore of the continent. He claimed for Great Britain what is now the Australian state of New South Wales. The settlement of Australia was unexpectedly influenced by 13 North American colonies gaining their independence from Britain as a result of winning the American revolution and signing a peace treaty with Britain in Paris in 1783.

Up to that time, Britain had sent many of its convicts to the American colonies. After the Americans defeated the British, Great Britain required another locale where prisoners could be sent. Australia proved ideal due to its great distance from England. However, prisoners had to be guarded; this required free workers. Other free citizens of Britain also wished for a better life and emigrated to Australia. The number was small until the discovery of gold in 1851 generated a mass migration, primarily from the British isles. People sought riches. The United States was 68 years old, but the colonies making up Australia were not much older; it had been only 81 years since Cook's discovery. The U.S. gold rush happened at almost the same time, gold being discovered in California in 1849. Although the U.S. gold rush attracted people from Europe, Australia also attracted gold seekers from similar areas.

A similarity between Australia and the United States is that, especially in the New England colonies, there was an early emphasis on education as a foundation to a strong moral society. In the United States, early school emphasis was on reading so that pupils could read the bible. In Australia, by 1810, the convicts were being released from prisons and becoming a free minority. This free minority realized that a successful community required principled behavior and moral restraint.[52]

Although Australia had established a small society of freemen by 1810, there had been attention to education prior to that time. Colonists who were not prisoners wanted their children, who increased in number after women arrived, to have education and faith. The Anglican church responded. A further strengthening of the Church's involvement in education resulted from the arrival of Anglican missionaries fleeing uprisings in Tahiti. These missionaries proselytized that religion was education.

The Australian colonies supported the Church's view that education was the vehicle for fostering belief and adherence to Christian church principles. The state firmly believed that religion was essential in the quest for social and moral order and religion had to be woven into the educational experience. However, not all Christian denominations were included. In 1838, the Church Acts legitimized the Anglican, Catholic, Methodist, and Presbyterian denominations as the accepted forms of Christian worship.[53]

In the 1830s and 1840s, churches increased their hold on Australian education to an extent that concerned the central administration of the Australian colonies. The government agreed to continue government support of the denominational schools under the aegis of the Denominational Schools' Board if the churches allowed the government to establish and fund a parallel board, the Board of National Education. It was agreed to by all parties, and the Board of National Education was established in 1848. Essentially, this arrangement laid the foundations for private and public education to exist in parallel tracks.

From the middle to the latter years of the 1800s, citizens and those persons in government began to realize that the Denominational Schools' Board furnished preference to the majority Anglican population. People questioned why religious schools should receive state funds. In 1851, South Australia became the first colony to terminate funding to denominational schools. Tasmania and Western Australia followed, as did Queensland and Victoria. In 1872, New South Wales finally followed as well.

The severing of governmental support during the period of 1880 through 1900 for denominational school systems stimulated free, compulsory, and secular education. Legislation was passed in the various states that strengthened departments of education.

The last two decades of the 19th century were a period of heightened economic activity. Certain individuals amassed great fortunes in mining and various industries. Education benefited in several ways from the philanthropy that resulted. Religiously based private colleges received endowments that assured their continued developments. In Australia, the term *college*, especially when referring to private schools, is what Americans identify as a high school, or, more specifically, a private high school or academy. During this period of largesse, there occurred a major expansion of Presbyterian and Methodist Ladies Colleges (private high schools). Accompanying this educational expansion at the college level was also a growth of the grammar school.[54]

During the entire 19th century, the Australian states were separate British colonies. However, with the various economic activities and the numerous growing educational systems, there arose among the Australian colonists a nascent desire to join the colonies. In 1885, a federal council was established to do just that. The desire for union had been planted, and on January 1, 1901, the Commonwealth of Australia was proclaimed. The new parliament had its first meeting on May 9, 1901.

## The Australian Educational System

From the very beginning of nationhood, education has been part of the national goal of attaining a highly functioning society. All Australian states have compulsory attendance laws, requiring children to attend school from K to grade 10, ages 5 to 15. Education is managed by the various State departments of Education. In the Northern Territory, education receives federal funding, and education programs are administered through the Northern Territory administration.

Australians describe their schools in some ways unfamiliar to Americans. Public schools in Australia are called *government schools*. Government schools classified as primary enroll the majority of K–6 pupils. There also are secondary government schools. However, private secondary schools, attracting an increasing number of secondary-age students, are part of a K–12 private school system. Adding to name confusion are the *greater public schools*. These are mostly church sponsored and are actually private corporations.

Also different from the U.S. system of public schools is the governmental funding of private schools. Additional private schools also exist in the "Catholic systemic schools and low-fee paying Christian schools."[55] For the past several years, some Australians have spoken against using public monies to support private school education.

**PRIMARY EDUCATION.**   State governments direct primary education, which ranges from pre–year 1 to year 7 in South Australia but pre–year 1 to year 6 in the other states. In the past, states' central Boards of Education played major roles in determining curriculum, educational materials, and instructional approaches. Currently, the Boards simply provide general educational guidelines, leaving the details of curriculum development and material selection to school districts and individual schools.

Teachers create curricula designed for specific pupil populations. Teachers and support staff also produce student assessments. External assessment systems are not utilized to any extent. This has been standard practice for more than 40 years.[56]

Primary school curricula in many ways resemble those offered in the United States: reading, language study (English), writing, mathematics, general sciences, social studies, Australian history, geography, and civics. Students also can study personal development/health, commerce, computer technology, and the visual arts. Foreign languages, especially Asian languages, are also offered: Indonesian, Japanese, and Chinese. The introduction of these languages has been rather slow. Other language offerings are Italian, Spanish, French, and German. In Aboriginal schools, especially in the states of Western Australia and Northern Queensland, the Aboriginal indigenous languages are offered; these languages are offered in the Northern Territory as well.[57]

**SECONDARY EDUCATION.**   As noted previously, secondary education occurs in government (public) educational institutions as well as private secondary education institutions (colleges). Both receive governmental funds from state and federal sources. Since the early 1980s at least, there has been competition between government and private schools for funds and students. The private secondary schools seem to be winning. As noted by David T. Gamage and Takeyuki Ueyama, in the early years of the first decade of this century, the private sector was receiving billions of dollars from the Liberal and National Party Coalition Government, whereas government schools were being financially starved.[58]

With more than sufficient funds, private schools, especially at the secondary level, have generated what many Australians deem superior curricula and learning experiences. Many Australians consider the teachers better prepared. Also driving parents to enroll their students in private secondary schools are current social dynamics. Australian society is becoming more diverse. Many cultural groups comfortable in a predominantly White culture are now retreating from the increasingly diverse public social scene. Australia has experienced an increase in violence in the general society and in schools, primarily secondary schools but also middle schools. Many communities have drug problems both within and outside school boundaries. Traditional Australian values are being challenged. Many secondary students in government schools are not graduating.

There has been and continues to be an exodus to the outer suburbs surrounding Australia's major cities. Communities of like-minded individuals, often exhibiting middle-class and upper-middle-class values, are congregating in somewhat identical communities. As White middle- and upper-class Australians exit the cities proper, private schools follow. Private schools in Australia receive public funding on a per student capita basis. With this formula, students can experience more intense educational programs.[59]

Although there may be differences in the quality of instruction and depth of content coverage, the curricula of secondary governmental and private schools are essentially the same. Both systems' schools stress the following disciplines: English, mathematics, science, history, geography, economics, personal development/health, computer science, modern technology, and visual arts. Some secondary schools offer technology courses. Students planning to attend a university must pass public matriculation exams.

## Teacher Education

Individuals wishing to be teachers, whether at the primary or secondary education level, must complete a 4-year university program. In the last year of study, students take courses focused on various methods courses and the history and context of education. For students desiring an edge in the job market, there are master's degree options in educational administration, general education, and curriculum design and development. Education curricula also address the technical aspects of modern society, offering courses in computer sciences designed specifically for educators. In their last year of university study, education students, both primary and secondary levels, engage in 6 weeks of supervised student teaching.

Students preparing to be primary school teachers usually take a broad liberal arts curriculum before their senior year. Those students focusing on the secondary school often concentrate on a particular discipline such as mathematics, science, English, or history.

As is well known, teachers never really complete their education upon graduation. One program in Australia that addresses this constant need to update knowledge and pedagogical skills is the Quality Teacher Programme. This program, available to all teachers throughout Australia, addresses both primary and secondary education. Under the direction of Teaching Australia, the program encourages the creation and implementation of novel instructional methods, orchestrates research relevant to teachers' concerns, and communicates research results to educators. Additionally, Teaching Australia furnishes hands-on guidance in creating professional development courses dealing with a range of educational responsibilities.[60]

The Australian central government, in cooperation with the various states, also coordinates various National Projects, which identify and promote best practice in both curriculum and instruction. Also addressed is acquainting teachers in the field with the best resources in various curricular fields. Further, these National Projects help establish national educational networks for teachers and support staff, including administrators and supervisors. Examples of such projects include school-based action research, workshops, distance learning sessions, and the education of school project leaders.[61] In Western Australia, there is a project termed Getting It Right (GIR), which educates teachers to become specialist teachers (ST). Teachers chosen for learning to be STs are actually recommended by fellow teachers in a particular school.

Teachers chosen by their colleagues experience seven 3-day workshops over 2 years, the length of their ST appointment. The STs usually focus on numeracy and literacy for at-risk pupils and work with the classroom teacher for a half-day each week. This enables STs to collaborate with a school's teachers over a week's time.

Specialist teachers also track particular students' learnings, becoming participant–observers. At times, they assist teachers in developing particular lessons to address specific students' needs. They also serve as sounding boards for the classroom teacher.[62]

## Lessons from Australia

The Australian education system, although somewhat similar to that in the United States, does have some major differences. One difference is a strong parallel private school system supported by the government that competes with the public government schools. Such strong government support of the private system seems to have created a continued distance between social classes. Perhaps a lesson for the United States, even though we do not finance private schools directly, is to nurture in our citizens an appreciation of all citizens and a recognition that all people are needed for a smoothly functioning society.

Another lesson for us is that much innovation and assessment are managed at the local level. State education boards trust their educators. The GIR project exemplifies a confidence that teachers in local schools possess the necessary expertise.

One lesson worth noting is that in Australia, educational innovation is being encouraged by fostering cooperation and collaboration among different schools and educators. The Quality Teacher Programme does not put schools and districts into competition for funds.

## CHINA

### Background

China's history extends back at least 4,000 years. Historians classify China as one of the four cradles of civilization. From its beginning as a political entity, it has viewed education as essential to its existence. Scholars were considered of greater importance than soldiers. Educational institutions were well established by 2000 BC. However, these institutions were only for the ruling and wealthy classes, often the same peoples.

Amazingly, China had established government schools and local schools beginning in 800 BC. These schools became more common up to 400 BC. During this period, China even had established civil service examinations. These examinations determined which civil servants were competent and also reflected the views of the highly respected philosopher Confucius, who scholars believe lived from 551 to 479 BC. Confucius's ideas and views greatly influenced Chinese thought regarding government, civil service, education, and basic personal behavior. He believed in a meritocracy in which the leader of a government should be the most qualified person, not necessarily the most powerful. Also, Confucius urged that individuals should strive for great civility and accept freely their societal obligations.

A flourishing society required citizens who were gentlemen. These persons did not come primarily from the wealthy. Once leaders, through their merit, had risen to positions of power, followers were required give due respect and reverence to those people. Appropriate for education, Confucius considered that a true gentleman engaged in continuous self-examination. Today, we interpret this to mean continuous inquiry as to a person's action, knowledge possessed, and inquiries enacted.[63]

Confucius did not advocate education for the masses; indeed, he believed that most common folks lacked the abilities to attain high merit. He considered that a gentlewoman, in contrast to a gentleman, should not receive any formal education. Followers of Confucius over the centuries noted that if men were to live peacefully, they had to be molded by education. This stress on formal education, even if only for the few, influenced Chinese cultural development in all its dimensions. This influence visibly lasted until the early 1900s.[64]

In the first half of the 20th century, not only did the influence of Confucius change, but the Chinese government and the systems of education went through convulsions. The last Emperor decreed that Chinese education should be accessible to greater numbers of Chinese and that education should strive to be more modern and Western. In 1905, the civil examination system was discontinued. In 1911, China's dynastic tradition ended, replaced with the new Nationalist Republic. China entered what many called a Golden Age, in which education was recognized in thought and deed. Education expanded its offerings to increasing numbers of citizens. However, the Sino-Japanese War (1937–1939) devastated Chinese educational strides. Military action essentially destroyed 70 percent of Chinese cultural institutions, including educational institutions. Then came World War II (1939–1945).

After these military conflicts, China, instead of rebuilding its educational institutions, became engaged in a civil war that lasted from 1946 until 1949. This war pitted the Chinese nationalists against the Chinese Communists. Education not only did not advance, it retreated. The Communists were victorious and in 1949 established the People's Republic of China. The new leaders rejected Western influence on Chinese education, drawing inspiration from the then Soviet Union.

Under Communist rule, China and its educational institutions experienced turmoil. In 1958, the Ministry of Education launched educational reforms that essentially ranked mental and manual labor at equal value. Productive labor had value and was essential for China's growth as a modern nation. Labor gained legitimacy and was melded into the Chinese curricula at primary, secondary, and higher education levels. Educational experiences were divided into half work and half study.[65]

This Cultural Revolution, many argue, stagnated the development of curricula requisite for functioning in the later 20th and early 21st centuries. With the death of Mao Zedong, the leader of China since the Communist victory in 1949, the Cultural Revolution ceased. What followed and continues to evolve is major and extensive innovation at all education levels. Further affecting China is the government's drive to rapidly modernize the nation. Education has been adapted, and, more surprisingly, the Communist government has integrated free-market approaches in building a modern economy.[66]

## The Chinese Education System

Throughout China's long history, education has been central in the people's thought, especially those among the privileged ranks and those in leadership positions. As noted before, Confucius's thought has had strong influence upon leaders' actions. And although Confucius's thought fell out of favor under Mao, it appears to have regained influence in more recent times.

Currently, the Chinese government elevates education as key to the country's economic growth and political world influence. Until the 1990s, the Chinese educational system was almost completely centralized under the directive of the National Ministry of Education. The Ministry had been established in 1952 and terminated in 1966 with the blessing of Mao Zedong. In 1975, it was reestablished. It again was abolished in 1985 and reemerged as the State Education Commission. This Commission, under direct central government control, the State Council, is responsible for all educational policies, the management of educational innovations, and the establishment of educational aims and goals, as well as educational standards and measures of assessment.[67]

## State Education Commission

Although the educational system is highly centralized, governmental and educational leaders realize that for China to gain its "rightful" place as a national world leader, there must be innovative education. In the 1990s, the Commission developed curricular guidelines that encouraged the Chinese education system to decentralize education at the primary and secondary levels and to develop a quality-oriented rather than a test-oriented approach to curricula and pedagogical strategies that focused on the learner rather than content covered. Finally, the Commission urged that schools at these levels provide more in-service education.[68]

Although the State Education Commission is attempting to loosen the central educational reins of the state, it is still functioning under the aegis of the Central Committee of the Chinese Communist Party and the State Council. To an outsider, the State Education Commission appears to be attempting to follow two contradictory directives: allow for more openness in educational matters to foster diversity of thinking among the populace, but not to the extent that divergence of political thought encourages protest and dissent.[69]

Still, the State Education Commission is lessening its grip on the curricula at all levels of education. It is encouraging states, local communities, and local schools to create more flexible curricula and allow students some choices among various curricula. The Commission encourages teachers in local schools and local and state governments to collaboratively develop curricular materials and select textbooks. The effort encourages educators to rely less on formalized testing and to employ more learner-centered educational activities.[70]

The State Education Commission directives have nurtured extensive changes regarding assessments in general and examinations in particular. The Commission urged the abolishment of the entrance examination for middle school, which had prevented some elementary students from continuing their education, at least at a quality school. The Commission strongly suggested that elementary and secondary schools create their own graduation examinations. The general public, parents, and students were to be involved in discussions of how to evaluate their schools.[71]

The primary purposes of these recommended changes were to "equip students with patriotism, collectivism, a love for socialism, and the Chinese cultural traditions, as well as moral-ethic values and a democratic spirit with Chinese characteristics."[72] "Furthermore, the new curriculum has as its goal fostering creativity, developing practical abilities, and cultivating scientific and humanistic spirits as well as environmental awareness."[73]

**PRIMARY EDUCATION.**    The Chinese primary school involves a 6-year program. Attendance is compulsory. In cities and urban areas, children often enter primary schools having experienced 1 year of kindergarten. Children in rural areas usually do not have kindergarten experience, or, if so, the experience is not a quality one.

As recently as 1999, primary schools were under the rigid control of the State Education Commission. Curricula were standardized, and instructional approaches were common throughout the nation. However, the central government pushed to encourage more local control in creating curricula, developing pedagogical approaches, constructing educational materials, and even selecting a variety of textbooks. All this is under the push for quality education.

Even with the encouragement of local curriculum development by teachers and local community members, the major subjects of the primary school—at least considered globally—are similar to the curricula of "preinnovation" primary schools. Chinese is offered, including reading, composition, and speaking. Other subject areas are arithmetic, natural science, politics, geography, history, music, art, and physical education. Since the mid-1990s, foreign languages have been offered, with English as a major offering; English is now mandatory, usually starting in grade 3. Some primary schools offer English in grade 1.[74]

Perhaps the greatest change in the primary school has been in instruction. Before the push for innovation, there was great stress on rote learning and memorization. The teacher expected uniformity of understanding. Pupils were to sit quietly listening to the teacher and repeating information presented. Today, primary schools exhibit a greatly altered picture.

Increasing numbers of primary school classrooms have pupils engaged in class discussions, various types of group work, and even role-playing.[75] Students are participating in cooperative learning, investigating problems in real-world situations in mathematics, environmental science, or social studies. Students are encouraged to engage in *challenge groups,* where student investigators have to defend and define their methodologies of investigation. Students also are, under teacher guidance, learning to write investigative reports. In science and mathematics, pupils derive formulas that explain and support their individual or collaborative work.[76]

In addition to innovative instruction, many primary school children also have access to the latest instructional technology. Computers are available for student use. Instructional computer programs engage students in their studies.

The preceding description of a modern primary school and its classrooms is not the norm in China. Such ideal schools exist primarily within cities. And, often, the students in these schools are from the wealthy and other privileged elites. There are more than 200 million students in primary and secondary schools. Approximately 80 percent of these students live in rural areas, where schools and educational services are scarce and, where available, not of high quality.

The State Education Commission's major challenge is bringing new educational ideas and excellence in teaching to all students throughout the country. Essentially, the aim is to have 9-year compulsory education adhered to and delivered with excellence. The aim has not been widely achieved in part because rural communities cannot afford to pay salaries for highly qualified teachers. Even if monies in rural communities were sufficient, which is not the case, many highly trained teachers do not wish to teach in rural communities, preferring city life.

Another difficulty for rural communities is that with about 600 million people, the average living wage is $2 per day. Families surviving on such meager wages cannot afford to pay teachers high salaries; nor can these parents afford to purchase high-quality educational materials. Often, the lack of electricity creates a roadblock to the use of educational technology.

Although the rural schools' curricula somewhat resemble that of urban schools, the curricula are taught mostly by teachers who have completed only a 2-year teacher-preparation program. In some rural communities, primary teachers have completed only primary school themselves. Those teachers who have earned a bachelor's degree usually have attained it through a distance education program.[77]

**SECONDARY EDUCATION.**    Compulsory-education laws require that students, upon completion of primary school, finish 3 years of secondary school. For students desiring to continue their education, some secondary schools offer an additional 3 years of education. China has had a tradition of dividing its secondary schools into *key* and *ordinary* schools. Key secondary schools offer a curriculum perceived as more rigorous academically than that offered in ordinary secondary schools. Initially, key schools were to educate students gifted in various knowledge areas deemed necessary for China's advance into the modern world.[78]

Key secondary schools are staffed by the best teachers. These schools also have first choice of the latest textbooks and educational materials. In some key schools, teachers and support staff actually create textbooks and support materials. Most frequently, key secondary schools are found in China's major cities. Often key students are children of the privileged classes: government workers, major Community Party members, business executives and other high-level employees, and others who have key contacts within the urban community.

It is not commonly known that these key schools, either 3-year or 6-year, accept only students whose parents have contacts within the city community. Exceptions are made for students with exceptional talents if they live within the city's boundaries. Students whose parents have migrated to the city to work cannot send their children to the city's public schools. These workers have to send their children back to their home communities for their education at the secondary level. In many cases, this is not possible. And, if it is possible, most likely the secondary school is classified as ordinary.[79] As Kam Wing Chan notes, "this is engineered by the discriminatory 'hukou,' or household registration system, which classifies them as 'outsiders.'"[80] This practice exists in most Chinese cities. In Shanghai, there are 3 million to 4 million people, essentially the working poor, but the city school system is not obligated to provide an education to these people's children. A problem of this policy, besides denying these students an education, is that it creates divides among various social strata. Also, it limits the development of talent.[81]

Because students who attend these select schools have the highest success rate in being accepted into elite colleges in China and even in distant countries, there is a major push among privileged children to do well in school in order to get into a prestigious college. A great deal of pressure is placed on these children to do well in school. In fact, most Chinese parents view education as their children's primary job.

Grouping key and ordinary secondary schools, we still find discrepancies in the offerings of secondary school education. At the end of the 20th century, 70 percent of the Chinese population lived in rural areas. However, for this vast rural population, the number of secondary schools available was only 20 percent of the total number of schools. Thus, 80 percent of secondary schools were available to serve a highly select 30 percent of the population.[82] Although the current percentages of schools available to particular populations may have changed somewhat, the general pattern continues.

It appears that the secondary school curricula in global terms focus on the same broad disciplined areas. It also appears that the State Education Commission has mandated that all secondary schools utilize innovative educational materials and pedagogical strategies. However, the city schools have superior materials and more-qualified teachers. In some rural secondary schools, there is even a lack of chairs and desks.

The curriculum offered at secondary schools, regardless of type, includes studies in Chinese, mathematics, English, political ideology and morality, political and legal knowledge, philosophy, economics, physics, chemistry, biology, geography, and history. Computer science is also offered where possible. Physical education, art, and music are also taught. Most curricular courses are studied for the duration of secondary school, either 3 or 6 years. Geography and history are offered for 3 years. Computer science requires 1 year of study.[83]

As noted, China in this century has created educational policies and offered structured encouragement to create more flexible curricula while still focusing on the key disciplines. It also has urged state and local school levels to facilitate utilization of novel pedagogies. In many cases, there has been success. However, one thrust has not attained the desired success level: the drive to deemphasize testing, especially objective standardized testing to rank and group students.

Betty Preus has noted that in China, parents, community members, and teachers realize that for pupils to maximize their potential for success, they must do well in school, and exams still reign supreme. Teachers realize that students must do well through both primary and secondary schools. Success in passing exams at the primary level increases students' odds of getting into a key secondary school. Students excelling at the secondary level must do well on the national university entrance examination. Even students at ordinary secondary schools must excel and pass exams to gain admission to vocational and technical schools.[84]

This attachment to testing, despite government urgings to view assessment as less central to quality education, has proved difficult to lessen. However, some progress is being made. In some schools, students are participating in developing their own means of evaluation. Yet this move to less attention on formal assessment, for example, examination, seems not to be having much impact on schooling in rural areas. In these areas, teacher tests and formal examinations are still widely used.

## Teacher Education

Teacher education is under the guidance of the Teacher Education Bureau, one of the many bureaus of the State Education Commission. This bureau is charged with creating teacher education policies and providing strong guidance to teacher education. Additionally, the Bureau manages directives for structuring the curriculum and the admission requirements of education students.[85]

In the last decade of the 20th century, the Teacher Education Bureau initiated a series of innovations to make teacher education more responsive to the then-approaching 21st century. The goal, which has essentially been attained, is for all education students to have 4 years of undergraduate education. As of 2007, there were some primary teachers who still had only 3 years of training. In the first decade of this century, an increasing number of teachers, especially those planning to teach in city schools, were obtaining graduate degrees.[86]

The improvement of teaching in China's schools not only addressed raising the quality of preservice education, but also attended to in-service education. Chinese authorities realized that practicing teachers at primary and secondary levels needed to be "retooled." Such education addressed specific needs of the teachers. Some in-service courses stimulated particular research projects aimed at ameliorating particular education problems.[87]

The Chinese government today, while ramping up attempts at bringing innovative and diverse teacher education programs into higher education, is constantly dealing with echoes from a past in which teacher education was rigidly regulated by the State and Communist Party. Chinese educational thinkers are attempting to be creative within state-mandated rigid confines. The quality-education movement, which is stressing creativity and innovation, applies only to the economy and technology. There exists a damper on innovation and creativity within the political realm.

In observing the curricula offered education students, there is a sameness of disciplined offerings: educational foundation courses, second languages, instructional strategies courses, psychology, philosophy, history of education, sociology, moral education, and physical education. At the secondary-level curriculum are the major academic disciplines: mathematics, history, sociology, biology, chemistry, and physics. Today, courses are offered in computer science for both primary and secondary teachers, especially those preparing to teach in urban schools. In some cases, primary teachers specialize in particular subject areas. All teacher education students have a teaching practicum. This practicum, usually 6 weeks long, occurs in the third and fourth years of the educational program.[88]

## Lessons from China

Perhaps the most important lesson for American educators, and especially American politicians and the American public, is that test scores on standardized tests that solely report a nation's students' achievement essentially offer no useful information. As we have learned, in China most test scores reported are very misleading. As Kam Wing Chan has noted, comparing U.S. students' scores with the scores attained by students in Shanghai's schools is like comparing the scores of students attending select schools in New York City with students of an entire other country.[89]

Another lesson to consider is that China is moving toward empowering local schools to assume more responsibility for their curricula, pedagogies, and means of assessment. American politicians and some educators are urging an opposite thrust.

Another lesson is that we must always consider the cultural, political, and geographic contexts of the nation to which we compare ourselves. In China, parents judge how well their children are doing in school by external indicators: "grades, test scores," and "admission to prestigious universities."[90] To Chinese parents, their child's number 1 job *is* school. This puts tremendous stress on children, particularly those attending city schools. Also, in China, conformity is the norm. A person must fit in with his or her group. The push for academic excellence often means that subjects and activities that American parents consider important to their children's total development, such as art, music, and sports, may be perceived as detrimental to serious study. As Zhao posits, many Chinese students, in attempting to reach high external standards of success, develop a loss of self-confidence and a belief in the value of external metrics of motivation.[91]

## BRAZIL

### Background

The Federative Republic of Brazil can be considered the United States of South America. Like the United States, it takes up a vast amount of the South American continent. Brazil touches the borders of all of the other South American countries save Ecuador and Chile.[92] Also, like the United States, it was once ruled by colonial masters, Portuguese in Brazil's case. During its colonial period and even after it gained its independence from Portugal, it was a slave society, ending the practice only in 1888. Another similarity with the United States is its vast wealth of natural resources. Further, Brazil is a land essentially occupied by immigrants.[93] Much like the United States, these various peoples have melded together, even those with ancestors who were slaves. Although there are various groups in Brazil, standings are determined more by social and economic rankings than by racial and ethnic backgrounds. Still, Brazil does have racial issues, which educational and other institutions are attempting to address.

Brazil's history is longer than the United States'. Although ours officially began in 1607 with the establishment of Jamestown in Virginia, Brazil's presence was established in 1549 with the arrival of Jesuit missionaries. They established an elementary school in a settlement named Salvador, in Bahia state. The Jesuits' aim was not only to educate the indigenous peoples, but also to bring the Christian faith to them. The Jesuits created and controlled the educational system in the Brazilian colony for 210 years. During this time, these missionaries established primary and secondary schools, primarily for the arriving settlers.[94]

The Jesuit educational system ended in 1759, when the Portuguese King José I's minister, the Marquis of Pombal, ordered all Jesuits expelled from Portugal and its colonies, including Brazil. Pombal believed that education in Portugal and the colonies should serve the state and not the church. Even though the edict was enacted, the new emphasis for education had little effect on the actual curriculum.

During the 1800s, there were some major changes in Brazilian education. From 1808 until the beginnings of the 1820s, Brazil actually became the Kingdom of Portugal. The Portuguese royal family went to Brazil to escape the invasion of French troops under Napoleon's command. The King authorized the creation of numerous schools and even some scientific centers.

All this abruptly ended in 1822, when Brazil declared its independence from Portugal. Brazil's Constitution, ratified in 1824, afforded free elementary education to all citizens. Secondary education seems to have escaped governmental concern. The new government decentralized the educational system, giving the various provinces authority to chart the direction of elementary education. This administrative arrangement lasted for a little more than 100 years. From the 1920s onward, Brazil's central government used its control of schools to address educational challenges.

For most of the 20th century, Brazil experienced turmoil—essentially two revolutions. In 1964, the military overthrew the government in a coup. This dictatorship lasted until 1980. Despite military rule with limited freedoms for the masses, government actions did favor education. In 1970, the government moved to eliminate adult illiteracy. In 1971, the government passed a law that altered the structure of elementary and secondary education, expanding basic education from 4 to 8 years and making attendance compulsory.[95] The law, although frequently amended, guided education well into the 1990s. The central government went into the 21st century not in the strongest position to exercise its authority. Captains of industry and the influence of international firms handicapped the federal government.

Despite its many problems, Brazil has evolved from an agricultural past into a major industrialized nation. Manufactured products make up 90 percent of its economy, agricultural products making up the remaining 10 percent. After Seattle, Washington, and Toulouse, France, Sao Paulo is the third major center of airplane production and design. Of 500 major companies throughout South America, 80 percent are Brazilian owned.[96]

## The Brazilian Education System

There are 26 states and a Federal District in Brazil. The management of Brazil's education involves a collaboration among federal, state, and municipal government organizations. At the federal level, the Ministry of Education creates legislation determining and implementing educational policy and furnishes financial assistance according to need. Educational policy is developed by an advisory panel to the Ministry of Education. Panel members are appointed educators having national stature. This council sets standards and offers recommendations as to appropriate curricula and pedagogical approaches.

In Brazil, there are four levels, or *cycles,* in the educational system: primary school, middle school, higher school, and advanced school. The primary school, offering 8 years of study, is similar to our American elementary school and middle or junior high school. The middle school, or middle education level, similar to our secondary school, engages students in 3 or 4 years of study. However, this level of schooling is often identified as college level, as is done in some secondary schools in Australia. The first two Brazilian levels of schooling are compulsory and free.[97]

**PRIMARY SCHOOL (ELEMENTARY EDUCATION).**    The primary school, mandatory for children aged 7 to 14, is managed by either state or local municipalities/townships. However, the direction of management is determined by educational policies mandated by the Ministry of Education. The Ministry, as previously noted, is guided in its actions by an advisory panel of recognized educational authorities. Educational standards and the basic structure of the schools' curriculum are shaped by this council.

The primary schools' curricula have two areas of emphasis: common and diversified. The common dimension serves as a mandatory core, defined specifically by the Ministry of

Education. The diversified areas of study are within the purview of the various state boards of education. Local or municipal school authorities also are authorized by the state boards to participate in designing and implementing curricula in the diversified realm.[98]

The common core furnishes students with basic disciplined knowledge and skills. Stressed throughout the total curriculum are reading, writing, and arithmetic. Upper grades include literature, language usage and composition, and the beginnings of more advanced mathematics. Also offered at increasingly age-appropriate levels of difficulty are earth science, contemporary Brazilian society, and civics.

The diversified realm concentrates on the specific needs of the local student populations. However, all schools teach the Portuguese language, emphasizing written- and spoken-language skills and concepts. Also, this area of the curriculum deals with geography, sociology, history, political science, general science (with special emphasis on earth science and biology), and in the upper grades, a more advanced mathematics.

Although the curriculum is divided into a common core and a diversified area, the pedagogy utilized in primary education is as varied as we would find in the United States. Ideally, instructional methods are personalized to students' specific and myriad needs. At the end of the 20th century and continuing in this century are attempts by teachers to engage students more actively in their learning.

A Brazilian educator, Paulo Freire, attempted to change the nature and purpose of Brazilian education, instruction included. This educator, whom your authors associate with radical educators, also influenced education in the United States to some degree. Freire firmly believed that Brazilian education, for most of its modern history, aimed at keeping the Brazilian populace oppressed. There is some truth to this view in that Brazil was ruled for extensive periods of time by the military. He believed, as did many teachers—especially at the primary school level—that educational methods should assist students in recognizing their oppression and freeing themselves via their studies and means of inquiry. Students should collaborate in teams to actively investigate curricular topics. Teachers should challenge students, not just present material.[99] Brazil is both a modern developed nation and an evolving, developing nation, and its schools and their curricular and pedagogical approaches reflect this duality.

**MIDDLE (SECONDARY) EDUCATION.**    Middle education involves students from ages 15 to 18 or 19, comparable to the U.S. high school. Attending middle education is not compulsory. At the end of the 20th century, less than 20 percent of secondary-age students attended middle schools. However, among those who did attend, significant numbers took evening classes. This was due to many students having to work during the day, which was especially true in rural areas. In this century, more secondary school students are taking these schools' offerings. Still, many young people are not receiving an education because of widespread poverty, not only in rural areas, but in Brazil's major cities.

As noted, Brazil is a developed (modern) nation and a developing (second-world) nation. These are many reasons for this duality. The rate of change in Brazil from developing- (second-world) to developed- (first-world) nation status has overwhelmed many aspects of Brazil's governmental and social management at all levels. As agriculture became mechanized, fewer people were needed in rural areas. These people flooded into the cities, usually without the skills for employment in the modern industrial and service industries sectors. Additionally, the various industries became more mechanized, thus requiring fewer workers.[100]

Major cities, such as Rio de Janeiro and Sao Paulo in the southeastern coastal area, were not able to accommodate the influx. Cities in northeastern Brazil, such as Recife and Salvador, faced and still face the same dilemma. These hoards of peoples created communities—actually, slums called *favelas*—in areas deemed unsuitable for settlement. People living in these *favelas* are mainly concerned with surviving. Faced with scraping together what little work they can and living in shacks, these individuals, especially the youths, do not consider education a high priority.[101]

Attracting the rural and urban poor to formal education is a major challenge for Brazil. These school-age children are viewed by their parents as necessary workers to assist the families in getting by. As recently as 2004, Crouch concluded that "the distribution of income and social opportunity" in Brazil is "among the most unequal in the world."[102]

The secondary school curriculum continues those subjects and disciplines introduced in the primary school, although at more advanced levels. The curriculum has dual aims: to prepare students to succeed in higher, or university, education or to succeed in advanced technical/ professional schools. All secondary school students must take a foreign language plus Portuguese, stressing communication, writing, grammar, and literature. The requirement for a foreign language may be a new requirement for some students, depending on the particular primary school they attended. Advanced mathematics is offered for students preparing for university education. Business/technical mathematics is designed for students planning to enter technical and professional fields. Chemistry, biology, physics, and earth science make up the science offerings. History, geography, sociology, and economics are the social science offerings. Students also have options in music and art. Although much of the curriculum is part of the common core, the diversified curriculum allows for variety in both content and methodology. As Brazil furthers its modern development, it is quite likely that this level will become compulsory.[103]

## Teacher Education

Teachers in Brazil were trained, if at all, in professional teaching schools, *Curso Normal,* very similar to the normal schools in the United States. In the mid-1930s, again somewhat similar to what occurred in the United States, the training of teachers attained a bit more structure. Students had to complete a specifically created teacher-certification course of study. However, students could enter this program if they had competed only primary education (elementary and middle school education in the United States). However, if students desired to teach at the primary school, they could gain entry into the profession with graduation from primary level education, bypassing the certification program. Individuals who wished to teach at the secondary level had to complete a teaching-certification course. This changed in the 1950s, with those planning to be secondary school teachers being required to possess a college degree. Primary teachers did not need a degree until later in the 20th century. Today, teachers at both levels must possess college degrees. Many students choosing education enroll in higher-education institutions, focusing on human and social sciences or applied social sciences. Along with courses that focus on various professions in these areas, students take courses specifically designed for careers in education.[104]

Most teachers in urban areas today have college degrees in some subject specialty. However, in rural areas not only is there a scarcity in actual schools, but a scarcity of well-educated teachers. Also there is a major problem in establishing schools within the urban slums, or *favelas.* "Many Brazilians consider the country's *favelas* too dangerous to enter—and thus do their best to ignore their existence altogether."[105] Teachers are included among those who fear these slums. However, the Brazilian government is not ignoring the challenges of education. Today, there is a National Institute for Pedagogical Studies conducting educational research and also establishing a repository of educational research done elsewhere.[106]

## Lessons from Brazil

Every nation has unique history, geography, demography, culture, sociology, economics, politics, and, more often than not, aspirations. This being the case, any lessons to be learned from considering Brazil, or any other country discussed in this chapter, should be carefully pondered.

Brazil is unique because in many ways it is similar to the United States in its size, its political and economic dominance, its cultural diversity, and, to some extent, its challenges of addressing educational opportunity and equity.[107] However, we must recognize that although both countries have numerous diverse cultures, there are major differences in these cultures, their interactions and their perceptions of themselves socially, culturally, and politically. Perhaps the central lesson to grasp in considering Brazil is to remember what Parag Khanna noted: "[A]s Brazil goes, so goes South America."[108] We can draw from this statement: As Brazil goes, so goes the U.S. relationship with the Western Hemisphere.

## REPUBLIC OF SOUTH AFRICA

### Background

Harm de Blij noted in 2005 that among Americans, the continent of Africa, especially the region south of the Sahara, is mostly in the realm of the unknown: *terra incognita.* The exception to our knowledge situation is the Republic of South Africa.[109]

American awareness of South Africa is largely due to it being the most economically developed and wealthiest African nation. Additionally, much of its history has been influenced by Dutch and British colonial rule. The British connection has motivated many Americans to consider this nation. Also, South Africa's 1948 separation of the White European citizens from all other non-White citizens, a policy called *apartheid,* brought international negative attention to South Africa.

Today, apartheid is no longer national policy. South Africa reigns as Africa's main economic powerhouse with strong economic and political connections with the global community.

South Africa's strategic location at the most southern part of the African continent has motivated various European groups over the centuries to engage in battles for control. In 1652, the Dutch established a base, now Cape Town, for the East India Company. The prime reason for the base was to supply provisions to Dutch ships rounding the Cape of Good Hope, destined to points east. The indigenous peoples, mainly people identified as the Khoi Khoi, early became concerned that these Whites had intentions of staying. This view was confirmed in 1658, when the Dutch East India Company established the first school, mainly for imported Black slaves.[110]

The Dutch were not alone in recognizing the value of this land. Indeed, Europeans, even during the 1500s, had sited trading posts along the west coast of Africa. However, these early posts and surrounding settlements remained primarily on the coastal areas,[111] but, early in the 1700s, Dutch traders and settlers increased their numbers pushing the native peoples from their lands. Following the Dutch came British, French, and Germans. In 1795, the British invaded the Cape area, pushing out the Dutch. The British returned it to the Dutch in 1803 and retook it in 1806. The 1820s saw increasing British settlement in a region about 800 miles east of Cape Town. Between the Dutch and the British, the indigenous peoples were pushed further from their historical lands. Toward the end of the 19th century, Europeans controlled all the African peoples' territories.

As increasing numbers of British emigrated to the region, the Dutch became alarmed at potentially being colonized by the British. Therefore, in 1836, the Dutch commenced what is now called the "Great Trek." In this trek, the Dutch migrated from the Cape region to the interior region. Here they discovered fertile lands and ample water. However, the region was also inhabited by native peoples. As they did in the Cape region, the Dutch pushed the indigenous peoples from their lands, often hiring them as laborers. In time, the Dutch established two republics in this area: the Transvaal and the Orange Free State. During this time, the Dutch had also created their own language, Afrikaans. Today, outside of Pretoria, there is a monument to the Afrikaans language, the only monument to a language in the world. Today, Africaans is still the major language in the country, with English a close second. There are nine other native languages spoken in the country.

With the Dutch vacated from the Cape region, the British established Cape Colony and Natal. However, with the discovery of diamonds in 1867 and gold in the 1870s in the two Dutch states, the British eventually declared war against the Dutch, resulting in the Anglo–Boer War, 1899–1902. The British were victorious, but they later realized that to maintain dominance over the native peoples, they needed to align themselves with the Dutch. In 1909, the Dutch (the Boers) and the British signed an agreement that essentially laid the foundation for combining the Dutch and British territories into one nation. In 1910, the nation, the Union of South Africa, became part of the British Empire.[112]

Although the new nation, actually a British colony, solidified European power, including the German and French settlers, the national arrangement still disadvantaged the Blacks, who made up more than 75 percent of the population. Schools, mostly organized and managed by church groups (primarily the Dutch Reformed Church) were established to serve different racial groups. Schools for the Europeans, primarily Dutch, British, French, and Germans, aimed to install in the White children that it was their right to have dominance over the indigenous peoples in all matters, social, economic, and political. Other schools, also primarily administered by religious organizations, did create curricula for the natives, stressing Western culture and Christianity.[113]

The indigenous Africans perhaps at first welcomed the inclusion of their lands under the rule of the British Empire, but they certainly were not content playing subordinate roles in what they perceived as their country. In 1912, the native Africans created the South African Native National Conference, later known as the African National Congress. What made this Congress unique was that it was the first ever organization on the African continent to have various indigenous tribes cooperate and collaborate to gain political dominance in their country.[114]

In 1931, Great Britain granted complete independence to South Africa. Independence did not bring peace and harmony to the various European settlers. Conflicts continued, primarily between the British and the Dutch—the Boers. Seeking to control the new nation, the Boers, identifying themselves as Afrikaaners, established the National Party in 1933. The National Party gained control of the nation in the 1948 election. Non-White South Africans were not allowed to vote. With the National Party in power, it introduced the policy of apartheid, the complete separation of Europeans and non-Europeans.[115]

The policy of apartheid not only prohibited the mixing of non-Europeans, the indigenous peoples, with Europeans, it further ruled that particular ethnic groups had to live separately in particular areas, called *homelands*. These homelands were developed in various parts of the country. Non-Whites had to commute from their homelands to their workplaces. If they worked in the cities, they were required to have passes and documentation to explain the reason they were within city boundaries.

Although schools in South Africa had essentially neglected the education of the natives in the past, the schools for the natives (Black), Coloreds (mixed race), and Asian Indians (people originally from India) were even more oppressive under apartheid. No longer was their education to make them Western. The Bantu Education Act was passed by the White government in 1953, putting the education of Blacks, Coloreds, and Indians under direct government control.

The government's stance on the education of non-Whites was made clear by the then Minister of Native Affairs, a Mr. Verwoerd:

> There is no place for him (the Black African), in the European community above the level of certain forms of labour . . . for that reason it is of no avail for him to receive a training which has as its aim absorption in the European community, where he cannot be absorbed.[116]

Almost as soon as the Bantu Education Act went into effect, there was resistance from the Blacks, Coloreds, and Indians of South Africa. Indeed, non-European South Africans had protested their conditions before the Bantu Act. The African National Congress became a thorn in the government's side, so much so that the national government outlawed the party in 1960. Resistance went underground. In the late 1960s, a "Black Consciousness" movement gained ground. To counter its effectiveness in rousing the people, including liberal White South Africans, the government outlawed the Black Consciousness movement in 1977. Violence had erupted the previous year, 1976, at schools in a homeland, Soweto (Southwest township). One trigger to the violence was the students' demand that the language of instruction not be the mother tongue of the particular students' ethnic group. The students felt that such instruction limited their learnings and options after school. Most students also shunned the official national language, Afrikaans. They wanted English. English was the high-status language; it had more utility both within and outside the country. The government ignored the demands. Students rioted in the streets of Soweto. Some students were shot and killed. Although the government quelled the uprising, the students did receive the option of having their instruction either in Afrikaans or English. Most students selected English.[117]

The masses continued to push for their rights as full citizens of South Africa. In February 1990, F. W. DeKlerk, the last White head of state, lifted the bans on the various political organizations. Political prisoners, the most famous being Nelson Mandela, were released. The nation was on a new path. A major waypoint was achieved in 1994 with South Africa's first democratic election. The people elected Nelson Mandela as the first indigenous president. The following year, an Education White Paper was produced that presented "the vision for a new racially integrated education system based upon the principles of democracy, equity and the redress of past inequalities."[118]

## The South African Education System

Today, the Republic of South Africa is a parliamentary democracy. Attaining this form of representative government has been challenging. Among all African nations, especially among those in Sub-Saharan Africa, South Africa is the most technologically developed and modern nation, as well as being a democracy. However, it confronts numerous challenges that have resulted from the region's past actions. The educational system is playing a major role in addressing many past inequities: educating all learners through the age of 15 or grade 9, ensuring quality educational experiences, fostering a strong belief in democracy, reducing racism and sexism, raising people out of poverty, developing appreciations of diverse cultures and languages, and fostering allegiance to the nation.[119]

## The Department of Education

South Africa's basic aims and goals are articulated by the Department of Education. Directives for enacting guidelines at the provincial and local levels also come from the department. The provincial educational departments oversee both public and private schools at the various levels: preprimary, primary, secondary, and higher education. The specific creation of curriculum and the organization of instruction are undertaken by local school authorities.[120]

Perhaps the department's greatest challenge is equalizing educational access and occasions for quality education. Throughout the nation, there is a great disparity among educational options for those living in both rural and urban areas. In urban areas, many children live in slum cities. Few slum cities have schools. Rural areas do have some schools, but they rank far below city schools in quality.

Adding to the problems of rural schools is the fact that few teachers wish to teach in them. Also, the rural poor have other issues besides having their children attend school. Daily chores usually carried out by rural school-age children take precedence over formal education. Schools in city slums also have difficulty attracting teachers.[121]

Despite slow progress, the Department of Education remains committed to improving education for all students. The movement to quality education did receive a boost, at least at the conceptual level, from a policy document, *Curriculum 2005,* which outlined a new national framework for curriculum development and implementation. Innovation in both curriculum and instruction was directed to start in grade 1 and continue through the various grade levels. The concept of outcomes-based learning was integral to the suggested innovation. The new curricula and instructional strategies were to be perfected by a decentralized educational system.[122]

*Curriculum 2005* called for a systems' break. No longer was education to fill up students' heads with knowledge and skills sets. No longer was the purpose of education just to pass tests to graduate to the next educational level. The educational experience was to develop in students the disposition of lifelong learning. This learning called for interactions among learners and between learners and teachers. Teachers were urged and educated to be facilitators, not just deliverers of information.

In this century, education has improved. The stress on outcomes-based education has been softened. The stress of interactive learning and putting students in control of their learning has been achieved in some schools, mostly urban schools. Some interpret the softening of outcomes-based education as meaning that it never really was introduced effectively. Certainly, South Africa at the primary and secondary levels still has a long way to travel before it overcomes the apartheid legacy: keeping the Whites privileged and denying the rest of the people their rights.

**PRIMARY EDUCATION.**   The primary school in South Africa engages students in 6 years of study starting at age 6. The curriculum in the first 3 years emphasizes reading, writing, and arithmetic. Additionally, study of a foreign language is introduced. Most instruction is given in either Afrikaans or English. Foreign languages are usually selected from one of the remaining nine national languages. However, students are not limited to these nine national languages. Because of the large numbers of Asian Indians, there is demand for Hindi and other major Indian languages.

In the remaining 3 years of primary school, students focus on the following discipline and subject areas: mathematics, general science, environmental studies, history, geography, health education, and language, including the student's first language and the foreign language previously selected. The curriculum also stresses physical education, art, and music, often reflecting the local cultural groups where the school is located.[123]

As noted before, teachers are urged to be facilitators rather than lecturers. On paper, it appears that instruction stresses inquiry and group investigations. However, many teachers still favor "teaching as telling." One issue confronting teachers in both urban and rural schools is the scarcity of quality educational materials.

**SECONDARY EDUCATION.**   Secondary education involves 6 years, grades 7 through 12. In the first 3 years, the curriculum has some flexibility, stressing a broad knowledge of the various disciplines, introduced in the later primary grades. In the last 3 years, students select a discipline area for concentrated study. The discipline areas offered are general and commercial education; natural sciences, such as biology and chemistry; social sciences, such as geography, anthropology, and sociology; history; technical studies, such as computer science; art; and, finally, agriculture. Primary language and foreign language studies continue. Essentially, the curricula in these last 3 years are offered to allow students to either enter the workforce with specific knowledge and skills or advance to higher education, either at the university or technical school levels.[124]

Pedagogical approaches in the first 3 years involve collaborative learning and an open-ended inquiry emphasis. During the last 3 years of secondary study, students engage in more apprentic-like and lablike learnings. Teachers assume more supervisory roles in their pedagogical methods. Of course, these methods are the ideal.

### Teacher Education

For most of South Africa's history, teacher education has been sporadic. As did most other professions, teacher education evolved as the demand for more-educated citizens increased. In South Africa's case, teacher education was hindered by the separation of the Whites from all other groups. This was commonplace well before the official implementation of apartheid. For those few Black, Colored, and Indian children who did attend school, the teachers often had little more education than the students being taught.

In the late 1800s, at least among the White population, the view that teachers should have some formal education to mold young minds arose. Early forms of formal teacher education were established in colleges that were quite similar to U.S. normal schools. These institutions followed a similar evolvement, becoming teacher-training colleges. Teacher-training colleges furnished the majority of teachers until 1998, at which time teacher education shifted from the college level to the university level.

Many teachers colleges did not wish to lose their identities and chose to become affiliated with particular universities. With this arrangement, teacher education students could apply their college credits toward particular university degrees. This connection strengthened in 2005 with the publication of the National Qualifications Framework. Today, in South Africa, education students do receive what can be defined as a basic liberal arts curriculum and then a specialty in education or a subject discipline.[125]

## Lessons from South Africa

In reflecting on lessons that might be learned from education in South Africa, it appears potential lessons may come not solely from the country's educational evolution, but from its actions writ large. From South Africa's initial settlement into modern times, the European settlers viewed the indigenous peoples as less than Whites. They enslaved some. They certainly took advantage of all native peoples.

Perhaps a major lesson for us is that although education can bring knowledge, education brings a change in values, attitudes, and actions only slowly. Curricula introduced often bring memories of past events that are irritating. Emotions are very challenging to direct into positive realms when injustices have been part of prior histories. South Africa and its educational system are still reaping the negative spoils of apartheid. Inequalities in education offered are very present still. The differences between the urban and the rural areas still create tension.

Certainly, South Africa's education has enabled the nation to become modern and rich. We have seen medical breakthroughs in many areas. Dr. Barnard, a South African, performed the first heart transplant in the world. South Africa has now rejoined the legitimate world family of nations. However, we must remember that it was not the nation's education that brought respectability to its shore; it was that the nation realized that apartheid was a cancer. The nation had to accept that basic rights are for all citizens.

However, education still has much to do to bring equity to all citizens. Although the nation is the richest in the African continent, it still has major economic and racial divisions within its borders. Whites still dominate the economy, even though they are the minority. The percentage of South Africans who live in poverty hovers around 50 percent. The range between the economic haves and have-nots continues to expand. The wealth of the few controls the lives of the many. Crime rates are among the highest in the world. The HIV/AIDS situation continues as a national crisis that has an impact not only on the country, but on the entire world.

Perhaps in ruminating about education in South Africa, we can view South Africans' actions as an ongoing experiment that has potential relevance to all nations. However, we must remember that education, even that deemed excellent and effective, cannot solve the world's problems. It might be well for the reader to recall the four myths of education that were discussed in Chapter 6.

## Conclusion

This chapter began with the statement, "We live in the 21st century." The chapter commenced the section Education in Particular Countries as follows: "No nation is an island unto itself. We are living at 'warp-speed' globalization." Truly, we are sharing the planet with others. Increasing numbers of us are recognizing that our times are uncertain and are confronting us with novel problems to which we do not have immediate answers—and perhaps never will.

This time situation must be recognized by all concerned with education. As noted by Robert Cooper, "when you have a problem you cannot solve, enlarge the context."[126] This is the reason for this last chapter—enlarging the context of education to acquaint ourselves with six countries. Considering these countries will not solve our problems, but such observations may provide new insights. Certainly, we cannot address challenges and generate educational solutions solely within the confines of our national borders. We are not an island.

To educate students for effective membership in the world community, we as educators and contributing members of the public must comprehend peoples living outside our borders. We require some grasp of their histories, their cultures, their aspirations, their world contributions, and even their problems. We must apprehend how they have addressed and currently address the challenges of education.

The six countries (Finland, Turkey, Australia, China, Brazil, and South Africa) were not chosen randomly. They are exemplars of regions. These countries are presented to stimulate our awarenesses and insights and to furnish us knowledge of their educational histories and current educational actions so that we can contemplate our own educational behaviors and challenges with expanded cognizance.

All nation-states educate their citizens. Yet some, if not all, nation–states at times mis-educate their citizens. From our purview of these six countries, we observe that all possess the commonplaces of schools: curricula, pedagogies, educational materials, and school personnel (teachers, administrators, supervisors, and so on). At least

currently, all schools have their students' interests at heart. These school systems draw curricular foci and pedagogical approaches from both within their countries and from the world community. The commonplaces of education, while common, are shaped in unique ways by the political and social cultures within which they function. From the stories of these countries, we can extract how they are preparing their student citizens to comprehend the world community—varied spaces outside their country. We must also query ourselves on this point.

All countries, including the six in this chapter, create educational institutions to pursue their interests, as do we. However, as Cooper articulates, the essential "question . . . is how they define" their interests. "Is their view wide or narrow? How do they want to shape the future? What sort of country do they want to be? What kind of world do they want to live in?"[127]

## Endnotes

1. Danny Westneat, "It's Time to School This Myth," *The Seattle Times* (February 16, 2011), pp. B1, B7.
2. Ibid.
3. Arne Duncan, cited in Westneat, "It's Time to School This Myth."
4. Monica Martinez, "Innovation: Imponderable or Ponderables?, *Phi Delta Kappan* (February 2010), pp. 72–73.
5. Ibid., p. 73
6. Ibid.
7. Ibid.
8. Tom Loveless, "How Well Are American Students Learning?," cited in Westneat, "It's Time to School This Myth."
9. R. Hanvey, "An Attainable Global Perspective," cited in Sadiq A. Abdullahi, "Rethinking Global Education in the Twenty-first Century," Chapter 2 in Joseph Zajda, ed., *Global Pedagogies: Schooling for the Future* (London: Springer Science & Business Media, 2010), pp. 23–34.
10. Sadiq A. Abdullahi, "Rethinking Global Education in the Twenty-first Century," Chapter 2 in Zajda, *Global Pedagogies: Schooling for the Future.*
11. Stephen David, Nadine Dolby, and Fazal Rizvi, "Globalization and Postnational Possibilities in Education for the Future: Rethinking Borders and Boundaries," Chapter 3 in Zajda, *Global Pedagogies: Schooling for the Future.*
12. Ibid.
13. K. McDonald, "Post-national Considerations for Curriculum," cited in Stephen David, Nadine Dolby, and Fazal Rizvi, "Globalization and Postnational Possibilities in Education for the Future: Rethinking Borders and Boundaries," in Joseph Zajda, ed., *Global Pedagogies: Schooling for the Future.*
14. J. Zajda, "The International Handbook of Globalisation, Education and Policy Research," cited in Sadiq A. Abdullahi,

"Rethinking Global Education in the Twenty-first Century," in Zajda, *Global Pedagogies: Schooling for the Future.*
15. David, Dolby, and Rizvi, "Globalization and Postnational Possibilities in Education for the Future: Rethinking Borders and Boundaries."
16. Albert Einstein, cited in Keith Baker, "Are International Tests Worth Anything?," *Phi Delta Kappan* (October 2007), p. 104.
17. Finland, Ministry of Education, cited in Linda Darling-Hammond, *The Flat World and Education* (New York: Teachers College Press, 2010), p. 163.
18. Finland, Ministry of Education, cited in Richard Morehouse, "Finland," in Rebecca Marlow-Ferguson, ed., *World Education Encyclopedia,* 2nd ed., Vol. 1 (Farmington Hills, MI: Gale Group, 2002), pp. 437–449.
19. Darling-Hammond, *The Flat World and Education.*
20. Ari Antikainen, "Global Transformation of a Nordic Learning Society: The Case of Finland," Chapter 8 in Zajda, *Global Pedagogies: Schooling for the Future,* pp. 129–143.
21. Ibid.
22. Keith Baker, "Are International Tests Worth Anything?," *Phi Delta Kappan* (October 2007), p. 101.
23. Ibid., p. 102.
24. Ibid.
25. Richard Morehouse, "Finland," in Rebecca Marlow-Ferguson, ed., *World Education Encyclopedia,* 2nd ed., Vol. 1 (Farmington Hills, MI: Gale Group, 2002), pp. 437–449.
26. Ibid.
27. Antikainen, "Global Transformation of a Nordic Learning Society: The Case of Finland."
28. M. Castells, *The Rise of Network Society,* cited in Antikainen, "Global Transformation of Nordic Learning Society: The Case of Finland," p. 132.

29. T. Husen, *Learning Society,* in Antikainen, "Global Transformation of a Nordic Learning Society: The Case of Finland," p. 130.
30. Morehouse, "Finland," p. 439.
31. Ibid.
32. W. Norton Grubb, "Dynamic Inequality and Intervention: Lessons from a Small Country," *Phi Delta Kappan* (October 2007), pp. 105–114.
33. Morehouse, "Finland."
34. Ibid.
35. Ibid., pp. 443–444.
36. Darling-Hammond, *The Flat World and Education*; and Morehouse, "Finland."
37. Ibid.
38. Morehouse, "Finland."
39. Darling-Hammond, *The Flat World and Education*.
40. Ibid.
41. Ibid.
42. Grubb, "Dynamic Inequality and Intervention: Lessons from a Small Country."
43. Ibid., p. 109.
44. Jo Anne R. Bryant, "Turkey," in Rebecca Marlow-Ferguson, ed., *World Education Encyclopedia,* 2nd ed., Vol. 3 (Farmington Hills, MI: Gale Group, 2002), pp. 1415–1425.
45. Ibid.
46. Abdullahi, "Rethinking Global Education in the Twenty-first Century."
47. Bryant, "Turkey."
48. Ibid.
49. Harriet Marshal and Madeleine Arnot, "The Gender Agenda: The Limits and Possibilities of Global and National Citizenship Education," Chapter 7 in Joseph Zajda, Lynn Davies, and Suzanne Majhanovich, eds., *Comparative and Global Pedagogies: Equity, Access and Democracy in Education* (London: Springer Science & Business Media, 2008), pp. 103–123.
50. Bryant, "Turkey."
51. Ibid., p. 1422.
52. Mark Hutchinson, "Australia," in Rebecca Marlow-Ferguson, ed., *World Education Encyclopedia,* 2nd ed., Vol. 1 (Farmington Hills, MI: Gale Group, 2002), pp. 55–68.
53. Ibid.
54. Ibid.
55. Ibid., p. 60.
56. Darling-Hammond, *The Flat World and Education*.
57. Hutchinson, "Australia."
58. David T. Gamage and Takeyuki Ueyama, "Values, Roles, Visions and Professional Development in the Twenty-first Century: Australian and Japanese Principals Voice Their Views," Chapter 5 in Zajda, *Global Pedagogies: Schooling for the Future.*
59. Hutchinson, "Australia."
60. Darling-Hammond, *The Flat World and Education*.
61. Ibid.
62. Ibid.
63. L. Ewen, *The Ascension of Confucianism to State Ideology and Its Downfall* (Shanghai, People's Republic of China: Shanghai Education Publishing House, 2006).
64. Ibid.
65. Ting Ni, "China," in Rebecca Marlow-Ferguson, ed., *World Education Encyclopedia,* 2nd ed., Vol. 1 (Farmington Hills, MI: Gale Group, 2002), pp. 236–255.
66. Ibid.
67. Ibid.
68. Betty Preus, "Educational Trends in China and the United States: Proverbial Pendulum or Potential for Balance?," *Phi Delta Kappan* (October 2007), pp. 115–118.
69. Jerry Large, "Clear View of China from Tibet," *The Seattle Times* (March 3, 2011), pp. B1, B8.
70. Preus, "Educational Trends in China and the United States: Proverbial Pendulum or Potential for Balance?"
71. Yong Zhao, *Catching Up or Leading the Way* (Alexandria, VA: Association for Supervision and Curriculum Development, 2009).
72. Jiaoyubu (Ministry of Education, 2001), cited in Zhao, *Catching Up or Leading the Way,* p. 61.
73. Zhao, *Catching Up or Leading the Way,* p. 61.
74. Edward G. Pultorak and Glenn C. Markle, "Snapshots of Chinese Classrooms Illustrate Disparities," *Phi Delta Kappan* (September 2008), pp. 45–49.
75. Preus, "Educational Trends in China and the United States: Proverbial Pendulum or Potential for Balance?"
76. Darling-Hammond, *The Flat World and Education*.
77. Pultorak and Markle, "Snapshots of Chinese Classrooms Illustrate Disparities."
78. Ting Ni, "China."
79. Ibid.
80. Kam Wing Chan, "Test Scores Notwithstanding, China Is Not 'Eating Our Lunch,'" *The Seattle Times* (January 3, 2011), p. 49.
81. Ibid.
82. Ting Ni, "China."
83. Ibid.
84. Preus, "Educational Trends in China and the United States: Proverbial Pendulum or Potential for Balance?"
85. Ting Ni, "China."
86. Preus, "Educational Trends in China and the United States: Proverbial Pendulum or Potential for Balance?"
87. Ting Ni, "China."
88. Ibid.
89. Chan, "Test Scores Notwithstanding, China Is Not 'Eating Our Lunch.'"
90. Zhao, *Catching Up or Leading the Way,* p. 94.
91. Ibid.
92. Parag Khanna, *The Second World* (New York: Random House, 2008).
93. Patricia K. Kubow and Paul R. Fossum, *Comparative Education: Exploring Issues in International Context,* 2nd ed. (Columbus, OH: Pearson Education Inc., 2007).

94. Monica Rector and Marco Silva, "Brazil," in Rebecca Marlow-Ferguson, *World Education Encyclopedia,* 2nd ed., Vol. 1 (Farmington Hills, MI: Gale Group, 2002).

95. Ibid.

96. Khanna, *The Second World.*

97. Kubow and Fossum, *Comparative Education: Exploring Issues in International Context.*

98. Ibid.

99. Rector and Silva, "Brazil."

100. Kubow and Fossum, *Comparative Education: Exploring Issues in International Context.*

101. N. P. Stromquist, *Literacy for Citizenship: Gender and Grassroots Dynamics in Brazil,* cited in Patricia K. Kubow and Paul R. Fossum, *Comparative Education: Exploring Issues in International Context.*

102. L. Crouch, *South Africa: Overcoming Past Injustice,* in Patricia K. Kubow and Paul R. Fossum, *Comparative Education: Exploring Issues in International Context,* p. 53.

103. Kubow and Fossum, *Comparative Education: Exploring Issues in International Context.*

104. Rector and Silva, "Brazil."

105. Khanna, *The Second World,* p. 157.

106. Rector and Silva, "Brazil."

107. Kubow and Fossum, *Comparative Education: Exploring Issues in International Context.*

108. Khanna, *The Second World,* p. 158.

109. Harm de Blij, *Why Geography Matters* (New York: Oxford University Press, Inc., 2005).

110. Clive Smith, "Africa," in Gary McCulloch and David Crook, eds., *The Routledge International Encyclopedia of Education* (New York: Routledge, 2008), pp. 557–559.

111. de Blij, *Why Geography Matters.*

112. Mbulelo Vizikhungo Mzamane and S. D. Berkowitz, "South Africa," in Rebecca Marlow-Ferguson, ed., *World Education Encyclopedia,* 2nd ed., Vol. 3 (Farmington Hills, MI: Gale Group, 2002), pp. 1230–1243.

113. Ibid.; and Smith, "Africa."

114. Mzamane and Berkowitz, "South Africa."

115. Ibid.

116. F. Molteno, "The Historical Foundations of Schooling of Black South Africans," in P. Kallaway, ed., *Apartheid and Education: The Marginalization of Black South Africans* (Johannesburg, S.A.: African Press, 1984), pp. 92–93, cited in Smith, "South Africa," *The Routledge International Encyclopedia of Education.*

117. Kubow and Fossum, *Comparative Education: Exploring Issues in International Context.*

118. Smith, "Africa," p. 558.

119. Mzamane and Berkowitz, "South Africa."

120. Ibid.

121. Kubow and Fossum, *Comparative Education: Exploring Issues in International Context.*

122. Smith, "Africa."

123. Kubow and Fossum, *Comparative Education: Exploring Issues in International Context.*

124. Ibid.

125. Ibid.

126. Robert Cooper, *The Breaking of Nations* (New York: Grove Press, 2003), p. 138.

127. Ibid., pp. 137–138.

# NAME INDEX

# SUBJECT INDEX